THE HISTORY
OF ENGLAND

VOLUME II

THE HISTORY
OF ENGLAND

from the Invasion of Julius Caesar

to The Revolution in 1688

IN SIX VOLUMES
BY DAVID HUME, ESQ.

VOLUME II

Based on the Edition of 1778, with the Author's

Last Corrections and Improvements

LibertyClassics

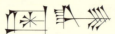
This Liberty*Classics* edition is based on the edition of 1778, containing the author's last corrections and improvements. The only two recorded sets of that edition in the United States were consulted. One is a complete set at the Humanities Research Center of the University of Texas at Austin. The other is an incomplete set in the Boston Public Library. The publisher acknowledges with thanks the cooperation of both institutions as well as the advice of Professors William B. Todd and David Levy.

Design by Martin Lubin/Betty Binns Graphics, New York, New York.
Editorial services provided by Harkavy Publishing Service, New York, New York.

Library of Congress Cataloging in Publication Data

Hume, David, 1711–1776.
 The history of England.

 "Based on the edition of 1778, with the author's last corrections and improvements."
 Reprint. Originally published: London: T. Cadell, 1778. With new foreword.
 1. Great Britain—History—To 1485. 2. Great Britain—History—Tudors, 1485–1603. 3. Great Britain—History—Stuarts, 1603–1714. I. Title.
DA30.H9 1983   942   82–25868
ISBN 0–86597–019–X (series)
ISBN 0–86597–020–3 (pbk. series)
ISBN 0–86597–026–2 (Volume II)
ISBN 0–86597–027–0 (Volume II pbk.)

10 9 8 7 6 5 4 3 2

C O N T E N T S

O F T H E S E C O N D V O L U M E

XII

H E N R Y I I I

*Settlement of the government –
General pacification – Death of the
protector – Some commotions – Hubert de Burgh
displaced – The bishop of Winchester minister –
King's partiality to foreigners – Grievances –
Ecclesiastical grievances – Earl of Cornwal
elected king of the Romans – Discontent
of the barons – Simon de Mountfort earl of Leicester –
Provisions of Oxford – Usurpation of the barons –
Prince Edward – Civil wars of the
barons – Reference to the king of France – Renewal of the
civil wars – Battle of Lewes – House of commons –
Battle of Evesham and death of Leicester –
Settlement of the government – Death –
and character of the king – Miscellaneous transactions
of this reign*

PAGE 3

XIII
EDWARD I

*Civil administration of the king –
Conquest of Wales – Affairs of Scotland –
Competitors for the crown of Scotland –
Reference to Edward – Homage of Scotland –
Award of Edward in favour of Baliol – War
with France – Digression concerning
the constitution of parliament – War with Scotland –
Scotland subdued – War with France – Dissensions
with the clergy – Arbitrary measures –
Peace with France – Revolt of Scotland –
That kingdom again subdued – again revolts –
is again subdued – Robert Bruce –
Third revolt of Scotland – Death –
and character of the king – Miscellaneous transactions
of this reign*

PAGE 73

XIV
EDWARD II

*Weakness of the king –
His passion for favourites – Piers
Gavaston – Discontent of the barons – Murder
of Gavaston – War with Scotland – Battle
of Bannockburn – Hugh le Despenser – Civil
commotions – Execution of the earl of Lancaster –*

Conspiracy against the king – Insurrection –
The king dethroned – Murdered – His character –
Miscellaneous transactions
in this reign

PAGE 147

X V

E D W A R D   I I I

War with Scotland –
Execution of the earl of Kent – Execution
of Mortimer, earl of March – State of Scotland – War
with that kingdom – King's claim to the crown of France –
Preparations for war with France – War –
Naval victory – Domestic disturbances – Affairs
of Britanny – Renewal of the war with France
– Invasion of France – Battle of Crecy –
War with Scotland – Captivity of the king
of Scots – Calais taken

PAGE 182

X V I

Institution of the garter –
State of France – Battle of Poictiers –
Captivity of the king of France – State
of that kingdom – Invasion of France – Peace
of Bretigni – State of France – Expedition

XVII
RICHARD II

XVIII
HENRY IV

XIX
HENRY V

XX
HENRY VI

King's marriage with the Lady Elizabeth Gray –
Warwic disgusted – Alliance with Burgundy –
Insurrection in Yorkshire – Battle of Banbury –
Warwic and Clarence banished – Warwic and Clarence
return – Edward IV expelled – Henry VI restored –
Edward IV returns – Battle of Barnet, and
death of Warwic – Battle of Teukesbury,
and murder of prince Edward – Death of
Henry VI – Invasion of France –
Peace of Pecquigni – Trial and execution
of the duke of Clarence – Death and character
of Edward IV

PAGE 455

XXIII

EDWARD V
AND RICHARD III

Edward V – State
of the court – The earl of Rivers
arrested – Duke of Glocester protector –
Execution of Lord Hastings – The protector
aims at the crown – Assumes the crown – Murder
of Edward V and of the duke of York – Richard III –
Duke of Buckingham discontented – The earl
of Richmond – Buckingham executed – Invasion
by the earl of Richmond – Battle
of Bosworth – Death and character
of Richard III

PAGE 494

THE HISTORY
OF ENGLAND

VOLUME II

XII

HENRY III

Settlement of the government – General pacification – Death of the Protector – Some commotions – Hubert de Burgh displaced – The bishop of Winchester minister – King's partiality to foreigners – Grievances – Ecclesiastical grievances – Earl of Cornwal elected king of the Romans – Discontent of the barons – Simon de Mountfort earl of Leicester – Provisions of Oxford – Usurpation of the barons – Prince Edward – Civil wars of the barons – Reference to the king of France – Renewal of the civil wars – Battle of Lewes – House of commons – Battle of Evesham and death of Leicester – Settlement of the government – Death – and character of the king – Miscellaneous transactions of this reign.

M OST SCIENCES, in proportion as they encrease and improve, *1216.* invent methods by which they facilitate their reasonings; and employing general theorems, are enabled to comprehend in a few propositions a great number of inferences and conclusions. History also, being a collection of facts which are multiplying without end, is obliged to adopt such arts of abridgment, to retain the more material events, and to drop all the minute circumstances, which are only interesting during the time, or to the persons engaged in the transactions. This truth is no where more evident than with regard to the reign, upon which we are going to enter. What mortal could have the patience to write or read a long detail of such frivolous events as those with which it is filled, or attend to a tedious narrative which would follow, through a series of fifty-six years, the caprices and weaknesses of so mean a prince as Henry? The chief reason, why protestant writers have been so anxious to spread out the incidents of this reign, is in order to expose the rapacity, ambition, and artifices of the court of Rome, and to prove, that the great dignitaries of the catholic church, while they pretended to have nothing in view but the salvation of souls, had bent all their attention to the acquisition of riches, and were restrained by no sense of justice or of honour, in the pursuit of that great object.[a] But this conclusion would readily be allowed them, though it were not illustrated by such a detail of uninteresting incidents; and follows indeed, by an evident necessity, from the very situation, in which that church was placed with regard to the rest of Europe. For, besides that ecclesiastical power, as it can always cover its operations under a cloak of sanctity, and attacks men on the side where they dare not employ their reason, lies less under controul than civil government; besides this general cause, I say, the pope and his courtiers were foreigners to most of the churches which they governed; they could not possibly have any other object than to pillage the provinces for present gain; and as they lived at a distance, they would be little awed by shame or remorse, in employing every lucrative expedient, which was suggested to them. England being one of the most remote provinces attached to the Romish hierarchy, as well as the most prone to superstition, felt severely, during this reign, while its patience was not yet fully exhausted, the influence of these causes; and we shall often have occasion to touch cursorily upon such incidents. But we shall not attempt to comprehend every transaction transmitted to us; and till the end of the reign, when the events become more

[a] M. Paris, p. 623.

CHAPTER XII

memorable, we shall not always observe an exact chronological order in our narration.

The earl of Pembroke, who, at the time of John's death, was mareschal of England, was by his office at the head of the armies, and consequently, during a state of civil wars and convulsions, at the head of the government; and it happened fortunately for the young monarch and for the nation, that the power could not have been intrusted into more able and more faithful hands. This nobleman, who had maintained his loyalty unshaken to John during the lowest fortune of that monarch, determined to support the authority of the infant prince; nor was he dismayed at the number and violence of his enemies. Sensible, that Henry, agreeably to the prejudices of the times, would not be deemed a sovereign, till crowned and anointed by a churchman; he immediately carried the young prince to Gloucester, where the ceremony of coronation was performed, in the presence of Gualo, the legate, and of a few noblemen, by the bishops of Winchester and Bath.[b] As the concurrence of the papal authority was requisite to support the tottering throne, Henry was obliged to swear fealty to the pope, and renew that homage, to which his father had already subjected the kingdom:[c] And in order to enlarge the authority of Pembroke, and to give him a more regular and legal title to it, a general council of the barons was soon after summoned at Bristol, where that nobleman was chosen protector of the realm.

Pembroke, that he might reconcile all men to the government of his pupil, made him grant a new charter of liberties, which, though mostly copied from the former concessions extorted from John, contains some alterations, which may be deemed remarkable.[d] The full privilege of elections in the clergy, granted by the late king, was not confirmed, nor the liberty of going out of the kingdom, without the royal consent: Whence we may conclude, that Pembroke and the barons, jealous of the ecclesiastical power, both were desirous of renewing the king's claim to issue a congè d'elire to the monks and chapters, and thought it requisite to put some check to the frequent appeals to Rome. But what may chiefly

Settlement of the government.

28th Oct.

11th Nov.

---

[b] M. Paris, p. 200. Hist. Croys. Cont. p. 474. W. Heming. p. 562. Trivet, p. 168. [c] M. Paris, p. 200. [d] Rymer, vol. i. p. 215.

surprize us is, that the obligation, to which John had subjected himself, of obtaining the consent of the great council before he levied any aids or scutages upon the nation, was omitted; and this article was even declared hard and severe, and was expressly left to future deliberation. But we must consider, that, though this limitation may perhaps appear to us the most momentous in the whole charter of John, it was not regarded in that light by the ancient barons, who were more jealous in guarding against particular acts of violence in the crown, than against such general impositions, which, unless they were evidently reasonable and necessary, could scarcely, without general consent, be levied upon men, who had arms in their hands, and who could repel any act of oppression, by which they were all immediately affected. We accordingly find, that Henry, in the course of his reign, while he gave frequent occasions for complaint, with regard to his violations of the Great Charter, never attempted, by his mere will, to levy any aids or scutages; though he was often reduced to great necessities, and was refused supply by his people. So much easier was it for him to transgress the law, when individuals alone were affected, than even to exert his acknowledged prerogatives, where the interest of the whole body was concerned.

This charter was again confirmed by the king in the ensuing year, with the addition of some articles to prevent the oppressions by sheriffs: And also with an additional charter of forests, a circumstance of great moment in those ages, when hunting was so much the occupation of the nobility, and when the king comprehended so considerable a part of the kingdom within his forests, which he governed by peculiar and arbitrary laws. All the forests, which had been enclosed since the reign of Henry II. were desaforested; and new perambulations were appointed for that purpose: Offences in the forests were declared to be no longer capital; but punishable by fine, imprisonment, and more gentle penalties: And all the proprietors of land recovered the power of cutting and using their own wood at their pleasure.

Thus, these famous charters were brought nearly to the shape, in which they have ever since stood; and they were, during many generations, the peculiar favourites of the English nation, and esteemed the most sacred rampart to national liberty and independance. As they secured the rights of all orders of men, they were anxiously defended by all, and became the basis, in a manner, of the English monarchy, and a kind of original contract, which both limited the authority of the king, and ensured the conditional allegiance of his subjects. Though often violated, they were still claimed by the nobility and people; and as no precedents were supposed valid, that infringed them, they rather acquired, than lost authority, from the frequent attempts, made against them in several ages, by regal and arbitrary power.

While Pembroke, by renewing and confirming the Great Charter, gave so much satisfaction and security to the nation in general, he also applied himself successfully to individuals: He wrote letters, in the king's name, to all the malcontent barons; in which he represented to them, that, whatever jealousy and animosity they might have entertained against the late king, a young prince, the lineal heir of their ancient monarchs, had now succeeded to the throne, without succeeding either to the resentments or principles of his predecessor: That the desperate expedient, which they had employed, of calling in a foreign potentate, had, happily for them as well as for the nation, failed of entire success, and it was still in their power, by a speedy return to their duty, to restore the independance of the kingdom, and to secure that liberty, for which they so zealously contended: That as all past offences of the barons were now buried in oblivion, they ought, on their part, to forget their complaints against their late sovereign, who, if he had been any wise blameable in his conduct, had left to his son the salutary warning, to avoid the paths, which had led to such fatal extremities: And that having now obtained a charter for their liberties, it was their interest to shew, by their conduct, that this acquisition was not incompatible with their allegiance, and that the rights of king and people, so far from being hostile and opposite, might mutually support and sustain each other.[e]

These considerations, enforced by the character of honour and constancy, which Pembroke had ever maintained, had a mighty influence on the barons; and most of them began secretly to negotiate with him, and many of them openly returned to their duty. The diffidence, which Lewis discovered, of their fidelity, forwarded this general propension towards the king; and when the

[e] Rymer, vol. i. p. 215. Brady's App. N°. 143.

French prince refused the government of the castle of Hertford to Robert Fitz-Walter, who had been so active against the late king, and who claimed that fortress as his property, they plainly saw, that the English were excluded from every trust, and that foreigners had engrossed all the confidence and affection of their new sovereign.[f] The excommunication too, denounced by the legate, against all the adherents of Lewis, failed not, in the turn which men's dispositions had taken, to produce a mighty effect upon them; and they were easily persuaded to consider a cause as impious, for which they had already entertained an unsurmountable aversion.[g] Though Lewis made a journey to France, and brought over succours from that kingdom,[h] he found, on his return, that his party was still more weakened by the desertion of his English confederates, and that the death of John had, contrary to his expectations, given an incurable wound to his cause. The earls of Salisbury, Arundel, and Warrenne, together with William Mareschal, eldest son of the protector, had embraced Henry's party; and every English nobleman was plainly watching for an opportunity of returning to his allegiance. Pembroke was so much strengthened by these accessions, that he ventured to invest Mount-sorel; though, upon the approach of the count of Perche with the French army, he desisted from his enterprize, and raised the siege.[i] The count, elated with this success, marched to Lincoln; and being admitted into the town, he began to attack the castle, which he soon reduced to extremity. The protector summoned all his forces from every quarter in order to relieve a place of such importance; and he appeared so much superior to the French, that they shut themselves up within the city, and resolved to act upon the defensive.[k] But the garrison of the castle, having received a strong reinforcement, made a vigorous sally upon the besiegers; while the English army, by concert, assaulted them in the same instant from without, mounted the walls by scalade, and bearing down all resistance, entered the city sword in hand. Lincoln was delivered over to be pillaged; the French army was totally routed; the count de Perche, with only two persons more, was killed, but many of the chief commanders and about 400 knights were made

[f] M. Paris, p. 200, 202.　[g] Ibid. p. 200. M. West. p. 277.　[h] Chron. Dunst. vol. i. p. 79. M. West. p. 277.　[i] M. Paris, p. 203.　[k] Chron. Dunst. vol. i. p. 81.

CHAPTER XII

prisoners by the English.[l] So little blood was shed in this important action, which decided the fate of one of the most powerful kingdoms in Europe; and such wretched soldiers were those ancient barons, who yet were unacquainted with every thing but arms!

Prince Lewis was informed of this fatal event, while employed in the siege of Dover, which was still valiantly defended against him by Hubert de Burgh. He immediately retreated to London, the center and life of his party; and he there received intelligence of a new disaster, which put an end to all his hopes. A French fleet, bringing over a strong reinforcement, had appeared on the coast of Kent; where they were attacked by the English under the command of Philip d'Albiney, and were routed with considerable loss. D'Albiney employed a stratagem against them, which is said to have contributed to the victory: Having gained the wind of the French, he came down upon them with violence; and throwing in their faces a great quantity of quicklime, which he purposely carried on board, he so blinded them, that they were disabled from defending themselves.[m]

After this second misfortune of the French, the English barons hastened every where to make peace with the protector, and by an early submission, to prevent those attainders, to which they were exposed on account of their rebellion. Lewis, whose cause was now totally desperate, began to be anxious for the safety of his person, and was glad, on any honourable conditions, to make his escape from a country, where, he found, every thing was now become hostile to him. He concluded a peace with Pembroke, promised to evacuate the kingdom, and only stipulated in return, an indemnity to his adherents, and a restitution of their honours and fortunes, together with the free and equal enjoyment of those liberties, which had been granted to the rest of the nation.[n] Thus was happily ended a civil war, which seemed to be founded on the most incurable hatred and jealousy, and had threatened the kingdom with the most fatal consequences. *General pacification.*

The precautions, which the king of France used in the conduct of this whole affair, are remarkable. He pretended, that his son

[l] M. Paris, p. 204, 205. Chron de Mullr. p. 195.   [m] M. Paris, p. 206. Ann. Waverl. p. 183. W. Heming. p. 563. Trivet, p. 169. M. West. p. 277. Knyghton, p. 2428.   [n] Rymer, vol. i. p. 221. M. Paris, p. 207. Chron. Dunst. vol. i. p. 83. M. West. p. 278. Knyghton, p. 2429.

had accepted of the offer from the English barons, without his advice, and contrary to his inclination: The armies sent to England were levied in Lewis's name: When that prince came over to France for aid, his father publicly refused to grant him any assistance, and would not so much as admit him to his presence: Even after Henry's party acquired the ascendant, and Lewis was in danger of falling into the hands of his enemies, it was Blanche of Castile his wife, not the king his father, who raised armies and equipped fleets for his succour.[o] All these artifices were employed, not to satisfy the pope; for he had too much penetration to be so easily imposed on: Nor yet to deceive the people; for they were too gross even for that purpose: They only served for a colouring to Philip's cause; and in public affairs, men are often better pleased, that the truth, though known to every body, should be wrapped up under a decent cover, than if it were exposed in open day-light to the eyes of all the world.

After the expulsion of the French, the prudence and equity of the protector's subsequent conduct, contributed to cure entirely those wounds, which had been made by intestine discord. He received the rebellious barons into favour; observed strictly the terms of peace, which he had granted them; restored them to their possessions; and endeavoured, by an equal behaviour, to bury all past animosities in perpetual oblivion. The clergy alone, who had adhered to Lewis, were sufferers in this revolution. As they had rebelled against their spiritual sovereign, by disregarding the interdict and excommunication, it was not in Pembroke's power to make any stipulations in their favour; and Gualo, the legate, prepared to take vengeance on them for their disobedience.[p] Many of them were deposed; many suspended; some banished; and all who escaped punishment, made atonement for their offence, by paying large sums to the legate, who amassed an immense treasure by this expedient.

Death of the protector. The earl of Pembroke did not long survive the pacification, which had been chiefly owing to his wisdom and valour;[q] and he was succeeded in the government by Peter des Roches, bishop of Winchester, and Hubert de Burgh, the justiciary. The councils of

[o] M. Paris, p. 256. Chron. Dunst. vol. i. p. 82.   [p] Brady's App. Nº. 144. Chron. Dunst. vol. i. p. 83.   [q] M. Paris, p. 210.

CHAPTER XII

the latter were chiefly followed; and had he possessed equal authority in the kingdom with Pembroke, he seemed to be every way
worthy of filling the place of that virtuous nobleman. But the
licentious and powerful barons, who had once broken the reins of
subjection to their prince, and had obtained by violence an en-
largement of their liberties and independance, could ill be restrained by laws under a minority; and the people, no less than the
king, suffered from their outrages and disorders. They retained by
force the royal castles, which they had seized during the past convulsions, or which had been committed to their custody by the
protector.[r] They usurped the king's demesnes:[s] They oppressed
their vassals: They infested their weaker neighbours: They invited
all disorderly people to enter in their retinue, and to live upon
their lands: And they gave them protection in all their robberies
and extortions.

Some com- motions.

No one was more infamous for these violent and illegal practices than the earl of Albemarle; who, though he had early returned to his duty, and had been serviceable in expelling the
French, augmented to the utmost the general disorder, and committed outrages in all the counties of the North. In order to reduce
him to obedience, Hubert seized an opportunity of getting possession of Rockingham castle, which Albemarle had garrisoned
with his licentious retinue: But this nobleman, instead of submitting, entered into a secret confederacy with Fawkes de Breauté,
Peter de Mauleon, and other barons, and both fortified the castle
of Biham for his defence, and made himself master by surprize of
that of Fotheringay. Pandulf, who was restored to his legateship,
was active in suppressing this rebellion; and with the concurrence
of eleven bishops, he pronounced the sentence of excommunication against Albemarle and his adherents:[t] An army was levied:
A scutage of ten shillings a knight's fee was imposed on all the
military tenants: Albemarle's associates gradually deserted him:
And he himself was obliged at last to sue for mercy. He received a
pardon, and was restored to his whole estate.

This impolitic lenity, too frequent in those times, was probably
the result of a secret combination among the barons, who never
could endure to see the total ruin of one of their own order: But

[r] Trivet, p. 174.　[s] Rymer, vol. i. p. 276.　[t] Chron. Dunst. vol. i. p. 102.

it encouraged Fawkes de Breauté, a man whom king John had raised from a low origin, to persevere in the course of violence, to which he had owed his fortune, and to set at naught all law and justice. When thirty-five verdicts were at one time found against him, on account of his violent expulsion of so many freeholders from their possessions; he came to the court of justice with an armed force, seized the judge who had pronounced the verdicts, and imprisoned him in Bedford castle. He then levied open war against the king; but being subdued, and taken prisoner, his life was granted him: but his estate was confiscated, and he was banished the kingdom.[u]

1222. Justice was executed with greater severity against disorders less premeditated, which broke out in London. A frivolous emulation in a match of wrestling, between the Londoners on the one hand, and the inhabitants of Westminster and those of the neighbouring villages on the other, occasioned this commotion. The former rose in a body, and pulled down some houses belonging to the abbot of Westminster: But this riot, which, considering the tumultuous disposition familiar to that capital, would have been little regarded, seemed to become more serious, by the symptoms which then appeared, of the former attachment of the citizens to the French interest. The populace, in the tumult, made use of the cry of war commonly employed by the French troops; *Mountjoy, mountjoy, God help us and our lord Lewis.* The justiciary made enquiry into the disorder; and finding one Constantine Fitz Arnulf to have been the ringleader, an insolent man, who justified his crime in Hubert's presence, he proceeded against him by martial law, and ordered him immediately to be hanged, without trial or form of process. He also cut off the feet of some of Constantine's accomplices.[w]

This act of power was complained of as an infringement of the Great Charter: Yet the justiciary, in a parliament, summoned at Oxford, (for the great councils about this time began to receive that appellation) made no scruple to grant in the king's name a renewal and confirmation of that charter. When the assembly made application to the crown for this favour; as a law in those

" Rymer, vol. i. p. 198. M. Paris, p. 221, 224. Ann. Waverl. p. 188. Chron. Dunst. vol. i. p. 141, 146. M. West. p. 283.   " M. Paris, p. 217, 218, 259. Ann. Waverl. p. 187. Chron. Dunst. vol. i. p. 129.

times seemed to lose its validity, if not frequently renewed; William de Briewere, one of the council of regency, was so bold as to say openly, that those liberties were extorted by force, and ought not to be observed: But he was reprimanded by the archbishop of Canterbury, and was not countenanced by the king or his chief ministers.[x] A new confirmation was demanded and granted two years after; and an aid, amounting to a fifteenth of all moveables, was given by the parliament, in return for this indulgence. The king issued writs anew to the sheriffs, enjoining the observance of the charter; but he inserted a remarkable clause in the writs, that those, who payed not the fifteenth, should not for the future be entitled to the benefit of those liberties.[y]

The low state, into which the crown was fallen, made it requisite for a good minister to be attentive to the preservation of the royal prerogatives, as well as to the security of public liberty. Hubert applied to the pope, who had always great authority in the kingdom, and was now considered as its superior lord; and desired him to issue a bull, declaring the king to be of full age, and entitled to exercise in person all the acts of royalty.[z] In consequence of this declaration, the justiciary resigned into Henry's hands the two important fortresses of the Tower and Dover castle, which had been entrusted to his custody; and he required the other barons to imitate his example. They refused compliance: The earls of Chester and Albemarle, John Constable of Chester, John de Lacy, Brian de l'Isle, and William de Cantel, with some others, even formed a conspiracy to surprize London, and met in arms at Waltham with that intention: But finding the king prepared for defence, they desisted from their enterprize. When summoned to court, in order to answer for their conduct, they scrupled not to appear, and to confess the design: But they told the king, that they had no bad intentions against his person, but only against Hubert de Burgh, whom they were determined to remove from his office.[a] They appeared too formidable to be chastised; and they were so little discouraged by the failure of their first enterprize, that they again met in arms at Leicester, in order to seize the king, who then resided at Northampton: But Henry, informed of their purpose,

[x] M. West. p. 282.   [y] Clause 9. H. 3. m. 9. and m. 6. d.   [z] M. Paris, p. 220.
[a] Chron. Dunst. vol. i. p. 137.

took care to be so well armed and attended, that the barons found it dangerous to make the attempt; and they sat down and kept Christmas in his neighbourhood.[b] The archbishop and the prelates, finding every thing tend towards a civil war, interposed with their authority, and threatened the barons with the sentence of excommunication, if they persisted in detaining the king's castles. This menace at last prevailed: Most of the fortresses were surrendered; though the barons complained, that Hubert's castles were soon after restored to him, while the king still kept theirs in his own custody. There are said to have been 1115 castles at that time in England.[c]

It must be acknowledged, that the influence of the prelates and the clergy was often of great service to the public. Though the religion of that age can merit no better name than that of superstition, it served to unite together a body of men who had great sway over the people, and who kept the community from falling to pieces, by the factions and independant power of the nobles. And what was of great importance; it threw a mighty authority into the hands of men, who by their profession were averse to arms and violence; who tempered by their mediation the general disposition towards military enterprizes; and who still maintained, even amidst the shock of arms, those secret links, without which it is impossible for human society to subsist.

Notwithstanding these intestine commotions in England, and the precarious authority of the crown, Henry was obliged to carry on war in France; and he employed to that purpose the fifteenth which had been granted him by parliament. Lewis VIII. who had succeeded to his father Philip, instead of complying with Henry's claim, who demanded the restitution of Normandy and the other provinces wrested from England, made an irruption into Poictou, took Rochelle[d] after a long siege, and seemed determined to expel the English from the few provinces which still remained to them. Henry sent over his uncle, the earl of Salisbury; together with his brother prince Richard, to whom he had granted the earldom of Cornwal, which had escheated to the crown. Salisbury stopped the progress of Lewis's arms, and retained the Poictevin and Gascon

[b] M. Paris, p. 221. Chron. Dunst. vol. i. p. 138. [c] Coke's Comment. on Magna Charta, chap. 17. [d] Rymer, vol. i. p. 269. Trivet, p. 179.

CHAPTER XII

vassals in their allegiance: But no military action of any moment was performed on either side. The earl of Cornwal, after two years' stay in Guienne, returned to England.

This prince was nowise turbulent or factious in his disposition: His ruling passion was to amass money, in which he succeeded so well as to become the richest subject in Christendom: Yet his attention to gain threw him sometimes into acts of violence, and gave disturbance to the government. There was a manor, which had formerly belonged to the earldom of Cornwal, but had been granted to Waleran de Ties, before Richard had been invested with that dignity, and while the earldom remained in the crown. Richard claimed this manor, and expelled the proprietor by force: Waleran complained: The king ordered his brother to do justice to the man, and restore him to his rights: The earl said, that he would not submit to these orders, till the cause should be decided against him by the judgment of his peers: Henry replied, that it was first necessary to re-instate Waleran in possession, before the cause could be tried; and he re-iterated his orders to the earl.[e] We may judge of the state of the government, when this affair had nearly produced a civil war. The earl of Cornwal, finding Henry peremptory in his commands, associated himself with the young earl of Pembroke, who had married his sister, and who was displeased on account of the king's requiring him to deliver up some royal castles which were in his custody. These two malcontents took into the confederacy the earls of Chester, Warenne, Glocester, Hereford, Warwic, and Ferrers, who were all disgusted on a like account.[f] They assembled an army, which the king had not the power or courage to resist; and he was obliged to give his brother satisfaction, by grants of much greater importance than the manor, which had been the first ground of the quarrel.[g]

The character of the king, as he grew to man's estate, became every day better known; and he was found in every respect unqualified for maintaining a proper sway among those turbulent barons, whom the feudal constitution subjected to his authority. Gentle, humane, and merciful even to a fault, he seems to have been steady in no other circumstance of his character; but to have received every impression from those who surrounded him, and whom he

_1227._

---

[e] M. Paris, p. 233. [f] Ibid. [g] Ibid.

loved, for the time, with the most imprudent and most unreserved affection. Without activity or vigour, he was unfit to conduct war; without policy or art, he was ill-fitted to maintain peace; His resentments, though hasty and violent, were not dreaded, while he was found to drop them with such facility; his friendships were little valued, because they were neither derived from choice, nor maintained with constancy. A proper pageant of state in a regular monarchy, where his ministers could have conducted all affairs in his name and by his authority; but too feeble in those disorderly times to sway a scepter, whose weight depended entirely on the firmness and dexterity of the hand which held it.

Hubert de Burgh displaced.

The ablest and most virtuous minister that Henry ever possessed, was Hubert de Burgh;[h] a man who had been steady to the crown in the most difficult and dangerous times, and who yet shewed no disposition, in the height of his power, to enslave or oppress the people. The only exceptionable part of his conduct is that which is mentioned by Matthew Paris,[i] if the fact be really true, and proceeded from Hubert's advice, namely, the recalling publicly and the annulling of the charter of forests, a concession so reasonable in itself, and so passionately claimed both by the nobility and people: But it must be confessed, that this measure is so unlikely, both from the circumstances of the times and character of the minister, that there is reason to doubt of its reality, especially as it is mentioned by no other historian. Hubert, while he enjoyed his authority, had an entire ascendant over Henry, and was loaded with honours and favours beyond any other subject. Besides acquiring the property of many castles and manors, he married the eldest sister of the king of Scots, was created earl of Kent, and by

1231.

an unusual concession, was made chief justiciary of England for life: Yet Henry, in a sudden caprice, threw off this faithful minister, and exposed him to the violent persecutions of his enemies. Among other frivolous crimes objected to him, he was accused of gaining the king's affections by enchantment, and of purloining from the royal treasury a gem, which had the virtue to render the wearer invulnerable, and of sending this valuable curiosity to the prince of Wales.[k] The nobility, who hated Hubert on account of his

---

[h] Ypod. Neustriae, p. 464. [i] P. 252. M. West. p. 216. ascribes this counsel to Peter Bishop of Winchester. [k] M. Paris, p. 259.

zeal in resuming the rights and possessions of the crown, no sooner saw the opportunity favourable, than they inflamed the king's animosity against him, and pushed him to seek the total ruin of his minister. Hubert took sanctuary in a church: The king ordered him to be dragged from thence: He recalled those orders: He afterwards renewed them: He was obliged by the clergy to restore him to the sanctuary: He constrained him soon after to surrender himself prisoner, and he confined him in the castle of the Devises. Hubert made his escape, was expelled the kingdom, was again received into favour, recovered a great share of the king's confidence, but never showed any inclination to reinstate himself in power and authority.[l]

The man, who succeeded him in the government of the king and kingdom, was Peter, bishop of Winchester, a Poictevin by birth, who had been raised by the late king, and who was no less distinguished by his arbitrary principles and violent conduct, than by his courage and abilities. This prelate had been left by king John justiciary and regent of the kingdom during an expedition which that prince made into France; and his illegal administration was one chief cause of that great combination among the barons, which finally extorted from the crown the charter of liberties, and laid the foundations of the English constitution. Henry, though incapable, from his character, of pursuing the same violent maxims, which had governed his father, had imbibed the same arbitrary principles; and in prosecution of Peter's advice, he invited over a great number of Poictevins and other foreigners, who, he believed, could more safely be trusted than the English, and who seemed useful to counterbalance the great and independant power of the nobility.[m] Every office and command was bestowed on these strangers; they exhausted the revenues of the crown, already too much impoverished;[n] they invaded the rights of the people; and their insolence, still more provoking than their power, drew on them the hatred and envy of all orders of men in the kingdom.[o]

Bishop of Winchester minister.

The barons formed a combination against this odious ministry, and withdrew from parliament; on pretence of the danger, to which they were exposed from the machinations of the Poictevins.

1233.

[l] Ibid. p. 259, 260, 261, 266. Chron. T. Wykes, p. 41, 42. Chron. Dunst. vol. i. p. 220, 221. M. West. p. 291, 301.   [m] M. Paris, p. 263.   [n] Chron. Dunst. vol. i. p. 151.   [o] M. Paris, p. 258.

When again summoned to attend, they gave for answer, that the king should dismiss his foreigners: Otherwise they would drive both him and them out of the kingdom, and put the crown on another head, more worthy to wear it:[p] Such was the style they used to their sovereign! They at last came to parliament, but so well attended, that they seemed in a condition to prescribe laws to the king and ministry. Peter des Roches, however, had in the interval found means of sowing dissention among them, and of bringing over to his party the earl of Cornwal, as well as the earls of Lincoln and Chester. The confederates were disconcerted in their measures: Richard, earl Mareschal, who had succeeded to that dignity on the death of his brother, William, was chased into Wales; he thence withdrew into Ireland; where he was treacherously murdered by the contrivance of the bishop of Winchester.[q] The estates of the more obnoxious barons were confiscated, without legal sentence or trial by their peers;[r] and were bestowed with a profuse liberality on the Poictevins. Peter even carried his insolence so far as to declare publickly, that the barons of England must not pretend to put themselves on the same foot with those of France, or assume the same liberties and privileges: The monarch in the former country had a more absolute power than in the latter. It had been more justifiable for him to have said, that men, so unwilling to submit to the authority of laws, could with the worse grace claim any shelter or protection from them.

When the king at any time was checked in his illegal practices, and when the authority of the Great Charter was objected to him, he was wont to reply; "Why should I observe this charter, which is neglected by all my grandees, both prelates and nobility?" It was very reasonably said to him: "You ought, sir, to set them the example."[s]

So violent a ministry, as that of the bishop of Winchester, could not be of long duration; but its fall proceeded at last from the influence of the church, not from the efforts of the nobles. Edmond, the primate, came to court, attended by many of the other prelates; and represented to the king the pernicious measures embraced by Peter des Roches, the discontents of his people, the

[p] Ibid. p. 265.   [q] Chron. Dunst. vol. i. p. 219.   [r] M. Paris, p. 265.   [s] Ibid. p. 609.

ruin of his affairs; and after requiring the dismission of the minister and his associates, threatened him with excommunication, in case of his refusal. Henry, who knew that an excommunication, so agreeable to the sense of the people, could not fail of producing the most dangerous effects, was obliged to submit: Foreigners were banished: The natives were restored to their place in council:[t] The primate, who was a man of prudence, and who took care to execute the laws and observe the charter of liberties, bore the chief sway in the government.

But the English in vain flattered themselves that they should be long free from the dominion of foreigners. The king, having married Eleanor, daughter of the count of Provence,[u] was surrounded by a great number of strangers from that country, whom he caressed with the fondest affection, and enriched by an imprudent generosity.[w] The bishop of Valence, a prelate of the house of Savoy, and maternal uncle to the queen, was his chief minister, and employed every art to amass wealth for himself and his relations. Peter of Savoy, a brother of the same family, was invested in the honour of Richmond, and received the rich wardship of earl Warrenne: Boniface of Savoy was promoted to the see of Canterbury: Many young ladies were invited over from Provence, and married to the chief noblemen in England, who were the king's wards:[x] And as the source of Henry's bounty began to fail, his Savoyard ministry applied to Rome, and obtained a bull; permitting him to resume all past grants; absolving him from the oath, which he had taken to maintain them; even enjoining him to make such a resumption, and representing those grants as invalid, on account of the prejudice which ensued from them to the Roman pontiff, in whom the superiority of the kingdom was vested.[y] The opposition, made to the intended resumption, prevented it from taking place; but the nation saw the indignities, to which the king was willing to submit, in order to gratify the avidity of his foreign favourites. About the same time, he published in England the sentence of excommunication pronounced against the emperor Frederic, his brother-in-law;[z] and said in excuse, that, being the pope's vassal, he was obliged by his allegiance to obey all the com-

1236.
14th
January.

King's partiality to foreigners.

---

[t] M. Paris, p. 271, 272.   [u] Rymer, vol. i. p. 448. M. Paris, p. 286.   [w] M. Paris, p. 236, 301, 305, 316, 541. M. West. p. 302, 304.   [x] M. Paris, p. 484. M. West. p. 338.   [y] M. Paris, p. 295, 301.   [z] Rymer, vol. i. p. 383.

mands of his holiness. In this weak reign, when any neighbouring potentate insulted the king's dominions, instead of taking revenge for the injury, he complained to the pope as his superior lord, and begged him to give protection to his vassal.[a]

*Griev-
ances.*

The resentment of the English barons rose high at the preference given to foreigners; but no remonstrance or complaint could ever prevail on the king to abandon them, or even to moderate his attachment towards them. After the Provençals and Savoyards might have been supposed pretty well satiated with the dignities and riches which they had acquired, a new set of hungry foreigners were invited over, and shared among them those favours, which the king ought in policy to have conferred on the English nobility, by whom his government could have been supported and defended. His mother, Isabella, who had been unjustly taken by the late king from the count de la Marche, to whom she was betrothed, was no sooner mistress of herself by the death of her husband, than she married that nobleman;[b] and she had born him four sons, Guy, William, Geoffrey, and Aymer, whom she sent over to England, in order to pay a visit to their brother. The good-natured and affectionate disposition of Henry was moved at the sight of such near relations; and he considered neither his own circumstances, nor the inclinations of his people, in the honours and riches which he conferred upon them.[c] Complaints rose as high against the credit of the Gascon as ever they had done against that of the Poictevin and of the Savoyard favourites; and to a nation prejudiced against them, all their measures appeared exceptionable and criminal. Violations of the Great Charter were frequently mentioned; and it is indeed more than probable, that foreigners, ignorant of the laws, and relying on the boundless affections of a weak prince, would, in an age, when a regular administration was not any where known, pay more attention to their present interest than to the liberties of the people. It is reported, that the Poictevins and other strangers, when the laws were at any time appealed to, in opposition to their oppressions, scrupled not to reply, *What did the English laws signify to them? They minded them not.* And as words are often more offensive than actions, this open contempt of the Eng-

1247.

[a] Chron. Dunst. vol. i. p. 150.   [b] Trivet, p. 174.   [c] M. Paris, p. 491. M. West. p. 338. Knyghton, p. 2436.

lish tended much to aggravate the general discontent, and made every act of violence, committed by the foreigners, appear not only an injury, but an affront to them.[d]

I reckon not among the violations of the Great Charter, some arbitrary exertions of prerogative, to which Henry's necessities pushed him, and which, without producing any discontent, were uniformly continued by all his successors, till the last century. As the parliament often refused him supplies, and that in a manner somewhat rude and indecent,[e] he obliged his opulent subjects, particularly the citizens of London, to grant him loans of money; and it is natural to imagine, that the same want of economy, which reduced him to the necessity of borrowing, would prevent him from being very punctual in the repayment.[f] He demanded benevolences or pretended voluntary contributions from his nobility and prelates.[g] He was the first king of England since the conquest, that could fairly be said to lie under the restraint of law; and he was also the first that practised the dispensing power, and employed the clause of *Non-obstante* in his grants and patents. When objections were made to this novelty, he replied, that the pope exercised that authority; and why might not he imitate the example? But the abuse, which the pope made of his dispensing power, in violating the canons of general councils, in invading the privileges and customs of all particular churches, and in usurping on the rights of patrons, was more likely to excite the jealousy of the people, than to reconcile them to a similar practice in their civil government. Roger de Thurkesby, one of the king's justices, was so displeased with the precedent, that he exclaimed, *Alas! what times are we fallen into? Behold, the civil court is corrupted in imitation of the ecclesiastical, and the river is poisoned from that fountain.*

The king's partiality and profuse bounty to his foreign relations, and to their friends and favourites, would have appeared more tolerable to the English, had any thing been done meanwhile for the honour of the nation, or had Henry's enterprizes in foreign countries, been attended with any success or glory to himself or to the public: At least, such military talents in the king would have served to keep his barons in awe, and have given weight and

---

[d] M. Paris, p. 566, 666. Ann. Waverl. p. 214. Chron. Dunst. vol. i. p. 335.
[e] M. Paris, p. 301.   [f] M. Paris, p. 406.   [g] M. Paris, p. 507.

authority to his government. But though he declared war against Lewis IX. in 1242, and made an expedition into Guienne, upon the invitation of his father-in-law, the count de la Marche, who promised to join him with all his forces; he was unsuccessful in his attempts against that great monarch, was worsted at Taillebourg, was deserted by his allies, lost what remained to him of Poictou, and was obliged to return, with loss of honour, into England.[h] The Gascon nobility were attached to the English government; because the distance of their sovereign allowed them to remain in a state of almost total independance: And they claimed, some time after, Henry's protection against an invasion, which the king of Castile made upon that territory. Henry returned into Guienne, and was more successful in this expedition; but he thereby involved himself and his nobility in an enormous debt, which both encreased their discontents, and exposed him to greater danger from their enterprizes.[i]

Want of economy and an ill-judged liberality were Henry's great defects; and his debts, even before this expedition, had become so troublesome, that he sold all his plate and jewels, in order to discharge them. When this expedient was first proposed to him, he asked, where he should find purchasers? It was replied, the citizens of London. *On my word,* said he, *if the treasury of Augustus were brought to sale, the citizens are able to be the purchasers: These clowns, who assume to themselves the name of barons, abound in every thing, while we are reduced to necessities.*[k] And he was thenceforth observed to be more forward and greedy in his exactions upon the citizens.[l]

Ecclesias-tical griev-ances. But the grievances, which the English during this reign had reason to complain of in the civil government, seem to have been still less burthensome than those which they suffered from the usurpations and exactions of the court of Rome. On the death of Langton in 1228, the monks of Christ-church elected Walter de Hemesham, one of their own body, for his successor: But as Henry refused to confirm the election, the pope, at his desire, annulled it;[m] and immediately appointed Richard, chancellor of Lincoln, for archbishop, without waiting for a new election. On the death of Richard in 1231, the monks elected Ralph de Neville bishop of

1253.

---

[h] M. Paris, p. 393, 394, 398, 399, 405. W. Heming. p. 574. Chron. Dunst. vol. i. p. 153.   [i] M. Paris, p. 614.   [k] M. Paris, p. 501.   [l] M. Paris, p. 501, 507, 518, 578, 606, 625, 648.   [m] M. Paris, p. 244.

CHAPTER XII

Chichester; and though Henry was much pleased with the election, the pope, who thought that prelate too much attached to the crown, assumed the power of annulling his election.[n] He rejected two clergymen more, whom the monks had successively chosen; and he at last told them, that, if they would elect Edmond, treasurer of the church of Salisbury, he would confirm their choice; and his nomination was complied with. The pope had the prudence to appoint both times very worthy primates; but men could not forbear observing his intention of thus drawing gradually to himself the right of bestowing that important dignity.

The avarice, however, more than the ambition of the see of Rome, seems to have been in this age the ground of general complaint. The papal ministers, finding a vast stock of power amassed by their predecessors, were desirous of turning it to immediate profit, which they enjoyed at home, rather than of enlarging their authority in distant countries, where they never intended to reside. Every thing was become venal in the Romish tribunals; simony was openly practised; no favours and even no justice could be obtained without a bribe; the highest bidder was sure to have the preference, without regard either to the merits of the person or of the cause; and besides the usual perversions of right in the decision of controversies, the pope openly assumed an absolute and uncontroled authority of setting aside, by the plenitude of his apostolic power, all particular rules and all privileges of patrons, churches, and convents. On pretence of remedying these abuses, pope Honorius, in 1226, complaining of the poverty of his see as the source of all grievances, demanded from every cathedral two of the best prebends, and from every convent two monks' portions, to be set apart as a perpetual and settled revenue of the papal crown: But all men being sensible, that the revenue would continue for ever, the abuses immediately return, his demand was unanimously rejected. About three years after, the pope demanded and obtained the tenth of all ecclesiastical revenues, which he levied in a very oppressive manner; requiring payment before the clergy had drawn their rents or tythes, and sending about usurers, who advanced them the money at exorbitant interest. In the year 1240, Otho, the legate, having in vain attempted the clergy in a body,

[n] Ibid. p. 254.

obtained separately, by intrigues and menaces, large sums from the prelates and convents, and on his departure is said to have carried more money out of the kingdom than he left in it. This experiment was renewed four years after with success by Martin the nuncio, who brought from Rome powers of suspending and excommunicating all clergymen, that refused to comply with his demands. The king, who relied on the pope for the support of his tottering authority, never failed to countenance those exactions.

Meanwhile, all the chief benefices of the kingdom were conferred on Italians; great numbers of that nation were sent over at one time to be provided for; non-residence and pluralities were carried to an enormous height; Mansel, the king's chaplain, is computed to have held at once seven hundred ecclesiastical livings; and the abuses became so evident as to be palpable to the blindness of superstition itself. The people, entering into associations, rose against the Italian clergy; pillaged their barns; wasted their lands; insulted the persons of such of them as they found in the kingdom;[o] and when the justices made enquiry into the authors of this disorder, the guilt was found to involve so many, and those of such high rank, that it passed unpunished. At last, when Innocent IV. in 1245, called a general council at Lyons, in order to excommunicate the emperor Frederic, the king and nobility sent over agents to complain before the council, of the rapacity of the Romish church. They represented, among many other grievances, that the benefices of the Italian clergy in England had been estimated, and were found to amount to 60,000 marks[p] a year, a sum which exceeded the annual revenue of the crown itself.[q] They obtained only an evasive answer from the pope; but as mention had been made before the council, of the feudal subjection of England to the see of Rome, the English agents, at whose head was Roger Bigod earl of Norfolk, exclaimed against the pretension, and insisted, that king John had no right, without the consent of

[o] Rymer, vol. i. p. 323. M. Paris, p. 255, 257.   [p] Innocent's bull in Rymer, vol. i. p. 471, says only 50,000 marks a year.   [q] M. Paris, p. 451. The customs were part of Henry's revenue, and amounted to 6000 pounds a year: They were at first small sums paid by the merchants for the use of the king's warehouses, measures, weights, &c. See Gilbert's history of the Exch. p. 214.

his barons, to subject the kingdom to so ignominious a servitude.[r] The popes indeed, afraid of carrying matters too far against England, seem thenceforth to have little insisted on that pretension.

This check, received at the council of Lyons, was not able to stop the court of Rome in its rapacity: Innocent exacted the revenues of all vacant benefices, the twentieth of all ecclesiastical revenues without exception; the third of such as exceeded a hundred marks a year; the half of such as were possessed by non-residents.[s] He claimed the goods of all intestate clergymen;[t] he pretended a title to inherit all money gotten by usury; he levied benevolences upon the people; and when the king, contrary to his usual practice, prohibited these exactions, he threatened to pronounce against him the same censures, which he had emitted against the emperor Frederic.[u]

But the most oppressive expedient, employed by the pope, was the embarking of Henry in a project for the conquest of Naples, or Sicily on this side the Fare, as it was called; an enterprize, which threw much dishonour on the king, and involved him, during some years, in great trouble and expence. The Romish church, taking advantage of favourable incidents, had reduced the kingdom of Sicily to the same state of feudal vassalage, which she pretended to extend over England, and which, by reason of the distance, as well as high spirit of this latter kingdom, she was not able to maintain. After the death of the emperor, Frederic II. the succession of Sicily devolved to Conradine, grandson of that monarch; and Mainfroy, his natural son, under pretence of governing the kingdom during the minority of the prince, had formed a scheme of establishing his own authority. Pope Innocent, who had carried on violent war against the emperor, Frederic, and had endeavoured to dispossess him of his Italian dominions, still continued hostilities against his grandson; but being disappointed in all his schemes by the activity and artifices of Mainfroy, he found, that his own force alone was not sufficient to bring to a happy issue so great an enterprize. He pretended to dispose of the Sicilian crown, both as superior lord of that particular kingdom, and as

1255.

[r] M. Paris, p. 460.   [s] M. Paris, p. 480. Ann. Burt. p. 305, 373.   [t] M. Paris, p. 474.   [u] M. Paris, p. 476.

vicar of Christ, to whom all kingdoms of the earth were subjected; and he made a tender of it to Richard earl of Cornwal, whose immense riches, he flattered himself, would be able to support the military operations against Mainfroy. As Richard had the prudence to refuse the present,[w] he applied to the king, whose levity and thoughtless disposition gave Innocent more hopes of success; and he offered him the crown of Sicily for his second son, Edmond.[x] Henry, allured by so magnificent a present, without reflecting on the consequences, without consulting either with his brother or the parliament, accepted of the insidious proposal; and gave the pope unlimited credit to expend whatever sums he thought necessary for compleating the conquest of Sicily. Innocent, who was engaged by his own interests to wage war with Mainfroy, was glad to carry on his enterprizes at the expence of his ally: Alexander IV. who succeeded him in the papal throne, continued the same policy: And Henry was surprized to find himself on a sudden involved in an immense debt, which he had never been consulted in contracting. The sum already amounted to 135,541 marks beside interest;[y] and he had the prospect, if he answered this demand, of being soon loaded with more exorbitant expences; if he refused it, of both incurring the pope's displeasure, and losing the crown of Sicily, which he hoped soon to have the glory of fixing on the head of his son.

He applied to the parliament for supply; and that he might be sure not to meet with opposition, he sent no writs to the more refractory barons: But even those who were summoned, sensible of the ridiculous cheat, imposed by the pope, determined not to lavish their money on such chimerical projects; and making a pretext of the absence of their brethren, they refused to take the king's demands into consideration.[z] In this extremity the clergy were his only resource; and as both their temporal and spiritual sovereign concurred in loading them, they were ill able to defend themselves against this united authority.

The pope published a crusade for the conquest of Sicily; and required every one, who had taken the cross against the Infidels, or had vowed to advance money for that service, to support the war

---

[w] M. Paris, p. 650.   [x] Rymer, vol. i. p. 502, 512, 530. M. Paris, p. 599, 613.   [y] Rymer, vol. i. p. 587. Chron. Dunst. vol. i. p. 319.   [z] M. Paris, p. 614.

CHAPTER XII

against Mainfroy, a more terrible enemy, as he pretended, to the
Christian faith than any Saracen.[a] He levied a tenth on all ecclesiastical benefices in England for three years; and gave orders
to excommunicate all bishops, who made not punctual payment.
He granted to the king the goods of intestate clergymen; the revenues of vacant benefices; the revenues of all non-residents.[b] But
these taxations, being levied by some rule, were deemed less grievous, than another imposition, which arose from the suggestion of
the bishop of Hereford, and which might have opened the door to
endless and intolerable abuses.

This prelate, who resided at the court of Rome by a deputation
from the English church, drew bills of different values, but
amounting on the whole to 150,540 marks, on all the bishops and
abbots of the kingdom; and granted these bills to Italian merchants, who, it was pretended, had advanced money for the service
of the war against Mainfroy.[c] As there was no likelihood of the
English prelates' submitting, without compulsion, to such an extraordinary demand, Rustand, the legate, was charged with the
commission of employing authority to that purpose; and he summoned an assembly of the bishops and abbots, whom he acquainted with the pleasure of the pope and of the king. Great were
the surprize and indignation of the assembly: The bishop of
Worcester exclaimed, that he would lose his life rather than comply: The bishop of London said, that the pope and king were more
powerful than he; but if his mitre were taken off his head, he
would clap on a helmet in its place.[d] The legate was no less violent
on the other hand; and he told the assembly, in plain terms, that
all ecclesiastical benefices were the property of the pope, and he
might dispose of them, either in whole or in part, as he saw
proper.[e] In the end, the bishops and abbots, being threatened with
excommunication, which made all their revenues fall into the
king's hands, were obliged to submit to the exaction: And the only
mitigation, which the legate allowed them, was, that the tenths,
already granted, should be accepted as a partial payment of the
bills. But the money was still insufficient for the pope's purpose:
The conquest of Sicily was as remote as ever: The demands which

[a] Rymer, vol. i. p. 547, 548, &c.   [b] Rymer, vol. i. p. 597, 598.   [c] M. Paris,
p. 612, 628. Chron. T. Wykes, p. 54.   [d] M. Paris, p. 614.   [e] M. Paris,
p. 619.

came from Rome were endless: Pope Alexander became so urgent a creditor, that he sent over a legate to England; threatening the kingdom with an interdict, and the king with excommunication, if the arrears, which he pretended to be due to him, were not instantly remitted.[f] And at last, Henry, sensible of the cheat, began to think of breaking off the agreement, and of resigning into the pope's hands that crown, which, it was not intended by Alexander, that he or his family should ever enjoy.[g]

Earl of Cornwal elected king of the Romans.

The earl of Cornwal had now reason to value himself on his foresight, in refusing the fraudulent bargain with Rome, and in preferring the solid honours of an opulent and powerful prince of the blood of England, to the empty and precarious glory of a foreign dignity. But he had not always firmness sufficient to adhere to this resolution: His vanity and ambition prevailed at last over his prudence and his avarice; and he was engaged in an enterprize no less expensive and vexatious than that of his brother, and not attended with much greater probability of success. The immense opulence of Richard having made the German princes cast their eye on him as a candidate for the empire; he was tempted to expend vast sums of money on his election, and he succeeded so far as to be chosen king of the Romans, which seemed to render his succession infallible to the imperial throne. He went over to Germany, and carried out of the kingdom no less a sum than seven hundred thousand marks, if we may credit the account given by some ancient authors,[h] which is probably much exaggerated.[i] His money, while it lasted, procured him friends and partizans: But it was soon drained from him by the avidity of the German princes;

[f] Rymer, vol. i. p. 624. M. Paris. p. 648.   [g] Rymer, vol. i. p. 630.   [h] M. Paris, p. 638. The same author, a few pages before, makes Richard's treasures amount to little more than half the sum, p. 634. The king's dissipations and expences, throughout his whole reign, according to the same author, had amounted only to about 940,000 marks, p. 638.   [i] The sums mentioned by ancient authors, who were almost all monks, are often improbable, and never consistent. But we know from an infallible authority, the public remonstrance to the council of Lyons, that the king's revenues were below 60,000 marks a year: His brother therefore could never have been master of 700,000 marks; especially as he did not sell his estates in England, as we learn from the same author: And we hear afterwards of his ordering all his woods to be cut, in order to satisfy the rapacity of the German princes: His son succeeded to the earldom of Cornwal and his other revenues.

CHAPTER XII

and, having no personal or family connexions in that country, and no solid foundation of power, he found at last, that he had lavished away the frugality of a whole life, in order to procure a splendid title, and that his absence from England, joined to the weakness of his brother's government, gave reins to the factious and turbulent dispositions of the English barons, and involved his own country and family in great calamities.

The successful revolt of the nobility from king John, and their imposing on him and his successors limitations of their royal power, had made them feel their own weight and importance, had set a dangerous precedent of resistance, and being followed by a long minority, had impoverished, as well as weakened that crown, which they were at last induced, from the fear of worse consequences, to re-place on the head of young Henry. In the king's situation, either great abilities and vigour were requisite to over-awe the barons, or great caution and reserve to give them no pretence for complaints; and it must be confessed, that this prince was possessed of neither of these talents. He had not prudence to chuse right measures, he wanted even that constancy, which sometimes gives weight to wrong ones; he was entirely devoted to his favourites, who were always foreigners; he lavished on them without discretion his diminished revenue; and finding, that his barons indulged their disposition towards tyranny, and observed not to their own vassals the same rules, which they had imposed on the crown, he was apt, in his administration, to neglect all the salutary articles of the Great Charter; which he remarked to be so little regarded by his nobility. This conduct had extremely lessened his authority in the kingdom; had multiplied complaints against him; and had frequently exposed him to affronts, and even to dangerous attempts upon his prerogative. In the year 1244, when he desired a supply from parliament, the barons, complaining of the frequent breaches of the Great Charter, and of the many fruitless applications which they had formerly made for the redress of this and other grievances, demanded in return, that he should give them the nomination of the great justiciary and of the chancellor, to whose hands chiefly the administration of justice was committed: And, if we may credit the historian,[k] they had formed the plan

Discontents of the barons.

[k] M. Paris, p. 432.

of other limitations, as well as of associations to maintain them, which would have reduced the king to be an absolute cypher, and have held the crown in perpetual pupillage and dependance. The king, to satisfy them, would agree to nothing but a renewal of the charter, and a general permission to excommunicate all the violaters of it: And he received no supply, except a scutage of twenty shillings on each knight's fee for the marriage of his eldest daughter to the king of Scotland; a burthen, which was expressly annexed to their feudal tenures.

Four years after, in a full parliament, when Henry demanded a new supply, he was openly reproached with the breach of his word, and the frequent violations of the charter. He was asked, whether he did not blush to desire any aid from his people, whom he professedly hated and despised, to whom on all occasions he preferred aliens and foreigners, and who groaned under the oppressions, which he either permitted or exercised over them. He was told, that, besides disparaging his nobility by forcing them to contract unequal and mean marriages with strangers, no rank of men was so low as to escape vexations from him or his ministers; that even the victuals consumed in his household, the clothes which himself and his servants wore, still more the wine which they used, were all taken by violence from the lawful owners, and no compensation was ever made them for the injury; that foreign merchants, to the great prejudice and infamy of the kingdom, shunned the English harbours, as if they were possessed by pirates, and the commerce with all nations was thus cut off by these acts of violence; that loss was added to loss, and injury to injury, while the merchants, who had been despoiled of their goods, were also obliged to carry them at their own charge to whatever place the king was pleased to appoint them; that even the poor fishermen on the coast could not escape his oppressions and those of his courtiers; and finding that they had not full liberty to dispose of their commodities in the English market, were frequently constrained to carry them to foreign ports, and to hazard all the perils of the ocean, rather than those which awaited them from his oppressive emissaries; and that his very religion was a ground of complaint to his subjects, while they observed, that the waxen tapers and splendid silks, employed in so many useful processions, were the spoils

CHAPTER XII

which he had forcibly ravished from the true owners.[l] Throughout this remonstrance, in which the complaints, derived from an abuse of the ancient right of purveyance, may be supposed to be somewhat exaggerated, there appears a strange mixture of regal tyranny in the practices which gave rise to it, and of aristocratical liberty or rather licentiousness in the expressions employed by the parliament. But a mixture of this kind is observable in all the ancient feudal governments; and both of them proved equally hurtful to the people.

As the king, in answer to their remonstrance, gave the parliament only good words and fair promises, attended with the most humble submissions, which they had often found deceitful, he obtained at that time no supply; and therefore, in the year 1253, when he found himself again under the necessity of applying to parliament, he had provided a new pretence, which he deemed infallible, and taking the vow of a Crusade, he demanded their assistance in that pious enterprize.[m] The parliament, however, for some time hesitated to comply; and the ecclesiastical order sent a deputation consisting of four prelates, the primate, and the bishops of Winchester, Salisbury, and Carlisle, in order to remonstrate with him on his frequent violations of their privileges, the oppressions with which he had loaded them and all his subjects,[n] and the uncanonical and forced elections, which were made to vacant dignities. "It is true," replied the king, "I have been somewhat faulty in this particular: I obtruded you my lord of Canterbury, upon your see: I was obliged to employ both entreaties and menaces, my lord of Winchester, to have you elected: My proceedings, I confess, were very irregular, my lords of Salisbury and Carlisle, when I raised you from the lowest stations to your present dignities: I am determined henceforth to correct these abuses; and it will also become you, in order to make a thorough reformation, to resign your present benefices; and try to enter again in a more regular and canonical manner."[o] The bishops, surprized at these unexpected sarcasms, replied, that the question was not at present how to correct past errors, but to avoid them for the future. The

[l] M. Paris, p. 498. See farther, p. 578. M. West. p. 348.   [m] M. Paris, p. 518, 558, 568. Chron. Dunst. vol. i. p. 293.   [n] M. Paris, p. 568.   [o] M. Paris, p. 579.

king promised redress both of ecclesiastical and civil grievances; and the parliament in return agreed to grant him a supply, a tenth of the ecclesiastical benefices, and a scutage of three marks on each knight's fee: But as they had experienced his frequent breach of promise, they required, that he should ratify the Great Charter in a manner still more authentic and more solemn than any which he had hitherto employed. All the prelates and abbots were assembled: They held burning tapers in their hands: The Great Charter was read before them: They denounced the sentence of excommunication against every one who should thenceforth violate that fundamental law: They threw their tapers on the ground, and exclaimed, *May the soul of every one, who incurs this sentence, so stink and corrupt in Hell!* The king bore a part in this ceremony; and subjoined: "So help me God, I will keep all these articles inviolate, as I am a man, as I am a christian, as I am a knight, and as I am a king crowned and anointed."[p] Yet was the tremendous ceremony no sooner finished, than his favourites, abusing his weakness, made him return to the same arbitrary and irregular administration; and the reasonable expectations of his people were thus perpetually eluded and disappointed.[q]

1258.
Simon de Mount-fort earl of Lei-cester.
All these imprudent and illegal measures afforded a pretence to Simon de Mountfort, earl of Leicester, to attempt an innovation in the government, and to wrest the scepter from the feeble and irresolute hand which held it. This nobleman was a younger son of that Simon de Mountfort, who had conducted with such valour and renown the Crusade against the Albigenses, and who, though he tarnished his famous exploits by cruelty and ambition, had left a name very precious to all the bigots of that age, particularly to the ecclesiastics. A large inheritance in England fell by succession to this family; but as the elder brother enjoyed still more opulent possessions in France, and could not perform fealty to two masters, he transferred his right to Simon, his younger brother, who came over to England, did homage for his lands, and was raised to the dignity of earl of Leicester. In the year 1238, he espoused Eleanor dowager of William earl of Pembroke, and sister to the king;[r] but the marriage of this princess with a subject and a foreigner, though

[p] M. Paris, p. 580. Ann. Burt. p. 323. Ann. Waverl. p. 210. W. Heming. p. 571. M. West. p. 353. [q] M. Paris, p. 597, 608. [r] Ibid. p. 314.

CHAPTER XII

contracted with Henry's consent, was loudly complained of by the earl of Cornwal, and all the barons of England; and Leicester was supported against their violence, by the king's favour and authority alone.[s] But he had no sooner established himself in his possessions and dignities, than he acquired, by insinuation and address, a strong interest with the nation, and gained equally the affections of all orders of men. He lost, however, the friendship of Henry from the usual levity and fickleness of that prince; he was banished the court; he was recalled; he was entrusted with the command of Guienne,[t] where he did good service and acquired honour; he was again disgraced by the king, and his banishment from court seemed now final and irrevocable. Henry called him traitor to his face; Leicester gave him the lye, and told him, that, if he were not his sovereign, he would soon make him repent of that insult. Yet was this quarrel accommodated either from the good-nature or timidity of the king; and Leicester was again admitted into some degree of favour and authority. But as this nobleman was become too great to preserve an entire complaisance to Henry's humours, and to act in subserviency to his other minions; he found more advantage in cultivating his interest with the public, and in inflaming the general discontents, which prevailed against the administration. He filled every place with complaints against the infringement of the Great Charter, the acts of violence committed on the people, the combination between the pope and the king in their tyranny and extortions, Henry's neglect of his native subjects and barons; and though himself a foreigner, he was more loud than any in representing the indignity of submitting to the dominion of foreigners. By his hypocritical pretensions to devotion, he gained the favour of the zealots and clergy: By his seeming concern for public good, he acquired the affections of the public: And besides the private friendships, which he had cultivated with the barons, his animosity against the favourites created an union of interests between him and that powerful order.

A recent quarrel, which broke out between Leicester and William de Valence, Henry's half brother, and chief favourite, brought matters to extremity,[u] and determined the former to give full scope to his bold and unbounded ambition, which the laws and

[s] Ibid. p. 315.   [t] Rymer, vol. i. p. 459, 513.   [u] M. Paris, p. 649.

the king's authority had hitherto with difficulty restrained. He secretly called a meeting of the most considerable barons, particularly Humphrey de Bohun, high constable, Roger Bigod, earl mareschal, and the earls of Warwic and Glocester; men, who by their family and possessions stood in the first rank of the English nobility. He represented to this company the necessity of reforming the state, and of putting the execution of the laws into other hands than those which had hitherto appeared, from repeated experience, so unfit for the charge with which they were entrusted. He exaggerated the oppressions exercised against the lower orders of the state, the violations of the barons' privileges, the continued depredations made on the clergy; and in order to aggravate the enormity of this conduct, he appealed to the Great Charter, which Henry had so often ratified, and which was calculated to prevent for ever the return of those intolerable grievances. He magnified the generosity of their ancestors, who, at a great expence of blood, had extorted that famous concession from the crown; but lamented their own degeneracy, who allowed so important an advantage, once obtained, to be wrested from them by a weak prince and by insolent strangers. And he insisted, that the king's word, after so many submissions and fruitless promises on his part, could no longer be relied on; and that nothing but his absolute inability to violate national privileges could henceforth ensure the regular observance of them.

These topics, which were founded in truth, and suited so well the sentiments of the company, had the desired effect, and the barons embraced a resolution of redressing the public grievances, by taking into their own hands the administration of government. Henry having summoned a parliament, in expectation of receiving supplies for his Sicilian project, the barons appeared in the hall, clad in complete armour, and with their swords by their side: The king on his entry, struck with the unusual appearance, asked them what was their purpose, and whether they pretended to make him their prisoner?[w] Roger Bigod replied in the name of the rest, that he was not their prisoner, but their sovereign; that they even intended to grant him large supplies, in order to fix his son on the throne of Sicily; that they only expected some return for this ex-

[w] Annal. Theokesbury.

pence and service; and that, as he had frequently made submissions to the parliament, had acknowledged his past errors, and had still allowed himself to be carried into the same path, which gave them such just reason of complaint, he must now yield to more strict regulations, and confer authority on those who were able and willing to redress the national grievances. Henry, partly allured by the hopes of supply, partly intimidated by the union and martial appearance of the barons, agreed to their demand; and promised to summon another parliament at Oxford, in order to digest the new plan of government, and to elect the persons, who were to be entrusted with the chief authority.

This parliament, which the royalists, and even the nation, from experience of the confusions that attended its measures, afterwards denominated the *mad parliament,* met on the day appointed; and as all the barons brought along with them their military vassals, and appeared with an armed force, the king, who had taken no precautions against them, was in reality a prisoner in their hands, and was obliged to submit to all the terms which they were pleased to impose upon him. Twelve barons were selected from among the king's ministers; twelve more were chosen by parliament: To these twenty-four, unlimited authority was granted to reform the state; and the king himself took an oath, that he would maintain whatever ordinances they should think proper to enact for that purpose.[x] Leicester was at the head of this supreme council, to which the legislative power was thus in reality transferred; and all their measures were taken by his secret influence and direction. Their first step bore a specious appearance, and seemed well calculated for the end, which they professed to be the object of all these innovations: They ordered that four knights should be chosen by each county; that they should make enquiry into the grievances of which their neighbourhood had reason to complain, and should attend the ensuing parliament, in order to give information to that assembly of the state of their particular counties:[y] A nearer approach to our present constitution than had been made by the barons in the reign of king John, when the knights were only appointed to meet in their several counties, and there to draw up

11 June. Provisions of Oxford.

---

[x] Rymer, vol. i. p. 655. Chron. Dunst. vol. i. p. 334. Knyghton, p. 2445.
[y] M. Paris, p. 657. Addit. p. 140. Ann. Burt. p. 412.

a detail of their grievances. Meanwhile the twenty-four barons proceeded to enact some regulations, as a redress of such grievances as were supposed to be sufficiently notorious. They ordered, that three sessions of parliament should be regularly held every year, in the months of February, June, and October; that a new sheriff should be annually elected by the votes of the freeholders in each county;[z] that the sheriffs should have no power of fining the barons who did not attend their courts, or the circuits of the justiciaries; that no heirs should be committed to the wardship of foreigners, and no castles intrusted to their custody; and that no new warrens or forests should be created, nor the revenues of any counties or hundreds be let to farm. Such were the regulations which the twenty-four barons established at Oxford, for the redress of public grievances.

But the earl of Leicester and his associates, having advanced so far to satisfy the nation, instead of continuing in this popular course, or granting the king that supply which they had promised him, immediately provided for the extension and continuance of their own authority. They rouzed anew the popular clamour, which had long prevailed against foreigners; and they fell with the utmost violence on the king's half-brothers, who were supposed to be the authors of all national grievances, and whom Henry had no longer any power to protect. The four brothers, sensible of their danger, took to flight, with an intention of making their escape out of the kingdom; they were eagerly pursued by the barons; Aymer, one of the brothers, who had been elected to the see of Winchester, took shelter in his episcopal palace, and carried the others along with him; they were surrounded in that place, and threatened to be dragged out by force, and to be punished for their crimes and misdemeanors; and the king, pleading the sacredness of an ecclesiastical sanctuary, was glad to extricate them from this danger by banishing them the kingdom. In this act of violence, as well as in the former usurpations of the barons, the queen and her uncles were thought to have secretly concurred; being jealous of the credit acquired by the brothers, which, they found, had eclipsed and annihilated their own.

[z] Chron. Dunst. vol. i. p. 336.

CHAPTER XII

But the subsequent proceedings of the twenty-four barons were sufficient to open the eyes of the nation, and to prove their intention of reducing for ever both the king and the people under the arbitrary power of a very narrow aristocracy, which must at last have terminated either in anarchy, or in a violent usurpation and tyranny. They pretended, that they had not yet digested all the regulations necessary for the reformation of the state, and for the redress of grievances; and that they must still retain their power, till that great purpose were thoroughly effected: In other words, that they must be perpetual governors, and must continue to reform, till they were pleased to abdicate their authority. They formed an association among themselves, and swore that they would stand by each other with their lives and fortunes: They displaced all the chief officers of the crown, the justiciary, the chancellor, the treasurer; and advanced either themselves or their own creatures in their place: Even the offices of the king's household were disposed of at their pleasure: The government of all the castles was put into hands in whom they found reason to confide: And the whole power of the state being thus transferred to them, they ventured to impose an oath; by which all the subjects were obliged to swear, under the penalty of being declared public enemies, that they would obey and execute all the regulations, both known and unknown, of the twenty-four barons: And all this, for the greater glory of God, the honour of the church, the service of the king, and the advantage of the kingdom.[a] No one dared to withstand this tyrannical authority: Prince Edward himself, the king's eldest son, a youth of eighteen, who began to give indications of that great and manly spirit, which appeared throughout the whole course of his life, was, after making some opposition, constrained to take that oath, which really deposed his father and his family from sovereign authority.[b] Earl Warrenne was the last person in the kingdom, that could be brought to give the confederated barons this mark of submission.

But the twenty-four barons, not content with the usurpation of the royal power, introduced an innovation in the constitution of parliament, which was of the utmost importance. They ordained,

Usurpations of the barons.

[a] Chron. T. Wykes, p. 52. [b] Ann. Burt. p. 411.

that this assembly should chuse a committee of twelve persons, who should, in the intervals of the sessions, possess the authority of the whole parliament, and should attend on a summons the person of the king, in all his motions. But so powerful were these barons, that this regulation was also submitted to; the whole government was overthrown or fixed on new foundations; and the monarchy was totally subverted, without its being possible for the king to strike a single stroke in defence of the constitution against the newly erected oligarchy.

1259.   The report, that the king of the Romans intended to pay a visit to England, gave alarm to the ruling barons, who dreaded lest the extensive influence and established authority of that prince would be employed to restore the prerogatives of his family, and overturn their plan of government.[c] They sent over the bishop of Worcester, who met him at St. Omars; asked him, in the name of the barons, the reason of his journey, and how long he intended to stay in England; and insisted, that, before he entered the kingdom, he should swear to observe the regulations established at Oxford. On Richard's refusal to take this oath, they prepared to resist him as a public enemy; they fitted out a fleet, assembled an army, and exciting the inveterate prejudices of the people against foreigners, from whom they had suffered so many oppressions, spread the report that Richard, attended by a number of strangers, meant to restore by force the authority of his exiled brothers, and to violate all the securities provided for public liberty. The king of the Romans was at last obliged to submit to the terms required of him.[d]

But the barons, in proportion to their continuance in power, began gradually to lose that popularity, which had assisted them in obtaining it; and men repined, that regulations, which were occasionally established, for the reformation of the state, were likely to become perpetual, and to subvert entirely the ancient constitution. They were apprehensive, lest the power of the nobles, always oppressive, should now exert itself without controul, by removing the counterpoise of the crown; and their fears were increased by some new edicts of the barons, which were plainly calculated to procure to themselves an impunity in all their violences. They appointed, that the circuits of the itinerant justices, the sole check on their

[c] M. Paris, p. 661.   [d] Ibid. p. 661, 662. Chron. T. Wykes, p. 53.

arbitrary conduct, should be held only once in seven years; and
men easily saw, that a remedy, which returned after such long
intervals, against an oppressive power, which was perpetual,
would prove totally insignificant and useless.[e] The cry became loud
in the nation, that the barons should finish their intended regulations. The knights of the shires, who seem now to have been
pretty regularly assembled, and sometimes in a separate house,
made remonstrances against the slowness of their proceedings.
They represented, that, though the king had performed all the
conditions required of him, the barons had hitherto done nothing
for the public good, and had only been careful to promote their
own private advantage, and to make inroads on royal authority;
and they even appealed to prince Edward, and claimed his interposition for the interests of the nation, and the reformation of the
government.[f] The prince replied, that, though it was from constraint, and contrary to his private sentiments, he had sworn to
maintain the provisions of Oxford, he was determined to observe
his oath: But he sent a message to the barons, requiring them to
bring their undertaking to a speedy conclusion, and fulfil their
engagements to the public: Otherwise, he menaced them, that, at
the expence of his life, he would oblige them to do their duty, and
would shed the last drop of his blood in promoting the interests,
and satisfying the just wishes of the nation.[g]

The barons, urged by so pressing a necessity, published at last
a new code of ordinances for the reformation of the state:[h] But the
expectations of the people were extremely disappointed, when
they found, that these consisted only of some trivial alterations in
the municipal law; and still more, when the barons pretended, that
the task was not yet finished, and that they must farther prolong
their authority, in order to bring the work of reformation to the
desired period. The current of popularity was now much turned to
the side of the crown; and the barons had little to rely on for their
support, besides the private influence and power of their families,
which, though exorbitant, was likely to prove inferior to the combination of king and people. Even this basis of power was daily
weakened by their intestine jealousies and animosities; their an-

---

[e] M. Paris, p. 667. Trivet, p. 209.   [f] Annal. Burt. p. 427.   [g] Annal. Burt.
p. 427.   [h] Ibid. p. 428, 439.

cient and inveterate quarrels broke out when they came to share the spoils of the crown; and the rivalship between the earls of Leicester and Glocester, the chief leaders among them, began to disjoint the whole confederacy. The latter, more moderate in his pretensions, was desirous of stopping or retarding the career of the barons' usurpations; but the former, enraged at the opposition which he met with in his own party, pretended to throw up all concern in English affairs; and he retired into France.[i]

The kingdom of France, the only state with which England had any considerable intercourse, was at this time governed by Lewis IX. a prince of the most singular character that is to be met with in all the records of history. This monarch united, to the mean and abject superstition of a monk, all the courage and magnanimity of the greatest hero; and, what may be deemed more extraordinary, the justice and integrity of a disinterested patriot, the mildness and humanity of an accomplished philosopher. So far from taking advantage of the divisions among the English, or attempting to expel those dangerous rivals from the provinces, which they still possessed in France; he had entertained many scruples with regard to the sentence of attainder pronounced against the king's father, had even expressed some intention of restoring the other provinces, and was only prevented from taking that imprudent resolution, by the united remonstrances of his own barons, who represented the extreme danger of such a measure,[k] and, what had a greater influence on Lewis, the justice of punishing by a legal sentence the barbarity and felony of John. Whenever this prince interposed in English affairs, it was always with an intention of composing the differences between the king and his nobility; he recommended to both parties every peaceable and reconciling measure; and he used all his authority with the earl of Leicester, his native subject, to bend him to a compliance with Henry. He made a treaty with England, at a time when the distractions of that kingdom were at the greatest height, and when the king's authority was totally annihilated; and the terms, which he granted, might, even in a more prosperous state of their affairs, be deemed reasonable and advantageous to the English. He yielded up some territories which had been conquered from Poictou and Guienne; he

20th
May.

[i] Chron. Dunst. vol. i. p. 348.   [k] M. Paris, p. 604.

ensured the peaceable possession of the latter province to Henry; he agreed to pay that prince a large sum of money; and he only required that the king should, in return, make a final cession of Normandy, and the other provinces, which he could never entertain any hopes of recovering by force of arms.[l] This cession was ratified by Henry, by his two sons, and two daughters, and by the king of the Romans and his three sons: Leicester alone, either moved by a vain arrogance, or desirous to ingratiate himself with the English populace, protested against the deed, and insisted on the right, however distant, which might accrue to his consort.[m] Lewis saw in his obstinacy the unbounded ambition of the man; and as the barons insisted, that the money, due by treaty, should be at their disposal, not at Henry's, he also saw, and probably with regret, the low condition, to which this monarch, who had more erred from weakness than from any bad intentions, was reduced by the turbulence of his own subjects.

But the situation of Henry soon after wore a more favourable aspect. The twenty-four barons had now enjoyed the sovereign power near three years; and had visibly employed it, not for the reformation of the state, which was their first pretence, but for the aggrandizement of themselves and of their families. The breach of trust was apparent to all the world: Every order of men felt it, and murmured against it: The dissensions among the barons themselves, which encreased the evil, made also the remedy more obvious and easy: And the secret desertion in particular of the earl of Glocester to the crown, seemed to promise Henry certain success in any attempt to resume his authority. Yet durst he not take that step, so reconcilable both to justice and policy, without making a previous application to Rome, and desiring an absolution from his oaths and engagements.[n]

The pope was at this time much dissatisfied with the conduct of the barons; who, in order to gain the favour of the people and clergy of England, had expelled all the Italian ecclesiastics, had confiscated their benefices, and seemed determined to maintain the liberties and privileges of the English church, in which the rights of patronage, belonging to their own families, were in-

1261.

---

[l] Rymer, vol. i. p. 675. M. Paris, p. 566. Chron. T. Wykes, p. 53. Trivet, p. 208. M. West. p. 371.   [m] Chron. T. Wykes, p. 53.   [n] Ann. Burt. p. 389.

cluded. The extreme animosity of the English clergy against the Italians was also a source of his disgust to this order; and an attempt, which had been made by them for farther liberty and greater independance on the civil power, was therefore less acceptable to the court of Rome.[o] About the same time, that the barons at Oxford had annihilated the prerogatives of the monarchy, the clergy met in a synod at Merton, and passed several ordinances, which were no less calculated to promote their own grandeur at the expence of the crown. They decreed, that it was unlawful to try ecclesiastics by secular judges; that the clergy were not to regard any prohibitions from civil courts; that lay-patrons had no right to confer spiritual benefices; that the magistrate was obliged, without farther enquiry, to imprison all excommunicated persons; and that ancient usage, without any particular grant or charter, was a sufficient authority for any clerical possessions or privileges.[p] About a century before, these claims would have been supported by the court of Rome beyond the most fundamental articles of faith: They were the chief points maintained by the great martyr, Becket; and his resolution in defending them had exalted him to the high station which he held in the catalogue of Romish saints. But principles were changed with the times: The pope was become somewhat jealous of the great independance of the English clergy, which made them stand less in need of his protection, and even emboldened them to resist his authority, and to complain of the preference given to the Italian courtiers, whose interests, it is natural to imagine, were the chief object of his concern. He was ready therefore, on the king's application, to annul these new constitutions of the church of England.[q] And, at the same time, he absolved the king and all his subjects from the oath which they had taken to observe the provisions of Oxford.[r]

Prince Edward.   Prince Edward, whose liberal mind, though in such early youth, had taught him the great prejudice, which his father had incurred, by his levity, inconstancy, and frequent breach of promise, refused for a long time to take advantage of this absolution; and declared that the provisions of Oxford, how unreasonable soever in themselves, and how much soever abused by the barons, ought still to

[o] Rymer, vol. i. p. 755.   [p] Ann. Burt. p. 389.   [q] Rymer, vol. i. p. 755. [r] Rymer, vol. i. p. 722. M. Paris, p. 666. W. Heming. p. 580. Ypod. Neust. p. 468. Knyghton, p. 2446.

CHAPTER XII

be adhered to by those who had sworn to observe them:[s] He himself had been constrained by violence to take that oath; yet was he determined to keep it. By this scrupulous fidelity, the prince acquired the confidence of all parties, and was afterwards enabled to recover fully the royal authority, and to perform such great actions both during his own reign and that of his father.

The situation of England, during this period, as well as that of most European kingdoms, was somewhat peculiar. There was no regular military force maintained in the nation: The sword, however, was not, properly speaking, in the hands of the people: The barons were alone entrusted with the defence of the community; and after any effort, which they made, either against their own prince, or against foreigners, as the military retainers departed home, the armies were disbanded, and could not speedily be reassembled at pleasure. It was easy therefore, for a few barons, by a combination, to get the start of the other party, to collect suddenly their troops, and to appear unexpectedly in the field with an army, which their antagonists, though equal or even superior in power and interest, would not dare to encounter. Hence the sudden revolutions, which often took place in those governments: Hence the frequent victories obtained without a blow by one faction over the other: And hence it happened, that the seeming prevalence of a party, was seldom a prognostic of its long continuance in power and authority.

The king, as soon as he received the pope's absolution from his oath, accompanied with menaces of excommunication against all opponents, trusting to the countenance of the church, to the support promised him by many considerable barons, and to the returning favour of the people, immediately took off the mask. After justifying his conduct by a proclamation, in which he set forth the private ambition, and the breach of trust, conspicuous in Leicester and his associates, he declared, that he had resumed the government, and was determined thenceforth to exert the royal authority for the protection of his subjects. He removed Hugh le Despenser and Nicholas de Ely, the justiciary and chancellor appointed by the barons; and put Philip Basset and Walter de Merton in their place. He substituted new sheriffs in all the counties, men

1262.

---

[s] M. Paris, p. 667.

of character and honour: He placed new governors in most of the castles: He changed all the officers of his household: He summoned a parliament, in which the resumption of his authority was ratified, with only five dissenting voices: And the barons, after making one fruitless effort, to take the king by surprize at Winchester, were obliged to acquiesce in those new regulations.[t]

23 April.

The king, in order to cut off every objection to his conduct, offered to refer all the differences between him and the earl of Leicester, to Margaret queen of France.[u] The celebrated integrity of Lewis gave a mighty influence to any decision which issued from his court; and Henry probably hoped, that the gallantry, on which all barons, as true knights, valued themselves, would make them ashamed not to submit to the award of that princess. Lewis merited the confidence reposed in him. By an admirable conduct, probably as political as just, he continually interposed his good offices to allay the civil discords of the English: He forwarded all healing measures, which might give security to both parties: And he still endeavoured, though in vain, to sooth by persuasion the fierce ambition of the earl of Leicester, and to convince him how much it was his duty to submit peaceably to the authority of his sovereign.

1263.

That bold and artful conspirator was nowise discouraged by the bad success of his past enterprizes. The death of Richard earl of locester, who was his chief rival in power, and who, before his decease, had joined the royal party, seemed to open a new field to his violence, and to expose the throne to fresh insults and injuries. It was in vain, that the king professed his intentions of observing strictly the great charter, even of maintaining all the regulations made by the reforming barons at Oxford or afterwards, except those which entirely annihilated the royal authority: These powerful chieftains, now obnoxious to the court, could not peaceably resign the hopes of entire independance and uncontrouled power, with which they had flattered themselves, and which they had so long enjoyed. Many of them engaged in Leicester's views, and among the rest, Gilbert, the young earl of Glocester, who brought him a mighty accession of power, from the extensive authority possessed by that opulent family. Even Henry, son of the king of

Civil wars of the barons.

[t] M. Paris, p. 668. Chron. T. Wykes, p. 55. [u] Rymer, vol. i. p. 724.

CHAPTER XII

the Romans, commonly called Henry d'Allmaine, though a prince of the blood, joined the party of the barons against the king, the head of his own family. Leicester himself, who still resided in France, secretly formed the links of this great conspiracy, and planned the whole scheme of operations.

The princes of Wales, notwithstanding the great power of the monarchs, both of the Saxon and Norman line, still preserved authority in their own country. Though they had often been constrained to pay tribute to the crown of England, they were with difficulty retained in subordination or even in peace; and almost through every reign since the conquest, they had infested the English frontiers with such petty incursions and sudden inroads, as seldom merit to have place in a general history. The English, still content with repelling their invasions, and chacing them back into their mountains, had never pursued the advantages obtained over them, nor been able, even under their greatest and most active princes, to fix a total, or so much as a feudal subjection on the country. This advantage was reserved to the present king, the weakest and most indolent. In the year 1237, Lewellyn, prince of Wales, declining in years and broken with infirmities, but still more harassed with the rebellion and undutiful behaviour of his younger son, Griffin, had recourse to the protection of Henry; and consenting to subject his principality, which had so long maintained, or soon recovered, its independance, to vassalage under the crown of England, had purchased security and tranquillity on these dishonourable terms. His eldest son and heir, David, renewed the homage to England; and having taken his brother prisoner, delivered him into Henry's hands, who committed him to custody in the Tower. That prince, endeavouring to make his escape, lost his life in the attempt; and the prince of Wales, freed from the apprehensions of so dangerous a rival, paid thenceforth less regard to the English monarch, and even renewed those incursions, by which the Welsh, during so many ages, had been accustomed to infest the English borders. Lewellyn, however, the son of Griffin, who succeeded to his uncle, had been obliged to renew the homage, which was now claimed by England as an established right; but he was well pleased to inflame those civil discords, on which he rested his present security, and founded his hopes of future independance. He entered into a confederacy with the earl of Leicester, and collecting all the force of his principality, invaded England with an army of 30,000 men. He ravaged the lands of Roger de Mortimer and of all the barons, who adhered to the crown;[w] he marched into Cheshire, and committed like depredations on prince Edward's territories; every place, where his disorderly troops appeared, was laid waste with fire and sword; and though Mortimer, a gallant and expert soldier, made stout resistance, it was found necessary, that the prince himself should head the army against this invader. Edward repulsed prince Lewellyn, and obliged him to take shelter in the mountains of North Wales: But he was prevented from making farther progress against the enemy, by the disorders, which soon after broke out in England.

The Welsh invasion was the appointed signal for the malcontent barons to rise in arms; and Leicester, coming over secretly from France, collected all the forces of his party, and commenced an open rebellion. He seized the person of the bishop of Hereford; a prelate obnoxious to all the inferior clergy, on account of his devoted attachment to the court of Rome.[x] Simon, bishop of Norwich, and John Mansel, because they had published the pope's bull, absolving the king and kingdom from their oaths to observe the provisions of Oxford, were made prisoners, and exposed to the rage of the party. The king's demesnes were ravaged with unbounded fury;[y] and as it was Leicester's interest to allure to his side, by the hopes of plunder, all the disorderly ruffians in England, he gave them a general licence to pillage the barons of the opposite party, and even all neutral persons. But one of the principal resources of his faction was the populace of the cities, particularly of London; and as he had, by his hypocritical pretensions to sanctity, and his zeal against Rome, engaged the monks and lower ecclesiastics in his party, his dominion over the inferior ranks of men became uncontroulable. Thomas Fitz-Richard, mayor of London, a furious and licentious man, gave the countenance of authority to these disorders in the capital; and having declared war against the substantial citizens, he loosened all the bands of government, by which that turbulent city was commonly but ill restrained. On the approach of Easter, the zeal of superstition, the appetite for plun-

---

[w] Chron. Dunst. vol. i. p. 354.   [x] Trivet, p. 211. M. West. p. 382, 392.
[y] Trivet, p. 211. M. West. p. 382.

CHAPTER XII

der, or what is often as prevalent with the populace as either of these motives, the pleasure of committing havoc and destruction, prompted them to attack the unhappy Jews, who were first pillaged without resistance, then massacred, to the number of five hundred persons.[z] The Lombard bankers were next exposed to the rage of the people; and though, by taking sanctuary in the churches, they escaped with their lives, all their money and goods became a prey to the licentious multitude. Even the houses of the rich citizens, though English, were attacked by night; and way was made by sword and by fire to the pillage of their goods, and often to the destruction of their persons. The queen, who, though defended by the Tower, was terrified by the neighbourhood of such dangerous commotions, resolved to go by water to the castle of Windsor; but as she approached the bridge, the populace assembled against her: The cry ran, *drown the witch;* and besides abusing her with the most opprobrious language, and pelting her with rotten eggs and dirt, they had prepared large stones to sink her barge, when she should attempt to shoot the bridge; and she was so frightened that she returned to the Tower.[a]

The violence and fury of Leicester's faction had risen to such a height in all parts of England, that the king, unable to resist their power, was obliged to set on foot a treaty of peace; and to make an accommodation with the barons on the most disadvantageous terms.[b] He agreed to confirm anew the provisions of Oxford, even those which entirely annihilated the royal authority; and the barons were again re-instated in the sovereignty of the kingdom. They restored Hugh le Despenser to the office of chief justiciary; they appointed their own creatures sheriffs in every county of England; they took possession of all the royal castles and fortresses; they even named all the officers of the king's household; and they summoned a parliament to meet at Westminister in order to settle more fully their plan of government. They here produced a new list of twenty-four barons, to whom they proposed, that the administration should be entirely committed; and they insisted, that the authority of this junto should continue, not only during the reign of the king, but also during that of prince Edward.

18th July.

14th Oct.

This prince, the life and soul of the royal party, had unhappily,

---

[z] Chron. T. Wykes, p. 59. [a] Chron. T. Wykes, p. 57. [b] Chron. Dunst. vol. i. p. 358. Trivet, p. 211.

before the king's accommodation with the barons, been taken prisoner by Leicester in a parley at Windsor;[c] and that misfortune,
more than any other incident, had determined Henry to submit to
the ignominious conditions imposed upon him. But Edward, having recovered his liberty by the treaty, employed his activity in
defending the prerogatives of his family; and he gained a great
part even among those who had at first adhered to the cause of
the barons. His cousin, Henry d'Allmaine, Roger Bigod earl mar-
eshal, earl Warrenne, Humphrey Bohun earl of Hereford, John
lord Basset, Ralph Basset, Hamond l'Estrange, Roger Mortimer,
Henry de Piercy, Robert de Brus, Roger de Leybourne, with almost all the Lords Marchers, as they were called, on the borders of
Wales and of Scotland, the most warlike parts of the kingdom,
declared in favour of the royal cause; and hostilities, which were
scarcely well composed, were again renewed in every part of England. But the near balance of the parties, joined to the universal
clamour of the people, obliged the king and barons to open anew
the negotiations for peace; and it was agreed by both sides to
submit their differences to the arbitration of the king of France.[d]

*Reference
to the
king of
France.*

This virtuous prince, the only man, who, in like circumstances,
could safely have been intrusted with such an authority by a neighbouring nation, had never ceased to interpose his good offices
between the English factions; and had even, during the short interval of peace, invited over to Paris both the king and the earl of
Leicester, in order to accommodate the differences between them;
but found, that the fears and animosities on both sides, as well as
the ambition of Leicester, were so violent, as to render all his
endeavours ineffectual. But when this solemn appeal, ratified by
the oaths and subscriptions of the leaders in both factions, was
made to his judgment, he was not discouraged from pursuing his
honourable purpose: He summoned the states of France at Ami-

1264.

ens; and there, in the presence of that assembly, as well as in that
of the king of England and Peter de Montfort, Leicester's son, he
brought this great cause to a trial and examination. It appeared to
him, that the provisions of Oxford, even had they not been extorted by force, had they not been so exorbitant in their nature and

---

[c] M. Paris, p. 669. Trivet, p. 213.   [d] M. Paris, p. 668. Chron. T. Wykes,
p. 58. W. Heming. p. 580. Chron. Dunst. vol. i. p. 363.

subversive of the ancient constitution, were expressly established as a temporary expedient, and could not, without breach of trust, be rendered perpetual by the barons. He therefore annulled these provisions; restored to the king the possession of his castles, and the power of nomination to the great offices; allowed him to retain what foreigners he pleased in his kingdom, and even to confer on them places of trust and dignity; and in a word, re-established the royal power in the same condition on which it stood before the meeting of the parliament at Oxford. But while he thus suppressed dangerous innovations, and preserved unimpaired the prerogatives of the English crown, he was not negligent of the rights of the people; and besides ordering that a general amnesty should be granted for all past offences, he declared, that his award was not any wise meant to derogate from the privileges and liberties which the nation enjoyed by any former concessions or charters of the crown.[e]

23d Jan.

This equitable sentence was no sooner known in England, than Leicester and his confederates determined to reject it, and to have recourse to arms, in order to procure to themselves more safe and advantageous conditions.[f] Without regard to his oaths and subscriptions, that enterprising conspirator directed his two sons, Richard and Peter de Montfort, in conjunction with Robert de Ferrars, earl of Derby, to attack the city of Worcester; while Henry and Simon de Montfort, two others of his sons, assisted by the prince of Wales, were ordered to lay waste the estate of Roger de Mortimer. He himself resided at London; and employing as his instrument, Fitz-Richard, the seditious mayor, who had violently and illegally prolonged his authority, he wrought up that city to the highest ferment and agitation. The populace formed themselves into bands and companies; chose leaders; practised all military exercises; committed violence on the royalists: And to give them greater countenance in their disorders, an association was entered into between the city and eighteen great barons, never to make peace with the king but by common consent and approbation. At the head of those who swore to maintain this association, were the earls of Leicester, Glocester, and Derby, with le

Renewal of the civil wars.

---

[e] Rymer, vol. i. p. 776, 777, &c. Chron. T. Wykes, p. 58. Knyghton, p. 2446.   [f] Chron. Dunst. vol. i. p. 363.

Despenser, the chief justiciary; men who had all previously sworn to submit to the award of the French monarch. Their only pretence for this breach of faith, was, that the latter part of Lewis's sentence was, as they affirmed, a contradiction to the former: He ratified the charter of liberties, yet annulled the provisions of Oxford; which were only calculated, as they maintained, to preserve that charter; and without which, in their estimation, they had no security for its observance.

The king and prince, finding a civil war inevitable, prepared themselves for defence; and summoning the military vassals from all quarters, and being reinforced by Baliol lord of Galloway, Brus lord of Annandale, Henry Piercy, John Comyn,[g] and other barons of the north, they composed an army, formidable as well from its numbers, as its military prowess and experience. The first enterprize of the royalists was the attack of Northampton, which was defended by Simon de Montfort, with many of the principal barons of that party: And a breach being made in the walls by Philip Basset, the place was carried by assault, and both the governor and the garrison were made prisoners. The royalists marched thence to Leicester and Nottingham; both which places having opened their gates to them, prince Edward proceeded with a detachment into the county of Derby, in order to ravage with fire and sword the lands of the earl of that name, and take revenge on him for his disloyalty. Like maxims of war prevailed with both parties throughout England; and the kingdom was thus exposed in a moment to greater devastation, from the animosities of the rival barons, than it would have suffered from many years of foreign or even domestic hostilities, conducted by more humane and more generous principles.

The earl of Leicester, master of London, and of the counties in the south-east of England, formed the siege of Rochester, which alone declared for the king in those parts, and which, besides earl Warrenne, the governor, was garrisoned by many noble and powerful barons of the royal party. The king and prince hastened from Nottingham, where they were then quartered, to the relief of the place; and on their approach, Leicester raised the siege and retreated to London, which, being the center of his power, he was

5th April.

[g] Rymer, vol. i. p. 772. M. West. p. 385. Ypod. Neust. p. 469.

afraid, might, in his absence, fall into the king's hands, either by force, or by a correspondence with the principal citizens, who were all secretly inclined to the royal cause. Reinforced by a great body of Londoners, and having summoned his partizans from all quarters, he thought himself strong enough to hazard a general battle with the royalists, and to determine the fate of the nation in one great engagement; which, if it proved successful, must be decisive against the king, who had no retreat for his broken troops in those parts; while Leicester himself, in case of any sinister accident, could easily take shelter in the city. To give the better colouring to his cause, he previously sent a message with conditions of peace to Henry, submissive in the language, but exorbitant in the demands;[h] and when the messenger returned with the lie and defiance from the king, the prince, and the king of the Romans, he sent a new message, renouncing, in the name of himself and of the associated barons, all fealty and allegiance to Henry. He then marched out of the city with his army, divided into four bodies: The first commanded by his two sons, Henry and Guy de Montfort, together with Humphrey de Bohun, earl of Hereford, who had deserted to the barons; the second led by the earl of Glocester, with William de Montchesney and John Fitz-John; the third, composed of Londoners, under the command of Nicholas de Segrave; the fourth headed by himself in person. The bishop of Chichester gave a general absolution to the army, accompanied with assurances, that, if any of them fell in the ensuing action, they would infallibly be received into heaven, as the reward of their suffering in so meritorious a cause.

Leicester, who possessed great talents for war, conducted his march with such skill and secrecy, that he had well nigh surprised the royalists in their quarters at Lewes in Sussex: But the vigilance and activity of prince Edward soon repaired this negligence; and he led out the king's army to the field in three bodies. He himself conducted the van, attended by earl Warrenne and William de Valence: The main body was commanded by the king of the Romans and his son Henry: The king himself was placed in the rear at the head of his principal nobility. Prince Edward rushed upon the Londoners, who had demanded the post of honour in leading

Battle of Lewes. 14th May.

---

[h] M. Paris, p. 669. W. Heming. p. 583.

the rebel army, but who, from their ignorance of discipline and want of experience, were ill fitted to resist the gentry and military men, of whom the prince's body was composed. They were broken in an instant; were chased off the field; and Edward, transported by his martial ardour, and eager to revenge the insolence of the Londoners against his mother,[i] put them to the sword for the length of four miles, without giving them any quarter, and without reflecting on the fate, which in the mean time attended the rest of the army. The earl of Leicester, seeing the royalists thrown into confusion by their eagerness in the pursuit, led on his remaining troops against the bodies commanded by the two royal brothers: He defeated with great slaughter the forces headed by the king of the Romans; and that prince was obliged to yield himself prisoner to the earl of Glocester: He penetrated to the body, where the king himself was placed, threw it into disorder, pursued his advantage, chased it into the town of Lewes, and obliged Henry to surrender himself prisoner.[k]

Prince Edward, returning to the field of battle from his precipitate pursuit of the Londoners, was astonished to find it covered with the dead bodies of his friends, and still more to hear, that his father and uncle were defeated and taken prisoners, and that Arundel, Comyn, Brus, Hamon l'Estrange, Roger Leybourne, and many considerable barons of his party, were in the hands of the victorious enemy. Earl Warrenne, Hugh Bigod, and William de Valence, struck with despair at this event, immediately took to flight, hurried to Pevencey, and made their escape beyond sea:[l] But the prince, intrepid amidst the greatest disasters, exhorted his troops to revenge the death of their friends, to relieve the royal captives, and to snatch an easy conquest from an enemy, disordered by their own victory.[m] He found his followers intimidated by their situation; while Leicester, afraid of a sudden and violent blow from the prince, amused him by a feigned negociation, till he was able to recal his troops from the pursuit, and to bring them into order.[n] There now appeared no farther resource to the royal party; surrounded by the armies and garrisons of the enemy, des-

[i] M. Paris, p. 670. Chron. T. Wykes, p. 62. W. Heming. p. 583. M. West. p. 387. Ypod. Neust. p. 469. H. Knyghton, p. 2450.   [k] M. Paris, p. 670. M. West. p. 387.   [l] Chron. T. Wykes, p. 63.   [m] W. Heming. p. 584. [n] W. Heming. p. 584.

titute of forage and provisions, and deprived of their sovereign, as well as of their principal leaders, who could alone inspirit them to an obstinate resistance. The prince, therefore, was obliged to submit to Leicester's terms, which were short and severe, agreeably to the suddenness and necessity of the situation. He stipulated, that he and Henry d'Allmaine should surrender themselves prisoners as pledges in lieu of the two kings; that all other prisoners on both sides should be released; [o] and that in order to settle fully the terms of agreement, application should be made to the king of France, that he should name six Frenchmen, three prelates, and three noblemen: These six to chuse two others of their own country: And these two to chuse one Englishman, who, in conjunction with themselves, were to be invested by both parties with full powers to make what regulations they thought proper for the settlement of the kingdom. The prince and young Henry accordingly delivered themselves into Leicester's hands, who sent them under a guard to Dover castle. Such are the terms of agreement, commonly called the *Mise* of Lewes, from an obsolete French term of that meaning: For it appears, that all the gentry and nobility of England, who valued themselves on their Norman extraction, and who disdained the language of their native country, made familiar use of the French tongue, till this period, and for some time after.

Leicester had no sooner obtained this great advantage, and gotten the whole royal family in his power, than he openly violated every article of the treaty, and acted as sole master, and even tyrant of the kingdom. He still detained the king in effect a prisoner, and made use of that prince's authority to purposes the most prejudicial to his interests, and the most oppressive of his people.[p] He every where disarmed the royalists, and kept all his own partizans in a military posture:[q] He observed the same partial conduct in the deliverance of the captives, and even threw many of the royalists into prison, besides those who were taken in the battle of Lewes: He carried the king from place to place, and obliged all the royal castles, on pretence of Henry's commands, to receive a governor and garrison of his own appointment: All the officers of the crown and of the household were named by him; and the whole author-

---

[o] M. Paris, p. 671. Knyghton, p. 2451.   [p] Rymer, vol. i. p. 790, 791, &c.
[q] Ibid. p. 795. Brady's appeals, N°. 211, 212. Chron. T. Wykes, p. 63.

ity, as well as arms of the state, was lodged in his hands: He instituted in the counties a new kind of magistracy, endowed with new and arbitrary powers, that of conservators of the peace:[r] His avarice appeared barefaced, and might induce us to question the greatness of his ambition, at least the largeness of his mind, if we had not reason to think, that he intended to employ his acquisitions as the instruments for attaining farther power and grandeur. He seized the estates of no less than eighteen barons, as his share of the spoil gained in the battle of Lewes: He engrossed to himself the ransom of all the prisoners; and told his barons, with a wanton insolence, that it was sufficient for them, that he had saved them by that victory from the forfeitures and attainders which hung over them:[s] He even treated the earl of Glocester in the same injurious manner, and applied to his own use the ransom of the king of the Romans, who in the field of battle had yielded himself prisoner to that nobleman. Henry, his eldest son, made a monopoly of all the wool in the kingdom, the only valuable commodity for foreign markets which it at that time produced.[t] The inhabitants of the cinque-ports, during the present dissolution of government, betook themselves to the most licentious piracy, preyed on the ships of all nations, threw the mariners into the sea, and by these practices soon banished all merchants from the English coasts and harbours. Every foreign commodity rose to an exorbitant price; and woollen cloth, which the English had not then the art of dying, was worn by them white, and without receiving the last hand of the manufacturer. In answer to the complaints which arose on this occasion, Leicester replied, that the kingdom could well enough subsist within itself, and needed no intercourse with foreigners. And it was found, that he even combined with the pyrates of the cinque-ports, and received as his share the third of their prizes.[u]

No farther mention was made of the reference to the king of France, so essential an article in the agreement of Lewes; and Leicester summoned a parliament, composed altogether of his own partizans, in order to rivet, by their authority, that power, which he had acquired by so much violence, and which he used with so much tyranny and injustice. An ordinance was there passed, to which the king's consent had been previously extorted,

[r] Rymer, vol. i. p. 792.   [s] Knyghton, p. 2451.   [t] Chron. T. Wykes, p. 65.
[u] Ibid.

CHAPTER XII

that every act of royal power should be exercised by a council of nine persons, who were to be chosen and removed by the majority of three, Leicester himself, the earl of Glocester, and the bishop of Chichester.[w] By this intricate plan of government, the scepter was really put into Leicester's hands; as he had the entire direction of the bishop of Chichester, and thereby commanded all the resolutions of the council of three, who could appoint or discard at pleasure every member of the supreme council.

But it was impossible that things could long remain in this strange situation. It behoved Leicester either to descend with some peril into the rank of a subject, or to mount up with no less into that of a sovereign; and his ambition, unrestrained either by fear or by principle, gave too much reason to suspect him of the latter intention. Mean while, he was exposed to anxiety from every quarter; and felt that the smallest incident was capable of overturning that immense and ill-cemented fabric, which he had reared. The queen, whom her husband had left abroad, had collected in foreign parts an army of desperate adventurers, and had assembled a great number of ships, with a view of invading the kingdom, and of bringing relief to her unfortunate family. Lewis, detesting Leicester's usurpations and perjuries, and disgusted at the English barons, who had refused to submit to his award, secretly favoured all her enterprizes, and was generally believed to be making preparations for the same purpose. An English army, by the pretended authority of the captive king, was assembled on the sea-coast to oppose this projected invasion;[x] but Leicester owed his safety more to cross winds, which long detained and at last dispersed and ruined the queen's fleet, than to any resistance, which, in their present situation, could have been expected from the English.

Leicester found himself better able to resist the spiritual thunders, which were leveled against him. The pope, still adhering to the king's cause against the barons, dispatched cardinal Guido as his legate into England, with orders to excommunicate by name the three earls, Leicester, Glocester, and Norfolk, and all others in general, who concurred in the oppression and captivity of their sovereign.[y] Leicester menaced the legate with death, if he set foot within the kingdom; but Guido, meeting in France the bishops of

[w] Rymer, vol. i. p. 793. Brady's App. N°. 213. [x] Brady's App. N°. 216, 217. Chron. Dunst. vol. i. p. 373. M. West. p. 385. [y] Rymer, vol. i. p. 798. Chron. Dunst. vol. i. p. 373.

Winchester, London, and Worcester, who had been sent thither on a negociation, commanded them, under the penalty of ecclesiastical censures, to carry his bull into England, and to publish it against the barons. When the prelates arrived off the coast, they were boarded by the pyratical mariners of the cinque-ports, to whom probably they gave a hint of the cargo, which they brought along with them: The bull was torn and thrown into the sea; which furnished the artful prelates with a plausible excuse for not obeying the orders of the legate. Leicester appealed from Guido to the pope in person; but before the ambassadors, appointed to defend his cause, could reach Rome, the pope was dead; and they found the legate himself, from whom they had appealed, seated on the papal throne, by the name of Urban IV. That daring leader was no wise dismayed with this incident; and as he found that a great part of his popularity in England was founded on his opposition to the court of Rome, which was now become odious, he persisted with the more obstinacy in the prosecution of his measures.

1265.
20th
Jan.

That he might both encrease, and turn to advantage his popularity, Leicester summoned a new parliament in London, where, he knew, his power was uncontrolable; and he fixed this assembly on a more democratical basis, than any which had ever been summoned since the foundation of the monarchy. Besides the barons of his own party, and several ecclesiastics, who were not

House of
commons.

immediate tenants of the crown; he ordered returns to be made of two knights from each shire, and what is more remarkable, of deputies from the boroughs, an order of men, which in former ages had always been regarded as too mean to enjoy a place in the national councils.[z] This period is commonly esteemed the epoch of the house of commons in England; and it is certainly the first time that historians speak of any representatives sent to parliament by the boroughs. In all the general accounts given in preceding times of those assemblies, the prelates and barons only are mentioned as the constituent members; and even in the most particular narratives delivered of parliamentary transactions, as in the trial of Thomas a Becket, where the events of each day, and almost of each hour, are carefully recorded by contemporary authors,[a] there is not, throughout the whole, the least appearance of a house of

[z] Rymer, vol. i. p. 802.   [a] Fitz-Stephen, Hist. Quadrip. Hoveden, &c.

CHAPTER XII

commons. But though that house derived its existence from so precarious and even so invidious an origin as Leicester's usurpation, it soon proved, when summoned by the legal princes, one of the most useful, and, in process of time, one of the most powerful members of the national constitution; and gradually rescued the kingdom from aristocratical as well as from regal tyranny. But Leicester's policy, if we must ascribe to him so great a blessing, only forwarded by some years an institution, for which the general state of things had already prepared the nation; and it is otherwise inconceivable, that a plant, set by so inauspicious a hand, could have attained to so vigorous a growth, and have flourished in the midst of such tempests and convulsions. The feudal system, with which the liberty, much more the power of the commons, was totally incompatible, began gradually to decline; and both the king and the commonalty, who felt its inconveniencies, contributed to favour this new power, which was more submissive than the barons to the regular authority of the crown, and at the same time afforded protection to the inferior orders of the state.

Leicester, having thus assembled a parliament of his own model, and trusting to the attachment of the populace of London, seized the opportunity of crushing his rivals among the powerful barons. Robert de Ferrars, earl of Derby, was accused in the king's name, seized, and committed to custody, without being brought to any legal trial.[b] John Gifford, menaced with the same fate, fled from London, and took shelter in the borders of Wales. Even the earl of Glocester, whose power and influence had so much contributed to the success of the barons, but who of late was extremely disgusted with Leicester's arbitrary conduct, found himself in danger from the prevailing authority of his ancient confederate; and he retired from parliament.[c] This known dissension gave courage to all Leicester's enemies and to the king's friends; who were now sure of protection from so potent a leader. Though Roger Mortimer, Hamon L'Estrange, and other powerful marchers of Wales, had been obliged to leave the kingdom, their authority still remained over the territories subjected to their jurisdiction; and there were many others who were disposed to give disturbance to

[b] Chron. T. Wykes, p. 66. Ann. Waverl. p. 216.   [c] M. Paris, p. 671. Ann. Waverl. p. 211.

the new government. The animosities, inseparable from the feudal aristocracy, broke out with fresh violence, and threatened the kingdom with new convulsions and disorders.

The earl of Leicester, surrounded with these difficulties, embraced a measure, from which he hoped to reap some present advantages, but which proved in the end the source of all his future calamities. The active and intrepid prince Edward had languished in prison ever since the fatal battle of Lewes; and as he was extremely popular in the kingdom, there arose a general desire of seeing him again restored to liberty.[d] Leicester finding, that he could with difficulty oppose the concurring wishes of the nation, stipulated with the prince, that, in return, he should order his adherents to deliver up to the barons, all their castles, particularly those on the borders of Wales; and should swear neither to depart the kingdom during three years, nor introduce into it any foreign forces.[e] The king took an oath to the same effect, and he also passed a charter, in which he confirmed the agreement or *Mise* of Lewes; and even permitted his subjects to rise in arms against him, if he should ever attempt to infringe it.[f] So little care did Leicester take, though he constantly made use of the authority of this captive prince, to preserve to him any appearance of royalty or kingly prerogatives!

In consequence of this treaty, prince Edward was brought into Westminster-hall, and was declared free by the barons: But instead of really recovering his liberty, as he had vainly expected, he found, that the whole transaction was a fraud on the part of Leicester; that he himself still continued a prisoner at large, and was guarded by the emissaries of that nobleman; and that, while the faction reaped all the benefit from the performance of his part of the treaty, care was taken that he should enjoy no advantage by it. As Glocester, on his rupture with the barons, had retired for safety to his estates on the borders of Wales; Leicester followed him with an army to Hereford,[g] continued still to menace and negotiate, and that he might add authority to his cause, he carried both the king and prince along with him. The earl of Glocester here concerted with young Edward the manner of that prince's escape. He found

11th March.

---

[d] Knyghton, p. 2457.   [e] Ann. Waverl. p. 216.   [f] Blackiston's Mag. Charta. Chron. Dunst. vol. i. p. 378.   [g] Chron. T. Wykes, p. 67. Ann. Waverl. p. 218. W. Heming. p. 585. Chron. Dunst. vol. i. p. 383, 384.

CHAPTER XII

means to convey to him a horse of extraordinary swiftness; and appointed Roger Mortimer, who had returned into the kingdom, to be ready at hand with a small party to receive the prince, and to guard him to a place of safety. Edward pretended to take the air with some of Leicester's retinue, who were his guards; and making matches between their horses, after he thought he had tired and blown them sufficiently, he suddenly mounted Glocester's horse, and called to his attendants, that he had long enough enjoyed the pleasure of their company, and now bid them adieu. They followed him for some time, without being able to overtake him; and the appearance of Mortimer with his company put an end to their pursuit. *28th May.*

The royalists, secretly prepared for this event, immediately flew to arms; and the joy of this gallant prince's deliverance, the oppressions under which the nation laboured, the expectation of a new scene of affairs, and the countenance of the earl of Glocester, procured Edward an army which Leicester was utterly unable to withstand. This nobleman found himself in a remote quarter of the kingdom; surrounded by his enemies; barred from all communication with his friends by the Severne, whose bridges Edward had broken down; and obliged to fight the cause of his party under these multiplied disadvantages. In this extremity he wrote to his son, Simon de Montfort, to hasten from London with an army for his relief; and Simon had advanced to Kenilworth with that view, where, fancying that all Edward's force and attention were directed against his father, he lay secure and unguarded. But the prince, making a sudden and forced march, surprized him in his camp, dispersed his army, and took the earl of Oxford, and many other noblemen prisoners, almost without resistance. Leicester, ignorant of his son's fate, passed the Severne in boats during Edward's absence, and lay at Evesham, in expectation of being every hour joined by his friends from London: When the prince, who availed himself of every favourable moment, appeared in the field before him. Edward made a body of his troops advance from the road which led to Kenilworth, and ordered them to carry the banners taken from Simon's army; while he himself, making a circuit with the rest of his forces, purposed to attack the enemy on the other quarter. Leicester was long deceived by this stratagem, and took one division of Edward's army for his friends; but at last, perceiving his mistake, and observing the great superiority and *Battle of Evesham, and death of Leicester. 4th August.*

excellent disposition of the royalists, he exclaimed, that they had learned from him the art of war; adding, "The Lord have mercy on our souls, for I see our bodies are the prince's." The battle immediately began, though on very unequal terms. Leicester's army, by living in the mountains of Wales without bread, which was not then much used among the inhabitants, had been extremely weakened by sickness and desertion, and was soon broken by the victorious royalists; while his Welsh allies, accustomed only to a desultory kind of war, immediately took to flight, and were pursued with great slaughter. Leicester himself, asking for quarter, was slain in the heat of the action, with his eldest son Henry, Hugh le Despenser, and about one hundred and sixty knights, and many other gentlemen of his party. The old king had been purposely placed by the rebels in the front of the battle; and being clad in armour, and thereby not known by his friends, he received a wound, and was in danger of his life: But crying out, *I am Henry of Winchester, your king,* he was saved; and put in a place of safety by his son, who flew to his rescue.

The violence, ingratitude, tyranny, rapacity and treachery of the earl of Leicester, gave a very bad idea of his moral character, and make us regard his death as the most fortunate event, which, in this conjuncture, could have happened to the English nation: Yet must we allow the man to have possessed great abilities, and the appearance of great virtues, who, though a stranger, could, at a time when strangers were the most odious, and the most universally decried, have acquired so extensive an interest in the kingdom, and have so nearly paved his way to the throne itself. His military capacity, and his political craft, were equally eminent: He possessed the talents both of governing men and conducting business: And though his ambition was boundless, it seems neither to have exceeded his courage nor his genius; and he had the happiness of making the low populace, as well as the haughty barons, co-operate towards the success of his selfish and dangerous purposes. A prince of greater abilities and vigour than Henry might have directed the talents of this nobleman either to the exaltation of his throne, or to the good of his people: But the advantages given to Leicester, by the weak and variable administration of the king, brought on the ruin of royal authority, and produced great confusions in the kingdom, which however in the end preserved

CHAPTER XII

and extremely improved national liberty, and the constitution. His popularity, even after his death, continued so great, that, though he was excommunicated by Rome, the people believed him to be a saint; and many miracles were said to be wrought upon his tomb.[h]

The victory of Evesham, with the death of Leicester, proved decisive in favour of the royalists, and made an equal, though an opposite impression on friends and enemies, in every part of England. The king of the Romans recovered his liberty: The other prisoners of the royal party were not only freed, but courted, by their keepers: Fitz-Richard, the seditious mayor of London, who had marked out forty of the most wealthy citizens for slaughter, immediately stopped his hand on receiving intelligence of this great event: And almost all the castles, garrisoned by the barons, hastened to make their submissions, and to open their gates to the king. The isle of Axholme alone, and that of Ely, trusting to the strength of their situation, ventured to make resistance; but were at last reduced, as well as the castle of Dover, by the valour and activity of prince Edward.[i] Adam de Gourdon, a courageous baron, maintained himself during some time in the forests of Hampshire, committed depredations in the neighbourhood, and obliged the prince to lead a body of troops into that country against him. Edward attacked the camp of the rebels; and being transported by the ardour of battle, leaped over the trench with a few followers, and encountered Gourdon in single combat. The victory was long disputed between these valiant combatants; but ended at last in the prince's favour, who wounded his antagonist, threw him from his horse, and took him prisoner. He not only gave him his life; but introduced him that very night to the queen at Guilford, procured him his pardon, restored him to his estate, received him into favour, and was ever after faithfully served by him.[k]

A total victory of the sovereign over so extensive a rebellion commonly produces a revolution of government, and strengthens, as well as enlarges, for some time, the prerogatives of the crown: Yet no sacrifices of national liberty were made on this occasion; the Great Charter remained still inviolate; and the king, sensible that his own barons, by whose assistance alone he had prevailed, were

Settlement of the government.

1266.

[h] Chron. de Mailr. p. 232.   [i] M. Paris, p. 676. W. Heming. p. 588.   [k] M. Paris, p. 675.

no less jealous of their independance than the other party, seems thenceforth to have more carefully abstained from all those exertions of power, which had afforded so plausible a pretence to the rebels. The clemency of this victory is also remarkable: No blood was shed on the scaffold: No attainders, except of the Mountfort family, were carried into execution: And though a parliament, assembled at Winchester, attainted all those, who had borne arms against the king, easy compositions were made with them for their lands;[l] and the highest sum, levied on the most obnoxious offenders, exceeded not five years rent of their estate. Even the earl of Derby, who again rebelled, after having been pardoned and restored to his fortune, was obliged to pay only seven years' rent, and was a second time restored. The mild disposition of the king, and the prudence of the prince, tempered the insolence of victory, and gradually restored order to the several members of the state, disjointed by so long a continuance of civil wars and commotions.

The city of London, which had carried farthest the rage and animosity against the king, and which seemed determined to stand upon its defence after almost all the kingdom had submitted, was, after some interval, restored to most of its liberties and privileges; and Fitz-Richard, the mayor, who had been guilty of so much illegal violence, was only punished by fine and imprisonment. The countess of Leicester, the king's sister, who had been extremely forward in all attacks on the royal family, was dismissed the kingdom with her two sons, Simon and Guy, who proved very ungrateful for this lenity. Five years afterwards, they assassinated, at Viterbo in Italy, their cousin Henry d'Allmaine, who at that very time was endeavouring to make their peace with the king; and by taking sanctuary in the church of the Franciscans, they escaped the punishment due to so great an enormity.[m]

1267. The merits of the earl of Glocester, after he returned to his allegiance, had been so great, in restoring the prince to his liberty, and assisting him in his victories against the rebellious barons, that it was almost impossible to content him in his demands; and his youth and temerity, as well as his great power, tempted him, on some new disgust, to raise again the flames of rebellion in the

---

[l] M. Paris, p. 675.　[m] Rymer, vol. i. p. 879, vol. ii. p. 4, 6. Chron. T. Wykes, p. 94. W. Heming. p. 589. Trivet, p. 240.

CHAPTER XII

kingdom. The mutinous populace of London, at his instigation, took to arms; and the prince was obliged to levy an army of 30,000 men, in order to suppress them. Even this second rebellion did not provoke the king to any act of cruelty; and the earl of Glocester himself escaped with total impunity. He was only obliged to enter into a bond of 20,000 marks, that he should never again be guilty of rebellion: A strange method of enforcing the laws, and a proof of the dangerous independance of the barons in those ages! These potent nobles were, from the danger of the precedent, averse to the execution of the laws of forfeiture and felony against any of their fellows; though they could not with a good grace refuse to concur in obliging them to fulfil any voluntary contract and engagement, into which they had entered.

The prince finding the state of the kingdom tolerably composed, was seduced, by his avidity for glory, and by the prejudices of the age, as well as by the earnest solicitations of the king of France, to undertake an expedition against the infidels in the Holy Land;[n] and he endeavoured previously to settle the state in such a manner, as to dread no bad effects from his absence. As the formidable power and turbulent disposition of the earl of Glocester gave him apprehensions, he insisted on carrying him along with him, in consequence of a vow, which that nobleman had made to undertake the same voyage: In the mean time, he obliged him to resign some of his castles, and to enter into a new bond not to disturb the peace of the kingdom.[o] He sailed from England with an army; and arrived in Lewis's camp before Tunis in Africa, where he found that monarch already dead, from the intemperance of the climate and the fatigues of his enterprize. The great, if not only weakness of this prince in his government was the imprudent passion for crusades; but it was this zeal chiefly that procured him from the clergy the title of St. Lewis, by which he is known in the French history; and if that appellation had not been so extremely prostituted, as to become rather a term of reproach, he seems, by his uniform probity and goodness, as well as his piety, to have fully merited the title. He was succeeded by his son, Philip, denominated the Hardy; a prince of some merit, though much inferior to that of his father.

1270.

[n] M. Paris, p. 677.   [o] Chron. T. Wykes, p. 90.

1271.

Prince Edward, not discouraged by this event, continued his voyage to the Holy Land, where he signalized himself by acts of valour: Revived the glory of the English name in those parts: And struck such terror into the Saracens, that they employed an assassin to murder him, who wounded him in the arm, but perished in the attempt.[p] Meanwhile, his absence from England was attended with many of those pernicious consequences, which had been dreaded from it. The laws were not executed: The barons oppressed the common people with impunity:[q] They gave shelter on their estates to bands of robbers, whom they employed in committing ravages on the estates of their enemies: The populace of London returned to their usual licentiousness: And the old king, unequal to the burthen of public affairs, called aloud for his gallant son to return,[r] and to assist him in swaying that scepter, which

1272.
16th
Nov.
Death

was ready to drop from his feeble and irresolute hands. At last, overcome by the cares of government, and the infirmities of age, he visibly declined, and he expired at St. Edmondsbury in the 64th year of his age, and 56th of his reign; the longest reign that is to be met with in the English annals. His brother, the king of the Romans (for he never attained the title of emperor) died about seven months before him.

and char-
acter of
the king.

The most obvious circumstance of Henry's character is his incapacity for government, which rendered him as much a prisoner in the hands of his own ministers and favourites, and as little at his own disposal, as when detained a captive in the hands of his enemies. From this source, rather than from insincerity or treachery, arose his negligence in observing his promises; and he was too easily induced, for the sake of present convenience, to sacrifice the lasting advantages arising from the trust and confidence of his people. Hence too were derived his profusion to favourites, his attachment to strangers, the variableness of his conduct, his hasty resentments, and his sudden forgiveness and return of affection. Instead of reducing the dangerous power of his nobles, by obliging them to observe the laws towards their inferiors, and setting them the salutary example in his own government; he was seduced to imitate their conduct, and to make his arbitrary will, or rather that

[p] M. Paris, p. 678, 679. W. Heming. p. 520.   [q] Chron. Dunst. vol. i. p. 404.   [r] Rymer, vol. i. p. 809. M. Paris, p. 678.

of his ministers, the rule of his actions. Instead of accommodating himself, by a strict frugality, to the embarrassed situation in which his revenue had been left, by the military expeditions of his uncle, the dissipations of his father, and the usurpations of the barons; he was tempted to levy money by irregular exactions, which, without enriching himself, impoverished, at least disgusted his people. Of all men, nature seemed least to have fitted him for being a tyrant; yet are there instances of oppression in his reign, which, though derived from the precedents, left him by his predecessors, had been carefully guarded against by the Great Charter, and are inconsistent with all rules of good government. And on the whole we may say, that greater abilities, with his good dispositions, would have prevented him from falling into his faults; or with worse dispositions, would have enabled him to maintain and defend them.

This prince was noted for his piety and devotion, and his regular attendance on public worship; and a saying of his on that head is much celebrated by ancient writers. He was engaged in a dispute with Lewis IX. of France, concerning the preference between sermons and masses: He maintained the superiority of the latter, and affirmed, that he would rather have one hour's conversation with a friend, than hear twenty the most elaborate discourses, pronounced in his praise.[s]

Henry left two sons, Edward his successor, and Edmond earl of Lancaster; and two daughters, Margaret queen of Scotland, and Beatrix dutchess of Britanny. He had five other children, who died in their infancy.

The following are the most remarkable laws enacted during this reign. There had been great disputes between the civil and ecclesiastical courts concerning bastardy. The common law had deemed all those to be bastards who were born before wedlock: By the canon law they were legitimate: And when any dispute of inheritance arose, it had formerly been usual for the civil courts to issue writs to the spiritual, directing them to enquire into the legitimacy of the person. The bishop always returned an answer agreeable to the canon law, though contrary to the municipal law of the kingdom. For this reason, the civil courts had changed the

Miscellaneous transactions of this reign.

---

[s] Walsing. Edw. I. p. 43.

terms of their writ; and instead of requiring the spiritual courts to make inquisition concerning the legitimacy of the person, they only proposed the simple question of fact, whether he were born before or after wedlock. The prelates complained of this practice to the parliament assembled at Merton in the twentieth of this king, and desired that the municipal law might be rendered conformable to the canon: But received from all the nobility the memorable reply, *Nolumus leges Angliae mutare,* We will not change the laws of England.[t]

After the civil wars, the parliament summoned at Marlebridge, gave their approbation to most of the ordinances, which had been established by the reforming barons, and which, though advantageous to the security of the people, had not received the sanction of a legal authority. Among other laws, it was there enacted, that all appeals from the courts of inferior lords should be carried directly to the king's courts, without passing through the courts of the lords immediately superior.[u] It was ordained, that money should bear no interest during the minority of the debtor.[w] This law was reasonable, as the estates of minors were always in the hands of their lords, and the debtors could not pay interest where they had no revenue. The charter of king John had granted this indulgence: It was omitted in that of Henry III. for what reason is not known; but it was renewed by the statute of Marlebridge. Most of the other articles of this statute are calculated to restrain the oppressions of sheriffs, and the violence and iniquities committed in distraining cattle and other goods. Cattle and the instruments of husbandry formed at that time the chief riches of the people.

In the 35th year of this king an assize was fixed of bread, the price of which was settled, according to the different prices of corn, from one shilling a quarter to seven shillings and sixpence,[x] money of that age. These great variations are alone a proof of bad tillage:[y] Yet did the prices often rise much higher, than any taken

---

[t] Statute of Merton, chap. 9. [u] Statute of Marlb. chap. 20. [w] Ibid. chap. 16. [x] Statutes at large, p. 6. [y] We learn from Cicero's orations against Verres, lib. iii. cap. 84, 92, that the price of corn in Sicily was, during the praetorship of Sacerdos, five Denarii a Modius; during that of Verres, which immediately succeeded, only two Sesterces: That is, ten times lower; a presumption, or rather a proof, of the very bad state of tillage in ancient times.

notice of by the statute. The chronicle of Dunstable tells us, that in this reign, wheat was once sold for a mark, nay for a pound a quarter; that is, three pounds of our present money.[z] The same law affords us a proof of the little communication between the parts of the kingdom, from the very different prices which the same commodity bore at the same time. A brewer, says the statute, may sell two gallons of ale for a penny in cities, and three or four gallons for the same price in the country. At present, such commodities, by the great consumption of the people, and the great stocks of the brewers, are rather cheapest in cities. The Chronicle above-mentioned observes, that wheat one year was sold in many places for eight shillings a quarter, but never rose in Dunstable above a crown.

Though commerce was still very low, it seems rather to have encreased since the Conquest; at least, if we may judge of the increase of money by the price of corn. The medium between the highest and lowest prices of wheat, assigned by the statute, is four shillings and three pence a quarter, that is, twelve shillings and nine pence of our present money. This is near half of the middling price in our time. Yet the middling price of cattle, so late as the reign of king Richard, we found to be above eight, near ten times lower than the present. Is not this the true inference, from comparing these facts, that, in all uncivilized nations, cattle, which propagate of themselves, bear always a lower price than corn, which requires more art and stock to render it plentiful, than those nations are possessed of? It is to be remarked, that Henry's assize of corn was copied from a preceding assize established by king John; consequently, the prices which we have here compared of corn and cattle may be looked on as contemporary; and they were drawn, not from one particular year, but from an estimation of the middling prices for a series of years. It is true, the prices, assigned by the assize of Richard, were meant as a standard for the accompts of sheriffs and escheators; and as considerable profits were allowed to these ministers, we may naturally suppose, that the common value of cattle was somewhat higher: Yet still, so great a difference between the prices of corn and cattle as that of four to one, compared to the present rates, affords important reflections

[z] See also Knyghton, p. 2444.

concerning the very different state of industry and tillage in the two periods.

Interest had in that age mounted to an enormous height, as might be expected from the barbarism of the times and men's ignorance of commerce. Instances occur of fifty per cent. payed for money.[a] There is an edict of Philip Augustus near this period, limiting the Jews in France to 48 per cent.[b] Such profits tempted the Jews to remain in the kingdom, notwithstanding the grievous oppressions, to which, from the prevalent bigotry and rapine of the age, they were continually exposed. It is easy to imagine how precarious their state must have been under an indigent prince, somewhat restrained in his tyranny over his native subjects, but who possessed an unlimited authority over the Jews, the sole pro-prietors of money in the kingdom, and hated on account of their riches, their religion, and their usury: Yet will our ideas scarcely come up to the extortions which in fact we find to have been practised upon them. In the year 1241, 20,000 marks were exacted from them:[c] Two years after, money was again extorted; and one Jew alone, Aaron of York, was obliged to pay above 4000 marks:[d] In 1250, Henry renewed his oppressions; and the same Aaron was condemned to pay him 30,000 marks upon an accusation of for-gery:[e] The high penalty imposed upon him, and which, it seems, he was thought able to pay, is rather a presumption of his inno-cence than of his guilt. In 1255, the king demanded 8000 marks from the Jews, and threatened to hang them, if they refused com-pliance. They now lost all patience, and desired leave to retire with their effects out of the kingdom. But the king replied: "How can I remedy the oppressions you complain of? I am myself a beggar. I am spoiled, I am stripped of all my revenues: I owe above 200,000 marks; and if I had said 300,000, I should not exceed the truth: I am obliged to pay my son, prince Edward, 15,000 marks a year: I have not a farthing; and I must have money, from any hand, from any quarter, or by any means." He then delivered over the Jews to the earl of Cornwal, that those whom the one brother had flead, the other might embowel, to make use of the words of the historian.[f] King John, his father, once demanded 10,000 marks

---

[a] M. Paris, p. 586.   [b] Brussel Traité des Fiefs, vol. i. p. 576.   [c] M. Paris, p. 372.   [d] Ibid. p. 410.   [e] Ibid. p. 525.   [f] Ibid. p. 606.

CHAPTER XII

from a Jew of Bristol; and on his refusal, ordered one of his teeth to be drawn every day till he should comply. The Jew lost seven teeth; and then paid the sum required of him.[g] One talliage laid upon the Jews in 1243 amounted to 60,000 marks;[h] a sum equal to the whole yearly revenue of the crown.

To give a better pretence for extortions, the improbable and absurd accusation, which has been at different times advanced against that nation, was revived in England, that they had crucified a child in derision of the sufferings of Christ. Eighteen of them were hanged at once for this crime:[i] Though it is no wise credible, that even the antipathy born them by the Christians, and the oppressions under which they laboured, would ever have pushed them to be guilty of that dangerous enormity. But it is natural to imagine, that a race, exposed to such insults and indignities both from king and people, and who had so uncertain an enjoyment of their riches, would carry usury to the utmost extremity, and by their great profits make themselves some compensation for their continual perils.

Though these acts of violence against the Jews proceeded much from bigotry, they were still more derived from avidity and rapine. So far from desiring in that age to convert them, it was enacted by law in France, that, if any Jew embraced Christianity, he forfeited all his goods, without exception, to the king or his superior lord. These plunderers were careful, lest the profits, accruing from their dominion over that unhappy race, should be diminished by their conversion.[k]

Commerce must be in a wretched condition, where interest was so high, and where the sole proprietors of money employed it in usury only, and were exposed to such extortion and injustice. But the bad police of the country was another obstacle to improvements; and rendered all communication dangerous, and all property precarious. The Chronicle of Dunstable says,[l] that men were never secure in their houses, and that whole villages were often plundered by bands of robbers, though no civil wars at that time prevailed in the kingdom. In 1249, some years before the insurrection of the barons, two merchants of Brabant came to the king

[g] Ibid. p. 160.   [h] Madox, p. 152.   [i] M. Paris, p. 613.   [k] Brussel, vol. i. p. 622. Du Cange verbo *Judaei*.   [l] Vol. i. p. 155.

at Winchester, and told him, that they had been spoiled of all their goods by certain robbers, whom they knew, because they saw their faces every day in his court; that like practices prevailed all over England, and travellers were continually exposed to the danger of being robbed, bound, wounded, and murdered; that these crimes escaped with impunity, because the ministers of justice themselves were in a confederacy with the robbers; and that they, for their part, instead of bringing matters to a fruitless trial by law, were willing, though merchants, to decide their cause with the robbers by arms and a duel. The king, provoked at these abuses, ordered a jury to be inclosed, and to try the robbers: The jury, though consisting of twelve men of property in Hampshire, were found to be also in a confederacy with the felons, and acquitted them. Henry in a rage committed the jury to prison, threatened them with severe punishment, and ordered a new jury to be inclosed, who, dreading the fate of their fellows, at last found a verdict against the criminals. Many of the king's own household were discovered to have participated in the guilt; and they said for their excuse, that they received no wages from him, and were obliged to rob for a maintenance.[m] *Knights and esquires,* says the Dictum of Kenelworth, *who were robbers, if they have no land, shall pay the half of their goods, and find sufficient security to keep henceforth the peace of the kingdom.* Such were the manners of the times!

One can the less repine, during the prevalence of such manners, at the frauds and forgeries of the clergy; as it gives less disturbance to society, to take men's money from them with their own consent, though by deceits and lies, than to ravish it by open force and violence. During this reign, the papal power was at its summit, and was even beginning insensibly to decline, by reason of the immeasurable avarice and extortions of the court of Rome, which disgusted the clergy as well as laity, in every kingdom of Europe. England itself, though sunk in the deepest abyss of ignorance and superstition, had seriously entertained thoughts of shaking off the papal yoke;[n] and the Roman pontiff was obliged to think of new expedients for rivetting it faster upon the Christian world. For this purpose, Gregory IX. published his decretals,[o]

[m] M. Paris, p. 509.   [n] M. Paris, p. 421.   [o] Trivet, p. 191.

CHAPTER XII

which are a collection of forgeries, favourable to the court of Rome, and consist of the supposed decrees of popes in the first centuries. But these forgeries are so gross, and confound so palpably all language, history, chronology, and antiquities; matters more stubborn than any speculative truths whatsoever; that even that church, which is not startled at the most monstrous contradictions and absurdities, has been obliged to abandon them to the critics. But in the dark period of the thirteenth century, they passed for undisputed and authentic; and men, entangled in the mazes of this false literature, joined to the philosophy, equally false, of the times, had nothing wherewithal to defend themselves, but some small remains of common sense, which passed for profaneness and impiety, and the indelible regard to self-interest, which, as it was the sole motive in the priests for framing these impostures, served also, in some degree, to protect the laity against them.

Another expedient, devised by the church of Rome, in this period, for securing her power, was the institution of new religious orders, chiefly the Dominicans and Franciscans, who proceeded with all the zeal and success that attend novelties; were better qualified to gain the populace than the old orders, now become rich and indolent; maintained a perpetual rivalship with each other in promoting their gainful superstitions; and acquired a great dominion over the minds, and consequently over the purses of men, by pretending a desire of poverty and a contempt for riches. The quarrels which arose between these orders, lying still under the controul of the sovereign pontiff, never disturbed the peace of the church, and served only as a spur to their industry in promoting the common cause; and though the Dominicans lost some popularity by their denial of the immaculate conception, a point in which they unwarily engaged too far to be able to recede with honour, they counterbalanced this disadvantage by acquiring more solid establishments, by gaining the confidence of kings and princes, and by exercising the jurisdiction assigned them, of ultimate judges and punishers of heresy. Thus, the several orders of monks became a kind of regular troops or garrisons of the Romish church; and though the temporal interests of society, still more the cause of true piety, were hurt, by their various devices to captivate the populace, they proved the chief supports of that mighty fabric of superstition, and, till the revival of true learning, secured it from any dangerous invasion.

The trial by ordeal was abolished in this reign by order of council: A faint mark of improvement in the age.[p]

Henry granted a charter to the town of Newcastle, in which he gave the inhabitants a licence to dig coal. This is the first mention of coal in England.

We learn from Madox,[q] that this king gave at one time 100 shillings to master Henry, his poet: Also the same year he orders this poet ten pounds.

It appears from Selden, that in the 47th of this reign a hundred and fifty temporal, and fifty spiritual barons were summoned to perform the service, due by their tenures.[r] In the 35th of the subsequent reign eighty-six temporal barons, twenty bishops, and forty-eight abbots, were summoned to a parliament convened at Carlisle.[s]

[p] Rymer, vol. i. p. 228. Spelman, p. 326. [q] Page 268. [r] Titles of honour, part 2. chap. 3. [s] Parliamentary Hist. vol. i. p. 151.

XIII
EDWARD I

---

*Civil administration of the king – Conquest
of Wales – Affairs of Scotland – Competitors
for the crown of Scotland – Reference to
Edward – Homage of Scotland – Award of Edward
in favour of Baliol – War with France –
Digression concerning the constitution of
parliament – War with Scotland – Scotland
subdued – War with France – Dissensions with
the clergy – Arbitrary measures – Peace with
France – Revolt of Scotland – That kingdom
again subdued – again revolts – is again
subdued – Robert Bruce – Third revolt of
Scotland – Death and character of the king –
Miscellaneous transactions of this reign.*

T HE ENGLISH were as yet so little enured to obedience under a   *1272.*
regular government, that the death of almost every king,
since the conquest, had been attended with disorders; and the
council, reflecting on the recent civil wars, and on the animosities
which naturally remain after these great convulsions, had reason
to apprehend dangerous consequences from the absence of the
son and successor of Henry. They therefore hastened to proclaim
prince Edward, to swear allegiance to him, and to summon the
states of the kingdom, in order to provide for the public peace in

this important conjuncture.[t] Walter Giffard, archbishop of York, the earl of Cornwal, son of Richard, king of the Romans, and the earl of Glocester, were appointed guardians of the realm, and proceeded peaceably to the exercise of their authority, without either meeting with opposition from any of the people, or being disturbed with emulation and faction among themselves. The high character acquired by Edward during the late commotions, his military genius, his success in subduing the rebels, his moderation in settling the kingdom, had procured him great esteem, mixed with affection, among all orders of men; and no one could reasonably entertain hopes of making any advantage of his absence, or of raising disturbance in the nation. The earl of Glocester himself, whose great power and turbulent spirit had excited most jealousy, was forward to give proofs of his allegiance; and the other malcontents, being destitute of a leader, were obliged to remain in submission to the government.

Prince Edward had reached Sicily in his return from the Holy Land, when he received intelligence of the death of his father; and he discovered a deep concern on the occasion. At the same time he learned the death of an infant son, John, whom his princess, Eleanor of Castile, had born him at Acre in Palestine, and as he appeared much less affected with that misfortune, the king of Sicily expressed a surprize at this difference of sentiment: But was told by Edward, that the death of a son was a loss which he might hope to repair; the death of a father was a loss irreparable.[u]

1273.

Edward proceeded homeward; but as he soon learned the quiet settlement of the kingdom, he was in no hurry to take possession of the throne, but spent near a year in France, before he made his appearance in England. In his passage by Chalons in Burgundy, he was challenged by the prince of the country to a tournament which he was preparing; and as Edward excelled in those martial and dangerous exercises, the true image of war, he declined not the opportunity of acquiring honour in that great assembly of the neighbouring nobles. But the image of war was here unfortunately turned into the thing itself. Edward and his retinue were so successful in the jousts, that the French knights, provoked at their

---

[t] Rymer, vol. ii. p. 1. Walsing p. 43. Trivet, p. 239. [u] Walsing. p. 44. Trivet, p. 240.

CHAPTER XIII

superiority, made a serious attack upon them, which was repulsed, and much blood was idly shed in the quarrel.[w] This rencounter received the name of the petty battle of Chalons.

Edward went from Chalons to Paris, and did homage to Philip for the dominions which he held in France.[x] He thence returned to Guienne, and settled that province, which was in some confusion. He made his journey to London through France; in his passage he accommodated at Montreuil a difference with Margaret, countess of Flanders, heiress of that territory;[y] he was received with joyful acclamations by his people, and was solemnly crowned at Westminster by Robert, archbishop of Canterbury.

1274.

19th Aug.

The king immediately applied himself to the re-establishment of his kingdom, and to the correcting of those disorders, which the civil commotions and the loose administration of his father had introduced into every part of government. The plan of his policy was equally generous and prudent. He considered the great barons both as the immediate rivals of the crown, and oppressors of the people; and he purposed, by an exact distribution of justice, and a rigid execution of the laws, to give at once protection to the inferior orders of the state, and to diminish the arbitrary power of the great, on which their dangerous authority was chiefly founded. Making it a rule in his own conduct to observe, except on extraordinary occasions, the privileges secured to them by the Great Charter, he acquired a right to insist upon their observance of the same charter towards their vassals and inferiors; and he made the crown be regarded by all the gentry and commonalty of the kingdom, as the fountain of justice, and the general asylum against oppression. Besides enacting several useful statutes, in a parliament which he summoned at Westminster, he took care to inspect the conduct of all his magistrates and judges, to displace such as were either negligent or corrupt, to provide them with sufficient force for the execution of justice, to extirpate all bands and confederacies of robbers, and to repress those more silent robberies, which were committed either by the power of the nobles, or under the countenance of public authority. By this rigid administration, the face of the kingdom was soon changed; and order and justice took place

Civil administration of the king.

1275.
16th Feb.

---

[w] Walsing, p. 44. Trivet, p. 241. M. West. p. 402. [x] Walsing. p. 45.
[y] Rymer, vol. ii. p. 32, 33.

of violence and oppression: But amidst the excellent institutions and public-spirited plans of Edward, there still appears somewhat both of the severity of his personal character and of the prejudices of the times.

As the various kinds of malefactors, the murderers, robbers, incendiaries, ravishers, and plunderers, had become so numerous and powerful, that the ordinary ministers of justice, especially in the western counties, were afraid to execute the laws against them, the king found it necessary to provide an extraordinary remedy for the evil; and he erected a new tribunal, which, however useful, would have been deemed, in times of more regular liberty, a great stretch of illegal and arbitrary power. It consisted of commissioners, who were empowered to enquire into disorders and crimes of all kinds, and to inflict the proper punishments upon them. The officers, charged with this unusual commission, made their circuits throughout the counties of England most infested with this evil, and carried terror into all those parts of the kingdom. In their zeal to punish crimes, they did not sufficiently distinguish between the innocent and guilty; the smallest suspicion became a ground of accusation and trial; the slightest evidence was received against criminals; prisons were crowded with malefactors, real or pretended; severe fines were levied for small offences; and the king, though his exhausted exchequer was supplied by this expedient, found it necessary to stop the course of so great rigour, and after terrifying and dissipating by this tribunal the gangs of disorderly people in England, he prudently annulled the commission;[z] and never afterwards renewed it.

Among the various disorders, to which the kingdom was subject, no one was more universally complained of than the adulteration of the coin; and as this crime required more art than the English of that age, who chiefly employed force and violence in their iniquities, were possessed of, the imputation fell upon the Jews.[a] Edward also seems to have indulged a strong prepossession against that nation; and this ill-judged zeal for Christianity being naturally augmented by an expedition to the Holy Land, he let

[z] Spellman's Gloss. in verbo *Trailbaston*. But Spellman was either mistaken in placing this commission in the fifth year of the king, or it was renewed in 1305. See Rymer, vol. ii. p. 960. Trivet, p. 338. M. West. p. 450.
[a] Walsing. p. 48. Heming. vol. i. p. 6.

CHAPTER XIII

loose the whole rigour of his justice against that unhappy people. Two hundred and eighty of them were hanged at once for this crime in London alone, besides those who suffered in other parts of the kingdom.[b] The houses and lands, (for the Jews had of late ventured to make purchases of that kind) as well as the goods of great multitudes, were sold and confiscated: And the king, lest it should be suspected that the riches of the sufferers were the chief part of their guilt, ordered a moiety of the money, raised by these confiscations, to be set apart, and bestowed upon such as were willing to be converted to Christianity. But resentment was more prevalent with them, than any temptation from their poverty; and very few of them could be induced by interest to embrace the religion of their persecutors. The miseries of this people did not here terminate. Though the arbitrary talliages and exactions, levied upon them, had yielded a constant and a considerable revenue to the crown; Edward, prompted by his zeal and his rapacity, resolved some time after[c] to purge the kingdom entirely of that hated race, and to seize to himself at once their whole property as the reward of his labour.[d] He left them only money sufficient to bear their charges into foreign countries, where new persecutions and extortions awaited them: But the inhabitants of the cinque-ports, imitating the bigotry and avidity of their sovereign, despoiled most of them of this small pittance, and even threw many of them into the sea: A crime, for which the king, who was determined to be the sole plunderer in his dominions, inflicted a capital punishment upon them. No less than fifteen thousand Jews were at this time robbed of their effects and banished the kingdom: Very few of that nation have since lived in England: And as it is impossible for a nation to subsist without lenders of money, and none will lend without a compensation, the practice of usury, as it was then called, was thenceforth exercised by the English themselves upon their fellow-citizens, or by Lombards and other foreigners. It is very much to be questioned, whether the dealings of these new usurers were equally open and unexceptionable with those of the old. By a law of Richard, it was enacted, that three copies should be made of every bond given to a Jew; one to be put

[b] T. Wykes, p. 107.   [c] In the year 1290.   [d] Walsing. p. 54. Heming. vol. i. p. 20. Trivet, p. 266.

into the hands of a public magistrate, another into those of a man of credit, and a third to remain with the Jew himself.[e] But as the canon law, seconded by the municipal, permitted no Christian to take interest, all transactions of this kind must, after the banishment of the Jews, have become more secret and clandestine, and the lender, of consequence, be paid both for the use of his money, and for the infamy and danger which he incurred by lending it.

The great poverty of the crown, though no excuse, was probably the cause of this egregious tyranny exercised against the Jews; but Edward also practised other more honourable means of remedying that evil. He employed a strict frugality in the management and distribution of his revenue: He engaged the parliament to vote him a fifteenth of all moveables; the pope to grant him the tenth of all ecclesiastical revenues for three years; and the merchants to consent to a perpetual imposition of half a mark on every sack of wool exported, and a mark on three hundred skins. He also issued commissions to enquire into all encroachments on the royal demesne; into the value of escheats, forfeitures, and wardships; and into the means of repairing or improving every branch of the revenue.[f] The commissioners, in the execution of their office, began to carry matters too far against the nobility, and to question titles to estates which had been transmitted from father to son for several generations. Earl Warrenne, who had done such eminent service in the late reign, being required to show his titles, drew his sword; and subjoined, that William, the Bastard, had not conquered the kingdom for himself alone: His ancestor was a joint adventurer in the enterprize; and he himself was determined to maintain what had from that period remained unquestioned in his family. The king, sensible of the danger, desisted from making farther enquiries of this nature.

1276.
Conquest
of Wales.
But the active spirit of Edward could not long remain without employment. He soon after undertook an enterprize more prudent for himself, and more advantageous to his people. Lewellyn, prince of Wales, had been deeply engaged with the Mountfort faction; had entered into all their conspiracies against the crown; had frequently fought on their side; and till the battle of

---

[e] Trivet, p. 128.   [f] Ann. Waverl. p. 235.

CHAPTER XIII

Evesham, so fatal to that party, had employed every expedient to depress the royal cause, and to promote the success of the barons. In the general accommodation, made with the vanquished, Lewellyn had also obtained his pardon; but as he was the most powerful, and therefore the most obnoxious vassal of the crown, he had reason to entertain anxiety about his situation, and to dread the future effects of resentment and jealousy in the English monarch. For this reason, he determined to provide for his security by maintaining a secret correspondence with his former associates; and he even made his addresses to a daughter of the earl of Leicester, who was sent to him from beyond sea, but being intercepted in her passage near the isles of Sicily, was detained in the court of England.[g] This incident encreasing the mutual jealousy between Edward and Lewellyn, the latter, when required to come to England, and do homage to the new king, scrupled to put himself in the hands of an enemy, desired a safe-conduct from Edward, insisted upon having the king's son and other noblemen delivered to him as hostages, and demanded, that his consort should previously be set at liberty.[h] The king, having now brought the state to a full settlement, was not displeased with this occasion of exercising his authority, and subduing entirely the principality of Wales. He refused all Lewellyn's demands, except that of a safe-conduct; sent him repeated summons to perform the duty of a vassal; levied an army to reduce him to obedience; obtained a new aid of a fifteenth from parliament; and marched out with certain assurance of success against the enemy. Besides the great disproportion of force between the kingdom and the principality, the circumstances of the two states were entirely reversed; and the same intestine dissentions, which had formerly weakened England, now prevailed in Wales, and had even taken place in the reigning family. David and Roderic, brothers to Lewellyn, dispossessed of their inheritance by that prince, had been obliged to have recourse to the protection of Edward, and they seconded with all their interest, which was extensive, his attempts to enslave their native country. The Welsh prince had no resource but in the inaccessible situation of his mountains, which had hitherto, through many ages, de-

1277.

[g] Walsing. p. 46, 47. Heming. vol. i. p. 5. Trivet, p. 248.   [h] Rymer, vol. ii. p. 68. Walsing. p. 46. Trivet, p. 247.

fended his forefathers against all attempts of the Saxon and Norman conquerors; and he retired among the hills of Snowdun, resolute to defend himself to the last extremity. But Edward, equally vigorous and cautious, entering by the north with a formidable army, pierced into the heart of the country; and having carefully explored every road before him, and secured every pass behind him, approached the Welsh army in its last retreat. He here avoided the putting to trial the valour of a nation, proud of its ancient independance, and enflamed with animosity against its hereditary enemies; and he trusted to the slow, but sure effects of famine, for reducing that people to subjection. The rude and simple manners of the natives, as well as the mountainous situation of their country, had made them entirely neglect tillage, and trust to pasturage alone for their subsistence: A method of life which had hitherto secured them against the irregular attempts of the English, but exposed them to certain ruin, when the conquest of the country was steddily pursued, and prudently planned by Edward. Destitute of magazines, cooped up in a narrow corner, they, as well as their cattle, suffered all the rigors of famine; and Lewellyn, without being able to strike a stroke for his independance, was at last obliged to submit at discretion, and receive the terms imposed upon him by the victor.[i] He bound himself to pay to Edmond 50,000 pounds, as a reparation of damages; to do homage to the crown of England; to permit all the other barons of Wales, except four near Snowdun, to swear fealty to the same crown; to relinquish the country between Cheshire and the river Conway; to settle on his brother Roderic a thousand marks a year, and on David five hundred; and to deliver ten hostages as security for his future submission.[k]

19th
Nov.

Edward, on the performance of the other articles, remitted to the prince of Wales the payment of the 50,000 pounds,[l] which were stipulated by treaty, and which, it is probable the poverty of the country made it absolutely impossible for him to levy. But notwithstanding this indulgence, complaints of iniquities soon arose on the side of the vanquished: The English, insolent on their easy and bloodless victory, oppressed the inhabitants of the dis-

[i] T. Wykes, p. 105. [k] Rymer, vol. ii. p. 88. Walsing. p. 47. Trivet, p. 251.
T. Wykes, p. 106. [l] Rymer, p. 92.

tricts which were yielded to them: The lords marchers committed with impunity all kinds of violence on their Welsh neighbours: New and more severe terms were imposed on Lewellyn himself; and Edward, when the prince attended him at Worcester, exacted a promise that he would retain no person in his principality who should be obnoxious to the English monarch.[m] There were other personal insults, which raised the indignation of the Welsh, and made them determine rather to encounter a force, which they had already experienced to be so much superior, than to bear oppression from the haughty victors. Prince David, seized with the national spirit, made peace with his brother, and promised to concur in the defence of public liberty. The Welsh flew to arms; and Edward, not displeased with the occasion of making his conquest final and absolute, assembled all his military tenants, and advanced into Wales with an army, which the inhabitants could not reasonably hope to resist. The situation of the country gave the Welsh at first some advantage over Luke de Tany, one of Edward's captains, who had passed the Menau with a detachment:[n] But Lewellyn, being surprized by Mortimer, was defeated and slain in an action, and 2000 of his followers were put to the sword.[o] David, who succeeded him in the principality, could never collect an army sufficient to face the English; and being chaced from hill to hill, and hunted from one retreat to another, was obliged to conceal himself under various disguises, and was at last betrayed in his lurking-place to the enemy. Edward sent him in chains to Shrewsbury; and bringing him to a formal trial before all the peers of England, ordered this sovereign prince to be hanged, drawn, and quartered, as a traitor, for defending by arms the liberties of his native country, together with his own hereditary authority.[p] All the Welsh nobility submitted to the conqueror; the laws of England, with the sheriffs and other ministers of justice, were established in that principality; and though it was long before national antipathies were extinguished, and a thorough union attained between the people, yet this important conquest, which it had required

1283.

---

[m] Dr. Powell's Hist. of Wales, p. 344, 345.   [n] Walsing. p. 50. Heming. vol. i. p. 9. Trivet, p. 258. T. Wykes, p. 110.   [o] Heming. vol. i. p. 11. Trivet, p. 257. Ann. Waverl. p. 235.   [p] Heming. vol. i. p. 12. Trivet, p. 259. Ann. Waverl. p. 238. T. Wykes, p. 111. M. West. p. 411.

eight hundred years fully to effect, was at last, through the abilities of Edward, completed by the English.

1284. The king, sensible that nothing kept alive the ideas of military valour and of ancient glory, so much as the traditional poetry of the people, which, assisted by the power of music, and the jollity of festivals, made deep impression on the minds of the youth, gathered together all the Welsh bards, and from a barbarous, though not absurd policy, ordered them to be put to death.[q]

There prevails a vulgar story, which, as it well suits the capacity of the monkish writers, is carefully recorded by them: That Edward, assembling the Welsh, promised to give them a prince of unexceptionable manners, a Welshman by birth, and one who could speak no other language. On their acclamations of joy, and promise of obedience, he invested in the principality his second son Edward, then an infant, who had been born at Carnarvon. The death of his eldest son Alfonso, soon after, made young Edward heir of the monarchy: The principality of Wales was fully annexed to the crown; and henceforth gives a title to the eldest son of the kings of England.

1286. The settlement of Wales appeared so complete to Edward, that, in less than two years after, he went abroad, in order to make peace between Alphonso, king of Arragon, and Philip the Fair, who had lately succeeded his father Philip the Hardy on the throne of France.[r] The difference between these two princes had arisen about the kingdom of Sicily, which the pope, after his hopes from England failed him, had bestowed on Charles, brother to St. Lewis, and which was claimed upon other titles, by Peter king of Arragon, father to Alphonso. Edward had powers from both princes to settle the terms of peace, and he succeeded in his endeavours; but as the controversy nowise regards England, we shall not enter into a detail of it. He stayed abroad above three years; and on his return, found many disorders to have prevailed, both from open violence, and from the corruption of justice.

Thomas Chamberlain, a gentleman of some note, had assembled several of his associates at Boston, in Lincolnshire, under pretence of holding a tournament, an exercise practised by the gentry only; but in reality with a view of plundering the rich fair

[q] Sir J. Wynne, p. 15.   [r] Rymer, vol. ii. p. 149, 150, 174.

CHAPTER XIII

of Boston, and robbing the merchants. To facilitate his purpose, he privately set fire to the town; and while the inhabitants were employed in quenching the flames, the conspirators broke into the booths, and carried off the goods. Chamberlain himself was detected and hanged, but maintained so steddily the point of honour to his accomplices, that he could not be prevailed on, by offers or promises, to discover any of them. Many other instances of robbery and violence broke out in all parts of England; though the singular circumstances attending this conspiracy have made it alone be particularly recorded by historians.[s]

But the corruption of the judges, by which the fountains of justice were poisoned, seemed of still more dangerous consequence. Edward, in order to remedy this prevailing abuse, summoned a parliament, and brought the judges to a trial; where all of them, except two, who were clergymen, were convicted of this flagrant iniquity, were fined, and deposed. The amount of the fines, levied upon them, is alone a sufficient proof of their guilt; being above one hundred thousand marks, an immense sum in those days, and sufficient to defray the charges of an expensive war between two great kingdoms. The king afterwards made all the new judges swear, that they would take no bribes; but his expedient, of deposing and fining the old ones, was the more effectual remedy. *1289.*

We now come to give an account of the state of affairs in Scotland, which gave rise to the most interesting transactions of this reign, and of some of the subsequent; though the intercourse of that kingdom with England, either in peace or war, had hitherto produced so few events of moment, that, to avoid tediousness, we have omitted many of them, and have been very concise in relating the rest. If the Scots had, before this period, any real history, worthy of the name, except what they glean from scattered passages in the English historians, those events, however minute, yet, being the only foreign transactions of the nation, might deserve a place in it.

Though the government of Scotland had been continually exposed to those factions and convulsions, which are incident to all barbarous, and to many civilized nations; and though the succes- *Affairs of Scotland.*

[s] Heming. vol. i. p. 16, 17.

sions of their kings, the only part of their history which deserves any credit, had often been disordered by irregularities and usurpations; the true heir of the royal family had still in the end prevailed, and Alexander III. who had espoused the sister of Edward, probably inherited, after a period of about eight hundred years, and through a succession of males, the scepter of all the Scottish princes, who had governed the nation, since its first establishment in the island. This prince died in 1286 by a fall from his horse at Kinghorn,[t] without leaving any male issue, and without any descendant, except Margaret, born of Eric, king of Norway, and of Margaret, daughter of the Scottish monarch. This princess, commonly called the maid of Norway, though a female, and an infant, and a foreigner, yet being the lawful heir of the kingdom, had, through her grandfather's care, been recognized successor by the states of Scotland;[u] and on Alexander's death, the dispositions, which had been previously made against that event, appeared so just and prudent, that no disorders, as might naturally be apprehended, ensued in the kingdom. Margaret was acknowledged queen of Scotland; five guardians, the bishops of St. Andrews and Glasgow, the earls of Fife and Buchan, and James, steward of Scotland, entered peaceably upon the administration; and the infant princess, under the protection of Edward, her great uncle, and Eric, her father, who exerted themselves on this occasion, seemed firmly seated on the throne of Scotland. The English monarch was naturally led to build mighty projects on this incident; and having lately, by force of arms, brought Wales under subjection, he attempted, by the marriage of Margaret with his eldest son Edward, to unite the whole island into one monarchy, and thereby to give it security both against domestic convulsions and foreign invasions. The amity, which had of late prevailed between the two nations, and which, even in former times, had never been interrupted by any violent wars or injuries, facilitated extremely the execution of this project, so favourable to the happiness and grandeur of both kingdoms; and the states of Scotland readily gave their assent to the English proposals, and even agreed, that their young sovereign should be educated in the court of Edward. Anxious, however, for the liberty and independancy of their country,

1290.

---

[t] Heming. vol. i. p. 29. Trivet, p. 267.   [u] Rymer, vol. ii. p. 266.

CHAPTER XIII

they took care to stipulate very equitable conditions, ere they entrusted themselves into the hands of so great and so ambitious a monarch. It was agreed, that they should enjoy all their ancient laws, liberties, and customs; that in case young Edward and Margaret should die without issue, the crown of Scotland should revert to the next heir, and should be inherited by him free and independant; that the military tenants of the crown should never be obliged to go out of Scotland, in order to do homage to the sovereign of the united kingdoms, nor the chapters of cathedral, collegiate, or conventual churches, in order to make elections; that the parliaments, summoned for Scottish affairs, should always be held within the bounds of that kingdom; and that Edward should bind himself, under the penalty of 100,000 marks, payable to the pope for the use of the holy wars, to observe all these articles.[w] It is not easy to conceive, that two nations could have treated more on a foot of equality than Scotland and England maintained during the whole course of this transaction: And though Edward gave his assent to the article, concerning the future independancy of the Scottish crown, with a *saving of his former rights;* this reserve gave no alarm to the nobility of Scotland, both because these rights, having hitherto been little heard of, had occasioned no disturbance, and because the Scots had so near a prospect of seeing them entirely absorbed in the rights of their sovereignty.

But this project, so happily formed and so amicably conducted, failed of success, by the sudden death of the Norvegian princess, who expired on her passage to Scotland,[x] and left a very dismal prospect to the kingdom. Though disorders were for the present obviated by the authority of the regency formerly established, the succession itself of the crown was now become an object of dispute; and the regents could not expect, that a controversy, which is not usually decided by reason and argument alone, would be peaceably settled by them, or even by the states of the kingdom, amidst so many powerful pretenders. The posterity of William, king of Scotland, the prince taken prisoner by Henry II. being all extinct by the death of Margaret of Norway; the right to the crown devolved on the issue of David, earl of Huntingdon, brother to William, whose male line, being also extinct, left the

1291.

Competitors for the crown of Scotland.

---

[w] Rymer, vol. ii. p. 482.   [x] Heming. vol. i. p. 30. Trivet, p. 268.

succession open to the posterity of his daughters. The earl of Huntingdon had three daughters; Margaret, married to Alan lord of Galloway, Isabella, wife of Robert Brus or Bruce, lord of Annandale, and Adama, who espoused Henry lord Hastings. Margaret, the eldest of the sisters, left one daughter, Devergilda, married to John Baliol, by whom she had a son of the same name, one of the present competitors for the crown: Isabella, the second, bore a son, Robert Bruce, who was now alive, and who also insisted on his claim: Adama the third left a son, John Hastings, who pretended, that the kingdom of Scotland, like many other inheritances, was divisible among the three daughters of the earl of Huntingdon, and that he, in right of his mother, had a title to a third of it. Baliol and Bruce united against Hastings, in maintaining that the kingdom was indivisible; but each of them, supported by plausible reasons, asserted the preference of his own title. Baliol was sprung from the elder branch: Bruce was one degree nearer the common stock: If the principle of representation was regarded, the former had the better claim: If propinquity was considered, the latter was entitled to the preference.[y] The sentiments of men were divided: All the nobility had taken part on one side or the other: The people followed implicitly their leaders: The two claimants themselves had great power and numerous retainers in Scotland: And it is no wonder, that, among a rude people, more accustomed to arms than enured to laws, a controversy of this nature, which could not be decided by any former precedent among them, and which is capable of exciting commotions in the most legal and best established governments, should threaten the state with the most fatal convulsions.

Each century has its peculiar mode in conducting business; and men, guided more by custom than by reason, follow, without enquiry, the manners, which are prevalent in their own time. The practice of that age, in controversies between states and princes, seems to have been to chuse a foreign prince, as an equal arbiter, by whom the question was decided, and whose sentence prevented those dismal confusions and disorders, inseparable at all times from war, but which were multiplied a hundred fold, and dispersed into every corner, by the nature of the feudal governments.

[y] Heming. vol. i. p. 36.

CHAPTER XIII

It was thus that the English king and barons, in the preceding reign, had endeavoured to compose their dissensions by a reference to the king of France; and the celebrated integrity of that monarch had prevented all the bad effects, which might naturally have been dreaded from so perilous an expedient. It was thus that the kings of France and Arragon, and afterwards other princes, had submitted their controversies to Edward's judgment; and the remoteness of their states, the great power of the princes, and the little interest which he had on either side, had induced him to acquit himself with honour in his decisions. The parliament of Scotland, therefore, threatened with a furious civil war, and allured by the great reputation of the English monarch, as well as by the present amicable correspondence between the kingdoms, agreed in making a reference to Edward; and Fraser, bishop of St. Andrews, with other deputies, was sent to notify to him their resolution, and to claim his good offices in the present dangers to which they were exposed.[2] His inclination, they flattered themselves, led him to prevent their dissensions, and to interpose with a power, which none of the competitors would dare to withstand: When this expedient was proposed by one party, the other deemed it dangerous to object to it: Indifferent persons thought that the imminent perils of a civil war would thereby be prevented: And no one reflected on the ambitious character of Edward, and the almost certain ruin, which must attend a small state, divided by faction, when it thus implicitly submits itself to the will of so powerful and encroaching a neighbour.

Reference to Edward.

The temptation was too strong for the virtue of the English monarch to resist. He purposed to lay hold of the present favourable opportunity, and if not to create, at least to revive, his claim of a feudal superiority over Scotland; a claim which had hitherto lain in the deepest obscurity, and which, if ever it had been an object of attention, or had been so much as suspected, would have effectually prevented the Scottish barons from chusing him for an umpire. He well knew, that, if this pretension were once submitted to, as it seemed difficult, in the present situation of Scotland, to oppose it, the absolute sovereignty of that kingdom (which had been the case with Wales) would soon follow; and that one great

Homage of Scotland.

[2] Heming. vol. i. p. 31.

vassal, cooped up in an island with his liege lord, without resource from foreign powers, without aid from any fellow vassals, could not long maintain his dominions against the efforts of a mighty kingdom, assisted by all the cavils which the feudal law afforded his superior against him. In pursuit of this great object, very advantageous to England, perhaps in the end no less beneficial to Scotland, but extremely unjust and iniquitous in itself, Edward busied himself in searching for proofs of his pretended superiority; and instead of looking into his own archives, which, if his claim had been real, must have afforded him numerous records of the homages done by the Scottish princes, and could alone yield him any authentic testimony, he made all the monasteries be ransacked for old chronicles and histories written by Englishmen, and he collected all the passages, which seemed anywise to favour his pretensions.[a] Yet even in this method of proceeding, which must have discovered to himself the injustice of his claim, he was far from being fortunate. He began his proofs from the time of Edward the elder, and continued them through all the subsequent Saxon and Norman times; but produced nothing to his purpose.[b] The whole amount of his authorities during the Saxon period, when stripped of the bombast and inaccurate style of the monkish historians, is, that the Scots had sometimes been defeated by the English, had received peace on disadvantageous terms, had made submissions to the English monarch, and had even perhaps fallen into some dependance on a power, which was so much superior, and which they had not at that time sufficient force to resist. His authorities from the Norman period were, if possible, still less conclusive: The historians indeed make frequent mention of homage done by the northern potentate; but no one of them says that it was done for his kingdom, and several of them declare, in express terms, that it was relative only to the fiefs which he enjoyed south of the Tweed;[c] in the same manner, as the king of England himself swore fealty to the French monarch, for the fiefs which he inherited in France. And to such scandalous shifts was Edward reduced, that he quotes a passage from Hoveden,[d] where it is asserted, that a Scottish king had done homage to England; but he purposely omits the latter

[a] Walsing. p. 55.   [b] Rymer, vol. ii. p. 559.   [c] Hoveden, p. 492, 662. M. Paris, p. 109. M. West. p. 256.   [d] P. 662.

part of the sentence, which expresses that this prince did homage for the lands which he held in England.

When William, king of Scotland, was taken prisoner in the battle of Alnwic, he was obliged, for the recovery of his liberty, to swear fealty to the victor for his crown itself. The deed was performed according to all the rites of the feudal law: The record was preserved in the English archives, and is mentioned by all the historians: But as it is the only one of the kind, and as historians speak of this superiority as a great acquisition gained by the fortunate arms of Henry II.[e] there can remain no doubt, that the kingdom of Scotland was, in all former periods, entirely free and independant. Its subjection continued a very few years: King Richard, desirous, before his departure for the Holy Land, to conciliate the friendship of William, renounced that homage, which, he says in express terms, had been extorted by his father; and he only retained the usual homage which had been done by the Scottish princes for the lands which they held in England.

But though this transaction rendered the independance of Scotland still more unquestionable, than if no fealty had ever been sworn to the English crown; the Scottish kings, apprized of the point aimed at by their powerful neighbours, seem for a long time to have retained some jealousy on that head, and in doing homage, to have anxiously obviated all such pretensions. When William in 1200 did homage to John at Lincoln, he was careful to insert a salvo for his royal dignity:[f] When Alexander III. sent assistance to his father-in-law, Henry III. during the wars of the barons, he previously procured an acknowledgment, that this aid was granted only from friendship, not from any right claimed by the English monarch:[g] And when the same prince was invited to assist at the coronation of this very Edward, he declined attendance, till he received a like acknowledgment.[h]

But as all these reasons (and stronger could not be produced) were but a feeble rampart against the power of the sword, Edward, carrying with him a great army, which was to enforce his proofs, advanced to the frontiers, and invited the Scottish parliament and all the competitors to attend him in the castle of Norham, a place

[e] Neubr. lib. ii. cap. 4. Knyghton, p. 2392. [f] Hoveden, p. 811. [g] Rymer, vol. ii. p. 844. [h] See note [A] at the end of the volume.

situated on the southern banks of the Tweed, in order to determine that cause, which had been referred to his arbitration. But though this deference seemed due to so great a monarch, and was no more than what his father and the English barons had, in similar circumstances, paid to Lewis IX. the king, careful not to give umbrage, and determined never to produce his claim, till it should be too late to think of opposition, sent the Scottish barons an acknowledgment, that, though at that time they passed the frontiers, this step should never be drawn into precedent, or afford the English kings a pretence for exacting a like submission in any

10th May.

future transaction.[i] When the whole Scottish nation had thus unwarily put themselves in his power, Edward opened the conferences at Norham: He informed the parliament, by the mouth of Roger le Brabançon, his chief justiciary, that he was come thither to determine the right among the competitors to their crown; that he was determined to do strict justice to all parties; and that he was intitled to this authority, not in virtue of the reference made to him, but in quality of superior and liege lord of the kingdom.[k] He then produced his proofs of this superiority, which he pretended to be unquestionable, and he required of them an acknowledgment of it; a demand, which was superfluous if the fact were already known and avowed, and which plainly betrays Edward's consciousness of his lame and defective title. The Scottish parliament was astonished at so new a pretension, and answered only by their silence. But the king, in order to maintain the appearance of free and regular proceedings, desired them to remove into their own country, to deliberate upon his claim, to examine his proofs, to propose all their objections, and to inform him of their resolution: And he appointed a plain at Upsettleton, on the northern banks of the Tweed, for that purpose.

When the Scottish barons assembled in this place, though moved with indignation at the injustice of this unexpected claim, and at the fraud with which it had been conducted, they found themselves betrayed into a situation, in which it was impossible for them to make any defence for the ancient liberty and independance of their country. The king of England, a martial and politic

[i] Rymer, vol. ii. p. 539, 845. Walsing. p. 56.   [k] Rymer, vol. ii. p. 543. See note [B] at the end of the volume.

prince, at the head of a powerful army, lay at a very small distance, and was only separated from them by a river fordable in many places. Though by a sudden flight some of them might themselves be able to make their escape; what hopes could they entertain of securing the kingdom against his future enterprizes? Without a head, without union among themselves, attached all of them to different competitors, whose title they had rashly submitted to the decision of this foreign usurper, and who were thereby reduced to an absolute dependance upon him; they could only expect by resistance to entail on themselves and their posterity a more grievous and more destructive servitude. Yet even in this desperate state of their affairs, the Scottish barons, as we learn from Walsingham,[l] one of the best historians of that period, had the courage to reply, that, till they had a king, they could take no resolution on so momentous a point: The journal of king Edward says, that they made no answer at all:[m] That is, perhaps, no *particular* answer or objection to Edward's claim: And by this solution it is possible to reconcile the journal with the historian. The king, therefore, interpreting their silence as consent, addressed himself to the several competitors, and previously to his pronouncing sentence, required their acknowledgment of his superiority.

It is evident from the genealogy of the royal family of Scotland, that there could only be two questions about the succession, that between Baliol and Bruce on the one hand, and lord Hastings on the other, concerning the partition of the crown; and that between Baliol and Bruce themselves, concerning the preference of their respective titles, supposing the kingdom indivisible: Yet there appeared on this occasion no less than nine claimants besides; John Comyn or Cummin lord of Badenoch, Florence earl of Holland, Patric Dunbar earl of March, William de Vescey, Robert de Pynkeni, Nicholas de Soules, Patric Galythly, Roger de Mandeville, Robert de Ross; not to mention the king of Norway, who claimed as heir to his daughter Margaret.[n] Some of these competitors were descended from more remote branches of the royal family; others were even sprung from illegitimate children; and as none of them

---

[l] Page 56. M. West. p. 436. It is said by Hemingford, vol. i. p. 33, that the king menaced violently the Scotch barons, and forced them to compliance, at least to silence.   [m] Rymer, vol. ii. p. 548.   [n] Walsing. p. 58.

had the least pretence of right, it is natural to conjecture, that Edward had secretly encouraged them to appear in the list of claimants, that he might sow the more division among the Scottish nobility, make the cause appear the more intricate, and be able to chuse, among a great number, the most obsequious candidate.

But he found them all equally obsequious on this occasion.[o] Robert Bruce was the first that acknowledged Edward's right of superiority over Scotland; and he had so far foreseen the king's pretensions, that even in his petition, where he set forth his claim to the crown, he had previously applied to him as liege lord of the kingdom; a step which was not taken by any of the other competitors.[p] They all, however, with seeming willingness, made a like acknowledgment when required; though Baliol, lest he should give offence to the Scottish nation, had taken care to be absent during the first days; and he was the last that recognized the king's title.[q] Edward next deliberated concerning the method of proceeding in the discussion of this great controversy. He gave orders, that Baliol, and such of the competitors as adhered to him, should chuse forty commissioners; Bruce and his adherents forty more: To these the king added twenty-four Englishmen: He ordered these hundred and four commissioners to examine the cause deliberately among themselves, and make their report to him:[r] And he promised in the ensuing year to give his determination. Mean while, he pretended, that it was requisite to have all the fortresses of Scotland delivered into his hands, in order to enable him, without opposition, to put the true heir in possession of the crown; and this exorbitant demand was complied with, both by the states and by the claimants.[s] The governors also of all the castles immediately resigned their command; except Umfreville earl of Angus, who refused, without a formal and particular acquittal from the parliament and the several claimants, to surrender his fortresses to so domineering an arbiter, who had given to Scotland so many just reasons of suspicion.[t] Before this assembly broke up, which had fixed such a mark of dishonour on the nation, all the prelates and barons there present swore fealty to Edward; and that prince ap-

[o] Rymer, vol. ii. p. 529, 545. Walsing. p. 56. Heming. vol. i. p. 33, 34. Trivet, p. 260. M. West. p. 415.   [p] Rymer, vol. ii. p. 577, 578, 579. [q] Ibid. p. 546.   [r] Ibid. p. 555, 556.   [s] Ibid. p. 529. Walsing. p. 56, 57. [t] Rymer, vol. ii. p. 531.

CHAPTER XIII

pointed commissioners to receive a like oath from all the other barons and persons of distinction in Scotland.[u]

The king, having finally made, as he imagined, this important acquisition, left the commissioners to sit at Berwic, and examine the titles of the several competitors, who claimed the precarious crown, which Edward was willing for some time to allow the lawful heir to enjoy. He went southwards, both in order to assist at the funeral of his mother, queen Eleanor, who died about this time, and to compose some differences which had arisen among his principal nobility. Gilbert earl of Glocester, the greatest baron of the kingdom, had espoused the king's daughter; and being elated by that alliance, and still more by his own power, which, he thought, set him above the laws, he permitted his bailiffs and vassals to commit violence on the lands of Humphrey Bohun earl of Hereford, who retaliated the injury by like violence. But this was not a reign in which such illegal proceedings could pass with impunity. Edward procured a sentence against the two earls, committed them both to prison, and would not restore them to their liberty, till he exacted a fine of 1000 marks from Hereford, and one of 10,000 from his son-in-law.

During this interval, the titles of John Baliol and of Robert *1292.* Bruce, whose claims appeared to be the best founded among the competitors for the crown of Scotland, were the subject of general disquisition, as well as of debate among the commissioners. Edward, in order to give greater authority to his intended decision, proposed this general question both to the commissioners, and to all the celebrated lawyers in Europe; Whether a person descended from the elder sister, but farther removed by one degree, were preferable, in the succession of kingdoms, fiefs, and other indivisible inheritances, to one descended from the younger sister, but one degree nearer to the common stock? This was the true state of the case; and the principle of representation had now gained such ground every where, that a uniform answer was returned to the king in the affirmative. He therefore pronounced sentence in favour of Baliol; and when Bruce, upon this disappointment, joined afterwards lord Hastings, and claimed a third of the kingdom, which he now pretended to be divisible, Edward, though his inter-

[u] Ibid. p. 573.

Award of
Edward
in favour
of Baliol.
ests seemed more to require the partition of Scotland, again pronounced sentence in favour of Baliol. That competitor, upon renewing his oath of fealty to England, was put in possession of the kingdom;[w] all his fortresses were restored to him,[x] and the conduct of Edward, both in the deliberate solemnity of the proceedings, and in the justice of the award, was so far unexceptionable.

1293.
Had the king entertained no other view than that of establishing his superiority over Scotland, though the iniquity of that claim was apparent, and was aggravated by the most egregious breach of trust, he might have fixed his pretensions, and have left that important acquisition to his posterity: But he immediately proceeded in such a manner, as made it evident, that, not content with this usurpation, he aimed also at the absolute sovereignty and dominion of the kingdom. Instead of gradually enuring the Scots to the yoke, and exerting his rights of superiority with moderation, he encouraged all appeals to England; required king John himself, by six different summons on trivial occasions, to come to London;[y] refused him the privilege of defending his cause by a procurator; and obliged him to appear at the bar of his parliament as a private person.[z] These humiliating demands were hitherto quite unknown to a king of Scotland: They are however the necessary consequence of vassalage by the feudal law; and as there was no preceding instance of such treatment submitted to by a prince of that country, Edward must, from that circumstance alone, had there remained any doubt, have been himself convinced, that his claim was altogether an usurpation.[*] But his intention plainly was, to enrage Baliol by these indignities, to engage him in rebellion, and to assume the dominion of the state as the punishment of his treason and felony. Accordingly Baliol, though a prince of a soft and gentle spirit, returned into Scotland highly provoked at this usage, and determined at all hazards to vindicate his liberty; and the war, which soon after broke out between France and England, gave him a favourable opportunity of executing his purpose.

The violence, robberies, and disorders, to which that age was so subject, were not confined to the licentious barons and their retainers at land: The sea was equally infested with piracy: The

[w] Rymer, vol. ii. p. 590, 591, 593, 600.   [x] Rymer, vol. ii. p. 590.   [y] Rymer, vol. ii. p. 603, 605, 606, 608, 615, 616.   [z] Ryley's Placit. Parl. p. 152, 153.
[*] See note [C] at the end of the volume.

CHAPTER XIII

feeble execution of the laws had given licence to all orders of men: And a general appetite for rapine and revenge, supported by a false point of honour, had also infected the merchants and mariners; and it pushed them, on any provocation, to seek redress, by immediate retaliation upon the aggressors. A Norman and an English vessel met off the coast near Bayonne; and both of them *War with France.* having occasion for water, they sent their boats to land, and the several crews came at the same time to the same spring: There ensued a quarrel for the preference: A Norman, drawing his dagger, attempted to stab an Englishman; who, grappling with him, threw his adversary on the ground; and the Norman, as was pretended, falling on his own dagger, was slain.[a] This scuffle between two seamen about water, soon kindled a bloody war between the two nations, and involved a great part of Europe in the quarrel. The mariners of the Norman ship carried their complaints to the French king: Philip, without enquiring into the fact, without demanding redress, bade them take revenge, and trouble him no more about the matter.[b] The Normans, who had been more regular than usual in applying to the crown, needed but this hint to proceed to immediate violence. They seized an English ship in the channel; and hanging, along with some dogs, several of the crew on the yard-arm, in presence of their companions, dismissed the vessel;[c] and bade the mariners inform their countrymen, that vengeance was now taken for the blood of the Norman killed at Bayonne. This injury, accompanied with so general and deliberate an insult, was resented by the mariners of the cinque ports, who, without carrying any complaint to the king, or waiting for redress, retaliated by committing like barbarities on all French vessels without distinction. The French, provoked by their losses, preyed on the ships of all Edward's subjects, whether English or Gascon: The sea became a scene of piracy between the nations: The sovereigns, without either seconding or repressing the violence of their subjects, seemed to remain indifferent spectators: The English made private associations with the Irish and Dutch seamen; the French with the Flemish and Genoese:[d] And the animosities of the people on both sides became every day more violent and barbarous. A

---

[a] Walsing. p. 58. Heming. vol. i. p. 39.   [b] Walsing. p. 58.   [c] Heming. vol. i. p. 40. M. West. p. 419.   [d] Heming. vol. i. p. 40.

fleet of two hundred Norman vessels set sail to the south for wine and other commodities; and in their passage, seized all the English ships which they met with; hanged the seamen, and seized the goods. The inhabitants of the English sea-ports, informed of this incident, fitted out a fleet of sixty sail, stronger and better manned than the others, and awaited the enemy on their return. After an obstinate battle, they put them to rout, and sunk, destroyed, or took the greater part of them.[e] No quarter was given; and it is pretended, that the loss of the French amounted to 15,000 men: Which is accounted for by this circumstance, that the Norman fleet was employed in transporting a considerable body of soldiers from the south.

The affair was now become too important to be any longer overlooked by the sovereigns. On Philip's sending an envoy to demand reparation and restitution, the king dispatched the bishop of London to the French court, in order to accommodate the quarrel. He first said, that the English courts of justice were open to all men; and if any Frenchman were injured, he might seek reparation by course of law.[f] He next offered to adjust the matter by private arbiters, or by a personal interview with the king of France, or by a reference either to the pope or the college of cardinals, or any particular cardinals, agreed on by both parties.[g] The French, probably the more disgusted, as they were hitherto losers in the quarrel, refused all these expedients: The vessels and the goods of merchants were confiscated on both sides: Depredations were continued by the Gascons on the western coast of France, as well as by the English in the channel: Philip cited the king, as duke of Guienne, to appear in his court at Paris, and answer for these offences: And Edward, apprehensive of danger to that province, sent John St. John, an experienced soldier, to Bourdeaux, and gave him directions to put Guienne in a posture of defence.[h]

1294. That he might however prevent a final rupture between the nations, the king dispatched his brother, Edmond, earl of Lancaster, to Paris; and as this prince had espoused the queen of Navarre, mother to Jane, queen of France, he seemed, on account

---

[e] Walsing. p. 60. Trivet, p. 274. Chron. Dunst. vol. ii. p. 609.   [f] Trivet, p. 275.   [g] Ibid.   [h] Trivet, p. 276.

CHAPTER XIII

of that alliance, the most proper person for finding expedients to accommodate the difference. Jane pretended to interpose with her good offices: Mary, the queen-dowager, feigned the same amicable disposition: And these two princesses told Edmond, that the circumstance, the most difficult to adjust, was the point of honour with Philip, who thought himself affronted by the injuries committed against him by his sub-vassals in Guienne: But if Edward would once consent to give him seizin and possession of that province, he would think his honour fully repaired, would engage to restore Guienne immediately, and would accept of a very easy satisfaction for all the other injuries. The king was consulted on the occasion; and as he then found himself in immediate danger of war with the Scots, which he regarded as the more important concern, this politic prince, blinded by his favourite passion for subduing that nation, allowed himself to be deceived by so gross an artifice.[i] He sent his brother orders to sign and execute the treaty with the two queens; Philip solemnly promised to execute his part of it; and the king's citation to appear in the court of France, was accordingly recalled: But the French monarch was no sooner put in possession of Guienne, than the citation was renewed; Edward was condemned for non-appearance; and Guienne, by a formal sentence, was declared to be forfeited and annexed to the crown.[k]

Edward, fallen into a like snare with that which he himself had spread for the Scots, was enraged; and the more so, as he was justly ashamed of his own conduct, in being so egregiously over-reached by the court of France. Sensible of the extreme difficulties, which he should encounter in the recovery of Gascony, where he had not retained a single place in his hands; he endeavoured to compensate that loss, by forming alliances with several princes, who, he projected, should attack France on all quarters, and make a diversion of her forces. Adolphus de Nassau, king of the Romans, entered into a treaty with him for that purpose;[l] as did also Amadaeus, count of Savoy, the archbishop of Cologne, the counts of Gueldre and Luxembourg; the duke of Brabant and count of Barre, who had married his two daughters, Margaret and Eleanor: But these alliances were extremely burdensome to his narrow rev-

[i] Rymer, vol. ii. p. 619, 620. Walsing. p. 61. Heming. vol. i. p. 42, 43. Trivet, p. 277. [k] Rymer, vol. ii. p. 620, 622. Walsing. p. 61. Trivet, p. 278. [l] Heming. vol. i. p. 51.

enues, and proved in the issue entirely ineffectual. More impression was made on Guienne by an English army, which he completed by emptying the jails of many thousand thieves and robbers, who had been confined there for their crimes. So low had the profession of arms fallen, and so much had it degenerated from the estimation in which it stood during the vigour of the feudal system!

1295. The king himself was detained in England, first by contrary winds;[m] then by his apprehensions of a Scottish invasion, and by a rebellion of the Welsh, whom he repressed and brought again under subjection.[n] The army, which he sent to Guienne, was commanded by his nephew, John de Bretagne, earl of Richmond, and under him by St. John, Tibetot, de Vere, and other officers of reputation;[o] who made themselves masters of the town of Bayonne, as well as of Bourg, Blaye, Reole, St. Severe, and other places, which straitened Bourdeaux, and cut off its communication both by sea and land. The favour, which the Gascon nobility bore to the English government, facilitated these conquests, and seemed to promise still greater successes; but this advantage was soon lost by the misconduct of some of the officers. Philip's brother, Charles de Valois, who commanded the French armies, having laid siege to Podensac, a small fortress near Reole, obliged Giffard, the governor, to capitulate; and the articles, though favourable to the English, left all the Gascons prisoners at discretion, of whom about fifty were hanged by Charles as rebels: A policy, by which he both intimidated that people, and produced an irreparable breach between them and the English.[p] That prince immediately attacked Reole, where the earl of Richmond himself commanded; and as the place seemed not tenable, the English general drew his troops to the water-side, with an intention of embarking with the greater part of the army. The enraged Gascons fell upon his rear, and at the same time opened their gates to the French, who, besides making themselves masters of the place, took many prisoners of distinction. St. Severe was more vigorously defended by Hugh de Vere, son of the earl of Oxford; but was at last obliged to capitulate. The French king, not content with these successes in

[m] Chron. Dunst. vol. ii. p. 622.　[n] Walsing. p. 62. Heming. vol. i. p. 55. Trivet, p. 282. Chron. Dunst. vol. ii. p. 622.　[o] Trivet, p. 279.　[p] Heming. vol. i. p. 49.

CHAPTER XIII

Gascony, threatened England with an invasion; and by a sudden attempt, his troops took and burnt Dover,[q] but were obliged soon after to retire. And in order to make a greater diversion of the English force, and engage Edward in dangerous and important wars, he formed a secret alliance with John Baliol, king of Scotland; the commencement of that strict union, which, during so many centuries, was maintained, by mutual interests and necessities, between the French and Scottish nations. John confirmed this alliance by stipulating a marriage between his eldest son and the daughter of Charles de Valois.[r]

The expences attending these multiplied wars of Edward, and his preparations for war, joined to alterations which had insensibly taken place in the general state of affairs, obliged him to have frequent recourse to parliamentary supplies, introduced the lower orders of the state into the public councils, and laid the foundations of great and important changes in the government. *Digression concerning the constitution of parliament.*

Though nothing could be worse calculated for cultivating the arts of peace or maintaining peace itself, than the long subordination of vassalage from the king to the meanest gentleman, and the consequent slavery of the lower people, evils inseparable from the feudal system; that system was never able to fix the state in a proper warlike posture, or give it the full exertion of its power for defence, and still less for offence, against a public enemy. The military tenants, unacquainted with obedience, unexperienced in war, held a rank in the troops by their birth, not by their merits or services; composed a disorderly and consequently a feeble army; and during the few days, which they were obliged by their tenures to remain in the field, were often more formidable to their own prince than to foreign powers, against whom they were assembled. The sovereigns came gradually to disuse this cumbersome and dangerous machine, so apt to recoil upon the hand which held it; and exchanging the military service for pecuniary supplies, inlisted forces by means of a contract with particular officers, (such as those the Italians denominate *Condottieri*) whom they dismissed at the end of the war.[s] The barons and knights themselves often entered into these engagements with the prince; and were enabled

---

[q] Trivet, p. 284. Chron. Dunst. vol. ii. p. 642.   [r] Rymer, vol. ii. p. 680, 681, 695, 697. Heming. vol. i. p. 76. Trivet, p. 285.   [s] Cotton's Abr. p. 11.

to fill their bands, both by the authority which they possessed over their vassals and tenants, and from the great numbers of loose, disorderly people, whom they found on their estates, and who willingly embraced an opportunity of gratifying their appetite for war and rapine.

Mean-while, the old Gothic fabric, being neglected, went gradually to decay. Though the Conqueror had divided all the lands of England into sixty thousand knights' fees, the number of these was insensibly diminished by various artifices; and the king at last found, that, by putting the law in execution, he could assemble a small part only of the ancient force of the kingdom. It was a usual expedient for men, who held of the king or great barons by military tenure, to transfer their land to the church, and receive it back by another tenure called frankalmoigne, by which they were not bound to perform any service.[t] A law was made against this practice; but the abuse had probably gone far before it was attended to, and probably was not entirely corrected by the new statute, which, like most laws of that age, we may conjecture to have been but feebly executed by the magistrate against the perpetual interest of so many individuals. The constable and mareschal, when they mustered the armies, often, in a hurry, and for want of better information, received the service of a baron for fewer knights' fees, than were due by him; and one precedent of this kind was held good against the king, and became ever after a reason for diminishing the service.[u] The rolls of knights' fees were inaccurately kept; no care was taken to correct them before the armies were summoned into the field;[w] it was then too late to think of examining records and charters; and the service was accepted on the footing which the vassal himself was pleased to acknowledge, after all the various subdivisions and conjunctions of property had thrown an obscurity on the nature and extent of his tenure.[x] It is easy to judge of the intricacies which would attend disputes of this kind with individuals; when even the number of military fees, belonging to the church, whose property was fixed and unalienable, became the subject of controversy; and we find in partic-

[t] Madox's Baronia Anglica, p. 114.   [u] Madox's Baronia Anglica, p. 115.
[w] We hear only of one king, Henry II. who took this pains; and the record, called Liber niger Scaccarii, was the result of it.   [x] Madox, Bar. Ang. p. 116.

CHAPTER XIII

ular, that, when the bishop of Durham was charged with seventy knights' fees for the aid levied on occasion of the marriage of Henry II.'s daughter to the duke of Saxony, the prelate acknowledged ten, and disowned the other sixty.[y] It is not known in what manner this difference was terminated; but had the question been concerning an armament to defend the kingdom, the bishop's service would probably have been received without opposition for ten fees; and this rate must also have fixed all his future payments. Pecuniary scutages, therefore, diminished as much as military services:[z] Other methods of filling the exchequer as well as the armies must be devised: New situations produced new laws and institutions: And the great alterations in the finances and military power of the crown, as well as in private property, were the source of equal innovations in every part of the legislature or civil government.

The exorbitant estates, conferred by the Norman on his barons and chieftains, remained not long entire and unimpaired. The landed property was gradually shared out into more hands; and those immense baronies were divided, either by provisions to younger children, by partitions among co-heirs, by sale, or by escheating to the king, who gratified a great number of his courtiers, by dealing them out among them in smaller portions. Such moderate estates, as they required economy, and confined the proprietors to live at home, were better calculated for duration; and the order of knights and small barons grew daily more numerous, and began to form a very respectable rank or order in the state. As they were all immediate vassals of the crown by military tenure, they were, by the principles of the feudal law, equally intitled with the greatest barons to a seat in the national or general councils; and this right, though regarded as a privilege, which the owners would not entirely relinquish, was also considered as a burthen, which they desired to be subjected to on extraordinary

[y] Ibid. p. 122. Hist. of Exch. p. 404. [z] In order to pay the sum of 100,000 marks, as king Richard's ransom, twenty shillings were imposed on each knight's fee. Had the fees remained on the original footing, as settled by the Conqueror, this scutage would have amounted to 90,000 marks, which was nearly the sum required: But we find, that other grievous taxes were imposed to complete it: A certain proof, that many frauds and abuses had prevailed in the roll of knights' fees.

occasions only. Hence it was provided in the charter of king John, that, while the great barons were summoned to the national council by a particular writ, the small barons, under which appellation the knights were also comprehended, should only be called by a general summons of the sheriff. The distinction between great and small barons, like that between rich and poor, was not exactly defined; but, agreeably to the inaccurate genius of that age and to the simplicity of ancient government, was left very much to be determined by the discretion of the king and his ministers. It was usual for the prince to require, by a particular summons, the attendance of a baron in one parliament, and to neglect him in future parliaments;[a] nor was this uncertainty ever complained of as an injury. He attended when required: He was better pleased on other occasions to be exempted from the burthen: And as he was acknowledged to be of the same order with the greatest barons, it gave them no surprize to see him take his seat in the great council, whether he appeared of his own accord, or by a particular summons from the king. The barons by *Writ,* therefore, began gradually to intermix themselves with the barons by *Tenure;* and, as Camden tells us,[b] from an ancient manuscript, now lost, that, after the battle of Evesham, a positive law was enacted, prohibiting every baron from appearing in parliament, who was not invited thither by a particular summons, the whole baronage of England held thenceforward their seat by writ, and this important privilege of their tenures was in effect abolished. Only, where writs had been regularly continued for some time in one great family, the omission of them would have been regarded as an affront, and even as an injury.

A like alteration gradually took place in the order of earls, who were the highest rank of barons. The dignity of an earl, like that of a baron, was anciently territorial and official:[c] He exercised jurisdiction within his county: He levied the third of the fines to his own profit: He was at once a civil and a military magistrate: And though his authority, from the time of the Norman conquest, was hereditary in England, the title was so much connected with the office, that, where the king intended to create a new earl, he had

[a] Chancellor West's enquiry into the manner of creating peers, p. 43, 46, 47, 55. [b] In Britann. p. 122. [c] Spellm. Gloss. in voce *Comes.*

no other expedient than to erect a certain territory into a county or earldom, and to bestow it upon the person and his family.[d] But as the sheriffs, who were the vice-gerents of the earls, were named by the king, and removeable at pleasure, he found them more dependant upon him; and endeavoured to throw the whole authority and jurisdiction of the office into their hands. This magistrate was at the head of the finances, and levied all the king's rents within the county. He assessed at pleasure the talliages of the inhabitants in royal demesne: He had usually committed to him the management of wards and often of escheats: He presided in the lower courts of judicature: And thus, though inferior to the earl in dignity, he was soon considered, by this union of the judicial and fiscal powers, and by the confidence reposed in him by the king, as much superior to him in authority, and undermined his influence within his own jurisdiction.[e] It became usual, in creating an earl, to give him a fixed salary, commonly about twenty pounds a year, in lieu of his third of the fines: The diminution of his power kept pace with the retrenchment of his profit: And the dignity of earl, instead of being territorial and official, dwindled into personal and titular. Such were the mighty alterations, which already had fully taken place, or were gradually advancing, in the house of peers; that is, in the parliament: For there seems anciently to have been no other house.

But though the introduction of barons by writ, and of titular earls, had given some encrease to royal authority; there were other causes, which counterbalanced those innovations, and tended in a higher degree to diminish the power of the sovereign. The disuse, into which the feudal militia had in a great measure fallen, made the barons almost entirely forget their dependence on the crown: By the diminution of the number of knights fees, the king had no reasonable compensation when he levied scutages and exchanged their service for money: The alienations of the crown lands had reduced him to poverty: And above all, the concession of the Great Charter had set bounds to royal power, and had rendered it more difficult and dangerous for the prince to exert any extraordinary

---

[d] Essays on British antiquities. This practice, however, seems to have been more familiar in Scotland and the kingdoms on the continent, than in England.   [e] There are instances of princes of the blood who accepted of the office of sheriff. Spellman in voce *Vicecomes*.

act of arbitrary authority. In this situation it was natural for the king to court the friendship of the lesser barons and knights, whose influence was no ways dangerous to him, and who, being exposed to oppression from their powerful neighbours, sought a legal protection under the shadow of the throne. He desired, therefore, to have their presence in parliament, where they served to controul the turbulent resolutions of the great. To exact a regular attendance of the whole body would have produced confusion, and would have imposed too heavy a burden upon them. To summon only a few by writ, though it was practised and had a good effect, served not entirely the king's purpose; because these members had no farther authority than attended their personal character, and were eclipsed by the appearance of the more powerful nobility. He therefore dispensed with the attendance of most of the lesser barons in parliament; and in return for this indulgence (for such it was then esteemed) required them to chuse in each county a certain number of their own body, whose charges they bore, and who, having gained the confidence, carried with them, of course, the authority, of the whole order. This expedient had been practised at different times, in the reign of Henry III.[f] and regularly, during that of the present king. The numbers sent up by each county varied at the will of the prince:[g] They took their seat among the other peers; because by their tenure they belonged to that order:[h] The introducing of them into that house scarcely appeared an innovation: And though it was easily in the king's power, by varying their number, to command the resolutions of the whole parliament, this circumstance was little attended to, in an age when force was more prevalent than laws, and when a resolution, though taken by the majority of a legal assembly, could not be executed, if it opposed the will of the more powerful minority.

But there were other important consequences, which followed the diminution and consequent disuse of the ancient feudal militia. The king's expence, in levying and maintaining a military force for every enterprize, was encreased beyond what his narrow reve-

[f] Rot. Claus. 38. Hen. III. m. 7. and 12 d.: As also Rot. Claus. 42. Hen. III. m. 1. d. Prynne's Pref. to Cotton's Abridgment.   [g] Brady's answer to Petyt, from the records, p. 151.   [h] Brady's Treatise of Boroughs, App. N°. 13.

CHAPTER XIII

nues were able to bear: As the scutages of his military tenants, which were accepted in lieu of their personal service, had fallen to nothing; there were no means of supply but from voluntary aids granted him by the parliament and clergy: Or from the talliages which he might levy upon the towns and inhabitants in royal demesne. In the preceding year, Edward had been obliged to exact no less than the sixth of all moveables from the laity, and a moiety of all ecclesiastical benefices[i] for his expedition into Poictou, and the suppression of the Welsh: And this distressful situation, which was likely often to return upon him and his successors, made him think of a new device, and summon the representatives of all the boroughs to parliament. This period, which is the twenty-third of his reign, seems to be the real and true epoch of the house of commons; and the faint dawn of popular government in England. For the representatives of the counties were only deputies from the smaller barons and lesser nobility: And the former precedent of representatives from the boroughs, who were summoned by the earl of Leicester, was regarded as the act of a violent usurpation, had been discontinued in all the subsequent parliaments, and if such a measure had not become necessary on other accounts, that precedent was more likely to blast than give credit to it.

During the course of several years, the kings of England, in imitation of other European princes, had embraced the salutary policy of encouraging and protecting the lower and more industrious orders of the state; whom they found well disposed to obey the laws and civil magistrate, and whose ingenuity and labour furnished commodities, requisite for the ornament of peace and support of war. Though the inhabitants of the country were still left at the disposal of their imperious lords; many attempts were made to give more security and liberty to citizens, and make them enjoy unmolested the fruits of their industry. Boroughs were erected by royal patent within the demesne lands: Liberty of trade was conferred upon them: The inhabitants were allowed to farm at a fixed rent their own tolls and customs:[k] They were permitted to elect their own magistrates: Justice was administered to them by these magistrates, without obliging them to attend the sheriff or county

---

[i] Ibid. p. 31. from the records. Heming. vol. i. p. 52. M. West. p. 422. Ryley, p. 462.   [k] Madox, Firma Burgi, p. 21.

court: And some shadow of independence, by means of these equitable privileges, was gradually acquired by the people.[l] The king, however, retained still the power of levying talliages or taxes upon them at pleasure;[m] and though their poverty and the customs of the age made these demands neither frequent nor exorbitant, such unlimited authority in the sovereign was a sensible check upon commerce, and was utterly incompatible with all the principles of a free government. But when the multiplied necessities of the crown produced a greater avidity for supply, the king, whose prerogative entitled him to exact it, found that he had not power sufficient to enforce his edicts, and that it was necessary, before he imposed taxes, to smooth the way for his demand, and to obtain the previous consent of the boroughs, by solicitations, remonstrances, and authority. The inconvenience of transacting this business with every particular borough was soon felt; and Edward became sensible, that the most expeditious way of obtaining supply, was to assemble the deputies of all the boroughs, to lay before them the necessities of the state, to discuss the matter in their presence, and to require their consent to the demands of their sovereign. For this reason, he issued writs to the sheriffs, enjoining them to send to parliament, along with two knights of the shire, two deputies from each borough within their county,[n] and these provided with sufficient powers from their community, to consent, in their name, to what he and his council should require of them. *As it is a most equitable rule,* says he, in his preamble to this writ, *that what concerns all should be approved of by all; and common dangers be repelled by united efforts ;*[o] a noble principle, which may seem to indicate a liberal mind in the king, and which laid the foundation of a free and an equitable government.

[l] Brady of Boroughs, App. N°. 1, 2, 3.   [m] The king had not only the power of talliating the inhabitants within his own demesnes, but that of granting to particular barons the power of talliating the inhabitants within theirs. See Brady's answer to Petyt, p. 118. Madox's Hist. of the Exchequer, p. 518.   [n] Writs were issued to about 120 cities and boroughs.   [o] Brady of Boroughs, p. 25, 33, from the records. The writs of the parliament immediately preceding, remain; and the return of knights is there required, but not a word of the boroughs: A demonstration, that this was the very year in which they commenced. In the year immediately preceding, the taxes were levied by a seeming free consent of each particular borough, beginning with London. Id. p. 31, 32, 33, from the records. Also his answer to Petyt, p. 40, 41.

CHAPTER XIII

After the election of these deputies, by the aldermen and common council, they gave sureties for their attendance before the king and parliament: Their charges were respectively borne by the borough, which sent them: And they had so little idea of appearing as legislators, a character extremely wide of their low rank and condition,[p] that no intelligence could be more disagreeable to any borough, than to find that they must elect, or to any individual than that he was elected, to a trust from which no profit or honour could possibly be derived.[q] They composed not, properly speaking, any essential part of the parliament: They sat apart both from the barons and knights,[r] who disdained to mix with such mean personages: After they had given their consent to the taxes required of them, their business being then finished, they separated, even though the parliament still continued to sit, and to canvass the national business:[s] And as they all consisted of men, who were real burgesses of the place from which they were sent, the sheriff, when he found no person of abilities or wealth sufficient for the office, often used the freedom of omitting particular boroughs in his returns; and as he received the thanks of the people for this indulgence, he gave no displeasure to the court, who levied on all the boroughs, without distinction, the tax agreed to by the majority of deputies.[t]

The union, however, of the representatives from the boroughs gave gradually more weight to the whole order; and it became customary for them, in return for the supplies which they granted, to prefer petitions to the crown for the redress of any particular grievance, of which they found reason to complain. The more the king's demands multiplied, the faster these petitions encreased both in number and authority; and the prince found it difficult to

[p] Reliquia Spellm. p. 64. Prynne's pref. to Cotton's Abridg. and the Abridg. passim.   [q] Brady of Boroughs, p. 59, 60.   [r] Ibid. p. 37, 38, from the records, and append. p. 19. Also his append. to his answ. to Petyt, Record. And his gloss. in Verb. *Communitas Regn.* p. 33.   [s] Ryley's Placit. Parl. p. 241, 242, &c. Cotton's Abridg. p. 14.   [t] Brady of Boroughs, p. 52. from the records. There is even an instance in the reign of Edward III. when the king named all the deputies. Id. answ. to Petyt, p. 161. If he fairly named the most considerable and creditable burgesses, little exception would be taken; as their business was not to check the king, but to reason with him, and consent to his demands. It was not till the reign of Richard II. that the sheriffs were deprived of the power of omitting boroughs at pleasure. See Stat. at large, 5th Richard II. cap. 4.

refuse men, whose grants had supported his throne, and to whose assistance he might so soon be again obliged to have recourse. The commons however were still much below the rank of legislators.[u] Their petitions, though they received a verbal assent from the throne, were only the rudiments of laws: The judges were afterwards entrusted with the power of putting them into form: And the king, by adding to them the sanction of his authority, and that sometimes without the assent of the nobles, bestowed validity upon them. The age did not refine so much as to perceive the danger of these irregularities. No man was displeased, that the sovereign, at the desire of any class of men, should issue an order, which appeared only to concern that class; and his predecessors were so near possessing the whole legislative power, that he gave no disgust by assuming it in this seemingly inoffensive manner. But time and farther experience gradually opened men's eyes and corrected these abuses. It was found, that no laws could be fixed for one order of men without affecting the whole; and that the force and efficacy of laws depended entirely on the terms employed in wording them. The house of peers, therefore, the most powerful order in the state, with reason expected, that their assent should be expressly granted to all public ordinances:[w] And in the reign of Henry V. the commons required, that no laws should be framed merely upon their petitions, unless the statutes were worded by themselves, and had passed their house in the form of a bill.[x]

But as the same causes, which had produced a partition of property, continued still to operate; the number of knights and lesser barons, or what the English call the gentry, perpetually encreased, and they sunk into a rank still more inferior to the great nobility. The equality of tenure was lost in the great inferiority of power and property; and the house of representatives from the counties was gradually separated from that of the peers, and formed a distinct order in the state.[y] The growth of commerce,

[u] See note [D] at the end of the volume.　[w] In those instances found in Cotton's abridgement, where the king appears to answer of himself the petitions of the commons, he probably exerted no more than that power, which was long inherent in the crown, of regulating matters by royal edicts or proclamations. But no durable or general statute seems ever to have been made by the king from the petition of the commons alone, without the assent of the peers. It is more likely that the peers alone, without the commons, would enact statutes.　[x] Brady's answ. to Petyt, p. 85. from the records.　[y] Cotton's abridgement, p. 13.

CHAPTER XIII

meanwhile, augmented the private wealth and consideration of the burgesses; the frequent demands of the crown encreased their public importance; and as they resembled the knights of shires in one material circumstance, that of representing particular bodies of men; it no longer appeared unsuitable to unite them together in the same house, and to confound their rights and privileges.[z] Thus the third estate, that of the commons, reached at last its present form; and as the country gentlemen made thenceforwards no scruple of appearing as deputies from the buroughs, the distinction between the members was entirely lost, and the lower house acquired thence a great accession of weight and importance in the kingdom. Still, however, the office of this estate was very different from that which it has since exercised with so much advantage to the public. Instead of checking and controuling the authority of the king, they were naturally induced to adhere to him, as the great fountain of law and justice, and to support him against the power of the aristocracy, which at once was the source of oppression to themselves, and disturbed him in the execution of the laws. The king, in his turn, gave countenance to an order of men, so useful and so little dangerous: The peers also were obliged to pay them some consideration: And by this means, the third estate, formerly so abject in England, as well as in all other European nations, rose by slow degrees to their present importance; and in their progress made arts and commerce, the necessary attendants of liberty and equality, flourish in the kingdom.[a]

What sufficiently proves, that the commencement of the house of burgesses, who are the true commons, was not an affair of chance, but arose from the necessities of the present situation, is, that Edward, at the very same time, summoned deputies from the inferior clergy, the first that ever met in England,[b] and he required them to impose taxes on their constituents for the public service. Formerly the ecclesiastical benefices bore no part of the burthens of the state: The pope indeed of late had often levied impositions upon them: He had sometimes granted this power to the sovereign:[c] The king himself had in the preceding year exacted, by menaces and violence, a very grievous tax of half the revenues of

---

[z] See note [E] at the end of the volume.   [a] See note [F] at the end of the volume.   [b] Archbishop Wake's State of the church of England, p. 235. Brady of Boroughs, p. 34. Gilbert's Hist. of the Exch. p. 46.   [c] Ann. Waverl. p. 227, 228. T. Wykes, p. 99, 120.

the clergy: But as this precedent was dangerous, and could not easily be repeated in a government which required the consent of the subject to any extraordinary resolution, Edward found it more prudent to assemble a lower house of convocation, to lay before them his necessities, and to ask some supply. But on this occasion he met with difficulties. Whether that the clergy thought themselves the most independant body in the kingdom, or were disgusted by the former exorbitant impositions, they absolutely refused their assent to the king's demand of a fifth of their moveables, and it was not till a second meeting, that, on their persisting in this refusal, he was willing to accept of a tenth. The barons and knights granted him, without hesitation, an eleventh; the burgesses, a seventh. But the clergy still scrupled to meet on the king's writ; lest by such an instance of obedience they should seem to acknowledge the authority of the temporal power: And this compromise was at last fallen upon, that the king should issue his writ to the archbishop; and that the archbishop should, in consequence of it, summon the clergy, who, as they then appeared to obey their spiritual superior, no longer hesitated to meet in convocation. This expedient, however, was the cause, why the ecclesiastics were separated into two houses of convocation, under their several archbishops, and formed not one estate, as in other countries of Europe; which was at first the king's intention.[d] We now return to the course of our narration.

Edward, conscious of the reasons of disgust which he had given to the king of Scots, informed of the dispositions of that people, and expecting the most violent effects of their resentment, which he knew he had so well merited; employed the supplies, granted him by his people, in making preparations against the hostilities of his northern neighbour. When in this situation, he received intelligence of the treaty secretly concluded between John and Philip; and though uneasy at this concurrence of a French and Scottish war, he resolved not to encourage his enemies by a pusillanimous behaviour, or by yielding to their united efforts. He summoned John to perform the duty of a vassal, and to send him a supply of forces against an invasion from France, with which he was then threatened: He next required, that the fortresses of Berwic, Jedbor-

1296.

---

[d] Gilbert's Hist. of Exch. p. 51, 54.

CHAPTER XIII

ough, and Roxborough, should be put into his hands as a security during the war:[e] He cited John to appear in an English parliament to be held at Newcastle: And when none of these successive demands were complied with, he marched northward with numerous forces, 30,000 foot, and 4000 horse, to chastise his rebellious vassal. The Scottish nation, who had little reliance on the vigour and abilities of their prince, assigned him a council of twelve noblemen, in whose hands the sovereignty was really lodged,[f] and who put the country in the best posture of which the present distractions would admit. A great army, composed of 40,000 infantry, though supported only by 500 cavalry, advanced to the frontiers; and after a fruitless attempt upon Carlisle, marched eastwards to defend those provinces which Edward was preparing to attack. But some of the most considerable of the Scottish nobles, Robert Bruce, the father and son, the earls of March and Angus, prognosticating the ruin of their country, from the concurrence of intestine divisions and a foreign invasion, endeavoured here to ingratiate themselves with Edward, by an early submission; and the king, encouraged by this favourable incident, led his army into the enemies' country, and crossed the Tweed without opposition at Coldstream. He then received a message from John, by which that prince, having now procured, for himself and his nation, pope Celestine's dispensation from former oaths, renounced the homage which had been done to England, and set Edward at defiance.[g] This bravado was but ill supported by the military operations of the Scots. Berwic was already taken by assault: Sir William Douglas, the governor, was made prisoner: Above 7000 of the garrison were put to the sword: And Edward, elated by this great advantage, dispatched earl Warrenne with 12,000 men, to lay siege to Dunbar, which was defended by the flower of the Scottish nobility.

28th March.

The Scots, sensible of the importance of this place, which, if taken, laid their whole country open to the enemy, advanced with their main army, under the command of the earls of Buchan, Lenox, and Marre, in order to relieve it. Warrenne, not dismayed at the great superiority of their number, marched out to give them

27th April.

---

[e] Rymer, vol. ii. p. 692. Walsing. p. 64. Heming. vol. i. p. 84. Trivet, p. 286.
[f] Heming. vol. i. p. 75.　[g] Rymer, vol. ii. p. 607. Walsing. p. 66. Heming. vol. i. p. 92.

battle. He attacked them with great vigour; and as undisciplined troops, when numerous, are but the more exposed to a panic upon any alarm, he soon threw them into confusion, and chased them off the field with great slaughter. The loss of the Scots is said to have amounted to 20,000 men: The castle of Dunbar, with all its garrison, surrendered next day to Edward, who, after the battle, had brought up the main body of the English, and who now proceeded with an assured confidence of success. The castle of Roxborough was yielded by James, steward of Scotland; and that nobleman, from whom is descended the royal family of Stuart, was again obliged to swear fealty to Edward. After a feeble resistance, the castles of Edinburgh and Stirling opened their gates to the enemy. All the southern parts were instantly subdued by the English; and to enable them the better to reduce the northern, whose inaccessible situation seemed to give them some more security, Edward sent for a strong reinforcement of Welsh and Irish, who, being accustomed to a desultory kind of war, were the best fitted *Scotland* to pursue the fugitive Scots into the recesses of their lakes and *subdued.* mountains. But the spirit of the nation was already broken by their misfortunes; and the feeble and timid Baliol, discontented with his own subjects, and over-awed by the English, abandoned all those resources, which his people might yet have possessed in this extremity. He hastened to make his submissions to Edward; he expressed the deepest penitence for his disloyalty to his liege lord; and he made a solemn and irrevocable resignation of his crown into the hands of that monarch.[h] Edward marched northwards to Aberdeen and Elgin, without meeting an enemy: No Scotchman approached him but to pay him submission and do him homage: Even the turbulent Highlanders, ever refractory to their own princes, and averse to the restraint of laws, endeavoured to prevent the devastation of their country, by giving him early proofs of obedience: And Edward, having brought the whole kingdom to a seeming state of tranquillity, returned to the south with his army. There was a stone, to which the popular superstition of the Scots paid the highest veneration: All their kings were seated on it, when they received the rite of inauguration: An ancient tradition assured them, that, wherever this stone was placed, their nation

[h] Rymer, vol. ii. p. 718. Walsing. p. 67. Heming. vol. i. p. 99. Trivet, p. 292.

CHAPTER XIII

should always govern: And it was carefully preserved at Scone, as the true palladium of their monarchy, and their ultimate resource amidst all their misfortunes. Edward got possession of it; and carried it with him to England.[i] He gave orders to destroy the records, and all those monuments of antiquity, which might preserve the memory of the independance of the kingdom, and refute the English claims of superiority. The Scots pretend, that he also destroyed all the annals preserved in their convents: But it is not probable, that a nation, so rude and unpolished, should be possessed of any history, which deserves much to be regretted. The great seal of Baliol was broken; and that prince himself was carried prisoner to London, and committed to custody in the Tower. Two years after, he was restored to liberty, and submitted to a voluntary banishment in France; where, without making any farther attempts for the recovery of his royalty, he died in a private station. Earl Warrenne was left governor of Scotland:[k] Englishmen were entrusted with the chief offices: And Edward, flattering himself that he had attained the end of all his wishes, and that the numerous acts of fraud and violence, which he had practised against Scotland, had terminated in the final reduction of that kingdom, returned with his victorious army into England.

An attempt, which he made about the same time, for the recovery of Guienne, was not equally successful. He sent thither an army of 7000 men, under the command of his brother the earl of Lancaster. That prince gained at first some advantages over the French at Bourdeaux: But he was soon after seized with a distemper, of which he died at Bayonne. The command devolved on the earl of Lincoln, who was not able to perform any thing considerable during the rest of the campaign.[l] *War with France.*

But the active and ambitious spirit of Edward, while his conquests brought such considerable accessions to the English monarchy, could not be satisfied, so long as Guienne, the ancient patrimony of his family, was wrested from him by the dishonest artifices of the French monarch. Finding, that the distance of that province rendered all his efforts against it feeble and uncertain, he purposed to attack France in a quarter where she appeared more

[i] Walsing. p. 68. Trivet, p. 299.   [k] Rymer, vol. ii. p. 726. Trivet, p. 295.
[l] Heming. vol. i. p. 72, 73, 74.

vulnerable; and with this view, he married his daughter, Elizabeth, to John earl of Holland, and at the same time contracted an alliance with Guy earl of Flanders, stipulated to pay him the sum of 75,000 pounds, and projected an invasion with their united forces upon Philip, their common enemy.[m] He hoped, that, when he himself, at the head of the English, Flemish, and Dutch armies, reinforced by his German allies, to whom he had promised or remitted considerable sums, should enter the frontiers of France, and threaten the capital itself, Philip would at last be obliged to relinquish his acquisitions, and purchase peace by the restitution of Guienne. But in order to set this great machine in movement, considerable supplies were requisite from the parliament; and Edward, without much difficulty, obtained from the barons and knights a new grant of a twelfth of all their moveables, and from the boroughs, that of an eighth. The great and almost unlimited power of the king over the latter, enabled him to throw the heavier part of the burthen on them; and the prejudices, which he seems always to have entertained against the church, on account of the former zeal of the clergy for the Mountfort faction, made him resolve to load them with still more considerable impositions, and he required of them a fifth of their moveables. But he here met with an opposition, which for some time disconcerted all his measures, and engaged him in enterprizes, that were somewhat dangerous to *him*; and would have proved fatal to any of his predecessors.

Dissen-tions with the clergy.   Boniface VIII. who had succeeded Celestine in the papal throne, was a man of the most lofty and enterprizing spirit; and though not endowed with that severity of manners, which commonly accompanies ambition in men of his order, he was determined to carry the authority of the tiara, and his dominion over the temporal power, to as great a height as it had ever attained in any former period. Sensible that his immediate predecessors, by oppressing the church in every province of Christendom, had extremely alienated the affections of the clergy, and had afforded the civil magistrate a pretence for laying like impositions on ecclesiastical revenues, he attempted to resume the former station of the sovereign pontiff, and to establish himself as the common

---

[m] Rymer, vol. ii. p. 761. Walsing. p. 68.

protector of the spiritual order against all invaders. For this purpose, he issued very early in his pontificate a general bull, prohibiting all princes from levying without his consent any taxes
upon the clergy, and all clergymen from submitting to such impositions; and he threatened both of them with the penalties of excommunication in case of disobedience.[n] This important edict is
said to have been procured by the solicitation of Robert de Winchelsey archbishop of Canterbury, who intended to employ it as a
rampart against the violent extortions, which the church had felt
from Edward, and the still greater, which that prince's multiplied
necessities gave them reason to apprehend. When a demand,
therefore, was made on the clergy of a fifth of their moveables, a
tax which was probably much more grievous than a fifth of their
revenue, as their lands were mostly stocked with their cattle, and
cultivated by their villains; the clergy took shelter under the bull of
pope Boniface, and pleaded conscience in refusing compliance.[o]
The king came not immediately to extremities on this repulse; but
after locking up all their granaries and barns, and prohibiting all
rent to be paid them, he appointed a new synod, to confer with him
upon his demand. The primate, not dismayed by these proofs of
Edward's resolution, here plainly told him, that the clergy owed
obedience to two sovereigns, their spiritual and their temporal; but
their duty bound them to a much stricter attachment to the former
than to the latter: They could not comply with his commands, (for
such, in some measure, the requests of the crown were then
deemed) in contradiction to the express prohibition of the sovereign pontiff.[p]

The clergy had seen in many instances, that Edward paid little   *1297.*
regard to those numerous privileges, on which they set so high a
value. He had formerly seized, in an arbitrary manner, all the
money and plate belonging to the churches and convents, and had
applied them to the public service;[q] and they could not but
expect more violent treatment of this sharp refusal, grounded on
such dangerous principles. Instead of applying to the pope for a
relaxation of his bull, he resolved immediately to employ the
power in his hands; and he told the ecclesiastics, that, since they

[n] Rymer, vol. ii. p. 706. Heming. vol. i. p. 104.   [o] Heming. vol. i. p. 107.
Trivet, p. 296. Chron. Dunst. vol. ii. p. 652.   [p] Heming. vol. i. p. 107.
[q] Walsing. p. 65. Heming. vol. i. p. 51.

refused to support the civil government, they were unworthy to receive any benefit from it; and he would accordingly put them out of the protection of the laws. This vigorous measure was immediately carried into execution.[r] Orders were issued to the judges to receive no cause brought before them by the clergy; to hear and decide all causes in which they were defendants: To do every man justice against them; to do them justice against no body.[s] The ecclesiastics soon found themselves in the most miserable situation imaginable. They could not remain in their own houses or convents for want of subsistence: If they went abroad, in quest of maintenance, they were dismounted, robbed of their horses and cloaths, abused by every ruffian, and no redress could be obtained by them for the most violent injury. The primate himself was attacked on the highway, was stripped of his equipage and furniture, and was at last reduced to board himself with a single servant in the house of a country clergyman.[t] The king, mean while, remained an indifferent spectator of all these violences; and without employing his officers in committing any immediate injury on the priests, which might have appeared invidious and oppressive, he took ample vengeance on them for their obstinate refusal of his demands. Though the archbishop issued a general sentence of excommunication against all who attacked the persons or property of ecclesiastics, it was not regarded: While Edward enjoyed the satisfaction of seeing the people become the voluntary instruments of his justice against them, and enure themselves to throw off that respect for the sacred order, by which they had so long been overawed and governed.

The spirits of the clergy were at last broken by this harsh treatment. Besides that the whole province of York, which lay nearest the danger that still hung over them from the Scots, voluntarily, from the first, voted a fifth of their moveables; the bishops of Salisbury, Ely, and some others, made a composition for the secular clergy within their dioceses; and they agreed, not to pay the fifth, which would have been an act of disobedience to Boniface's bull, but to deposit a sum equivalent to some church appointed them; whence it was taken by the king's officers.[u] Many particular

[r] Walsing. p. 69. Heming. vol. i. p. 107. [s] M. West. p. 429. [t] Heming. vol. i. p. 109. [u] Heming. vol. i. p. 108, 109. Chron. Dunst. p. 653.

CHAPTER XIII

convents and clergymen made payment of a like sum, and received the king's protection.[w] Those who had not ready money, entered into recognizances for the payment. And there was scarcely found one ecclesiastic in the kingdom, who seemed willing to suffer, for the sake of religious privileges, this new species of martyrdom, the most tedious and languishing of any, the most mortifying to spiritual pride, and not rewarded by that crown of glory, which the church holds up, with such ostentation, to her devoted adherents.

But as the money, granted by parliament, though considerable, was not sufficient to supply the king's necessities, and that levied by compositions with the clergy came in slowly, Edward was obliged, for the obtaining of farther supply, to exert his arbitrary power, and to lay an oppressive hand on all orders of men in the kingdom. He limited the merchants in the quantity of wool allowed to be exported; and at the same time forced them to pay him a duty of forty shillings a sack, which was computed to be above the third of the value.[x] He seized all the rest of the wool, as well as all the leather of the kingdom, into his hands, and disposed of these commodities for his own benefit:[y] He required the sheriffs of each county to supply him with 2000 quarters of wheat, and as many of oats, which he permitted them to seize wherever they could find them. The cattle and other commodities, necessary for supplying his army, were laid hold of without the consent of the owners:[z] And though he promised to pay afterwards the equivalent of all these goods, men saw but little probability that a prince, who submitted so little to the limitations of law, could ever, amidst his multiplied necessities, be reduced to a strict observance of his engagements. He showed at the same time an equal disregard to the principles of the feudal law, by which all the lands of his kingdom were held: In order to encrease his army, and enable him to support that great effort, which he intended to make against France, he required the attendance of every proprietor of land, possessed of twenty pounds a year, even though he held not of the crown, and was not obliged by his tenure to perform any such service.[a]

These acts of violence and of arbitrary power, notwithstanding

Arbitrary measures.

---

[w] Chron. Dunst. vol. ii. p. 654.   [x] Walsing. p. 69. Trivet, p. 296.
[y] Heming. vol. i. p. 52, 110.   [z] Heming. vol. i. p. 111.   [a] Walsing. p. 69.

the great personal regard generally borne to the king, bred murmurs in every order of men; and it was not long, ere some of the great nobility, jealous of their own privileges, as well as of national liberty, gave countenance and authority to these complaints. Edward assembled on the sea-coast an army, which he purposed to send over to Gascony, while he himself should in person make an impression on the side of Flanders; and he intended to put these forces under the command of Humphrey Bohun, earl of Hereford, the constable, and Roger Bigod, earl of Norfolk, the Mareschal of England. But these two powerful earls refused to execute his commands, and affirmed, that they were only obliged by their office to attend his person in the wars. A violent altercation ensued; and the king, in the height of his passion, addressing himself to the constable, exclaimed, *Sir earl, by God, you shall either go or hang. By God, Sir King,* replied Hereford, *I will neither go nor hang.*[b] And he immediately departed, with the mareschal, and above thirty other considerable barons.

Upon this opposition, the king laid aside the project of an expedition against Guienne; and assembled the forces, which he himself purposed to transport into Flanders. But the two earls, irritated in the contest and elated by impunity, pretending that none of their ancestors had ever served in that country, refused to perform the duty of their office in mustering the army.[c] The king, now finding it adviseable to proceed with moderation, instead of attainting the earls, who possessed their dignities by hereditary right, appointed Thomas de Berkeley, and Geoffrey de Geyneville, to act in that emergence, as constable and mareschal.[d] He endeavoured to reconcile himself with the church; took the primate again into favour;[e] made him, in conjunction with Reginald de Grey, tutor to the prince, whom he intended to appoint guardian of the kingdom during his absence; and he even assembled a great number of the nobility in Westminster-hall, to whom he deigned to make an apology for his past conduct. He pleaded the urgent necessities of the crown; his extreme want of money; his engagements from honour as well as interest to support his foreign allies: And he promised, if ever he returned in safety, to redress all

---

[b] Heming. vol. i. p. 112. [c] Rymer, vol. ii. p. 783. Walsing. p. 70. [d] M. West. p. 430. [e] Heming. vol. i. p. 113.

CHAPTER XIII

their grievances, to restore the execution of the laws, and to make all his subjects compensation for the losses which they had sustained. Meanwhile, he begged them to suspend their animosities; to judge of him by his future conduct, of which, he hoped, he should be more master; to remain faithful to his government, or if he perished in the present war, to preserve their allegiance to his son and successor.[f]

There were certainly, from the concurrence of discontents among the great, and grievances of the people, materials sufficient, in any other period, to have kindled a civil war in England: But the vigour and abilities of Edward kept every one in awe; and his dexterity, in stopping on the brink of danger, and retracting the measures, to which he had been pushed by his violent temper and arbitrary principles, saved the nation from so great a calamity. The two great earls dared not to break out into open violence: They proceeded no farther than framing a remonstrance, which was delivered to the king at Winchelsea, when he was ready to embark for Flanders. They there complained of the violations of the great charter and that of forests; the violent seizure of corn, leather, cattle, and above all, of wool, a commodity, which they affirmed to be equal in value to half the lands of the kingdom; the arbitrary imposition of forty shillings a sack on the small quantity of wool allowed to be exported by the merchants; and they claimed an immediate redress of all these grievances.[g] The king told them, that the greater part of his council were now at a distance, and without their advice he could not deliberate on measures of so great importance.[h]

But the constable and mareschal, with the barons of their party, resolved to take advantage of Edward's absence, and to obtain an explicit assent to their demands. When summoned to attend the parliament at London, they came with a great body of cavalry and infantry; and before they would enter the city, required that the gates should be put into their custody.[i] The primate, who secretly favoured all their pretensions, advised the council to comply; and thus they became masters both of the young prince and of the resolutions of parliament. Their demands, however, were mod-

Dissensions with th barons.

[f] Heming. vol. i. p. 114. M. West. p. 430.   [g] Walsing. p. 72. Heming. vol. i. p. 115. Trivet, p. 302.   [h] Walsing. p. 72. Heming. vol. i. p. 117. Trivet, p. 304.   [i] Heming. vol. i. p. 138.

erate; and such as sufficiently justify the purity of their intentions in all their past measures: They only required, that the two charters should receive a solemn confirmation; that a clause should be added to secure the nation for ever against all impositions and taxes without consent of parliament; and that they themselves and their adherents, who had refused to attend the king into Flanders, should be pardoned for the offence, and should be again received into favour.[k] The prince of Wales and his council assented to these terms; and the charters were sent over to the king in Flanders to be there confirmed by him. Edward felt the utmost reluctance to this measure, which, he apprehended, would for the future impose fetters on his conduct, and set limits to his lawless authority. On various pretences, he delayed three days giving any answer to the deputies; and when the pernicious consequences of his refusal were represented to him, he was at last obliged, after many internal struggles, to affix his seal to the charters, as also to the clause that bereaved him of the power, which he had hitherto assumed, of imposing arbitrary taxes upon the people.[l]

That we may finish at once this interesting transaction concerning the settlement of the charters, we shall briefly mention the subsequent events which relate to it. The constable and mareschal, informed of the king's compliance, were satisfied; and not only ceased from disturbing the government, but assisted the regency with their power against the Scots, who had risen in arms, and had thrown off the yoke of England.[m] But being sensible, that the smallest pretence would suffice to make Edward retract these detested laws, which, though they had often received the sanction both of king and parliament, and had been acknowledged during three reigns, were never yet deemed to have sufficient validity; they insisted, that he should again confirm them on his return to England, and should thereby renounce all plea which he might derive from his residing in a foreign country, when he formerly affixed his seal to them.[n] It appeared, that they judged aright of Edward's character and intentions: He delayed this confirmation as long as possible; and when the fear of worse consequences obliged him again to comply, he expressly added a salvo for his

[k] Walsing. p. 73. Heming. vol. i. p. 138, 139, 140, 141. Trivet, p. 308.
[l] Walsing. p. 74. Heming. vol. i. p. 143.   [m] Heming. vol. i. p. 143.
[n] Heming. vol. i. p. 159.

CHAPTER XIII

royal dignity or prerogative, which in effect enervated the whole force of the charters.[o] The two earls and their adherents left the parliament in disgust; and the king was constrained, on a future occasion, to grant to the people, without any subterfuge, a pure and absolute confirmation of those laws,[p] which were so much the object of their passionate affection. Even farther securities were then provided for the establishment of national privileges. Three knights were appointed to be chosen in each county, and were invested with the power of punishing, by fine and imprisonment, every transgression or violation of the charters:[q] A precaution, which, though it was soon disused, as encroaching too much on royal prerogative, proves the attachment, which the English in that age bore to liberty, and their well-grounded jealousy of the arbitrary disposition of Edward.

The work, however, was not yet entirely finished and complete. In order to execute the lesser charter, it was requisite, by new perambulations, to set bounds to the royal forests, and to disafforest all land which former encroachments had comprehended within their limits. Edward discovered the same reluctance to comply with this equitable demand; and it was not till after many delays on his part, and many solicitations and requests, and even menaces of war and violence,[r] on the part of the barons, that the perambulations were made, and exact boundaries fixed, by a jury in each county, to the extent of his forests.[s] Had not his ambitious and active temper raised him so many foreign enemies, and obliged him to have recourse so often to the assistance of his subjects, it is not likely that those concessions could ever have been extorted from him.

But while the people, after so many successful struggles, deemed themselves happy in the secure possession of their privileges; they were surprized in 1305 to find, that Edward had secretly applied to Rome, and had procured, from that mercenary

---

[o] Heming. vol. i. p. 167, 168.   [p] Heming. vol. i. p. 168.   [q] Hemingford, vol. i. p. 170.   [r] Walsing. p. 80. We are told by Tyrrel, vol. ii. p. 145. from the Chronicle of St. Albans, that the barons not content with the execution of the charter of forests, demanded of Edward as high terms as had been imposed on his father by the earl of Leicester: But no other historian mentions this particular.   [s] Heming. vol. i. p. 171. M. West. p. 431, 433.

court, an absolution from all the oaths and engagements, which he had so often reiterated, to observe both the charters. There are some historians[t] so credulous as to imagine, that this perilous step was taken by him for no other purpose than to acquire the merit of granting a new confirmation of the charters, as he did soon after; and a confirmation so much the more unquestionable, as it could never after be invalidated by his successors, on pretence of any force or violence which had been imposed upon him. But besides, that this might have been done with a better grace, if he had never applied for any such absolution, the whole tenor of his conduct proves him to be little susceptible of such refinements in patriotism; and this very deed itself, in which he anew confirmed the charters, carries on the face of it a very opposite presumption. Though he ratified the charters in general, he still took advantage of the papal bull so far as to invalidate the late perambulations of the forests, which had been made with such care and attention, and to reserve to himself the power, in case of favourable incidents, to extend as much as formerly those arbitrary jurisdictions. If the power was not in fact made use of, we can only conclude, that the favourable incidents did not offer.

Thus, after the contests of near a whole century, and these ever accompanied with violent jealousies, often with public convulsions, the Great Charter was finally established; and the English nation have the honour of extorting, by their perseverance, this concession from the ablest, the most warlike, and the most ambitious of all their princes.[u] It is computed, that above thirty confirmations of the charter were at different times required of several kings, and granted by them, in full parliament; a precaution, which, while it discovers some ignorance of the true nature of law and government, proves a laudable jealousy of national privileges in the people, and an extreme anxiety, lest contrary precedents should ever be pleaded as an authority for infringing them. Accordingly we find, that, though arbitrary practices often

---

[t] Brady, vol. ii. p. 84. Carte, vol. ii. p. 292. [u] It must however be remarked, that the king never forgave the chief actors in this transaction, and he found means afterwards to oblige both the constable and mareschal to resign their offices into his hands. The former received a new grant of it: But the office of mareschal was given to Thomas of Brotherton, the king's second son.

CHAPTER XIII

prevailed, and were even able to establish themselves into settled customs, the validity of the Great Charter was never afterwards formally disputed; and that grant was still regarded as the basis of English government, and the sure rule by which the authority of every custom was to be tried and canvassed. The jurisdiction of the Star-chamber, martial law, imprisonment by warrants from the privy-council, and other practices of a like nature, though established for several centuries, were scarcely ever allowed by the English to be parts of their constitution: The affection of the nation for liberty still prevailed over all precedent, and even all political reasoning: The exercise of these powers, after being long the source of secret murmurs among the people, was, in fulness of time, solemnly abolished, as illegal, at least as oppressive, by the whole legislative authority.

To return to the period from which this account of the charters has led us: Though the king's impatience to appear at the head of his armies in Flanders made him overlook all considerations, either of domestic discontents or of commotions among the Scots; his embarkation had been so long retarded by the various obstructions thrown in his way, that he lost the proper season for action, and after his arrival made no progress against the enemy. The king of France, taking advantage of his absence, had broken into the Low Countries; had defeated the Flemings in the battle of Furnes; had made himself master of Lisle, St. Omer, Courtrai, and Ypres; and seemed in a situation to take full vengeance on the earl of Flanders, his rebellious vassal. But Edward, seconded by an English army of 50,000 men (for this is the number assigned by historians[w]) was able to stop the career of his victories; and Philip, finding all the weak resources of his kingdom already exhausted, began to dread a reverse of fortune, and to apprehend an invasion on France itself. The king of England, on the other hand, disappointed of assistance from Adolph, king of the Romans, which he had purchased at a very high price, and finding many urgent calls for his presence in England, was desirous of ending on any honourable terms a war, which served only to divert his force from the execution of more important projects. This disposition in both monarchs soon produced a cessation of hostilities for two years;

[w] Heming. vol. i. p. 146.

and engaged them to submit their differences to the arbitration of pope Boniface.

1298.   Boniface was among the last of the sovereign pontiffs that exercised an authority over the temporal jurisdiction of princes; and these exorbitant pretensions, which he had been tempted to assume from the successful example of his predecessors, but of which the season was now past, involved him in so many calamities, and were attended with so unfortunate a catastrophe, that they have been secretly abandoned, though never openly relinquished, by his successors in the apostolic chair. Edward and Philip, equally jealous of papal claims, took care to insert in their reference, that Boniface was made judge of the difference by their consent, as a private person, not by any right of his pontificate; and the pope, without seeming to be offended at this mortifying clause, proceeded to give a sentence between them, in which they both acquiesced.[x] He brought them to agree, that their union should be cemented by a double marriage; that of Edward himself, who was now a widower, with Margaret, Philip's sister, and that of the prince of Wales, with Isabella, daughter of that monarch.[y] Philip was likewise willing to restore Guienne to the English, which he had indeed no good pretence to detain; but he insisted, that the Scots and their king, John Baliol, should, as his allies, be comprehended in the treaty, and should be restored to their liberty. The

Peace with France. difference, after several disputes, was compromised, by their making mutual sacrifices to each other. Edward agreed to abandon his ally the earl of Flanders, on condition that Philip should treat in like manner his ally the king of Scots. The prospect of conquering these two countries, whose situation made them so commodious an acquisition to the respective kingdoms, prevailed over all other considerations; and though they were finally disappointed in their hopes, their conduct was very reconcilable to the principles of an interested policy. This was the first specimen which the Scots had of the French alliance, and which was exactly conformable to what a smaller power must always expect, when it blindly attaches itself to the will and fortunes of a greater. That unhappy people, now engaged in a brave, though unequal contest

---

[x] Rymer, vol. ii. p. 817. Heming. vol. i. p. 149. Trivet, p. 310.   [y] Rymer, vol. ii. p. 823.

CHAPTER XIII

for their liberties, were totally abandoned by the ally, in whom
they reposed their final confidence, to the will of an imperious
conqueror.

Though England, as well as other European countries, was, in *Revolt of*
its ancient state, very ill qualified for making, and still worse for *Scotland.*
maintaining conquests, Scotland was so much inferior in its internal force, and was so ill situated for receiving foreign succours, that
it is no wonder Edward, an ambitious monarch, should have cast
his eye on so tempting an acquisition, which brought both security
and greatness to his native country. But the instruments, whom he
employed to maintain his dominion over the northern kingdom,
were not happily chosen; and acted not with the requisite prudence and moderation, in reconciling the Scottish nation to a yoke,
which they bore with such extreme reluctance. Warrenne, retiring
into England, on account of his bad state of health, left the administration entirely in the hands of Ormesby, who was appointed
justiciary of Scotland, and Cressingham, who bore the office of
treasurer; and a small military force remained, to secure the precarious authority of those ministers. The latter had no other object
than the amassing of money by rapine and injustice: The former
distinguished himself by the rigour and severity of his temper:
And both of them, treating the Scots as a conquered people, made
them sensible, too early, of the grievous servitude into which they
had fallen. As Edward required, that all the proprietors of land
should swear fealty to him; every one, who refused or delayed
giving this testimony of submission, was outlawed and imprisoned,
and punished without mercy; and the bravest and most generous
spirits of the nation were thus exasperated to the highest degree
against the English government.[z]

There was one William Wallace, of a small fortune, but descended of an ancient family, in the west of Scotland, whose courage prompted him to undertake, and enabled him finally to accomplish, the desperate attempt of delivering his native country from
the dominion of foreigners. This man, whose valorous exploits are
the object of just admiration, but have been much exaggerated by
the traditions of his countrymen, had been provoked by the insolence of an English officer to put him to death; and finding

[z] Walsing. p. 70. Heming. vol. i. p. 118. Trivet, p. 299.

himself obnoxious on that account to the severity of the administration, he fled into the woods, and offered himself as a leader to
all those whom their crimes, or bad fortune, or avowed hatred of
the English, had reduced to a like necessity. He was endowed with
gigantic force of body, with heroic courage of mind, with disinterested magnanimity, with incredible patience, and ability to bear
hunger, fatigue, and all the severities of the seasons; and he soon
acquired, among those desperate fugitives, that authority, to
which his virtues so justly intitled him. Beginning with small attempts, in which he was always successful, he gradually proceeded
to more momentous enterprizes; and he discovered equal caution
in securing his followers, and valour in annoying the enemy. By his
knowledge of the country, he was enabled, when pursued, to ensure a retreat among the morasses or forests or mountains; and
again, collecting his dispersed associates, he unexpectedly appeared in another quarter, and surprized and routed and put to
the sword the unwary English. Every day brought accounts of his
great actions, which were received with no less favour by his countrymen than terror by the enemy: All those, who thirsted after
military fame, were desirous to partake of his renown: His successful valour seemed to vindicate the nation from the ignominy, into
which it had fallen, by its tame submission to the English: And
though no nobleman of note ventured as yet to join his party, he
had gained a general confidence and attachment, which birth and
fortune are not alone able to confer.

Wallace, having, by many fortunate enterprizes, brought the
valour of his followers to correspond to his own, resolved to strike
a decisive blow against the English government; and he concerted
the plan of attacking Ormesby at Scone, and of taking vengeance
on him, for all the violence and tyranny, of which he had been
guilty. The justiciary, apprized of his intentions, fled hastily into
England: All the other officers of that nation imitated his example:
Their terror added alacrity and courage to the Scots, who betook
themselves to arms in every quarter: Many of the principal barons,
and among the rest Sir William Douglas,[a] openly countenanced
Wallace's party: Robert Bruce secretly favoured and promoted
the same cause: And the Scots, shaking off their fetters, prepared themselves to defend, by an united effort, that liberty

[a] Walsing. p. 70. Heming. vol. i. p. 118.

CHAPTER XIII

which they had so unexpectedly recovered from the hands of their oppressors.

But Warrenne, collecting an army of 40,000 men in the north of England, determined to re-establish his authority; and he endeavoured, by the celerity of his armament and of his march, to compensate for his past negligence, which had enabled the Scots to throw off the English government. He suddenly entered Annandale, and came up with the enemy at Irvine, before their forces were fully collected, and before they had put themselves in a posture of defence. Many of the Scottish nobles, alarmed with their dangerous situation, here submitted to the English, renewed their oaths of fealty, promised to deliver hostages for their good behaviour, and received a pardon for past offences.[b] Others who had not yet declared themselves, such as the steward of Scotland and the earl of Lenox, joined, though with reluctance, the English army; and waited a favourable opportunity for embracing the cause of their distressed countrymen. But Wallace, whose authority over his retainers was more fully confirmed by the absence of the great nobles, persevered obstinately in his purpose; and finding himself unable to give battle to the enemy, he marched northwards, with an intention of prolonging the war, and of turning to his advantage the situation of that mountainous and barren country. When Warrenne advanced to Stirling, he found Wallace encamped at Cambuskenneth, on the opposite banks of the Forth; and being continually urged by the impatient Cressingham, who was actuated both by personal and national animosities against the Scots,[c] he prepared to attack them in that position, which Wallace, no less prudent than courageous, had chosen for his army.[d] In spite of the remonstrances of Sir Richard Lundy, a Scotchman of birth and family, who sincerely adhered to the English, he ordered his army to pass a bridge which lay over the Forth; but he was soon convinced, by fatal experience, of the error of his conduct. Wallace, allowing such numbers of the English to pass as he thought proper, attacked them before they were fully formed, put them to rout, pushed part of them into the river, destroyed the rest by the edge of the sword, and gained a complete victory over them.[e] Among the slain was Cressingham himself, whose memory was so

[b] Heming. vol. i. p. 121, 122.　[c] Heming. vol. i. p. 127.　[d] On the 11th of September 1297.　[e] Walsing. p. 73. Heming. vol. i. p. 127, 128, 129. Trivet, p. 307.

extremely odious to the Scots, that they flea'd his dead body, and made saddles and girths of his skin.[f] Warrenne, finding the remainder of his army much dismayed by this misfortune, was obliged again to evacuate the kingdom, and retire into England. The castles of Roxborough and Berwic, ill fortified and feebly defended, fell soon after into the hands of the Scots.

Wallace, universally revered as the deliverer of his country, now received, from the hands of his followers, the dignity of regent or guardian under the captive Baliol; and finding that the disorders of war, as well as the unfavourable seasons, had produced a famine in Scotland, he urged his army to march into England, to subsist at the expence of the enemy, and to revenge all past injuries, by retaliating on the hostile nation. The Scots, who deemed every thing possible under such a leader, joyfully attended his call. Wallace, breaking into the northern counties during the winter season, laid every place waste with fire and sword; and after extending on all sides, without opposition, the fury of his ravages, as far as the bishopric of Durham, he returned, loaded with spoils, and crowned with glory, into his own country.[g] The disorders, which at that time prevailed in England, from the refractory behaviour of the constable and mareschal, made it impossible to collect an army sufficient to resist the enemy, and exposed the nation to this loss and dishonour.

But Edward, who received in Flanders intelligence of these events, and had already concluded a truce with France, now hastened over to England, in certain hopes, by his activity and valour, not only of wiping off this disgrace, but of recovering the important conquest of Scotland, which he always regarded as the chief glory and advantage of his reign. He appeased the murmurs of his people by concessions and promises: He restored to the citizens of London the election of their own magistrates, of which they had been bereaved in the later part of his father's reign: He ordered strict enquiry to be made concerning the corn and other goods, which had been violently seized before his departure, as if he intended to pay the value to the owners:[h] And making public professions of confirming and observing the charters, he regained

---

[f] Heming. vol. i. p. 130.   [g] Heming. vol. i. p. 131, 132, 133.   [h] Rymer, vol. ii. p. 813.

CHAPTER XIII

the confidence of the discontented nobles. Having by all these popular arts rendered himself entirely master of his people, he collected the whole military force of England, Wales, and Ireland; and marched with an army of near a hundred thousand combatants to the northern frontiers.

Nothing could have enabled the Scots to resist, but for one season, so mighty a power, except an entire union among themselves; but as they were deprived of their king, whose personal qualities, even when he was present, appeared so contemptible, and had left among his subjects no principle of attachment to him or his family; factions, jealousies, and animosities unavoidably arose among the great, and distracted all their councils. The elevation of Wallace, though purchased by so great merit, and such eminent services, was the object of envy to the nobility, who repined to see a private gentleman raised above them by his rank, and still more by his glory and reputation. Wallace himself, sensible of their jealousy, and dreading the ruin of his country from those intestine discords, voluntarily resigned his authority, and retained only the command over that body of his followers, who, being accustomed to victory under his standard, refused to follow into the field any other leader. The chief power devolved on the steward of Scotland, and Cummin of Badenoch; men of eminent birth, under whom the great chieftains were more willing to serve in defence of their country. The two Scottish commanders, collecting their several forces from every quarter, fixed their station at Falkirk, and purposed there to abide the assault of the English. Wallace was at the head of a third body, which acted under his command. The Scottish army placed their pikemen along their front: Lined the intervals between the three bodies with archers: And dreading the great superiority of the English in cavalry, endeavoured to secure their front by palisadoes, tied together by ropes.[i] In this disposition, they expected the approach of the enemy.

The king, when he arrived in sight of the Scots, was pleased with the prospect of being able, by one decisive stroke, to determine the fortune of the war; and dividing his army also into three bodies, he led them to the attack. The English archers, who began

22d July. Battle of Falkirk.

[i] Walsing. p. 75. Heming. vol. i. p. 163.

about this time to surpass those of other nations, first chased the Scottish bowmen off the field; then pouring in their arrows among the pikemen, who were cooped up within their intrenchments, threw them into disorder, and rendered the assault of the English pikemen and cavalry more easy and successful. The whole Scottish army was broken, and chased off the field with great slaughter; which the historians, attending more to the exaggerated relations of the populace, than to the probability of things, make amount to fifty or sixty thousand men.[k] It is only certain, that the Scots never suffered a greater loss in any action, nor one which seemed to threaten more inevitable ruin to their country.

In this general rout of the army, Wallace's military skill and presence of mind enabled him to keep his troops entire; and retiring behind the Carron, he marched leisurely along the banks of that small river, which protected him from the enemy. Young Bruce, who had already given many proofs of his aspiring genius, but who served hitherto in the English army, appeared on the opposite banks; and distinguishing the Scottish chief, as well by his majestic port, as by the intrepid activity of his behaviour, called out to him, and desired a short conference. He here represented to Wallace the fruitless and ruinous enterprize in which he was engaged; and endeavoured to bend his inflexible spirit to submission under superior power and superior fortune: He insisted on the unequal contest between a weak state, deprived of its head and agitated by intestine discord, and a mighty nation, conducted by the ablest and most martial monarch of the age, and possessed of every resource either for protracting the war, or for pushing it with vigour and activity: If the love of his country were his motive for perseverance, his obstinacy tended only to prolong her misery; if he carried his views to private grandeur and ambition, he might reflect, that, even if Edward should withdraw his armies, it appeared from past experience, that so many haughty nobles, proud of the pre-eminence of their families, would never submit to personal merit, whose superiority they were less inclined to regard as an object of admiration, than as a reproach and injury to themselves. To these exhortations Wallace replied, that, if he had hith-

[k] Walsing. p. 76. T. Wykes, p. 127. Heming. vol. i. p. 163, 164, 165. Trivet, p. 313, says only 20,000. M. West. p. 431, says 40,000.

erto acted alone, as the champion of his country, it was solely because no second or competitor, or what he rather wished, no leader had yet appeared to place himself in that honourable station: That the blame lay entirely on the nobility, and chiefly on Bruce himself, who, uniting personal merit to dignity of family, had deserted the post, which both nature and fortune, by such powerful calls, invited him to assume: That the Scots, possessed of such a head, would, by their unanimity and concord, have surmounted the chief difficulty under which they now laboured, and might hope, notwithstanding their present losses, to oppose successfully all the power and abilities of Edward: That Heaven itself could not set a more glorious prize before the eyes either of virtue or ambition, than to join in one object, the acquisition of royalty with the defence of national independance: And that as the interests of his country, more than those of a brave man, could never be sincerely cultivated by a sacrifice of liberty, he himself was determined, as far as possible, to prolong, not her misery, but her freedom, and was desirous, that his own life, as well as the existence of the nation, might terminate, when they could no otherwise be preserved than by receiving the chains of a haughty victor. The gallantry of these sentiments, though delivered by an armed enemy, struck the generous mind of Bruce: The flame was conveyed from the breast of one hero to that of another: He repented of his engagements with Edward; and opening his eyes to the honourable path, pointed out to him by Wallace, secretly determined to seize the first opportunity of embracing the cause, however desperate, of his oppressed country.[l]

The subjection of Scotland, notwithstanding this great victory of Edward, was not yet entirely completed. The English army, after reducing the southern provinces, was obliged to retire for want of provisions; and left the northern counties in the hands of the natives. The Scots, no less enraged at their present defeat, than elated by their past victories, still maintained the contest for liberty; but being fully sensible of the great inferiority of their force, they endeavoured, by applications to foreign courts, to procure to themselves some assistance. The supplications of the Scottish min- *1299.*

[l] This story is told by all the Scotch writers; though it must be owned that Trivet and Hemingford, authors of good credit, both agree that Bruce was not at that time in Edward's army.

isters were rejected by Philip; but were more successful with the court of Rome. Boniface, pleased with an occasion of exerting his authority, wrote a letter to Edward, exhorting him to put a stop to his oppressions on Scotland, and displaying all the proofs, such as they had probably been furnished him by the Scots themselves, for the ancient independance of that kingdom.[m] Among other arguments, hinted at above, he mentioned the treaty conducted and finished by Edward himself, for the marriage of his son with the heiress of Scotland; a treaty which would have been absurd, had he been superior lord of the kingdom, and had possessed by the feudal law the right of disposing of his ward in marriage. He mentioned several other striking facts, which fell within the compass of Edward's own knowledge; particularly, that Alexander, when he did homage to the king, openly and expressly declared in his presence, that he swore fealty not for his crown, but for the lands which he held in England: And the pope's letter might have passed for a reasonable one, had he not subjoined his own claim to be liege lord of Scotland; a claim which had not once been heard of, but which, with a singular confidence, he asserted to be full, entire, and derived from the most remote antiquity. The affirmative style, which had been so successful with him and his predecessors in spiritual contests, was never before abused after a more egregious manner in any civil controversy.

*1300.
Scotland
again
subdued.*

1301.

The reply, which Edward made to Boniface's letter, contains particulars, no less singular and remarkable.[n] He there proves the superiority of England by historical facts, deduced from the period of Brutus, the Trojan, who, he said, founded the British monarchy in the age of Eli and Samuel: He supports his position by all the events which passed in the island before the arrival of the Romans: And after laying great stress on the extensive dominions and heroic victories of king Arthur, he vouchsafes at last to descend to the time of Edward the elder, with which, in his speech to the states of Scotland, he had chosen to begin his claim of superiority. He asserts it to be a fact, *notorious and confirmed by the records of antiquity,* that the English monarchs had often conferred the kingdom of Scotland on their own subjects; had dethroned these vassal kings when unfaithful to them; and had substituted others in their stead.

[m] Rymer, vol. ii. p. 844.   [n] Ibid. p. 863.

CHAPTER XIII

He displays with great pomp the full and complete homage which William had done to Henry II.; without mentioning the formal abolition of that *extorted* deed by king Richard, and the renunciation of all future claims of the same nature. Yet this paper he begins with a solemn appeal to the Almighty, the searcher of hearts, for his own firm persuasion of the justice of his claim; and no less than a hundred and four barons, assembled in parliament at Lincoln, concur, in maintaining before the pope, under their seals, the validity of these pretensions.[o] At the same time, however, they take care to inform Boniface, that, though they had justified their cause before him, they did not acknowledge him for their judge: The crown of England was free and sovereign: They had sworn to maintain all its royal prerogatives, and would never permit the king himself, were he willing, to relinquish its independancy.

That neglect, almost total, of truth and justice, which sovereign states discover in their transactions with each other, is an evil universal and inveterate; is one great source of the misery to which the human race is continually exposed; and it may be doubted, whether in many instances it be found in the end to contribute to the interests of those princes themselves, who thus sacrifice their integrity to their politics. As few monarchs have lain under stronger temptations to violate the principles of equity, than Edward in his transactions with Scotland; so never were they violated with less scruple and reserve: Yet his advantages were hitherto precarious and uncertain; and the Scots, once roused to arms and enured to war, began to appear a formidable enemy, even to this military and ambitious monarch. They chose John Cummin for their regent; *Scotland again revolts.* and not content with maintaining their independance in the northern parts, they made incursions into the southern counties, which, Edward imagined, he had totally subdued. John de Segrave, whom he had left guardian of Scotland, led an army to oppose them; and lying at Roslin near Edinburgh, sent out his forces in three *1303.* divisions, to provide themselves with forage and subsistence from *24th Feb.* the neighbourhood. One party was suddenly attacked by the regent and Sir Simon Fraser; and being unprepared, was immedi-

[o] Rymer, vol. ii. p. 873. Walsing. p. 85. Heming. vol. i. p. 186. Trivet, p. 330. M. West. p. 443.

ately routed and pursued with great slaughter. The few that escaped, flying to the second division, gave warning of the approach of the enemy: The soldiers ran to their arms: And were immediately led on to take revenge for the death of their countrymen. The Scots, elated with the advantage already obtained, made a vigorous impression upon them: The English, animated with a thirst of vengeance, maintained a stout resistance: The victory was long undecided between them; but at last declared itself entirely in favour of the former, who broke the English, and chaced them to the third division, now advancing with a hasty march to support their distressed companions. Many of the Scots had fallen in the two first actions; most of them were wounded; and all of them extremely fatigued by the long continuance of the combat: Yet were they so transported with success and military rage, that, having suddenly recovered their order, and arming the followers of their camp with the spoils of the slaughtered enemy, they drove with fury upon the ranks of the dismayed English. The favourable moment decided the battle; which the Scots, had they met with a steady resistance, were not long able to maintain: The English were chaced off the field: Three victories were thus gained in one day:[p] And the renown of these great exploits, seconded by the favourable dispositions of the people, soon made the regent master of all the fortresses in the south; and it became necessary for Edward to begin anew the conquest of the kingdom.

The king prepared himself for this enterprize with his usual vigour and abilities. He assembled both a great fleet and a great army; and entering the frontiers of Scotland, appeared with a force, which the enemy could not think of resisting in the open field: The English navy, which sailed along the coast, secured the army from any danger of famine: Edward's vigilance preserved it from surprizes: And by this prudent disposition they marched victorious from one extremity of the kingdom to the other, ravaging the open country, reducing all the castles,[q] and receiving the submissions of all the nobility, even those of Cummin the regent. The most obstinate resistance was made by the castle of Brechin, defended by Sir Thomas Maule; and the place opened not its gates, till the death of the governor, by discouraging the garrison,

[p] Heming. vol. i. p. 197.   [q] Ibid. p. 205.

CHAPTER XIII

obliged them to submit to the fate, which had overwhelmed the *Is again* rest of the kingdom. Wallace, though he attended the English *subdued.* army in their march, found but few opportunities of signalizing that valour, which had formerly made him so terrible to his enemies.

Edward, having completed his conquest, which employed him *1304.* during the space of near two years, now undertook the more difficult work of settling the country, of establishing a new form of government, and of making his acquisition durable to the crown of England. He seems to have carried matters to extremity against the natives: He abrogated all the Scottish laws and customs:[r] He endeavoured to substitute the English in their place: He entirely razed or destroyed all the monuments of antiquity: Such records or histories as had escaped his former search were now burnt or dispersed: And he hastened, by too precipitate steps, to abolish entirely the Scottish name, and to sink it finally in the English.

Edward, however, still deemed his favourite conquest ex- *1305.* posed to some danger, so long as Wallace was alive: and being prompted both by revenge and policy, he employed every art to discover his retreat, and become master of his person. At last, that hardy warrior, who was determined, amidst the universal slavery of his countrymen, still to maintain his independancy, was betrayed into Edward's hands by Sir John Monteith, his friend, whom he had made acquainted with the place of his concealment. The king, whose natural bravery and magnanimity should have induced him to respect like qualities in an enemy, enraged at some acts of violence committed by Wallace during the fury of war, resolved to overawe the Scots by an example of severity: He or- dered Wallace to be carried in chains to London; to be tried as a *23d Au-* rebel and traitor, though he had never made submissions or sworn *gust.* fealty to England; and to be excuted on Tower-hill. This was the unworthy fate of a hero, who, through a course of many years, had, with signal conduct, intrepidity, and perseverance, defended, against a public and oppressive enemy, the liberties of his native country.

But the barbarous policy of Edward failed of the purpose to which it was directed. The Scots, already disgusted at the great

---

[r] Ryley, p. 506.

innovations introduced by the sword of a conqueror into their laws and government, were farther enraged at the injustice and cruelty exercised upon Wallace; and all the envy, which, during his lifetime, had attended that gallant chief, being now buried in his grave, he was universally regarded as the champion of Scotland, and the patron of her expiring independancy. The people, inflamed with resentment, were every where disposed to rise against the English government, and it was not long ere a new and more fortunate leader presented himself, who conducted them to liberty, to victory, and to vengeance.

1306.
Robert
Bruce.

Robert Bruce, grandson of that Robert, who had been one of the competitors for the crown, had succeeded, by his grandfather's and father's death, to all their rights; and the demise of John Baliol, together with the captivity of Edward, eldest son of that prince, seemed to open a full career to the genius and ambition of this young nobleman. He saw, that the Scots, when the title to their crown had expired in the males of their ancient royal family, had been divided into parties nearly equal between the houses of Bruce and Baliol; and that every incident, which had since happened, had tended to wean them from any attachment to the latter. The slender capacity of John had proved unable to defend them against their enemies: He had meanly resigned his crown into the hands of the conqueror: He had, before his deliverance from captivity, re-iterated that resignation in a manner seemingly voluntary; and had in that deed thrown out many reflections extremely dishonourable to his ancient subjects, whom he publicly called traitors, ruffians, and rebels, and with whom, he declared, he was determined to maintain no farther correspondence:[s] He had, during the time of his exile, adhered strictly to that resolution; and his son, being a prisoner, seemed ill qualified to revive the rights, now fully abandoned, of his family. Bruce therefore hoped, that the Scots, so long exposed, from the want of a leader, to the oppressions of their enemies, would unanimously fly to his standard, and would seat him on the vacant throne, to which he brought such plausible pretensions. His aspiring spirit, inflamed by the fervor of youth, and buoyed up by his natural courage, saw the glory alone of the enterprize, or regarded the prodigious difficulties, which

[s] Brady's hist. vol. ii. App. N°. 27.

CHAPTER XIII

attended it, as the source only of farther glory. The miseries and
oppressions, which he had beheld his countrymen suffer in their
unequal contest; the repeated defeats and misfortunes, which they
had undergone; proved to him so many incentives to bring them
relief, and conduct them to vengeance against the haughty victor.
The circumstances, which attended Bruce's first declaration, are
variously related; but we shall rather follow the account given by
the Scottish historians; not that their authority is in general anywise comparable to that of the English; but because they may be
supposed sometimes better informed concerning facts, which so
nearly interested their own nation.

Bruce, who had long harboured in his breast the design of
freeing his enslaved country, ventured at last to open his mind to
John Cummin, a powerful nobleman, with whom he lived in strict
intimacy. He found his friend, as he imagined, fully possessed with
the same sentiments; and he needed to employ no arts of persuasion to make him embrace the resolution of throwing off, on the
first favourable opportunity, the usurped dominion of the English. But on the departure of Bruce, who attended Edward to
London, Cummin, who either had all along dissembled with him,
or began to reflect more coolly in his absence on the desperate
nature of the undertaking, resolved to atone for his crime in as-
senting to this rebellion, by the merit of revealing the secret to the
king of England. Edward did not immediately commit Bruce to
custody; because he intended, at the same time, to seize his three
brothers, who resided in Scotland; and he contented himself with
secretly setting spies upon him, and ordering all his motions to be
strictly watched. A nobleman of Edward's court, Bruce's intimate
friend, was apprized of his danger; but not daring, amidst so many
jealous eyes, to hold any conversation with him, he fell on an
expedient to give him warning, that it was full time he should make
his escape. He sent him, by a servant, a pair of gilt spurs and a
purse of gold, which he pretended to have borrowed from him;
and left it to the sagacity of his friend to discover the meaning of
the present. Bruce immediately contrived the means of his escape;
and as the ground was at that time covered with snow, he had the
precaution, it is said, to order his horses to be shod with their shoes
inverted, that he might deceive those, who should track his path
over the open fields or cross roads, through which he purposed to

travel. He arrived in a few days at Dumfries in Annandale, the chief seat of his family interest; and he happily found a great number of the Scottish nobility there assembled, and among the rest, John Cummin, his former associate.

10th Feb.
The noblemen were astonished at the appearance of Bruce among them; and still more when he discovered to them the object of his journey. He told them, that he was come to live or die with them in defence of the liberties of his country, and hoped, with their assistance, to redeem the Scottish name from all the indignities, which it had so long suffered from the tyranny of their imperious masters: That the sacrifice of the rights of his family was the first injury, which had prepared the way for their ensuing slavery; and by resuming them, which was his firm purpose, he opened to them the joyful prospect of recovering from the fraudulent usurper their ancient and hereditary independance: That all past misfortunes had proceeded from their disunion; and they would soon appear no less formidable than of old to their enemies, if they now deigned to follow into the field their rightful prince, who knew no medium between death and victory: That their mountains and their valour, which had, during so many ages, protected their liberty from all the efforts of the Roman empire, would still be sufficient, were they worthy of their generous ancestors, to defend them against the utmost violence of the English tyrant: That it was unbecoming men, born to the most ancient independance known in Europe, to submit to the will of any masters; but fatal to receive those, who, being irritated by such persevering resistance, and inflamed with the highest animosity, would never deem themselves secure in their usurped dominion but by exterminating all the ancient nobility, and even all the ancient inhabitants: And that, being reduced to this desperate extremity, it were better for them at once to perish, like brave men, with swords in their hands, than to dread long, and at last undergo, the fate of the unfortunate Wallace, whose merits, in the brave and obstinate defence of his country, were finally rewarded by the hands of an English executioner.

The spirit with which this discourse was delivered, the bold sentiments which it conveyed, the novelty of Bruce's declaration, assisted by the graces of his youth and manly deportment, made deep impression on the minds of his audience, and rouzed all those principles of indignation and revenge, with which they had long been secretly actuated. The Scottish nobles declared their unanimous resolution to use the utmost efforts in delivering their country from bondage, and to second the courage of Bruce, in asserting his and their undoubted rights, against their common oppressors. Cummin alone, who had secretly taken his measures with the king, opposed this general determination; and by representing the great power of England, governed by a prince of such uncommon vigour and abilities, he endeavoured to set before them the certain destruction, which they must expect, if they again violated their oaths of fealty, and shook off their allegiance to the victorious Edward.[t] Bruce, already apprized of his treachery, and foreseeing the certain failure of all his own schemes of ambition and glory from the opposition of so potent a leader, took immediately his resolution; and moved partly by resentment, partly by policy, followed Cummin on the dissolution of the assembly, attacked him in the cloysters of the Grey Friars through which he passed, and running him through the body, left him for dead. Sir Thomas Kirkpatric, one of Bruce's friends, asking him soon after, if the traitor were slain; *I believe so,* replied Bruce. *And is that a matter,* cried Kirkpatric, *to be left to conjecture? I will secure him.* Upon which he drew his dagger, ran to Cummin, and stabbed him to the heart. This deed of Bruce and his associates, which contains circumstances justly condemned by our present manners, was regarded in that age, as an effort of manly vigour and just policy. The family of Kirkpatric took for the crest of their arms, which they still wear, a hand with a bloody dagger; and chose for their motto these words, *I will secure him;* the expression employed by their ancestor, when he executed that violent action.

The murder of Cummin affixed the seal to the conspiracy of the Scottish nobles: They had now no resource left but to shake off the yoke of England, or to perish in the attempt: The genius of the nation rouzed itself from its present dejection: And Bruce, flying to different quarters, excited his partizans to arms, attacked with success the dispersed bodies of the English, got possession of many of the castles, and having made his authority be acknowledged in most parts of the kingdom, was solemnly crowned and inau-

Third revolt of Scotland.

[t] M. West. p. 453.

gurated in the abbey of Scone by the bishop of St. Andrews, who had zealously embraced his cause. The English were again chased out of the kingdom, except such as took shelter in the fortresses that still remained in their hands; and Edward found, that the Scots, twice conquered in his reign, and often defeated, must yet be anew subdued. Not discouraged with these unexpected difficulties, he sent Aymer de Valence with a considerable force into Scotland to check the progress of the malcontents; and that nobleman falling unexpectedly upon Bruce at Methven in Perthshire, threw his army into such disorder, as ended in a total defeat.[u] Bruce fought with the most heroic courage, was thrice dismounted in the action, and as often recovered himself; but was at last obliged to yield to superior fortune, and take shelter, with a few followers, in the western isles. The earl of Athole, Sir Simon Fraser, and Sir Christopher Seton, who had been taken prisoners, were ordered by Edward to be executed as rebels and traitors.[w]

1307. Many other acts of rigour were exercised by him; and that prince, vowing revenge against the whole Scottish nation, whom he deemed incorrigible in their aversion to his government, assembled a great army, and was preparing to enter the frontiers, secure of success, and determined to make the defenceless Scots the vic-

7th July, Death, tims of his severity; when he unexpectedly sickened and died near Carlisle; enjoining with his last breath his son and successor to prosecute the enterprize, and never to desist till he had finally subdued the kingdom of Scotland. He expired in the sixty-ninth year of his age, and the thirty-fifth of his reign, hated by his neighbours, but extremely respected and revered by his own subjects.

and character of the king. The enterprizes, finished by this prince, and the projects, which he formed and brought near to a conclusion, were more prudent, more regularly conducted, and more advantageous to the solid interests of his kingdom, than those which were undertaken in any reign either of his ancestors or his successors. He restored authority to the government, disordered by the weakness of his father; he maintained the laws against all the efforts of his turbulent barons; he fully annexed to his crown the principality of

---

[u] Walsing. p. 91. Heming. vol. i. p. 222, 223. Trivet, p. 344. [w] Heming. vol. i. p. 223. M. West. p. 456.

Wales; he took many wise and vigorous measures for reducing Scotland to a like condition; and though the equity of this latter enterprize may reasonably be questioned, the circumstances of the two kingdoms promised such certain success, and the advantage was so visible of uniting the whole island under one head, that those who give great indulgence to reasons of state in the measures of princes, will not be apt to regard this part of his conduct with much severity. But Edward, however exceptionable his character may appear on the head of justice, is the model of a politic and warlike king: He possessed industry, penetration, courage, vigilance, and enterprize: He was frugal in all expences that were not necessary; he knew how to open the public treasures on a proper occasion; he punished criminals with severity; he was gracious and affable to his servants and courtiers: and being of a majestic figure, expert in all military exercises, and in the main well-proportioned in his limbs, notwithstanding the great length and the smallness of his legs, he was as well qualified to captivate the populace by his exterior appearance, as to gain the approbation of men of sense by his more solid virtues.

But the chief advantage, which the people of England reaped, and still continue to reap, from the reign of this great prince, was the correction, extension, amendment, and establishment of the laws, which Edward maintained in great vigour, and left much improved to posterity: For the acts of a wise legislator commonly remain; while the acquisitions of a conqueror often perish with him. This merit has justly gained to Edward the appellation of the English Justinian. Not only the numerous statutes, passed in his reign, touch the chief points of jurisprudence, and, according to Sir Edward Coke,[x] truly deserve the name of establishments, because they were more constant, standing, and durable laws than any made since; but the regular order, maintained in his administration, gave an opportunity to the common law to refine itself, and brought the judges to a certainty in their determinations, and the lawyers to a precision in their pleadings. Sir Matthew Hale has remarked the sudden improvement of English law during this reign; and ventures to assert, that, till his own time, it had never received any considerable encrease.[y] Edward settled the jurisdic-

Miscellaneous transactions of this reign.

---

[x] Institute, p. 156.   [y] History of the English law, p. 158, 163.

tion of the several courts; first established the office of justice of peace; abstained from the practice, too common before him, of interrupting justice by mandates from the privy-council;[z] repressed robberies and disorders;[a] encouraged trade by giving merchants an easy method of recovering their debts;[b] and, in short, introduced a new face of things by the vigour and wisdom of his administration. As law began now to be well established, the abuse of that blessing began also to be remarked. Instead of their former associations for robbery and violence, men entered into formal combinations to support each other in law-suits; and it was found requisite to check this iniquity by act of parliament.[c]

There happened in this reign a considerable alteration in the execution of the laws: The king abolished the office of chief justiciary, which, he thought, possessed too much power, and was dangerous to the crown:[d] He completed the division of the court of exchequer into four distinct courts, which managed, each, its several branch, without dependance on any one magistrate; and as the lawyers afterwards invented a method, by means of their fictions, of carrying business from one court to another, the several courts became rivals and checks to each other; a circumstance which tended much to improve the practice of the law in England.

But though Edward appeared thus, throughout his whole reign, a friend to law and justice, it cannot be said, that he was an enemy to arbitrary power; and in a government more regular and legal than was that of England in his age, such practices, as those which may be remarked in his administration, would have given sufficient ground of complaint, and sometimes were even in his age the object of general displeasure. The violent plunder and banishment of the Jews; the putting of the whole clergy, at once, and by an arbitrary edict, out of the protection of law; the seizing

---

[z] Articuli super Cart. cap. 6. Edward enacted a law to this purpose; but it is doubtful, whether he ever observed it. We are sure that scarcely any of his successors did. The multitude of these letters of protection were the ground of a complaint by the commons in 3 Edward II. See Ryley, p. 525. This practice is declared illegal by the statute of Northampton passed in the second of Edward III. but it still continued, like many other abuses. There are instances of it so late as the reign of queen Elizabeth.   [a] Statute of Winton.   [b] Statute of Acton Burnel.   [c] Statute of conspirators.
[d] Spelman. Gloss. in verbo *justiciarius*. Gilbert's Hist. of the Exchequer, p. 8.

of all the wool and leather of the kingdom; the heightening of the impositions on the former valuable commodity; the new and illegal commission of Trailbaston; the taking of all the money and plate of monasteries and churches, even before he had any quarrel with the clergy; the subjecting of every man possessed of twenty pounds a year to military service, though not bound to it by his tenure; his visible reluctance to confirm the great charter, as if that concession had no validity from the deeds of his predecessors; the captious clause which he at last annexed to his confirmation; his procuring of the pope's dispensation from the oaths which he had taken to observe that charter; and his levying of talliages at discretion even after the statute, or rather charter, by which he had renounced that prerogative; these are so many demonstrations of his arbitrary disposition, and prove with what exception and reserve we ought to celebrate his love of justice. He took care that his subjects should do justice to each other; but he desired always to have his own hands free in all his transactions, both with them and with his neighbours.

The chief obstacle to the execution of justice in those times was the power of the great barons; and Edward was perfectly qualified, by his character and abilities, for keeping these tyrants in awe, and restraining their illegal practices. This salutary purpose was accordingly the great object of his attention; yet was he imprudently led into a measure which tended to encrease and confirm their dangerous authority. He passed a statute, which, by allowing them to entail their estates, made it impracticable to diminish the property of the great families, and left them every means of encrease and acquisition.[e]

Edward observed a contrary policy with regard to the church: He seems to have been the first Christian prince that passed a statute of mortmain; and prevented by law the clergy from making new acquisitions of lands, which by the ecclesiastical canons they were for ever prohibited from alienating. The opposition between his maxims with regard to the nobility and to the ecclesiastics, leads us to conjecture, that it was only by chance he passed the beneficial statute of mortmain, and that his sole object was, to maintain the number of knights' fees, and to prevent the superiors from being defrauded of the profits of wardship, marriage, livery, and other

[e] Brady of Boroughs, p. 25, from the records.

emoluments arising from the feudal tenures. This is indeed the reason assigned in the statute itself, and appears to have been his real object in enacting it. The author of the annals of Waverly ascribes this act chiefly to the king's anxiety for maintaining the military force of the kingdom; but adds that he was mistaken in his purpose; for that the Amalekites were overcome more by the prayers of Moses than by the sword of the Israelites.*[f]* The statute of mortmain was often evaded afterwards by the invention of *Uses*.

Edward was active in restraining the usurpations of the church; and excepting his ardour for Crusades, which adhered to him during his whole life, seems, in other respects, to have been little infected with superstition, the vice chiefly of weak minds. But the passion for Crusades was really in that age the passion for glory. As the pope now felt himself somewhat more restrained in his former practice of pillaging the several churches in Europe, by laying impositions upon them, he permitted the generals of particular orders, who resided at Rome, to levy taxes on the convents subjected to their jurisdiction; and Edward was obliged to enact a law against this new abuse. It was also become a practice of the court of Rome to provide successors to benefices before they became vacant: Edward found it likewise necessary to prevent by law this species of injustice.

The tribute of 1000 marks a year, to which king John, in doing homage to the pope, had subjected the kingdom, had been pretty regularly paid since his time, though the vassalage was constantly denied, and indeed, for fear of giving offence, had been but little insisted on. The payment was called by a new name of *census*, not by that of tribute. King Edward seems to have always paid this money with great reluctance, and he suffered the arrears, at one time, to run on for six years,*[g]* at another for eleven:*[h]* But as princes in that age stood continually in need of the pope's offices, for dispensations of marriage and for other concessions, the court of Rome always found means, sooner or later, to catch the money. The levying of first-fruits was also a new device, begun in this reign, by which his holiness thrust his fingers very frequently into the purses of the faithful; and the king seems to have unwarily given way to it.

---

[f] P. 234. See also M. West, p. 409. *[g]* Rymer, vol. ii. p. 77, 107. *[h]* Id. p. 862.

CHAPTER XIII

In the former reign, the taxes had been partly scutages, partly such a proportional part of the moveables, as was granted by parliament: In this, scutages were entirely dropped; and the assessment on moveables was the chief method of taxation. Edward in his fourth year had a fifteenth granted him; in his fifth year a twelfth; in his eleventh year a thirtieth from the laity, a twentieth from the clergy; in his eighteenth year a fifteenth; in his twenty-second year a tenth from the laity, a sixth from London and other corporate towns, half of their benefices from the clergy; in his twenty-third year an eleventh from the barons and others, a tenth from the clergy, a seventh from the burgesses; in his twenty-fourth year a twelfth from the barons and others, an eighth from the burgesses, from the clergy, nothing, because of the pope's inhibition; in his twenty-fifth year an eighth from the laity, a tenth from the clergy of Canterbury, a fifth from those of York; in his twenty-ninth year a fifteenth from the laity, on account of his confirming the perambulations of the forests; the clergy granted nothing; in his thirty-third year, first a thirtieth from the barons and others, and a twentieth from the burgesses, then a fifteenth from all his subjects; in his thirty-fourth year a thirtieth from all his subjects for knighting his eldest son.

These taxes were moderate; but the king had also duties upon exportation and importation granted him from time to time: The heaviest were commonly upon wool. Poundage, or a shilling a pound, was not regularly granted the kings for life till the reign of Henry V.

In 1296, the famous mercantile society, called the *Merchant Adventurers*, had its first origin: It was instituted for the improvement of the woollen manufacture, and the vending of the cloth abroad, particularly at Antwerp.[i] For the English at this time scarcely thought of any more distant commerce.

This king granted a charter or declaration of protection and privileges to foreign merchants, and also ascertained the customs or duties which those merchants were in return to pay on merchandize imported and exported. He promised them security; allowed them a jury on trials, consisting half of natives, half of foreigners; and appointed them a justiciary in London for their protection. But notwithstanding this seeming attention to foreign

[i] Anderson's history of commerce, vol. i. p. 137.

merchants, Edward did not free them from the cruel hardship, of making one answerable for the debts, and even for the crimes of another, that came from the same country.[k] We read of such practices among the present barbarous nations. The king also imposed on them a duty of two shillings on each tun of wine imported, over and above the old duty; and forty pence on each sack of wool exported, besides half a mark, the former duty.[l]

In the year 1303, the Exchequer was robbed, and of no less a sum than 100,000 pounds, as is pretended.[m] The abbot and monks of Westminster were indicted for this robbery, but acquitted. It does not appear, that the king ever discovered the criminals with certainty; though his indignation fell on the society of Lombard merchants, particularly the Frescobaldi, very opulent Florentines.

The pope having in 1307 collected much money in England, the king enjoined the nuncio not to export it in specie but in bills of exchange.[n] A proof that commerce was but ill understood at that time.

Edward had by his first wife, Eleanor of Castile, four sons, but Edward, his heir and successor, was the only one that survived him. She also bore him eleven daughters, most of whom died in their infancy: Of the surviving, Joan was married first to the earl of Glocester, and after his death, to Ralph de Monthermer: Margaret espoused John duke of Brabant: Elizabeth espoused first John earl of Holland; and afterwards the earl of Hereford; Mary was a nun at Ambresbury. He had by his second wife, Margaret of France, two sons and a daughter; Thomas created earl of Norfolk, and Mareschal of England; and Edmond who was created earl of Kent by his brother when king. The princess died in her infancy.

---

[k] Anderson's hist. of commerce, vol. i. p. 146.   [l] Rymer, vol. iv. p. 361. It is the charter of Edw. I. which is there confirmed by Edw. III.   [m] Rymer, vol. ii. p. 530.   [n] Rymer, vol. ii. p. 1092.

XIV

EDWARD II

---

*Weakness of the king – His passion
for favourites – Piers Gavaston –
Discontent of the barons – Murder of
Gavaston – War with Scotland – Battle of
Bannockburn – Hugh le Despenser – Civil
commotions – Execution of the earl of
Lancaster – Conspiracy against the king –
Insurrection – The king dethroned –
Murdered – His Character – Miscellaneous
transactions in this reign.*

THE PREPOSSESSIONS, entertained in favour of young Edward, *1307.* kept the English from being fully sensible of the extreme loss, which they had sustained by the death of the great monarch, who filled the throne; and all men hastened with alacrity to take the oath of allegiance to his son and successor. This prince was in the twenty-third year of his age, was of an agreeable figure, of a mild and gentle disposition, and having never discovered a propensity to any dangerous vice, it was natural to prognosticate tranquillity and happiness from his government. But the first act of his reign blasted all these hopes, and shewed him to be totally unqualified *Weakness* for that perilous situation, in which every English monarch, dur- *of the* ing those ages, had, from the unstable form of the constitution, *king.* and the turbulent dispositions of the people, derived from it, the misfortune to be placed. The indefatigable Robert Bruce, though his army had been dispersed and he himself had been obliged to take shelter in the western isles, remained not long unactive; but before the death of the late king, had sallied from his retreat, had again collected his followers, had appeared in the field, and had obtained by surprize an important advantage over Aymer de Valence, who commanded the English forces.[o] He was now become so considerable as to have afforded the king of England sufficient glory in subduing him, without incurring any danger of seeing all those mighty preparations, made by his father, fail in the enterprize. But Edward, instead of pursuing his advantages, marched but a little way into Scotland; and having an utter incapacity, and equal aversion, for all application or serious business, he immediately returned upon his footsteps, and disbanded his army. His grandees perceived from this conduct, that the authority of the crown, fallen into such feeble hands, was no longer to be dreaded, and that every insolence might be practised by them with impunity.

His passion for favourites. Piers Gavaston.

The next measure, taken by Edward, gave them an inclination to attack those prerogatives, which no longer kept them in awe. There was one Piers Gavaston, son of a Gascon knight of some distinction, who had honourably served the late king, and who, in reward of his merits, had obtained an establishment for his son in the family of the prince of Wales. This young man soon insinuated himself into the affections of his master, by his agreeable behaviour, and by supplying him with all those innocent, though frivolous amusements, which suited his capacity and his inclinations. He was endowed with the utmost elegance of shape and person, was noted for a fine mien and easy carriage, distinguished himself in all warlike and genteel exercises, and was celebrated for those quick sallies of wit, in which his countrymen usually excel. By all these accomplishments he gained so entire an ascendant over young Edward, whose heart was strongly disposed to friendship and confidence, that the late king, apprehensive of the consequences, had banished him the kingdom, and had, before he died, made his son promise never to recall him. But no sooner did he find himself master, as he vainly imagined, than he sent for Gavaston; and even before his arrival at court, endowed him with

[o] Trivet, p. 346.

the whole earldom of Cornwal, which had escheated to the crown, by the death of Edmond, son of Richard king of the Romans.[p] Not content with conferring on him those possessions, which had sufficed as an appanage for a prince of the blood, he daily loaded him with new honours and riches; married him to his own niece, sister of the earl of Glocester; and seemed to enjoy no pleasure in his royal dignity, but as it enabled him to exalt to the highest splendor this object of his fond affections.

The haughty barons, offended at the superiority of a minion, whose birth, though reputable, they despised, as much inferior to their own, concealed not their discontent; and soon found reasons to justify their animosity in the character and conduct of the man they hated. Instead of disarming envy by the moderation and modesty of his behaviour, Gavaston displayed his power and influence with the utmost ostentation; and deemed no circumstance of his good fortune so agreeable as its enabling him to eclipse and mortify all his rivals. He was vain-glorious, profuse, rapacious; fond of exterior pomp and appearance, giddy with prosperity; and as he imagined, that his fortune was now as strongly rooted in the kingdom, as his ascendant was uncontrouled over the weak monarch, he was negligent in engaging partizans, who might support his sudden and ill-established grandeur. At all tournaments, he took delight in foiling the English nobility, by his superior address: In every conversation, he made them the object of his wit and raillery: Every day his enemies multiplied upon him; and naught was wanting but a little time to cement their union, and render it fatal, both to him and to his master.[q]

It behoved the king to take a journey to France, both in order to do homage for the dutchy of Guienne, and to espouse the princess Isabella, to whom he had long been affianced, though unexpected accidents had hitherto retarded the completion of the marriage.[r] Edward left Gavaston guardian of the realm,[s] with more ample powers, than had usually been conferred;[t] and on his return with his young queen, renewed all the proofs of that fond attachment to the favourite, of which every one so loudly complained.

Discontent of the barons.

[p] Rymer, vol. iii. p. 1. Heming, vol. i. p. 243. Walsing. p. 96.   [q] T. de la More, p. 593. Walsing. p. 97.   [r] T. de la More, p. 593. Trivet, cont. p. 3.   [s] Rymer, vol. iii. p. 47. Ypod. Neust. p. 499.   [t] Brady's App. N°. 49.

This princess was of an imperious and intriguing spirit; and find-ing, that her husband's capacity required, as his temper inclined, him to be governed, she thought herself best intitled, on every account, to perform the office, and she contracted a mortal hatred against the person, who had disappointed her in these ex-pectations. She was well pleased, therefore, to see a combination of the nobility forming against Gavaston, who, sensible to her hatred, had wantonly provoked her by new insults and injuries.

1308.

Thomas, earl of Lancaster, cousin-german to the king, and first prince of the blood, was by far the most opulent and power-ful subject in England, and possessed in his own right, and soon after in that of his wife, heiress of the family of Lincoln, no less than six earldoms, with a proportionable estate in land, attended with all the jurisdictions and power, which commonly in that age were annexed to landed property. He was turbulent and factious in his disposition; mortally hated the favourite, whose influence over the king exceeded his own; and he soon became the head of that party among the barons, who desired the depression of this insolent stranger. The confederated nobles bound themselves by oath to expel Gavaston: Both sides began already to put them-selves in a warlike posture: The licentiousness of the age broke out in robberies and other disorders, the usual prelude of civil war: And the royal authority, despised in the king's own hands, and hated in those of Gavaston, became insufficient for the execution of the laws, and the maintenance of peace in the kingdom. A parliament being summoned at Westminster, Lancaster and his party came thither with an armed retinue; and were there enabled to impose their own terms on the sovereign. They required the banishment of Gavaston, imposed an oath on him never to return, and engaged the bishops, who never failed to interpose in all civil concerns, to pronounce him excommunicated, if he remained any longer in the kingdom.[u] Edward was obliged to submit;[w] but even in his compliance, gave proofs of his fond attachment to his fa-vourite. Instead of removing all umbrage, by sending him to his own country, as was expected, he appointed him lord lieutenant of Ireland,[x] attended him to Bristol on his journey thither, and before

---

[u] Trivet, cont. p. 5.   [w] Rymer, vol. iii. p. 80.   [x] Ibid. p. 92. Murimuth, p. 39.

CHAPTER XIV

his departure conferred on him new lands and riches both in Gascony and England.[y] Gavaston, who did not want bravery, and possessed talents for war,[z] acted, during his government, with vigour against some Irish rebels, whom he subdued.

Meanwhile, the king, less shocked with the illegal violence which had been imposed upon him, than unhappy in the absence of his minion, employed every expedient to soften the opposition of the barons to his return; as if success in that point were the chief object of his government. The high office of hereditary steward was conferred on Lancaster: His father-in-law, the earl of Lincoln, was bought off by other concessions: Earl Warrenne was also mollified by civilities, grants, or promises: The insolence of Gavaston, being no longer before men's eyes, was less the object of general indignation: And Edward, deeming matters sufficiently prepared for his purpose, applied to the court of Rome, and obtained for Gavaston a dispensation from that oath, which the barons had compelled him to take, that he would for ever abjure the realm.[a] He went down to Chester, to receive him on his first landing from Ireland; flew into his arms with transports of joy; and having obtained the formal consent of the barons in parliament to his re-establishment, set no longer any bounds to his extravagant fondness and affection. Gavaston himself, forgetting his past misfortunes, and blind to their causes, resumed the same ostentation and insolence; and became more than ever the object of general detestation among the nobility.

The barons first discovered their animosity by absenting themselves from parliament; and finding that this expedient had not been successful, they began to think of employing sharper and more effectual remedies. Though there had scarcely been any national ground of complaint, except some dissipation of the public treasure: Though all the acts of mal-administration, objected to the king and his favourite, seemed of a nature more proper to excite heart-burnings in a ball or assembly, than commotions in a great kingdom: Yet such was the situation of the times, that the barons were determined, and were able, to make them the reasons of a total alteration in the constitution and civil government. Hav- *7th Feb.*

[y] Rymer, vol. iii. p. 87.   [z] Heming. vol. i. p. 248. T. de la More, p. 593.
[a] Rymer, vol. iii, p. 167.

ing come to parliament, in defiance of the laws and the king's prohibition, with a numerous retinue of armed followers, they found themselves entirely masters; and they presented a petition, which was equivalent to a command, requiring Edward to devolve on a chosen junto the whole authority both of the crown and of the parliament. The king was obliged to sign a commission, empowering the prelates and barons to elect twelve persons, who should, till the term of Michaelmas in the year following, have authority to enact ordinances for the government of the kingdom, and regulation of the king's household; consenting that these ordinances should, thenceforth, and for ever, have the force of laws; allowing the ordainers to form associations among themselves and their friends, for their strict and regular observance; and all this for the greater glory of God, the security of the church, and the honour and advantage of the king and kingdom.[b] The barons in return signed a declaration, in which they acknowledged, that they owed these concessions merely to the king's free grace; promised that this commission should never be drawn into precedent; and engaged, that the power of the ordainers should expire at the time appointed.[c]

16th March.

The chosen junto accordingly framed their ordinances, and presented them to the king and parliament, for their confirmation in the ensuing year. Some of these ordinances were laudable, and tended to the regular execution of justice: Such as those, requiring sheriffs to be men of property, abolishing the practice of issuing privy seals for the suspension of justice, restraining the practice of purveyance, prohibiting the adulteration and alteration of the coin, excluding foreigners from the farms of the revenue, ordering all payments to be regularly made into the exchequer, revoking all late grants of the crown, and giving the parties damages in the case of vexatious prosecutions. But what chiefly grieved the king, was the ordinance for the removal of evil counsellors, by which a great number of persons were by name excluded from every office of power and profit; and Piers Gavaston himself was for ever banished the king's dominions, under the penalty, in case of disobedience, of being declared a public enemy. Other persons, more

1311.

[b] Brady's App. N°. 50. Heming, vol. i. p. 247. Walsing. p. 97. Ryley, p. 526.
[c] Brady's App. N°. 51.

CHAPTER XIV

agreeable to the barons, were substituted in all the offices. And it was ordained, that, for the future, all the considerable dignities in the household, as well as in the law, revenue, and military governments, should be appointed by the *baronage* in parliament; and the power of making war, or assembling his military tenants, should no longer be vested solely in the king, nor be exercised without the consent of the nobility.

Edward, from the same weakness both in his temper and situation, which had engaged him to grant this unlimited commission to the barons, was led to give a parliamentary sanction to their ordinances: But as a consequence of the same character, he *secretly* made a protest against them, and declared, that, since the commission was granted only for the making of ordinances to the advantage of king and kingdom, such articles as should be found prejudicial to both, were to be held as not ratified and confirmed.[d] It is no wonder, indeed, that he retained a firm purpose to revoke ordinances, which had been imposed on him by violence, which entirely annihilated the royal authority, and above all, which deprived him of the company and society of a person, whom, by an unusual infatuation, he valued above all the world, and above every consideration of interest or tranquillity.

As soon, therefore, as Edward, removing to York, had freed himself from the immediate terror of the barons' power, he invited back Gavaston from Flanders, which that favourite had made the place of his retreat; and declaring his banishment to be illegal, and contrary to the laws and customs of the kingdom,[e] openly reinstated him in his former credit and authority. The barons, highly provoked at this disappointment, and apprehensive of danger to themselves from the declared animosity of so powerful a minion, saw, that either his or their ruin was now inevitable; and they renewed with redoubled zeal their former confederacies against him. The earl of Lancaster was a dangerous head of this alliance: Guy, earl of Warwic, entered into it with a furious and precipitate passion: Humphrey Bohun, earl of Hereford, the constable, and Aymer de Valence, earl of Pembroke, brought to it a great accession of power and interest: Even earl Warrenne deserted the royal cause, which he had hitherto supported, and was induced to em-

1312.

---

[d] Ryley's Placit. Parl. p. 530, 541.   [e] Brady's App. N°. 53. Walsing. p. 98.

brace the side of the confederates:[f] And as Robert de Winchelsey, archbishop of Canterbury, professed himself of the same party, he determined the body of the clergy, and consequently the people, to declare against the king and his minion. So predominant, at that time, was the power of the great nobility, that the combination of a few of them was always able to shake the throne; and such an universal concurrence became irresistible. The earl of Lancaster suddenly raised an army, and marched to York, where he found the king already removed to Newcastle:[g] He flew thither in pursuit of him; and Edward had just time to escape to Tinmouth, where he embarked, and sailed with Gavaston to Scarborough. He left his favourite in that fortress, which, had it been properly supplied with provisions, was deemed impregnable; and he marched forward to York, in hopes of raising an army, which might be able to support him against his enemies. Pembroke was sent by the confederates to besiege the castle of Scarborough; and Gavaston, sensible of the bad condition of his garrison, was obliged to capitulate, and to surrender himself prisoner.[h] He stipulated, that he should remain in Pembroke's hands for two months; that endeavours should, during that time, be mutually used for a general accommodation; that if the terms proposed by the barons were not accepted, the castle should be restored to him in the same condition as when he surrendered it; and that the earl of Pembroke, and Henry Piercy should, by contract, pledge all their lands for the fulfilling of these conditions.[i] Pembroke, now master of the person of this public enemy, conducted him to the castle of Dedington, near Banbury; where, on pretence of other business, he left him, protected by a feeble guard.[k] Warwic, probably in concert with Pembroke, attacked the castle: The garrison refused to make any resistance: Gavaston was yielded up to him, and conducted to Warwic castle: The earls of Lancaster, Hereford, and Arundel, immediately repaired thither:[l] And without any regard, either to the laws or the military capitulation, they ordered the head of the obnoxious favourite to be struck off, by the hands of the executioner.[m]

19th May.

Murder of Gavaston. 1st July.

[f] Trivet, cont. p. 4.   [g] Walsing. p. 101.   [h] Walsing. p. 101.   [i] Rymer, vol. ii. p. 324.   [k] T. de la More, p. 593.   [l] Dugd. Baron. vol. ii. p. 44.   [m] Walsing. p. 101. T. de la More, p. 593. Trivet, cont. p. 9.

CHAPTER XIV

The king had retired northward to Berwic, when he heard of Gavaston's murder; and his resentment was proportioned to the affection which he had ever borne him, while living. He threatened vengeance on all the nobility, who had been active in that bloody scene, and he made preparations for war in all parts of England. But being less constant in his enmities than in his friendships, he soon after hearkened to terms of accommodation; granted the barons a pardon of all offences; and as they stipulated to ask him publicly pardon on their knees,[n] he was so pleased with these vain appearances of submission, that he seemed to have sincerely forgiven them all past injuries. But as they still pretended, notwithstanding their lawless conduct, a great anxiety for the maintenance of law, and required the establishment of their former ordinances as a necessary security for that purpose; Edward told them, that he was willing to grant them a free and legal confirmation of such of these ordinances as were not entirely derogatory to the prerogative of the crown. This answer was received for the present as satisfactory. The king's person, after the death of Gavaston, was now become less obnoxious to the public; and as the ordinances, insisted on, appeared to be nearly the same with those which had formerly been extorted from Henry III. by Mountfort, and which had been attended with so many fatal consequences, they were, on that account, demanded with less vehemence by the nobility and people. The minds of all men seemed to be much appeased: The animosities of faction no longer prevailed: And England, now united under its head, would henceforth be able, it was hoped, to take vengeance on all its enemies; particularly on the Scots, whose progress was the object of general resentment and indignation.

Immediately after Edward's retreat from Scotland, Robert Bruce left his fastnesses, in which he intended to have sheltered his feeble army; and supplying his defect of strength by superior vigour and abilities, he made deep impression on all his enemies, foreign and domestic. He chased lord Argyle and the chieftain of the Macdowals from their hills, and made himself entirely master of the high country: He thence invaded with success the Cummins

War with Scotland.

[n] Ryley, p. 538. Rymer, vol. iii. p. 366.

in the low countries of the north: He took the castles of Inverness, Forfar, and Brechin: He daily gained some new accession of territory; and what was a more important acquisition, he daily reconciled the minds of the nobility to his dominion, and inlisted under his standard every bold leader, whom he enriched by the spoils of his enemies. Sir James Douglas, in whom commenced the greatness and renown of that warlike family, seconded him in all his enterprizes: Edward Bruce, Robert's own brother, distinguished himself by acts of valour: And the terror of the English power being now abated by the feeble conduct of the king, even the least sanguine of the Scots began to entertain hopes of recovering their independence; and the whole kingdom, except a few fortresses, which he had not the means to attack, had acknowledged the authority of Robert.

In this situation, Edward had found it necessary to grant a truce to Scotland; and Robert successfully employed the interval in consolidating his power, and introducing order into the civil government, disjointed by a long continuance of wars and factions. The interval was very short: The truce, ill observed on both sides, was at last openly violated; and war recommenced with greater fury than ever. Robert, not content with defending himself, had made successful inroads into England, subsisted his needy followers by the plunder of that country, and taught them to despise the military genius of a people, who had long been the object of their terror. Edward, at last, rouzed from his lethargy, had marched an army into Scotland; and Robert, determined not to risque too much against an enemy so much superior, retired again into the mountains. The king advanced beyond Edinburgh; but being destitute of provisions, and being ill supported by the English nobility, who were then employed in framing their ordinances, he was soon obliged to retreat, without gaining any advantage over the enemy. But the appearing union of all the parties in England, after the death of Gavaston, seemed to restore that kingdom to its native force, opened again the prospect of reducing Scotland, and promised a happy conclusion to a war, in which both the interests and passions of the nation were so deeply engaged.

1314. Edward assembled forces from all quarters, with a view of finishing at one blow this important enterprize. He summoned the most warlike of his vassals from Gascony: He inlisted troops from

Flanders and other foreign countries: He invited over great numbers of the disorderly Irish as to a certain prey: He joined to them a body of the Welsh, who were actuated by like motives: And assembling the whole military force of England, he marched to the frontiers with an army, which, according to the Scotch writers, amounted to a hundred thousand men.

The army, collected by Robert, exceeded not thirty thousand combatants; but being composed of men, who had distinguished themselves by many acts of valour, who were rendered desperate by their situation, and who were enured to all the varieties of fortune, they might justly, under such a leader, be deemed formidable to the most numerous and best appointed armies. The castle of Stirling, which, with Berwic, was the only fortress in Scotland, that remained in the hands of the English, had long been besieged by Edward Bruce: Philip de Mowbray, the governor, after an obstinate defence, was at last obliged to capitulate, and to promise, that, if, before a certain day, which was now approaching, he were not relieved, he should open his gates to the enemy.[o] Robert therefore, sensible that here was the ground on which he must expect the English, chose the field of battle with all the skill and prudence imaginable, and made the necessary preparations for their reception. He posted himself at Bannockburn, about two miles from Stirling; where he had a hill on his right flank, and a morass on his left: And not content with having taken these precautions to prevent his being surrounded by the more numerous army of the English; he foresaw the superior strength of the enemy in cavalry, and made provision against it. Having a rivulet in front, he commanded deep pits to be dug along its banks, and sharp stakes to be planted in them; and he ordered the whole to be carefully covered over with turf.[p] The English arrived in sight on the evening, and a bloody conflict immediately ensued between two bodies of cavalry; where Robert, who was at the head of the Scots, engaged in single combat with Henry de Bohun, a gentleman of the family of Hereford; and at one stroke cleft his adversary to the chin with a battle-ax, in sight of the two armies. The English horse fled with precipitation to their main body.

The Scots, encouraged by this favourable event, and glorying

[o] Rymer, vol. iii. p. 481.   [p] T. de la More, p. 594.

in the valour of their prince, prognosticated a happy issue to the combat on the ensuing day: The English, confident in their numbers, and elated with former successes, longed for an opportunity of revenge: And the night, though extremely short in that season and in that climate, appeared tedious to the impatience of the several combatants. Early in the morning, Edward drew out his army, and advanced towards the Scots. The earl of Glocester, his nephew, who commanded the left wing of the cavalry, impelled by the ardour of youth, rushed on to the attack without precaution, and fell among the covered pits, which had been prepared by Bruce for the reception of the enemy.[q] This body of horse was disordered: Glocester himself was overthrown and slain: Sir James Douglas, who commanded the Scottish cavalry, gave the enemy no leisure to rally, but pushed them off the field with considerable loss, and pursued them in sight of their whole line of infantry. While the English army was alarmed with this unfortunate beginning of the action, which commonly proves decisive, they observed an army on the heights towards the left, which seemed to be marching leisurely in order to surround them; and they were distracted by their multiplied fears. This was a number of waggoners and sumpter boys, whom Robert had collected; and having supplied them with military standards, gave them the appearance at a distance of a formidable body. The stratagem took effect: A panic seized the English: They threw down their arms and fled: They were pursued with great slaughter, for the space of ninety miles, till they reached Berwic: And the Scots, besides an inestimable booty, took many persons of quality prisoners, and above 400 gentlemen, whom Robert treated with great humanity,[r] and whose ransom was a new accession of wealth to the victorious army. The king himself narrowly escaped by taking shelter in Dunbar, whose gates were opened to him by the earl of March; and he thence passed by sea to Berwic.

Such was the great and decisive battle of Bannockburn, which secured the independance of Scotland, fixed Bruce on the throne of that kingdom, and may be deemed the greatest overthrow that the English nation, since the conquest, has ever received. The number of slain on those occasions is always uncertain, and is

Battle of Bannockburn. 25th June.

[q] Ibid.   [r] Ypod. Neust. p. 501.

commonly much magnified by the victors: But this defeat made a deep impression on the minds of the English; and it was remarked, that, for some years, no superiority of numbers could encourage them to keep the field against the Scots. Robert, in order to avail himself of his present success, entered England, and ravaged all the northern counties without opposition: He besieged Carlisle; but that place was saved by the valour of Sir Andrew Harcla, the governor: He was more successful against Berwic, which he took by assault: And this prince, elated by his continued prosperity, now entertained hopes of making the most important conquests *1315.* on the English. He sent over his brother Edward, with an army of 6000 men, into Ireland; and that nobleman assumed the title of King of that island: He himself followed soon after with more numerous forces: The horrible and absurd oppressions, which the Irish suffered under the English government, made them, at first, fly to the standard of the Scots, whom they regarded as their deliverers: But a grievous famine, which at that time desolated both Ireland and Britain, reduced the Scottish army to the greatest extremities; and Robert was obliged to return, with his forces much diminished, into his own country. His brother, after having experienced a variety of fortune, was defeated and slain near Dundalk by the English, commanded by lord Bermingham: And these projects, too extensive for the force of the Scottish nation, thus vanished into smoke.

Edward, besides suffering those disasters from the invasion of the Scots and the insurrection of the Irish, was also infested with a rebellion in Wales; and above all, by the factions of his own nobility, who took advantage of the public calamities, insulted his fallen fortunes, and endeavoured to establish their own independance on the ruins of the throne. Lancaster and the barons of his party, who had declined attending him on his Scottish expedition, no sooner saw him return with disgrace, than they insisted on the renewal of their ordinances, which, they still pretended, had validity; and the king's unhappy situation obliged him to submit to their demands. The ministry was now modeled by the direction of Lancaster:[s] That prince was placed at the head of the council: It was declared, that all the offices should be filled, from time to time, by

[s] Ryley, p. 560. Rymer, vol. iii. p. 722.

the votes of parliament, or rather, by the will of the great barons:[t] And the nation, under this new model of government, endeavoured to put itself in a better posture of defence against the Scots. But the factious nobles were far from being terrified with the progress of these public enemies: On the contrary, they founded the hopes of their own future grandeur on the weakness and distresses of the crown: Lancaster himself was suspected, with great appearance of reason, of holding a secret correspondence with the king of Scots: And though he was entrusted with the command of the English armies, he took care that every enterprize should be disappointed, and every plan of operations prove unsuccessful.

All the European kingdoms, especially that of England, were at this time unacquainted with the office of a prime minister, so well understood at present in all regular monarchies; and the people could form no conception of a man, who, though still in the rank of a subject, possessed all the power of a sovereign, eased the prince of the burthen of affairs, supplied his want of experience or capacity, and maintained all the rights of the crown, without degrading the greatest nobles by their submission to his temporary authority. Edward was plainly by nature unfit to hold himself the reins of government: He had no vices; but was unhappy in a total incapacity for serious business: He was sensible of his own defects, and necessarily sought to be governed: Yet every favourite, whom he successively chose, was regarded as a fellow-subject, exalted above his rank and station: He was the object of envy to the great nobility: His character and conduct were decryed with the people: His authority over the king and kingdom was considered as an usurpation: And unless the prince had embraced the dangerous expedient, of devolving his power on the earl of Lancaster or some mighty baron, whose family interest was so extensive as to be able alone to maintain his influence, he could expect no peace or tranquillity upon the throne.

Hugh le Despenser. The king's chief favourite, after the death of Gavaston, was Hugh le Despenser or Spenser, a young man of English birth, of high rank, and of a noble family.[u] He possessed all the exterior

---

[t] Brady, vol. ii. p. 122. from the records, app. No. 61. Ryley, p. 560.
[u] Dugd. Baron. vol. i. p. 389.

CHAPTER XIV

accomplishments of person and address, which were fitted to engage the weak mind of Edward; but was destitute of that moderation and prudence, which might have qualified him to mitigate
the envy of the great, and conduct him through all the perils of
that dangerous station, to which he was advanced. His father, who
was of the same name, and who, by means of his son, had also
attained great influence over the king, was a nobleman venerable
from his years, respected through all his past life for wisdom,
valour, and integrity, and well fitted, by his talents and experience,
could affairs have admitted of any temperament, to have supplied
the defects both of the king and of his minion.[w] But no sooner was
Edward's attachment declared for young Spenser, than the turbulent Lancaster, and most of the great barons, regarded him as
their rival, made him the object of their animosity, and formed
violent plans for his ruin.[x] They first declared their discontent by
withdrawing from parliament; and it was not long ere they found
a pretence for preceeding to greater extremities against him.

The king, who set no limits to his bounty towards his minions, had married the younger Spenser to his niece, one of the
co-heirs of the earl of Glocester, slain at Bannockburn. The favourite, by his succession to that opulent family, had inherited
great possessions in the marches of Wales,[y] and being desirous of
extending still farther his influence in those quarters, he is accused
of having committed injustice on the barons of Audley and Ammori, who had also married two sisters of the same family. There
was likewise a baron in the neighbourhood, called William de
Braouse, lord of Gower, who had made a settlement of his estate
on John de Mowbray, his son-in-law; and in case of failure of that
nobleman and his issue, had substituted the earl of Hereford, in
the succession to the barony of Gower. Mowbray, on the decease
of his father-in-law, entered immediately in possession of the estate, without the formality of taking livery and seizin from the
crown: But Spenser, who coveted that barony, persuaded the king
to put in execution the rigour of the feudal law, to seize Gower as
escheated to the crown, and to confer it upon him.[z] This transaction, which was the proper subject of a lawsuit, immediately

1321.
Civil
commo-
tions.

---

[w] T. de la More, p. 594.   [x] Walsingham, p. 113. T. de la More, p. 595.
Murimuth, p. 55.   [y] Trivet, cont. p. 25.   [z] Monach. Malmes.

excited a civil war in the kingdom. The earls of Lancaster and Hereford flew to arms: Audley and Ammori joined them with all their forces: The two Rogers de Mortimer and Roger de Clifford, with many others, disgusted for private reasons at the Spensers, brought a considerable accession to the party: And their army being now formidable, they sent a message to the king, requiring him immediately to dismiss or confine the younger Spenser; and menacing him in case of refusal, with renouncing their allegiance to him, and taking revenge on that minister by their own authority. They scarcely waited for an answer; but immediately fell upon the lands of young Spenser, which they pillaged and destroyed; murdered his servants, drove off his cattle, and burned his houses.[a] They thence proceeded to commit like devastations on the estates of Spenser, the father, whose character they had hitherto seemed to respect. And having drawn and signed a formal association among themselves,[b] they marched to London with all their forces, stationed themselves in the neighbourhood of that city, and demanded of the king the banishment of both the Spensers. These noblemen were then absent; the father abroad, the son at sea; and both of them employed in different commissions: The king therefore replied, that his coronation oath, by which he was bound to observe the laws, restrained him from giving his assent to so illegal a demand, or condemning noblemen who were accused of no crime, nor had any opportunity afforded them of making answer.[c] Equity and reason were but a feeble opposition to men, who had arms in their hands, and who, being already involved in guilt, saw no safety but in success and victory. They entered London with their troops; and giving in to the parliament, which was then sitting, a charge against the Spensers, of which they attempted not to prove one article, they procured, by menaces and violence, a sentence of attainder and perpetual exile against these ministers.[d] This sentence was voted by the lay barons alone: For the commons, though now an estate in parliament, were yet of so little consideration, that their assent was not demanded; and even the votes of the prelates were neglected amidst the present disorders. The only symptom, which these turbulent barons gave of their regard to

[a] Murimuth, p. 55.   [b] Tyrrel, vol. ii. p. 280. from the register of C. C. Canterbury.   [c] Walsing. p. 114.   [d] Tottle's collect. part 2. p. 50. Walsing. p. 114.

CHAPTER XIV

law, was their requiring from the king an indemnity for their illegal proceedings;[e] after which they disbanded their army, and separated, in security, as they imagined, to their several castles.

This act of violence, in which the king was obliged to acquiesce, rendered his person and his authority so contemptible, that every one thought himself entitled to treat him with neglect. The queen, having occasion soon after to pass by the castle of Leeds in Kent, which belonged to the lord Badlesmere, desired a night's lodging; but was refused admittance, and some of her attendants, who presented themselves at the gate, were killed.[f] The insult upon this princess, who had always endeavoured to live on good terms with the barons, and who joined them heartily in their hatred of the young Spenser, was an action which no body pretended to justify; and the king thought, that he might, without giving general umbrage, assemble an army, and take vengeance on the offender. No one came to the assistance of Badlesmere; and Edward prevailed:[g] But having now some forces on foot, and having concerted measures with his friends throughout England, he ventured to take off the mask, to attack all his enemies, and to recall the two Spensers, whose sentence he declared illegal, unjust, contrary to the tenor of the Great Charter, passed without the assent of the prelates, and extorted by violence from him and the estate of barons.[h] Still the commons were not mentioned by either party.

The king had now got the start of the barons; an advantage, which, in those times, was commonly decisive: And he hastened with his army to the marches of Wales, the chief seat of the power of his enemies, whom he found totally unprepared for resistance. Many of the barons in those parts endeavoured to appease him by submission:[i] Their castles were seized, and their persons committed to custody. But Lancaster, in order to prevent the total ruin of his party, summoned together his vassals and retainers; declared his alliance with Scotland, which had long been suspected; received the promise of a reinforcement from that country, under the command of Randolf, earl of Murray, and Sir James Douglas;[k] and being joined by the earl of Hereford, ad-

1322.

---

[e] Tottle's collect. part 2. p. 54. Rymer, vol. iii p. 891.   [f] Rymer, vol. iii. p. 89. Walsing. p. 114, 115. T. de la More, p. 595. Murimuth, p. 56.
[g] Walsing. p. 115.   [h] Rymer, vol. iii. p. 907. T. de la More, p. 595.
[i] Walsing. p. 115.   Murimuth, p. 57.   [k] Rymer, vol. iii. p. 958.

vanced with all his forces against the king, who had collected an army of 30,000 men, and was superior to his enemies. Lancaster posted himself at Burton upon Trent, and endeavoured to defend the passages of the river:[l] But being disappointed in that plan of operations; this prince, who had no military genius, and whose personal courage was even suspected, fled with his army to the north, in expectation of being there joined by his Scottish allies.[m] He was pursued by the king; and his army diminished daily; till he came to Boroughbridge, where he found Sir Andrew Harcla posted with some forces on the opposite side of the river, and ready to dispute the passage with him. He was repulsed in an

16th March.

attempt which he made to force his way; the earl of Hereford was killed; the whole army of the rebels was disconcerted; Lancaster himself was become incapable of taking any measures either for flight or defence; and he was seized without resistance by Harcla, and conducted to the king.[n] In those violent times, the laws were so much neglected on both sides, that, even where they might, without any sensible inconvenience, have been observed, the conquerors deemed it unnecessary to pay any regard to them. Lancaster, who was guilty of open rebellion, and was taken in arms against his sovereign, instead of being tried by the laws of his country, which pronounced the sentence of death against him, was

23d March, Execution of the earl of Lancaster.

condemned by a court-martial,[o] and led to execution. Edward, however little vindictive in his natural temper, here indulged his revenge, and employed against the prisoner the same indignities, which had been exercised by his orders against Gavaston. He was clothed in a mean attire, placed on a lean jade without a bridle, a hood was put on his head, and in this posture, attended by the acclamations of the people, this prince was conducted to an eminence near Pomfret, one of his own castles, and there beheaded.[p]

Thus perished Thomas earl of Lancaster, prince of the blood, and one of the most potent barons that had ever been in England. His public conduct sufficiently discovers the violence and turbulence of his character: His private deportment appears not to have been more innocent: And his hypocritical devotion, by which

[l] Walsing. p. 115.   [m] Ypod. Neust. p. 504.   [n] T. de la More, p. 596. Walsing. p. 116.   [o] Tyrrel, vol. ii. p. 291. from the records.   [p] Leland's Coll. vol. i. p. 668.

CHAPTER XIV

he gained the favour of the monks and populace, will rather be regarded as an aggravation than an alleviation of his guilt. Badlesmere, Giffard, Barret, Cheyney, Fleming, and about eighteen of the most notorious offenders, were afterwards condemned by a legal trial and were executed. Many were thrown into prison: Others made their escape beyond sea: Some of the king's servants were rewarded from the forfeitures: Harcla received for his services the earldom of Carlisle, and a large estate, which he soon after forfeited with his life, for a treasonable correspondence with the king of Scotland. But the greater part of those vast escheats was seized by young Spenser, whose rapacity was insatiable. Many of the barons of the king's party were disgusted with this partial division of the spoils: The envy against Spenser rose higher than ever: The usual insolence of his temper, enflamed by success, impelled him to commit many acts of violence: The people, who always hated him, made him still more the object of aversion: All the relations of the attainted barons and gentlemen secretly vowed revenge: And though tranquillity was in appearance restored to the kingdom, the general contempt of the king and odium against Spenser, bred dangerous humours, the source of future revolutions and convulsions.

In this situation no success could be expected from foreign wars; and Edward, after making one more fruitless attempt against Scotland, whence he retreated with dishonour, found it necessary to terminate hostilities with that kingdom, by a truce of thirteen years.[q] Robert, though his title to the crown was not acknowledged in the treaty, was satisfied with ensuring his possession of it during so long a time. He had repelled with gallantry all the attacks of England: He had carried war both into that kingdom and into Ireland: He had rejected with disdain the pope's authority, who pretended to impose his commands upon him, and oblige him to make peace with his enemies: His throne was firmly established, as well in the affections of his subjects, as by force of arms: Yet there naturally remained some inquietude in his mind, while at war with a state, which, however at present disordered by faction, was of itself so much an over-match for him both in riches and in num-

[q] Rymer, vol. iii. p. 1022. Murimuth, p. 60.

bers of people. And this truce was, at the same time, the more seasonable for England; because the nation was at that juncture threatened with hostilities from France.

1324.   Philip the fair, king of France, who died in 1315, had left the crown to his son Lewis Hutin, who, after a short reign, dying without male issue, was succeeded by Philip the Long, his brother, whose death soon after made way for Charles the Fair, the youngest brother of that family. This monarch had some grounds of complaint against the king's ministers in Guienne; and as there was no common or equitable judge in that strange species of sovereignty, established by the feudal law, he seemed desirous to take advantage of Edward's weakness, and under that pretence, to confiscate all his foreign dominions.[r] After an embassy by the earl of Kent, the king's brother, had been tried in vain, queen Isabella obtained permission to go over to Paris, and endeavour to adjust, in an amicable manner, the difference with her brother: But while she was making some progress in this negociation, Charles started a new pretension, the justice of which could not be disputed, that Edward himself should appear in his court, and do homage for the fees which he held in France. But there occurred many difficulties in complying with this demand. Young Spenser, by whom the king was implicitly governed, had unavoidably been engaged in many quarrels with the queen, who aspired to the same influence; and though that artful princess, on her leaving England, had dissembled her animosity, Spenser, well acquainted with her secret sentiments, was unwilling to attend his master to Paris, and appear in a court, where her credit might expose him to insults, if not to danger. He hesitated no less on allowing the king to make the journey alone; both fearing, lest that easy prince should in his absence fall under other influence, and foreseeing the perils, to which he himself should be exposed, if, without the protection of royal authority, he remained in England, where he was so generally hated. While these doubts occasioned delays and difficulties, Isabella proposed, that Edward should resign the dominion of Guienne to his son, now thirteen years of age; and that the prince should come to Paris, and do the homage which every vassal owed to his superior lord. This expedient, which seemed so happily to

1325.

---

[r] Rymer, vol. iv. p. 74, 98.

remove all difficulties, was immediately embraced: Spenser was charmed with the contrivance: Young Edward was sent to Paris: And the ruin, covered under this fatal snare, was never perceived or suspected, by any of the English council.

The queen on her arrival in France, had there found a great number of English fugitives, the remains of the Lancastrian faction; and their common hatred of Spenser soon begat a secret friendship and correspondence between them and that princess. Among the rest was young Roger Mortimer, a potent baron in the Welsh marches, who had been obliged, with others, to make his submissions to the king, had been condemned for high treason; but having received a pardon for his life, was afterwards detained in the Tower, with an intention of rendering his confinement perpetual. He was so fortunate as to make his escape into France;[s] and being one of the most considerable persons now remaining of the party, as well as distinguished by his violent animosity against Spenser, he was easily admitted to pay his court to queen Isabella. The graces of his person and address advanced him quickly in her affections: He became her confident and counsellor in all her measures: And gaining ground daily upon her heart, he engaged her to sacrifice at last, to her passion, all the sentiments of honour and of fidelity to her husband.[t] Hating now the man, whom she had injured, and whom she never valued, she entered ardently into all Mortimer's conspiracies; and having artfully gotten into her hands the young prince, and heir of the monarchy, she resolved on the utter ruin of the king, as well as of his favourite. She engaged her brother to take part in the same criminal purpose: Her court was daily filled with the exiled barons: Mortimer lived in the most declared intimacy with her: A correspondence was secretly carried on with the malcontent party in England: And when Edward, informed of those alarming circumstances, required her speedily to return with the prince, she publicly replied, that she would never set foot in the kingdom, till Spenser was for ever removed from his presence and councils: A declaration, which procured her great popularity in England, and threw a decent veil over all her treasonable enterprizes.

Con-spiracy against the king.

[s] Rymer, vol. iv. p. 7, 8, 20. T. de la More, p. 596. Walsing. p. 120. Ypod. Neust. p. 506. [t] T. de la More, p. 598. Murimuth, p. 65.

Edward endeavoured to put himself in a posture of defence;[u] but, besides the difficulties arising from his own indolence and slender abilities, and the want of authority, which of consequence attended all his resolutions, it was not easy for him, in the present state of the kingdom and revenue, to maintain a constant force ready to repel an invasion, which he knew not at what time or place *Insurrec-* he had reason to expect. All his efforts were unequal to the trai- *tions.* terous and hostile conspiracies, which, both at home and abroad, were forming against his authority, and which were daily penetrating farther even into his own family. His brother, the earl of Kent, a virtuous but weak prince, who was then at Paris, was engaged by his sister-in-law, and by the king of France, who was also his cousin-german, to give countenance to the invasion, whose sole object, he believed, was the expulsion of the Spensers: He prevailed on his elder brother, the earl of Norfolk, to enter secretly into the same design: The earl of Leicester, brother and heir of the earl of Lancaster, had too many reasons for his hatred of these ministers, to refuse his concurrence. Walter de Reynel, archbishop of Canterbury, and many of the prelates, expressed their approbation of the queen's measures: Several of the most potent barons, envying the authority of the favourite, were ready to fly to arms: The minds of the people, by means of some truths and many calumnies, were strongly disposed to the same party: And there needed but the appearance of the queen and prince, with such a body of foreign troops, as might protect her against immediate violence, to turn all this tempest, so artfully prepared, against the unhappy Edward.

1326. Charles, though he gave countenance and assistance to the faction, was ashamed openly to support the queen and prince, against the authority of a husband and father; and Isabella was obliged to court the alliance of some other foreign potentate, from whose dominions she might set out on her intended enterprize. For this purpose, she affianced young Edward, whose tender age made him incapable to judge of the consequences, with Philippa, daughter of the count of Holland and Hainault;[w] and having, by the open assistance of this prince, and the secret protection of her brother, inlisted in her service near 3000 men, she set sail from the

[u] Rymer, vol. iv. p. 184, 188, 225. [w] T. de la More, p. 598.

harbour of Dort, and landed safely, and without opposition, on the coast of Suffolk. The earl of Kent was in her company: Two other princes of the blood, the earl of Norfolk, and the earl of Leicester, joined her soon after her landing with all their followers: Three prelates, the bishops of Ely, Lincoln, and Hereford, brought her both the force of their vassals and the authority of their character:[x] Even Robert de Watteville, who had been sent by the king to oppose her progress in Suffolk, deserted to her with all his forces. To render her cause more favourable, she renewed her declaration, that the sole purpose of her enterprize was to free the king and kingdom from the tyranny of the Spensers, and of chancellor Baldoc, their creature.[y] The populace were allured by her specious pretences: The barons thought themselves secure against forfeitures by the appearance of the prince in her army: And a weak irresolute king, supported by ministers generally odious, was unable to stem this torrent, which bore with such irresistible violence against him.

24th
Sept.

Edward, after trying in vain to rouze the citizens of London to some sense of duty,[z] departed for the west, where he hoped to meet with better reception; and he had no sooner discovered his weakness by leaving the city, than the rage of the populace broke out without controul against him and his ministers. They first plundered, then murdered all those who were obnoxious to them: They seized the bishop of Exeter, a virtuous and loyal prelate, as he was passing through the streets; and having beheaded him, they threw his body into the river.[a] They made themselves masters of the Tower by surprize; then entered into a formal association to put to death, without mercy, every one who should dare to oppose the enterprize of queen Isabella, and of the prince.[b] A like spirit was soon communicated to all other parts of England; and threw the few servants of the king, who still entertained thoughts of performing their duty, into terror and astonishment.

Edward was hotly pursued to Bristol by the earl of Kent, seconded by the foreign forces under John de Hainault. He found himself disappointed in his expectations with regard to the loyalty of those parts; and he passed over to Wales, where, he flattered

---

[x] Walsing. p. 123. Ypod. Neust. p. 507. T. de la More, p. 598. Murimuth, p. 66. [y] Ypod. Neust. p. 508. [z] Walsing. p. 123. [a] Walsing. p. 124. T. de la More, p. 599. Murimuth, p. 66. [b] Walsing, p. 124.

himself, his name was more popular, and which he hoped to find uninfected with the contagion of general rage, which had seized the English.[c] The elder Spenser, created earl of Winchester, was left governor of the castle of Bristol; but the garrison mutinied against him, and he was delivered into the hands of his enemies. This venerable noble, who had nearly reached his ninetieth year, was instantly, without trial, or witness, or accusation, or answer, condemned to death by the rebellious barons: He was hanged on a gibbet; his body was cut in pieces, and thrown to the dogs;[d] and his head was sent to Winchester, the place whose title he bore, and was there set on a pole, and exposed to the insults of the populace.

The king, disappointed anew in his expectations of succour from the Welsh, took shipping for Ireland; but being driven back by contrary winds, he endeavoured to conceal himself in the mountains of Wales: He was soon discovered, was put under the custody of the earl of Leicester, and was confined in the castle of Kenilworth. The younger Spenser, his favourite, who also fell into the hands of his enemies, was executed, like his father, without any appearance of a legal trial:[e] The earl of Arundel, almost the only man of his rank in England, who had maintained his loyalty, was, without any trial, put to death at the instigation of Mortimer: Baldoc, the chancellor, being a priest, could not with safety be so suddenly dispatched; but being sent to the bishop of Hereford's palace in London, he was there, as his enemies probably foresaw, seized by the populace, was thrown into Newgate, and soon after expired, from the cruel usage which he had received.[f] Even the usual reverence, paid to the sacerdotal character, gave way, with every other consideration, to the present rage of the people.

The king dethroned.

The queen, to avail herself of the prevailing delusion, summoned, in the king's name, a parliament at Westminster; where, together with the power of her army, and the authority of her partizans among the barons, who were concerned to secure their past treasons by committing new acts of violence against their sovereign, she expected to be seconded by the fury of the populace, the most dangerous of all instruments, and the least answerable for their excesses. A charge was drawn up against the king, in which, even though it was framed by his inveterate ene-

*1327.
13th
Jan.*

[c] Murimuth, p. 67.   [d] Leland's Coll. vol. i. p. 673. T. de la More, p. 599. Walsing. p. 125. M. Froissart, liv. i. chap. 13.   [e] Walsing. p. 125. Ypod. Neust. p. 508.   [f] Walsing, p. 126. Murimuth, p. 68.

mies, nothing but his narrow genius, or his misfortunes were objected to him: For the greatest malice found no particular crime with which it could reproach this unhappy prince. He was accused of incapacity for government, of wasting his time in idle amusements, of neglecting public business, of being swayed by evil counsellors, of having lost, by his misconduct, the kingdom of Scotland, and part of Guienne; and to swell the charge, even the death of some barons, and the imprisonment of some prelates, convicted of treason, were laid to his account.[g] It was in vain, amidst the violence of arms and tumult of the people, to appeal either to law or to reason: The deposition of the king, without any appearing opposition, was voted by parliament: The prince, already declared regent by his party,[h] was placed on the throne: And a deputation was sent to Edward at Kenilworth, to require his resignation, which menaces and terror soon extorted from him.

But it was impossible, that the people, however corrupted by the barbarity of the times, still farther enflamed by faction, could for ever remain insensible to the voice of nature. Here, a wife had first deserted, next invaded, and then dethroned her husband; had made her minor son an instrument in this unnatural treatment of his father; had by lying pretences seduced the nation into a rebellion against their sovereign; had pushed them into violence and cruelties, that had dishonoured them: All those circumstances were so odious in themselves, and formed such a complicated scene of guilt, that the least reflection sufficed to open men's eyes, and make them detest this flagrant infringement of every public and private duty. The suspicions which soon arose of Isabella's criminal commerce with Mortimer, the proofs which daily broke out of this part of her guilt, encreased the general abhorrence against her; and her hyprocrisy, in publicly bewailing with tears the king's unhappy fate,[i] was not able to deceive even the most stupid and most prejudiced of her adherents. In proportion as the queen became the object of public hatred, the dethroned monarch, who had been the victim of her crimes and her ambition, was regarded with pity, with friendship, with veneration: And men became sensible, that all his misconduct, which faction had so much exaggerated, had been owing to the unavoidable weakness, not

---

[g] Knyghton, p. 2765, 2766. Brady's App. N°. 72. [h] Rymer, vol. iv. p. 137. Walsing. p. 125. [i] Walsing. p. 126.

to any voluntary depravity of his character. The earl of Leicester, now earl of Lancaster, to whose custody he had been committed, was soon touched with those generous sentiments; and besides using his prisoner with gentleness and humanity, he was suspected to have entertained still more honourable intentions in his favour. The king, therefore, was taken from his hands, and delivered over to lord Berkeley, and Mautravers, and Gournay, who were entrusted alternately, each for a month, with the charge of guarding him. While he was in the custody of Berkeley, he was still treated with the gentleness due to his rank and his misfortunes; but when the turn of Mautravers and Gournay came, every species of indignity was practised against him, as if their intention had been to break entirely the prince's spirit, and to employ his sorrows and afflictions, instead of more violent and more dangerous expedients, for the instruments of his murder.[k] It is reported, that one day, when Edward was to be shaved, they ordered cold and dirty water to be brought from the ditch for that purpose; and when he desired it to be changed, and was still denied his request, he burst into tears, which bedewed his cheeks; and he exclaimed, that, in spite of their insolence, he should be shaved with clean and warm water.[l] But as this method of laying Edward in his grave appeared still too slow to the impatient Mortimer, he secretly sent orders to the two keepers, who were at his devotion, instantly to dispatch him; and these ruffians contrived to make the manner of his death as cruel and barbarous as possible. Taking advantage of Berkeley's sickness, in whose custody he then was, and who was thereby incapacitated from attending his charge;[m] they came to Berkeley-castle, and put themselves in possession of the king's person. They threw him on a bed; held him down violently with a table, which they flung over him; thrust into his fundament a red-hot iron, which they inserted through a horn; and though the outward marks of violence upon his person were prevented by this expedient, the horrid deed was discovered to all the guards and attendants by the screams, with which the agonizing king filled the castle, while his bowels were consuming.

Gournay and Mautravers were held in general detestation; and

21st Sept. The king murdered.

---

[k] Anonymi Hist. p. 838. [l] T. de la More, p. 602. [m] Cotton's Abridg. p. 8.

when the ensuing revolution in England threw their protectors from power, they found it necessary to provide for their safety by flying the kingdom. Gournay was afterwards seized at Marseilles, delivered over to the seneschal of Guienne, put on board a ship with a view of carrying him to England; but he was beheaded at sea, by secret orders, as was supposed, from some nobles and prelates in England, anxious to prevent any discovery, which he might make of his accomplices. Mautravers concealed himself for several years in Germany; but having found means of rendering some service to Edward III. he ventured to approach his person, threw himself on his knees before him, submitted to mercy, and received a pardon.[n]

It is not easy to imagine a man more innocent and inoffensive than the unhappy king, whose tragical death we have related; nor a prince less fitted for governing that fierce and turbulent people, subjected to his authority. He was obliged to devolve on others the weight of government, which he had neither ability nor inclination to bear: The same indolence and want of penetration led him to make choice of ministers and favourites, who were not always the best qualified for the trust committed to them: The seditious grandees, pleased with his weakness, yet complaining of it; under pretence of attacking his ministers, insulted his person and invaded his authority: And the impatient populace, mistaking the source of their grievances, threw all the blame upon the king, and encreased the public disorders by their faction and violence. It was in vain to look for protection from the laws, whose voice, always feeble in those times, was not heard amidst the din of arms: What could not defend the king was less able to give shelter to any of the people: The whole machine of government was torne in pieces with fury and violence: And men, instead of regretting the manners of their age, and the form of their constitution, which required the most steady and most skilful hand to conduct them, imputed all errors to the person who had the misfortune to be entrusted with the reins of empire.

His character.

But though such mistakes are natural and almost unavoidable while the events are recent, it is a shameful delusion in modern historians, to imagine, that all the ancient princes, who were un-

[n] Cotton's Abridg. p. 66, 81. Rymer, vol. v. p. 600.

fortunate in their government, were also tyrannical in their conduct, and that the seditions of the people always proceeded from some invasion of their privileges by the monarch. Even a great and a good king was not in that age secure against faction and rebellion, as appears in the case of Henry II.; but a great king had the best chance, as we learn from the history of the same period, for quelling and subduing them. Compare the reigns and characters of Edward I. and II. The father made several violent attempts against the liberties of the people: His barons opposed him: He was obliged, at least found it prudent, to submit: But as they dreaded his valour and abilities, they were content with reasonable satisfaction, and pushed no farther their advantages against him. The facility and weakness of the son, not his violence, threw every thing into confusion: The laws and government were overturned: An attempt to reinstate them was an unpardonable crime: And no atonement, but the deposition and tragical death of the king himself, could give those barons contentment. It is easy to see, that a constitution, which depended so much on the personal character of the prince, must necessarily, in many of its parts, be a government of will, not of laws. But always to throw, without distinction, the blame of all disorders upon the sovereign, would introduce a fatal error in politics, and serve as a perpetual apology for treason and rebellion: As if the turbulence of the great, and madness of the people, were not, equally with the tyranny of princes, evils incident to human society, and no less carefully to be guarded against in every well regulated constitution.

Miscellaneous transactions during this reign. While these abominable scenes passed in England, the theatre of France was stained with a wickedness equally barbarous, and still more public and deliberate. The order of knights templars had arisen during the first fervour of the Crusades; and uniting the two qualities the most popular in that age, devotion and valour, and exercising both in the most popular of all enterprizes, the defence of the Holy Land, they had made rapid advances in credit and authority, and had acquired, from the piety of the faithful, ample possessions in every country of Europe, especially in France. Their great riches, joined to the course of time, had, by degrees, relaxed the severity of these virtues; and the templars had in a great measure lost that popularity, which first raised them to honour and distinction. Acquainted from experience with the fatigues and

CHAPTER XIV

dangers of those fruitless expeditions to the East, they rather chose
to enjoy in ease their opulent revenues in Europe: And being all
men of birth, educated, according to the custom of that age, without any tincture of letters, they scorned the ignoble occupations of
a monastic life, and passed their time wholly in the fashionable
amusements of hunting, gallantry, and the pleasures of the table.
Their rival order, that of St. John of Jerusalem, whose poverty had
as yet preserved them from like corruptions, still distinguished
themselves by their enterprizes against the Infidels, and succeeded
to all the popularity, which was lost by the indolence and luxury of
the templars. But though these reasons had weakened the foundations of this order, once so celebrated and revered, the immediate
cause of their destruction proceeded from the cruel and vindictive
spirit of Philip the Fair, who, having entertained a private disgust
against some eminent templars, determined to gratify at once his
avidity and revenge, by involving the whole order in an undistinguished ruin. On no better information, than that of two
knights, condemned by their superiors to perpetual imprisonment
for their vices and profligacy; he ordered on one day all the templars in France to be committed to prison, and imputed to them
such enormous and absurd crimes, as are sufficient of themselves
to destroy all the credit of the accusation. Besides their being
universally charged with murder, robbery, and vices the most
shocking to nature, every one, it was pretended, whom they received into their order, was obliged to renounce his Saviour, to spit
upon the cross,[o] and to join to this impiety the superstition of
worshipping a gilded head, which was secretly kept in one of their
houses at Marseilles. They also initiated, it was said, every candidate by such infamous rites, as could serve to no other purpose,
than to degrade the order in his eyes, and destroy for ever the
authority of all his superiors over him.[p] Above a hundred of these
unhappy gentlemen were put to the question, in order to extort
from them a confession of their guilt: The more obstinate perished
in the hands of their tormentors. Several, to procure immediate
ease in the violence of their agonies, acknowledged whatever was
required of them: Forged confessions were imputed to others:

[o] Rymer, vol. iii. p. 31, 101.   [p] It was pretended, that he kissed the knights
who received him on the mouth, navel, and breech. Dupuy, p. 15, 16.
Wals. p. 99.

And Philip, as if their guilt were now certain, proceeded to a confiscation of all their treasures. But no sooner were the templars relieved from their tortures, than, preferring the most cruel execution to a life with infamy, they disavowed their confessions, exclaimed against the forgeries, justified the innocence of their order, and appealed to all the gallant actions, performed by them in ancient or later times, as a full apology for their conduct. The tyrant, enraged at this disappointment, and thinking himself now engaged in honour to proceed to extremities, ordered fifty-four of them, whom he branded as relapsed heretics, to perish by the punishment of fire in his capital: Great numbers expired after a like manner in other parts of the kingdom: And when he found, that the perseverance of these unhappy victims, in justifying to the last their innocence, had made deep impression on the spectators, he endeavoured to overcome the constancy of the templars by new inhumanities. The grand master of the order, John de Molay, and another great officer, brother to the sovereign of Dauphiny, were conducted to a scaffold, erected before the church of Notredame, at Paris: A full pardon was offered them on the one hand: The fire, destined for their execution, was shown them on the other: These gallant nobles still persisted in the protestations of their own innocence and that of their order; and were instantly hurried into the flames by the executioner.[q]

In all this barbarous injustice, Clement V. who was the creature of Philip, and then resided in France, fully concurred; and without examining a witness, or making any enquiry into the truth of facts, he, summarily, by the plenitude of his apostolic power, abolished the whole order. The templars all over Europe were thrown into prison; their conduct underwent a strict scrutiny; the power of their enemies still pursued and oppressed them; but no where, except in France, were the smallest traces of their guilt pretended to be found. England sent an ample testimony of their piety and morals; but as the order was now annihilated, the knights were distributed into several convents, and their possessions were, by command of the pope, transferred to the order of St. John.[r] We now proceed to relate some other detached transactions of the present period.

[q] Vertot, vol. ii. p. 142.　　[r] Rymer, vol. iii. p. 323, 956. vol. iv. p. 47. Ypod. Neust. p. 506.

CHAPTER XIV

The kingdom of England was afflicted with a grievous famine during several years of this reign. Perpetual rains and cold weather, not only destroyed the harvest, but bred a mortality among the cattle, and raised every kind of food to an enormous price.[s] The parliament, in 1315, endeavoured to fix more moderate rates to commodities; not sensible that such an attempt was impracticable, and that, were it possible to reduce the price of provisions by any other expedient than by introducing plenty, nothing could be more pernicious and destructive to the public. Where the produce of a year, for instance, falls so far short, as to afford full subsistance only for nine months, the only expedient for making it last all the twelve, is to raise the prices, to put the people by that means on short allowance, and oblige them to save their food, till a more plentiful season. But in reality, the encrease of prices is a necessary consequence of scarcity; and laws, instead of preventing it, only aggravate the evil, by cramping and restraining commerce. The parliament accordingly, in the ensuing year, repealed their ordinance, which they had found useless and burdensome.[t]

The prices affixed by the parliament are somewhat remarkable: Three pounds twelve shillings of our present money for the best stalled ox; for other oxen, two pounds eight shillings: A fat hog of two years old, ten shillings: A fat wether unshorn, a crown; if shorn, three shillings and six-pence: A fat goose, seven-pence halfpenny: A fat capon, six-pence: A fat hen, three-pence: Two chickens, three-pence: Four pigeons, three-pence: Two dozen of eggs, three-pence.[u] If we consider these prices, we shall find, that butcher's meat, in this time of great scarcity, must still have been sold, by the parliamentary ordinance, three times cheaper than our middling prices at present: Poultry somewhat lower; because, being now considered as a delicacy, it has risen beyond its proportion. In the country places of Ireland and Scotland, where delicacies bear no price, poultry is at present as cheap, if not cheaper, than butcher's meat. But the inference I would draw from the comparison of prices is still more considerable: I suppose that the rates, affixed by parliament, were inferior to the usual market prices in those years of famine and mortality of cattle; and that

[s] Trivet, cont. p. 17, 18.   [t] Wals. p. 107.   [u] Rot. Parl. 7 Edw. II. n. 35, 36. Ypod. Neust. p. 502.

these commodities, instead of a third, had really risen to a half of the present value. But the famine at that time was so consuming, that wheat was sometimes sold for above four pounds ten shillings a quarter,[w] usually for three pounds;[x] that is, twice our middling prices. A certain proof of the wretched state of tillage in those ages. We formerly found, that the middling price of corn in that period was half of the present price; while the middling price of cattle was only an eighth part: We here find the same immense disproportion in years of scarcity. It may thence be inferred with certainty, that the raising of corn was a species of manufactory, which few in that age could practise with advantage: And there is reason to think, that other manufactures more refined, were sold even beyond their present prices: At least there is a demonstration for it in the reign of Henry VII. from the rates affixed to scarlet and other broad cloth by act of parliament. During all those times, it was usual for the princes and great nobility to make settlements of their velvet beds and silken robes, in the same manner as of their estates and manors.[y] In the list of jewels and plate, which had belonged to the ostentatious Gavaston, and which the king recovered from the earl of Lancaster after the murder of that favourite, we find some embroidered girdles, flowered shirts, and silk waistcoats.[z] It was afterwards one article of accusation against that potent and opulent earl, when he was put to death, that he had purloined some of that finery of Gavaston's. The ignorance of those ages in manufactures, and still more, their unskilful husbandry, seem a clear proof that the country was then far from being populous.

All trade and manufactures indeed were then at a very low ebb. The only country in the northern parts of Europe, where they seem to have risen to any tolerable degree of improvement, was Flanders. When Robert, earl of that country, was applied to by the king, and was desired to break off commerce with the Scots, whom Edward called his rebels, and represented as excommunicated on that account by the church, the earl replied, that Flanders was always considered as common, and free and open to all nations.[a]

The petition of the elder Spenser to parliament, complaining of the devastation committed on his lands by the barons, contains

[w] Murimuth, p. 48. Walsingham, p. 108, says it rose to six pounds. [x] Ypod. Neust. p. 502. Trivet, cont. p. 18. [y] Dugdale passim. [z] Rymer, vol. iii. p. 388. [a] Rymer, vol. iii. p. 770.

several particulars, which are curious, and discover the manners of the age.[b] He affirms, that they had ravaged sixty-three manors belonging to him, and he makes his losses amount to 46,000 pounds; that is, to 138,000 of our present money. Among other particulars, he enumerates 28,000 sheep, 1000 oxen and heifers, 1200 cows with their breed for two years, 560 cart horses, 2000 hogs, together with 600 bacons, 80 carcasses of beef, and 600 muttons in the larder; ten tuns of cyder, arms for 200 men, and other warlike engines and provisions. The plain inference is, that the greater part of Spenser's vast estate, as well as the estates of the other nobility, was farmed by the landlord himself, managed by his stewards or bailiffs, and cultivated by his villains. Little or none of it was let on lease to husbandmen: Its produce was consumed in rustic hospitality by the baron or his officers: A great number of idle retainers, ready for any disorder or mischief, were maintained by him: All who lived upon his estate were absolutely at his disposal: Instead of applying to courts of justice, he usually sought redress by open force and violence: The great nobility were a kind of independant potentates, who, if they submitted to any regulations at all, were less governed by the municipal law, than by a rude species of the law of nations. The method, in which we find they treated the king's favourites and ministers, is a proof of their usual way of dealing with each other. A party, which complains of the arbitrary conduct of ministers, ought naturally to affect a great regard for the laws and constitution, and maintain at least the appearance of justice in their proceedings: Yet those barons, when discontented, came to parliament with an armed force, constrained the king to assent to their measures, and without any trial or witness or conviction, passed, from the pretended notoriety of facts, an act of banishment or attainder against the minister, which, on the first revolution of fortune, was reversed by like expedients. The parliament, during factious times, was nothing but the organ of present power. Though the persons, of whom it was chiefly composed, seemed to enjoy great independance, they really possessed no true liberty; and the security of each individual among them, was not so much derived from the general protection of law, as from his own private power and that of his confederates. The authority of the monarch, though far from absolute, was

[b] Brady's hist. vol. ii. p. 143, from Claus. 15 Edw. II. M. 14. Dors. in cedula.

irregular, and might often reach him: The current of a faction might overwhelm him: A hundred considerations, of benefits and injuries, friendships and animosities, hopes and fears, were able to influence his conduct; and amidst these motives a regard to equity and law and justice was commonly, in those rude ages, of little moment. Nor did any man entertain thoughts of opposing present power, who did not deem himself strong enough to dispute the field with it by force, and was not prepared to give battle to the sovereign or the ruling party.

Before I conclude this reign, I cannot forbear making another remark, drawn from the detail of losses given in by the elder Spenser; particularly, the great quantity of salted meat which he had in his larder, 600 bacons, 80 carcasses of beef, 600 muttons. We may observe that the outrage, of which he complained, began after the third of May, or the eleventh new style, as we learn from the same paper. It is easy therefore to conjecture what a vast store of the same kind he must have laid up at the beginning of winter; and we may draw a new conclusion with regard to the wretched state of ancient husbandry, which could not provide subsistance for the cattle during winter, even in such a temperate climate as the south of England: For Spenser had but one manor so far north as Yorkshire. There being few or no inclosures, except perhaps for deer, no sown grass, little hay, and no other resource for feeding cattle; the barons, as well as the people, were obliged to kill and salt their oxen and sheep in the beginning of winter, before they became lean upon the common pasture: A precaution still practised with regard to oxen in the least cultivated parts of this island. The salting of mutton is a miserable expedient, which has every where been long disused. From this circumstance, however trivial in appearance, may be drawn important inferences, with regard to the domestic economy and manner of life in those ages.

The disorders of the times, from foreign wars and intestine dissentions, but above all, the cruel famine, which obliged the nobility to dismiss many of their retainers, encreased the number of robbers in the kingdom; and no place was secure from their incursions.[c] They met in troops like armies, and over-ran the country. Two cardinals, themselves, the pope's legates, notwithstanding

[c] Ypod. Neust. p. 502. Wals. p. 107.

CHAPTER XIV

the numerous train, which attended them, were robbed, and de-spoiled of their goods and equipage, when they travelled on the high-way.[d]

Among the other wild fancies of the age, it was imagined, that the persons affected with leprosy, a disease at that time very com-mon, probably from bad diet, had conspired with the Saracens to poison all the springs and fountains; and men being glad of any pretence to get rid of those who were a burthen to them, many of those unhappy people were burnt alive on this chimerical im-putation. Several Jews also were punished in their persons, and their goods were confiscated on the same account.[e]

Stowe, in his survey of London, gives us a curious instance of the hospitality of the ancient nobility in this period: It is taken from the accounts of the cofferer or steward of Thomas earl of Lancaster, and contains the expences of that earl during the year 1313, which was not a year of famine. For the pantry, buttery, and kitchen, 3405 pounds. For 369 pipes of red wine, and two of white, 104 pounds, &c. The whole 7309 pounds; that, is near 22,000 pounds of our present money; and making allowance for the cheapness of commodities, near a hundred thousand pounds.

I have seen a French manuscript, containing accounts of some private disbursements of this king. There is an article, among others, of a crown paid to one for making the king laugh. To judge by the events of the reign, this ought not to have been an easy undertaking.

This king left four children, two sons and two daughters: Ed-ward, his eldest son and successor; John, created afterwards earl of Cornwal, who died young at Perth; Jane, afterwards married to David Bruce, king of Scotland; and Eleanor, married to Reginald, count of Gueldres.

[d] Ypod. Neust. p. 503. T. de la More, p. 594. Trivet, cont. p. 22. Murimuth, p. 51. [e] Ypod. Neust. p. 504.

XV
EDWARD III

*War with Scotland – Execution of the Earl
of Kent – Execution of Mortimer, earl of
March – State of Scotland – War with that
kingdom – King's claim to the crown of France –
Preparations for war with France – War –
Naval victory – Domestic disturbances –
Affairs of Britanny – Renewal of the war with
France – Invasion of France – Battle of Crecy –
War with Scotland – Captivity of the king
of Scots – Calais taken.*

1327.
20th
Jan. THE VIOLENT PARTY, which had taken arms against Edward II. and finally deposed that unfortunate monarch, deemed it requisite for their future security to pay so far an exterior obeisance to the law, as to desire a parliamentary indemnity for all their illegal proceedings; on account of the necessity, which, it was pretended, they lay under, of employing force against the Spensers and other evil counsellors, enemies of the kingdom. All the attainders also, which had passed against the earl of Lancaster and his adherents, when the chance of war turned against them, were easily reversed during the triumph of their party;[f] and the Spensers, whose former attainder had been reversed by parliament, were now again, in this change of fortune, condemned by the votes

[f] Rymer, vol. iv. p. 245, 257, 258, &c.

182

CHAPTER XV

of their enemies. A council of regency was likewise appointed by parliament, consisting of twelve persons; five prelates, the arch-bishops of Canterbury and York, the bishops of Winchester, Worcester, and Hereford; and seven lay peers, the earls of Nor-folk, Kent, and Surrey, and the lords Wake, Ingham, Piercy, and Ross. The earl of Lancaster was appointed guardian and protector of the king's person. But though it was reasonable to expect, that, as the weakness of the former king had given reins to the licen-tiousness of the barons, great domestic tranquillity would not pre-vail during the present minority; the first disturbance arose from an invasion by foreign enemies.

The king of Scots, declining in years and health, but retaining *War with* still that martial spirit, which had raised his nation from the lowest *Scotland.* ebb of fortune, deemed the present opportunity favourable for infesting England. He first made an attempt on the castle of Nor-ham, in which he was disappointed; he then collected an army of 25,000 men on the frontiers, and having given the command to the earl of Murray and lord Douglas, threatened an incursion into the northern counties. The English regency, after trying in vain every expedient to restore peace with Scotland, made vigorous prepara-tions for war, and besides assembling an English army of near sixty thousand men, they invited back John Hainault, and some foreign cavalry, whom they had dismissed, and whose discipline and arms had appeared superior to those of their own country. Young Ed-ward himself, burning with a passion for military fame, appeared at the head of these numerous forces; and marched from Durham, the appointed place of rendezvous, in quest of the enemy, who had already broken into the frontiers, and were laying every thing waste around them.

Murray and Douglas were the two most celebrated warriors, bred in the long hostilities between the Scots and English; and their forces, trained in the same school, and enured to hardships, fatigues, and dangers, were perfectly qualified, by their habits and manner of life, for that desultory and destructive war, which they carried into England. Except a body of about 4000 cavalry, well armed, and fit to make a steady impression in battle, the rest of the army were light-armed troops, mounted on small horses, which found subsistance every where, and carried them with rapid and unexpected marches, whether they meant to commit depredations on the peaceable inhabitants, or to attack an armed enemy, or to retreat into their own country. Their whole equipage consisted of a bag of oat-meal, which, as a supply in case of necessity, each soldier carried behind him; together with a light plate of iron, on which he instantly baked the meal into a cake, in the open fields. But his chief subsistance was the cattle which he seized; and his cookery was as expeditious as all his other operations. After fleaing the animal, he placed the skin, loose and hanging in the form of a bag, upon some stakes; he poured water into it, kindled a fire below, and thus made it serve as a caldron for the boiling of his victuals.[g]

The chief difficulty which Edward met with, after composing some dangerous frays, which broke out between his foreign forces and the English,[h] was to come up with an army so rapid in its marches, and so little incumbered in its motions. Though the flame and smoke of burning villages directed him sufficiently to the place of their encampment, he found, upon hurrying thither, that they had already dislodged; and he soon discovered, by new marks of devastation, that they had removed to some distant quarter. After harassing his army during some time in this fruitless chace, he advanced northwards, and crossed the Tyne, with a resolution of awaiting them on their return homewards, and taking vengeance for all their depredations.[i] But that whole country was already so much wasted by their frequent incursions, that it could not afford subsistance to his army; and he was obliged again to return southwards, and change his plan of operations. He had now lost all track of the enemy; and though he promised the reward of a hundred pounds a year to any one who should bring him an account of their motions, he remained unactive some days, before he received any intelligence of them.[k] He found at last, that they had fixed their camp on the southern banks of the Were, as if they intended to await a battle; but their prudent leaders had chosen the ground with such judgment, that the English, on their approach, saw it impracticable, without temerity, to cross the river in their front, and attack them in their present situation. Edward, impatient for revenge and glory, here sent them a defiance, and

[g] Froissard, liv. iv. chap. 18.   [h] Ibid. liv. i. chap. 17.   [i] Ibid. liv. iv. chap 19.   [k] Rymer, vol. iv. p. 312. Froissard, liv. iv. chap. 19.

challenged them, if they dared, to meet him in an equal field, and try the fortune of arms. The bold spirit of Douglas could ill brook this bravadoe, and he advised the acceptance of the challenge; but he was over-ruled by Murray, who replied to Edward, that he never took the counsel of an enemy in any of his operations. The king, therefore, kept still his position opposite to the Scots; and daily expected, that necessity would oblige them to change their quarters, and give him an opportunity of overwhelming them with superior forces. After a few days, they suddenly decamped, and marched farther up the river; but still posted themselves in such a manner, as to preserve the advantage of the ground, if the enemy should venture to attack them.[l] Edward insisted, that all hazards should be run, rather than allow these ravagers to escape with impunity; but Mortimer's authority prevented the attack, and opposed itself to the valour of the young monarch. While the armies lay in this position, an incident happened which had well nigh proved fatal to the English. Douglas, having gotten the word, and surveyed exactly the situation of the English camp, entered it secretly in the night-time, with a body of two hundred determined soldiers, and advanced to the royal tent, with a view of killing or carrying off the king, in the midst of his army. But some of Edward's attendants, awaking in that critical moment, made resistance; his chaplain and chamberlain sacrificed their lives for his safety; the king himself, after making a valorous defence, escaped in the dark: And Douglas, having lost the greater part of his followers, was glad to make a hasty retreat with the remainder.[m] Soon after, the Scottish army decamped without noise in the dead of night; and having thus gotten the start of the English, arrived without farther loss in their own country. Edward, on entering the place of the Scottish encampment, found only six Englishmen, whom the enemy, after breaking their legs, had tied to trees, in order to prevent their carrying any intelligence to their countrymen.[n]

The king was highly incensed at the disappointment, which he had met with, in his first enterprize, and at the head of so gallant an army. The symptoms, which he had discovered of bravery and

[l] Froissard, liv. iv. chap. 19.   [m] Froissard, liv. iv. chap. 19. Hemingford, p. 268. Ypod. Neust. p. 509. Knyghton, p. 2552.   [n] Froissard, liv. iv. chap. 19.

spirit, gave extreme satisfaction, and were regarded as sure prognostics of an illustrious reign: But the general displeasure fell violently on Mortimer, who was already the object of public odium: And every measure, which he pursued, tended to aggravate, beyond all bounds, the hatred of the nation both against him and queen Isabella.

When the council of regency was formed, Mortimer, though in the plenitude of his power, had taken no care to ensure a place in it; but this semblance of moderation was only a cover to the most iniquitous and most ambitious projects. He rendered that council entirely useless by usurping to himself the whole sovereign authority; he settled on the queen-dowager the greater part of the royal revenues; he never consulted either the princes of the blood, or the nobility in any public measure; the king himself was so besieged by his creatures, that no access could be procured to him; and all the envy, which had attended Gavaston and Spenser, fell much more deservedly on the new favourite.

1328. Mortimer, sensible of the growing hatred of the people, thought it requisite, on any terms, to secure peace abroad; and he entered into a negociation with Robert Bruce for that purpose. As the claim of superiority in England, more than any other cause, had tended to inflame the animosities between the two nations, Mortimer, besides stipulating a marriage between Jane, sister of Edward, and David, the son and heir of Robert, consented to resign absolutely this claim, to give up all the homages done by the Scottish parliament and nobility, and to acknowledge Robert as independant sovereign of Scotland.[o] In return for these advantages, Robert stipulated the payment of 30,000 marks to England. This treaty was ratified by parliament;[p] but was nevertheless the source of great discontent among the people, who, having entered zealously into the pretensions of Edward I. and deeming themselves disgraced by the successful resistance made by so inferior a nation, were disappointed by this treaty, in all future hopes both of conquest and of vengeance.

The princes of the blood, Kent, Norfolk, and Lancaster, were much united in their councils; and Mortimer entertained great

[o] Rymer, p. 337. Heming. p. 270. Anon. Hist. p. 392.   [p] Ypod. Neust. p. 510.

suspicions of their designs against him. In summoning them to parliament, he strictly prohibited them, in the king's name, from coming attended by an armed force, an illegal but usual practice in that age. The three earls, as they approached to Salisbury, the place appointed for the meeting of parliament, found, that, though they themselves, in obedience to the king's command, had brought only their usual retinue with them, Mortimer and his party were attended by all their followers in arms; and they began with some reason to apprehend a dangerous design against their persons. They retreated, assembled their retainers, and were returning with an army to take vengeance on Mortimer; when the weakness of Kent and Norfolk, who deserted the common cause, obliged Lancaster also to make his submissions.[q] The quarrel, by the interposition of the prelates, seemed for the present to be appeased.

But Mortimer, in order to intimidate the princes, determined to have a victim; and the simplicity, with the good intentions of the earl of Kent, afforded him soon after an opportunity of practising upon him. By himself and his emissaries, he endeavoured to persuade that prince, that his brother, king Edward, was still alive, and detained in some secret prison in England. The earl, whose remorses for the part which he had acted against the late king, probably inclined him to give credit to this intelligence, entered into a design of restoring him to liberty, of re-instating him on the throne, and of making thereby some atonement for the injuries which he himself had unwarily done him.[r] After this harmless contrivance had been allowed to proceed a certain length, the earl was seized by Mortimer, was accused before the parliament, and condemned by those slavish, though turbulent barons, to lose his life and fortune. The queen and Mortimer, apprehensive of young Edward's lenity towards his uncle, hurried on the execution, and the prisoner was beheaded next day: But so general was the affection borne him, and such pity prevailed for his unhappy fate, that, though peers had been easily found to condemn him, it was evening before his enemies could find an executioner to perform the office.[s]

1329.

1330.

9th March. Execution of the earl of Kent.

---

[q] Knyghton, p. 2554.   [r] Avesbury, p. 8. Anon. Hist. p. 395.   [s] Heming. p. 271. Ypod. Neust. p. 510. Knyghton, p. 2555.

The earl of Lancaster, on pretence of his having assented to this conspiracy, was soon after thrown into prison: Many of the prelates and nobility were prosecuted: Mortimer employed this engine to crush all his enemies, and to enrich himself and his family by the forfeitures. The estate of the earl of Kent was seized for his younger son, Geoffrey: The immense fortunes of the Spensers and their adherents were mostly converted to his own use: He affected a state and dignity equal or superior to the royal: His power became formidable to every one: His illegal practices were daily complained of: And all parties, forgetting past animosities, conspired in their hatred of Mortimer.

It was impossible, that these abuses could long escape the observation of a prince, endowed with so much spirit and judgment as young Edward, who, being now in his eighteenth year, and feeling himself capable of governing, repined at being held in fetters by this insolent minister. But so much was he surrounded by the emissaries of Mortimer, that it behoved him to conduct the project for subverting him, with the same secrecy and precaution, as if he had been forming a conspiracy against his sovereign. He communicated his intentions to lord Mountacute, who engaged the lords Molins and Clifford, Sir John Nevil of Hornby, Sir Edward Bohun, Ufford, and others, to enter into their views; and the castle of Nottingham was chosen for the scene of the enterprize. The queen-dowager and Mortimer lodged in that fortress: The king also was admitted, though with a few only of his attendants: And as the castle was strictly guarded, the gates locked every evening, and the keys carried to the queen, it became necessary to communicate the design to Sir William Eland, the governor, who zealously took part in it. By his direction, the king's associates were admitted through a subterraneous passage, which had formerly been contrived for a secret outlet from the castle, but was now buried in rubbish; and Mortimer, without having it in his power to make resistance, was suddenly seized in an apartment adjoining to the queen's.[t] A parliament was immediately summoned for his condemnation. He was accused before that assembly of having usurped regal power from the council of regency, appointed by parliament; of having procured the death of the late king; of

[t] Avesbury, p. 9.

CHAPTER XV

having deceived the earl of Kent into a conspiracy to restore that prince; of having solicited and obtained exorbitant grants of the royal demesnes; of having dissipated the public treasure; of secreting 20,000 marks of the money paid by the king of Scotland; and of other crimes and misdemeanors.[u] The parliament condemned him, from the supposed notoriety of the facts, without trial, or hearing his answer, or examining a witness; and he was hanged on a gibbet at the Elmes, in the neighbourhood of London. It is remarkable, that this sentence was near twenty years after reversed by parliament, in favour of Mortimer's son; and the reason assigned was the illegal manner of proceeding.[w] The principles of law and justice were established in England, not in such a degree as to prevent any iniquitous sentence against a person obnoxious to the ruling party; but sufficient, on the return of his credit, or that of his friends, to serve as a reason or pretence for its reversal.

Execution of Mortimer. 29th Nov.

Justice was also executed by a sentence of the house of peers, on some of the inferior criminals, particularly on Simon de Bereford: But the Barons, in that act of jurisdiction, entered a protest, that though they had tried Bereford, who was none of their peers, they should not for the future be obliged to receive any such indictment. The queen was confined to her own house at Risings near London: Her revenue was reduced to 4000 pounds a year:[x] And though the king, during the remainder of her life, paid her a decent visit once or twice a year, she never was able to reinstate herself in any credit or authority.

1331.

Edward, having now taken the reins of government into his own hands, applied himself, with industry and judgment, to redress all those grievances, which had proceeded either from want of authority in the crown, or from the late abuses of it. He issued writs to the judges, enjoining them to administer justice, without paying any regard to arbitrary orders from the ministers: And as the robbers, thieves, murderers, and criminals of all kinds, had, during the course of public convulsions, multiplied to an enormous degree, and were openly protected by the great barons, who made use of them against their enemies, the king, after exacting from the peers a solemn promise in parliament, that they would

[u] Brady's App. No. 83. Anon. Hist. p. 397, 398. Knyghton, p. 2556.
[w] Cotton's Abridg. p. 85, 86.   [x] Cotton's Abridg. p. 10.

break off all connexions with such malefactors,[y] set himself in earnest to remedy the evil. Many of these gangs had become so numerous, as to require his own presence to disperse them; and he exerted both courage and industry in executing this salutary office. The ministers of justice, from his example, employed the utmost diligence in discovering, pursuing, and punishing the criminals; and this disorder was by degrees corrected, at least palliated; the utmost that could be expected with regard to a disease, hitherto inherent in the constitution.

In proportion as the government acquired authority at home, it became formidable to the neighbouring nations; and the ambitious spirit of Edward sought, and soon found, an opportunity of *State of* exerting itself. The wise and valiant Robert Bruce, who had recov- *Scotland.* ered by arms the independance of his country, and had fixed it by the last treaty of peace with England, soon after died, and left David his son, a minor, under the guardianship of Randolf, earl of Murray, the companion of all his victories. It had been stipulated in this treaty, that both the Scottish nobility, who, before the commencement of the wars, enjoyed lands in England, and the English who inherited estates in Scotland, should be restored to their respective possessions:[z] But though this article had been executed pretty regularly on the part of Edward, Robert, who observed that the estates, claimed by Englishmen, were much more numerous and valuable than the others, either thought it dangerous to admit so many secret enemies into the kingdom, or found it difficult to wrest from his own followers the possessions bestowed on them as the reward of former services: And he had protracted the performance of his part of the stipulation. The English nobles, disappointed in their expectations, began to think of a remedy; and as their influence was great in the north, their enmity alone, even though unsupported by the king of England, became dangerous to the minor prince, who succeeded to the Scottish throne.

1332. Edward Baliol, the son of that John, who was crowned king of Scotland, had been detained some time a prisoner in England after his father was released; but having also obtained his liberty, he went over to France, and resided in Normandy, on his patrimonial estate in that country, without any thoughts of reviving the claims of his family to the crown of Scotland. His pretensions,

[y] Cotton's Abridg.   [z] Rymer, vol. iv. p. 384.

CHAPTER XV

however plausible, had been so strenuously abjured by the Scots, and rejected by the English, that he was universally regarded as a private person; and he had been thrown into prison on account of some private offence, of which he was accused. Lord Beaumont, a great English baron, who, in the right of his wife, claimed the earldom of Buchan in Scotland,[a] found him in this situation; and deeming him a proper instrument for his purpose, made such interest with the king of France, who was not aware of the consequences, that he recovered him his liberty, and brought him over with him to England.

The injured nobles, possessed of such a head, began to think of vindicating their rights by force of arms; and they applied to Edward for his concurrence and assistance. But there were several reasons, which deterred the king from openly avowing their enterprize. In his treaty with Scotland, he had entered into a bond of 20,000 pounds, payable to the pope, if within four years he violated the peace; and as the term was not yet elapsed, he dreaded the exacting of that penalty by the sovereign pontiff, who possessed so many means of forcing princes to make payment. He was also afraid, that violence and injustice would every where be imputed to him, if he attacked with superior force a minor king, and a brother-in-law, whose independant title had so lately been acknowledged by a solemn treaty. And as the regent of Scotland, on every demand which had been made of restitution to the English barons, had always confessed the justice of their claim, and had only given an evasive answer, grounded on plausible pretences, Edward resolved not to proceed by open violence, but to employ like artifices against him. He secretely encouraged Baliol in his enterprize; connived at his assembling forces in the north; and gave countenance to the nobles, who were disposed to join in the attempt. A force of near 2500 men was inlisted under Baliol, by Umfreville earl of Angus, the lords Beaumont, Ferrars, Fitz-warin, Wake, Stafford, Talbot, and Moubray. As these adventurers apprehended, that the frontiers would be strongly armed and guarded, they resolved to make their attack by sea; and having embarked at Ravenspur, they reached in a few days the coast of Fife.

Scotland was at that time in a very different situation from that

[a] Rymer, vol. iv. p. 251.

in which it had appeared under the victorious Robert. Besides the loss of that great monarch, whose genius and authority preserved entire the whole political fabric, and maintained an union among the unruly barons, Lord Douglas, impatient of rest, had gone over to Spain in a crusade against the Moors, and had there perished in battle:[b] The earl of Murray, who had long been declining through age and infirmities, had lately died, and had been succeeded in the regency by Donald earl of Marre, a man of much inferior talents: The military spirit of the Scots, though still unbroken, was left without a proper guidance and direction: And a minor king seemed ill qualified to defend an inheritance, which it had required all the consummate valour and abilities of his father to acquire and maintain. But as the Scots were apprized of the intended invasion, great numbers, on the appearance of the English fleet, immediately ran to the shore, in order to prevent the landing of the enemy. Baliol had valour and activity, and he drove back the Scots with considerable loss.[c] He marched westward into the heart of the country; flattering himself that the ancient partizans of his family would declare for him. But the fierce animosities, which had been kindled between the two nations, inspiring the Scots with a strong prejudice against a prince supported by the English, he was regarded as a common enemy; and the regent found no difficulty in assembling a great army to oppose him. It is pretended, that Marre had no less than 40,000 men under his banners; but the same hurry and impatience, that made him collect a force, which from its greatness was so disproportioned to the occasion, rendered all his motions unskilful and imprudent. The river Erne ran between the two armies; and the Scots, confiding in that security, as well as in their great superiority of numbers, kept no order in their encampment. Baliol passed the river in the night-time; attacked the unguarded and undisciplined Scots; threw them into confusion, which was encreased by the darkness and by their very numbers to which they trusted; and he beat them off the field with great slaughter.[d] But in the morning, when the Scots were at some distance, they were ashamed of having yielded the victory to so weak a foe, and they hurried back to recover the honour of the day.

*11th
Aug.*

---

[b] Froissard, liv. i. chap. 21.   [c] Heming. p. 272. Walsing. p. 131. Knyghton, p. 2560.   [d] Knyghton, p. 2561.

CHAPTER XV

Their eager passions urged them precipitately to battle, without regard to some broken ground, which lay between them and the enemy, and which disordered and confounded their ranks. Baliol seized the favourable opportunity, advanced his troops upon them, prevented them from rallying, and anew chaced them off the field with redoubled slaughter. There fell above 12,000 Scots in this action; and among these the flower of their nobility; the regent himself, the earl of Carric, a natural son of their late king, the earls of Athole and Monteith, lord Hay of Errol, constable, and the lords Keith and Lindsey. The loss of the English scarcely exceeded thirty men; a strong proof, among many others, of the miserable state of military discipline in those ages.[e]

Baliol soon after made himself master of Perth; but still was not able to bring over any of the Scots to his party. Patric Dunbar, earl of March, and Sir Archibald Douglas, brother to the lord of that name, appeared at the head of the Scottish armies, which amounted still to near 40,000 men; and they purposed to reduce Baliol and the English by famine. They blockaded Perth by land; they collected some vessels with which they invested it by water: But Baliol's ships, attacking the Scottish fleet, gained a complete victory; and opened the communication between Perth and the sea.[f] The Scotch armies were then obliged to disband for want of pay and subsistence: The nation was in effect subdued by a handful of men: Each nobleman, who found himself most exposed to danger, successively submitted to Baliol: That prince was crowned at Scone: David, his competitor, was sent over to France with his betrothed wife, Jane, sister to Edward: And the heads of his party sued to Baliol for a truce, which he granted them, in order to assemble a parliament in tranquillity, and have his title recognized by the whole Scottish nation. *27th Sept.*

But Baliol's imprudence or his necessities making him dismiss the greater part of his English followers, he was, notwithstanding the truce, attacked of a sudden near Annan by Sir Archibald Douglas, and other chieftains of the party; he was routed; his brother John Baliol was slain; he himself was chaced into England *1333.*

[e] Heming. p. 273. Walsing. p. 131. Knyghton, p. 2561.   [f] Heming. p. 273. Knyghton, p. 2561.

in a miserable condition; and thus lost his kingdom by a revolution as sudden as that by which he had acquired it.

While Baliol enjoyed his short-lived and precarious royalty, he had been sensible, that, without the protection of England, it would be impossible for him to maintain possession of the throne; and he had secretly sent a message to Edward, offering to acknowledge his superiority, to renew the homage for his crown, and to espouse the princess Jane, if the pope's consent could be obtained, for dissolving her former marriage, which was not yet consummated. Edward, ambitious of recovering that important concession, made by Mortimer during his minority, threw off all scruples, and willingly accepted the offer; but as the dethroning of Baliol had rendered this stipulation of no effect, the king prepared to re-instate him in possession of the crown; an enterprize, which appeared from late experience so easy and so little hazardous. As he possessed many popular arts, he consulted his parliament on the occasion; but that assembly, finding the resolution already taken, declined giving any opinion, and only granted him, in order to support the enterprize, an aid of a fifteenth, from the personal estates of the nobility and gentry, and a tenth of the moveables of boroughs. And they added a petition, that the king would thenceforth live on his own revenue, without grieving his subjects by illegal taxes, or by the outrageous seizure of their goods in the shape of purveyance.[g]

War with Scotland.

As the Scots expected, that the chief brunt of the war would fall upon Berwic, Douglas, the regent, threw a strong garrison into that place under the command of Sir William Keith, and he himself assembled a great army on the frontiers, ready to penetrate into England, as soon as Edward should have invested that place. The English army was less numerous, but better supplied with arms and provisions, and retained in stricter discipline; and the king, notwithstanding the valiant defence made by Keith, had in two months reduced the garrison to extremities, and had obliged them to capitulate: They engaged to surrender, if they were not relieved within a few days by their countrymen.[h] This intelligence, being conveyed to the Scottish army, which was preparing to invade Northumberland, changed their plan of operations, and en-

[g] Cotton's Abridg.　[h] Rymer, vol. iv. p. 564, 565, 566.

gaged them to advance towards Berwic, and attempt the relief of that important fortress. Douglas, who had ever purposed to decline a pitched battle, in which he was sensible of the enemy's superiority, and who intended to have drawn out the war by small skirmishes, and by mutually ravaging each other's country, was forced, by the impatience of his troops, to put the fate of the kingdom upon the event of one day. He attacked the English at *19th* Halidown-hill, a little north of Berwic; and though his heavy- *July.* armed cavalry dismounted, in order to render the action more steady and desperate, they were received with such valour by Edward, and were so galled by the English archers, that they were soon thrown into disorder, and on the fall of Douglas, their general, were totally routed. The whole army fled in confusion, and the English, but much more the Irish, gave little quarter in the pursuit: All the nobles of chief distinction were either slain or taken prisoners: Near thirty thousand of the Scots fell in the action: While the loss of the English amounted only to one knight, one esquire, and thirteen private soldiers: An inequality almost incredible.[i]

After this fatal blow, the Scottish nobles had no other resource than instant submission; and Edward, leaving a considerable body with Baliol to complete the conquest of the kingdom, returned with the remainder of his army to England. Baliol was acknowledged king by a parliament assembled at Edinburgh;[k] the superiority of England was again recognized; many of the Scottish nobility swore fealty to Edward; and to complete the misfortunes of that nation, Baliol ceded Berwic, Dunbar, Roxborough, Edinburgh, and all the south-east counties of Scotland, which were declared to be for ever annexed to the English monarchy.[l]

If Baliol, on his first appearance, was dreaded by the Scots, *1334.* as an instrument employed by England for the subjection of the kingdom, this deed confirmed all their suspicions, and rendered him the object of universal hatred. Whatever submissions they might be obliged to make, they considered him, not as their prince, but as the delegate and confederate of their determined enemy: And neither the manners of the age, nor the state of Edward's

[i] Heming. p. 275, 276, 277. Knyghton, p. 2559. Otterborne, p. 115.
[k] Rymer, vol. iv. p. 590. [l] Ibid. p. 614.

revenue permitting him to maintain a standing army in Scotland, the English forces were no sooner withdrawn, than the Scots revolted from Baliol, and returned to their former allegiance under Bruce. Sir Andrew Murray, appointed regent by the party of this latter prince, employed with success his valour and activity in many small but decisive actions against Baliol; and in a short time had almost wholly expelled him the kingdom. Edward was *1335.* obliged again to assemble an army and to march into Scotland: The Scots, taught by experience, withdrew into their hills and fastnesses: He destroyed the houses and ravaged the estates of those whom he called rebels: But this confirmed them still farther in their obstinate antipathy to England and to Baliol; and being now rendered desperate, they were ready to take advantage, on the first opportunity, of the retreat of their enemy, and they soon re-conquered their country from the English. Edward made anew *1336.* his appearance in Scotland with like success: He found every thing hostile in the kingdom, except the spot on which he was encamped: And though he marched uncontrouled over the low countries, the nation itself was farther than ever from being broken and subdued. Besides being supported by their pride and anger, passions difficult to tame, they were encouraged, amidst all their calamities, by daily promises of relief from France; and as a war was now likely to break out between that kingdom and England, they had reason to expect from this incident a great diversion of that force, which had so long oppressed and overwhelmed them.

1337.
King's
claim to
the crown
of France.
We now come to a transaction, on which depended the most memorable events, not only of this long and active reign, but of the whole English and French history, during more than a century; and it will therefore be necessary to give a particular account of the springs and causes of it.

It had long been a prevailing opinion, that the crown of France could never descend to a female; and in order to give more authority to this maxim, and assign it a determinate origin, it had been usual to derive it from a clause in the Salian Code, the law of an ancient tribe among the Franks: though that clause, when strictly examined, carries only the appearance of favouring this principle, and does not really, by the confession of the best anti-

CHAPTER XV

quaries, bear the sense commonly imposed upon it. But though positive law seems wanting among the French for the exclusion of females, the practice had taken place; and the rule was established beyond controversy on some ancient as well as some modern precedents. During the first race of the monarchy, the Franks were so rude and barbarous a people, that they were incapable of submitting to a female reign; and in that period of their history there were frequent instances of kings advanced to royalty in prejudice of females, who were related to the crown by nearer degrees of consanguinity. These precedents, joined to like causes, had also established the male succession in the second race; and though the instances were neither so frequent nor so certain during that period, the principle of excluding the female line seems still to have prevailed, and to have directed the conduct of the nation. During the third race, the crown had descended from father to son for eleven generations, from Hugh Capet to Lewis Hutin; and thus, in fact, during the course of nine hundred years, the French monarchy had always been governed by males, and no female and none who founded his title on a female had ever mounted the throne. Philip the Fair, father of Lewis Hutin, left three sons, this Lewis, Philip the Long, and Charles the Fair, and one daughter, Isabella, queen of England. Lewis Hutin, the eldest, left at his death one daughter, by Margaret sister to Eudes, duke of Burgundy; and as his queen was then pregnant, Philip, his younger brother, was appointed regent, till it should appear whether the child proved a son or a daughter. The queen bore a male, who lived only a few days: Philip was proclaimed king: And as the duke of Burgundy made some opposition, and asserted the rights of his niece, the states of the kingdom, by a solemn and deliberate decree, gave her an exclusion, and declared all females for ever incapable of succeeding to the crown of France. Philip died after a short reign, leaving three daughters; and his brother, Charles, without dispute or controversy, then succeeded to the crown. The reign of Charles was also short: He left one daughter; but as his queen was pregnant, the next male heir was appointed regent, with a declared right of succession, if the issue should prove female. This prince was Philip de Valois, cousin German to the deceased king; being the son of Charles de Valois, brother of

Philip the Fair. The queen of France was delivered of a daughter: The regency ended; and Philip de Valois was unanimously placed on the throne of France.

The king of England, who was at that time a youth of fifteen years of age, embraced a notion, that he was intitled, in right of his mother, to the succession of the kingdom, and that the claim of the nephew was preferable to that of the cousin german. There could not well be imagined a notion weaker or worse grounded. The principle of excluding females was of old an established opinion in France, and had acquired equal authority with the most express and positive law: It was supported by ancient precedents: It was confirmed by recent instances, solemnly and deliberately decided: And what placed it still farther beyond controversy; if Edward was disposed to question its validity, he thereby cut off his own pretensions; since the three last kings had all left daughters, who were still alive, and who stood before him in the order of succession. He was therefore reduced to assert, that, though his mother, Isabella, was, on account of her sex, incapable of succeeding, he himself, who inherited through her, was liable to no such objection, and might claim by the right of propinquity. But, besides that this pretension was more favourable to Charles, king of Navarre, descended from the daughter of Lewis Hutin, it was so contrary to the established principles of succession in every country of Europe,[m] was so repugnant to the practice both in private and public inheritances, that no body in France thought of Edward's claim: Philip's title was universally recognized:[n] And he never imagined, that he had a competitor; much less, so formidable a one as the king of England.

But though the youthful and ambitious mind of Edward had rashly entertained this notion, he did not think proper to insist on his pretensions, which must have immediately involved him, on very unequal terms, in a dangerous and implacable war with so powerful a monarch. Philip was a prince of mature years, of great experience, and at that time of an established character both for prudence and valour; and by these circumstances, as well as by the internal union of his people, and their acquiescence in his undoubted right, he possessed every advantage above a raw youth,

[m] Froissard, liv. 1. chap. 4.　　[n] Id. liv. i. chap. 22.

CHAPTER XV

newly raised, by injustice and violence, to the government of the most intractable and most turbulent subjects in Europe. But there immediately occurred an incident, which required, that Edward should either openly declare his pretensions, or for ever renounce and abjure them. He was summoned to do homage for Guienne: Philip was preparing to compel him by force of arms: That country was in a very bad state of defence: And the forfeiture of so rich an inheritance was, by the feudal law, the immediate consequence of his refusing or declining to perform the duty of a vassal. Edward therefore thought it prudent to submit to present necessity: He went over to Amiens: Did homage to Philip: And as there had arisen some controversy concerning the terms of this submission, he afterwards sent over a formal deed, in which he acknowledged that he owed liege homage to France;[o] which was in effect ratifying, and that in the strongest terms, Philip's title to the crown of that kingdom. His own claim indeed was so unreasonable, and so thoroughly disavowed by the whole French nation, that to insist on it was no better than pretending to the violent conquest of the kingdom; and it is probable that he would never have farther thought of it, had it not been for some incidents, which excited an animosity between the monarchs.

Robert of Artois was descended from the blood royal of France, was a man of great character and authority, had espoused Philip's sister, and by his birth, talents, and credit was entitled to make the highest figure, and fill the most important offices, in the monarchy. This prince had lost the county of Artois, which he claimed as his birthright, by a sentence, commonly deemed iniquitous, of Philip the Fair; and he was seduced to attempt recovering possession by an action, so unworthy of his rank and character as a forgery.[p] The detection of this crime covered him with shame and confusion: His brother-in-law not only abandoned him, but prosecuted him with violence: Robert, incapable of bearing disgrace, left the kingdom, and hid himself in the Low Countries: Chaced from that retreat, by the authority of Philip, he came over to England; in spite of the French king's menaces

[o] Rymer, vol. iv. p. 477, 481. Froissard, liv. 1. chap. 25. Anon. Hist. p. 394. Walsing. p. 130. Murimuth, p. 73.   [p] Froissard, liv. 1. chap. 29.

and remonstrances, he was favourably received by Edward;[q] and was soon admitted into the councils and shared the confidence of that monarch. Abandoning himself to all the movements of rage and despair, he endeavoured to revive the prepossession entertained by Edward in favour of his title to the crown of France, and even flattered him, that it was not impossible for a prince of his valour and abilities, to render his claim effectual. The king was the more disposed to hearken to suggestions of this nature, because he had, in several particulars, found reason to complain of Philip's conduct with regard to Guienne, and because that prince had both given protection to the exiled David Bruce, and supported, at least encouraged the Scots in their struggles for independance. Thus resentment gradually filled the breasts of both monarchs, and made them incapable of hearkening to any terms of accommodation, proposed by the pope, who never ceased interposing his good offices between them. Philip thought, that he should be wanting to the first principles of policy, if he abandoned Scotland: Edward affirmed, that he must relinquish all pretensions to generosity, if he withdrew his protection from Robert. The former, informed of some preparations for hostilities, which had been made by his rival, issued a sentence of felony and attainder against Robert, and declared, that every vassal of the crown, whether *within* or *without* the kingdom, who gave countenance to that traitor, would be involved in the same sentence; a menace easy to be understood: The latter, resolute not to yield, endeavoured to form alliances in the Low Countries and on the frontiers of Germany, the only places from which he either could make an effectual attack upon France, or produce such a diversion as might save the province of Guienne, which lay so much exposed to the power of Philip.

Preparations for war with France.

The king began with opening his intentions to the count of Hainault, his father-in-law; and having engaged him in his interests, he employed the good offices and councils of that prince in drawing into his alliance the other sovereigns of that neighbourhood. The duke of Brabant was induced, by his mediation, and by large remittances of money from England, to promise his concurrence:[r] The archbishop of Cologn, the duke of Gueldres, the marquis of Juliers, the count of Namur, the lords of Fauque-

[q] Rymer, vol. iv. p. 747. Froissard, liv. 1. chap. 27.   [r] Rymer, vol. iv. p. 777.

mont and Baquen, were engaged by like motives to embrace the English alliance.[s] These sovereign princes could supply, either from their own states or from the bordering countries, great numbers of warlike troops; and naught was wanting to make the force on that quarter very formidable but the accession of Flanders; which Edward procured by means somewhat extraordinary and unusual.

As the Flemings were the first people in the northern parts of Europe, that cultivated arts and manufactures, the lower ranks of men among them had risen to a degree of opulence unknown elsewhere to those of their station in that barbarous age; had acquired privileges and independance; and began to emerge from that state of vassalage, or rather of slavery, into which the common people had been universally thrown by the feudal institutions. It was probably difficult for them to bring their sovereign and their nobility to conform themselves to the principles of law and civil government, so much neglected in every other country: It was impossible for them to confine themselves within the proper bounds in their opposition and resentment against any instance of tyranny: They had risen in tumults: Had insulted the nobles: Had chaced their earl into France: And delivering themselves over to the guidance of a seditious leader, had been guilty of all that insolence and disorder, to which the thoughtless and enraged populace are so much inclined, wherever they are unfortunate enough to be their own masters.[t]

Their present leader was James d'Arteville, a brewer in Ghent, who governed them with a more absolute sway than had ever been assumed by any of their lawful sovereigns: He placed and displaced the magistrates at pleasure: He was accompanied by a guard, who, on the least signal from him, instantly assassinated any man that happened to fall under his displeasure: All the cities of Flanders were full of his spies; and it was immediate death to give him the smallest umbrage: The few nobles, who remained in the country, lived in continual terror from his violence: He seized the estates of all those whom he had either banished or murdered; and bestowing a part on their wives and children, converted the remainder to his own use.[u] Such were the first effects, that Europe

---

[s] Froissard, liv. 4. chap. 29, 33, 36. [t] Froissard, liv. 1. chap. 30. Meyerus.
[u] Froissard, liv. I. chap. 30.

saw, of popular violence; after having groaned, during so many ages, under monarchical and aristocratical tyranny.

James d'Arteville was the man, to whom Edward addressed himself for bringing over the Flemings to his interests; and that prince, the most haughty and most aspiring of the age, never courted any ally with so much assiduity and so many submissions, as he employed towards this seditious and criminal tradesman. D'Arteville, proud of these advances from the king of England, and sensible that the Flemings were naturally inclined to maintain connexions with the English, who furnished them the materials of their woollen manufactures, the chief source of their opulence, readily embraced the interests of Edward, and invited him over into the Low Countries. Edward, before he entered on this great enterprize, affected to consult his parliament, asked their advice, and obtained their consent.[w] And the more to strengthen his hands, he procured from them a grant of 20,000 sacks of wool; which might amount to about a hundred thousand pounds: This commodity was a good instrument to employ with the Flemings; and the price of it with his German allies. He completed the other necessary sums by loans, by pawning the crown jewels, by confiscating or rather robbing at once all the Lombards, who now exercised the invidious trade, formerly monopolized by the Jews, of lending on interest;[x] and being attended by a body of English forces, and by several of his nobility, he sailed over to Flanders.

1338.   The German princes, in order to justify their unprovoked hostilities against France, had required the sanction of some legal authority; and Edward, that he might give them satisfaction on this head, had applied to Lewis of Bavaria, then emperor, and had been created by him *vicar of the empire;* an empty title, but which seemed to give him a right of commanding the service of the princes of Germany.[y] The Flemings, who were vassals of France, pretending like scruples with regard to the invasion of their liege lord; Edward, by the advice of d'Arteville, assumed, in his commissions, the title of king of France, and, in virtue of this right, claimed their assistance for dethroning Philip de Valois, the usurper of his kingdom.[z] This step, which, he feared, would de-

---

[w] Cotton's Abridg.   [x] Dugd. Baron. vol. ii. p. 146.   [y] Froissard, liv. i. chap. 35.   [z] Heming. p. 303. Walsingham, p. 143.

CHAPTER XV

stroy all future amity between the kingdoms, and beget endless and implacable jealousies in France, was not taken by him without much reluctance and hesitation: And not being in itself very justifiable, it has in the issue been attended with many miseries to both kingdoms. From this period we may date the commencement of that great animosity, which the English nation have ever since born to the French, which has so visible an influence on all future transactions, and which has been, and continues to be the spring of many rash and precipitate resolutions among them. In all the preceding reigns since the conquest, the hostilities between the two crowns had been only casual and temporary; and as they had never been attended with any bloody or dangerous event, the traces of them were easily obliterated by the first treaty of pacification. The English nobility and gentry valued themselves on their French or Norman extraction: They affected to employ the language of that country in all public transactions, and even in familiar conversation: And both the English court and camp being always full of nobles, who came from different provinces of France, the two people were, during some centuries, more intermingled together than any two distinct nations, whom we meet with in history. But the fatal pretensions of Edward III. dissolved all these connexions, and left the seeds of great animosity in both countries, especially among the English. For it is remarkable, that this latter nation, though they were commonly the aggressors, and by their success and situation were enabled to commit the most cruel injuries on the other, have always retained a stronger tincture of national antipathy; nor is their hatred retaliated on them to an equal degree by the French. That country lies in the middle of Europe, has been successively engaged in hostilities with all its neighbours, the popular prejudices have been diverted into many channels, and, among a people of softer manners, they never rose to a great height against any particular nation.

Philip made great preparations against the attack from the English, and such as seemed more than sufficient to secure him from the danger. Besides the concurrence of all the nobility in his own populous and warlike kingdom, his foreign alliances were both more cordial and more powerful than those which were formed by his antagonist. The pope, who, at this time, lived in Avignon, was dependant on France, and being disgusted at the connexions between Edward and Lewis of Bavaria, whom he had excommunicated, he embraced with zeal and sincerity the cause of the French monarch. The king of Navarre, the duke of Britanny, the count of Bar, were in the same interests; and on the side of Germany, the king of Bohemia, the Palatine, the dukes of Lorraine and Austria, the bishop of Liege, the counts of Deuxpont, Vaudemont, and Geneva. The allies of Edward were in themselves weaker; and having no object, but his money, which began to be exhausted, they were slow in their motions and irresolute in their measures. The duke of Brabant, the most powerful among them, seemed even inclined to withdraw himself wholly from the alliance; and the king was necessitated, both to give the Brabanters new privileges in trade, and to contract his son Edward with the daughter of that prince, ere he could bring him to fulfil his engagements. The summer was wasted in conferences and negociations before Edward could take the field; and he was obliged, in order to allure his German allies into his measures, to pretend that the first attack should be made upon Cambray, a city of the empire which had been garrisoned by Philip.[a] But finding, upon trial, the difficulty of the enterprize, he conducted them towards the frontiers of France; and he there saw, by a sensible proof, the vanity of his expectations: The count of Namur, and even the count of Hainault, his brother-in-law, (for the old count was dead) refused to commence hostilities against their liege lord, and retired with their troops.[b] So little account did they make of Edward's pretensions to the crown of France!

War with France.   The king, however, entered the enemy's country, and encamped on the fields of Vironfosse near Capelle, with an army of near 50,000 men, composed almost entirely of foreigners: Philip approached him with an army of near double the force, composed chiefly of native subjects; and it was daily expected that a battle would ensue. But the English monarch was averse to engage against so great a superiority: The French thought it sufficient if he eluded the attacks of his enemy, without running any unnecessary hazard. The two armies faced each other for some days: Mu-

---

[a] Froissard, liv. i. chap. 39. Heming. p. 305.   [b] Froissard, liv. i. chap. 30.

CHAPTER XV

tual defiances were sent: And Edward, at last, retired into Flanders, and disbanded his army.[c]

Such was the fruitless and almost ridiculous conclusion of Edward's mighty preparations; and as his measures were the most prudent, that could be embraced in his situation, he might learn from experience in what a hopeless enterprize he was engaged. His expences, though they had led to no end, had been consuming and destructive: He had contracted near 300,000 pounds of debt;[d] he had anticipated all his revenue; he had pawned every thing of value, which belonged either to himself or his queen; he was obliged in some measure even to pawn himself to his creditors, by not sailing to England, till he obtained their permission, and by promising on his word of honour to return in person, if he did not remit their money.

But he was a prince of too much spirit to be discouraged by the first difficulties of an undertaking; and he was anxious to retrieve his honour by more successful and more gallant enterprizes. For this purpose, he had, during the course of the campaign, sent orders to summon a parliament by his son Edward, whom he had left with the title of guardian, and to demand some supply in his urgent necessities. The barons seemed inclined to grant his request; but the knights, who often, at this time, acted as a separate body from the burgesses, made some scruple of taxing their constituents, without their consent; and they desired the guardian to summon a new parliament, which might be properly impowered for that purpose. The situation of the king and parliament was, for the time, nearly similar to that which they constantly fell into about the beginning of the last century, and similar consequences began visibly to appear. The king, sensible of the frequent demands which he should be obliged to make on his people, had been anxious to ensure to his friends a seat in the house of commons, and at his instigation, the sheriffs and other placemen had made interest to be elected into that assembly; an abuse which the knights desired the king to correct by the tenor of his writ of summons, and which was accordingly

[c] Froissard, liv. i. chap. 41, 42, 43. Heming. p. 307. Walsing. p. 143.
[d] Cotton's Abridg. p. 17.

remedied. On the other hand, the knights had professedly annexed conditions to their intended grant, and required a considerable retrenchment of the royal prerogatives, particularly with regard to purveyance, and the levying of the ancient feudal aids for knighting the king's eldest son, and marrying his eldest daughter. The new parliament, called by the guardian, retained the same free spirit; and though they offered a large supply of 30,000 sacks of wool, no business was concluded; because the conditions, which they annexed, appeared too high to be compensated by a temporary concession. But when Edward himself came over to England, he summoned another parliament, and he had the interest to procure a supply on more moderate terms. A confirmation of the two charters and of the privileges of boroughs, a pardon for old debts and trespasses, and a remedy for some abuses in the execution of common law, were the chief conditions insisted on, and the king, in return for his concessions on these heads, obtained from the barons and knights an unusual grant for two years of the ninth sheaf, lamb, and fleece on their estates, and from the burgesses, a ninth of their moveables at their true value. The whole parliament also granted a duty of forty shillings on each sack of wool exported, on each three hundred wool-fells, and on each last of leather for the same term of years; but dreading the arbitrary spirit of the crown, they expressly declared, that this grant was to continue no longer, and was not to be drawn into precedent. Being soon after sensible, that this supply, though considerable and very unusual in that age, would come in slowly, and would not answer the king's urgent necessities, proceeding both from his debts, and his preparations for war; they agreed, that 20,000 sacks of wool should immediately be granted him, and their value be deducted from the ninths, which were afterwards to be levied.

But there appeared, at this time, another jealousy in the parliament, which was very reasonable, and was founded on a sentiment that ought to have engaged them rather to check than support the king in all those ambitious projects, so little likely to prove successful, and so dangerous to the nation, if they did. Edward, who, before the commencement of the former campaign, had, in several commissions, assumed the title of king of France, now

CHAPTER XV

more openly, in all public deeds, gave himself that appellation, and always quartered the arms of France with those of England in his seals and ensigns. The parliament thought proper to obviate the consequences of this measure, and to declare, that they owed him no obedience as king of France, and that the two kingdoms must for ever remain distinct and independant.[e] They undoubtedly foresaw, that France, if subdued, would in the end prove the seat of government; and they deemed this previous protestation necessary, in order to prevent their becoming a province to that monarchy. A frail security, if the event had really taken place!

As Philip was apprized, from the preparations which were making both in England and the Low Countries, that he must expect another invasion from Edward, he fitted out a great fleet of 400 vessels; manned with 40,000 men; and he stationed them off Sluise, with a view of intercepting the king in his passage. The English navy was much inferior in number, consisting only of 240 sail; but whether it were by the superior abilities of Edward, or the greater dexterity of his seamen, they gained the wind of the enemy, and had the sun in their backs; and with these advantages began the action. The battle was fierce and bloody: The English archers, whose force and address were now much celebrated, galled the French on their approach: And when the ships grappled together, and the contest became more steady and furious, the example of the king, and of so many gallant nobles, who accompanied him, animated to such a degree the seamen and soldiery, that they maintained every where a superiority over the enemy. The French also had been guilty of some imprudence in taking their station so near the coast of Flanders, and chusing that place for the scene of action. The Flemings, descrying the battle, hurried out of their harbours, and brought a reinforcement to the English; which, coming unexpectedly, had a greater effect than in proportion to its power and numbers. Two hundred and thirty French ships were taken: Thirty thousand Frenchmen were killed, with two of their admirals: The loss of the English was inconsiderable, compared to the greatness and importance of the victory.[f] None of Philip's courtiers, it is said, dared to inform him of the

1340.

Naval victory. 13th June.

[e] 14 Edward III. [f] Froissard, liv. i. chap. 51. Avesbury, p. 56. Heming. p. 321.

event; till his fool or jester gave him a hint, by which he discovered the loss that he had sustained.[g]

The lustre of this great success encreased the king's authority among his allies, who assembled their forces with expedition, and joined the English army. Edward marched to the frontiers of France at the head of above 100,000 men, consisting chiefly of foreigners, a more numerous army than, either before or since, has ever been commanded by any king of England.[h] At the same time, the Flemings, to the number of 50,000 men, marched out under the command of Robert of Artois, and laid siege to St. Omer; but this tumultuary army, composed entirely of tradesmen, unexperienced in war, was routed by a sally of the garrison, and notwithstanding the abilities of their leader, was thrown into such a panic, that they were instantly dispersed, and never more appeared in the field. The enterprizes of Edward, though not attended with so inglorious an issue, proved equally vain and fruitless. The king of France had assembled an army more numerous than the English; was accompanied by all the chief nobility of his kingdom; was attended by many foreign princes, and even by three monarchs, the kings of Bohemia, Scotland, and Navarre:[i] Yet he still adhered to the prudent resolution of putting nothing to hazard, and after throwing strong garrisons into all the frontier towns, he retired backwards, persuaded, that the enemy, having wasted their force in some tedious and unsuccessful enterprize, would afford him an easy victory.

Tournay was at that time one of the most considerable cities of Flanders, containing above 60,000 inhabitants of all ages, who were affectionate to the French government; and as the secret of Edward's design had not been strictly kept, Philip learned, that the English, in order to gratify their Flemish allies, had intended to open the campaign with the siege of this place: He took care therefore to supply it with a garrison of 14,000 men, commanded by the bravest nobility of France; and he reasonably expected, that these forces, joined to the inhabitants, would be able to defend the city against all the efforts of the enemy. Accordingly, Edward, when he commenced the siege about the end of July, found every where an obstinate resistance: The valour of one side was encoun-

[g] Walsing. p. 148.   [h] Rymer, vol. v. p. 197.   [i] Froissard, liv. i. chap. 57.

CHAPTER XV

tered with equal valour by the other: Every assault was repulsed
and proved unsuccessful: And the king was at last obliged to turn
the siege into a blockade, in hopes that the great numbers of the
garrison and citizens, which had enabled them to defend themselves against his attacks, would but expose them to be the more
easily reduced by famine.[k] The count of Eu, who commanded in
Tournay, as soon as he perceived that the English had formed this
plan of operations, endeavoured to save his provisions, by expelling all the useless mouths; and the duke of Brabant, who
wished no success to Edward's enterprizes, gave every one a free
passage through his quarters.

After the siege had continued ten weeks, the city was reduced
to distress; and Philip, recalling all his scattered garrisons, advanced towards the English camp at the head of a mighty army,
with an intention of still avoiding any decisive action, but of
seeking some opportunity for throwing relief into the place. Here
Edward, irritated with the small progress he had hitherto made,
and with the disagreeable prospect that lay before him, sent Philip
a defiance by a herald; and challenged him to decide their claims
for the crown of France, either by single combat, or by an action
of a hundred against a hundred, or by a general engagement.
But Philip replied, that Edward having done homage to him for
the dutchy of Guienne, and having solemnly acknowledged him
for his superior, it by no means became him to send a defiance
to his liege lord and sovereign: That he was confident, notwithstanding all Edward's preparations, and his conjunction with the
rebellious Flemings, he himself should soon be able to chace him
from the frontiers of France: That as the hostilities from England
had prevented him from executing his purposed crusade against
the infidels, he trusted in the assistance of the Almighty, who
would reward his pious intentions, and punish the aggressor,
whose ill-grounded claims had rendered them abortive: That
Edward proposed a duel on very unequal terms, and offered to
hazard only his own person, against both the kingdom of France,
and the person of the king: But that, if he would encrease the
stake, and put also the kingdom of England on the issue of the
duel, he would, notwithstanding that the terms would still be

[k] Froissard, liv. i. chap. 54.

unequal, very willingly accept of the challenge.[l] It was easy to see, that these mutual bravadoes were intended only to dazzle the populace, and that the two kings were too wise to think of executing their pretended purpose.

While the French and English armies lay in this situation, and a general action was every day expected, Jane, countess dowager of Hainault, interposed with her good offices, and endeavoured to conciliate peace between the contending monarchs, and to prevent any farther effusion of blood. This princess was mother-in-law to Edward, and sister to Philip; and though she had taken the vows in a convent, and had renounced the world, she left her retreat on this occasion, and employed all her pious efforts to allay those animosities, which had taken place between persons so nearly related to her, and to each other. As Philip had no material claims on his antagonist, she found that he hearkened willingly to the proposals; and even the haughty and ambitious Edward, convinced of his fruitless attempt, was not averse to her negociation. He was sensible from experience, that he had engaged in an enterprize which far exceeded his force; and that the power of England was never likely to prevail over that of a superior kingdom, firmly united under an able and prudent monarch. He discovered, that all the allies, whom he could gain by negociation, were at bottom averse to his enterprize; and though they might second it to a certain length, would immediately detach themselves, and oppose its final accomplishment, if ever they could be brought to think, that there was seriously any danger of it. He even saw, that their chief purpose was to obtain money from him; and as his supplies from England came in very slowly, and had much disappointed his expectations, he perceived their growing indifference in his cause, and their desire of embracing all plausible terms of accommodation. Convinced at last, that an undertaking must be imprudent, which could only be supported by means so unequal to the end, he *31 Sept.* concluded a truce, which left both parties in possession of their present acquisitions, and stopped all farther hostilities on the side of the Low Countries, Guienne, and Scotland, till Midsummer next.[m] A negociation was soon after opened at Arras, under the

[l] Du Tillet, Recueil de Traitéz, &c. Heming. p. 325, 326. Walsing. p. 149.
[m] Froissard, liv. i. chap. 64. Avesbury, p. 65.

CHAPTER XV

mediation of the pope's legates; and the truce was attempted to be converted into a solid peace. Edward here required, that Philip should free Guienne from all claims of superiority, and entirely withdraw his protection from Scotland: But as he seemed not any wise entitled to make such high demands, either from his past successes, or future prospects, they were totally rejected by Philip, who agreed only to a prolongation of the truce.

The king of France soon after detached the emperor Lewis from the alliance of England, and engaged him to revoke the title of imperial vicar, which he had conferred on Edward.[n] The king's other allies on the frontiers of France, disappointed in their hopes, gradually withdrew from the confederacy. And Edward himself, harassed by his numerous and importunate creditors, was obliged to make his escape by stealth into England.

The unusual tax of a ninth sheaf, lamb, and fleece, imposed by parliament, together with the great want of money, and still more, of credit in England, had rendered the remittances to Flanders extremely backward; nor could it be expected, that any expeditious method of collecting an imposition, which was so new in itself, and which yielded only a gradual produce, could possibly be contrived by the king or his ministers. And though the parliament, foreseeing the inconvenience, had granted, as a present resource, 20,000 sacks of wool, the only English goods that bore a sure price in foreign markets, and were the next to ready money; it was impossible, but the getting possession of such a bulky commodity, the gathering of it from different parts of the kingdom, and the disposing of it abroad, must take up more time than the urgency of the king's affairs would permit, and must occasion all the disappointments complained of, during the course of the campaign. But though nothing had happened, which Edward might not reasonably have foreseen, he was so irritated with the unfortunate issue of his military operations, and so much vexed and affronted by his foreign creditors, that he was determined to throw the blame somewhere off himself, and he came in very bad humour into England. He discovered his peevish disposition by the first act which he performed after his arrival: As he landed unexpectedly, he found the Tower negligently guarded; and he immediately committed to prison, the constable

Domestic disturbances.

[n] Heming. p. 352. Ypod. Neust. p. 514. Knyghton, p. 2580.

and all others who had the charge of that fortress, and he treated them with unusual rigour.[o] His vengeance fell next on the officers of the revenue, the sheriffs, the collectors of the taxes, the undertakers of all kinds; and besides dismissing all of them from their employments, he appointed commissions to enquire into their conduct; and these men, in order to gratify the king's humour, were sure not to find any person innocent, who came before them.[p] Sir John St. Paul, keeper of the privy seal, Sir John Stonore, chief justice, Andrew Aubrey, mayor of London, were displaced and imprisoned; as were also the bishop of Chichester, chancellor, and the bishop of Lichfield, treasurer. Stratford, archbishop of Canterbury, to whom the charge of collecting the new taxes had been chiefly entrusted, fell likewise under the king's displeasure; but being absent at the time of Edward's arrival, he escaped feeling the immediate effects of it.

There were strong reasons, which might discourage the kings of England, in those ages, from bestowing the chief offices of the crown on prelates and other ecclesiastical persons. These men had so entrenched themselves in privileges and immunities, and so openly challenged an exemption from all secular jurisdiction, that no civil penalty could be inflicted on them for any malversation in office; and as even treason itself was declared to be no canonical offence, nor was allowed to be a sufficient reason for deprivation or other spiritual censures, that order of men had ensured to themselves an almost total impunity, and were not bound by any political law or statute. But, on the other hand, there were many peculiar causes which favoured their promotion. Besides that they possessed almost all the learning of the age, and were best qualified for civil employments; the prelates enjoyed equal dignity with the greatest barons, and gave weight, by their personal authority, to the powers entrusted with them: While, at the same time, they did not endanger the crown by accumulating wealth or influence in their families, and were restrained, by the decency of their character, from that open rapine and violence, so often practised by the nobles. These motives had induced Edward, as well as many of his predecessors, to entrust the chief departments of govern-

[o] Ypod. Neust. p. 513.   [p] Avesbury, p. 70. Heming. p. 326. Walsingham, p. 150.

CHAPTER XV

ment in the hands of ecclesiastics; at the hazard of seeing them disown his authority as soon as it was turned against them.

This was the case with archbishop Stratford. That prelate, *1341.* informed of Edward's indignation against him, prepared himself for the storm; and not content with standing upon the defensive, he resolved, by beginning the attack, to show the king, that he knew the privileges of his character, and had courage to maintain them. He issued a general sentence of excommunication against all, who, on any pretext, exercised violence on the person or goods of clergymen; who infringed those privileges secured by the great charter, and by ecclesiastical canons; or who accused a prelate of treason or any other crime, in order to bring him under the king's displeasure.[q] Even Edward had reason to think himself struck at by this sentence; both on account of the imprisonment of the two bishops and that of other clergymen concerned in levying the taxes, and on account of his seizing their lands and moveables, that he might make them answerable for any balance, which remained in their hands. The clergy, with the primate at their head, were now formed into a regular combination against the king; and many calumnies were spread against him, in order to deprive him of the confidence and affections of his people. It was pretended, that he meant to recal the general pardon, and the remission which he had granted of old debts, and to impose new and arbitrary taxes without consent of parliament. The archbishop went so far, in a letter to the king himself, as to tell him, that there were two powers, by which the world was governed, the holy pontifical apostolic dignity, and the royal subordinate authority: That of these two powers, the clerical was evidently the supreme; since the priests were to answer, at the tribunal of the divine judgment, for the conduct of kings themselves: That the clergy were the spiritual fathers of all the faithful, and amongst others of kings and princes; and were intitled, by a heavenly charter, to direct their wills and actions, and to censure their transgressions: And that prelates had heretofore cited emperors before their tribunal, had sitten in judgment on their life and behaviour, and had anathematized them for their obstinate offences.[r] These topics were not well calculated to

[q] Heming. p. 339. Ang. Sacra, vol. i. p. 21, 22. Walsingham, p. 153.
[r] Anglia Sacra, vol. i. p. 27.

appease Edward's indignation; and when he called a parliament, he sent not to the primate, as to the other peers, a summons to attend it. Stratford was not discouraged at this mark of neglect or anger: He appeared before the gates, arrayed in his pontifical robes, holding the crosier in his hand, and accompanied by a pompous train of priests and prelates; and he required admittance as the first and highest peer in the realm. During two days, the king rejected his application: But sensible, either that this affair might be attended with dangerous consequences, or that in his impatience he had groundlessly accused the primate of malversation in his office, which seems really to have been the case; he at last permitted him to take his seat, and was reconciled to him.[s]

Edward now found himself in a bad situation both with his own people and with foreign states; and it required all his genius and capacity to extricate himself from such multiplied difficulties and embarrassments. His unjust and exorbitant claims on France and Scotland had engaged him in an implacable war with these two kingdoms, his nearest neighbours: He had lost almost all his foreign alliances by his irregular payments: He was deeply involved in debts, for which he owed a consuming interest: His military operations had vanished into smoke; and except his naval victory, none of them had been attended even with glory or renown, either to himself or to the nation: The animosity between him and the clergy was open and declared: The people were discontented on account of many arbitrary measures, in which he had been engaged: And what was more dangerous, the nobility, taking advantage of his present necessities, were determined to retrench his power, and by encroaching on the ancient prerogatives of the crown, to acquire to themselves independance and authority. But the aspiring genius of Edward, which had so far transported him beyond the bounds of discretion, proved at last sufficient to reinstate him in his former authority, and finally to render his reign the most triumphant that is to be met with in English story: Though for the present he was obliged, with some loss of honour, to yield to the current, which bore so strongly against him.

The parliament framed an act, which was likely to produce considerable innovations in the government. They premised,

[s] Anglia Sacra, vol. i. p. 38, 39, 40, 41.

that, whereas the great charter had, to the manifest peril and slander of the king and damage of his people, been violated in many points, particularly by the imprisonment of free men and the seizure of their goods, without suit, indictment, or trial, it was necessary to confirm it anew, and to oblige all the chief officers of the law, together with the steward and chamberlain of the household, the keeper of the privy-seal, the controller and treasurer of the wardrobe, and those who were entrusted with the education of the young prince, to swear to the regular observance of it. They also remarked, that the peers of the realm had formerly been arrested and imprisoned, and dispossessed of their temporalities and lands, and even some of them put to death, without judgment or trial; and they therefore enacted that such violences should henceforth cease, and no peer be punished but by the award of his peers *in parliament*. They required, that, whenever any of the great offices above mentioned became vacant, the king should fill it by the advice of his council, and the consent of such barons as should at that time be found to reside in the neighbourhood of the court. And they enacted, that, on the third day of every session, the king should resume into his own hand all these offices, except those of justices of the two benches and the barons of exchequer; that the ministers should for the time be reduced to private persons; that they should in that condition answer before parliament to any accusation brought against them; and that, if they were found any wise guilty, they should finally be dispossessed of their offices, and more able persons be substituted in their place.[t] By these last regulations, the barons approached as near as they durst to those restrictions, which had formerly been imposed on Henry III. and Edward II. and which, from the dangerous consequences attending them, had become so generally odious, that they did not expect to have either the concurrence of the people in demanding them, or the assent of the present king in granting them.

In return for these important concessions, the parliament offered the king a grant of 20,000 sacks of wool; and his wants were so urgent, from the clamours of his creditors, and the demands of his foreign allies, that he was obliged to accept of the supply

[t] 15 Edw. III.

on these hard conditions. He ratified this statute in full parliament; but he *secretly* entered a protest of such a nature, as were sufficient, one should imagine, to destroy all future trust and confidence with his people: He declared, that, as soon as his convenience permitted, he would, from his own authority, revoke what had been extorted from him.[u] Accordingly, he was no sooner possessed of the parliamentary supply, than he issued an edict, which contains many extraordinary positions and pretensions. He first asserts, that that statute had been enacted contrary to law; as if a free legislative body could ever do any thing illegal. He next affirms, that, as it was hurtful to the prerogatives of the crown which he had sworn to defend, he had only dissembled, when he seemed to ratify it, but that he had never in his own breast given his assent to it. He does not pretend, that either he or the parliament lay under force; but only that some inconvenience would have ensued, had he not seemingly affixed his sanction to that pretended statute. He therefore, with the advice of his council and of *some* earls and barons, abrogates and annuls it; and though he professes himself willing and determined to observe such articles of it as were formerly law, he declares it to have thenceforth no force or authority.[w] The parliaments, that were afterwards assembled, took no notice of this arbitrary exertion of royal power, which, by a parity of reason, left all their laws at the mercy of the king; and during the course of two years, Edward had so far reestablished his influence, and freed himself from his present necessities, that he then obtained from his parliament a legal repeal of the obnoxious statute.[x] This transaction certainly contains remarkable circumstances, which discover the manners and sentiments of the age, and may prove what inaccurate work might be expected from such rude hands, when employed in legislation, and in rearing the delicate fabric of laws and a constitution.

But though Edward had happily recovered his authority at home, which had been impaired by the events of the French war, he had undergone so many mortifications from that attempt, and

[u] Statutes at Large, 15 Edw. III. That this protest of the king's was *secret* appears evidently, since otherwise it would have been ridiculous in the parliament to have accepted of his assent: Besides the king owns that he *dissembled*, which would not have been the case, had his protest been public.
[w] Statutes at Large, 15 Edw. III.   [x] Cotton's Abridgm. p. 38, 39.

CHAPTER XV

saw so little prospect of success, that he would probably have dropped his claim, had not a revolution in Britanny opened to him more promising views, and given his enterprizing genius a full opportunity of displaying itself.

John III. duke of Britanny, had, during some years, found himself declining through age and infirmities; and having no issue, he was solicitous to prevent those disorders, to which, on the event of his demise, a disputed succession might expose his subjects. His younger brother, the count of Penthievre, had left only one daughter, whom the duke deemed his heir; and as his family had inherited the dutchy by a female succession, he thought her title preferable to that of the count of Mountfort, who, being his brother by a second marriage, was the male heir of that principality.[y] He accordingly purposed to bestow his niece in marriage on some person, who might be able to defend her rights; and he cast his eye on Charles of Blois, nephew of the king of France, by his mother, Margaret of Valois, sister to that monarch. But as he both loved his subjects and was beloved by them, he determined not to take this important step without their approbation; and having assembled the states of Britanny, he represented to them the advantages of that alliance, and the prospect, which it gave, of an entire settlement of the succession. The Bretons willingly concurred in his choice: The marriage was concluded: All his vassals, and among the rest, the count of Mountfort, swore fealty to Charles and to his consort as to their future sovereigns: And every danger of civil commotions seemed to be obviated, as far as human prudence could provide a remedy against them.

But on the death of this good prince, the ambition of the count of Mountfort broke through all these regulations, and kindled a war, not only dangerous to Britanny, but to a great part of Europe. While Charles of Blois was soliciting at the court of France the investiture of the dutchy, Mountfort was active in acquiring immediate possession of it; and by force or intrigue he made himself master of Rennes, Nantz, Brest, Hennebonne, and all the most important fortresses, and engaged many considerable barons to acknowledge his authority.[z] Sensible that he could expect no favour from Philip, he made a voyage to England, on pretence of

Affairs of Britanny.

[y] Froissard, liv. i. chap. 64.   [z] Froissard, liv. i. chap. 65, 66, 67, 68.

soliciting his claim to the earldom of Richmond, which had devolved to him by his brother's death; and there, offering to do homage to Edward, as king of France, for the dutchy of Britanny, he proposed a strict alliance for the support of their mutual pretensions. Edward saw immediately the advantages attending this treaty: Mountfort, an active and valiant prince, closely united to him by interest, opened at once an entrance into the heart of France, and afforded him much more flattering views, than his allies on the side of Germany and the Low Countries, who had no sincere attachment to his cause, and whose progress was also obstructed by those numerous fortifications, which had been raised on that frontier. Robert of Artois was zealous in inforcing these considerations: The ambitious spirit of Edward was little disposed to sit down under those repulses which he had received, and

Renewal of the war with France. which, he thought, had so much impaired his reputation: And it required a very short negociation to conclude a treaty of alliance between two men; who, though their pleas with regard to the preference of male or female succession were directly opposite, were intimately connected by their immediate interests.[a]

As this treaty was still a secret, Mountfort, on his return, ventured to appear at Paris, in order to defend his cause before the court of peers; but observing Philip and his judges to be prepossessed against his title, and dreading their intentions of arresting him, till he should restore what he had seized by violence, he suddenly made his escape; and war immediately commenced between him and Charles of Blois.[b] Philip sent his eldest son, the duke of Normandy, with a powerful army, to the assistance of the latter; and Mountfort, unable to keep the field against his rival, remained in the city of Nantz, where he was besieged. The city was taken by the treachery of the inhabitants; Mountfort fell into the hands of his enemies; was conducted as a prisoner to Paris; and was shut up in the tower of the Louvre.[c]

1342. This event seemed to put an end to the pretensions of the count of Mountfort; but his affairs were immediately retrieved by an unexpected incident, which inspired new life and vigour into his party. Jane of Flanders, countess of Mountfort, the most extraordinary woman of the age, was rouzed, by the

[a] Froissard, liv. i. chap. 69.   [b] Ibid. chap. 70, 71.   [c] Ibid. chap. 73.

CHAPTER XV

captivity of her husband, from those domestic cares, to which she had hitherto limited her genius; and she courageously undertook to support the falling fortunes of her family. No sooner did she receive the fatal intelligence, than she assembled the inhabitants of Rennes, where she then resided; and carrying her infant son in her arms, deplored to them the calamity of their sovereign. She recommended to their care the illustrious orphan, the sole male remaining of their ancient princes, who had governed them with such indulgence and lenity, and to whom they had ever professed the most zealous attachment. She declared herself willing to run all hazards with them in so just a cause; discovered the resources which still remained in the alliance of England; and entreated them to make one effort against an usurper, who, being imposed on them by the arms of France, would in return make a sacrifice to his protector of the ancient liberties of Britanny. The audience, moved by the affecting appearance, and inspirited by the noble conduct, of the princess, vowed to live and die with her in defending the rights of her family: All the other fortresses of Britanny embraced the same resolution: The countess went from place to place, encouraging the garrisons, providing them with every thing necessary for subsistance, and concerting the proper plans of defence; and after she had put the whole province in a good posture, she shut herself up in Hennebonne, where she waited with impatience the arrival of those succours, which Edward had promised her. Mean while, she sent over her son to England, that she might both put him in a place of safety, and engage the king more strongly, by such a pledge, to embrace with zeal the interests of her family.

Charles of Blois, anxious to make himself master of so important a fortress as Hennebone, and still more to take the countess prisoner, from whose vigour and capacity all the difficulties to his succession in Britanny now proceeded, sat down before the place, with a great army, composed of French, Spaniards, Genoese, and some Bretons; and he conducted the attack with indefatigable industry.[d] The defence was no less vigorous: The besiegers were repulsed in every assault: Frequent sallies were made with success by the garrison: And the countess herself being the

_____

[d] Froissard, liv. i. chap. 81.

most forward in all military operations, every one was ashamed not to exert himself to the utmost in this desperate situation. One day she perceived, that the besiegers, entirely occupied in an attack, had neglected a distant quarter of their camp; and she immediately sallied forth at the head of a body of 200 cavalry, threw them into confusion, did great execution upon them, and set fire to their tents, baggage, and magazines: But when she was preparing to return, she found that she was intercepted, and that a considerable body of the enemy had thrown themselves between her and the gates. She instantly took her resolution: She ordered her men to disband, and to make the best of their way by flight to Brest: She met them at the appointed place of rendezvous, collected another body of 500 horse, returned to Hennebonne, broke unexpectedly through the enemy's camp, and was received with shouts and acclamations by the garrison, who, encouraged by this reinforcement, and by so rare an example of female valour, determined to defend themselves to the last extremity.

The reiterated attacks, however, of the besiegers had at length made several breaches in the walls; and it was apprehended, that a general assault, which was every hour expected, would overpower the garrison, diminished in numbers, and extremely weakened with watching and fatigue. It became necessary to treat of a capitulation; and the bishop of Leon was already engaged, for that purpose, in a conference with Charles of Blois; when the countess, who had mounted to a high tower, and was looking towards the sea with great impatience, descried some sails at a distance. She immediately exclaimed: *Behold the succours! the English succours! No capitulation.*[e] This fleet had on board a body of heavy-armed cavalry, and six thousand archers, whom Edward had prepared for the relief of Hennebonne, but who had been long detained by contrary winds. They entered the harbour under the command of Sir Walter Manny, one of the bravest captains of England; and having inspired fresh courage into the garrison, immediately sallied forth, beat the besiegers from all their posts, and obliged them to decamp.

But notwithstanding this success, the countess of Mountfort found that her party, overpowerd by numbers, was declining in

[e] Froissard, liv. i. chap. 81.

CHAPTER XV

every quarter; and she went over to solicit more effectual succours from the king of England. Edward granted her a considerable reinforcement under Robert of Artois; who embarked on board a fleet of forty-five ships, and sailed to Britanny. He was met in his passage by the enemy; an action ensued, where the countess behaved with her wonted valour, and charged the enemy sword in hand; but the hostile fleets, after a sharp action, were separated by a storm, and the English arrived safely in Britanny. The first exploit of Robert was the taking of Vannes, which he mastered by conduct and address:[f] But he survived a very little time this prosperity. The Breton noblemen of the party of Charles assembled secretly in arms, attacked Vannes of a sudden, and carried the place; chiefly by reason of a wound received by Robert, of which he soon after died at sea on his return to England.[g]

After the death of this unfortunate prince, the chief author of all the calamities, with which his country was overwhelmed for more than a century, Edward undertook in person the defence of the countess of Mountfort; and as the last truce with France was now expired, the war, which the English and French had hitherto carried on as allies to the competitors for Britanny, was thenceforth conducted in the name and under the standard of the two monarchs. The king landed at Morbian near Vannes, with an army of 12,000 men; and being master of the field, he endeavoured to give a lustre to his arms, by commencing at once three important sieges, that of Vannes, of Rennes, and of Nantz. But by undertaking too much, he failed of success in all his enterprizes. Even the siege of Vannes, which Edward in person conducted with vigour, advanced but slowly;[h] and the French had all the leisure requisite for making preparations against him. The duke of Normandy, eldest son of Philip, appeared in Britanny at the head of an army of 30,000 infantry, and 4000 cavalry; and Edward was now obliged to draw together all his forces, and to entrench himself strongly before Vannes, where the duke of Normandy soon after arrived, and in a manner invested the besiegers. The garrison and the French camp were plentifully supplied with provisions; while the English, who durst not make any attempt upon the place in the presence of a superior army, drew all their subsistance from

[f] Ibid. chap. 93.   [g] Ibid. chap. 94.   [h] Froissard, liv. i. chap. 95.

England, exposed to the hazards of the sea, and sometimes to those which arose from the fleet of the enemy. In this dangerous situation, Edward willingly hearkened to the mediation of the pope's legates, the cardinals of Palestrine and Frescati, who endeavoured to negociate, if not a peace, at least a truce between the two kingdoms. A treaty was concluded for a cessation of arms during three years;[i] and Edward had the abilities, notwithstanding his present dangerous situation, to procure to himself very equal and honourable terms. It was agreed, that Vannes should be sequestered, during the truce, in the hands of the legates, to be disposed of afterwards as they pleased; and though Edward knew the partiality of the court of Rome towards his antagonists, he saved himself by this device from the dishonour of having undertaken a fruitless enterprize. It was also stipulated, that all prisoners should be released, that the places in Britanny should remain in the hands of the present possessors, and that the allies on both sides should be comprehended in the truce.[k] Edward, soon after concluding this treaty, embarked with his army for England.

The truce, though calculated for a long time, was of very short duration; and each monarch endeavoured to throw on the other the blame of its infraction. Of course, the historians of the two countries differ in their account of the matter. It seems probable, however, as is affirmed by the French writers, that Edward, in consenting to the truce, had no other view than to extricate himself from a perilous situation, into which he had fallen, and was afterwards very careless in observing it. In all the memorials which remain on this subject, he complains chiefly of the punishment inflicted on Oliver de Clisson, John de Montauban, and other Breton noblemen, who, he says, were partizans of the family of Mountfort, and consequently under the protection of England.[l] But it appears, that, at the conclusion of the truce, those noblemen had openly, by their declarations and actions, embraced the cause of Charles of Blois;[m] and if they had entered into any secret correspondence and engagements with Edward, they were traitors to their party, and were justly punishable by Philip and Charles, for

[i] Ibid. chap. 99. Avesbury, p. 102.   [k] Heming. p. 359.   [l] Rymer, vol. v. p. 453, 454, 459, 466, 496. Heming. p. 376.   [m] Froissard, liv. x. chap. 96. p. 100.

CHAPTER XV

their breach of faith; nor had Edward any ground of complaint against France for such severities. But when he laid these pretended injuries before the parliament, whom he affected to consult *1344.* on all occasions, that assembly entered into the quarrel, advised the king not to be amused by a fraudulent truce, and granted him supplies for the renewal of the war: The counties were charged with a fifteenth for two years, and the boroughs with a tenth. The clergy consented to give a tenth for three years.

These supplies enabled the king to complete his military preparations; and he sent his cousin, Henry earl of Derby, son of the earl of Lancaster, into Guienne, for the defence of that province.[n] This prince, the most accomplished in the English court, possessed to a high degree the virtues of justice and humanity, as well as those of valour and conduct,[o] and not content with protecting and cherishing the province committed to his care, he made a successful invasion on the enemy. He attacked the count of Lisle, the French general, at Bergerac, beat him from his entrenchments, and took the place. He reduced a great part of Perigord, and continually advanced in his conquests, till the count of Lisle, having collected an army of ten or twelve thousand men, sat down *1345.* before Auberoche, in hopes of recovering that place, which had fallen into the hands of the English. The earl of Derby came upon him by surprize with only a thousand cavalry, threw the French into disorder, pushed his advantage, and obtained a complete victory. Lisle himself, with many considerable nobles, was taken prisoner.[p] After this important success, Derby made a rapid progress in subduing the French provinces. He took Monsegur, Monpesat, Villefranche, Miremont, and Tonnins, with the fortress of Damassen. Aiguillon, a fortress deemed impregnable, fell into his hands from the cowardice of the governor. Angouleme was surrendered after a short siege. The only place, where he met with considerable resistance, was Reole, which, however, was at last

---

[n] Froissard, liv. i. chap. 103. Avesbury, p. 121.   [o] It is reported of this prince, that, having once, before the attack of a town, promised the soldiers the plunder, one private man happened to fall upon a great chest full of money, which he immediately brought to the earl, as thinking it too great for himself to keep possession of it. But Derby told him, that his promise did not depend on the greatness or smallness of the sum; and ordered him to keep it all for his own use.   [p] Froissard, liv. i. chap. 104.

reduced after a siege of above nine weeks.[q] He made an attempt on Blaye, but thought it more prudent to raise the siege, than waste his time before a place of small importance.[r]

1346. The reason, why Derby was permitted to make, without opposition, such progress on the side of Guienne, was the difficulties under which the French finances then laboured, and which had obliged Philip to lay on new impositions, particularly the duty on salt, to the great discontent, and almost mutiny of his subjects. But after the court of France was supplied with money, great preparations were made; and the duke of Normandy, attended by the duke of Burgundy, and other great nobility, led towards Guienne a powerful army, which the English could not think of resisting in the open field. The earl of Derby stood on the defensive, and allowed the French to carry on at leisure the siege of Angouleme, which was their first enterprize. John lord Norwich, the governor, after a brave and vigorous defence, found himself reduced to such extremities, as obliged him to employ a stratagem, in order to save his garrison, and to prevent his being reduced to surrender at discretion. He appeared on the walls, and desired a parley with the duke of Normandy. The prince there told Norwich, that he supposed he intended to capitulate. "Not at all," replied the governor: "But as to-morrow is the feast of the Virgin, to whom, I know, that you, Sir, as well as myself, bear a devotion, I desire a cessation of arms for that day." The proposal was agreed to; and Norwich, having ordered his forces to prepare all their baggage, marched out next day, and advanced towards the French camp. The besiegers, imagining they were to be attacked, ran to their arms; but Norwich sent a messenger to the duke, reminding him of his engagement. The duke, who piqued himself on faithfully keeping his word, exclaimed, *I see the governor has outwitted me: But let us be content with gaining the place:* And the English were allowed to pass through the camp unmolested.[s] After some other successes, the duke of Normandy laid siege to Aiguillon; and as the natural strength of the fortress, together with a brave garrison under the command of the earl of Pembroke, and Sir Walter Manny, rendered it impossible to take the place by assault, he purposed, after making several fruitless attacks,[t] to reduce it by

[q] Ibid. chap. 110. [r] Ibid. chap. 112. [s] Froissard, liv. i. chap. 120.
[t] Ibid. chap. 121.

CHAPTER XV

famine: But before he could finish this enterprize, he was called to another quarter of the kingdom, by one of the greatest disasters that ever befel the French monarchy.[u]

Edward, informed by the earl of Derby of the great danger to which Guienne was exposed, had prepared a force with which he intended in person to bring it relief. He embarked at Southampton on board a fleet of near a thousand sail of all dimensions; and carried with him, besides all the chief nobility of England, his eldest son the prince of Wales, now fifteen years of age. The winds proved long contrary;[w] and the king, in despair of arriving in time at Guienne, was at last persuaded by Geoffry d'Harcourt, to change the destination of his enterprize. This nobleman was a Norman by birth, had long made a considerable figure in the court of France, and was generally esteemed for his personal merit and his valour; but being disobliged and persecuted by Philip, he had fled into England; had recommended himself to Edward, who was an excellent judge of men; and had succeeded to Robert of Artois in the invidious office of exciting and assisting the king in every enterprize against his native country. He had long insisted, that an expedition to Normandy promised, in the present circumstances, more favourable success, than one to Guienne; that Edward would find the northern provinces almost destitute of military force, which had been drawn to the south; that they were full of flourishing cities, whose plunder would enrich the English; that their cultivated fields, as yet unspoiled by war, would supply them with plenty of provisions; and that the neighbourhood of the capital rendered every event of importance in those quarters.[x] These reasons, which had not before been duly weighed by Edward, began to make more impression after the disappointments which he had met with in his voyage to Guienne: He ordered his fleet to sail to Normandy, and safely disembarked his army at la Hogue. *12th July.*

This army, which, during the course of the ensuing campaign, was crowned with the most splendid success, consisted of four thousand men at arms, ten thousand archers, ten thousand Welsh infantry, and six thousand Irish. The Welsh and the Irish were light, disorderly troops, fitter for doing execution in a pursuit, or scouring the country, than for any stable action. The bow was always esteemed a frivolous weapon, where true military discipline *Invasion of France.*

[u] Ibid. chap. 134.   [w] Avesbury, p. 123.   [x] Froissard, liv. i. chap. 121.

was known, and regular bodies of well-armed foot maintained. The only solid force in this army were the men at arms; and even these, being cavalry, were, on that account, much inferior, in the shock of battle, to good infantry: And as the whole were new levied troops, we are led to entertain a very mean idea of the military force of those ages, which, being ignorant of every other art, had not properly cultivated the art of war itself, the sole object of general attention.

The king created the earl of Arundel constable of his army, and the earls of Warwic and Harcourt, mareschals: He bestowed the honour of knighthood on the prince of Wales and several of the young nobility, immediately upon his landing. After destroying all the ships in la Hogue, Barfleur, and Cherbourg, he spread his army over the whole country, and gave them an unbounded licence of burning, spoiling, and plundering every place, of which they became masters. The loose discipline, then prevalent, could not be much hurt by these disorderly practices; and Edward took care to prevent any surprize, by giving orders to his troops, however they might disperse themselves in the day-time, always to quarter themselves at night near the main body. In this manner, Montebourg, Carentan, St. Lo, Valognes, and other places in the Cotentin, were pillaged without resistance; and an universal consternation was spread over the province.[y]

The intelligence of this unexpected invasion soon reached Paris; and threw Philip into great perplexity. He issued orders, however, for levying forces in all quarters, and dispatched the count of Eu, constable of France, and the count of Tancarville, with a body of troops, to the defence of Caën, a populous and commercial but open city, which lay in the neighbourhood of the English army. The temptation of so rich a prize soon allured Edward to approach it; and the inhabitants, encouraged by their numbers, and by the reinforcements which they daily received from the country, ventured to meet him in the field. But their courage failed them on the first shock: They fled with precipitation: The counts of Eu and Tancarville were taken prisoners: The victors entered the city along with the vanquished, and a furious massacre commenced, without distinction of age, sex, or

[y] Froissard, liv. i. chap. 122.

CHAPTER XV

condition. The citizens, in despair, barricadoed their houses, and assaulted the English with stones, bricks, and every missile weapon: The English made way by fire to the destruction of the citizens: Till Edward, anxious to save both his spoil and his soldiers, stopped the massacre; and having obliged the inhabitants to lay down their arms, gave his troops licence to begin a more regular and less hazardous plunder of the city. The pillage continued for three days: The king reserved for his own share the jewels, plate, silks, fine cloth, and fine linen; and he bestowed all the remainder of the spoil on his army. The whole was embarked on board the ships, and sent over to England; together with three hundred of the richest citizens of Caën, whose ransom was an additional profit, which he expected afterwards to levy.[z] This dismal scene passed in the presence of two cardinal legates, who had come to negociate a peace between the kingdoms.

The king moved next to Roüen in hopes of treating that city in the same manner; but found, that the bridge over the Seine was already broken down, and that the king of France himself was arrived there with his army. He marched along the banks of that river towards Paris, destroying the whole country, and every town and village, which he met with on his road.[a] Some of his light troops carried their ravages even to the gates of Paris; and the royal palace of St. Germans, together with Nanterre, Ruelle, and other villages, was reduced to ashes within sight of the capital. The English intended to pass the river at Poissy, but found the French army encamped on the opposite banks, and the bridge at that place, as well as all others over the Seine, broken down by orders from Philip. Edward now saw, that the French meant to enclose him in their country, in hopes of attacking him with advantage on all sides: But he saved himself by a stratagem from this perilous situation. He gave his army orders to dislodge, and to advance farther up the Seine; but immediately returning by the same road, he arrived at Poissy, which the enemy had already quitted, in order to attend his motions. He repaired the bridge with incredible celerity, passed over his army, and having thus disengaged himself from the enemy, advanced by quick marches towards Flanders. His vanguard, commanded by Harcourt, met with the townsmen of

[z] Froissard, liv. i. chap. 124.   [a] Ibid. chap. 125.

Amiens, who were hastening to reinforce their king, and defeated them with great slaughter:[b] He passed by Beauvais, and burned the suburbs of that city: But as he approached the Somme, he found himself in the same difficulty as before: All the bridges on that river were either broken down, or strongly guarded: An army, under the command of Godemar de Faye, was stationed on the opposite banks: Philip was advancing on him from the other quarter, with an army of a hundred thousand men: And he was thus exposed to the danger of being enclosed, and of starving in an enemy's country. In this extremity, he published a reward to any one, that should bring him intelligence of a passage over the Somme. A peasant, called Gobin Agace, whose name has been preserved by the share which he had in these important transactions, was tempted on this occasion to betray the interests of his country; and he informed Edward of a ford below Abbeville, which had a sound bottom, and might be passed without difficulty at low water.[c] The king hastened thither, but found Godemar de Faye on the opposite banks. Being urged by necessity, he deliberated not a moment; but threw himself into the river, sword in hand, at the head of his troops; drove the enemy from their station; and pursued them to a distance on the plain.[d] The French army under Philip arrived at the ford, when the rear-guard of the English were passing. So narrow was the escape, which Edward, by his prudence and celerity, made from this danger! The rising of the tide prevented the French king from following him over the ford, and obliged that prince to take his route over the bridge at Abbeville; by which some time was lost.

It is natural to think, that Philip, at the head of so vast an army, was impatient to take revenge on the English, and to prevent the disgrace, to which he must be exposed, if an inferior enemy should be allowed, after ravaging so great a part of his kingdom, to escape with impunity. Edward also was sensible, that such must be the object of the French monarch; and as he had advanced but a little way before his enemy, he saw the danger of precipitating his march over the plains of Picardy, and of exposing his rear to the insults of the numerous cavalry, in which the French camp

[b] Froissard, liv. i. chap. 125.   [c] Ibid. chap. 126, 127.   [d] Froissard, liv. i. chap. 127.

CHAPTER XV

abounded. He took therefore a prudent resolution: He chose his ground with advantage near the village of Crecy; he disposed his army in excellent order; he determined to await in tranquillity the arrival of the enemy; and he hoped, that their eagerness to engage, and to prevent his retreat, after all their past disappointments, would hurry them on to some rash and ill-concerted action. He drew up his army on a gentle ascent, and divided them into three lines: The first was commanded by the prince of Wales, and under him, by the earls of Warwic and Oxford, by Harcourt, and by the lords Chandos, Holland, and other noblemen: The earls of Arundel and Northampton, with the lords Willoughby, Basset, Roos, and Sir Lewis Tufton, were at the head of the second line: He took to himself the command of the third division, by which he purposed either to bring succour to the two first lines, or to secure a retreat in case of any misfortune, or to push his advantages against the enemy. He had likewise the precaution to throw up trenches on his flanks, in order to secure himself from the numerous bodies of the French, who might assail him from that quarter; and he placed all his baggage behind him in a wood, which he also secured by an intrenchment.[e]

Battle of Crecy, 25th Aug.

The skill and order of this disposition, with the tranquillity in which it was made, served extremely to compose the minds of the soldiers; and the king, that he might farther inspirit them, rode through the ranks with such an air of cheerfulness and alacrity, as conveyed the highest confidence into every beholder. He pointed out to them the necessity to which they were reduced, and the certain and inevitable destruction which awaited them, if, in their present situation, enclosed on all hands in an enemy's country, they trusted to any thing but their own valour, or gave that enemy an opportunity of taking revenge for the many insults and indignities, which they had of late put upon him. He reminded them of the visible ascendant, which they had hitherto maintained, over all the bodies of French troops that had fallen in their way; and assured them, that the superior numbers of the army, which at present hovered over them, gave them not greater force, but was an advantage easily compensated by the order in which he had placed his own army, and the resolution which he expected from

[e] Froissard, liv. i. chap. 128.

them. He demanded nothing, he said, but that they would imitate his own example, and that of the prince of Wales; and as the honour, the lives, the liberties of all, were now exposed to the same danger, he was confident, that they would make one common effort to extricate themselves from the present difficulties, and that their united courage would give them the victory over all their enemies.

It is related by some historians,[f] that Edward, besides the resources, which he found in his own genius and presence of mind, employed also a new invention against the enemy, and placed in his front some pieces of artillery, the first that had yet been made use of on any remarkable occasion in Europe. This is the epoch of one of the most singular discoveries, that has been made among men; a discovery, which changed by degrees the whole art of war: and by consequence many circumstances in the political government of Europe. But the ignorance of that age, in the mechanical arts, rendered the progress of this new invention very slow. The artillery, first framed, were so clumsy and of such difficult management, that men were not immediately sensible of their use and efficacy: And even to the present times, improvements have been continually making on this furious engine, which, though it seemed contrived for the destruction of mankind, and the overthrow of empires, has in the issue rendered battles less bloody, and has given greater stability to civil societies. Nations, by its means, have been brought more to a level: Conquests have become less frequent and rapid: Success in war has been reduced nearly to be a matter of calculation: And any nation, overmatched by its enemies, either yields to their demands, or secures itself by alliances against their violence and invasion.

The invention of artillery was at this time known in France as well as in England;[g] but Philip, in his hurry to overtake the enemy, had probably left his cannon behind him, which he regarded as a useless incumbrance. All his other movements discovered the same imprudence and precipitation. Impelled by anger, a dangerous counsellor, and trusting to the great superiority of his numbers, he thought that all depended on forcing an engagement with the English, and that, if he could once reach the enemy in their

[f] Jean Villani, lib. 12. cap. 66.   [g] Du Gange Gloss. in verb. *Bombarda*.

CHAPTER XV

retreat, the victory on his side was certain and inevitable. He made a hasty march in some confusion from Abbeville; but after he had advanced above two leagues, some gentlemen, whom he had sent before to take a view of the enemy, returned to him, and brought him intelligence, that they had seen the English drawn up in great order, and awaiting his arrival. They therefore advised him to defer the combat till the ensuing day, when his army would have recovered from their fatigue, and might be disposed into better order, than their present hurry had permitted them to observe. Philip assented to this counsel; but the former precipitation of his march, and the impatience of the French nobility, made it impracticable for him to put it in execution. One division pressed upon another: Orders to stop were not seasonably conveyed to all of them; This immense body was not governed by sufficient discipline to be manageable: And the French army, imperfectly formed into three lines, arrived, already fatigued and disordered, in presence of the enemy. The first line, consisting of 15,000 Genoese cross-bow men, was commanded by Anthony Doria, and Charles Grimaldi: The second was led by the count of Alençon, brother to the king: The king himself was at the head of the third. Besides the French monarch, there were no less than three crowned heads in this engagement: The king of Bohemia, the king of the Romans, his son, and the king of Majorca; with all the nobility and great vassals of the crown of France. The army now consisted of above 120,000 men, more than three times the number of the enemy. But the prudence of one man was superior to the advantage of all this force and splendor.

The English, on the approach of the enemy, kept their ranks firm and immoveable; and the Genoese first began the attack. There had happened, a little before the engagement, a thundershower, which had moistened and relaxed the strings of the Genoese cross-bows; their arrows for this reason fell short of the enemy. The English archers, taking their bows out of their cases, poured in a shower of arrows upon this multitude who were opposed to them; and soon threw them into disorder. The Genoese fell back upon the heavy-armed cavalry of the count of Alençon;[h] who, enraged at their cowardice, ordered his troops to put them to the

[h] Froissard, liv. i. chap. 130.

sword. The artillery fired amidst the crowd; the English archers continued to send in their arrows among them; and nothing was to be seen in that vast body but hurry and confusion, terror and dismay. The young prince of Wales had the presence of mind to take advantage of this situation, and to lead on his line to the charge. The French cavalry, however, recovering somewhat their order, and encouraged by the example of their leader, made a stout resistance; and having at last cleared themselves of the Genoese runaways, advanced upon their enemies, and by their superior numbers began to hem them round. The earls of Arundel and Northampton now advanced their line to sustain the prince, who, ardent in his first feats of arms, set an example of valour, which was imitated by all his followers. The battle became for some time hot and dangerous, and the earl of Warwic, apprehensive of the event from the superior numbers of the French, dispatched a messenger to the king, and entreated him to send succours to the relief of the prince. Edward had chosen his station on the top of the hill; and he surveyed in tranquillity the scene of action. When the messenger accosted him, his first question was, whether the prince were slain or wounded. On receiving an answer in the negative, *Return,* said he, *to my son, and tell him that I reserve the honour of the day to him: I am confident that he will show himself worthy of the honour of knighthood, which I so lately conferred upon him: He will be able without my assistance to repel the enemy.*[i] This speech, being reported to the prince and his attendants, inspired them with fresh courage: They made an attack with redoubled vigour on the French, in which the count of Alençon was slain: That whole line of cavalry was thrown into disorder: The riders were killed or dismounted: The Welsh infantry rushed into the throng, and with their long knives cut the throats of all who had fallen; nor was any quarter given that day by the victors.[k]

The king of France advanced in vain with the rear to sustain the line commanded by his brother: He found them already discomfited; and the example of their rout encreased the confusion, which was before but too prevalent in his own body. He had himself a horse killed under him: He was remounted; and, though left almost alone, he seemed still determined to maintain the combat; when John of Hainault seized the reins of his bridle, turned about

[i] Froissard, liv. i. chap. 130.   [k] Ibid.

CHAPTER XV

his horse, and carried him off the field of battle. The whole French army took to flight, and was followed and put to the sword without mercy by the enemy; till the darkness of the night put an end to the pursuit. The king, on his return to the camp, flew into the arms of the prince of Wales, and exclaimed; *My brave son: Persevere in your honourable cause: You are my son; for valiantly have you acquitted yourself to-day: You have shewn yourself worthy of empire.*[l]

This battle, which is known by the name of the battle of Crecy, began after three o'clock in the afternoon, and continued till evening. The next morning was foggy; and as the English observed, that many of the enemy had lost their way in the night and in the mist, they employed a stratagem to bring them into their power: They erected on the eminences some French standards which they had taken in the battle; and all, who were allured by this false signal, were put to the sword, and no quarter given them. In excuse for this inhumanity, it was alleged that the French king had given like orders to his troops; but the real reason probably was, that the English, in their present situation, did not chuse to be encumbered with prisoners. On the day of battle, and on the ensuing, there fell, by a moderate computation, 1200 French knights, 1400 gentlemen, 4000 men at arms, besides about 30,000 of inferior rank:[m] Many of the principal nobility of France, the dukes of Lorraine and Bourbon, the earls of Flanders, Blois, Vaudemont, Aumale, were left on the field of battle. The kings also of Bohemia and Majorca were slain: The fate of the former was remarkable: He was blind from age; but being resolved to hazard his person, and set an example to others, he ordered the reins of his bridle to be tied on each side to the horses of two gentlemen of his train; and his dead body, and those of his attendants, were afterwards found among the slain, with their horses standing by them in that situation.[n] His crest was three ostrich feathers; and his motto these German words, *Ich dien, I serve:* Which the prince of Wales and his successors adopted in memorial of this great victory. The action may seem no less remarkable for the small loss sustained by the English than for the great slaughter of the French: There were killed in it only one esquire and three knights,[o] and very few of inferior rank; a demonstration, that the prudent disposition

[l] Ibid. chap. 131. [m] Froissard, liv. i. chap. 131. Knyghton, p. 2588. [n] Froissard, liv. i. chap. 130. Walsingham, p. 166. [o] Knyghton, p. 2588.

planned by Edward, and the disorderly attack made by the French, had rendered the whole rather a rout than a battle, which was indeed the common case with engagements in those times.

The great prudence of Edward appeared not only in obtaining this memorable victory, but in the measures which he pursued after it. Not elated by his present prosperity, so far as to expect the total conquest of France, or even that of any considerable provinces; he purposed only to secure such an easy entrance into that kingdom, as might afterwards open the way to more moderate advantages. He knew the extreme distance of Guienne: He had experienced the difficulty and uncertainty of penetrating on the side of the Low Countries, and had already lost much of his authority over Flanders by the death of d'Arteville, who had been murdered by the populace themselves, his former partizans, on his attempting to transfer the sovereignty of that province to the prince of Wales.[p] The king, therefore, limited his ambition to the conquest of Calais; and after the interval of a few days, which he employed in interring the slain, he marched with his victorious army, and presented himself before the place.

John of Vienne, a valiant knight of Burgundy, was governor of Calais, and being supplied with every thing necessary for defence, he encouraged the townsmen to perform to the utmost their duty to their king and country. Edward therefore, sensible from the beginning that it was in vain to attempt the place by force, purposed only to reduce it by famine: He chose a secure station for his camp; drew entrenchments around the whole city; raised huts for his soldiers, which he covered with straw or broom; and provided his army with all the conveniences, necessary to make them endure the winter season, which was approaching. As the governor soon perceived his intention, he expelled all the useless mouths; and the king had the generosity to allow these unhappy people to pass through his camp, and he even supplied them with money for their journey.[q]

While Edward was engaged in this siege, which employed him near a twelvemonth, there passed in different places many other events; and all to the honour of the English arms.

The retreat of the duke of Normandy from Guienne left the earl of Derby master of the field; and he was not negligent in

[p] Froissard, liv. i. chap. 116.   [q] Froissard, liv. i. chap. 133.

making his advantage of the superiority. He took Mirebeau by assault: He made himself master of Lusignan in the same manner: Taillebourg and St. Jean d'Angeli fell into his hands: Poictiers opened its gates to him; and Derby having thus broken into the frontiers on that quarter, carried his incursions to the banks of the Loire, and filled all the southern provinces of France with horror and devastation.[r]

The flames of war were at the same time kindled in Britanny. Charles of Blois invaded that province with a considerable army, and invested the fortress of Roche de Rien; but the countess of Mountfort, reinforced by some English troops under Sir Thomas Dagworth, attacked him during the night in his entrenchments, dispersed his army, and took Charles himself prisoner.[s] His wife, by whom he enjoyed his pretensions to Britanny, compelled by the present necessity, took on her the government of the party, and proved herself a rival in every shape, and an antagonist to the countess of Mountfort, both in the field and in the cabinet. And while these heroic dames presented this extraordinary scene to the world, another princess in England, of still higher rank, showed herself no less capable of exerting every manly virtue.

The Scottish nation, after long defending, with incredible perseverance, their liberties against the superior force of the English, recalled their king, David Bruce, in 1342. Though that prince, neither by his age nor capacity, could bring them great assistance, he gave them the countenance of sovereign authority; and as Edward's wars on the continent proved a great diversion to the force of England, they rendered the balance more equal between the kingdoms. In every truce which Edward concluded with Philip, the king of Scotland was comprehended; and when Edward made his last invasion upon France, David was strongly solicited by his ally to begin also hostilities, and to invade the northern counties of England. The nobility of his nation being always forward in such incursions, David soon mustered a great army, entered Northumberland at the head of above 50,000 men, and carried his ravages and devastations to the gates of Durham.[t] But queen Philippa, assembling a body of little more than 12,000 men,[u] which she entrusted to the command of Lord Piercy, ventured to approach

War with Scotland.

---

[r] Ibid. chap. 136.   [s] Ibid. chap. 143. Walsingham, p. 168. Ypod. Neust. p. 517, 518.   [t] Froissard, liv. i. chap. 137.   [u] Ibid. chap. 138.

him at Neville's Cross near that city; and riding through the ranks of her army, exhorted every man to do his duty, and to take revenge on these barbarous ravagers.[w] Nor could she be persuaded to leave the field, till the armies were on the point of engaging. The Scots have often been unfortunate in the great pitched battles which they fought with the English; even though they commonly declined such engagements where the superiority of numbers was not on their side: But never did they receive a more fatal blow than the present. They were broken and chaced off the field: Fifteen thousand of them, some historians say twenty thousand, were slain; among whom were Edward Keith, earl Mareschal, and Sir Thomas Charteris, chancellor: And the king himself was taken prisoner, with the earls of Southerland, Fife, Monteith, Carrie, lord Douglas, and many other noblemen.[x]

17th Oct.

Captivity of the king of Scots.

Philippa, having secured her royal prisoner in the Tower,[y] crossed the sea at Dover; and was received in the English camp before Calais with all the triumph due to her rank, her merit, and her success. This age was the reign of chivalry and gallantry: Edward's court excelled in these accomplishments as much as in policy and arms: And if any thing could justify the obsequious devotion then professed to the fair sex, it must be the appearance of such extraordinary women as shone forth during that period.

1347. Calais taken.

The town of Calais had been defended with remarkable vigilance, constancy, and bravery by the townsmen, during a siege of unusual length: But Philip, informed of their distressed condition, determined at last to attempt their relief; and he approached the English with an immense army, which the writers of that age make amount to 200,000 men. But he found Edward so surrounded with morasses, and secured by entrenchments, that, without running on inevitable destruction, he concluded it impossible to make an attempt on the English camp. He had no other resource than to send his rival a vain challenge to meet him in the open field; which being refused, he was obliged to decamp with his army, and disperse them into their several provinces.[z]

John of Vienne, governor of Calais, now saw the necessity of surrendering his fortress, which was reduced to the last extremity,

[w] Ibid. chap. 138.   [x] Froissard, liv. 1. chap. 139.   [y] Rymer, vol. v. p. 537.
[z] Froissard, liv. 1. chap. 144, 145. Avesbury, p. 161, 162.

CHAPTER XV

by famine and the fatigue of the inhabitants. He appeared on the walls, and made a signal to the English centinels that he desired a parley. Sir Walter Manny was sent to him by Edward. "Brave knight," cried the governor, "I have been entrusted by my sovereign with the command of this town: It is almost a year since you besieged me; and I have endeavoured, as well as those under me, to do our duty. But you are acquainted with our present condition: We have no hopes of relief; we are perishing with hunger; I am willing therefore to surrender, and desire, as the sole condition, to ensure the lives and liberties of these brave men, who have so long shared with me every danger and fatigue."[a]

Manny replied, that he was well acquainted with the intentions of the king of England; that that prince was incensed against the townsmen of Calais for their pertinacious resistance, and for the evils which they had made him and his subjects suffer; that he was determined to take exemplary vengeance on them; and would not receive the town on any condition which should confine him in the punishment of these offenders. "Consider," replied Vienne, "that this is not the treatment to which brave men are intitled: If any English knight had been in my situation, your king would have expected the same conduct from him. The inhabitants of Calais have done for their sovereign what merits the esteem of every prince; much more of so gallant a prince as Edward. But I inform you, that, if we must perish, we shall not perish unrevenged; and that we are not yet so reduced, but we can sell our lives at a high price to the victors. It is the interest of both sides to prevent these desperate extremities; and I expect, that you yourself, brave knight, will interpose your good offices with your prince in our behalf."

Manny was struck with the justness of these sentiments, and represented to the king the danger of reprisals, if he should give such treatment to the inhabitants of Calais. Edward was at last persuaded to mitigate the rigour of the conditions demanded: He only insisted, that six of the most considerable citizens should be sent to him to be disposed of as he thought proper; that they should come to his camp carrying the keys of the city in their hands, bareheaded and barefooted, with ropes about their necks:

[a] Froissard, liv. 1. chap. 146.

HISTORY OF ENGLAND

And on these conditions, he promised to spare the lives of all the remainder.[b]

When this intelligence was conveyed to Calais, it struck the inhabitants with new consternation. To sacrifice six of their fellow-citizens to certain destruction, for signalizing their valour in a common cause, appeared to them even more severe than that general punishment, with which they were before threatened; and they found themselves incapable of coming to any resolution in so cruel and distressful a situation. At last one of the principal inhabitants called Eustace de St. Pierre, whose name deserves to be recorded, stepped forth, and declared himself willing to encounter death for the safety of his friends and companions: Another, animated by his example, made a like generous offer: A third and a fourth presented themselves to the same fate; and the whole number was soon completed. These six heroic burgesses appeared before Edward in the guise of malefactors, laid at his feet the keys of their city, and were ordered to be led to execution. It is surprizing, that so generous a prince should ever have entertained such a barbarous purpose against such men; and still more that he should seriously persist in the resolution of executing it.* But the entreaties of his queen saved his memory from that infamy: She threw herself on her knees before him, and with tears in her eyes begged the lives of these citizens. Having obtained her request, she carried them into her tent, ordered a repast to be set before them, and after making them a present of money and clothes, dismissed them in safety.[c]

4th August.
The king took possession of Calais; and immediately executed an act of rigor, more justifiable because more necessary, than that which he had before resolved on. He knew, that, notwithstanding his pretended title to the crown of France, every Frenchman regarded him as a mortal enemy: He therefore ordered all the inhabitants of Calais to evacuate the town, and he peopled it anew with English; a policy which probably preserved so long to his successors the dominion of that important fortress. He made it the staple of wool, leather, tin, and lead; the four chief, if not the sole commodities of the kingdom, for which there was any considerable

---

[b] Froissard, liv. 1. chap. 146. *See note [G] at the end of the volume.
[c] Froissard, liv. 1. chap. 146.

CHAPTER XV

demand in foreign markets. All the English were obliged to bring thither these goods: Foreign merchants came to the same place in order to purchase them: And at a period, when posts were not established, and when the communication between states was so imperfect, this institution, though it hurt the navigation of England, was probably of advantage to the kingdom.

Through the mediation of the pope's legates, Edward concluded a truce with France; but even during this cessation of arms, he had very nearly lost Calais, the sole fruit of all his boasted victories. The king had entrusted that place to Aimery de Pavie, an Italian, who had discovered bravery and conduct in the wars, but was utterly destitute of every principle of honour and fidelity. This man agreed to deliver up Calais for the sum of 20,000 crowns; and Geoffrey de Charni, who commanded the French forces in those quarters, and who knew, that, if he succeeded in this service, he should not be disavowed, ventured, without consulting his master, to conclude the bargain with him. Edward, informed of this treachery, by means of Aimery's secretary, summoned the governor to London on other pretences; and having charged him with the guilt, promised him his life, but on condition that he would turn the contrivance to the destruction of the enemy. The Italian easily agreed to this double treachery. A day was appointed for the admission of the French; and Edward, having prepared a force of about a thousand men, under Sir Walter Manny, secretly departed from London, carrying with him the prince of Wales; and without being suspected, arrived the evening before at Calais. He made a proper disposition for the reception of the enemy; and kept all his forces and the garrison under arms. On the appearance of Charni, a chosen band of French soldiers was admitted at the postern, and Aimery, receiving the stipulated sum, promised, that, with their assistance, he would immediately open the great gate to the troops, who were waiting with impatience for the fulfilling of his engagement. All the French who entered were immediately slain or taken prisoners: The great gate opened: Edward rushed forth with cries of battle and of victory: The French, though astonished at the event, behaved with valour: A fierce and bloody engagement ensued. As the morning broke, the king, who was not distinguished by his arms, and who fought as a private man under the standard of Sir Walter Manny, remarked a French gentleman,

1348.

1349.
1st Jan.

called Eustace de Ribaumont, who exerted himself with singular
vigour and bravery; and he was seized with a desire of trying a
single combat with him. He stepped forth from his troop, and
challenging Ribaumont by name, (for he was known to him) began
a sharp and dangerous encounter. He was twice beaten to the
ground by the valour of the Frenchman: He twice recovered himself: Blows were redoubled with equal force on both sides: The
victory was long undecided: Till Ribaumont, perceiving himself
to be left almost alone, called out to his antagonist, *Sir knight, I
yield myself your prisoner;* and at the same time delivered his sword
to the king. Most of the French, being overpowered by numbers,
and intercepted in their retreat, lost either their lives or their
liberty.[d]

The French officers, who had fallen into the hands of the
English, were conducted into Calais; where Edward discovered to
them the antagonist with whom they had had the honour to be
engaged, and treated them with great regard and courtesy. They
were admitted to sup with the prince of Wales, and the English
nobility; and after supper, the king himself came into the apartment, and went about, conversing familiarly with one or other of
his prisoners. He even addressed himself to Charni, and avoided
reproaching him, in too severe terms, with the treacherous attempt, which he had made upon Calais during the truce: But he
openly bestowed the highest encomiums on Ribaumont; called
him the most valorous knight that he had ever been acquainted
with; and confessed, that he himself had at no time been in so great
danger as when engaged in combat with him. He then took a string
of pearls, which he wore about his own head, and throwing it over
the head of Ribaumont, he said to him, "Sir Eustace, I bestow this
present upon you, as a testimony of my esteem for your bravery:
And I desire you to wear it a year for my sake: I know you to be gay
and amorous; and to take delight in the company of ladies and
damsels: Let them all know from what hand you had the present:
You are no longer a prisoner; I acquit you of your ransom; and you
are at liberty to-morrow to dispose of yourself as you think
proper."

[d] Froissard, liv. 1. chap. 140, 141, 142.

CHAPTER XV

Nothing proves more evidently the vast superiority assumed by the nobility and gentry above all the other orders of men during those ages, than the extreme difference which Edward made in his treatment of these French knights, and that of the six citizens of Calais, who had exerted more signal bravery in a cause more justifiable and more honourable.

XVI

EDWARD III

Institution of the garter – State of France – Battle of Poictiers – Captivity of the king of France – State of that kingdom – Invasion of France – Peace of Bretigni – State of France – Expedition into Castile – Rupture with France – Ill success of the English – Death of the prince of Wales – Death – and character of the king – Miscellaneous transactions in this reign.

1349.

Institution of the garter.

THE PRUDENT CONDUCT and great success of Edward in his foreign wars had excited a strong emulation and a military genius among the English nobility; and these turbulent barons, over-awed by the crown, gave now a more useful direction to their ambition, and attached themselves to a prince who led them to the acquisition of riches and of glory. That he might farther promote the spirit of emulation and obedience, the king instituted the order of the garter, in imitation of some orders of a like nature, religious as well as military, which had been established in different parts of Europe. The number received into this order consisted of twenty-five persons, besides the sovereign; and as it has never been enlarged, this badge of distinction continues as honourable as at its first institution, and is still a valuable, though a cheap, present, which the prince can confer on his greatest subjects. A vulgar story prevails, but is not supported by any ancient authority, that, at a court-ball, Edward's mistress, commonly supposed to be the countess of Salisbury, dropped her garter; and the king, taking it up, observed some of the courtiers to smile, as if they thought that he had not obtained this favour merely by accident: Upon which he called out, *Honi soit qui mal y pense,* Evil to him that evil thinks; and as every incident of gallantry among those ancient warriors was magnified into a matter of great importance,* he instituted the order of the garter in memorial of this event, and gave these words as the motto of the order. This origin, though frivolous, is not unsuitable to the manners of the times; and it is indeed difficult by any other means to account, either for the seemingly unmeaning terms of the motto, or for the peculiar badge of the garter, which seems to have no reference to any purpose either of military use or ornament.

But a sudden damp was thrown over this festivity and triumph of the court of England, by a destructive pestilence, which invaded that kingdom as well as the rest of Europe; and is computed to have swept away near a third of the inhabitants in every country, which it attacked. It was probably more fatal in great cities than in the country; and above fifty thousand souls are said to have perished by it in London alone.ᵉ This malady first discovered itself in the north of Asia, was spread over all that country, made its progress from one end of Europe to the other, and sensibly depopulated every state through which it passed. So grievous a calamity, more than the pacific disposition of the princes, served to maintain and prolong the truce between France and England.

During this truce, Philip de Valois died, without being able to re-establish the affairs of France, which his bad success against England had thrown into extreme disorder. This monarch, during the first years of his reign, had obtained the appellation of *Fortunate,* and acquired the character of prudent; but he ill maintained either the one or the other; less from his own fault, than because he was overmatched by the superior fortune and superior genius of Edward. But the incidents in the reign of his son John, gave the

1350.

---

* See note [H] at the end of the volume. ᵉ Stowe's Survey, p. 478. There were buried 50,000 bodies in one churchyard, which Sir Walter Manny had bought for the use of the poor. The same author says, that there died above 50,000 persons of the plague in Norwich, which is quite incredible.

French nation cause to regret even the calamitous times of his predecessor. John was distinguished by many virtues, particularly a scrupulous honour and fidelity: He was not deficient in personal courage: But as he wanted that masterly prudence and foresight, which his difficult situation required, his kingdom was at the same time disturbed by intestine commotions, and oppressed with foreign wars. The chief source of its calamities, was Charles king of Navarre, who received the epithet of the *bad* or *wicked,* and whose conduct fully entitled him to that appellation. This prince was descended from males of the blood royal of France; his mother was daughter of Lewis Hutin; he had himself espoused a daughter of king John: But all these ties, which ought to have connected him with the throne, gave him only greater power to shake and overthrow it. With regard to his personal qualities, he was courteous, affable, engaging, eloquent; full of insinuation and address; inexhaustible in his resources; active and enterprising. But these splendid accomplishments were attended with such defects, as rendered them pernicious to his country, and even ruinous to himself: He was volatile, inconstant, faithless, revengeful, malicious: Restrained by no principle or duty: Insatiable in his pretensions: And whether successful or unfortunate in one enterprize, he immediately undertook another, in which he was never deterred from employing the most criminal and most dishonourable expedients.

The constable of Eu, who had been taken prisoner by Edward at Caen, recovered his liberty, on the promise of delivering as his ransom, the town of Guisnes, near Calais, of which he was superior lord: But as John was offended at this stipulation, which, if fulfilled, opened still farther that frontier to the enemy, and as he suspected the constable of more dangerous connexions with the king of England, he ordered him to be seized, and without any legal or formal trial, put him to death in prison. Charles de la Cerda was appointed constable in his place; and had a like fatal end: The king of Navarre ordered him to be assassinated; and such was the weakness of the crown, that this prince, instead of dreading punishment, would not even agree to ask pardon for his offence, but on condition that he should receive an accession of territory: And he had also John's second son put into his hands, as

1354.
State of
France.

a security for his person, when he came to court, and performed this act of mock penitence and humiliation before his sovereign.[f]

The two French princes seemed entirely reconciled; but this dissimulation, to which John submitted from necessity, and Charles from habit, did not long continue; and the king of Navarre knew, that he had reason to apprehend the most severe vengeance for the many crimes and treasons, which he had already committed, and the still greater, which he was meditating. To ensure himself of protection, he entered into a secret correspondence with England, by means of Henry earl of Derby, now earl of Lancaster, who at that time was employed in fruitless negociations for peace at Avignon, under the mediation of the pope. John detected this correspondence; and to prevent the dangerous effects of it, he sent forces into Normandy, the chief seat of the king of Navarre's power, and attacked his castles and fortresses. But hearing that Edward had prepared an army to support his ally, he had the weakness to propose an accommodation with Charles, and even to give this traiterous subject the sum of a hundred thousand crowns, as the purchase of a feigned reconcilement, which rendered him still more dangerous. The king of Navarre, insolent from past impunity, and desperate from the dangers which he apprehended, continued his intrigues; and associating himself with Geoffrey d'Harcourt, who had received his pardon from Philip de Valois, but persevered still in his factious disposition, he encreased the number of his partizans in every part of the kingdom. He even seduced by his address, Charles, the king of France's eldest son, a youth of seventeen years of age, who was the first that bore the appellation of Dauphin, by the re-union of the province of Dauphiny to the crown. But this prince, being made sensible of the danger and folly of these connexions, promised to make atonement for the offence by the sacrifice of his associates; and in concert with his father, he invited the king of Navarre, and other noblemen of the party, to a feast at Roüen, where they were betrayed into the hands of John. Some of the most obnoxious were immediately led to execution; the king of Navarre was thrown into prison:[g] But this stroke of severity in the king, and of treachery in

1355.

[f] Froissard, liv. I. chap. 144.   [g] Froissard, liv. i. chap. 146. Avesbury, p. 243.

the Dauphin, was far from proving decisive in maintaining the royal authority. Philip of Navarre, brother to Charles, and Geoffrey d'Harcourt, put all the towns and castles belonging to that prince in a posture of defence; and had immediate recourse to the protection of England in this desperate extremity.

The truce between the two kingdoms, which had always been ill observed on both sides, was now expired; and Edward was entirely free to support the French malcontents. Well pleased, that the factions in France had at length gained him some partizans in that kingdom, which his pretensions to the crown had never been able to accomplish, he purposed to attack his enemy both on the side of Guienne, under the command of the prince of Wales, and on that of Calais, in his own person.

Young Edward arrived in the Garronne with his army, on board a fleet of three hundred sail, attended by the earls of Warwic, Salisbury, Oxford, Suffolk, and other English noblemen. Being joined by the vassals of Gascony, he took the field; and as the present disorders in France prevented every proper plan of defence, he carried on with impunity his ravages and devastations, according to the mode of war in that age. He reduced all the villages and several towns in Languedoc to ashes: He presented himself before Toulouse; passed the Garronne, and burned the suburbs of Carcassonne; advanced even to Narbonne, laying every place waste around him: And after an incursion of six weeks, returned with a vast booty and many prisoners to Guienne, where he took up his winter-quarters.[h] The constable of Bourbon, who commanded in those provinces, received orders, though at the head of a superior army, on no account to run the hazard of a battle.

The king of England's incursion from Calais was of the same nature, and attended with the same issue. He broke into France at the head of a numerous army; to which he gave a full licence of plundering and ravaging the open country. He advanced to St. Omer, where the king of France was posted; and on the retreat of that prince, followed him to Hesdin.[i] John still kept at a distance, and declined an engagement: But in order to save his reputation,

---

[h] Froissard, liv. I. chap. 144, 146.   [i] Froissard, liv. I. chap. 144. Avesbury, p. 206. Walsing. p. 171.

CHAPTER XVI

he sent Edward a challenge to fight a pitched battle with him; a usual bravadoe in that age, derived from the practice of single combat, and ridiculous in the art of war. The king, finding no sincerity in this defiance, retired to Calais, and thence went over to England, in order to defend that kingdom against a threatened invasion of the Scots.

The Scots, taking advantage of the king's absence, and that of the military power of England, had surprized Berwic; and had collected an army with a view of committing ravages upon the northern provinces: But on the approach of Edward, they abandoned that place, which was not tenable, while the castle was in the hands of the English; and retiring to their mountains, gave the enemy full liberty of burning and destroying the whole country from Berwic to Edinburgh.[k] Baliol attended Edward on this expedition; but finding, that his constant adherence to the English had given his countrymen an unconquerable aversion to his title, and that he himself was declining through age and infirmities, he finally resigned into the king's hands his pretensions to the crown of Scotland,[l] and received in lieu of them an annual pension of 2000 pounds, with which he passed the remainder of his life in privacy and retirement.

During these military operations, Edward received information of the encreasing disorders in France, arising from the imprisonment of the king of Navarre; and he sent Lancaster at the head of a small army, to support the partizans of the prince in Normandy. The war was conducted with various success; but chiefly to the disadvantage of the French malcontents; till an important event happened in the other quarter of the kingdom, which had well nigh proved fatal to the monarchy of France, and threw every thing into the utmost confusion.

The prince of Wales, encouraged by the success of the preceding campaign, took the field with an army, which no historian makes amount to above 12,000 men, and of which not a third were English; and with this small body, he ventured to penetrate into the heart of France. After ravaging the Agenois, Quercy, and the Limousin, he entered the province of Berry; and made some attacks, though without success, on the towns of Bourges and Is-

1356.

[k] Walsing. p. 171.   [l] Rymer, vol. v. p. 823. Ypod. Neust. p. 521.

soudun. It appeared, that his intentions were to march into Normandy, and to join his forces with those of the earl of Lancaster, and the partizans of the king of Navarre; but finding all the bridges on the Loire broken down, and every pass carefully guarded, he was obliged to think of making his retreat into Guienne.[m] He found this resolution the more necessary, from the intelligence which he received of the king of France's motions. That monarch, provoked at the insult offered him by this incursion, and entertaining hopes of success from the young prince's temerity, collected a great army of above 60,000 men, and advanced by hasty marches to intercept his enemy. The prince, not aware of John's near approach, lost some days, on his retreat, before the castle of Remorantin;[n] and thereby gave the French an opportunity of overtaking him. They came within sight at Maupertuis near Poictiers; and Edward, sensible that his retreat was now become impracticable, prepared for battle with all the courage of a young hero, and with all the prudence of the oldest and most experienced commander.

Battle of Poictiers.

But the utmost prudence and courage would have proved insufficient to save him in this extremity, had the king of France known how to make use of his present advantages. His great superiority in numbers enabled him to surround the enemy; and by intercepting all provisions, which were already become scarce in the English camp, to reduce this small army, without a blow, to the necessity of surrendering at discretion. But such was the impatient ardour of the French nobility, and so much had their thoughts been bent on overtaking the English as their sole object, that this idea never struck any of the commanders; and they immediately took measures for the assault, as for a certain victory. While the French army was drawn up in order of battle, they were stopped by the appearance of the cardinal of Perigord; who having learned the approach of the two armies to each other, had hastened, by interposing his good offices, to prevent any farther effusion of Christian blood. By John's permission, he carried proposals to the prince of Wales; and found him so sensible of the bad posture of his affairs, that an accommodation seemed not impracticable. Edward told him, that he would agree to any terms consistent with his

[m] Walsing. p. 171.   [n] Froissard, liv. I. chap. 158. Walsing. p. 171.

CHAPTER XVI

own honour and that of England; and he offered to purchase a retreat by ceding all the conquests, which he had made during this and the former campaign, and by stipulating not to serve against France during the course of seven years. But John, imagining that he had now got into his hands a sufficient pledge for the restitution of Calais, required that Edward should surrender himself prisoner with a hundred of his attendants; and offered on these terms a safe retreat to the English army. The prince rejected the proposal with disdain; and declared, that, whatever fortune might attend him, England should never be obliged to pay the price of his ransom. This resolute answer cut off all hopes of accommodation; but as the day was already spent in negociating, the battle was delayed till the next morning.[o]

The cardinal of Perigord, as did all the prelates of the court of Rome, bore a great attachment to the French interest; but the most determined enemy could not, by any expedient, have done a greater prejudice to John's affairs, than he did them by this delay. The prince of Wales had leisure, during the night, to strengthen, by new intrenchments, the post which he had before so judiciously chosen; and he contrived an ambush of 300 men at arms, and as many archers, whom he put under the command of the Captal de Buche, and ordered to make a circuit, that they might fall on the flank or rear of the French army during the engagement. The van of his army was commanded by the earl of Warwic, the rear by the earls of Salisbury and Suffolk, the main body by the prince himself. The lords Chandos, Audeley, and many other brave and experienced commanders, were at the head of different corps of his army. *19th Sept.*

John also arranged his forces in three divisions, nearly equal: The first was commanded by the duke of Orleans, the king's brother; the second by the Dauphin attended by his two younger brothers; the third by the king himself, who had by his side Philip, his fourth son and favourite, then about fourteen years of age. There was no reaching the English army but through a narrow lane, covered on each side by hedges; and in order to open this passage, the mareschals, Andrehen and Clermont, were ordered to advance with a separate detachment of men at arms. While they

[o] Froissard, liv. I. chap. 161.

marched along the lane, a body of English archers, who lined the hedges, plyed them on each side with their arrows; and being very near them, yet placed in perfect safety, they coolly took their aim against the enemy, and slaughtered them with impunity. The French detachment, much discouraged by the unequal combat, and diminished in their number, arrived at the end of the lane, where they met on the open ground the prince of Wales himself, at the head of a chosen body, ready for their reception. They were discomfited and overthrown: One of the mareschals was slain; the other taken prisoner: And the remainder of the detachment, who were still in the lane, and exposed to the shot of the enemy, without being able to make resistance, recoiled upon their own army, and put every thing into disorder.[p] In that critical moment, the Captal de Buche unexpectedly appeared, and attacked in flank the Dauphin's line, which fell into some confusion. Landas, Bodenai, and St. Venant, to whom the care of the young prince and his brothers had been committed, too anxious for their charge or for their own safety, carried them off the field, and set the example of flight, which was followed by that whole division. The duke of Orleans, seized with a like panic, and imagining all was lost, thought no longer of fighting, but carried off his division by a retreat, which soon turned into a flight. Lord Chandos called out to the prince, that the day was won; and encouraged him to attack the division, under king John, which, though more numerous than the whole English army, were somewhat dismayed with the precipitate flight of their companions. John here made the utmost efforts to retrieve by his valour, what his imprudence had betrayed; and the only resistance made that day was by his line of battle. The prince of Wales fell with impetuosity on some German cavalry placed in the front, and commanded by the counts of Sallebruche, Nydo, and Nosto: A fierce battle ensued: One side were encouraged by the near prospect of so great a victory: The other were stimulated by the shame of quitting the field to an enemy so much inferior: But the three German generals, together with the duke of Athens, constable of France, falling in battle, that body of cavalry gave way, and left the king himself exposed to the whole fury of the enemy. The ranks were every moment thinned around him: The nobles

[p] Froissard, liv. I. chap. 162.

fell by his side, one after another: His son, scarce fourteen years of age, received a wound, while he was fighting valiantly, in defence of his father: The king himself, spent with fatigue, and overwhelmed by numbers, might easily have been slain; but every English gentleman, ambitious of taking alive the royal prisoner, spared him in the action, exhorted him to surrender, and offered him quarter: Several who attempted to seize him, suffered for their temerity. He still cried out, *Where is my cousin, the prince of Wales?* and seemed unwilling to become prisoner to any person of inferior rank. But being told, that the prince was at a distance on the field, he threw down his gauntlet, and yielded himself to Dennis de Morbec, a knight of Arras, who had been obliged to fly his country for murder. His son was taken with him.[q]

Captivity of the king of France.

The prince of Wales, who had been carried away in pursuit of the flying enemy, finding the field entirely clear, had ordered a tent to be pitched, and was reposing himself after the toils of battle; enquiring still with great anxiety concerning the fate of the French monarch. He dispatched the earl of Warwic to bring him intelligence; and that nobleman came happily in time to save the life of the captive prince, which was exposed to greater danger than it had been during the heat of action. The English had taken him by violence from Morbec: The Gascons claimed the honour of detaining the royal prisoner. And some brutal soldiers, rather than yield the prize to their rivals, had threatened to put him to death.[r] Warwic overawed both parties, and approaching the king with great demonstrations of respect, offered to conduct him to the prince's tent.

Here commences the real and truly admirable heroism of Edward: For victories are vulgar things in comparison of that moderation and humanity displayed by a young prince of twenty-seven years of age, not yet cooled from the fury of battle, and elated by as extraordinary and as unexpected success as had ever crowned the arms of any commander. He came forth to meet the captive king with all the marks of regard and sympathy; administered comfort to him amidst his misfortunes; paid him the tribute of praise due to his valour; and ascribed his own victory merely to the

[q] Rymer, vol. vi. p. 72, 154. Froissard, liv. I. chap. 164. [r] Froissard, liv. I. chap. 164.

blind chance of war or to a superior providence, which controuls all the efforts of human force and prudence.[s] The behaviour of John showed him not unworthy of this courteous treatment: His present abject fortune never made him forget a moment that he was a king: More touched by Edward's generosity than by his own calamities, he confessed, that, notwithstanding his defeat and captivity, his honour was still unimpaired; and that, if he yielded the victory, it was at least gained by a prince of such consummate valour and humanity.

Edward ordered a repast to be prepared in his tent for the prisoner; and he himself served at the royal captive's table, as if he had been one of his retinue: He stood at the king's back during the meal; constantly refused to take a place at table; and declared, that, being a subject, he was too well acquainted with the distance between his own rank, and that of royal majesty, to assume such freedom. All his father's pretensions to the crown of France were now buried in oblivion: John in captivity received the honours of a king, which were refused him when seated on the throne: His misfortunes, not his title, were respected; and the French prisoners, conquered by this elevation of mind, more than by their late discomfiture, burst into tears of admiration; which were only checked by the reflection, that such genuine and unaltered heroism in an enemy must certainly in the issue prove but the more dangerous to their native country.[t]

1357.

All the English and Gascon knights imitated the generous example set them by their prince. The captives were every where treated with humanity, and were soon after dismissed on paying moderate ransoms to the persons into whose hands they had fallen. The extent of their fortunes was considered; and an attention was given, that they should still have sufficient means left to perform their military service in a manner suitable to their rank and quality. Yet so numerous were the noble prisoners, that these ransoms, added to the spoils, gained in the field, were sufficient to enrich the prince's army; and as they had suffered very little in the action, their joy and exultation was complete.

The prince of Wales conducted his prisoner to Bourdeaux; and not being provided with forces so numerous as might enable him

[s] Poul. Cemil. p. 197.   [t] Froissard, liv. I. chap. 168.

CHAPTER XVI

to push his present advantages, he concluded a two years' truce with France,[u] which was also become requisite, that he might conduct the captive king with safety into England. He landed at Southwark, and was met by a great concourse of people, of all ranks and stations. The prisoner was clad in royal apparel, and mounted on a white steed, distinguished by its size and beauty, and by the richness of its furniture. The conqueror rode by his side in a meaner attire, and carried by a black palfry. In this situation, more glorious than all the insolent parade of a Roman triumph, he passed through the streets of London, and presented the king of France to his father, who advanced to meet him, and received him with the same courtesy, as if he had been a neighbouring potentate, that had voluntarily come to pay him a friendly visit.[w] It is impossible, in reflecting on this noble conduct, not to perceive the advantages, which resulted from the otherwise whimsical principles of chivalry, and which gave men, in those rude times, some superiority even over people of a more cultivated age and nation. *24th May.*

The king of France, besides the generous treatment which he met with in England, had the melancholy consolation of the wretched, to see companions in affliction. The king of Scots had been eleven years a captive in Edward's hands; and the good fortune of this latter monarch had reduced at once the two neighbouring potentates, with whom he was engaged in war, to be prisoners in his capital. But Edward, finding that the conquest of Scotland was nowise advanced by the captivity of its sovereign, and that the government, conducted by Robert Stuart, his nephew and heir, was still able to defend itself, consented to restore David Bruce to his liberty, for the ransom of 100,000 marks sterling; and that prince delivered the sons of all his principal nobility, as hostages for the payment.[x]

Meanwhile, the captivity of John, joined to the preceding disorders of the French government, had produced in that country, a dissolution, almost total, of civil authority, and had occasioned confusions, the most horrible and destructive that had ever been experienced in any age or in any nation. The dauphin, now about eighteen years of age, naturally assumed the royal power *1358. State of France.*

[u] Rymer, vol. vi. p. 3.   [w] Froissard, liv. i. chap. 173.   [x] Rymer, vol. vi. p. 45, 46, 52, 56. Froissard, liv. i. chap. 174. Walsing. p. 173.

during his father's captivity; but though endowed with an excellent capacity, even in such early years, he possessed neither experience nor authority sufficient to defend a state, assailed at once by foreign power and shaken by intestine faction. In order to obtain supply, he assembled the states of the kingdom: That assembly, instead of supporting his administration, were themselves seized with the spirit of confusion; and laid hold of the present opportunity to demand limitations of the prince's power, the punishment of past malversations, and the liberty of the king of Navarre. Marcel, provost of the merchants, and first magistrate of Paris, put himself at the head of the unruly populace; and from the violence and temerity of his character, pushed them to commit the most criminal outrages against the royal authority. They detained the dauphin in a fort of captivity; they murdered in his presence Robert de Clermont and John de Conflans, mareschals, the one of Normandy, the other of Burgundy; they threatened all the other ministers with a like fate; and when Charles, who was obliged to temporize and dissemble, made his escape from their hands, they levied war against him, and openly erected the standard of rebellion. The other cities of the kingdom, in imitation of the capital, shook off the dauphin's authority; took the government into their own hands; and spread the disorder into every province. The nobles, whose inclinations led them to adhere to the crown, and were naturally disposed to check these tumults, had lost all their influence; and being reproached with cowardice on account of the base desertion of their sovereign in the battle of Poictiers, were treated with universal contempt by the inferior orders. The troops, who, from the deficiency of pay, were no longer retained in discipline, threw off all regard to their officers, sought the means of subsistance by plunder and robbery, and associating to them all the disorderly people, with whom that age abounded, formed numerous bands, which infested all parts of the kingdom. They desolated the open country; burned and plundered the villages; and by cutting off all means of communication or subsistance, reduced even the inhabitants of the walled towns to the most extreme necessity. The peasants, formerly oppressed, and now left unprotected, by their masters, became desperate from their present misery; and rising every where in arms, carried to the last extremity those disorders, which were derived from the sedi-

CHAPTER XVI

tion of the citizens and disbanded soldiers.[y] The gentry, hated for their tyranny, were every where exposed to the violence of popular rage; and instead of meeting with the regard due to their past dignity, became only, on that account, the object of more wanton insult to the mutinous peasants. They were hunted like wild beasts, and put to the sword without mercy: Their castles were consumed with fire, and levelled to the ground: Their wives and daughters were first ravished, then murdered: The savages proceeded so far as to impale some gentlemen, and roast them alive before a slow fire: A body of nine thousand of them broke into Meaux, where the wife of the dauphin with above 300 ladies had taken shelter: The most brutal treatment and most atrocious cruelty were justly dreaded by this helpless company: But the Captal de Buche, though in the service of Edward, yet moved by generosity and by the gallantry of a true knight, flew to their rescue, and beat off the peasants with great slaughter. In other civil wars, the opposite factions, falling under the government of their several leaders, commonly preserve still the vestige of some rule and order: But here the wild state of nature seemed to be renewed: Every man was thrown loose and independant of his fellows: And the populousness of the country, derived from the preceding police of civil society, served only to encrease the horror and confusion of the scene.

Amidst these disorders, the king of Navarre made his escape from prison, and presented a dangerous leader to the furious malcontents.[z] But the splendid talents of this prince qualified him only to do mischief, and to encrease the public distractions: He wanted the steadiness and prudence requisite for making his intrigues subservient to his ambition, and forming his numerous partizans into a regular faction. He revived his pretensions, somewhat obsolete, to the crown of France: But while he advanced this claim, he relied entirely on his alliance with the English, who were concerned in interest to disappoint his pretensions, and who, being public and inveterate enemies to the state, served only, by the friendship which they seemingly bore him, to render his cause the more odious. And in all his operations, he acted more like a leader of banditti, than one who aspired to be the head of a regular

---

[y] Froissard, liv. i. chap. 182, 183, 184. [z] Froissard, liv. i. chap. 181.

government, and who was engaged by his station to endeavour the re-establishment of order in the community.

The eyes, therefore, of all the French, who wished to restore peace to their miserable and desolated country, were turned towards the dauphin; and that young prince, though not remarkable for his military talents, possessed so much prudence and spirit, that he daily gained the ascendant over all his enemies. Marcel, the seditious provost of Paris, was slain, while he was attempting to deliver the city to the king of Navarre and the English; and the capital immediately returned to its duty.[a] The most considerable bodies of the mutinous peasants were dispersed, and put to the sword: Some bands of military robbers underwent the same fate: And though many grievous disorders still remained, France began gradually to assume the face of a regular civil government, and to form some plan for its defence and security.

During the confusion in the dauphin's affairs, Edward seemed to have a favourable opportunity for pushing his conquests: But besides that his hands were tied by the truce, and he could only assist underhand the faction of Navarre; the state of the English finances and military power, during those ages, rendered the kingdom incapable of making any regular or steady effort, and obliged it to exert its force at very distant intervals, by which all the projected ends were commonly disappointed. Edward employed himself, during a conjuncture so inviting, chiefly in negociations with his prisoner; and John had the weakness to sign terms of peace, which, had they taken effect, must have totally ruined and dismembered his kingdom. He agreed to restore all the provinces which had been possessed by Henry II. and his two sons, and to annex them for ever to England, without any obligation of homage or fealty on the part of the English monarch. But the dauphin and the states of France rejected this treaty, so dishonourable and pernicious to the kingdom;[b] and Edward, on the expiration of the truce, having now, by subsidies and frugality, collected some treasure, prepared himself for a new invasion of France.

The great authority and renown of the king and the prince of Wales, the splendid success of their former enterprizes, and the certain prospect of plunder from the defenceless provinces of

[a] Ibid. chap. 187.   [b] Froissard, liv. i. chap. 201.

CHAPTER XVI

France, soon brought together the whole military power of England; and the same motives invited to Edward's standard all the hardy adventurers of the different countries of Europe.[c] He passed over to Calais, where he assembled an army of near a hundred thousand men; a force which the dauphin could not pretend to withstand in the open field: That prince therefore prepared himself to elude a blow, which it was impossible for him to resist. He put all the considerable towns in a posture of defence; ordered them to be supplied with magazines and provisions; distributed proper garrisons in all places; secured every thing valuable in the fortified cities; and chose his own station at Paris, with a view of allowing the enemy to vent their fury on the open country.

The king, aware of this plan of defence, was obliged to carry along with him six thousand waggons, loaded with the provisions necessary for the subsistance of his army. After ravaging the province of Picardy, he advanced into Champagne; and having a strong desire of being crowned king of France at Rheims, the usual place in which this ceremony is performed, he laid seige to that city, and carried on his attacks, though without success, for the space of seven weeks.[d] The place was bravely defended by the inhabitants, encouraged by the exhortations of the archbishop, John de Craon; till the advanced season (for this expedition was entered upon in the beginning of winter) obliged the king to raise the seige. The province of Champagne, meanwhile, was desolated by his incursions; and he thence conducted his army, with a like intent, into Burgundy. He took and pillaged Tonnerre, Gaillon, Avalon, and other small places; but the duke of Burgundy, that he might preserve his country from farther ravages, consented to pay him the sum of 100,000 nobles.[e] Edward then bent his march towards the Nivernois, which saved itself by a like composition: He laid waste Brie and the Gatinois; and after a long march, very destructive to France, and somewhat ruinous to his own troops, he appeared before the gates of Paris, and taking up his quarters at Bourg-la-Reine, extended his army to Long-jumeau, Mont-rouge, and Vaugirard. He tried to provoke the dauphin to hazard a battle,

1359.
4th Nov.

*Invasion
of France.*

1360.

---

[c] Ibid. chap. 205.   [d] Froissard, liv. i. chap. 208. Walsing. p. 174.
[e] Rymer, vol. vi p. 461. Walsing. p. 174.

by sending him a defiance; but could not make that prudent prince change his plan of operations. Paris was safe from the danger of an assault by its numerous garrison; from that of a blockade by its well supplied magazines: And as Edward himself could not subsist his army in a country, wasted by foreign and domestic enemies, and left also empty by the precaution of the dauphin, he was obliged to remove his quarters; and he spread his troops into the provinces of Maine, Beausse, and the Chartraine, which were abandoned to the fury of their devastations.[f] The only repose, which France experienced, was during the festival of Easter, when the king stopped the course of his ravages. For superstition can sometimes restrain the rage of men, which neither justice nor humanity is able to controul.

While the war was carried on in this ruinous manner, the negociations for peace were never interrupted: But as the king still insisted on the full execution of the treaty, which he had made with his prisoner at London, and which was strenuously rejected by the dauphin, there appeared no likelihood of an accommodation. The earl, now duke of Lancaster (for this title was introduced into England during the present reign), endeavoured to soften the rigour of these terms, and to finish the war on more equal and reasonable conditions. He insisted with Edward, that, notwithstanding his great and surprising successes, the object of the war, if such were to be esteemed the acquisition of the crown of France, was not become any nearer than at the commencement of it; or rather, was set at a greater distance, by those very victories and advantages, which seemed to lead to it. That his claim of succession had not from the first procured him one partizan in the kingdom; and the continuance of these destructive hostilities had united every Frenchman in the most implacable animosity against him. That though intestine faction had creeped into the government of France, it was abating every moment; and no party, even during the greatest heat of the contest, when subjection under a foreign enemy usually appears preferable to the dominion of fellow-citizens, had ever adopted the pretensions of the king of England. That the king of Navarre himself, who alone was allied with the English, instead of being a cordial friend, was Edward's most dan-

[f] Walsing. p. 175.

CHAPTER XVI

gerous rival, and in the opinion of his partizans possessed a much preferable title to the crown of France. That the prolongation of the war, however it might enrich the English soldiers, was ruinous to the king himself, who bore all the charges of the armament without reaping any solid or durable advantage from it. That if the present disorders of France continued, that kingdom would soon be reduced to such a state of desolation that it would afford no spoils to its ravagers; if it could establish a more steady government, it might turn the chance of war in its favour, and by its superior force and advantages, be able to repel the present victors. That the dauphin, even during his greatest distresses, had yet conducted himself with so much prudence as to prevent the English from acquiring one foot of land in the kingdom; and it were better for the king to accept by a peace what he had in vain attempted to acquire by hostilities, which, however hitherto successful, had been extremely expensive, and might prove very dangerous. And that Edward having acquired so much glory by his arms, the praise of moderation was the only honour, to which he could now aspire; an honour so much the greater, as it was durable, was united with that of prudence, and might be attended with the most real advantages.[g]

These reasons induced Edward to accept of more moderate terms of peace; and it is probable, that, in order to palliate this change of resolution, he ascribed it to a vow made during a dreadful tempest, which attacked his army on their march, and which ancient historians represent as the cause of this sudden accommodation.[h] The conferences between the English and French commissioners were carried on during a few days at Bretigni in the Chartraine, and the peace was at last concluded on the following conditions:[i] It was stipulated that king John should be restored to his liberty, and should pay as his ransom three millions of crowns of gold, about 1,500,000 pounds of our present money;[k] which was to be discharged at different payments: That Edward should for ever renounce all claim to the crown of France, and to the provinces of Normandy, Maine, Touraine, and Anjou, possessed by his ancestors; and should receive in exchange the provinces of Poic-

Peace of Bretigni.

8th May.

[g] Froissard, liv. i. chap. 211.   [h] Froissard, liv. i. chap. 211.   [i] Rymer, vol. vi. p. 178. Froissard, liv. i. chap. 212.   [k] See note [I] at the end of the volume.

tou, Xaintonge, l'Agenois, Perigort, the Limousin, Quercy, Rovergue, l'Angoumois, and other districts in that quarter, together with Calais, Guisnes, Montreuil, and the county of Ponthieu, on the other side of France: That the full sovereignty of all these provinces, as well as that of Guienne, should be vested in the crown of England, and that France should renounce all title to feudal jurisdiction, homage, or appeal from them: That the king of Navarre should be restored to all his honours and possessions: That Edward should renounce his confederacy with the Flemings, John his connexions with the Scots: That the disputes concerning the succession of Britanny, between the families of Blois and Mountfort, should be decided by arbiters, appointed by the two kings; and if the competitors refused to submit to the award, the dispute should no longer be a ground of war between the kingdoms: And that forty hostages, such as should be agreed on, should be sent to England as a security for the execution of all these conditions.[l]

8th July.　　In consequence of this treaty, the king of France was brought over to Calais; whither Edward also soon after repaired: And there, both princes solemnly ratified the treaty. John was sent to Boulogne; the king accompanied him a mile on his journey; and the two monarchs parted, with many professions, probably cordial and sincere, of mutual amity.[m] The good disposition of John made him fully sensible of the generous treatment which he had received in England, and obliterated all memory of the ascendant gained over him by his rival. There seldom has been a treaty of so great importance so faithfully executed by both parties. Edward had scarcely from the beginning entertained any hopes of acquiring the crown of France: By restoring John to his liberty, and making peace at a juncture so favourable to his arms, he had now plainly renounced all pretensions of this nature: He had sold at a very high price that chimerical claim: And had at present no other

---

[l] The hostages were the two sons of the French king, John and Lewis; his brother Philip duke of Orleans, the duke of Bourbon, James de Bourbon count de Ponthieu, the counts d'Eu, de Longueville, de St. Pol, de Harcourt, de Vendome, de Couci, de Craon, de Montmorenci, and many of the chief nobility of France. The princes were mostly released on the fulfilling of certain articles: Others of the hostages, and the duke of Berry among the rest, were permitted to return upon their parole, which they did not keep. Rymer, vol. vi. p. 278, 285, 287.　　[m] Froissard, liv. i. chap. 213.

CHAPTER XVI

interest than to retain those acquisitions which he had made with such singular prudence and good fortune. John, on the other hand, though the terms were severe, possessed such fidelity and honour, that he was determined at all hazards to execute them, and to use every expedient for satisfying a monarch, who had indeed been his greatest political enemy, but had treated him personally with singular humanity and regard. But, notwithstanding his endeavours, there occurred many difficulties in fulfilling his purpose; chiefly from the extreme reluctance, which many towns and vassals in the neighbourhood of Guienne, expressed against submitting to the English dominion;[n] and John, in order to adjust these differences, took a resolution of coming over himself to England. His council endeavoured to dissuade him from this rash design; and probably would have been pleased to see him employ more chicanes for eluding the execution of so disadvantageous a treaty: But John replied to them, that, though good faith were banished from the rest of the earth, she ought still to retain her habitation in the breasts of princes. Some historians would detract from the merit of this honourable conduct, by representing John as enamoured of an English lady, to whom he was glad, on this pretence, to pay a visit: But besides, that this surmise is not founded on any good authority, it appears somewhat unlikely on account of the advanced age of that prince, who was now in his fifty-sixth year. He was lodged in the Savoy; the palace where he had resided during his captivity, and where he soon after sickened and died. Nothing can be a stronger proof of the great dominion of fortune over men, than the calamities which pursued a monarch of such eminent valour, goodness, and honour, and which he incurred merely by reason of some slight imprudences, which, in other situations, would have been of no importance. But though both his reign and that of his father proved extremely unfortunate to their kingdom, the French crown acquired, during their time, very considerable accessions, those of Dauphiny and Burgundy. This latter province, however, John had the imprudence again to dismember by bestowing it on Philip his fourth son, the object of his most tender affections;[o] a deed, which was afterwards the source of many calamities to the kingdom.

John was succeeded in the throne by Charles, the Dauphin, a

1363.

1364.
8th
April.

[n] Froissard, liv. i. chap. 214.   [o] Rymer, vol. vi. p. 421.

prince educated in the school of adversity, and well qualified, by his consummate prudence and experience, to repair all the losses, which the kingdom had sustained from the errors of his two predecessors. Contrary to the practice of all the great princes of those times, which held nothing in estimation but military courage, he seems to have fixed it as a maxim never to appear at the head of his armies; and he was the first king in Europe, that showed the advantage of policy, foresight, and judgment, above a rash and precipitate valour. The events of his reign, compared with those of the preceding, are a proof, how little reason kingdoms have to value themselves on their victories, or to be humbled by their defeats; which in reality ought to be ascribed chiefly to the good or bad conduct of their rulers, and are of little moment towards determining national characters and manners.

State of France. Before Charles could think of counterbalancing so great a power as England, it was necessary for him to remedy the many disorders, to which his own kingdom was exposed. He turned his arms against the king of Navarre, the great disturber of France during that age: He defeated this prince by the conduct of Bertrand du Guesclin, a gentleman of Britanny, one of the most accomplished characters of the age, whom he had the discernment to chuse as the instrument of all his victories:[p] And he obliged his enemy to accept of moderate terms of peace. Du Guesclin was less fortunate in the wars of Britanny, which still continued, notwithstanding the mediation of France and England: He was defeated and taken prisoner at Auray by Chandos: Charles of Blois was there slain, and the young count of Mountfort soon after got entire possession of that dutchy.[q] But the prudence of Charles broke the force of this blow: He submitted to the decision of fortune: He acknowledged the title of Mountfort, though a zealous partizan of England; and received the proffered homage for his dominions. But the chief obstacle which the French king met with in the settlement of the state, proceeded from obscure enemies, whom their crimes alone rendered eminent, and their number dangerous.

On the conclusion of the treaty of Bretigni, the many military

---

[p] Froissard, liv. i. chap. 119, 120.   [q] Froissard, liv. i. chap. 227, 228, &c. Walsing. p. 180.

adventurers, who had followed the standard of Edward, being dispersed into the several provinces, and possessed of strong holds, refused to lay down their arms, or relinquish a course of life, to which they were now accustomed, and by which alone they could gain a subsistance.[r] They associated themselves with the banditti, who were already enured to the habits of rapine and violence; and under the name of the *companies* and *companions*, became a terror to all the peaceable inhabitants. Some English and Gascon gentlemen of character, particularly Sir Matthew Gournay, Sir Hugh Calverly, the chevalier Verte, and others, were not ashamed to take the command of these ruffians, whose numbers amounted on the whole to near 40,000, and who bore the appearance of regular armies, rather than bands of robbers. These leaders fought pitched battles with the troops of France, and gained victories; in one of which Jaques de Bourbon, a prince of the blood, was slain:[s] And they proceeded to such a height, that they wanted little but regular establishments to become princes, and thereby sanctify, by the maxims of the world, their infamous profession. The greater spoil they committed on the country, the more easy they found it to recruit their number: All those, who were reduced to misery and despair, flocked to their standard: The evil was every day encreasing: And though the pope declared them excommunicated, these military plunderers, however deeply affected with the sentence, to which they paid a much greater regard than to any principles of morality, could not be induced by it to betake themselves to peaceable or lawful professions.

As Charles was not able by power to redress so enormous a grievance, he was led by necessity, and by the turn of his character, to correct it by policy, and to contrive some method of discharging into foreign countries this dangerous and intestine evil. *1366.*

Peter, king of Castile, stigmatized by his contemporaries and by posterity, with the epithet of *Cruel,* had filled with blood and murder his kingdom and his own family; and having incurred the universal hatred of his subjects, he kept, from present terror alone, an anxious and precarious possession of the throne. His nobles fell every day the victims of his severity: He put to death several of his natural brothers from groundless jealousy: Each murder, by mul-

---

[r] Froissard, liv. I. chap. 214.   [s] Ibid. chap. 214, 215.

tiplying his enemies, became the occasion of fresh barbarities: And as he was not destitute of talents, his neighbours, no less than his own subjects, were alarmed at the progress of his violence and injustice. The ferocity of his temper, instead of being softened by his strong propensity to love, was rather inflamed by that passion, and took thence new occasion to exert itself. Instigated by Mary de Padilla, who had acquired the ascendant over him, he threw into prison Blanche de Bourbon, his wife, sister to the queen of France; and soon after made way by poison for the espousing of his mistress.

Henry, count of Transtamare, his natural brother, seeing the fate of every one who had become obnoxious to this tyrant, took arms against him; but being foiled in the attempt, he sought for refuge in France, where he found the minds of men extremely inflamed against Peter, on account of his murder of the French princess. He asked permission of Charles to enlist the *companies* in his service, and to lead them into Castile; where, from the concurrence of his own friends and the enemies of his brother, he had the prospect of certain and immediate success. The French king, charmed with the project, employed du Guesclin in negociating with the leaders of these banditti. The treaty was soon concluded. The high character of honour, which that general possessed, made every one trust to his promises: Though the intended expedition was kept a secret, the companies implicity inlisted under his standard: And they required no other condition before their engagement, than an assurance, that they were not to be led against the prince of Wales in Guienne. But that prince was so little averse to the enterprize, that he allowed some gentlemen of his retinue to enter into the service under du Guesclin.

Du Guesclin, having completed his levies, led the army first to Avignon, where the pope then resided, and demanded, sword in hand, an absolution for his soldiers, and the sum of 200,000 livres. The first was readily promised him; some more difficulty was made with regard to the second. "I believe, that my fellows," replied du Guesclin, "may make a shift to do without your absolution; but the money is absolutely necessary." The pope then extorted from the inhabitants in the city and neighbourhood the sum of a hundred thousand livres, and offered it to du Guesclin. "It is not my purpose," cried that generous warrior, "to oppress the

CHAPTER XVI

innocent people. The pope and his cardinals themselves can well spare me that sum from their own coffers. This money, I insist, must be restored to the owners. And should they be defrauded of it, I shall myself return from the other side of the Pyrenees, and oblige you to make them restitution." The pope found the necessity of submitting, and paid him, from his treasury, the sum demanded.[t] The army, hallowed by the blessings, and enriched by the spoils of the church, proceeded on their expedition.

These experienced and hardy soldiers, conducted by so able a general, easily prevailed over the king of Castile, whose subjects, instead of supporting their oppressor, were ready to join the enemy against him.[u] Peter fled from his dominions, took shelter in Guienne, and craved the protection of the prince of Wales, whom his father had invested with the sovereignty of these conquered provinces, by the title of the principality of Aquitaine.[w] The prince seemed now to have entirely changed his sentiments with regard to the Spanish transactions: Whether that he was moved by the generosity of supporting a distressed prince, and thought, as is but too usual among sovereigns, that the rights of the people were a matter of much less consideration; or dreaded the acquisition of so powerful a confederate to France as the new king of Castile; or what is most probable, was impatient of rest and ease, and sought only an opportunity for exerting his military talents, by which he had already acquired so much renown. He promised his assistance to the dethroned monarch; and having obtained the consent of his father, he levied a great army, and set out upon his enterprize. He was accompanied by his younger brother, John of Gaunt, created duke of Lancaster, in the room of the good prince of that name, who had died without any male issue, and whose daughter he had espoused. Chandos also, who bore among the English the same character, which du Guesclin had acquired among the French, commanded under him in this expedition.

1367. Expedition into Castile.

The first blow, which the prince of Wales gave to Henry of Transtamare, was the recalling of all the *companies* from his service; and so much reverence did they bear to the name of Edward, that great numbers of them immediately withdrew from Spain, and

---

[t] Hist. du Guesclin. [u] Froissard, liv. I. chap. 230. [w] Rymer, vol. vi. p. 384. Froissard, liv. I. chap. 231.

inlisted under his banners. Henry however, beloved by his new subjects, and supported by the king of Arragon and others of his neighbours, was able to meet the enemy with an army of 100,000 men; forces three times more numerous than those which were commanded by Edward. Du Guesclin, and all his experienced officers, advised him to delay any decisive action, to cut off the prince of Wales's provisions, and to avoid every engagement with a general, whose enterprizes had hitherto been always conducted with prudence, and crowned with success. Henry trusted too much to his numbers; and ventured to encounter the English prince at

3d April. Najara.[x] Historians of that age are commonly very copious in describing the shock of armies in battle, the valour of the combatants, the slaughter and various successes of the day: But though small rencounters in those times were often well disputed, military discipline was always too imperfect to preserve order in great armies; and such actions deserve more the name of routs than of battles. Henry was chaced off the field, with the loss of above 20,000 men: There perished only four knights and forty private men on the side of the English.

Peter, who so well merited the infamous epithet which he bore, purposed to murder all his prisoners in cool blood; but was restrained from this barbarity by the remonstrances of the prince of Wales. All Castile now submitted to the victor: Peter was restored to the throne: And Edward finished this perilous enterprize with his usual glory. But he had soon reason to repent his connexions with a man like Peter, abandoned to all sense of virtue and honour. The ungrateful tyrant refused the stipulated pay to the English forces; and Edward, finding his soldiers daily perish by sickness, and even his own health impaired by the climate, was obliged, without receiving any satisfaction on this head, to return into Guienne.[y]

The barbarities, exercised by Peter over his helpless subjects, whom he now regarded as vanquished rebels, revived all the animosity of the Castilians against him; and on the return of Henry of Transtamare, together with du Guesclin, and some forces levied anew in France, the tyrant was again dethroned, and was taken

---

[x] Froissard, liv. I. chap. 241.   [y] Froissard, liv. i. chap. 242, 243. Walsingham, p. 182.

prisoner. His brother, in resentment of his cruelties, murdered him with his own hand; and was placed on the throne of Castile, which he transmitted to his posterity. The duke of Lancaster, who espoused in second marriage the eldest daughter of Peter, inherited only the empty title of that sovereignty, and, by claiming the succession, encreased the animosity of the new king of Castile against England.

But the prejudice, which the affairs of prince Edward received from this splendid, though imprudent expedition, ended not with it. He had involved himself in so much debt by his preparations and the pay of his troops, that he found it necessary, on his return, to impose on his principality a new tax, to which some of the nobility consented with extreme reluctance, and to which others absolutely refused to submit.[z] This incident revived the animosity which the inhabitants bore to the English, and which all the amiable qualities of the prince of Wales were not able to mitigate or assuage. They complained, that they were considered as a conquered people, that their privileges were disregarded, that all trust was given to the English alone, that every office of honour and profit was conferred on these foreigners, and that the extreme reluctance, which most of them had expressed, to receive the new yoke, was likely to be long remembered against them. They cast, therefore, their eyes towards their ancient sovereign, whose prudence, they found, had now brought the affairs of his kingdom into excellent order; and the counts of Armagnac, Comminge, and Perigord, and Lord d'Albret, with other nobles, went to Paris, and were encouraged to carry their complaints to Charles, as to their lord paramount, against these oppressions of the English government.[a]

In the treaty of Bretigni it had been stipulated, that the two

*1368.
Rupture
with
France.*

---

[z] This tax was a livre upon a hearth; and it was imagined, that the imposition would have yielded 1,200,000 livres a year, which supposes so many hearths in the provinces possessed by the English. But such loose conjectures have commonly no manner of authority, much less in such ignorant times. There is a strong instance of it in the present reign. The house of commons granted the king a tax of twenty-two shillings on each parish, supposing that the amount of the whole would be 50,000 pounds. But they were found to be in a mistake of near five to one. Cotton, p. 3. And the council assumed the power of augmenting the tax upon each parish.
[a] Froissard, liv. I. chap. 244.

kings should make renunciations; Edward of his claim to the crown of France and to the provinces of Normandy, Maine, and Anjou; John of the homage and fealty due for Guienne and the other provinces ceded to the English. But when that treaty was confirmed and renewed at Calais, it was found necessary, as Edward was not yet in possession of all the territories, that the mutual renunciations should for some time be deferred; and it was agreed, that the parties, mean-while, should make no use of their respective claims against each other.[b] Though the failure in exchanging these renunciations had still proceeded from France,[c] Edward appears to have taken no umbrage at it; both because this clause seemed to give him entire security, and because some reasonable apology had probably been made to him for each delay. It was, however, on this pretence, though directly contrary to treaty, that Charles resolved to ground his claim, of still considering himself as superior lord of those provinces, and of receiving the appeals of his sub-vassals.[d]

1369. But as views of policy, more than those of justice, enter into the deliberations of princes; and as the mortal injuries received from the English, the pride of their triumphs, the severe terms imposed by the treaty of peace, seemed to render every prudent means of revenge honourable against them; Charles was determined to take this measure, less by the reasonings of his civilians and lawyers, than by the present situation of the two monarchies. He considered the declining years of Edward, the languishing state of the prince of Wales's health, the affection which the inhabitants of all these provinces bore to their ancient master, their distance from England, their vicinity to France, the extreme animosity expressed by his own subjects against these invaders, and their ardent thirst of vengeance; and having silently made all the necessary preparations, he sent to the prince of Wales a summons to appear in his court at Paris, and there to justify his conduct towards his vassals. The prince replied, that he would come to Paris; but it should be at the head of sixty thousand men.[e] The unwarlike character of Charles kept prince Edward, even yet, *1370.* from thinking, that the monarch was in earnest, in this bold and hazardous attempt.

[b] Rymer, vol. vi. p. 219, 230, 234, 237, 243.   [c] Rot. Franc. 35 Edw. III. m. 3. from Tyrrel, vol. iii. p. 643.   [d] Froissard, liv. I. chap. 245.   [e] Ibid. chap. 247, 248.

CHAPTER XVI

It soon appeared what a poor return the king had received by his distant conquests for all the blood and treasure expended in the quarrel, and how impossible it was to retain acquisitions, in an age when no regular force could be maintained sufficient to defend them against the revolt of the inhabitants, especially if that danger was joined with the invasion of a foreign enemy. Charles fell first upon Ponthieu, which gave the English an inlet into the heart of France: The citizens of Abbeville opened their gates to him:[f] Those of St. Valori, Rue, and Crotoy imitated the example, and the whole country was in a little time reduced to submission. The dukes of Berri and Anjou, brothers to Charles, being assisted by du Guesclin, who was recalled from Spain, invaded the southern provinces; and by means of their good conduct, the favourable dispositions of the people, and the ardour of the French nobility, they made every day considerable progress against the English. The state of the prince of Wales's health did not permit him to mount on horseback, or exert his usual activity: Chandos, the constable of Guienne, was slain in one action:[g] The Captal de Buche, who succeeded him in that office, was taken prisoner in another:[h] And when young Edward himself was obliged by his encreasing infirmities to throw up the command, and return to his native country, the affairs of the English in the south of France seemed to be menaced with total ruin.

Ill success of the English.

The king, incensed at these injuries, threatened to put to death all the French hostages, who remained in his hands; but on reflection abstained from that ungenerous revenge. After resuming, by advice of parliament, the vain title of king of France,[i] he endeavoured to send succours into Gascony; but all his attempts, both by sea and land, proved unsuccessful. The earl of Pembroke was intercepted at sea, and taken prisoner with his whole army near Rochelle by a fleet, which the king of Castile had fitted out for that purpose:[k] Edward himself embarked for Bourdeaux with another army; but was so long detained by contrary winds, that he was obliged to lay aside the enterprize.[l] Sir Robert Knolles, at the head of 30,000 men, marched out of Calais, and continued his ravages to the gates of Paris, without being able to provoke the

[f] Walsingham, p. 183. [g] Froissard, liv. I. chap. 277. Walsingham, p. 185.
[h] Froissard, liv. I. chap. 310. [i] Rymer, vol. vi. p. 621. Cotton's Abridg.
p. 108. [k] Froissard, liv. I. chap. 302, 303, 304. Walsingham, p. 186.
[l] Froissard, liv. I. chap. 311. Walsingham, p. 187.

enemy to an engagement: He proceeded in his march to the provinces of Maine and Anjou, which he laid waste; but part of his army being there defeated by the conduct of du Guesclin, who was now created constable of France, and who seems to have been the first consummate general that had yet appeared in Europe, the rest were scattered and dispersed, and the small remains of the English forces, instead of reaching Guienne, took shelter in Britanny, whose sovereign had embraced the alliance of England.[m] The duke of Lancaster, some time after, made a like attempt with an army of 25,000 men; and marched the whole length of France from Calais to Bourdeaux; but was so much harassed by the flying parties which attended him, that he brought not the half of his army to the place of their destination. Edward, from the necessity of his affairs, was at last obliged to conclude a truce with the enemy;[n] after almost all his ancient possessions in France had been ravished from him, except Bourdeaux and Bayonne, and all his conquests, except Calais.

The decline of the king's life was exposed to many mortifications, and corresponded not to the splendid and noisy scenes, which had filled the beginning and the middle of it. Besides seeing the loss of his foreign dominions, and being baffled in every attempt to defend them; he felt the decay of his authority at home, and experienced, from the sharpness of some parliamentary remonstrances, the great inconstancy of the people, and the influence of present fortune over all their judgments.[o] This prince, who, during the vigour of his age, had been chiefly occupied in the pursuits of war and ambition, began, at an unseasonable period, to indulge himself in pleasure; and being now a widower, he attached himself to a lady of sense and spirit, one Alice Pierce, who acquired a great ascendant over him, and by her influence gave such general disgust, that, in order to satisfy the parliament, he was obliged to remove her from court.[p] The indolence also, naturally attending old age and infirmities, had made him, in a great measure, resign the administration into the hands of his son, the duke of Lancaster, who, as he was far from being popular, weakened extremely the affection, which the English bore to the person and government of

[m] Froissard, liv. I. chap. 291. Walsingham, p. 185.   [n] Froissard, liv. I. chap. 311. Walsingham, p. 187.   [o] Walsingham, p. 189. Ypod. Neust. p. 530.   [p] Walsingham, p. 189.

CHAPTER XVI

the king. Men carried their jealousies very far against the duke; and as they saw with much regret, the death of the prince of Wales every day approaching, they apprehended, lest the succession of his son, Richard, now a minor, should be defeated by the intrigues of Lancaster, and by the weak indulgence of the old king. But Edward, in order to satisfy both the people and the prince on this head, declared in parliament his grandson heir and successor to the crown; and thereby cut off all the hopes of the duke of Lancaster, if he ever had the temerity to entertain any.

The prince of Wales, after a lingering illness, died in the forty-sixth year of his age; and left a character, illustrious for every eminent virtue, and from his earliest youth till the hour he expired, unstained by any blemish. His valour and military talents formed the smallest part of his merit: His generosity, humanity, affability, moderation, gained him the affections of all men; and he was qualified to throw a lustre, not only on that rude age, in which he lived, and which nowise infected him with its vices, but on the most shining period of ancient or modern history. The king survived about a year this melancholy incident: England was deprived at once of both these princes, its chief ornament and support: He expired in the sixty-fifth year of his age and the fifty-first of his reign; and the people were then sensible, though too late, of the irreparable loss, which they had sustained.

1376. 8th June. Death of the prince of Wales.

1377. 21st June. Death and character of the king.

The English are apt to consider with peculiar fondness the history of Edward III. and to esteem his reign, as it was one of the longest, and most glorious also, that occurs in the annals of their nation. The ascendant which they then began to acquire over France, their rival and supposed national enemy, makes them cast their eyes on this period with great complacency, and sanctifies every measure, which Edward embraced for that end. But the domestic government of this prince is really more admirable than his foreign victories; and England enjoyed, by the prudence and vigour of his administration, a longer interval of domestic peace and tranquillity than she had been blest with in any former period, or than she experienced for many ages after. He gained the affections of the great, yet curbed their licentiousness: He made them feel his power, without their daring, or even being inclined, to murmur at it: His affable and obliging behaviour, his munificence and generosity, made them submit with pleasure to his dominion;

his valour and conduct made them successful in most of their enterprizes; and their unquiet spirits, directed against a public enemy, had no leisure to breed those disturbances, to which they were naturally so much inclined, and which the frame of the government seemed so much to authorize. This was the chief benefit, which resulted from Edward's victories and conquests. His foreign wars were, in other respects, neither founded in justice, nor directed to any salutary purpose. His attempt against the king of Scotland, a minor and a brother-in-law, and the revival of his grandfather's claim of superiority over that kingdom, were both unreasonable and ungenerous; and he allowed himself to be too easily seduced, by the glaring prospect of French conquests, from the acquisition of a point, which was practicable, and which, if attained, might really have been of lasting utility to his country and his successors. The success, which he met with in France, though chiefly owing to his eminent talents, was unexpected; and yet, from the very nature of things, not from any unforeseen accidents, was found, even during his life-time, to have procured him no solid advantages. But the glory of a conqueror is so dazzling to the vulgar, the animosity of nations is so violent, that the fruitless desolation of so fine a part of Europe as France, is totally disregarded by us, and is never considered as a blemish in the character or conduct of this prince. And indeed, from the unfortunate state of human nature, it will commonly happen, that a sovereign of genius, such as Edward, who usually finds every thing easy in his domestic government, will turn himself towards military enterprizes, where alone he meets with opposition, and where he has full exercise for his industry and capacity.

Edward had a numerous posterity by his queen, Philippa of Hainault. His eldest son was the heroic Edward, usually denominated the Black Prince, from the colour of his armour. This prince espoused his cousin Joan, commonly called the *Fair Maid of Kent,* daughter and heir of his uncle, the earl of Kent, who was beheaded in the beginning of this reign. She was first married to Sir Thomas Holland, by whom she had children. By the prince of Wales, she had a son, Richard, who alone survived his father.

The second son of king Edward (for we pass over such as died in their childhood) was Lionel duke of Clarence, who was first married to Elizabeth de Burgh, daughter and heir of the earl of

CHAPTER XVI

Ulster, by whom he left only one daughter, married to Edmund Mortimer, earl of Marche. Lionel espoused in second marriage, Violante, the daughter of the duke of Milan,[q] and died in Italy soon after the consummation of his nuptials, without leaving any posterity by that princess. Of all the family, he resembled most his father and older brother in his noble qualities.

Edward's third son was John of Gaunt, so called from the place of his birth: He was created duke of Lancaster; and from him sprang that branch which afterwards possessed the crown. The fourth son of this royal family was Edmund, created earl of Cambridge by his father, and duke of York by his nephew. The fifth son was Thomas, who received the title of earl of Buckingham from his father, and that of duke of Glocester from his nephew. In order to prevent confusion, we shall always distinguish these two princes by the titles of York and Glocester, even before they were advanced to them.

There were also several princesses born to Edward by Philippa; to wit, Isabella, Joan, Mary, and Margaret, who espoused, in the order of their names, Ingelram de Coucy earl of Bedford, Alphonso king of Castile, John of Mountfort duke of Britanny, and John Hastings earl of Pembroke. The princess Joan died at Bourdeaux before the consummation of her marriage.

It is remarked by an elegant historian,[r] that Conquerors, though usually the bane of human kind, proved often in those feudal times, the most indulgent of sovereigns: They stood most in need of supplies from their people; and not being able to compel them by force to submit to the necessary impositions, they were obliged to make them some compensation, by equitable laws and popular concessions. This remark is, in some measure, though imperfectly, justified by the conduct of Edward III. He took no steps of moment without consulting his parliament, and obtaining their approbation, which he afterwards pleaded as a reason for their supporting his measures.[s] The parliament, therefore, rose into greater consideration during his reign, and acquired more regular authority than in any former time; and even the house of commons, which, during turbulent and factious periods, was natu-

Miscellaneous transactions of this reign.

---

[q] Rymer, vol. vi. p. 564.   [r] Dr. Robertson's Hist. of Scotland, B. I.
[s] Cotton's Abridg. p. 108, 120.

rally depressed by the greater power of the crown and barons, began to appear of some weight in the constitution. In the later years of Edward, the king's ministers were impeached in parliament, particularly lord Latimer, who fell a sacrifice to the authority of the commons;[t] and they even obliged the king to banish his mistress by their remonstrances. Some attention was also paid to the election of their members; and lawyers, in particular, who were, at that time, men of a character somewhat inferior, were totally excluded the house during several parliaments.[u]

One of the most popular laws, enacted by any prince, was the statute, which passed in the twenty-fifth of this reign,[w] and which limited the cases of high treason, before vague and uncertain, to three principal heads, conspiring the death of the king, levying war against him, and adhering to his enemies; and the judges were prohibited, if any other cases should occur, from inflicting the penalty of treason, without an application to parliament. The bounds of treason were indeed so much limited by this statute, which still remains in force without any alteration, that the lawyers were obliged to enlarge them, and to explain a conspiracy for levying war against the king to be equivalent to a conspiracy against his life; and this interpretation, seemingly forced, has, from the necessity of the case, been tacitly acquiesced in. It was also ordained, that a parliament should be held once a year or oftener, if need be: A law which, like many others, was never observed, and lost its authority by disuse.[x]

Edward granted above twenty parliamentary confirmations of the Great Charter; and these concessions are commonly appealed to as proofs of his great indulgence to the people, and his tender regard for their liberties. But the contrary presumption is more natural. If the maxims of Edward's reign had not been in general somewhat arbitrary, and if the Great Charter had not been frequently violated, the parliament would never have applied for these frequent confirmations, which could add no force to a deed regularly observed, and which could serve to no other purpose, than to prevent the contrary precedents from turning into a rule, and acquiring authority. It was indeed the effect of the irregular

---

[t] Ibid. p. 122.   [u] Cotton's Abridg. p. 18.   [w] Chap. 2.   [x] 4 Edw. III. chap. 14.

CHAPTER XVI

government during those ages, that a statute, which had been enacted some years, instead of acquiring, was imagined to lose force, by time, and needed to be often renewed by recent statutes of the same sense and tenor. Hence likewise that general clause, so frequent in old acts of parliament, that the statutes, enacted by the king's progenitors, should be observed;[y] a precaution, which, if we do not consider the circumstances of the times, might appear absurd and ridiculous. The frequent confirmations in general terms of the privileges of the church proceeded from the same cause.

It is a clause in one of Edward's statutes, *that no man, of what estate or condition soever, shall be put out of land or tenement, nor taken nor imprisoned, nor disherited, nor put to death, without being brought in answer by due process of the law.*[z] This privilege was sufficiently secured by a clause of the Great Charter, which had received a general confirmation in the first chapter of the same statute. Why then is the clause so anxiously, and, as we may think, so superfluously repeated? Plainly, because there had been some late infringements of it, which gave umbrage to the commons.[a]

But there is no article, in which the laws are more frequently repeated during this reign, almost in the same terms, than that of purveyance, which the parliament always calls an *outrageous* and *intolerable* grievance, and the source of *infinite* damage to the people.[b] The parliament tried to abolish this prerogative altogether, by prohibiting any one from taking goods without the consent of the owners,[c] and by changing the *heinous name* of *purveyors*, as they term it, into that of *buyers:*[d] But the arbitrary conduct of Edward still brought back the grievance upon them; though contrary both to the Great Charter, and to many statutes. This disorder was in a great measure derived from the state of the public finances and of the kingdom; and could therefore the less admit of remedy. The prince frequently wanted ready money; yet his family must be subsisted: He was therefore obliged to employ force and violence for the purpose, and to give tallies, at what rate he pleased, to the owners of the goods which he laid hold of. The kingdom also abounded so little in commodities, and the interior commu-

---

[y] 36 Edw. III. cap. 1. 37 Edw. III. cap. 1, &c.   [z] 28 Edw. III. cap. 3.
[a] They assert, in the 15th of this reign, that there had been such instances. Cotton's Abridg. p. 31. They repeat the same in the 21st year. See p. 59.
[b] 36 Edw. III. &c.   [c] 14 Edw. III. cap. 19.   [d] 36 Edw. III. cap. 2.

nication was so imperfect, that, had the owners been strictly protected by law, they could easily have exacted any price from the king; especially in his frequent progresses, when he came to distant and poor places, where the court did not usually reside, and where a regular plan for supplying it could not easily be established. Not only the king, but several great lords, insisted upon this right of purveyance within certain districts.[e]

The magnificent castle of Windsor was built by Edward III. and his method of conducting the work may serve as a specimen of the condition of the people in that age. Instead of engaging workmen by contracts and wages, he assessed every county in England to send him a certain number of masons, tilers, and carpenters, as if he had been levying an army.[f]

They mistake, indeed, very much the genius of this reign, who imagine that it was not extremely arbitrary. All the high prerogatives of the crown were to the full exerted in it; but what gave some consolation, and promised in time some relief to the people, they were always complained of by the commons: Such as the dispensing power;[g] the extension of the forests;[h] erecting monopolies;[i] exacting loans;[k] stopping justice by particular warrants;[l] the renewal of the commission of *trailbaton;*[m] pressing men and ships into the public service;[n] levying arbitrary and exorbitant fines;[o] extending the authority of the privy council or star-chamber to the decision of private causes;[p] enlarging the power of the mareschal's and other arbitrary courts;[q] imprisoning members for freedom of speech in parliament;[r] obliging people without any rule to send recruits of men at arms, archers, and hoblers to the army.[s]

But there was no act of arbitrary power more frequently repeated in this reign, than that of imposing taxes without consent of parliament. Though that assembly granted the king greater supplies than had ever been obtained by any of his predecessors, his great undertakings and the necessity of his affairs obliged him to levy still more; and after his splendid success against France had

[e] 7 Rich. II. cap. 8. [f] Ashmole's hist. of the garter, p. 129. [g] Cotton's Abridg. p. 148. [h] Cotton, p. 71. [i] Cotton's Abridg. p. 56, 61, 122. [k] Rymer, vol. v. p. 491, 574. Cotton's Abridg. p. 56. [l] Cotton, p. 114. [m] Ibid. p. 67. [n] Cotton's Abridg. p. 47, 79, 113. [o] Ibid. p. 32. [p] Ibid. p. 74. [q] Ibid. [r] Walsing. p. 189, 190. [s] Tyrrel's Hist. vol. viii. p. 554. from the records.

CHAPTER XVI

added weight to his authority, these arbitrary impositions became almost annual and perpetual. Cotton's Abridgment of the records affords numerous instances of this kind, in the first[t] year of his reign, in the thirteenth year,[u] in the fourteenth,[w] in the twentieth,[x] in the twenty-first,[y] in the twenty-second,[z] in the twenty-fifth,[a] in the thirty-eighth,[b] in the fiftieth,[c] and in the fifty-first.[d]

The king openly avowed and maintained this power of levying taxes at pleasure. At one time, he replied to the remonstrance made by the commons against it, that the impositions had been exacted from great necessity, and had been assented to by the prelates, earls, barons, and *some* of the commons;[e] at another, that he would advise with his council.[f] When the parliament desired, that a law might be enacted for the punishment of such as levied these arbitrary impositions, he refused compliance.[g] In the subsequent year, they desired that the king might renounce this pretended prerogative; but his answer was, that he would levy no taxes without necessity, for the defence of the realm, and where he reasonably might use that authority.[h] This incident passed a few days before his death; and these were, in a manner, his last words to his people. It would seem, that the famous charter or statute of Edward I. *de tallagio non concedendo,* though never repealed, was supposed to have already lost by age all its authority.

These facts can only show the *practice* of the times: For as to the *right,* the continual remonstrances of the commons may seem to prove that it rather lay on their side: At least, these remonstrances served to prevent the arbitrary practices of the court from becoming an established part of the constitution. In so much a better condition were the privileges of the people even during the arbitrary reign of Edward III. than during some subsequent ones, particularly those of the Tudors, where no tyranny or abuse of power ever met with any check or opposition, or so much as a remonstrance, from parliament.

In this reign we find, according to the sentiments of an ingenious and learned author, the first strongly marked and probably

---

[t] Rymer, vol. iv. p. 363. [u] P. 17, 18. [w] Rymer, vol. iv. p. 39. [x] P. 47.
[y] P. 52, 53, 57, 58. [z] P. 69. [a] P. 76. [b] P. 101. [c] P. 38. [d] P. 152.
[e] Cotton, p. 53. He repeats the same answer in p. 60. *Some of the commons* were such as he should be pleased to consult with. [f] Cotton, p. 57.
[g] Ibid. p. 138. [h] Ibid. p. 132.

contested distinction between a proclamation by the king and his privy-council, and a law which had received the assent of the lords and commons.[i]

It is easy to imagine, that a prince of so much sense and spirit as Edward, would be no slave to the court of Rome. Though the old tribute was paid during some years of his minority,[k] he afterwards withheld it; and when the pope in 1367 threatened to cite him to the court of Rome, for default of payment, he laid the matter before his parliament. That assembly unanimously declared, that king John could not, without a national consent, subject his kingdom to a foreign power: And that they were therefore determined to support their sovereign against this unjust pretension.[l]

During this reign, the statute of provisors was enacted, rendering it penal to procure any presentations to benefices from the court of Rome, and securing the rights of all patrons and electors, which had been extremely encroached on by the pope.[m] By a subsequent statute, every person was out-lawed who carried any cause by appeal to the court of Rome.[n]

The laity at this time seem to have been extremely prejudiced against the papal power, and even somewhat against their own clergy, because of their connexions with the Roman pontiff. The parliament pretended, that the usurpations of the pope were the cause of all the plagues, injuries, famine, and poverty of the realm; were more destructive to it than all the wars; and were the reason why it contained not a third of the inhabitants and commodities, which it formerly possessed: That the taxes, levied by him, exceeded five times those which were paid to the king: That every thing was venal in that sinful city of Rome; and that even the patrons in England had thence learned to practise simony without shame or remorse.[o] At another time, they petition the king to employ no churchman in any office of state;[p] and they even speak in plain terms, of expelling by force the papal authority, and thereby providing a remedy against oppressions, which they neither could nor would any longer endure.[q] Men who talked in this strain, were not far from the reformation: But Edward did not think proper to second all this zeal. Though he passed the statute of provisors, he

[i] Observations on the statutes, p. 193.   [k] Rymer, vol. iv. p. 434.
[l] Cotton's Abridg. p. 110.   [m] 25 Edw. III. 27 Edw. III.   [n] 27 Edw. III. 38 Edw. III.   [o] Cotton, p. 74, 128, 129.   [p] Ibid. p. 112.   [q] Cotton, p. 41.

CHAPTER XVI

took little care of its execution; and the parliament made frequent complaints of his negligence on this head.[r] He was content with having reduced such of the Romish ecclesiastics, as possessed revenues in England, to depend entirely upon him by means of that statute.

As to the police of the kingdom during this period, it was certainly better than during times of faction, civil war, and disorder, to which England was so often exposed: Yet were there several vices in the constitution, the bad consequences of which all the power and vigilance of the king could not prevent. The barons, by their confederacies with those of their own order, and by supporting and defending their retainers in every iniquity,[s] were the chief abettors of robbers, murderers, and ruffians of all kinds; and no law could be executed against those criminals. The nobility were brought to give their promise in parliament, that they would not avow, retain, or support any felon or breaker of the law;[t] yet this engagement, which we may wonder to see exacted from men of their rank, was never regarded by them. The commons make continual complaints of the multitude of robberies, murders, rapes, and other disorders, which, they say, were become numberless in every part of the kingdom, and which they always ascribe to the protection that the criminals received from the great.[u] The king of Cyprus, who paid a visit to England in this reign, was robbed and stripped on the highway with his whole retinue.[w] Edward himself contributed to this dissolution of law, by his facility in granting pardons to felons from the solicitation of the courtiers. Laws were made to retrench this prerogative,[x] and remonstrances of the commons were presented against the abuse of it:[y] But to no purpose. The gratifying of a powerful nobleman continued still to be of more importance than the protection of the people. The king also granted many franchises, which interrupted the course of justice and the execution of the laws.[z]

Commerce and industry were certainly at a very low ebb during this period. The bad police of the country alone affords a sufficient reason. The only exports were wool, skins, hydes, leather, butter,

[r] Ibid. p. 119, 128, 129, 130, 148. [s] 11 Edw. III. cap. 14. 4 Edw. III. cap. 2. 15 Edw. III. cap. 4. [t] Cotton, p. 10. [u] Ibid. p. 51, 62, 64, 70, 160. [w] Walsing. p. 170. [x] 10 Edw. III. cap. 2. 27 Edw. III. cap. 2. [y] Cotton, p. 75. [z] Ibid. p. 54.

tin, lead, and such unmanufactured goods, of which wool was by
far the most considerable. Knyghton has asserted, that 100,000
sacks of wool were annually exported, and sold at twenty pounds
a sack, money of that age. But he is widely mistaken both in the
quantity exported and in the value. In 1349, the parliament remonstrate, that the king, by an illegal imposition of forty shillings
on each sack exported, had levied 60,000 pounds a year:[a] Which
reduces the annual exports to 30,000 sacks. A sack contained
twenty-six stone, and each stone fourteen pounds;[b] and at a medium was not valued at above five pounds a sack,[c] that is, fourteen
or fifteen pounds of our present money. Knyghton's computation
raises it to sixty pounds, which is near four times the present price
of wool in England. According to this reduced computation, the
export of wool brought into the kingdom about 450,000 pounds of
our present money, instead of six millions, which is an extravagant
sum. Even the former sum is so high, as to afford a suspicion of
some mistake in the computation of the parliament with regard to
the number of sacks exported. Such mistakes were very usual in
those ages.

Edward endeavoured to introduce and promote the woollen
manufacture by giving protection and encouragement to foreign
weavers,[d] and by enacting a law, which prohibited every one from
wearing any cloth but of English fabric.[e] The parliament prohibited the exportation of woollen goods, which was not so well
judged, especially while the exportation of unwrought wool was so
much allowed and encouraged. A like injudicious law was made
against the exportation of manufactured iron.[f]

It appears from a record in the Exchequer, that in 1354 the
exports of England amounted to 294,184 pounds seventeen shillings and two-pence: The imports to 38,970 pounds three shillings
and six-pence money of that time. This is a great balance, considering that it arose wholly from the exportation of raw wool and
other rough materials. The import was chiefly linen and fine cloth,
and some wine. England seems to have been extremely drained at
this time by Edward's foreign expeditions and foreign subsidies,
which probably was the reason, why the exports so much exceed
the imports.

[a] Ibid. p. 48, 69.   [b] 34 Edw. III. cap. 5.   [c] Cotton, p. 29.   [d] 11 Edw. III.
cap. 5. Rymer, vol. iv. p. 723. Murimuth, p. 88.   [e] 11 Edw. III. cap. 2.
[f] 28 Edw. III. cap. 5

CHAPTER XVI

The first toll we read of in England, for mending the highways, was imposed in this reign: It was that for repairing the road between St. Giles's and Temple-Bar.[g]

In the first of Richard II. the parliament complains extremely of the decay of shipping during the preceding reign, and assert, that one sea-port formerly contained more vessels than were then to be found in the whole kingdom. This calamity, they ascribe to the arbitrary seizure of ships by Edward, for the service of his frequent expeditions.[h] The parliament in the fifth of Richard renew the same complaint,[i] and we likewise find it made in the forty-sixth of Edward III. So false is the common opinion, that this reign was favourable to commerce.

There is an order of this king, directed to the mayor and sheriffs of London, to take up all ships of forty tun and upwards to be converted into ships of war.[k]

The parliament attempted the impracticable scheme of reducing the price of labour after the pestilence, and also that of poultry.[l] A reaper, in the first week of August, was not allowed above two pence a day, or near six pence of our present money; in the second week a third more. A master carpenter was limited through the whole year to three pence a day, a common carpenter to two pence, money of that age.[m] It is remarkable, that, in the same reign, the pay of a common soldier, an archer, was six-pence a day; which, by the change, both in denomination and value, would be equivalent to near five shillings of our present money.[n] Soldiers were then inlisted only for a very short time: They lived idle all the rest of the year, and commonly all the rest of their lives: One successful campaign, by pay and plunder, and the ransom of prisoners, was supposed to be a small fortune to a man; which was a great allurement to enter into the service.[o]

[g] Rymer, vol. v. p. 520. [h] Cotton, p. 155, 164. [i] Cap. 3. [k] Rymer, vol. iv. p. 664. [l] 37 Edw. III. cap. 3. [m] 25 Edw. III. cap. 1, 3. [n] Dugdale's Baronage, vol. i. p. 784. Brady's hist. vol. ii. App. N°. 92. The pay of a man at arms was quadruple. We may therefore conclude, that the numerous armies, mentioned by historians in those times, consisted chiefly of ragamuffins, who followed the camp, and lived by plunder. Edward's army before Calais consisted of 31,094 men; yet its pay for sixteen months was only 127,201 pounds. Brady, ibid. [o] Commodities seem to have risen since the Conquest. Instead of being ten times cheaper than at present, they were in the age of Edward III. only three or four times. This change seems to have taken place in a great measure since Edward I. The allow-

The staple of wool, wool-fells, leather, and lead, was fixed by act of parliament in particular towns of England.[p] Afterwards it was removed by law to Calais: But Edward, who commonly deemed his prerogative above law, paid little regard to these statutes; and when the parliament remonstrated with him on account of those acts of power, he plainly told them, that he would proceed in that matter as he thought proper.[q] It is not easy to assign the reason of this great anxiety for fixing a staple; unless perhaps it invited foreigners to a market, when they knew beforehand, that they should there meet with great choice of any particular species of commodity. This policy of inviting foreigners to Calais was carried so far, that all English merchants were prohibited by law from exporting any English goods from the staple; which was in a manner the total abandoning of all foreign navigation, except that to Calais.[r] A contrivance seemingly extraordinary.

It was not till the middle of this century that the English began to extend their navigation even to the Baltic;[s] nor till the middle of the subsequent, that they sailed to the Mediterranean.[t]

Luxury was complained of in that age, as well as in others of more refinement; and attempts were made by parliament to restrain it, particularly on the head of apparel, where surely it is the most obviously innocent and inoffensive. No man under a hundred a year was allowed to wear gold, silver, or silk in his clothes: Servants also were prohibited from eating flesh meat, or fish, above once a day.[u] By another law it was ordained, that no one should be allowed, either for dinner or supper, above three dishes in each course, and not above two courses: And it is likewise expressly declared, that *soused* meat is to count as one of these dishes.[w] It was easy to foresee that such ridiculous laws must prove ineffectual, and could never be executed.

The use of the French language, in pleadings and public deeds, was abolished.[x] It may appear strange, that the nation should so

---

ance granted by Edward III. to the earl of Murray, then a prisoner in Nottingham castle, is one pound a week; whereas the bishop of St. Andrews, the primate of Scotland, had only six-pence a day allowed him by Edward I. [p] 27 Edw. III. [q] Cotton, p. 117. [r] 27 Edw. III. cap. 7. [s] Anderson, vol. i. p. 151. [t] Id. p. 177. [u] 37 Edw. III. cap. 8, 9, 10, &c. [w] 10. Edw. III. [x] 36 Edw. III cap. 15.

CHAPTER XVI

long have worn this badge of conquest: But the king and nobility seem never to have become thoroughly English, or to have forgotten their French extraction, till Edward's wars with France gave them an antipathy to that nation. Yet still, it was long before the use of the English tongue came into fashion. The first English paper which we meet with in Rymer is in the year 1386, during the reign of Richard II.[y] There are Spanish papers in that collection of more ancient date.[z] And the use of the Latin and French still continued.

We may judge of the ignorance of this age in geography, from a story told by Robert of Avesbury. Pope Clement VI. having, in 1344, created Lewis of Spain prince of *the fortunate Islands,* meaning the Canaries, then newly discovered; the English ambassador at Rome and his retinue were seized with an alarm, that Lewis had been created king of England; and they immediately hurried home, in order to convey this important intelligence. Yet such was the ardour for study at this time, that Speed in his Chronicle informs us, there were then 30,000 students in the university of Oxford alone. What was the occupation of all these young men? To learn very bad Latin, and still worse Logic.

In 1364, the commons petitioned, that, in consideration of the preceding pestilence, such persons as possessed manors holding of the king in chief, and had let different leases without obtaining licences, might continue to exercise the same power, till the country were become more populous.[a] The commons were sensible, that this security of possession was a good means for rendering the kingdom prosperous and flourishing; yet durst not apply, all at once, for a greater relaxation of their chains.

There is not a reign among those of the ancient English monarchs, which deserves more to be studied than that of Edward III. nor one where the domestic transactions will better discover the true genius of that kind of mixed government, which was then established in England. The struggles, with regard to the validity and authority of the great charter, were now over: The king was acknowledged to lie under some limitations: Edward himself was a prince of great capacity, not governed by favourites, not led

[y] Rymer, vol. vii. p. 526. This paper, by the style, seems to have been drawn by the Scots, and was signed by the wardens of the marches only. [z] Rymer, vol. vi. p. 554. [a] Cotton, p. 97.

astray by any unruly passion, sensible that nothing could be more essential to his interests than to keep on good terms with his people: Yet on the whole it appears, that the government, at best, was only a barbarous monarchy, not regulated by any fixed maxims, or bounded by any certain undisputed rights, which in practice were regularly observed. The king conducted himself by one set of principles; the barons by another; the commons by a third; the clergy by a fourth. All these systems of government were opposite and incompatible. Each of them prevailed in its turn, as incidents were favourable to it: A great prince rendered the monarchical power predominant: The weakness of a king gave reins to the aristocracy: A superstitious age saw the clergy triumphant: The people, for whom chiefly government was instituted, and who chiefly deserve consideration, were the weakest of the whole. But the commons, little obnoxious to any other order; though they sunk under the violence of tempests, silently reared their head in more peaceable times; and while the storm was brewing, were courted by all sides, and thus received still some accession to their privileges, or, at worst, some confirmation of them.

It has been an established opinion, that gold coin was not struck till this reign: But there has lately been found proof that it is as ancient as Henry III.[b]

[b] See Observations on the more ancient Statutes, p. 375. 2d edit.

XVII

RICHARD II

---

*Government during the minority –
Insurrection of the common people –
Discontents of the barons – Civil
commotions – Expulsion or execution of
the king's ministers – Cabals of
the duke of Glocester – Murder of the duke
of Glocester – Banishment of Henry
duke of Hereford – Return of Henry –
General insurrection – Deposition of the
king – His murder – His character –
Miscellaneous transactions
during this reign*

THE parliament, which was summoned soon after the king's accession, was both elected and assembled in tranquillity; and the great change, from a sovereign of consummate wisdom and experience to a boy of eleven years of age, was not immediately felt by the people. The habits of order and obedience, which the barons had been taught during the long reign of Edward, still influenced them; and the authority of the king's three uncles, the dukes of Lancaster, York, and Glocester, sufficed to repress, for a time, the turbulent spirit, to which that order, in a weak reign, was so often subject. The dangerous ambition too of these princes them-

*1377.
Government during the minority.*

selves was checked, by the plain and undeniable title of Richard, by
the declaration of it made in parliament, and by the affectionate
regard, which the people bore to the memory of his father, and
which was naturally transferred to the young sovereign upon the
throne. The different characters also of these three princes rendered them a counterpoize to each other; and it was natural to
expect, that any dangerous designs, which might be formed by one
brother, would meet with opposition from the others. Lancaster,
whose age and experience, and authority under the late king, gave
him the ascendant among them; though his integrity seemed not
proof against great temptations, was neither of an enterprizing
spirit, nor of a popular and engaging temper. York was indolent,
unactive, and of slender capacity. Glocester was turbulent, bold,
and popular; but being the youngest of the family, was restrained
by the power and authority of his elder brothers. There appeared,
therefore, no circumstance in the domestic situation of England,
which might endanger the public peace, or give any immediate
apprehensions to the lovers of their country.

But as Edward, though he had fixed the succession to the
crown, had taken no care to establish a plan of government during
the minority of his grandson; it behoved the parliament to supply
this defect: And the house of commons distinguished themselves,
by taking the lead on the occasion. This house, which had been
rising to consideration during the whole course of the late reign,
naturally received an accession of power during the minority; and
as it was now becoming a scene of business, the members chose for
the first time a speaker, who might preserve order in their debates,
and maintain those forms, which are requisite in all numerous
assemblies. Peter de la Mare was the man pitched on; the same
person that had been imprisoned and detained in custody by the
late king for his freedom of speech, in attacking the mistress and
the ministers of that prince. But though this election discovered a
spirit of liberty in the commons, and was followed by farther attacks both on these ministers, and on Alice Pierce,[c] they were still
too sensible of their great inferiority, to assume at first any immediate share in the administration of government, or the care of the
king's person. They were content to apply by petition to the lords

[c] Walsing. p. 150.

CHAPTER XVII

for that purpose, and desire them, both to appoint a council of nine, who might direct the public business, and to chuse men of virtuous life and conversation, who might inspect the conduct and education of the young prince. The lords complied with the first part of this request, and elected the bishops of London, Carlisle, and Salisbury, the earls of Marche and Stafford, Sir Richard de Stafford, Sir Henry le Scrope, Sir John Devereux, and Sir Hugh Segrave, to whom they gave authority for a year to conduct the ordinary course of business.[d] But as to the regulation of the king's household, they declined interposing in an office, which, they said, both was invidious in itself, and might prove disagreeable to his majesty.

The commons, as they acquired more courage, ventured to proceed a step farther in their applications. They presented a petition, in which they prayed the king to check the prevailing custom among the barons of forming illegal confederacies, and supporting each other, as well as men of inferior rank, in the violations of law and justice. They received from the throne a general and an obliging answer to this petition: But another part of their application, that all the great officers should, during the king's minority, be appointed by parliament, which seemed to require the concurrence of the commons, as well as that of the upper house, in the nomination, was not complied with: The lords alone assumed the power of appointing these officers: The commons tacitly acquiesced in the choice; and thought, that, for the present, they themselves had proceeded a sufficient length, if they but advanced their pretensions, though rejected, of interposing in these more important matters of state.

On this foot then the government stood. The administration was concluded entirely in the king's name: No regency was expressly appointed: The nine counsellors and the great officers, named by the peers, did their duty, each in his respective department: And the whole system was for some years kept together, by the secret authority of the king's uncles, especially of the duke of Lancaster, who was in reality the regent.

The parliament was dissolved, after the commons had represented the necessity of their being re-assembled once every year, as

[d] Rymer, vol. vii. p. 161.

appointed by law; and after having elected two citizens as their treasurers, to receive and disburse the produce of two fifteenths and tenths, which they had voted to the crown. In the other parliaments called during the minority, the commons still discover a strong spirit of freedom and a sense of their own authority, which, without breeding any disturbance, tended to secure their independance and that of the people.[e]

Edward had left his grandson involved in many dangerous wars. The pretensions of the duke of Lancaster to the crown of Castile, made that kingdom still persevere in hostilities against England. Scotland, whose throne was now filled by Robert Stuart, nephew to David Bruce, and the first prince of that family, maintained such close connections with France, that war with one crown almost inevitably produced hostilities with the other. The French monarch, whose prudent conduct had acquired him the sirname of *wise,* as he had already baffled all the experience and valour of the two Edwards, was likely to prove a dangerous enemy to a minor king: But his genius, which was not naturally enterprizing, led him not, at present, to give any disturbance to his neighbours; and he laboured, besides, under many difficulties at home, which it was necessary for him to surmount, before he could think of making conquests in a foreign country. England was master of Calais, Bourdeaux, and Bayonne; had lately acquired possession of Cherbourg, from the cession of the king of Navarre, and of Brest from that of the duke of Britanny;[f] and having thus an easy entrance into France from every quarter, was able, even in its present situation, to give disturbance to his government. Before Charles could remove the English from these important posts, he died in the flower of his age, and left his kingdom to a minor son, who bore the name of Charles VI.

1378. Meanwhile, the war with France was carried on in a manner somewhat languid, and produced no enterprize of great lustre or renown. Sir Hugh Calverly, governor of Calais, making an inroad into Picardy, with a detachment of the garrison, set fire to Boulogne.[g] The duke of Lancaster conducted an army into Britanny, but returned without being able to perform any thing memorable.

[e] See note [J] at the end of the volume.   [f] Rymer, vol. vii. p. 190.
[g] Walsing. p. 209.

CHAPTER XVII

In a subsequent year, the duke of Glocester marched out of Calais   *1380.*
with a body of 2000 cavalry, and 8000 infantry; and scrupled not,
with his small army, to enter into the heart of France, and to
continue his ravages, through Picardy, Champaigne, the Brie, the
Beausse, the Gatinois, the Orleanois, till he reached his allies in the
province of Britanny.[h] The duke of Burgundy, at the head of a
more considerable army, came within sight of him; but the French
were so over-awed by the former successes of the English, that no
superiority of numbers could tempt them to venture a pitched
battle with the troops of that nation. As the duke of Britanny, soon
after the arrival of these succours, formed an accommodation with
the court of France; this enterprize also proved in the issue unsuccessful, and made no durable impression upon the enemy.

The expences of these armaments, and the usual want of
oeconomy attending a minority, much exhausted the English treasury, and obliged the parliament, besides making some alterations
in the council, to impose a new and unusual tax of three groats on
every person, male and female, above fifteen years of age; and
they ordained, that, in levying that tax, the opulent should relieve
the poor by an equitable compensation. This imposition produced
a mutiny, which was singular in its circumstances. All history
abounds with examples, where the great tyrannize over the
meaner sort: But here the lowest populace rose against their rulers, committed the most cruel ravages upon them, and took vengeance for all former oppressions.

The faint dawn of the arts and of good government in that   *1381.*
age, had excited the minds of the populace, in different states of
Europe, to wish for a better condition, and to murmur against
those chains, which the laws, enacted by the haughty nobility and
gentry, had so long imposed upon them. The commotions of the
people in Flanders, the mutiny of the peasants in France, were the
natural effects of this growing spirit of independence; and the
report of these events, being brought into England, where personal slavery, as we learn from Froissard,[i] was more general than
in any other country in Europe, had prepared the minds of the
multitude for an insurrection. One John Ball also, a seditious
preacher, who affected low popularity, went about the country,

[h] Froissard, liv. 2. chap. 50, 51. Walsing. p. 239.   [i] Liv. 2. chap. 74.

and inculcated on his audience the principles of the first origin of mankind from one common stock, their equal right to liberty and to all the goods of nature, the tyranny of artificial distinctions, and the abuses which had arisen from the degradation of the more considerable part of the species, and the aggrandizement of a few insolent rulers.[k] These doctrines, so agreeable to the populace, and so conformable to the ideas of primitive equality, which are engraven in the hearts of all men, were greedily received by the multitude; and scattered the sparks of that sedition, which the present tax raised into a conflagration.[l]

Insurrections of the common people.

The imposition of three groats a head had been farmed out to tax-gatherers in each county, who levied the money on the people with rigour; and the clause, of making the rich ease their poorer neighbours of some share of the burden, being so vague and undeterminate, had doubtless occasioned many partialities, and made the people more sensible of the unequal lot, which fortune had assigned them in the distribution of her favours. The first disorder was raised by a black-smith in a village of Essex. The tax-gatherers came to this man's shop, while he was at work; and they demanded payment for his daughter, whom he asserted to be below the age assigned by the statute. One of these fellows offered to produce a very indecent proof to the contrary, and at the same time laid hold of the maid: Which the father resenting, immediately knocked out the ruffian's brains with his hammer. The by-standers applauded the action, and exclaimed, that it was full time for the people to take vengeance on their tyrants, and to vindicate their native liberty. They immediately flew to arms: The whole neighbourhood joined in the sedition: The flame spread in an instant over the county: It soon propagated itself into that of Kent, of Hertford, Surrey, Sussex, Suffolk, Norfolk, Cambridge, and Lincoln. Before the government had the least warning of the danger, the disorder had grown beyond controul or opposition: The populace had shaken off all regard to their former masters: And being headed by the most audacious and criminal of their

---

[k] Froissard, liv. 2. chap. 74. Walsingham, p. 275.   [l] There were two verses at that time in the mouths of all the common people, which, in spite of prejudice, one cannot but regard with some degree of approbation:
When Adam delv'd and Eve span,
Where was then the gentleman?

CHAPTER XVII

associates, who assumed the feigned names of Wat Tyler, Jack Straw, Hob Carter, and Tom Miller, by which they were fond of denoting their mean origin, they committed every where the most outrageous violence on such of the gentry or nobility as had the misfortune to fall into their hands.

The mutinous populace, amounting to a hundred thousand men, assembled on Black-heath, under their leaders, Tyler and Straw; and as the princess of Wales, the king's mother, returning from a pilgrimage to Canterbury, passed through the midst of them, they insulted her attendants, and some of the most insolent among them, to show their purpose of levelling all mankind, forced kisses from her; but they allowed her to continue her journey, without attempting any farther injury.[m] They sent a message to the king, who had taken shelter in the Tower; and they desired a conference with him. Richard sailed down the river in a barge for that purpose; but on his approaching the shore, he saw such symptoms of tumult and insolence, that he put back and returned to that fortress.[n] The seditious peasants, meanwhile, favoured by the populace of London, had broken into the city; had burned the duke of Lancaster's palace of the Savoy; cut off the heads of all the gentlemen whom they laid hold of; expressed a particular animosity against the lawyers and attornies; and pillaged the warehouses of the rich merchants.[o] A great body of them quartered themselves at Mile-end; and the king, finding no defence in the Tower, which was weakly garrisoned, and ill supplied with provisions, was obliged to go out to them, and ask their demands. They required a general pardon, the abolition of slavery, freedom of commerce in market-towns without toll or impost, and a fixed rent on lands instead of the services due by villenage. These requests, which, though extremely reasonable in themselves, the nation was not sufficiently prepared to receive, and which it was dangerous to have extorted by violence, were however complied with; charters to that purpose were granted them; and this body immediately dispersed and returned to their several homes.[p]

During this transaction, another body of the rebels had broken into the Tower; had murdered Simon Sudbury, the primate, and

12th June.

---

[m] Froissard, liv. 2. chap. 74.   [n] Ibid. chap. 75.   [o] Ibid. chap. 76. Walsingham, p. 248, 249.   [p] Froissard, liv. 2. chap. 77.

chancellor, with Sir Robert Hales, the treasurer, and some other persons of distinction; and continued their ravages in the city.[q] The king, passing along Smithfield, very slenderly guarded, met with Wat Tyler, at the head of these rioters, and entered into a conference with him. Tyler, having ordered his companions to retire till he should give them a signal, after which they were to murder all the company except the king himself, whom they were to detain prisoner, feared not to come into the midst of the royal retinue. He there behaved himself in such a manner, that Walworth, the mayor of London, not able to bear his insolence, drew his sword, and struck him so violent a blow as brought him to the ground, where he was instantly dispatched by others of the king's attendants. The mutineers, seeing their leader fall, prepared themselves for revenge; and this whole company, with the king himself, had undoubtedly perished on the spot, had it not been for an extraordinary presence of mind, which Richard discovered on the occasion. He ordered his company to stop; he advanced alone towards the enraged multitude; and accosting them with an affable and intrepid countenance, he asked them, "What is the meaning of this disorder, my good people? Are ye angry that ye have lost your leader? I am your king: I will be your leader." The populace, overawed by his presence, implicitly followed him: He led them into the fields, to prevent any disorder which might have arisen by their continuing in the city: Being there joined by Sir Robert Knolles and a body of well armed veteran soldiers, who had been secretly drawn together, he strictly prohibited that officer from falling on the rioters, and committing an undistinguished slaughter upon them; and he peaceably dismissed them with the same charters, which had been granted to their fellows.[r] Soon after, the nobility and gentry, hearing of the king's danger, in which they were all involved, flocked to London, with their adherents and retainers; and Richard took the field at the head of an army 40,000 strong.[s] It then behoved all the rebels to submit: The charters of enfranchisement and pardon were revoked by parliament; the low people were reduced to the same slavish condition as before; and several of the ringleaders were severely punished for the late disor-

---

[q] Walsingham, p. 250, 251.   [r] Froissard, vol. ii. chap. 77. Walsingham, p. 252. Knyghton, p. 2637.   [s] Walsingham, p. 267.

CHAPTER XVII

ders. Some were even executed without process or form of law.[t] It was pretended, that the intentions of the mutineers had been to seize the king's person, to carry him through England at their head, to murder all the nobility, gentry, and lawyers, and even all the bishops and priests, except the mendicant friars; to dispatch afterwards the king himself; and having thus reduced all to a level, to order the kingdom at their pleasure.[u] It is not impossible, but many of them, in the delirium of their first success, might have formed such projects: But of all the evils incident to human society, the insurrections of the populace, when not raised and supported by persons of higher quality, are the least to be dreaded: The mischiefs, consequent to an abolition of all rank and distinction, become so great, that they are immediately felt, and soon bring affairs back to their former order and arrangement.

A youth of sixteen, (which was at this time the king's age) who had discovered so much courage, presence of mind, and address, and had so dexterously eluded the violence of this tumult, raised great expectations in the nation; and it was natural to hope, that he would, in the course of his life, equal the glories, which had so uniformly attended his father and his grandfather, in all their undertakings. But in proportion as Richard advanced in years, *1385.* these hopes vanished; and his want of capacity, at least of solid judgment, appeared in every enterprize, which he attempted. The Scots, sensible of their own deficiency in cavalry, had applied to the regency of Charles VI.; and John de Vienne, admiral of France, had been sent over with a body of 1500 men at arms, to support them in their incursions against the English. The danger was now deemed by the king's uncles somewhat serious; and a numerous army of 60,000 men was levied; and they marched into Scotland, with Richard himself at their head. The Scots did not pretend to make resistance against so great a force: They abandoned without scruple their country to be pillaged and destroyed by the enemy: And when de Vienne expressed his surprize at this plan of operations, they told him, that all their cattle was driven into the forests and fastnesses; that their houses and other goods were of small value; and that they well knew how to compensate any losses which

---

[t] 5 Rich. II. cap. ult. as quoted in the observations on ancient statutes, p. 262. [u] Walsingham, p. 265.

they might sustain in that respect, by making an incursion into England. Accordingly, when Richard entered Scotland by Berwic and the east coast, the Scots, to the number of 30,000 men, attended by the French, entered the borders of England by the west, and carrying their ravages through Cumberland, Westmoreland, and Lancashire, collected a rich booty, and then returned in tranquillity to their own country. Richard meanwhile advanced towards Edinburgh, and destroyed in his way all the towns and villages on each side of him: He reduced that city to ashes: He treated in the same manner, Perth, Dundee, and other places in the low countries; but when he was advised to march towards the west coast, to await there the return of the enemy, and to take revenge on them for their devastations, his impatience to return to England, and enjoy his usual pleasures and amusements, outweighed every consideration; and he led back his army without effecting any thing by all these mighty preparations. The Scots, soon after, finding the heavy bodies of French cavalry very useless in that desultory kind of war, to which they confined themselves, treated their allies so ill, that the French returned home; much disgusted with the country, and with the manners of its inhabitants.[w] And the English, though they regretted the indolence and levity of their king, saw themselves for the future secured against any dangerous invasion from that quarter.

1386. But it was so material an interest of the French court to wrest the sea-port towns from the hands of their enemy, that they resolved to attempt it by some other expedient, and found no means so likely as an invasion of England itself. They collected a great fleet and army at Sluise; for the Flemings were now in alliance with them: All the nobility of France were engaged in this enterprize: The English were kept in alarm: Great preparations were made for the reception of the invaders: And though the dispersion of the French ships by a storm, and the taking of many of them by the English, before the embarkation of the troops, freed the kingdom from the present danger, the king and council were fully sensible, that this perilous situation might every moment return upon them.[x]

---

[w] Froissard, liv. 2. chap. 149, 150, &c. liv. 3. chap. 52. Walsingham, p. 316, 317.   [x] Froissard, liv. 3. chap. 41, 53. Walsingham, p. 322, 323.

CHAPTER XVII

There were two circumstances chiefly, which engaged the French at this time to think of such attempts. The one was the absence of the duke of Lancaster, who had carried into Spain the flower of the English military force, in prosecution of his vain claim to the crown of Castile; an enterprize, in which, after some promising success, he was finally disappointed: The other was, the violent dissentions and disorders, which had taken place in the English government.

The subjection, in which Richard was held by his uncles, particularly by the duke of Glocester, a prince of ambition and genius, though it was not unsuitable to his years and slender capacity, was extremely disagreeable to his violent temper; and he soon attempted to shake off the yoke imposed upon him. Robert de Vere, earl of Oxford, a young man of a noble family, of an agreeable figure, but of dissolute manners, had acquired an entire ascendant over him; and governed him with an absolute authority. The king set so little bounds to his affection, that he first created his favourite marquis of Dublin, a title before unknown in England, then duke of Ireland; and transferred to him by patent, which was confirmed in parliament, the entire sovereignty for life of that island.[y] He gave him in marriage his cousin-german, the daughter of Ingelram de Couci, earl of Bedford; but soon after he permitted him to repudiate that lady, though of an unexceptionable character, and to marry a foreigner, a Bohemian, with whom he had become enamoured.[z] These public declarations of attachment turned the attention of the whole court towards the minion: All favours passed through his hands: Access to the king could only be obtained by his mediation: And Richard seemed to take no pleasure in royal authority, but so far as it enabled him to load with favours and titles and dignities this object of his affections.

The jealousy of power immediately produced an animosity between the minion and his creatures on the one hand, and the princes of the blood and chief nobility on the other; and the usual complaints against the insolence of favourites were loudly echoed, and greedily received, in every part of the kingdom. Moubray earl of Nottingham, the mareschal, Fitz-Alan earl of Arundel, Piercy

Discontent of the barons.

---

[y] Cotton, p. 310, 311. Cox's Hist. of Ireland, p. 129. Walsingham, p. 324.
[z] Walsingham, p. 328.

earl of Northumberland, Montacute earl of Salisbury, Beauchamp earl of Warwic, were all connected with each other, and with the princes, by friendship or alliance, and still more by their common antipathy to those who had eclipsed them in the king's favour and confidence. No longer kept in awe by the personal character of the prince, they scorned to submit to his ministers; and the method, which they took to redress the grievance complained of, well suited the violence of the age, and proves the desperate extremities, to which every opposition was sure to be instantly carried.

Michael de la Pole, the present chancellor, and lately created earl of Suffolk, was the son of an eminent merchant; but had risen by his abilities and valour during the wars of Edward III. had acquired the friendship of that monarch, and was esteemed the person of greatest experience and capacity among those who were attached to the duke of Ireland and the king's secret council. The duke of Glocester, who had the house of commons at his devotion, impelled them to exercise that power which they seem first to have assumed against lord Latimer during the declining years of the late king; and an impeachment against the chancellor was carried up by them to the house of peers, which was no less at his devotion. The king foresaw the tempest preparing against him and his ministers. After attempting in vain to rouse the Londoners to his defence, he withdrew from parliament, and retired with his court to Eltham. The parliament sent a deputation, inviting him to return, and threatening, that, if he persisted in absenting himself, they would immediately dissolve, and leave the nation, though at that time in imminent danger of a French invasion, without any support or supply for its defence. At the same time, a member was encouraged to call for the record, containing the parliamentary deposition of Edward II.; a plain intimation of the fate, which Richard, if he continued refractory, had reason to expect from them. The king, finding himself unable to resist, was content to stipulate, that, except finishing the present impeachment against Suffolk, no attack should be made upon any other of his ministers; and on that condition, he returned to the parliament.[a]

Nothing can prove more fully the innocence of Suffolk, than the frivolousness of the crimes, which his enemies, in the present

[a] See note [K] at the end of the volume.

plenitude of their power, thought proper to object against him.[b] It was alledged, that being chancellor, and obliged by his oath to consult the king's profit, he had purchased lands of the crown below their true value; that he had exchanged with the king a perpetual annuity of 400 marks a year, which he inherited from his father, and which was assigned upon the customs of the port of Hull, for lands of an equal income; that having obtained for his son the priory of St. Anthony, which was formerly possessed by a Frenchman, an enemy, and a schismatic, and a new prior being at the same time named by the pope, he had refused to admit this person, whose title was not legal, till he made a composition with his son, and agreed to pay him a hundred pounds a year from the income of the benefice; that he had purchased, from one Tydeman of Limborch, an old and forfeited annuity of fifty pounds a-year upon the crown, and had engaged the king to admit that bad debt; and that, when created earl of Suffolk, he had obtained a grant of 500 pounds a-year, to support the dignity of that title.[c] Even the proof of these articles, frivolous as they are, was found very deficient upon the trial: It appeared, that Suffolk had made no purchase from the crown while he was chancellor, and that all his bargains of that kind were made before he was advanced to that dignity.[d] It is almost needless to add, that he was condemned, notwithstanding his defence; and that he was deprived of his office.

Glocester and his associates observed their stipulation with the king, and attacked no more of his ministers: But they immediately attacked himself and his royal dignity, and framed a commission after the model of those, which had been attempted almost in every reign since that of Richard I. and which had always been attended with extreme confusion.[e] By this commission, which was ratified by parliament, a council of fourteen persons was ap-

---

[b] Cotton, p. 315. Knyghton, p. 2683.   [c] It is probable that the earl of Suffolk was not rich, nor able to support the dignity without the bounty of the crown: For his father, Michael de la Pole, though a great merchant, had been ruined by lending money to the late king. See Cotton, p. 194. We may remark that the dukes of Glocester and York, though vastly rich, received at the same time each of them a thousand pounds a year, to support their dignity. Rymer, vol. vii. p. 481. Cotton, p. 310.   [d] Cotton, p. 315.   [e] Knyghton, p. 2686. Statutes at large, 10 Rich. II. chap. i.

pointed, all of Glocester's faction, except Nevil, archbishop of York: The sovereign power was transferred to these men for a twelvemonth: The king, who had now reached the twenty-first year of his age, was in reality dethroned: The aristocracy was rendered supreme: And though the term of the commission was limited, it was easy to foresee, that the intentions of the party were to render it perpetual, and that power would with great difficulty be wrested from those grasping hands, to which it was once committed. Richard, however, was obliged to submit: He signed the commission, which violence had extorted from him; he took an oath never to infringe it; and though at the end of the session he *publickly* entered a protest, that the prerogatives of the crown, notwithstanding his late concession, should still be deemed entire and unimpaired,*f* the new commissioners, without regarding this declaration, proceeded to the exercise of their authority.

1387.
Civil
com-
motions.
 The king, thus dispossessed of royal power, was soon sensible of the contempt, into which he was fallen. His favourites and ministers, who were as yet allowed to remain about his person, failed not to aggravate the injury, which, without any demerit on his part, had been offered to him. And his eager temper was of itself sufficiently inclined to seek the means, both of recovering his authority, and of revenging himself on those who had invaded it. As the house of commons appeared now of weight in the constitution, he secretly tried some expedients for procuring a favourable election: He sounded some of the sheriffs, who, being at that time both the returning officers, and magistrates of great power in the counties, had naturally considerable influence in elections.*g* But as most of them had been appointed by his uncles, either during his minority, or during the course of the present commission, he found them in general averse to his enterprize. The sentiments and inclinations of the judges were more favourable to him. He met at Nottingham Sir Robert Tresilian, chief justice of the King's Bench, Sir Robert Belknappe, chief justice of the Common Pleas, Sir John Cary, chief baron of the Exchequer, Holt, Fulthorpe, and Bourg, inferior justices, and Lockton, serjeant at law;

---

f Cotton, p. 318. *g* In the preamble to 5 Henry IV. cap. vii. it is implied, that the sheriffs in a manner appointed the members of the house of commons, not only in this parliament, but in many others.

CHAPTER XVII

and he proposed to them some queries, which these lawyers, either from the influence of his authority or of reason, made no scruple of answering in the way he desired. They declared, that the late commission was derogatory to the royalty and prerogative of the king; that those who procured it, or advised the king to consent to it, were punishable with death; that those who necessitated and compelled him were guilty of treason; that those were equally criminal who should persevere in maintaining it; that the king has the right of dissolving parliaments at pleasure; that the parliament, while it sits, must first proceed upon the king's business; and that this assembly cannot without his consent impeach any of his ministers and judges.[h] Even according to our present strict maxims with regard to law and the royal prerogative, all these determinations, except the two last, appear justifiable: And as the great privileges of the commons, particularly that of impeachment, were hitherto new, and supported by few precedents, there want not plausible reasons to justify these opinions of the judges.[i] They signed therefore their answer to the king's queries before the archbishops of York and Dublin, the bishops of Durham, Chichester, and Bangor, the duke of Ireland, the earl of Suffolk, and two other counsellors of inferior quality.

The duke of Glocester, and his adherents, soon got intelligence of this secret consultation, and were naturally very much alarmed

---

[h] Knyghton, p. 2694. Ypod. Neust. p. 541.   [i] The parliament in 1341, exacted of Edward III. that, on the third day of every session, the king should resume all the great offices; and that the ministers should then answer to any accusation that should be brought against them: Which plainly implies, that, while ministers, they could not be accused or impeached in parliament. Henry IV. told the commons, that the usage of parliament required them to go first through the king's business in granting supplies; which order the king intended not to alter, Parl. Hist. vol. ii. p. 65. Upon the whole, it must be allowed, that, according to ancient practice and principles, there are at least plausible grounds for all these opinions of the Judges. It must be remarked, that this affirmation of Henry IV. was given deliberately, after consulting the house of peers, who were much better acquainted with the usage of parliament than the ignorant commons. And it has the greater authority, because Henry IV. had made this very principle a considerable article of charge against his predecessor; and that a very few years before. So ill grounded were most of the imputations thrown on the unhappy Richard!

at it. They saw the king's intentions; and they determined to prevent the execution of them. As soon as he came to London, which, they knew, was well disposed to their party, they secretly assembled their forces, and appeared in arms at Haringay-park, near Highgate, with a power, which Richard and his ministers were not able to resist. They sent him a message by the archbishop of Canterbury, and the lords Lovel, Cobham, and Devereux, and demanded, that the persons who had seduced him by their pernicious counsel, and were traitors both to him and to the kingdom, should be delivered up to them. A few days after, they appeared in his presence, armed and attended with armed followers; and they accused by name the archbishop of York, the duke of Ireland, the earl of Suffolk, Sir Robert Tresilian, and Sir Nicholas Brembre, as public and dangerous enemies to the state. They threw down their gauntlets before the king, and fiercely offered to maintain the truth of their charge by duel. The persons accused, and all the other obnoxious ministers, had withdrawn or had concealed themselves.

The duke of Ireland fled to Cheshire, and levied some forces, with which he advanced to relieve the king from the violence of the nobles. Glocester encountered him in Oxfordshire with much superior forces; routed him, dispersed his followers, and obliged him to fly into the Low-Countries, where he died in exile a few years after. The lords then appeared at London with an army of 40,000 men; and having obliged the king to summon a parliament, which was entirely at their devotion, they had full power, by observing a few legal forms, to take vengeance on all their enemies. Five great peers, men whose combined power was able at any time to shake the throne, the duke of Glocester, the king's uncle; the earl of Derby, son of the duke of Lancaster; the earl of Arundel; the earl of Warwic, and the earl of Nottingham, mareschal of England, entered before the parliament an accusation or appeal, as it was called, against the five counsellors, whom they had already accused before the king. The parliament, who ought to have been judges, were not ashamed to impose an oath on all their members, by which they bound themselves to live and die with the lords appellants, and to defend them against all opposition with their lives and fortunes.[k]

1388.
3d Feb.

Expulsion or execution of the king's ministers.

[k] Cotton, p. 322.

CHAPTER XVII

The other proceedings were well suited to the violence and iniquity of the times. A charge, consisting of thirty-nine articles, was delivered in by the appellants; and as none of the accused counsellors, except Sir Nicholas Brembre, was in custody, the rest were cited to appear; and upon their absenting themselves, the house of peers, after a very short interval, without hearing a witness, without examining a fact, or deliberating on one point of law, declared them guilty of high treason. Sir Nicholas Brembre, who was produced in court, had the appearance, and but the appearance, of a trial: The peers, though they were not by law his proper judges, pronounced, in a very summary manner, sentence of death upon him; and he was executed, together with Sir Robert Tresilian, who had been discovered and taken in the interval.

It would be tedious to recite the whole charge delivered in against the five counsellors; which is to be met with in several collections.[l] It is sufficient to observe in general, that, if we reason upon the supposition, which is the true one, that the royal prerogative was invaded by the commission extorted by the duke of Glocester and his associates, and that the king's person was afterwards detained in custody by rebels, many of the articles will appear, not only to imply no crime in the duke of Ireland and the ministers, but to ascribe to them actions, which were laudable, and which they were bound by their allegiance to perform. The few articles, impeaching the conduct of these ministers before that commission, which subverted the constitution, and annihilated all justice and legal authority, are vague and general; such as their engrossing the king's favour, keeping his barons at a distance from him, obtaining unreasonable grants for themselves or their creatures, and dissipating the public treasure by useless expences. No violence is objected to them; no particular illegal act;* no breach of any statute; and their administration may therefore be concluded to have been so far innocent and inoffensive. All the disorders indeed seem to have proceeded, not from any violation of the laws, or any ministerial tyranny; but merely from a rivalship of power, which the duke of Glocester, and the great nobility, agreeably to the genius of the times, carried to the utmost extremity

---

[l] Knyghton, p. 2715. Tyrrel, vol. iii. part 2. p. 919. from the records. Parliamentary History, vol. i. p. 414.   * See note [L] at the end of the volume.

against their opponents, without any regard to reason, justice, or humanity.

But these were not the only deeds of violence committed during the triumph of the party. All the other judges, who had signed the extrajudicial opinions at Nottingham, were condemned to death, and were, as a grace of favour, banished to Ireland; though they pleaded the fear of their lives, and the menaces of the king's ministers as their excuse. Lord Beauchamp of Holt, Sir James Berners, and John Salisbury, were also tried and condemned for high treason; merely because they had attempted to defeat the late commission: But the life of the latter was spared. The fate of Sir Simon Burley was more severe: This gentleman was much beloved for his personal merit, had distinguished himself by many honourable actions,*m* was created knight of the garter, and had been appointed governor to Richard, by the choice of the late king and of the Black Prince: He had attended his master from the earliest infancy of that prince, and had ever remained extremely attached to him: Yet all these considerations could not save him from falling a victim to Glocester's vengeance. This execution, more than all the others, made a deep impression on the mind of Richard: His queen too (for he was already married to the sister of the emperor Winceslaus, king of Bohemia) interested herself in behalf of Burley: She remained three hours on her knees before the duke of Glocester, pleading for that gentleman's life; but though she was become extremely popular by her amiable qualities, which had acquired her the appellation of *the good queen Anne;* her petition was sternly rejected by the inexorable tyrant.

The parliament concluded this violent scene by a declaration, that none of the articles, decided on these trials to be treason, should ever afterwards be drawn into precedent by the judges, who were still to consider the statute of the twenty-fifth of Edward as the rule of their decisions. The house of lords seem not at that time to have known or acknowledged the principle, that they

---

m At least this is the character given of him by Froissard, liv. 2. who knew him personally: Walsingham, p. 334. gives a very different character of him; but he is a writer somewhat passionate and partial; and the choice made of this gentleman by Edward III. and the Black Prince for the education of Richard, makes the character given him by Froissard, much more probable.

themselves were bound, in their judicial capacity, to follow the rules, which they, in conjunction with the king and commons, had established in their legislative.* It was also enacted, that every one should swear to the perpetual maintenance and support of the forfeitures and attainders, and of all the other acts passed during this parliament. The archbishop of Canterbury added the penalty of excommunication, as a farther security to these violent transactions.

It might naturally be expected, that the king, being reduced to such slavery by the combination of the princes and chief nobility, and having appeared so unable to defend his servants from the cruel effects of their resentment, would long remain in subjection to them; and never would recover the royal power, without the most violent struggles and convulsions: But the event proved contrary. In less than a twelvemonth, Richard, who was in his twenty-third year, declared in council, that, as he had now attained the full age, which entitled him to govern by his own authority his kingdom and household, he resolved to exercise his right of sovereignty; and when no one ventured to contradict so reasonable an intention, he deprived Fitz-Alan archbishop of Canterbury of the dignity of chancellor, and bestowed that high office on William of Wickham, bishop of Winchester; the bishop of Hereford was displaced from the office of treasurer, the earl of Arundel from that of admiral; even the duke of Glocester and the earl of Warwic were removed for a time from the council: And no opposition was made to these great changes. The history of this reign is imperfect, and little to be depended on; except where it is supported by public records: And it is not easy for us to assign the reason of this unexpected event. Perhaps, some secret animosities, naturally to be expected in that situation, had creeped in among the great men, and had enabled the king to recover his authority. Perhaps, the violence of their former proceedings had lost them the affections of the people, who soon repent of any cruel extremities, to which they are carried by their leaders. However this may be, Richard exercised with moderation the authority which he had resumed. He seemed to be entirely reconciled to his uncles[n] and the other great men, of whom he had so much reason to complain: He never

1389.

---

* See note [M] at the end of the volume.   [n] Dugdale, vol. ii. p. 170.

attempted to recal from banishment the duke of Ireland, whom he found so obnoxious to them: He confirmed by proclamation the general pardon, which the parliament had passed for all offences: And he courted the affections of the people, by voluntarily remitting some subsidies, which had been granted him; a remarkable, and almost singular instance of such generosity.

After this composure of domestic differences, and this restoration of the government to its natural state, there passes an interval of eight years, which affords not many remarkable events. The duke of Lancaster returned from Spain; having resigned to his rival all pretensions to the crown of Castile upon payment of a large sum of money,[o] and having married his daughter, Philippa, to the king of Portugal. The authority of this prince served to counterbalance that of the duke of Glocester, and secured the power of Richard, who paid great court to his eldest uncle, by whom he had never been offended, and whom he found more moderate in his temper than the younger. He made a cession to him for life of the dutchy of Guienne,[p] which the inclinations and changeable humour of the Gascons had restored to the English government; but as they remonstrated loudly against this deed, it was finally, with the duke's consent, revoked by Richard.[q] There happened an incident, which produced a dissention between Lancaster and his two brothers. After the death of the Spanish princess, he espoused Catharine Swineford, daughter of a private knight of Hainault, by whose alliance, York and Glocester thought the dignity of their family much injured: But the king gratified his uncle by passing in parliament a charter of legitimation to the children whom that lady had born him before marriage, and by creating the eldest earl of Somerset.[r]

The wars, meanwhile, which Richard had inherited with his crown, still continued; though interrupted by frequent truces, according to the practice of that age, and conducted with little vigour, by reason of the weakness of all parties. The French war was scarcely heard of; the tranquillity of the northern borders was only interrupted by one inroad of the Scots, which proceeded more from a rivalship between the two martial families of Piercy and

[o] Knyghton, p. 2677. Walsingham, p. 342.   [p] Rymer, vol. vii. p. 659.
[q] Ibid. p. 687.   [r] Cotton, p. 365. Walsingham, p. 352.

CHAPTER XVII

Douglas, than from any national quarrel: A fierce battle or skirmish was fought at Otterborne,[s] in which young Piercy, sirnamed *Hotspur,* from his impetuous valour, was taken prisoner, and Douglas slain, and the victory remained undecided.[t] Some insurrections of the Irish obliged the king to make an expedition into that country, which he reduced to obedience; and he recovered, in some degree, by this enterprize, his character of courage, which had suffered a little by the inactivity of his reign. At last, the English and French courts began to think in earnest of a lasting peace; but found it so difficult to adjust their opposite pretensions, that they were content to establish a truce of twenty-five years:[u] Brest and Cherbourg were restored, the former to the duke of Britanny, the latter to the king of Navarre: Both parties were left in possession of all the other places which they held at the time of concluding the truce: And to render the amity between the two crowns more durable, Richard, who was now a widower, was affianced to Isabella, the daughter of Charles.[w] This princess was only seven years of age; but the king agreed to so unequal a match, chiefly that he might fortify himself by this alliance, against the enterprizes of his uncles and the incurable turbulence as well as inconstancy of his barons.

The administration of the king, though it was not, in this interval, sullied by any unpopular act, except the seizing of the charter of London,[x] which was soon after restored, tended not much to corroborate his authority, and his personal character brought him into contempt, even while his public government appeared, in a good measure, unexceptionable. Indolent, profuse, addicted to low pleasures; he spent his whole time in feasting and jollity, and dissipated, in idle show, or in bounties to favourites of no reputation, that revenue which the people expected to see him employ in enterprizes directed to public honour and advantage. He forgot his rank by admitting all men to his familiarity; and he was not sensible, that their acquaintance with the qualities of his mind was not able to impress them with the respect, which he neglected to preserve from his birth and station. The earls of Kent and Hunt-

1396.

---

[s] 15th August, 1388.   [t] Froissard, liv. 3. chap. 124, 125, 126. Walsingham, p. 355.   [u] Rymer, vol. vii. p. 820.   [w] Ibid. p. 811.   [x] Ibid. p. 727. Walsingham, p. 347.

ingdon, his half brothers, were his chief confidents and favourites; and though he never devoted himself to them with so profuse an affection as that with which he had formerly been attached to the duke of Ireland, it was easy for men to see, that every grace passed through their hands, and that the king had rendered himself a mere cypher in the government. The small regard, which the public bore to his person, disposed them to murmur against his administration, and to receive with greedy ears every complaint, which the discontented or ambitious grandees suggested to them.

1397.
Cabals
of the
duke of
Glocester.

Glocester soon perceived the advantages, which this dissolute conduct gave him; and finding, that both resentment and jealousy on the part of his nephew still prevented him from acquiring any ascendant over that prince, he determined to cultivate his popularity with the nation, and to revenge himself on those who eclipsed him in favour and authority. He seldom appeared at court or in council: He never declared his opinion but in order to disapprove of the measures embraced by the king and his favourites: And he courted the friendship of every man, whom disappointment or private resentment had rendered an enemy to the administration. The long truce with France was unpopular with the English, who breathed nothing but war against that hostile nation; and Glocester took care to encourage all the vulgar prejudices, which prevailed on this subject. Forgetting the misfortunes, which attended the English arms during the later years of Edward; he made an invidious comparison between the glories of that reign and the inactivity of the present, and he lamented that Richard should have degenerated so much from the heroic virtues by which his father and his grandfather were distinguished. The military men were inflamed with a desire of war, when they heard him talk of the signal victories formerly obtained, and of the easy prey which might be made of French riches by the superior valour of the English: The populace readily embraced the same sentiments: And all men exclaimed, that this prince, whose counsels were so much neglected, was the true support of English honour, and alone able to raise the nation to its former power and splendor. His great abilities, his popular manners, his princely extraction, his immense riches, his high office of constable;[y] all these advantages,

[y] Rymer, vol. vii. p. 152.

not a little assisted by his want of court-favour, gave him a mighty authority in the kingdom, and rendered him formidable to Richard and his ministers.

Froissard,[z] a contemporary writer and very impartial, but whose credit is somewhat impaired by his want of exactness in material facts, ascribes to the duke of Glocester more desperate views, and such as were totally incompatible with the government and domestic tranquillity of the nation. According to that historian, he proposed to his nephew, Roger Mortimer, earl of Marche, whom Richard had declared his successor, to give him immediate possession of the throne, by the deposition of a prince, so unworthy of power and authority: And when Mortimer declined the project, he resolved to make a partition of the kingdom between himself, his two brothers, and the earl of Arundel; and entirely to dispossess Richard of the crown. The king, it is said, being informed of these designs, saw that either his own ruin or that of Glocester was inevitable; and he resolved, by a hasty blow, to prevent the execution of such destructive projects. This is certain, that Glocester, by his own confession, had often affected to speak contemptuously of the king's person and government; had deliberated concerning the lawfulness of throwing off allegiance to him; and had even born part in a secret conference, where his deposition was proposed, and talked of, and determined.[a] But it is reasonable to think, that his schemes were not so far advanced as to make him resolve on putting them immediately in execution. The danger, probably, was still too distant to render a desperate remedy entirely necessary for the security of government.

But whatever opinion we may form of the danger arising from Glocester's conspiracies, his aversion to the French truce and alliance was public and avowed; and that court, which had now a great influence over the king, pushed him to provide for his own safety, by punishing the traiterous designs of his uncle. The resentment

---

[z] Liv. 4. chap. 86.   [a] Cotton, p. 378. Tyrrel, vol. iii. part 2. p. 972, from the records. Parliamentary History, vol. i. p. 473. That this confession was genuine, and obtained without violence, may be entirely depended on. Judge Rickhill, who brought it over from Calais, was tried on that account, and acquitted in the first parliament of Henry IV. when Glocester's party was prevalent. His acquittal, notwithstanding his innocence, may even appear marvellous, considering the times. See Cotton, p. 393.

against his former acts of violence revived; the sense of his refractory and uncompliant behaviour was still recent; and a man, whose
ambition had once usurped royal authority, and who had murdered all the faithful servants of the king, was thought capable, on
a favourable opportunity, of renewing the same criminal enterprizes. The king's precipitate temper admitted of no deliberation:
He ordered Glocester to be unexpectedly arrested; to be hurried
on board a ship which was lying in the river; and to be carried over
to Calais, where alone, by reason of his numerous partizans, he
could safely be detained in custody.[b] The earls of Arundel and
Warwic were seized at the same time: The malcontents, so suddenly deprived of their leaders, were astonished and overawed:
And the concurrence of the dukes of Lancaster and York in those
measures, together with the earls of Derby and Rutland, the eldest
sons of these princes,[c] bereaved them of all possibility of resistance.

A parliament was immediately summoned at Westminster; and
the king doubted not to find the peers, and still more the commons, very compliant with his will. This house had in a former
parliament given him very sensible proofs of their attachment;[*]
and the present suppression of Glocester's party made him still
more assured of a favourable election. As a farther expedient for
that purpose, he is also said to have employed the influence of the
sheriffs; a practice which, though not unusual, gave umbrage, but
which the established authority of that assembly rendered afterwards still more familiar to the nation. Accordingly, the parliament passed whatever acts the king was pleased to dictate to them:[d]
They annulled for ever the commission which usurped upon the
royal authority, and they declared it treasonable to attempt, in any
future period, the revival of any similar commission:[e] They abrogated all the acts, which attainted the king's ministers, and which
that parliament who passed them, and the whole nation, had
sworn inviolably to maintain: And they declared the general par-

[b] Froissard, liv. 4. chap. 90. Walsing. p. 354.   [c] Rymer, vol. viii. p. 7.
[*] See note [N] at the end of the volume.   [d] The nobles brought numerous
retainers with them to give them security, as we are told by Walsingham,
p. 354. The king had only a few Cheshire men for his guard.   [e] Statutes
at Large, 21 Richard II.

CHAPTER XVII

don then granted to be invalid, as extorted by force, and never ratified by the free consent of the king. Though Richard, after he resumed the government, and lay no longer under constraint, had voluntarily, by proclamation, confirmed that general indemnity; this circumstance seemed not, in their eyes, to merit any consideration. Even a particular pardon granted six years after to the earl of Arundel, was annulled by parliament; on pretence, that it had been procured by surprize, and that the king was not then fully apprized of the degree of guilt incurred by that nobleman.

The commons then preferred an impeachment against Fitz-Alan, archbishop of Canterbury, and brother to Arundel, and accused him for his concurrence in procuring the illegal commission, and in attainting the king's ministers. The primate pleaded guilty; but as he was protected by the ecclesiastical privileges, the king was satisfied with a sentence, which banished him the kingdom, and sequestered his temporalities.[f] An appeal or accusation was presented against the duke of Glocester, and the earls of Arundel and Warwic, by the earls of Rutland, Kent, Huntingdon, Somerset, Salisbury, and Nottingham, together with the lords Spencer and Scrope, and they were accused of the same crimes which had been imputed to the archbishop, as well as of their appearance against the king in a hostile manner at Haringay-park. The earl of Arundel, who was brought to the bar, wisely confined all his defence to the pleading of both the general and particular pardon of the king; but his plea being over-ruled, he was condemned, and executed.[g] The earl of Warwic, who was also convicted of high treason, was, on account of his submissive behaviour, pardoned as to his life, but doomed to perpetual banishment in the Isle of Man. No new acts of treason were imputed to either of these noblemen. The only crimes, for which they were condemned, were the old attempts against the crown, which seemed to be obliterated, both by the distance of time, and by repeated pardons.[h] The reasons of this method of proceeding, it is difficult to conjecture. The recent conspiracies of Glocester seem certain from his own confession: But, perhaps, the king and ministry had not, at that time, in their hands, any satisfactory proof of their

---

[f] Cotton, p. 368.   [g] Ibid. p. 377. Froissard, liv. 4. chap. 90. Walsing. p. 354.   [h] Tyrrel, vol. iii. part 2. p. 968. from the records.

reality; perhaps, it was difficult to convict Arundel and Warwic, of any participation in them; perhaps, an enquiry into these conspiracies would have involved in the guilt some of those great noblemen, who now concurred with the crown, and whom it was necessary to cover from all imputation; or perhaps, the king, according to the genius of the age, was indifferent about maintaining even the appearance of law and equity, and was only solicitous by any means to ensure success in these prosecutions. This point, like many others in ancient history, we are obliged to leave altogether undetermined.

Murder of the duke of Glocester. A warrant was issued to the earl Marshal, governor of Calais, to bring over the duke of Glocester, in order to his trial; but the governor returned for answer, that the duke had died suddenly of an apoplexy in that fortress. Nothing could be more suspicious, from the time, than the circumstances of that prince's death: It became immediately the general opinion, that he was murdered by orders from his nephew: In the subsequent reign undoubted proofs were produced in parliament, that he had been suffocated with pillows by his keepers:[i] And it appeared, that the king, apprehensive lest the public trial and execution of so popular a prince, and so near a relation, might prove both dangerous and invidious, had taken this base method of gratifying, and, as he fancied, concealing, his revenge upon him. Both parties, in their successive triumphs, seem to have had no farther concern than that of retaliating upon their adversaries; and neither of them were aware, that, by imitating, they indirectly justified, as far as it lay in their power, all the illegal violence of the opposite party.

This session concluded with the creation or advancement of several peers: The earl of Derby was made duke of Hereford; the earl of Rutland, duke of Albemarle; the earl of Kent, duke of Surrey; the earl of Huntingdon, duke of Exeter; the earl of Nottingham, duke of Norfolk; the earl of Somerset, marquis of Dorset; lord Spenser, earl of Glocester; Ralph Nevil, earl of Westmoreland; Thomas Piercy, earl of Worcester; William Scrope, earl of Wiltshire.[k] The parliament, after a session of twelve days, was adjourned to Shrewsbury. The king, before the departure of the members, exacted from them an oath for the perpetual mainte-

[i] Cotton, p. 399, 400. Dugdale, vol. ii. p. 171.   [k] Cotton, p. 370, 371.

nance and establishment of all their acts; an oath, similar to that which had formerly been required by the duke of Glocester and his party, and which had already proved so vain and fruitless.

Both king and parliament met in the same dispositions at Shrewsbury. So anxious was Richard for the security of these acts, that he obliged the lords and commons to swear anew to them on the cross of Canterbury;[l] and he soon after procured a bull from the pope, by which they were, as he imagined, perpetually secured and established.[m] The parliament, on the other hand, conferred on him *for life* the duties on wool, wool-fells, and leather, and granted him besides, a subsidy of one tenth and a half, and one fifteenth and a half. They also reversed the attainder of Tresilian and the other judges; and with the approbation of the present judges, declared the answers, for which these magistrates had been impeached, to be just and legal:[n] And they carried so far their retrospect as to reverse, on the petition of lord Spenser, earl of Glocester, the attainder pronounced against the two Spensers in the reign of Edward II.[o] The ancient history of England is nothing but a catalogue of reversals: Every thing is in fluctuation and movement: One faction is continually undoing what was established by another: And the multiplied oaths, which each party exacted for the security of the present acts, betray a perpetual consciousness of their instability.

The parliament, before they were dissolved, elected a committee of twelve lords and six commoners,[p] whom they invested with the whole power both of lords and commons, and endowed with full authority to finish all business, which had been laid before the houses, and which they had not had leisure to bring to a conclusion.[q] This was an unusual concession; and though it was limited in the object, might, either immediately or as a precedent, have

1398.
28th
Jan.

---

[l] Ibid. p. 371.   [m] Walsing. p. 355.   [n] Statutes at large, 21 Rich. II.
[o] Cotton, p. 372.   [p] The names of the commissioners were, the dukes of Lancaster, York, Albemarle, Surrey, and Exeter, the marquis of Dorset, the earls of March, Salisbury, Northumberland, Glocester, Winchester, and Wiltshire, John Bussey, Henry Green, John Russel, Robert Teyne, Henry Chelmeswicke, and John Golofre. It is to be remarked, that the duke of Lancaster always concurred with the rest in all their proceedings, even in the banishment of his son, which was afterwards so much complained of.
[q] Cotton, p. 372. Walsing. p. 355.

proved dangerous to the constitution: But the cause of that extraordinary measure was an event singular and unexpected, which engaged the attention of the parliament.

After the destruction of the duke of Glocester and the heads of that party, a misunderstanding broke out among those noblemen, who had joined in the prosecution; and the king wanted either authority sufficient to appease it, or foresight to prevent it. The duke of Hereford appeared in parliament, and accused the duke of Norfolk of having spoken to him, in private, many slanderous words of the king, and of having imputed to that prince an intention of subverting and destroying many of his principal nobility.[r] Norfolk denied the charge, gave Hereford the lie, and offered to prove his own innocence by duel. The challenge was accepted: The time and place of combat were appointed: And as the event of this important trial by arms might require the interposition of legislative authority, the parliament thought it more suitable to delegate their power to a committee, than to prolong the session beyond the usual time which custom and general convenience had prescribed to it.[s]

The duke of Hereford was certainly very little delicate in the point of honour, when he revealed a private conversation to the ruin of the person who had entrusted him; and we may thence be more inclined to believe the duke of Norfolk's denial, than the other's asseveration. But Norfolk had in these transactions betrayed an equal neglect of honour, which brings him entirely on a level with his antagonist. Though he had publicly joined with the duke of Glocester and his party in all the former acts of violence against the king; and his name stands among the appellants who accused the duke of Ireland and the other ministers: Yet was he not ashamed publicly to impeach his former associates for the very crimes, which he had concurred with them in committing; and his name encreases the list of those appellants who brought them to a trial. Such were the principles and practices of those ancient

---

[r] Cotton, p. 372. Parliamentary history, vol. i. p. 490. [s] In the first year of Henry VI. when the authority of parliament was great, and when that assembly could least be suspected of lying under violence, a like concession was made to the privy council from like motives of convenience. See Cotton, p. 564.

CHAPTER XVII

knights and barons during the prevalence of the aristocratical government, and the reign of chivalry.

The lists for this decision of truth and right were appointed at Coventry before the king: All the nobility of England bandied into parties, and adhered either to the one duke or the other: The whole nation was held in suspence with regard to the event: But when the two champions appeared in the field, accoutered for the combat, the king interposed, to prevent both the present effusion of such noble blood, and the future consequences of the quarrel. By the advice and authority of the parliamentary commissioners, he stopped the duel; and to show his impartiality, he ordered, by the same authority, both the combatants to leave the kingdom;[1] assigning one country for the place of Norfolk's exile, which he declared perpetual, another for that of Hereford, which he limited to ten years.

Hereford was a man of great prudence and command of temper; and he behaved himself with so much submission in these delicate circumstances, that the king, before his departure, promised to shorten the term of his exile four years; and he also granted him letters patent, by which he was empowered, in case any inheritance should in the interval accrue to him, to enter immediately in possession, and to postpone the doing of homage till his return.

The weakness and fluctuation of Richard's counsels appear no where more evident than in the conduct of this affair. No sooner had Hereford left the kingdom, than the king's jealousy of the power and riches of that prince's family revived; and he was sensible, that, by Glocester's death, he had only removed a counterpoise to the Lancastrian interest, which was now become formidable to his crown and kingdom. Being informed, that Hereford had entered into a treaty of marriage with the daughter of the duke of Berry, uncle to the French king, he determined to prevent the finishing of an alliance, which would so much extend the interest of his cousin in foreign countries; and he sent over the earl of Salisbury to Paris with a commission for that purpose. The death of the duke of Lancaster, which happened soon after, called upon him to take new resolutions with regard to that opulent succession. The present duke, in consequence of the king's patent, desired to

Banishment of Henry duke of Hereford.

1399. 3d Feb.

[1] Cotton, p. 380. Walsingham, p. 356.

be put in possession of the estate and jurisdictions of his father: But Richard, afraid of strengthening the hands of a man, whom he had already so much offended, applied to the parliamentary commissioners, and persuaded them, that this affair was but an appendage to that business which the parliament had delegated to them. By their authority, he revoked his letters patent, and retained possession of the estate of Lancaster: And by the same authority, he seized and tried the duke's attorney, who had procured and insisted on the letters, and he had him condemned as a traitor, for faithfully executing that trust to his master.[u] An extravagant act of power! even though the king changed, in favour of the attorney, the penalty of death into that of banishment.

Henry, the new duke of Lancaster, had acquired, by his conduct and abilities, the esteem of the public; and having served with distinction against the infidels in Lithuania, he had joined to his other praises those of piety and valour, virtues which have at all times a great influence over mankind, and were, during those ages, the qualities chiefly held in estimation.[w] He was connected with most of the principal nobility by blood, alliance, or friendship; and as the injury, done him by the king, might in its consequences affect all of them, he easily brought them, by a sense of common interest, to take part in his resentment. The people, who must have an object of affection, who found nothing in the king's person, which they could love or revere, and who were even disgusted with many parts of his conduct,[x] easily transferred to Henry that attachment, which the death of the duke of Glocester had left without any fixed direction. His misfortunes were lamented; the injustice, which he had suffered, was complained of; and all men turned their eyes towards him, as the only person that could retrieve the lost honour of the nation, or redress the supposed abuses in the government.

[u] Tyrrel, vol. iii. part 2. p. 991, from the records.   [w] Walsingham, p. 343.
[x] He levied fines upon those who had ten years before joined the duke of Glocester and his party: They were obliged to pay him money, before he would allow them to enjoy the benefit of the indemnity; and in the articles of charge against him, it is asserted, that the payment of one fine did not suffice. It is indeed likely, that his ministers would abuse the power put into their hands; and this grievance extended to very many people. Historians agree in representing this practice as a great oppression. See Otterburne, p. 199.

CHAPTER XVII

While such were the dispositions of the people, Richard had the *Return of* imprudence to embark for Ireland, in order to revenge the death *Henry.* of his cousin, Roger earl of Marche, the presumptive heir of the crown, who had lately been slain in a skirmish by the natives; and he thereby left the kingdom of England open to the attempts of his provoked and ambitious enemy. Henry, embarking at Nantz with *4th July.* a retinue of sixty persons, among whom were the archbishop of Canterbury and the young earl of Arundel, nephew to that prelate, landed at Ravenspur in Yorkshire; and was immediately joined by the earls of Northumberland and Westmoreland, two of the most potent barons in England. He here took a solemn oath, that he had no other purpose in this invasion, than to recover the dutchy of Lancaster, unjustly detained from him; and he invited all his friends in England, and all lovers of their country, to second him in this reasonable and moderate pretension. Every place was in commotion: The malcontents in all quarters flew to arms: London discovered the strongest symptoms of its disposition to mutiny and rebellion: And Henry's army, encreasing on every day's march, soon amounted to the number of 60,000 combatants.

The duke of York was left guardian of the realm; a place to *General* which his birth intitled him, but which both his slender abilities, *insur-* and his natural connexions with the duke of Lancaster, rendered *rection.* him utterly incapable of filling in such a dangerous emergency. Such of the chief nobility, as were attached to the crown, and could either have seconded the guardian's good intentions, or have over-awed his infidelity, had attended the king into Ireland; and the efforts of Richard's friends were every where more feeble than those of his enemies. The duke of York, however, appointed the rendezvous of his forces at St. Albans, and soon assembled an army of 40,000 men, but found them entirely destitute of zeal and at-tachment to the royal cause, and more inclined to join the party of the rebels. He hearkened therefore very readily to a message from Henry, who entreated him not to oppose a loyal and humble sup-plicant in the recovery of his legal patrimony; and the guardian even declared publicly that he would second his nephew in so reasonable a request. His army embraced with acclamations the same measures; and the duke of Lancaster, reinforced by them, was now entirely master of the kingdom. He hastened to Bristol, into which some of the king's ministers had thrown themselves; and soon obliging that place to surrender, he yielded to the popular wishes, and without giving them a trial, ordered the earl of Wiltshire, Sir John Bussy, and Sir Henry Green, whom he there took prisoners, to be led to immediate execution.

The king, receiving intelligence of this invasion and insurrection, hastened over from Ireland, and landed in Milford Haven with a body of 20,000 men: But even this army, so much inferior to the enemy, was either overawed by the general combination of the kingdom, or seized with the same spirit of disaffection; and they gradually deserted him, till he found that he had not above 6000 men, who followed his standard. It appeared, therefore, necessary to retire secretly from this small body, which served only to expose him to danger; and he fled to the isle of Anglesea, where he purposed to embark either for Ireland or France, and there await the favourable opportunities, which the return of his subjects to a sense of duty, or their future discontents against the duke of Lancaster, would probably afford him. Henry, sensible of the danger, sent to him the earl of Northumberland with the strongest professions of loyalty and submission; and that nobleman, by treachery and false oaths, made himself master of the king's person, and carried him to his enemy at Flint Castle. Richard was
1st Sept. conducted to London, by the duke of Lancaster, who was there received with the acclamations of the mutinous populace. It is pretended, that the recorder met him on the road; and in the name of the city, entreated him, for the public safety, to put Richard to death, with all his adherents who were prisoners;[y] but the duke prudently determined to make many others participate in his guilt, before he would proceed to those extremities. For this purpose, he issued writs of election in the king's name, and appointed the immediate meeting of a parliament at Westminster.

Such of the peers, as were most devoted to the king, were either fled or imprisoned; and no opponents, even among the barons, dared to appear against Henry, amidst that scene of outrage and violence, which commonly attends revolutions, especially in England during those turbulent ages. It is also easy to imagine, that a house of commons, elected during this universal ferment, and this triumph of the Lancastrian party, would be extremely attached to that cause, and ready to second every suggestion of their

---

[y] Walsingham.

CHAPTER XVII

leaders. That order, being as yet of too little weight to stem the torrent, was always carried along with it, and served only to encrease the violence, which the public interest required it should endeavour to controul. The duke of Lancaster therefore, sensible that he should be entirely master, began to carry his views to the crown itself; and he deliberated with his partizans concerning the most proper means of effecting his daring purpose. He first extorted a resignation from Richard;[z] but as he knew, that this deed would plainly appear the result of force and fear, he also purposed, notwithstanding the danger of the precedent to himself and his posterity, to have him solemnly deposed in parliament for his pretended tyranny and misconduct. A charge, consisting of thirty-three articles, was accordingly drawn up against him, and presented to that assembly.[a]

Deposition of the king.

28th Sept.

If we examine these articles, which are expressed with extreme acrimony against Richard, we shall find, that, except some rash speeches which are imputed to him,[b] and of whose reality, as they are said to have passed in private conversation, we may reasonably entertain some doubt; the chief amount of the charge is contained in his violent conduct during the two last years of his reign, and naturally divides itself into two principal heads. The first and most considerable is the revenge, which he took on the princes and great barons, who had formerly usurped, and still persevered in controuling and threatening, his authority; the second is the violation of the laws and general privileges of his people. But the former, however irregular in many of its circumstances, was fully supported by authority of parliament, and was but a copy of the violence, which the princes and barons themselves, during their former triumph, had exercised against him and his party. The detention of Lancaster's estate was, properly speaking, a revocation, by parliamentary authority, of a grace, which the king himself had formerly granted him. The murder of Glocester (for the secret execution, however merited, of that prince, certainly deserves this appellation) was a private deed, formed not any precedent, and implied not any usurped or arbitrary power of the crown, which could justly give umbrage to the people. It really

---

[z] Knyghton, p. 2744. Otterburne, p. 212.   [a] Tyrrel, vol. iii. part 2. p. 1008, from the records. Knyghton, p. 2746. Otterburne, p. 214.   [b] Art. 16, 26.

proceeded from a defect of power in the king, rather than from his ambition; and proves, that, instead of being dangerous to the constitution, he possessed not even the authority necessary for the execution of the laws.

Concerning the second head of accusation, as it mostly consists of general facts, as framed by Richard's inveterate enemies, and was never allowed to be answered by him or his friends; it is more difficult to form a judgment. The greater part of these grievances, imputed to Richard, seems to be the exertion of arbitrary prerogatives; such as the dispensing power,[c] levying purveyance,[d] employing the marshal's court,[e] extorting loans,[f] granting protections from law-suits;[g] prerogatives, which, though often complained of, had often been exercised by his predecessors, and still continued to be so by his successors. But whether his irregular acts of this kind were more frequent, and injudicious, and violent than usual, or were only laid hold of and exaggerated, by the factions, to which the weakness of his reign had given birth, we are not able at this distance to determine with certainty. There is however one circumstance, in which his conduct is visibly different from that of his grandfather: He is not accused of having imposed one arbitrary tax, without consent of parliament, during his whole reign:[h] Scarcely a year passed during the reign of Edward, which was free from complaints with regard to this dangerous exertion of authority. But, perhaps, the ascendant, which Edward had acquired over the people, together with his great prudence, enabled him to make a life very advantageous to his subjects of this and other arbitrary prerogatives, and rendered them a smaller grievance in his hands, than a less absolute authority in those of his grandson. This is a point, which it would be rash for us to decide positively on either side; but it is certain, that a charge, drawn up by the duke of Lancaster, and assented to by a parliament, situated in those

---

[c] Art. 13, 17, 18.   [d] Art. 22.   [e] Art. 27.   [f] Art. 14.   [g] Art. 16.   [h] We learn from Cotton, p. 362, that the king, by his chancellor, told the commons, *that they were sunderly bound to him, and namely in forbearing to charge them with dismes and fifteens, the which he meant* no more *to charge them in his own person.* These words *no more* allude to the practice of his predecessors: He had not himself imposed any arbitrary taxes: Even the parliament, in the articles of his deposition, though they complain of heavy taxes, affirm not, that they were imposed illegally or by arbitrary will.

CHAPTER XVII

circumstances, forms no manner of presumption with regard to the unusual irregularity or violence of the king's conduct in this particular.[i]

When the charge against Richard was presented to the parliament, though it was liable, almost in every article, to objections, it was not canvassed, nor examined, nor disputed in either house, and seemed to be received with universal approbation. One man alone, the bishop of Carlisle, had the courage, amidst this general disloyalty and violence, to appear in defence of his unhappy master, and to plead his cause against all the power of the prevailing party. Though some topics, employed by that virtuous prelate, may seem to favour too much the doctrine of passive obedience, and to make too large a sacrifice of the rights of mankind; he was naturally pushed into that extreme by his abhorrence of the present licentious factions; and such intrepidity, as well as disinterestedness of behaviour, proves, that, whatever his speculative principles were, his heart was elevated far above the meanness and abject submission of a slave. He represented to the parliament, that all the abuses of government, which could justly be imputed to Richard, instead of amounting to tyranny, were merely the result of error, youth, or misguided counsel, and admitted of a remedy, more easy and salutary, than a total subversion of the constitution. That even had they been much more violent and dangerous than they really were, they had chiefly proceeded from former examples of resistance, which, making the prince sensible of his precarious situation, had obliged him to establish his throne by irregular and arbitrary expedients. That a rebellious disposition in subjects was the principal cause of tyranny in kings: Laws could never secure the subject which did not give security to the sovereign: And if the maxim of inviolable loyalty, which formed the basis of the English government, were once rejected, the privileges, belonging to the several orders of the state, instead of being fortified by that licentiousness, would thereby lose the surest foundation of their force and stability. That the parliamentary deposition of Edward II. far from making a precedent, which could controul this maxim, was only an example of successful violence; and it was sufficiently to be lamented, that crimes were so often

[i] See note [O] at the end of the volume.

committed in the world, without establishing principles which might justify and authorize them. That even that precedent, false and dangerous as it was, could never warrant the present excesses, which were so much greater, and which would entail distraction and misery on the nation, to the latest posterity. That the succession, at least, of the crown, was then preserved inviolate: The lineal heir was placed on the throne: And the people had an opportunity, by their legal obedience to him, of making atonement for the violence, which they had committed against his predecessor. That a descendant of Lionel, duke of Clarence, the elder brother of the late duke of Lancaster, had been declared in parliament successor to the crown: He had left posterity: And their title, however it might be overpowered by present force and faction, could never be obliterated from the minds of the people. That if the turbulent disposition alone of the nation had overturned the well-established throne of so good a prince as Richard; what bloody commotions must ensue, when the same cause was united to the motive of restoring the legal and undoubted heir to his authority? That the new government, intended to be established, would stand on no principle; and would scarcely retain any pretence, by which it could challenge the obedience of men of sense and virtue. That the claim of lineal descent was so gross as scarcely to deceive the most ignorant of the populace: Conquest could never be pleaded by a rebel against his sovereign: The consent of the people had no authority in a monarchy not derived from consent, but established by hereditary right; and however the nation might be justified, in deposing the misguided Richard, it could never have any reason for setting aside his lawful heir and successor, who was plainly innocent. And that the duke of Lancaster would give them but a bad specimen of the legal moderation, which might be expected from his future government, if he added, to the crime of his past rebellion, the guilt of excluding the family, which, both by right of blood, and by declaration of parliament, would, in case of Richard's demise, or voluntary resignation, have been received as the undoubted heirs of the monarchy.[k]

All the circumstances of this event, compared to those which attended the late revolution in 1688, show the difference between

[k] Sir John Heywarde, p. 101.

CHAPTER XVII

a great and civilized nation, deliberately vindicating its established privileges, and a turbulent and barbarous aristocracy, plunging headlong from the extremes of one faction into those of another. This noble freedom of the bishop of Carlisle, instead of being applauded, was not so much as tolerated: He was immediately arrested, by order of the duke of Lancaster, and sent a prisoner to the abbey of St. Albans. No farther debate was attempted: Thirty-three long articles of charge were, in one meeting, voted against Richard; and voted unanimously by the same peers and prelates, who, a little before, had, voluntarily and unanimously, authorized those very acts of violence, of which they now complained. That prince was deposed by the suffrages of both houses; and the throne being now vacant, the duke of Lancaster stepped forth, and having crossed himself on the forehead, and on the breast, and called upon the name of Christ,[l] he pronounced these words, which we shall give in the original language, because of their singularity.

In the name of Fadher, Son, and Holy Ghost, I Henry of Lancaster, challenge this rewme of Ynglande, and the croun, with all the membres, and the appurtenances; als I that am descendit by right line of the blode, coming fro the gude king Henry therde, and throge that right that God of his grace hath sent me, with helpe of kyn, and of my frendes to recover it; the which rewme was in poynt to be ondone by defaut of governance, and ondoying of the gude lawes.[m]

In order to understand this speech, it must be observed, that there was a silly story, received among some of the lowest vulgar, that Edmond, earl of Lancaster, son of Henry III. was really the elder brother of Edward I.; but that, by reason of some deformity in his person, he had been postponed in the succession, and his younger brother imposed on the nation in his stead. As the present duke of Lancaster inherited from Edmond by his mother, this genealogy made him the true heir of the monarchy; and it is therefore insinuated in Henry's speech: But the absurdity was too gross to be openly avowed either by him, or by the parliament. The case is the same with regard to his right of conquest: He was a subject who rebelled against his sovereign: He entered the kingdom with a retinue of no more than sixty persons: He could not

[l] Cotton, p. 389.   [m] Knyghton, p. 2757.

therefore be the conqueror of England; and this right is accordingly insinuated, not avowed. Still there is a third claim, derived from his merits in saving the nation from tyranny and oppression; and this claim is also insinuated: But as it seemed, by its nature, better calculated as a reason for his being *elected* king by a free choice, than for giving him an immediate right of possession, he durst not speak openly even on this head; and to obviate any notion of election, he challenges the crown as his due, either by acquisition or inheritance. The whole forms such a piece of jargon and nonsense, as is almost without example: No objection however was made to it in parliament: The unanimous voice of lords and commons placed Henry on the throne: He became king, nobody could tell how or wherefore: The title of the house of Marche, formerly recognized by parliament, was neither invalidated nor repealed; but passed over in total silence: And as a concern for the liberties of the people seems to have had no hand in this revolution, their right to dispose of the government, as well as all their other privileges, was left precisely on the same footing as before. But Henry having, when he claimed the crown, dropped some obscure hint concerning conquest, which, it was thought, might endanger these privileges, he soon after made a public declaration, that he did not thereby intend to deprive any other of his franchises or liberties:[n] Which was the only circumstance, where we shall find meaning or common sense, in all these transactions.

6th Oct.   The subsequent events discover the same headlong violence of conduct, and the same rude notions of civil government. The deposition of Richard dissolved the parliament: It was necessary to summon a new one: And Henry, in six days after, called together, without any new election, the same members; and this assembly he denominated a new parliament. They were employed in the usual task of reversing every deed of the opposite party. All the acts of the last parliament of Richard, which had been confirmed by their oaths, and by a papal bull, were abrogated: All the acts, which had passed in the parliament where Glocester prevailed, which had also been confirmed by their oaths, but which had been abrogated by Richard, were anew established:[o] The answers of Tresilian, and

[n] Knyghton, p. 2759. Otterborn, p. 220.   [o] Cotton, p. 390.

the other judges, which a parliament had annulled, but which a new parliament and new judges had approved, here received a second condemnation. The peers, who had accused Glocester, Arundel and Warwic, and who had received higher titles for that piece of service, were all of them degraded from their new dignities: Even the practice of prosecuting appeals in parliament, which bore the air of a violent confederacy against an individual, rather than of a legal indictment, was wholly abolished; and trials were restored to the course of common law.[p] The natural effect of this conduct was to render the people giddy with such rapid and perpetual changes, and to make them lose all notions of right and wrong in the measures of government.

The earl of Northumberland made a motion, in the house of peers, with regard to the unhappy prince whom they had deposed. He asked them, what advice they would give the king for the future treatment of him; since Henry was resolved to spare his life. They unanimously replied, that he should be imprisoned under a secure guard, in some secret place, and should be deprived of all commerce with any of his friends or partizans. It was easy to foresee, that he would not long remain alive in the hands of such barbarous and sanguinary enemies. Historians differ with regard to the manner in which he was murdered. It was long the prevailing opinion, that Sir Piers Exton, and others of his guards, fell upon him in the castle of Pomfret, where he was confined, and dispatched him with their halberts. But it is more probable, that he was starved to death in prison; and after all sustenance was denied him, he prolonged his unhappy life, it is said, for a fortnight, before he reached the end of his miseries. This account is more consistent with the story, that his body was exposed in public, and that no marks of violence were observed upon it. He died in the thirty-fourth year of his age, and the twenty-third of his reign. He left no posterity, either legitimate or illegitimate.

All the writers, who have transmitted to us the history of Richard, lived during the reigns of the Lancastrian princes; and candor requires, that we should not give entire credit to the reproaches, which they have thrown upon his memory. But after making all proper allowances, he still appears to have been a weak prince, and

23d Oct.

Murder of the king.

His character.

[p] Henry iv. cap. 14.

unfit for government, less for want of natural parts and capacity, than of solid judgment and a good education. He was violent in his temper; profuse in his expence; fond of idle show and mag- nificence; devoted to favourites; and addicted to pleasure: Pas- sions, all of them, the most inconsistent with a prudent oeconomy, and consequently dangerous in a limited and mixed government. Had he possessed the talents of gaining, and still more those of overawing, his great barons, he might have escaped all the misfor- tunes of his reign, and been allowed to carry much farther his oppressions over the people, if he really was guilty of any, without their daring to rebel, or even to murmur against him. But when the grandees were tempted, by his want of prudence and of vigour, to resist his authority, and execute the most violent enterprizes upon him, he was naturally led to seek an opportunity of retali- ation; justice was neglected; the lives of the chief nobility were sacrificed; and all these enormities seem to have proceeded less from a settled design of establishing arbitrary power, than from the insolence of victory, and the necessities of the king's situation. The manners indeed of the age were the chief source of such violence: Laws, which were feebly executed in peaceable times, lost all their authority during public convulsions: Both parties were alike guilty: Or if any difference may be remarked between them, we shall find, that the authority of the crown, being more legal, was commonly carried, when it prevailed, to less desperate extremities, than was that of the aristocracy.

On comparing the conduct and events of this reign, with those of the preceding, we shall find equal reason to admire Edward, and to blame Richard; but the circumstance of opposition, surely, will not lie in the strict regard paid by the former to national privileges, and the neglect of them by the latter. On the contrary, the prince of small abilities, as he felt his want of power, seems to have been more moderate in this respect than the other. Every parliament, assembled during the reign of Edward, remonstrates against the exertion of some arbitrary prerogative or other: We hear not any complaints of that kind during the reign of Richard, till the assem- bling of his last parliament, which was summoned by his inveterate enemies, which dethroned him, which framed their complaints during the time of the most furious convulsions, and whose testi- mony must therefore have, on that account, much less authority with every equitable judge.[q] Both these princes experienced the encroachment of the Great upon their authority. Edward, reduced to necessities, was obliged to make an express bargain with his parliament, and to sell some of his prerogatives for present supply; but as they were acquainted with his genius and capacity, they ventured not to demand any exorbitant concessions, or such as were incompatible with regal and sovereign power: The weakness of Richard tempted the parliament to extort a commission, which, in a manner, dethroned the prince, and transferred the sceptre into the hands of the nobility. The events of these encroachments were also suitable to the character of each. Edward had no sooner gotten the supply, than he departed from the engagements, which had induced the parliament to grant it; he openly told his people, that he had but *dissembled* with them when he seemed to make them these concessions; and he resumed and retained all his prerogatives. But Richard, because he was detected in consulting and deliberating with the judges on the lawfulness of restoring the constitution, found his barons immediately in arms against him; was deprived of his liberty; saw his favourites, his ministers, his tutor, butchered before his face, or banished and attainted; and was obliged to give way to all this violence. There cannot be a more remarkable contrast between the fortunes of two princes: It were happy for society, did this contrast always depend on the justice or injustice of the measures which men embrace, and not rather on the different degrees of prudence and vigour, with which those measures are supported.

There was a sensible decay of ecclesiastical authority during this period. The disgust, which the laity had received from the numerous usurpations both of the court of Rome, and of their own clergy, had very much weaned the kingdom from superstition; and strong symptoms appeared, from time to time, of a general desire to shake off the bondage of the Romish church. In the committee of eighteen, to whom Richard's last parliament delegated their whole power, there is not the name of one ecclesiastic to be found; a neglect which is almost without example, while the catholic religion subsisted in England.[r]

Miscellaneous transactions during this reign.

[q] Peruse, in this view, the abridgment of the records, by Sir Robert Cotton, during these two reigns. [r] See note [P] at the end of the volume.

The aversion entertained against the established church soon found principles and tenets and reasonings, by which it could justify and support itself. John Wickliffe, a secular priest, educated at Oxford, began in the latter end of Edward III. to spread the doctrine of reformation by his discourses, sermons, and writings; and he made many disciples among men of all ranks and stations. He seems to have been a man of parts and learning, and has the honour of being the first person in Europe, that publicly called in question those principles, which had universally passed for certain and undisputed during so many ages. Wickliffe himself, as well as his disciples, who received the name of Wickliffites, or Lollards, was distinguished by a great austerity of life and manners, a circumstance common to almost all those who dogmatize in any new way, both because men, who draw to them the attention of the public, and expose themselves to the odium of great multitudes, are obliged to be very guarded in their conduct, and because few, who have a strong propensity to pleasure or business, will enter upon so difficult and laborious an undertaking. The doctrines of Wickliffe, being derived from his search into the scriptures and into ecclesiastical antiquity, were nearly the same with those which were propagated by the reformers in the sixteenth century: He only carried some of them farther than was done by the more sober part of these reformers. He denied the doctrine of the real presence, the supremacy of the church of Rome, the merit of monastic vows: He maintained, that the scriptures were the sole rule of faith; that the church was dependant on the state, and should be reformed by it; that the clergy ought to possess no estates; that the begging friars were a nuisance, and ought not to be supported;[s] that the numerous ceremonies of the church were hurtful to true piety: He asserted, that oaths were unlawful, that dominion was founded in grace, that every thing was subject to fate and destiny, and that all men were pre-ordained either to eternal salvation or reprobation.[t] From the whole of his doctrines, Wickliffe appears to have been strongly tinctured with enthusiasm, and to have been

---

[s] Walsingham, p. 191, 208, 283, 284. Spelman Concil. vol. ii. p. 630. Knyghton, p. 2657. [t] Harpsfield, p. 668, 673, 674. Waldens. tom. i. lib. 3. art. I. cap. 8.

thereby the better qualified to oppose a church, whose chief characteristic is superstition.

The propagation of these principles gave great alarm to the clergy; and a bull was issued by pope Gregory XI. for taking Wickliffe into custody, and examining into the scope of his opinions.[u] Courteney, bishop of London, cited him before his tribunal; but the reformer had now acquired powerful protectors, who screened him from the ecclesiastical jurisdiction. The duke of Lancaster, who then governed the kingdom, encouraged the principles of Wickliffe; and he made no scruple, as well as lord Piercy, the mareschal, to appear openly in court with him, in order to give him countenance upon his trial: He even insisted, that Wickliffe should sit in the bishop's presence, while his principles were examined: Courteney exclaimed against the insult: The Londoners, thinking their prelate affronted, attacked the duke and mareschal, who escaped from their hands with some difficulty.[w] And the populace, soon after, broke into the houses of both these noblemen, threatened their persons, and plundered their goods. The bishop of London had the merit of appeasing their fury and resentment.

The duke of Lancaster, however, still continued his protection to Wickliffe, during the minority of Richard; and the principles of that reformer had so far propagated themselves, that, when the pope sent to Oxford a new bull against these doctrines, the university deliberated for some time, whether they should receive the bull; and they never took any vigorous measures in consequence of the papal orders.[x] Even the populace of London were at length brought to entertain favourable sentiments of this reformer: When he was cited before a synod at Lambeth, they broke into the assembly, and so overawed the prelates, who found both the people and the court against them, that they dismissed him without any farther censure.

The clergy, we may well believe, were more wanting in power than in inclination to punish this new heresy, which struck at all their credit, possessions, and authority. But there was hitherto no

[u] Spelm. Conc. vol. ii. p. 621. Walsingham, p. 201, 202, 203.
[w] Harpsfield in Hist. Wickl. p. 683.   [x] Wood's Ant. Oxon. lib. I. p. 191, &c. Walsingham, p. 201.

law in England, by which the secular arm was authorised to support orthodoxy; and the ecclesiastics endeavoured to supply the defect by an extraordinary and unwarrantable artifice. In the year 1381, there was an act passed, requiring sheriffs to apprehend the preachers of heresy and their abettors; but this statute had been surreptitiously obtained by the clergy, and had the formality of an enrolment without the consent of the commons. In the subsequent session, the lower house complained of the fraud; affirmed, that they had no intention to bind themselves to the prelates farther than their ancestors had done before them; and required that the pretended statute should be repealed, which was done accordingly.[y] But it is remarkable, that, notwithstanding this vigilance of the commons, the clergy had so much art and influence, that the repeal was suppressed, and the act, which never had any legal authority, remains to this day upon the statute book:[z] Though the clergy still thought proper to keep it in reserve, and not proceed to the immediate execution of it.

But besides this defect of power in the church, which saved Wickliffe, that reformer himself, notwithstanding his enthusiasm, seems not to have been actuated by the spirit of martyrdom; and in all subsequent trials before the prelates, he so explained away his doctrine by tortured meanings, as to render it quite innocent and inoffensive.[a] Most of his followers imitated his cautious disposition, and saved themselves either by recantations or explanations. He died of a palsy in the year 1385 at his rectory of Lutterworth in the county of Leicester; and the clergy, mortified that he should have escaped their vengeance, took care, besides assuring the people of his eternal damnation, to represent his last distemper as a visible judgment of heaven upon him for his multiplied heresies and impieties.[b]

The proselytes, however, of Wickliffe's opinions still encreased in England:[c] Some monkish writers represent one half of the kingdom as infected by those principles: They were carried over to Bohemia by some youth of that nation, who studied at Oxford: But though the age seemed strongly disposed to receive them, affairs

---

[y] Cotton's abridgment, p. 285. [z] 5 Rich. II chap. 5. [a] Walsingham, p. 206. Knyghton, p. 2655, 2656. [b] Walsingham, p. 312. Ypod. Neust. p. 337. [c] Knyghton, p. 2663.

were not yet fully ripe for this great revolution; and the finishing blow to ecclesiastical power was reserved to a period of more curiosity, literature, and inclination for novelties.

Meanwhile the English parliament continued to check the clergy and the court of Rome, by more sober and more legal expedients. They enacted anew the statute of *provisors,* and affixed higher penalties to the transgression of it, which, in some instances, was even made capital.[d] The court of Rome had fallen upon a new device, which encreased their authority over the prelates: The pope, who found that the expedient of arbitrarily depriving them was violent, and liable to opposition, attained the same end by transferring such of them, as were obnoxious, to poorer sees, and even to nominal sees, *in partibus infidelium.* It was thus that the archbishop of York, and the bishops of Durham and Chichester, the king's ministers, had been treated after the prevalence of Glocester's faction: The bishop of Carlisle met with the same fate after the accession of Henry IV. For the pope always joined with the prevailing powers, when they did not thwart his pretensions. The parliament, in the reign of Richard, enacted a law against this abuse: And the king made a general remonstrance to the court of Rome against all those usurpations, which he calls *horrible excesses* of that court.[e]

It was usual for the church, that they might elude the mortmain act, to make their votaries leave lands in trust to certain persons, under whose name the clergy enjoyed the benefit of the bequest: The parliament also stopped the progress of this abuse.[f] In the 17th of the king, the commons prayed, *that remedy might be had against such religious persons as cause their villains to marry free women inheritable, whereby the estate comes to those religious hands by collusion.*[g] This was a new device of the clergy.

The papacy was at this time somewhat weakened by a schism, which lasted during forty years, and gave great scandal to the devoted partizans of the holy see. After the pope had resided many years at Avignon, Gregory XI. was persuaded to return to Rome; and upon his death, which happened in 1380, the Romans, resolute to fix, for the future, the seat of the papacy in Italy, besieged

---

[d] 13 Rich. II. cap. 3. 16 Rich. II. cap. 4.   [e] Rymer, vol. vii. p. 672.
[f] Knyghton, p. 27, 38. Cotton, p. 355.   [g] Cotton, p. 355.

the cardinals in the conclave, and compelled them, though they were mostly Frenchmen, to elect Urban VI. an Italian, into that high dignity. The French cardinals, as soon as they recovered their liberty, fled from Rome, and protesting against the forced election, chose Robert, son of the count of Geneva, who took the name of Clement VII. and resided at Avignon. All the kingdoms of Christendom, according to their several interests and inclinations, were divided between these two pontiffs. The court of France adhered to Clement, and was followed by its allies, the king of Castile, and the king of Scotland: England of course was thrown into the other party, and declared for Urban. Thus the appellation of *Clementines* and *Urbanists* distracted Europe for several years; and each party damned the other as schismatics, and as rebels to the true vicar of Christ. But this circumstance, though it weakened the papal authority, had not so great an effect as might naturally be imagined. Though any king could easily, at first, make his kingdom embrace the party of one pope or the other, or even keep it some time in suspence between them, he could not so easily transfer his obedience at pleasure: The people attached themselves to their own party, as to a religious opinion; and conceived an extreme abhorrence to the opposite party, whom they regarded as little better than Saracens or infidels. Crusades were even undertaken in this quarrel; and the zealous bishop of Norwich, in particular, led over, in 1382, near 60,000 bigots into Flanders against the Clementines; but after losing a great part of his followers, he returned with disgrace into England.[h] Each pope, sensible, from this prevailing spirit among the people, that the kingdom, which once embraced his cause, would always adhere to him, boldly maintained all the pretensions of his see, and stood not much more in awe of the temporal sovereigns, than if his authority had not been endangered by a rival.

We meet with this preamble to a law enacted at the very beginning of this reign: "Whereas divers persons of small garrison of land or other possessions do make great retinue of people, as well of esquires as of others, in many parts of the realm, giving to them hats and other livery of one suit by year, taking again towards them

[h] Froissard, lib. 2. chap. 133, 134. Walsingham, p. 298, 299, 300, &c. Knyghton, p. 2671.

CHAPTER XVII

the value of the same livery or percase the double value, by such covenant and assurance, that every of them shall maintain other in all quarrels, be they reasonable or unreasonable, to the great mischief and oppression of the people, &c.[i]" This preamble contains a true picture of the state of the kingdom. The laws had been so feebly executed, even during the long, active, and vigilant reign of Edward III. that no subject could trust to their protection. Men openly associated themselves, under the patronage of some great baron, for their mutual defence. They wore public badges, by which their confederacy was distinguished. They supported each other in all quarrels, iniquities, extortions, murders, robberies, and other crimes. Their chief was more their sovereign than the king himself; and their own band was more connected with them than their country. Hence the perpetual turbulence, disorders, factions, and civil wars of those times: Hence the small regard paid to a character or the opinion of the public: Hence the large discretionary prerogatives of the crown, and the danger which might have ensued from the too great limitation of them. If the king had possessed no arbitrary powers, while all the nobles assumed and exercised them, there must have ensued an absolute anarchy in the state.

One great mischief, attending these confederacies, was the extorting from the king pardons for the most enormous crimes. The parliament often endeavoured, in the last reign, to deprive the prince of this prerogative; but, in the present, they were content with an abridgment of it. They enacted, that no pardon for rapes or for murder from malice prepense should be valid, unless the crime were particularly specified in it.[k] There were also some other circumstances required for passing any pardon of this kind: An excellent law; but ill observed, like most laws that thwart the manners of the people, and the prevailing customs of the times.

It is easy to observe, from these voluntary associations among the people, that the whole force of the feudal system was in a manner dissolved, and that the English had nearly returned in that particular to the same situation, in which they stood before the Norman conquest. It was indeed impossible, that that system could long subsist under the perpetual revolutions, to which landed

[i] Rich. II. chap. 7.   [k] 13 Rich. II. chap. 1.

property is every where subject. When the great feudal baronies were first erected, the lord lived in opulence in the midst of his vassals: He was in a situation to protect and cherish and defend them: The quality of patron naturally united itself to that of superior: And these two principles of authority mutually supported each other. But when, by the various divisions and mixtures of property, a man's superior came to live at a distance from him, and could no longer give him shelter or countenance; the tie gradually became more fictitious than real: New connexions from vicinity or other causes were formed: Protection was sought by voluntary services and attachment: The appearance of valour, spirit, abilities in any great man extended his interest very far: And if the sovereign were deficient in these qualities, he was no less, if not more exposed to the usurpations of the aristocracy, than even during the vigour of the feudal system.

The greatest novelty introduced into the civil government during this reign was the creation of peers by patent. Lord Beauchamp of Holt was the first peer, that was advanced to the house of lords in this manner. The practice of levying benevolences is also first mentioned in the present reign.

This prince lived in a more magnificent manner than perhaps any of his predecessors or successors. His household consisted of 10,000 persons: He had 300 in his kitchen; and all the other offices were furnished in proportion.[1] It must be remarked, that this enormous train had tables supplied them at the king's expence, according to the mode of that age. Such prodigality was probably the source of many exactions, by purveyors, and was one chief reason of the public discontents.

---

[1] Harding: This poet says, that he speaks from the authority of a clerk of the green cloth.

XVIII

HENRY IV

Title of the king –
An insurrection – An insurrection
in Wales – The earl of Northumberland
rebels – Battle of Shrewsbury – State of
Scotland – Parliamentary
transactions – Death – and character
of the king

THE ENGLISH had so long been familiarized to the hereditary succession of their monarchs, the instances of departure
from it had always born such strong symptoms of injustice and
violence, and so little of a national choice or election, and the
returns to the true line had ever been deemed such fortunate
incidents in their history, that Henry was afraid, lest, in resting his
title on the consent of the people, he should build on a foundation,
to which the people themselves were not accustomed, and whose
solidity they would with difficulty be brought to recognize. The
idea too of choice seemed always to imply that of conditions, and
a right of recalling the consent upon any supposed violation of
them; an idea which was not naturally agreeable to a sovereign,
and might in England be dangerous to the subjects, who, lying so
much under the influence of turbulent nobles, had ever paid but
an imperfect obedience even to their hereditary princes. For these
reasons Henry was determined never to have recourse to this
claim; the only one, on which his authority could consistently

1399.
Title of
the king.

333

stand: He rather chose to patch up his title in the best manner he could, from other pretensions: And in the end, he left himself, in the eyes of men of sense, no ground of right, but his present possession; a very precarious foundation, which, by its very nature, was liable to be overthrown by every faction of the great, or prejudice of the people. He had indeed a present advantage over his competitor: The heir of the house of Mortimer, who had been declared in parliament heir to the crown, was a boy of seven years of age:[m] His friends consulted his safety by keeping silence with regard to his title: Henry detained him and his younger brother in an honourable custody at Windsor castle: But he had reason to dread, that, in proportion as that nobleman grew to man's estate, he would draw to him the attachment of the people, and make them reflect on the fraud, violence, and injustice, by which he had been excluded from the throne. Many favourable topics would occur in his behalf: He was a native of England; possessed an extensive interest from the greatness and alliances of his family; however criminal the deposed monarch, this youth was entirely innocent; he was of the same religion, and educated in the same manners with the people, and could not be governed by any separate interest: These views would all concur to favour his claim; and though the abilities of the present prince might ward off any dangerous revolution, it was justly to be apprehended, that his authority could with difficulty be brought to equal that of his predecessors.

Henry in his very first parliament had reason to see the danger attending that station, which he had assumed, and the obstacles which he would meet with in governing an unruly aristocracy, always divided by faction, and at present inflamed with the resentments, consequent on such recent convulsions. The peers, on their assembling, broke out into violent animosities against each other; forty gauntlets, the pledges of furious battle, were thrown on the floor of the house by noblemen who gave mutual challenges; and *liar* and *traitor* resounded from all quarters. The king had so much authority with these doughty champions, as to prevent all the combats, which they threatened; but he was not able to bring them to a proper composure, or to an amicable disposition towards each other.

[m] Dugdale, vol. i. p. 151.

CHAPTER XVIII

It was not long before these passions broke into action. The earls of Rutland, Kent, and Huntingdon, and lord Spencer, who were now degraded from the respective titles of Albemarle, Surrey, Exeter, and Glocester, conferred on them by Richard, entered into a conspiracy, together with the earl of Salisbury and lord Lumley, for raising an insurrection, and for seizing the king's person at Windsor;[n] but the treachery of Rutland gave him warning of the danger. He suddenly withdrew to London; and the conspirators, who came to Windsor with a body of 500 horse, found that they had missed this blow, on which all the success of their enterprize depended. Henry appeared, next day, at Kingston upon Thames, at the head of 20,000 men, mostly drawn from the city; and his enemies, unable to resist his power, dispersed themselves, with a view of raising their followers in the several counties, which were the seat of their interest. But the adherents of the king were hot in the pursuit, and every where opposed themselves to their progress. The earls of Kent and Salisbury were seized at Cirencester by the citizens; and were next day beheaded without farther ceremony, according to the custom of the times.[o] The citizens of Bristol treated Spencer and Lumley in the same manner. The earl of Huntingdon, Sir Thomas Blount, and Sir Benedict Sely, who were also taken prisoners, suffered death, with many others of the conspirators, by orders from Henry. And when the quarters of these unhappy men were brought to London, no less than eighteen bishops and thirty-two mitred abbots, joined the populace, and met them with the most indecent marks of joy and exultation.

But the spectacle the most shocking to every one, who retained any sentiment either of honour or humanity, still remained. The earl of Rutland appeared, carrying on a pole the head of lord Spencer, his brother-in-law, which he presented in triumph to Henry, as a testimony of his loyalty. This infamous man, who was soon after duke of York by the death of his father, and first prince of the blood, had been instrumental in the murder of his uncle, the duke of Glocester;[p] had then deserted Richard, by whom he was trusted; had conspired against the life of Henry, to whom he had sworn allegiance; had betrayed his associates, whom he had se-

1400.
An insurrection.

---

[n] Walsingham, p. 362. Otterbourne, p. 224.   [o] Walsingham, p. 363. Ypod. Neust. 556.   [p] Dugdale, vol. ii. p. 171.

duced into this enterprize; and now displayed, in the face of the world, these badges of his multiplied dishonour.

1401.   Henry was sensible, that, though the execution of these conspirators might seem to give security to his throne, the animosities, which remain after such bloody scenes, are always dangerous to royal authority; and he therefore determined not to encrease, by any hazardous enterprize, those numerous enemies, with whom he was every where environed. While a subject, he was believed to have strongly imbibed all the principles of his father, the duke of Lancaster, and to have adopted the prejudices which the Lollards inspired against the abuses of the established church: But finding himself possessed of the throne by so precarious a title, he thought superstition a necessary implement of public authority; and he resolved, by every expedient, to pay court to the clergy. There were hitherto no penal laws enacted against heresy; an indulgence which had proceeded, not from a spirit of toleration in the Romish church, but from the ignorance and simplicity of the people, which had rendered them unfit either for starting or receiving any new or curious doctrines, and which needed not to be restrained by rigorous penalties. But when the learning and genius of Wickliffe had once broken, in some measure, the fetters of prejudice, the ecclesiastics called aloud for the punishment of his disciples; and the king, who was very little scrupulous in his conduct, was easily induced to sacrifice his principles to his interest, and to acquire the favour of the church by that most effectual method, the gratifying of their vengeance against opponents. He engaged the parliament to pass a law for that purpose: It was enacted, that, when any heretic, who relapsed or refused to abjure his opinions, was delivered over to the secular arm by the bishop or his commissaries, he should be committed to the flames by the civil magistrate before the whole people.[q] This weapon did not long remain unemployed in the hands of the clergy: William Sautré, rector of St. Osithes in London, had been condemned by the convocation of Canterbury; his sentence was ratified by the house of peers; the king issued his writ for the execution;[r] and the unhappy man atoned for his erroneous opinions by the penalty of fire. This is the first instance of that kind in England; and thus one horror more was added to

[q] 2 Henry IV. chap. vii.   [r] Rymer, vol. viii. p. 178.

those dismal scenes, which at that time were already but too familiar to the people.

But the utmost precaution and prudence of Henry could not shield him from those numerous inquietudes, which assailed him from every quarter. The connexions of Richard with the royal family of France made that court exert its activity to recover his authority, or revenge his death;[s] but though the confusions in England tempted the French to engage in some enterprize, by which they might distress their ancient enemy, the greater confusions, which they experienced at home, obliged them quickly to accommodate matters; and Charles, content with recovering his daughter from Henry's hands, laid aside his preparations, and renewed the truce between the kingdoms.[t] The attack of Guienne was also an inviting attempt, which the present factions, that prevailed among the French, obliged them to neglect. The Gascons, affectionate to the memory of Richard, who was born among them, refused to swear allegiance to a prince that had dethroned and murdered him; and the appearance of a French army on their frontiers, would probably have tempted them to change masters.[u] But the earl of Worcester, arriving with some English troops, gave countenance to the partizans of Henry, and overawed their opponents. Religion too was here found a cement to their union with England. The Gascons had been engaged by Richard's authority to acknowledge the pope of Rome; and they were sensible, that, if they submitted to France, it would be necessary for them to pay obedience to the pope of Avignon, whom they had been taught to detest as a schismatic. Their principles on this head were too fast rooted to admit of any sudden or violent alteration.

The revolution in England proved likewise the occasion of an insurrection in Wales. Owen Glendour, or Glendourduy, descended from the ancient princes of that country, had become obnoxious on account of his attachment to Richard; and Reginald, lord Gray of Ruthyn, who was closely connected with the new king, and who enjoyed a great fortune in the marches of Wales, thought the opportunity favourable for oppressing his neighbour, and taking possession of his estate.[w] Glendour, provoked at the injustice,

Insurrection in Wales.

[s] Rymer, vol. viii. p. 123.   [t] Ibid. vol. viii. p. 142, 152, 219.   [u] Ibid. vol. viii. p. 110, 111.   [w] Vita Ric. sec. p. 171, 172.

and still more at the indignity, recovered possession by the sword:[x] Henry sent assistance to Gray;[y] the Welsh took part with Glendour: A troublesome and tedious war was kindled, which Glendour long sustained by his valour and activity, aided by the natural strength of the country, and the untamed spirit of its inhabitants.

As Glendour committed devastations promiscuously on all the English, he infested the estate of the earl of Marche; and Sir Edmund Mortimer, uncle to that nobleman, led out the retainers of the family, and gave battle to the Welsh chieftain: His troops were routed, and he was taken prisoner:[z] At the same time, the earl himself, who had been allowed to retire to his castle of Wigmore, and who, though a mere boy, took the field with his followers, fell also into Glendour's hands, and was carried by him into Wales.[a] As Henry dreaded and hated all the family of Marche, he allowed the earl to remain in captivity; and though that young nobleman was nearly allied to the Piercies, to whose assistance he himself had owed his crown, he refused to the earl of Northumberland permission to treat of his ransom with Glendour.

The uncertainty in which Henry's affairs stood during a long time with France, as well as the confusions incident to all great changes in government, tempted the Scots to make incursions into England; and Henry, desirous of taking revenge upon them, but afraid of rendering his new government unpopular by requiring great supplies from his subjects, summoned at Westminster a council of the peers, without the commons, and laid before them the state of his affairs.[b] The military part of the feudal constitution was now much decayed: There remained only so much of that fabric as affected the civil rights and properties of men: And the peers here undertook, but voluntarily, to attend the king in an expedition against Scotland, each of them at the head of a certain number of his retainers.[c] Henry conducted this army to Edinburgh, of which he easily made himself master; and he there summoned Robert III. to do homage to him for his crown.[d] But finding that the Scots would neither submit nor give him battle, he returned in three weeks, after making this useless bravadoe; and he disbanded his army.

1402.

[x] Walsingham, p. 364.   [y] Vita Ric. sec. p. 172, 173.   [z] Dugdale, vol. i. p. 150.   [a] Ibid. vol. i. p. 151.   [b] Rymer, vol. viii. p. 125, 126.   [c] Ibid. p. 125.   [d] Ibid. p. 155, 156, &c.

CHAPTER XVIII

In the subsequent season, Archibald earl of Douglas, at the head of 12,000 men, and attended by many of the principal nobility of Scotland, made an irruption into England, and committed devastations on the northern counties. On his return home, he was overtaken by the Piercies, at Homeldon on the borders of England, and a fierce battle ensued, where the Scots were totally routed. Douglas himself was taken prisoner; as was Mordac earl of Fife, son of the duke of Albany, and nephew of the Scottish king, with the earls of Angus, Murray, and Orkney, and many others of the gentry and nobility.[e] When Henry received intelligence of this victory, he sent the earl of Northumberland orders not to ransom his prisoners, which that nobleman regarded as his right, by the laws of war, received in that age. The king intended to detain them, that he might be able by their means to make an advantageous peace with Scotland; but by this policy he gave a fresh disgust to the family of Piercy.

The obligations, which Henry had owed to Northumberland, were of a kind the most likely to produce ingratitude on the one side, and discontent on the other. The sovereign naturally became jealous of that power, which had advanced him to the throne; and the subject was not easily satisfied in the returns which he thought so great a favour had merited. Though Henry, on his accession, had bestowed the office of constable on Northumberland for life,[f] and conferred other gifts on that family, these favours were regarded as their due; the refusal of any other request was deemed an injury. The impatient spirit of Harry Piercy, and the factious disposition of the earl of Worcester, younger brother of Northumberland, inflamed the discontents of that nobleman; and the precarious title of Henry tempted him to seek revenge, by overturning that throne, which he had at first established. He entered into a correspondence with Glendour: He gave liberty to the earl of Douglas, and made an alliance with that martial chief: He rouzed up all his partizans to arms; and such unlimited authority at that time belonged to the great families, that the same men, whom, a few years before, he had conducted against Richard, now followed his standard in opposition to Henry. When war was ready to break out, Northumberland was seized with a sudden illness at

1403.
The earl of Northumberland rebels.

[e] Walsingham, p. 336. Vita Ric. sec. p. 180. Chron. Otterbourne, p. 237.
[f] Rymer, vol. viii. p. 89.

Berwic; and young Piercy, taking the command of the troops, marched towards Shrewsbury, in order to join his forces with those of Glendour. The king had happily a small army on foot, with which he had intended to act against the Scots; and knowing the importance of celerity in all civil wars, he instantly hurried down, that he might give battle to the rebels. He approached Piercy near Shrewsbury, before that nobleman was joined by Glendour; and the policy of one leader, and impatience of the other, made them hasten to a general engagement.

The evening before the battle, Piercy sent a manifesto to Henry, in which he renounced his allegiance, set that prince at defiance, and in the name of his father and uncle, as well as his own, enumerated all the grievances, of which, he pretended, the nation had reason to complain. He upbraided him with the perjury, of which he had been guilty, when, on landing at Ravenspur, he had sworn upon the gospels, before the earl of Northumberland, that he had no other intention than to recover the dutchy of Lancaster, and that he would ever remain a faithful subject to king Richard. He aggravated his guilt in first dethroning, then murdering that prince, and in usurping on the title of the house of Mortimer, to whom, both by lineal succession, and by declarations of parliament, the throne, when vacant by Richard's demise, did of right belong. He complained of his cruel policy, in allowing the young earl of Marche, whom he ought to regard as his sovereign, to remain a captive in the hands of his enemies, and in even refusing to all his friends permission to treat of his ransom. He charged him again with perjury in loading the nation with heavy taxes, after having sworn, that, without the utmost necessity, he would never levy any impositions upon them. And he reproached him with the arts employed in procuring favourable elections into parliament; arts, which he himself had before imputed as a crime to Richard, and which he had made one chief reason of that prince's arraignment and deposition.[g] This manifesto was well calculated to inflame the quarrel between the parties: The bravery of the two leaders promised an obstinate engagement: And the equality of the armies, being each about 12,000 men, a number which was not unmanageable by the com-

[g] Hall, fol. 21, 22, &c.

CHAPTER XVIII

manders, gave reason to expect a great effusion of blood on both sides, and a very doubtful issue to the combat.

We shall scarcely find any battle in those ages, where the shock was more terrible and more constant. Henry exposed his person in the thickest of the fight: His gallant son, whose military atchievements were afterwards so renowned, and who here performed his noviciate in arms, signalized himself on his father's footsteps, and even a wound, which he received in the face with an arrow, could not oblige him to quit the field.[h] Piercy supported that fame, which he had acquired in many a bloody combat. And Douglas, his ancient enemy and now his friend, still appeared his rival, amidst the horror and confusion of the day. This nobleman performed feats of valour, which are almost incredible: He seemed determined that the king of England should that day fall by his arm: He fought him all over the field of battle: And as Henry, either to elude the attacks of the enemy upon his person, or to encourage his own men by the belief of his presence every where, had accoutered several captains in the royal garb, the sword of Douglas rendered this honour fatal to many.[i] But while the armies were contending in this furious manner, the death of Piercy, by an unknown hand, decided the victory, and the royalists prevailed. There are said to have fallen that day on both sides near two thousand three hundred gentlemen; but the persons of greatest distinction were on the king's; the earl of Stafford, Sir Hugh Shirley, Sir Nicholas Gausel, Sir Hugh Mortimer, Sir John Massey, Sir John Calverly. About six thousand private men perished, of whom two thirds were of Piercy's army.[k] The earls of Worcester and Douglas were taken prisoners: The former was beheaded at Shrewsbury; the latter was treated with the courtesy due to his rank and merit.

The earl of Northumberland, having recovered from his sickness, had levyed a fresh army, and was on his march to join his son; but being opposed by the earl of Westmoreland, and hearing of the defeat at Shrewsbury, he dismissed his forces, and came with a small retinue to the king at York.[l] He pretended, that his sole intention in arming was to mediate between the parties: Henry

21st July: Battle of Shrewsbury.

[h] T. Livii, p. 3.   [i] Walsingham, p. 366, 367. Hall, fol. 22.   [k] Chron. Otterbourne, p. 224. Ypod. Neust. p. 560.   [l] Chron. Otterbourne, p. 225.

thought proper to accept of the apology, and even granted him a pardon for his offence: All the other rebels were treated with equal lenity; and except the earl of Worcester and Sir Richard Vernon, who were regarded as the chief authors of the insurrection, no person, engaged in this dangerous enterprize, seems to have perished by the hands of the executioner.[m]

1405. But Northumberland, though he had been pardoned, knew, that he never should be trusted, and that he was too powerful to be cordially forgiven by a prince, whose situation gave him such reasonable grounds of jealousy. It was the effect either of Henry's vigilance or good fortune, or of the narrow genius of his enemies, that no proper concert was ever formed among them: They rose in rebellion one after another; and thereby afforded him an opportunity of suppressing singly those insurrections, which, had they been united, might have proved fatal to his authority. The earl of Nottingham, son of the duke of Norfolk, and the archbishop of York, brother to the earl of Wiltshire, whom Henry, then duke of Lancaster, had beheaded at Bristol, though they had remained quiet while Piercy was in the field, still harboured in their breast a violent hatred against the enemy of their families; and they determined, in conjunction with the earl of Northumberland, to seek revenge against him. They be took themselves to arms before that powerful nobleman was prepared to join them; and publishing a manifesto, in which they reproached Henry with his usurpation of the crown and the murder of the late king, they required, that the right line should be restored, and all public grievances be redressed. The earl of Westmoreland, whose power lay in the neighbourhood, approached them with an inferior force at Shipton near York; and being afraid to hazard an action, he attempted to subdue them by a stratagem, which nothing but the greatest folly and simplicity on their part could have rendered successful. He desired a conference with the archbishop and earl between the armies: He heard their grievances with great patience. He begged them to propose the remedies: He approved of every expedient which they suggested: He granted them all their demands: He also engaged that Henry should give them entire satisfaction: And when he saw them pleased with the facility of his

[m] Rymer. vol. viii. p. 353.

concessions, he observed to them, that, since amity was now in effect restored between them, it were better on both sides to dismiss their forces, which otherwise would prove an unsupportable burthen to the country. The archbishop and the earl of Nottingham immediately gave directions to that purpose: Their troops disbanded upon the field: But Westmoreland, who had secretly issued contrary orders to *his* army, seized the two rebels without resistance, and carried them to the king, who was advancing with hasty marches to suppress the insurrection.[n] The trial and punishment of an archbishop might have proved a troublesome and dangerous undertaking, had Henry proceeded regularly, and allowed time for an opposition to form itself against that unusual measure: The celerity of the execution alone could here render it safe and prudent. Finding that Sir William Gascoigne, the chief justice, made some scruple of acting on this occasion, he appointed Sir William Fulthorpe for judge; who, without any indictment, trial, or defence, pronounced sentence of death upon the prelate, which was presently executed. This was the first instance in England of a capital punishment inflicted on a bishop; whence the clergy of that rank might learn, that their crimes, more than those of laics, were not to pass with impunity. The earl of Nottingham was condemned and executed in the same summary manner: But though many other persons of condition, such as lord Falconberg, Sir Ralph Hastings, Sir John Colville, were engaged in this rebellion, no others seem to have fallen victims to Henry's severity.

The earl of Northumberland, on receiving this intelligence, fled into Scotland, together with lord Bardolf;[o] and the king, without opposition, reduced all the castles and fortresses belonging to these noblemen. He thence turned his arms against Glendour, over whom his son, the prince of Wales, had obtained some advantages. But that enemy, more troublesome than dangerous, still found means of defending himself in his fastnesses, and of eluding, though not resisting, all the force of England. In a subsequent   *1407.* season, the earl of Northumberland and lord Bardolf, impatient of their exile, entered the North, in hopes of raising the people to arms; but found the country in such a posture as rendered all their

[n] Walsingham, p. 373. Otterbourne, p. 255.   [o] Walsingham, p. 374.

attempts unsuccessful. Sir Thomas Rokesby, sheriff of Yorkshire, levied some forces, attacked the invaders at Bramham, and gained a victory, in which both Northumberland and Bardolf were slain.[p] This prosperous event, joined to the death of Glendour, which happened soon after, freed Henry from all his domestic enemies; and this prince, who had mounted the throne by such unjustifiable means, and held it by such an exceptionable title, had yet, by his valour, prudence, and address, accustomed the people to the yoke, and had obtained a greater ascendant over his haughty barons, than the law alone, not supported by these active qualities, was ever able to confer.

About the same time, fortune gave Henry an advantage over that neighbour, who, by his situation, was most enabled to disturb his government. Robert III. king of Scots, was a prince, though of slender capacity, extremely innocent and inoffensive in his conduct: But Scotland, at that time, was still less fitted than England for cherishing, or even enduring, sovereigns of that character. The duke of Albany, Robert's brother, a prince of more abilities, at least of a more boisterous and violent disposition, had assumed the government of the state; and not satisfied with present authority, he entertained the criminal purpose of extirpating his brother's children, and of acquiring the crown to his own family. He threw in prison David, his eldest nephew; who there perished by hunger: James alone, the younger brother of David, stood between that tyrant and the throne; and king Robert, sensible of his son's danger, embarked him on board a ship, with a view of sending him to France, and entrusting him to the protection of that friendly power. Unfortunately, the vessel was taken by the English; prince James, a boy about nine years of age, was carried to London; and though there subsisted at that time a truce between the kingdoms, Henry refused to restore the young prince to his liberty. Robert, worn out with cares and infirmities, was unable to bear the shock of this last misfortune; and he soon after died, leaving the government in the hands of the duke of Albany.[q] Henry was now more sensible than ever of the importance of the acquisition, which he had made: While he retained such a pledge, he was sure of keeping the duke of Albany in dependance; or if offended, he could easily

[p] Ibid. p. 377. Chron. Otterb. p. 261.   [q] Buchanan, lib. 10.

CHAPTER XVIII

by restoring the true heir, take ample revenge upon the usurper. But though the king, by detaining James in the English court, had shown himself somewhat deficient in generosity, he made ample amends, by giving that prince an excellent education, which afterwards qualified him, when he mounted the throne, to reform, in some measure, the rude and barbarous manners of his native country.

The hostile dispositions, which of late had prevailed between France and England, were restrained, during the greater part of this reign, from appearing in action. The jealousies and civil commotions, with which both nations were disturbed, kept each of them from taking advantage of the unhappy situation of its neighbour. But as the abilities and good fortune of Henry had sooner been able to compose the English factions, this prince began, in the later part of his reign, to look abroad, and to foment the animosities between the families of Burgundy and Orleans, by which the government of France was, during that period, so much distracted. He knew, that one great source of the national discontent against his predecessor, was the inactivity of his reign; and he hoped, by giving a new direction to the restless and unquiet spirits of his people, to prevent their breaking out in domestic wars and disorders. That he might unite policy with force, he first entered into treaty with the duke of Burgundy, and sent that prince a small body of troops, which supported him against his enemies.[r] Soon after, he hearkened to more advantageous proposals made him by the duke of Orleans, and dispatched a greater body to support that party.[s] But the leaders of the opposite factions having made a temporary accommodation, the interests of the English were sacrificed and this effort of Henry proved, in the issue, entirely vain and fruitless. The declining state of his health and the shortness of his reign, prevented him from renewing the attempt, which his more fortunate son carried to so great a length against the French monarchy.

Such were the military and foreign transactions of this reign: The civil and parliamentary are somewhat more memorable, and more worthy of our attention. During the two last reigns, the elections of the commons had appeared a circumstance of govern-

1411.

1412.

Parliamentary transactions.

[r] Walsingham, p. 380.   [s] Rymer, vol. viii. p. 715, 738.

ment not to be neglected; and Richard was even accused of using unwarrantable methods for procuring to his partizans a seat in that house. This practice formed one considerable article of charge against him in his deposition; yet Henry scrupled not to tread in his footsteps, and to encourage the same abuses in elections. Laws were enacted against such undue influence, and even a sheriff was punished for an iniquitous return, which he had made:[t] But laws were commonly, at that time, very ill executed; and the liberties of the people, such as they were, stood on a surer basis than on laws and parliamentary elections. Though the house of commons was little able to withstand the violent currents, which perpetually ran between the monarchy and the aristocracy, and though that house might easily be brought, at a particular time, to make the most unwarrantable concessions to either; the general institutions of the state still remained invariable; the interests of the several members continued on the same footing; the sword was in the hands of the subject; and the government, though thrown into temporary disorder, soon settled itself on its ancient foundations.

During the greater part of this reign, the king was obliged to court popularity; and the house of commons, sensible of their own importance, began to assume powers which had not usually been exercised by their predecessors. In the first year of Henry, they procured a law, that no judge, in concurring with any iniquitous measure should be excused by pleading the orders of the king, or even the danger of his own life from the menaces of the sovereign.[u] In the second year, they insisted on maintaining the practice of not granting any supply before they received an answer to their petitions; which was a tacit manner of bargaining with the prince.[w] In the fifth year, they desired the king to remove from his household four persons who had displeased them, among whom was his own confessor; and Henry, though he told them, that he knew of no offence which these men had committed, yet, in order to gratify them, complied with their request.[x] In the sixth year, they voted the king supplies, but appointed treasurers of their own, to see the money disbursed for the purposes intended, and required them to deliver in their accounts to the house.[y] In the

[t] Cotton, p. 429. [u] Cotton, p. 364. [w] Ibid. p. 406. [x] Ibid. p. 426.
[y] Ibid. p. 438.

eighth year, they proposed, for the regulation of the government and household, thirty important articles, which were all agreed to; and they even obliged all the members of council, all the judges, and all the officers of the household, to swear to the observance of them.[z] The abridger of the records remarks the unusual liberties taken by the speaker and the house during this period.[a] But the great authority of the commons was but a temporary advantage, arising from the present situation. In a subsequent parliament, when the speaker made his customary application to the throne for liberty of speech, the king, having now overcome all his domestic difficulties, plainly told him, that he would have no novelties introduced, and would enjoy his prerogatives. But on the whole, the limitations of the government seem to have been more sensibly felt, and more carefully maintained by Henry, than by any of his predecessors.

During this reign, when the house of commons were, at any time, brought to make unwary concessions to the crown, they also shewed their freedom by a speedy retraction of them. Henry, though he entertained a perpetual and well-grounded jealousy of the family of Mortimer, allowed not their name to be once mentioned in parliament; and as none of the rebels had ventured to declare the earl of Marche king, he never attempted to procure, what would not have been refused him, an express declaration against the claim of that nobleman; because he knew that such a declaration, in the present circumstances, would have no authority, and would only serve to revive the memory of Mortimer's title in the minds of the people. He proceeded in his purpose after a more artful and covert manner. He procured a settlement of the crown on himself and his heirs-male,[b] thereby tacitly excluding the females, and transferring the Salic law into the English government. He thought, that, though the house of Plantagenet had at first derived their title from a female, this was a remote event, unknown to the generality of the people; and if he could once accustom them to the practice of excluding women, the title of the earl of Marche would gradually be forgotten and neglected by them. But he was very unfortunate in this attempt. During the long contests with France, the injustice of the Salic law had been so

---

[z] Ibid. p. 456, 457.   [a] Ibid. p. 462.   [b] Cotton, p. 454.

much exclaimed against by the nation, that a contrary principle had taken deep root in the minds of men; and it was now become impossible to eradicate it. The same house of commons, therefore, in a subsequent session, apprehensive that they had overturned the foundations of the English government, and that they had opened the door to more civil wars than might ensue even from the irregular elevation of the house of Lancaster, applied with such earnestness for a new settlement of the crown, that Henry yielded to their request, and agreed to the succession of the princesses of his family.[c] A certain proof, that nobody was, in his heart, satisfied with the king's title to the crown, or knew on what principle to rest it.

But though the commons, during this reign, showed a laudable zeal for liberty in their transactions with the crown; their efforts against the church were still more extraordinary, and seemed to anticipate very much the spirit which became so general in little more than a century afterwards. I know, that the credit of these passages rests entirely on one ancient historian;[d] but that historian was contemporary, was a clergyman, and it was contrary to the interests of his order to preserve the memory of such transactions, much more to forge precedents, which posterity might, some time, be tempted to imitate. This is a truth so evident, that the most likely way of accounting for the silence of the records on this head, is by supposing, that the authority of some churchmen was so great as to procure a razure, with regard to these circumstances, which the indiscretion of one of the order has happily preserved to us.

In the sixth of Henry, the commons, who had been required to grant supplies, proposed in plain terms to the king, that he should seize all the temporalities of the church, and employ them as a perpetual fund to serve the exigencies of the state. They insisted, that the clergy possessed a third of the lands of the kingdom; that they contributed nothing to the public burdens; and that their riches tended only to disqualify them from performing their ministerial functions with proper zeal and attention. When this address was presented, the archbishop of Canterbury, who then attended the king, objected, that the clergy, though they went not in person to the wars, sent their vassals and tenants in all cases of

[c] Rymer, vol. viii. p. 462.　[d] Walsingham.

necessity; while at the same time they themselves, who staid at home, were employed, night and day, in offering up their prayers for the happiness and prosperity of the state. The speaker smiled, and answered without reserve, that he thought the prayers of the church but a very slender supply. The archbishop however prevailed in the dispute: The king discouraged the application of the commons: And the lords rejected the bill which the lower house had framed for stripping the church of her revenues.[e]

The commons were not discouraged by this repulse: In the eleventh of the king they returned to the charge with more zeal than before: They made a calculation of all the ecclesiastical revenues, which, by their account, amounted to 485,000 marks a-year, and contained 18,400 ploughs of land. They proposed to divide this property among fifteen new earls, 1500 knights, 6000 esquires, and a hundred hospitals; besides 20,000 pounds a-year, which the king might take for his own use. And they insisted, that the clerical functions would be better performed than at present, by 15,000 parish priests, paid at the rate of seven marks a-piece of yearly stipend.[f] This application was accompanied with an address for mitigating the statutes enacted against the Lollards, which shows from what source the address came. The king gave the commons a severe reply; and farther to satisfy the church, and to prove that he was quite in earnest, he ordered a Lollard to be burned before the dissolution of the parliament.[g]

We have now related almost all the memorable transactions of this reign, which was busy and active; but produced few events, that deserve to be transmitted to posterity. The king was so much employed in defending his crown, which he had obtained by unwarrantable means, and possessed by a bad title, that he had little leisure to look abroad, or perform any action, which might redound to the honour and advantage of the nation. His health declined some months before his death: He was subject to fits, which bereaved him, for the time, of his senses: And though he was yet in the flower of his age, his end was visibly approaching. He expired at Westminster in the forty-sixth year of his age, and the thirteenth of his reign.

1413.

20th March. Death,

[e] Walsingham, p. 371. Ypod. Neust. p. 563. [f] Walsingham, p. 379. Tit. Livius. [g] Rymer, vol. viii. p. 627. Otterbourne, p. 267.

and char-
acter of
the king.

The great popularity, which Henry enjoyed before he attained the crown, and which had so much aided him in the acquisition of it, was entirely lost many years before the end of his reign; and he governed his people more by terror than by affection, more by his own policy than by their sense of duty or allegiance. When men came to reflect in cool blood on the crimes which had led him to the throne; the rebellion against his prince, the deposition of a lawful king, guilty sometimes perhaps of oppression, but more frequently of indiscretion; the exclusion of the true heir; the murder of his sovereign and near relation; these were such enormities as drew on him the hatred of his subjects, sanctified all the rebellious against him, and made the executions, though not remarkably severe, which he found necessary for the maintenance of his authority, appear cruel as well as iniquitous to the people. Yet without pretending to apologize for these crimes, which must ever be held in detestation, it may be remarked, that he was insensibly led into this blameable conduct by a train of incidents, which few men possess virtue enough to withstand. The injustice with which his predecessor had treated him, in first condemning him to banishment, then despoiling him of his patrimony, made him naturally think of revenge, and of recovering his lost rights; the headlong zeal of the people hurried him into the throne; the care of his own security, as well as his ambition, made him an usurper; and the steps have always been so few between the prisons of princes and their graves, that we need not wonder, that Richard's fate was no exception to the general rule. All these considerations make Henry's situation, if he retained any sense of virtue, much to be lamented; and the inquietude, with which he possessed his envied greatness, and the remorses, by which, it is said, he was continually haunted, render him an object of our pity, even when seated upon the throne. But it must be owned, that his prudence and vigilance and foresight, in maintaining his power, were admirable: His command of temper remarkable: His courage, both military and political, without blemish. And he possessed many qualities, which fitted him for his high station, and which rendered his usurpation of it, though pernicious in after-times, rather salutary, during his own reign, to the English nation.

Henry was twice married: By his first wife, Mary de Bohun, daughter and co-heir of the earl of Hereford, he had four sons,

CHAPTER XVIII

Henry, his successor in the throne, Thomas duke of Clarence, John duke of Bedford, and Humphrey duke of Glocester; and two daughters, Blanche and Philippa, the former married to the duke of Bavaria, the latter to the king of Denmark. His second wife, Jane, whom he married after he was king, and who was daughter of the king of Navarre, and widow of the duke of Britanny, brought him no issue.

By an act of the fifth of this reign, it is made felony to cut out any person's tongue or put out his eyes; crimes, which, the act says, were very frequent. This savage spirit of revenge denotes a barbarous people; though perhaps it was encreased by the prevailing factions and civil commotions.

Commerce was very little understood in this reign, as in all the preceding. In particular, a great jealousy prevailed against *merchant strangers;* and many restraints were by law imposed upon them; namely, that they should lay out in English manufactures or commodities all the money acquired by the sale of their goods; that they should not buy or sell with one another, and that all their goods should be disposed of three months after importation.[h] This last clause was found so inconvenient, that it was soon after repealed by parliament.

It appears that the expence of this king's household amounted to the yearly sum of 19,500 l. money of that age.[i]

Guicciardin tells us, that the Flemings in this century learned from Italy all the refinements in arts, which they taught the rest of Europe. The progress, however, of the arts were still very slow and backward in England.

[h] 4 Hen. IV. cap. 15. and 5 Hen. IV. cap. 9.   [i] Rymer, tom. viii. p. 610.

XIX

HENRY V

The king's former disorders –
His reformation – The Lollards –
Punishment of lord Cobham – State
of France – Invasion of that kingdom –
Battle of Azincour – State of France –
New invasion of France – Assassination
of the duke of Burgundy – Treaty of
Troye – Marriage of the king – His
death – and character – Miscellaneous
transactions during this reign

1413.
The
king's
former
disorders.
THE MANY JEALOUSIES, to which Henry IV.'s situation naturally exposed him, had so infected his temper, that he had entertained unreasonable suspicions with regard to the fidelity of his eldest son; and during the latter years of his life, he had excluded that prince from all share in public business, and was even displeased to see him at the head of armies, where his martial talents, though useful to the support of government, acquired him a renown, which, he thought, might prove dangerous to his own authority. The active spirit of young Henry, restrained from its proper exercise, broke out in extravagancies of every kind; and the riot of pleasure, the frolic of debauchery, the outrage of wine, filled the vacancies of a mind, better adapted to the pursuits of ambition, and the cares of government. This course of life threw

CHAPTER XIX

him among companions, whose disorders, if accompanied with spirit and humour, he indulged and seconded; and he was detected in many sallies, which, to severer eyes, appeared totally unworthy of his rank and station. There even remains a tradition, that, when heated with liquor and jollity, he scrupled not to accompany his riotous associates in attacking the passengers on the streets and highways, and despoiling them of their goods; and he found an amusement in the incidents, which the terror and regret of these defenceless people produced on such occasions. This extreme of dissoluteness proved equally disagreeable to his father, as that eager application to business, which had at first given him occasion of jealousy; and he saw in his son's behaviour the same neglect of decency, the same attachment to low company, which had degraded the personal character of Richard, and which, more than all his errors in government, had tended to overturn his throne. But the nation in general considered the young prince with more indulgence; and observed so many gleams of generosity, spirit, and magnanimity, breaking continually through the cloud, which a wild conduct threw over his character, that they never ceased hoping for his amendment; and they ascribed all the weeds, which shot up in that rich soil, to the want of proper culture and attention in the king and his ministers. There happened an incident which encouraged these agreeable views, and gave much occasion for favourable reflections to all men of sense and candour. A riotous companion of the prince's had been indicted before Gascoigne, the chief justice, for some disorders; and Henry was not ashamed to appear at the bar with the criminal, in order to give him countenance and protection. Finding, that his presence had not over-awed the chief justice, he proceeded to insult that magistrate on his tribunal; but Gascoigne, mindful of the character which he then bore, and the majesty of the sovereign and of the laws, which he sustained, ordered the prince to be carried to prison for his rude behaviour.[k] The spectators were agreeably disappointed, when they saw the heir of the crown submit peaceably to this sentence, make reparation for his error by acknowledging it, and check his impetuous nature in the midst of its extravagant career.

[k] Hall, fol. 33.

The memory of this incident, and of many others of a like nature, rendered the prospect of the future reign nowise disagreeable to the nation, and encreased the joy, which the death of so unpopular a prince as the late king naturally occasioned. The first steps taken by the young prince confirmed all those prepossessions, entertained in his favour.[l] He called together his former companions, acquainted them with his intended reformation, exhorted them to imitate his example, but strictly inhibited them, till they had given proofs of their sincerity in this particular, from appearing any more in his presence; and he thus dismissed them with liberal presents.[m] The wise ministers of his father, who had checked his riots, found that they had unknowingly been paying the highest court to him; and were received with all the marks of favour and confidence. The chief justice himself, who trembled to approach the royal presence, met with praises instead of reproaches, for his past conduct, and was exhorted to persevere in the same rigorous and impartial execution of the laws. The surprize of those who expected an opposite behaviour, augmented their satisfaction; and the character of the young king appeared brighter than if it had never been shaded by any errors.

But Henry was anxious not only to repair his own misconduct, but also to make amends for those iniquities, into which policy or the necessity of affairs had betrayed his father. He expressed the deepest sorrow for the fate of the unhappy Richard, did justice to the memory of that unfortunate prince, even performed his funeral obsequies with pomp and solemnity, and cherished all those who had distinguished themselves by their loyalty and attachment towards him.[n] Instead of continuing the restraints which the jealousy of his father had imposed on the earl of Marche, he received that young nobleman with singular courtesy and favour; and by this magnanimity so gained on the gentle and unambitious nature of his competitor, that he remained ever after sincerely attached to him, and gave him no disturbance in his future government. The family of Piercy was restored to its fortune and honours.[o] The king seemed ambitious to bury all party-distinctions in oblivion: The

---

[l] Walsing. p. 382. [m] Hall, fol. 33. Holingshed, p. 543. Goodwin's Life of Henry V. p. 1. [n] Hist. Croyland. contin. Hall, fol. 34. Holingshed, p. 544. [o] Holingshed, p. 545.

CHAPTER XIX

instruments of the preceding reign, who had been advanced from their blind zeal for the Lancastrian interests, more than from their merits, gave place every where to men of more honourable characters: Virtue seemed now to have an open career, in which it might exert itself: The exhortations, as well as example, of the prince gave it encouragement: All men were unanimous in their attachment to Henry; and the defects of his title were forgotten, amidst the personal regard, which was universally paid to him.

There remained among the people only one party distinction, which was derived from religious differences, and which, as it is of a peculiar and commonly a very obstinate nature, the popularity of Henry was not able to overcome. The Lollards were every day encreasing in the kingdom, and were become a formed party, which appeared extremely dangerous to the church, and even formidable to the civil authority.[p] The enthusiasm by which these sectaries were generally actuated, the great alterations which they pretended to introduce, the hatred which they expressed against the established hierarchy, gave an alarm to Henry; who, either from a sincere attachment to the ancient religion, or from a dread of the unknown consequences, which attend all important changes, was determined to execute the laws against such bold innovators. The head of this sect was Sir John Oldcastle, lord Cobham, a nobleman, who had distinguished himself by his valour and his military talents, and had, on many occasions, acquired the esteem both of the late and of the present king.[q] His high character and his zeal for the new sect pointed him out to Arundel, archbishop of Canterbury, as the proper victim of ecclesiastical severity; whose punishment would strike a terror into the whole party, and teach them that they must expect no mercy under the present administration. He applied to Henry for a permission to indict lord Cobham;[r] but the generous nature of the prince was averse to such sanguinary methods of conversion. He represented to the primate, that reason and conviction were the best expedients for supporting truth; that all gentle means ought first to be tried, in order to reclaim men from error; and that he himself would endeavour, by a conversation with Cobham, to reconcile him to the catholic faith.

The Lollards.

[p] Walsingham, p. 382. [q] Walsingham, p. 382. [r] Fox's Acts and Monuments, p. 513.

But he found that nobleman obstinate in his opinions, and determined not to sacrifice truths of such infinite moment to his complaisance for sovereigns.[s] Henry's principles of toleration, or rather his love of the practice, could carry him no farther; and he then gave full reins to ecclesiastical severity against the inflexible heresiarch. The primate indicted Cobham; and with the assistance of his three suffragans, the bishops of London, Winchester, and St. David's, condemned him to the flames for his erroneous opinions. Cobham, who was confined in the Tower, made his escape before the day appointed for his execution. The bold spirit of the man, provoked by persecution and stimulated by zeal, was urged to attempt the most criminal enterprizes; and his unlimited authority over the new sect proved, that he well merited the attention of the civil magistrate. He formed in his retreat very violent designs against his enemies; and dispatching his emissaries to all quarters, appointed a general rendezvous of the party, in order to seize the person of the king at Eltham, and put their persecutors to the

*1414.
6th Jan.* sword.[t] Henry, apprized of their intention, removed to Westminster: Cobham was not discouraged by this disappointment; but changed the place of rendezvous to the field near St. Giles's: The king, having shut the gates of the city, to prevent any reinforcement to the Lollards from that quarter, came into the fields in the night-time, seized such of the conspirators as appeared and afterwards laid hold of the several parties, who were hastening to the place appointed. It appeared, that a few only were in the secret of the conspiracy: The rest implicitly followed their leaders: But upon the trial of the prisoners, the treasonable designs of the sect were rendered certain, both from evidence and from the confession of the criminals themselves.[u] Some were executed, the greater number pardoned.[w] Cobham, himself, who made his escape by

*Punishment
of lord
Cobham.* flight, was not brought to justice, till four years after; when he was hanged as a traitor; and his body was burnt on the gibbet, in execution of the sentence pronounced against him as a heretic.[x] This criminal design, which was perhaps somewhat aggravated by

[s] Rymer, vol. ix. p. 61. Walsingham, p. 383.   [t] Walsingham, p. 385.
[u] Cotton, p. 554. Hall, fol. 35. Holingshed, p. 544.   [w] Rymer, vol. ix. p. 119,
129, 193.   [x] Walsingham, p. 400. Otterbourne, p. 280, Holingshed, p. 561.

CHAPTER XIX

the clergy, brought discredit upon the party, and checked the progress of that sect, which had embraced the speculative doctrines of Wickliffe, and at the same time aspired to a reformation of ecclesiastical abuses.

These two points were the great objects of the Lollards; but the bulk of the nation was not affected in the same degree by both of them. Common sense and obvious reflection had discovered to the people the advantages of a reformation in discipline; but the age was not yet so far advanced as to be seized with the spirit of controversy, or to enter into those abstruse doctrines, which the Lollards endeavoured to propagate throughout the kingdom. The very notion of heresy alarmed the generality of the people: Innovation in fundamental principles was suspicious: Curiosity was not, as yet, a sufficient counterpoize to authority: And even many, who were the greatest friends to the reformation of abuses, were anxious to express their detestation of the speculative tenets of the Wickliffites, which, they feared, threw disgrace on so good a cause. This turn of thought appears evidently in the proceedings of the parliament, which was summoned immediately after the detection of Cobham's conspiracy. That assembly passed severe laws against the new heretics: They enacted, that whoever was convicted of Lollardy before the Ordinary, besides suffering capital punishment according to the laws formerly established, should also forfeit his lands and goods to the king; and that the chancellor, treasurer, justices of the two benches, sheriffs, justices of the peace, and all the chief magistrates in every city and borough, should take an oath to use their utmost endeavours for the extirpation of heresy.[y] Yet this very parliament, when the king demanded supply, renewed the offer formerly pressed upon his father, and entreated him to seize all the ecclesiastical revenues, and convert them to the use of the crown.[z] The clergy were alarmed: They could offer the king no bribe which was equivalent: They only agreed to confer on him all the priories alien, which depended on capital abbies in Normandy, and had been bequeathed to these abbies, when that province remained united to England: And Chicheley, now archbishop of Canterbury, endeavoured to

[y] 2 Hen. V. chap. 7.   [z] Hall, fol. 35.

divert the blow, by giving occupation to the king, and by persuading him to undertake a war against France, in order to recover his lost rights to that kingdom.[a]

It was the dying injunction of the late king to his son, not to allow the English to remain long in peace, which was apt to breed intestine commotions; but to employ them in foreign expeditions, by which the prince might acquire honour; the nobility, in sharing his dangers, might attach themselves to his person; and all the restless spirits find occupation for their inquietude. The natural disposition of Henry sufficiently inclined him to follow this advice, and the civil disorders of France, which had been prolonged beyond those of England, opened a full career to his ambition.

1415.
State of
France.
The death of Charles V. which followed soon after that of Edward III. and the youth of his son, Charles VI. put the two kingdoms for some time in a similar situation; and it was not to be apprehended, that either of them, during a minority, would be able to make much advantage of the weakness of the other. The jealousies also between Charles's three uncles, the dukes of Anjou, Berri, and Burgundy, had distracted the affairs of France rather more than those between the dukes of Lancaster, York, and Gloucester, Richard's three uncles, disordered those of England; and had carried off the attention of the French nation from any vigorous enterprize against foreign states. But in proportion as Charles advanced in years, the factions were composed; his two uncles, the dukes of Anjou and Burgundy, died; and the king himself, assuming the reins of government, discovered symptoms of genius and spirit, which revived the drooping hopes of his country. This promising state of affairs was not of long duration: The unhappy prince fell suddenly into a fit of frenzy, which rendered him incapable of exercising his authority; and though he recovered from this disorder, he was so subject to relapses, that his judgment was gradually, but sensibly impaired, and no steady plan of government could be pursued by him. The administration of affairs was disputed between his brother, Lewis duke of Orleans, and his cousin-german, John duke of Burgundy: The propinquity to the crown pleaded in favour of the former: The latter, who, in right of his mother, had inherited the county of Flanders, which he

[a] Hall, fol. 35, 36.

CHAPTER XIX

annexed to his father's extensive dominions, derived a lustre from his superior power: The people were divided between these contending princes: And the king, now resuming, now dropping his authority, kept the victory undecided, and prevented any regular settlement of the state, by the final prevalence of either party.

At length, the dukes of Orleans and Burgundy, seeming to be moved by the cries of the nation and by the interposition of common friends, agreed to bury all past quarrels in oblivion, and to enter into strict amity: They swore before the altar the sincerity of their friendship; the priest administered the sacrament to both of them; they gave to each other every pledge, which could be deemed sacred among men: But all this solemn preparation was only a cover for the basest treachery, which was deliberately premeditated by the duke of Burgundy. He procured his rival to be assassinated in the streets of Paris: He endeavoured for some time to conceal the part which he took in the crime: But being detected, he embraced a resolution still more criminal and more dangerous to society, by openly avowing and justifying it.[b] The parliament itself of Paris, the tribunal of Justice, heard the harangues of the duke's advocate in defence of assassination, which he termed tyrannicide; and that assembly partly influenced by faction, partly overawed by power, pronounced no sentence of condemnation against this detestable doctrine.[c] The same question was afterwards agitated before the council of Constance; and it was with difficulty, that a feeble decision, in favour of the contrary opinion, was procured from these fathers of the church, the ministers of peace and of religion. But the mischievous effects of that tenet, had they been before anywise doubtful, appeared sufficiently from the present incidents. The commission of this crime, which destroyed all trust and security, rendered the war implacable between the French parties, and cut off every means of peace and accommodation. The princes of the blood, combining with the young duke of Orleans and his brothers, made violent war on the duke of Burgundy; and the unhappy king, seized sometimes by one party, sometimes by the other, transferred alternately to each of them the appearance of legal authority. The provinces were laid

---

[b] Le Laboureur, liv. xxvii. chap. 23, 24.　[c] Ibid. liv. 27. chap. 27. Monstrelet, chap. 39.

waste by mutual depredations: Assassinations were every where committed from the animosity of the several leaders; or what was equally terrible, executions were ordered, without any legal or free trial, by pretended courts of judicature. The whole kingdom was distinguished into two parties, the Burgundians, and the Armagnacs; so the adherents of the young duke of Orleans were called, from the count of Armagnac, father-in-law to that prince. The city of Paris, distracted between them, but inclining more to the Burgundians, was a perpetual scene of blood and violence; the king and royal family were often detained captives in the hands of the populace; their faithful ministers were butchered or imprisoned before their face; and it was dangerous for any man, amidst these enraged factions, to be distinguished by a strict adherence to the principles of probity and honour.

During this scene of general violence, there rose into some consideration a body of men, which usually makes no figure in public transactions even during the most peaceful times; and that was the university of Paris, whose opinion was sometimes demanded, and more frequently offered, in the multiplied disputes between the parties. The schism, by which the church was at that time divided, and which occasioned frequent controversies in the university, had raised the professors to an unusual degree of importance; and this connection between literature and superstition had bestowed on the former a weight, to which reason and knowledge are not, of themselves, any wise entitled among men. But there was another society whose sentiments were much more decisive at Paris, the fraternity of butchers, who, under the direction of their ringleaders, had declared for the duke of Burgundy, and committed the most violent outrages against the opposite party. To counterbalance their power, the Armagnacs made interest with the fraternity of carpenters; the populace ranged themselves on one side or the other; and the fate of the capital depended on the prevalence of either party.

The advantage, which might be made of these confusions, was easily perceived in England; and according to the maxims, which usually prevail among nations, it was determined to lay hold of the favourable opportunity. The late king, who was courted by both the French parties, fomented the quarrel, by alternately sending assistance to each; but the present sovereign, impelled by the vig-

CHAPTER XIX

our of youth and the ardour of ambition, determined to push his advantages to a greater length, and to carry violent war into that distracted kingdom. But while he was making preparations for this end, he tried to effect his purpose by negotiation; and he sent over embassadors to Paris, offering a perpetual peace and alliance; but demanding Catharine, the French king's daughter, in marriage, two millions of crowns as her portion, one million six hundred thousand as the arrears of king John's ransom, and the immediate possession and full sovereignty of Normandy and of all the other provinces, which had been ravished from England by the arms of Philip Augustus; together with the superiority of Britanny and Flanders.[d] Such exorbitant demands show, that he was sensible of the present miserable condition of France; and the terms, offered by the French court, though much inferior, discover their consciousness of the same melancholy truth. They were willing to give him the princess in marriage, to pay him eight hundred thousand crowns, to resign the entire sovereignty of Guienne, and to annex to that province the country of Perigord, Rovergue, Xaintonge, the Angoumois, and other territories.[e] As Henry rejected these conditions, and scarcely hoped that his own demands would be complied with, he never intermitted a moment his preparations for war, and having assembled a great fleet and army at Southampton, having invited all the nobility and military men of the kingdom to attend him by the hopes of glory and of conquest, he came to the sea-side, with a purpose of embarking on his expedition.

But while Henry was meditating conquests upon his neighbours, he unexpectedly found himself in danger from a conspiracy at home, which was happily detected in its infancy. The earl of Cambridge, second son of the late duke of York, having espoused the sister of the earl of Marche, had zealously embraced the interests of that family; and had held some conferences with lord

[d] Rymer, vol. ix. p. 208.   [e] Ibid. p. 211. It is reported by some historians (see Hist. Croyl. Cont. p. 500) that the Dauphin, in derision of Henry's claims and dissolute character, sent him a box of tennis balls; intimating that these implements of play were better adapted to him than the instruments of war. But this story is by no means credible; the great offers made by the court of France, show that they had already entertained a just idea of Henry's character, as well as of their own situation.

Scrope of Masham, and Sir Thomas Grey of Heton, about the means of recovering to that nobleman his right to the crown of England. The conspirators, as soon as detected, acknowledged their guilt to the king;[f] and Henry proceeded without delay to their trial and condemnation. The utmost that could be expected of the best king in those ages, was, that he would so far observe the essentials of justice, as not to make an innocent person a victim to his severity: But as to the formalities of law, which are often as material as the essentials themselves, they were sacrificed without scruple to the least interest or convenience. A jury of commoners was summoned: The three conspirators were indicted before them: The constable of Southampton castle swore, that they had separately confessed their guilt to him: Without other evidence, Sir Thomas Grey was condemned and executed: But as the earl of Cambridge and lord Scrope, pleaded the privilege of their peerage, Henry thought proper to summon a court of eighteen barons, in which the duke of Clarence presided: The evidence, given before the jury, was read to them: The prisoners, though one of them was a prince of the blood, were not examined, nor produced in court, nor heard in their own defence; but received sentence of death upon this proof, which was every way irregular and unsatisfactory; and the sentence was soon after executed. The earl of Marche was accused of having given his approbation to the conspiracy, and received a general pardon from the king.[g] He was probably either innocent of the crime imputed to him, or had made reparation by his early repentance and discovery.[h]

Invasion of France. The successes, which the arms of England have, in different ages, obtained over those of France, have been much owing to the favourable situation of the former kingdom. The English, happily seated in an island, could make advantage of every misfortune which attended their neighbours, and were little exposed to the danger of reprizals. They never left their own country, but when they were conducted by a king of extraordinary genius, or found their enemy divided by intestine factions, or were supported by a powerful alliance on the continent; and as all these circumstances concurred at present to favour their enterprize, they had reason to

[f] Rymer, vol. ix. p. 300. T. Livii, p. 8.   [g] Rymer, vol. ix. p. 303.   [h] St. Remi, chap. lv. Goodwin, p. 65.

expect from it proportionable success. The duke of Burgundy, expelled France by a combination of the princes, had been secretly soliciting the alliance of England;[i] and Henry knew, that this prince, though he scrupled at first to join the inveterate enemy of his country, would willingly, if he saw any probability of success, both assist him with his Flemish subjects, and draw over to the same side all his numerous partizans in France. Trusting therefore to this circumstance, but without establishing any concert with the duke, he put to sea, and landed near Harfleur, at the head of an army of 6000 men at arms, and 24,000 foot, mostly archers. He immediately began the siege of that place, which was valiantly defended by d'Estoûteville, and under him by de Guitri, de Gaucourt, and others of the French nobility: But as the garrison was weak, and the fortifications in bad repair, the governor was at last obliged to capitulate; and he promised to surrender the place if he received no succour before the eighteenth of September. The day came, and there was no appearance of a French army to relieve him. Henry, taking possession of the town, placed a garrison in it, and expelled all the French inhabitants, with an intention of peopling it anew with English.

14th Aug.

The fatigues of this siege, and the unusual heat of the season, had so wasted the English army, that Henry could enter on no farther enterprize; and was obliged to think of returning into England. He had dismissed his transports, which could not anchor in an open road upon the enemy's coasts: And he lay under a necessity of marching by land to Calais, before he could reach a place of safety. A numerous French army of 14,000 men at arms and 40,000 foot was by this time assembled in Normandy under the constable d'Albret; a force, which, if prudently conducted, was sufficient either to trample down the English in the open field, or to harass and reduce to nothing their small army, before they could finish so long and difficult a march. Henry, therefore, cautiously offered to sacrifice his conquest of Harfleur for a safe passage to Calais; but his proposal being rejected, he determined to make his way by valour and conduct through all the opposition of the enemy.[k] That he might not discourage his army by the appearance of flight, or expose them to those hazards which natu-

---

[i] Rymer, vol. ix. p. 137, 138.   [k] Le Laboureur, liv. 35. chap. 6.

rally attend precipitate marches, he made slow and deliberate journies,[l] till he reached the Somme, which he purposed to pass at the ford of Blanquetague, the same place where Edward, in a like situation, had before escaped from Philip de Valois. But he found the ford rendered impassable by the precaution of the French general, and guarded by a strong body on the opposite bank;[m] and he was obliged to march higher up the river, in order to seek for a safe passage. He was continually harassed on his march by flying parties of the enemy; saw bodies of troops on the other side ready to oppose every attempt; his provisions were cut off; his soldiers languished with sickness and fatigue; and his affairs seemed to be reduced to a desperate situation: When he was so dexterous or so fortunate as to seize by surprize a passage near St. Quintin, which had not been sufficiently guarded; and he safely carried over his army.[n]

Battle of Azincour.

25th Oct.

Henry then bent his march northwards to Calais; but he was still exposed to great and imminent danger from the enemy, who had also passed the Somme, and threw themselves full in his way, with a purpose of intercepting his retreat. After he had passed the small river of Ternois at Blangi, he was surprized to observe from the heights the whole French army drawn up in the plains of Azincour, and so posted that it was impossible for him to proceed on his march, without coming to an engagement. Nothing in appearance could be more unequal than the battle, upon which his safety and all his fortunes now depended. The English army was little more than half the number, which had disembarked at Harfleur; and they laboured under every discouragement and necessity. The enemy was four times more numerous, was headed by the dauphin and all the princes of the blood; and was plentifully supplied with provisions of every kind. Henry's situation was exactly similar to that of Edward at Cressy, and that of the Black Prince at Poictiers; and the memory of these great events, inspiring the English with courage, made them hope for a like deliverance from their present difficulties. The king likewise observed the same prudent conduct which had been followed by these great commanders: He drew up his army on a narrow ground between two

[l] T. Livii, p. 12.   [m] St. Remi, chap. 58.   [n] T. Livii, p. 13.

woods, which guarded each flank; and he patiently expected in that posture the attack of the enemy.[o]

Had the French constable been able, either to reason justly upon the present circumstances of the two armies, or to profit by past experience, he had declined a combat, and had waited, till necessity, obliging the English to advance, had made them relinquish the advantages of their situation. But the impetuous valour of the nobility, and a vain confidence in superior numbers, brought on this fatal action, which proved the source of infinite calamities to their country. The French archers on horseback and their men at arms, crowded in their ranks, advanced upon the English archers, who had fixed pallisadoes in their front to break the impression of the enemy, and who safely plyed them, from behind that defence, with a shower of arrows, which nothing could resist.[p] The clay soil, moistened by some rain, which had lately fallen, proved another obstacle to the force of the French cavalry: The wounded men and horses discomposed their ranks: The narrow compass, in which they were pent, hindered them from recovering any order: The whole army was a scene of confusion, terror, and dismay: And Henry, perceiving his advantage, ordered the English archers, who were light and unincumbered, to advance upon the enemy, and seize the moment of victory. They fell with their battle-axes upon the French, who, in their present posture, were incapable either of flying or of making defence: They hewed them in pieces without resistance:[q] And being seconded by the men at arms, who also pushed on against the enemy, they covered the field with the killed, wounded, dismounted, and overthrown. After all appearance of opposition was over, the English had leisure to make prisoners; and having advanced with uninterrupted success to the open plain, they there saw the remains of the French rear guard, which still maintained the appearance of a line of battle. At the same time, they heard an alarm from behind: Some gentlemen of Picardy, having collected about 600 peasants, had fallen upon the English baggage, and were doing execution on the

---

[o] St. Remi, chap. 62.　　[p] Walsingham, p. 392. T. Livii, p. 19. Le Laboureur, liv. 35. chap. 7. Monstrelet, chap. 147.　　[q] Walsingham, p. 393. Ypod. Neust. p. 584.

unarmed followers of the camp, who fled before them. Henry, seeing the enemy on all sides of him, began to entertain apprehensions from his prisoners; and he thought it necessary to issue general orders for putting them to death: But on discovering the truth, he stopped the slaughter, and was still able to save a great number.

No battle was ever more fatal to France, by the number of princes and nobility, slain or taken prisoners. Among the former were the constable himself, the count of Nevers and the duke of Brabant, brothers to the duke of Burgundy, the count of Vaudemont, brother to the duke of Lorraine, the duke of Alençon, the duke of Barre, the count of Marle. The most eminent prisoners were the dukes of Orleans and Bourbon, the counts d'Eu, Vendôme, and Richemont, and the mareschal of Boucicaut. An archbishop of Sens also was slain in this battle. The killed are computed on the whole to have amounted to ten thousand men; and as the slaughter fell chiefly upon the cavalry, it is pretended, that, of these, eight thousand were gentlemen. Henry was master of 14,000 prisoners. The person of chief note, who fell among the English, was the duke of York, who perished fighting by the king's side, and had an end more honourable than his life. He was succeeded in his honours and fortune by his nephew, son of the earl of Cambridge, executed in the beginning of the year. All the English, who were slain, exceeded not forty; though some writers, with greater probability, make the number more considerable.

The three great battles of Cressy, Poictiers, and Azincour bear a singular resemblance to each other, in their most considerable circumstances. In all of them, there appears the same temerity in the English princes, who, without any object of moment, merely for the sake of plunder, had ventured so far into the enemies' country as to leave themselves no retreat; and unless saved by the utmost imprudence in the French commanders, were, from their very situation, exposed to inevitable destruction. But allowance being made for this temerity, which, according to the irregular plans of war, followed in those ages, seems to have been, in some measure, unavoidable; there appears, in the day of action, the same presence of mind, dexterity, courage, firmness, and precaution on the part of the English: The same precipitation, confusion, and vain confidence on the part of the French: And the

CHAPTER XIX

events were such as might have been expected from such opposite conduct. The immediate consequences too of these three great victories were similar: Instead of pushing the French with vigour, and taking advantage of their consternation, the English princes, after their victory, seem rather to have relaxed their efforts, and to have allowed the enemy leisure to recover from his losses. Henry interrupted not his march a moment after the battle of Azincour; he carried his prisoners to Calais, thence to England; he even concluded a truce with the enemy; and it was not till after an interval of two years that any body of English troops appeared in France.

The poverty of all the European princes, and the small resources of their kingdoms, were the cause of these continual interruptions in their hostilities; and though the maxims of war were in general destructive, their military operations were mere incursions, which, without any settled plan, they carried on against each other. The lustre, however, attending the victory of Azincour, procured some supplies from the English parliament; though still unequal to the expences of a campaign. They granted Henry an entire fifteenth of moveables; and they conferred on him *for life* the duties of tonnage and poundage, and the subsidies on the exportation of wool and leather. This concession is more considerable than that which had been granted to Richard II. by his last parliament, and which was afterwards, on his deposition, made so great an article of charge against him.

But during this interruption of hostilities from England, France was exposed to all the furies of civil war; and the several parties became every day more enraged against each other. The duke of Burgundy, confident that the French ministers and generals were entirely discredited by the misfortune at Azincour, advanced with a great army to Paris, and attempted to re-instate himself in possession of the government, as well as of the person of the king. But his partizans in that city were overawed by the court, and kept in subjection: The duke despaired of success; and he retired with his forces, which he immediately disbanded in the Low-Countries.[r] He was soon after invited to make a new attempt, by some violent quarrels, which broke out in the royal family. The

State of France.

1417.

<hr>

[r] Le Laboureur, liv. 35. chap. 10.

queen, Isabella, daughter of the duke of Bavaria, who had been hitherto an inveterate enemy to the Burgundian faction, had received a great injury from the other party, which the implacable spirit of that princess was never able to forgive. The public necessities obliged the count of Armagnac, created constable of France in the place of d'Albret, to seize the great treasures which Isabella had amassed: and when she expressed her displeasure at this injury, he inspired into the weak mind of the king some jealousies concerning her conduct, and pushed him to seize, and put to the torture, and afterwards throw into the Seine, Bois-bourdon, her favourite, whom he accused of a commerce of gallantry with that princess. The queen herself was sent to Tours, and confined under a guard;[s] and after suffering these multiplied insults, she no longer scrupled to enter into a correspondence with the duke of Burgundy. As her son, the dauphin Charles, a youth of sixteen, was entirely governed by the faction of Armagnac, she extended her animosity to him, and sought his destruction with the most unrelenting hatred. She had soon an opportunity of rendering her unnatural purpose effectual. The duke of Burgundy, in concert with her, entered France at the head of a great army: He made himself master of Amiens, Abbeville, Dourlens, Montreüil, and other towns in Picardy; Senlis, Rheims, Chalons, Troye, and Auxerre, declared themselves of his party.[t] He got possession of Beaumont, Pontoise, Vernon, Meulant, Montlheri, towns in the neighbourhood of Paris; and carrying farther his progress towards the west, he seized Etampes, Chartres, and other fortresses; and was at last able to deliver the queen, who fled to Troye, and openly declared against those ministers, who, she said, detained her husband in capitivity.[u]

Meanwhile, the partizans of Burgundy raised a commotion in Paris, which always inclined to that faction. Lile-Adam, one of the duke's captains, was received into the city in the night-time, and headed the insurrection of the people, which in a moment became so impetuous, that nothing could oppose it. The person of the king was seized: The dauphin made his escape with difficulty: Great numbers of the faction of Armagnac were immediately butchered:

---

[s] St. Remi, chap. 74. Monstrelet, chap. 167.   [t] St. Remi, chap. 79.   [u] Ibid. chap. 81. Monstrelet, chap. 178, 179.

The count himself, and many persons of note, were thrown into prison: Murders were daily committed from private animosity, under pretence of faction: And the populace, not satiated with their fury, and deeming the course of public justice too dilatory, broke into the prisons, and put to death the count of Armagnac, and all the other nobility who were there confined.[w]

While France was in such furious combustion, and was so ill prepared to resist a foreign enemy, Henry, having collected some treasure, and levied an army, landed in Normandy at the head of 25,000 men; and met with no considerable opposition from any quarter. He made himself master of Falaise; Evreux and Caen submitted to him; Pont de l'Arche opened its gates; and Henry, having subdued all the lower Normandy, and having received a reinforcement of 15,000 men from England,[x] formed the siege of Roüen, which was defended by a garrison of 4000 men, seconded by the inhabitants, to the number of 15,000.[y] The cardinal des Ursins here attempted to incline him towards peace, and to moderate his pretensions: But the king replied to him in such terms as shewed that he was fully sensible of all his present advantages: "Do you not see," said he, "that God has led me hither as by the hand? France has no sovereign: I have just pretensions to that kingdom: Every thing is here in the utmost confusion: No one thinks of resisting me. Can I have a more sensible proof, that the Being, who disposes of empires, has determined to put the crown of France upon my head?"[z]

New invasion of France. 1st August. 1418.

But though Henry had opened his mind to this scheme of ambition, he still continued to negotiate with his enemies, and endeavoured to obtain more secure, though less considerable advantages. He made, at the same time, offers of peace to both parties; to the queen and duke of Burgundy on the one hand, who, having possession of the king's person, carried the appearance of legal authority;[a] and to the dauphin on the other, who, being the undoubted heir of the monarchy, was adhered to by every one that payed any regard to the true interests of their country.[b] These two parties also carried on a continual negotiation with each other.

[w] St. Remi, chap. 85, 86. Monstrelet, chap. 118.   [x] Walsingham, p. 400.
[y] St. Remi, chap. 91.   [z] Juvenal des Ursins.   [a] Rymer, vol. ix. p. 717, 749.
[b] Ibid. p. 626, &c.

The terms proposed on all sides were perpetually varying: The events of the war, and the intrigues of the cabinet, intermingled with each other: And the fate of France remained long in this uncertainty. After many negotiations, Henry offered the queen and the duke of Burgundy to make peace with them, to espouse the princess Catharine, and to accept of all the provinces ceded to Edward III. by the treaty of Bretigni, with the addition of Normandy, which he was to receive in full and entire sovereignty.[c] These terms were submitted to: There remained only some circumstances to adjust, in order to the entire completion of the treaty: But in this interval the duke of Burgundy secretly finished his treaty with the Dauphin; and these two princes agreed to share the royal authority during King Charles's lifetime, and to unite their arms in order to expel foreign enemies.[d]

This alliance, which seemed to cut off from Henry all hopes of farther success, proved in the issue the most favourable event that could have happened for his pretensions. Whether the Dauphin and the duke of Burgundy were ever sincere in their mutual engagements is uncertain; but very fatal effects resulted from their momentary and seeming union. The two princes agreed to an interview, in order to concert the means of rendering effectual their common attack on the English; but how both or either of them could with safety venture upon this conference, it seemed somewhat difficult to contrive. The assassination, perpetrated by the duke of Burgundy, and still more, his open avowal of the deed, and defence of the doctrine, tended to dissolve all the bands of civil society; and even men of honour, who detested the example, might deem it just, on a favourable opportunity, to retaliate upon the author. The duke, therefore, who neither dared to give, nor could pretend to expect any trust, agreed to all the contrivances for mutual security, which were proposed by the ministers of the dauphin. The two princes came to Montereau: The duke lodged in the castle: the dauphin in the town, which was divided from the castle by the river Yonne: The bridge between them was chosen for the place of interview: Two high rails were drawn across the bridge: The gates on each side were guarded, one by the officers of the dauphin, the other by those of the duke: The princes were to enter

[c] Ibid. p. 762.   [d] Ibid. p. 776. St. Remi, chap. 95.

into the intermediate space by the opposite gates, accompanied each by ten persons; and with all these marks of dissidence, to conciliate their mutual friendship. But it appeared, that no precautions are sufficient, where laws have no place, and where all principles of honour are utterly abandoned. Tannegui de Chatel, and others of the dauphin's retainers, had been zealous partizans of the late duke of Orleans; and they determined to seize the opportunity of revenging on the assassin the murder of that prince: They no sooner entered the rails, than they drew their swords and attacked the duke of Burgundy: His friends were astonished, and thought not of making any defence; and all of them either shared his fate, or were taken prisoners by the retinue of the dauphin.[e]

Assassination of the duke of Burgundy.

The extreme youth of this prince made it doubtful whether he had been admitted into the secret of the conspiracy: But as the deed was committed under his eye, by his most intimate friends, who still retained their connexions with him, the blame of the action, which was certainly more imprudent than criminal, fell entirely upon him. The whole state of affairs was every where changed by this unexpected incident. The city of Paris, passionately devoted to the family of Burgundy, broke out into the highest fury against the dauphin. The court of king Charles entered from interest into the same views; and as all the ministers of that monarch had owed their preferment to the late duke, and foresaw their downfal if the dauphin should recover possession of his father's person, they were concerned to prevent by any means the success of his enterprize. The queen, persevering in her unnatural animosity against her son, encreased the general flame, and inspired into the king, as far as he was susceptible of any sentiment, the same prejudices by which she herself had long been actuated. But above all, Philip count of Charolois, now duke of Burgundy, thought himself bound by every tie of honour and of duty, to revenge the murder of his father, and to prosecute the assassin to the utmost extremity. And in this general transport of rage, every consideration of national and family interest was buried in oblivion by all parties: The subjection to a foreign enemy, the expulsion of the lawful heir, the slavery of the kingdom,

[e] St. Remi, chap. 97. Monstrelet, chap. 211.

appeared but small evils, if they led to the gratification of the present passion.

The king of England had, before the death of the duke of Burgundy, profited extremely by the distractions of France, and was daily making a considerable progress in Normandy. He had taken Roüen after an obstinate siege:[f] He had made himself master of Pontoise and Gisors: He even threatened Paris, and by the terror of his arms, had obliged the court to remove to Troye: And in the midst of his successes, he was agreeably surprised, to find his enemies, instead of combining against him for their mutual defence, disposed to rush into his arms, and to make him the instrument of their vengeance upon each other. A league was immediately concluded at Arras between him and the duke of Burgundy. This prince, without stipulating any thing for himself, except the prosecution of his father's murder, and the marriage of the duke of Bedford with his sister, was willing to sacrifice the kingdom to Henry's ambition; and he agreed to every demand, made by that monarch. In order to finish this astonishing treaty, which was to transfer the crown of France to a stranger, Henry went to Troye, accompanied by his brothers, the dukes of Clarence and Glocester; and was there met by the duke of Burgundy. The imbecility, into which Charles had fallen, made him incapable of seeing any thing but through the eyes of those who attended him; as they, on their part, saw every thing through the medium of their passions. The treaty, being already concerted among the parties, was immediately drawn, and signed, and ratified: Henry's will seemed to be a law throughout the whole negotiation: Nothing was attended to but his advantages.

1420.

Treaty of Troye. The principal articles of the treaty were, that Henry should espouse the princess Catharine: That king Charles, during his lifetime, should enjoy the title and dignity of king of France: That Henry should be declared and acknowledged heir of the monarchy, and be entrusted with the present administration of the government: That that kingdom should pass to his heirs general: That France and England should for ever be united under one king; but should still retain their several usages, customs, and privileges: That all the princes, peers, vassals, and communities of

[f] T. Livii, p. 69. Monstrelet, chap. 201.

CHAPTER XIX

France, should swear, that they would both adhere to the future succession of Henry, and pay him present obedience as regent: That this prince should unite his arms to those of king Charles and the duke of Burgundy, in order to subdue the adherents of Charles, the pretended dauphin: And that these three princes should make no peace or truce with him but by common consent and agreement.[g]

Such was the tenor of this famous treaty; a treaty, which, as nothing but the most violent animosity could dictate it, so nothing but the power of the sword could carry into execution. It is hard to say, whether its consequences, had it taken effect, would have proved more pernicious to England or to France. It must have reduced the former kingdom to the rank of a province: It would have entirely disjointed the succession of the latter, and have brought on the destruction of every descendant of the royal family; as the houses of Orleans, Anjou, Alençon, Britanny, Bourbon, and of Burgundy itself, whose titles were preferable to that of the English princes, would on that account have been exposed to perpetual jealousy and persecution from the sovereign. There was even a palpable deficiency in Henry's claim, which no art could palliate. For besides the insuperable objections, to which Edward IIId's pretensions were exposed, *he* was not heir to that monarch: If female succession were admitted, the right had devolved on the house of Mortimer: Allowing, that Richard II. was a tyrant, and that Henry IVth's merits, in deposing him, were so great towards the English, as to justify that nation in placing him on the throne; Richard had nowise offended France, and his rival had merited nothing of that kingdom: It could not possibly be pretended, that the crown of France was become an appendage to that of England; and that a prince, who, by any means, got possession of the latter was, without farther question, entitled to the former. So that on the whole it must be allowed, that Henry's claim to France was, if possible, still more unintelligible, than the title, by which his father had mounted the throne of England.

But though all these considerations were overlooked, amidst the hurry of passion, by which the courts of France and Burgundy were actuated, they would necessarily revive during times of more

[g] Rymer, vol. ix. p. 895. St. Remi, chap. 101. Monstrelet, chap. 223.

Marriage of the king.

tranquillity; and it behoved Henry to push his present advantages, and allow men no leisure for reason or reflection. In a few days after, he espoused the princess Catharine: He carried his father-in-law to Paris, and put himself in possession of that capital: He obtained from the parliament and the three estates a ratification of the treaty of Troye: He supported the duke of Burgundy in procuring a sentence against the murderers of his father: And he immediately turned his arms with success against the adherents of the dauphin, who, as soon as he heard of the treaty of Troye, took on him the style and authority of regent, and appealed to God and his sword for the maintenance of his title.

The first place that Henry subdued, was Sens, which opened its gates after a slight resistance. With the same facility, he made himself master of Montereau. The defence of Melun was more obstinate: Barbasan, the governor, held out for the space of four months against the besiegers; and it was famine alone which obliged him to capitulate. Henry stipulated to spare the lives of all the garrison, except such as were accomplices in the murder of the duke of Burgundy; and as Barbasan himself was suspected to be of the number, his punishment was demanded by Philip: But the king had the generosity to intercede for him, and to prevent his execution.[h]

1421.

The necessity of providing supplies both of men and money obliged Henry to go over to England; and he left the duke of Exeter, his uncle, governor of Paris during his absence. The authority, which naturally attends success, procured from the English parliament a subsidy of a fifteenth; but, if we may judge by the scantiness of the supply, the nation was nowise sanguine on their king's victories; and in proportion as the prospect of their union with France became nearer, they began to open their eyes, and to see the dangerous consequences, with which that event must necessarily be attended. It was fortunate for Henry, that he had other resources, besides pecuniary supplies from his native subjects. The provinces, which he had already conquered, maintained his troops; and the hopes of farther advantages allured to his standard all men of ambitious spirits in England, who desired to signalize themselves by arms. He levied a new army of 24,000

[h] Holingshed, p. 577.

CHAPTER XIX

archers, and 4000 horsemen,[i] and marched them to Dover, the place of rendezvous. Every thing had remained in tranquillity at Paris, under the duke of Exeter; but there had happened in another quarter of the kingdom a misfortune, which hastened the king's embarkation.

The detention of the young king of Scots in England had hitherto proved advantageous to Henry; and by keeping the regent in awe, had preserved, during the whole course of the French war, the northern frontier in tranquillity. But when intelligence arrived in Scotland, of the progress made by Henry, and the near prospect of his succession to the crown of France, the nation was alarmed, and foresaw their own inevitable ruin, if the subjection of their ally left them to combat alone a victorious enemy, who was already so much superior in power and riches. The regent entered into the same views; and though he declined an open rupture with England, he permitted a body of seven thousand Scots, under the command of the earl of Buchan, his second son, to be transported into France for the service of the dauphin. To render this aid ineffectual, Henry had, in his former expedition, carried over the king of Scots, whom he obliged to send orders to his countrymen to leave the French service; but the Scottish general replied, that he would obey no commands which came from a king in captivity, and that a prince, while in the hands of his enemy, was nowise entitled to authority. These troops, therefore, continued still to act under the earl of Buchan; and were employed by the dauphin to oppose the progress of the duke of Clarence in Anjou. The two armies encountered at Baugé: The English were defeated: The duke himself was slain by Sir Allan Swinton, a Scotch knight, who commanded a company of men at arms: And the earls of Somerset,[k] Dorset, and Huntingdon, were taken prisoners.[l] This was the first action that turned the tide of success against the English; and the dauphin, that he might both attach the Scotch to his service, and reward the valour and conduct of the earl of Buchan, honoured that nobleman with the office of constable.

---

[i] Monstrelet, chap. 242. [k] His name was John, and he was afterwards created duke of Somerset. He was grandson of John of Gaunt duke of Lancaster. The earl of Dorset was brother to Somerset, and succeeded him in that title. [l] St. Remi, chap. 110. Monstrelet, chap. 239. Hall, fol. 76.

But the arrival of the king of England, with so considerable an army, was more than sufficient to repair this loss. Henry was received at Paris with great expressions of joy; so obstinate were the prejudices of the people: And he immediately conducted his army to Chartres, which had long been besieged by the dauphin. That prince raised the siege on the approach of the English; and being resolved to decline a battle, he retired with his army.[m] Henry made himself master of Dreux without a blow: He laid siege to Meaux at the solicitation of the Parisians, who were much incommoded by the garrison of that place. This enterprize employed the English arms during the space of eight months: The bastard of Vaurus, governor of Meaux, distinguished himself by an obstinate defence; but was at last obliged to surrender at discretion. The cruelty of this officer was equal to his bravery: He was accustomed to hang without distinction all the English and Burgundians who fell into his hands: And Henry, in revenge of his barbarity, ordered him immediately to be hanged on the same tree, which he had made the instrument of his inhuman executions.[n]

This success was followed by the surrender of many other places in the neighbourhood of Paris, which held for the dauphin: That prince was chased beyond the Loire, and he almost totally abandoned all the northern provinces: He was even pursued into the south by the united arms of the English and Burgundians, and threatened with total destruction. Notwithstanding the bravery and fidelity of his captains, he saw himself unequal to his enemies in the field; and found it necessary to temporize, and to avoid all hazardous actions with a rival, who had gained so much the ascendant over him. And to crown all the other prosperities of Henry, his queen was delivered of a son, who was called by his father's name, and whose birth was celebrated by rejoicings no less pompous, and no less sincere at Paris than at London. The infant prince seemed to be universally regarded as the future heir of both monarchies.

But the glory of Henry, when it had nearly reached the summit, *1422.* was stopped short by the hand of nature; and all his mighty *Death,* projects vanished into smoke. He was seized with a fistula, a malady, which the surgeons at that time had not skill enough to cure;

[m] St. Remi, chap. 3. [n] Rymer, vol. x. p. 212. T. Livii, p. 92, 93. St. Remi, chap. 116. Monstrelet, chap. 260.

CHAPTER XIX

and he was at last sensible, that his distemper was mortal, and that his end was approaching. He sent for his brother the duke of Bedford, the earl of Warwic, and a few noblemen more, whom he had honoured with his friendship; and he delivered to them, in great tranquillity, his last will with regard to the government of his kingdom and family. He entreated them to continue, towards his infant son, the same fidelity and attachment, which they had always professed to himself during his lifetime, and which had been cemented by so many mutual good offices. He expressed his indifference on the approach of death; and though he regretted, that he must leave unfinished a work so happily begun, he declared himself confident, that the final acquisition of France would be the effect of their prudence and valour. He left the regency of that kingdom to his elder brother, the duke of Bedford; that of England to his younger, the duke of Glocester; and the care of his son's person to the earl of Warwic. He recommended to all of them a great attention to maintain the friendship of the duke of Burgundy; and advised them never to give liberty to the French princes taken at Azincour, till his son were of age, and could himself hold the reins of government. And he conjured them, if the success of their arms should not enable them to place young Henry on the throne of France, never at least to make peace with that kingdom, unless the enemy, by the cession of Normandy, and its annexation to the crown of England, made compensation for all the hazard and expence of his enterprize.[o]

He next applied himself to his devotions, and ordered his chaplain to recite the seven penitential psalms. When that passage of the fifty-first psalm was read *build thou the walls of Jerusalem;* he interrupted the chaplain, and declared his serious intention, after he should have fully subdued France, to conduct a crusade against the infidels, and recover possession of the Holy Land.[p] So ingenious are men in deceiving themselves, that Henry forgot, in those moments, all the blood spilt by his ambition; and received comfort from this late and feeble resolve, which, as the mode of these enterprizes was now past, he certainly would never have carried into execution. He expired in the thirty-fourth year of his age and the tenth of his reign.

31st Aug.

---

[o] Monstrelet, chap. 265. Hall, fol. 80.   [p] St. Remi, chap. 118. Monstrelet, chap. 265.

and char-
acter of
the king.

This prince possessed many eminent virtues; and if we give indulgence to ambition in a monarch, or rank it, as the vulgar are inclined to do, among his virtues, they were unstained by any considerable blemish. His abilities appeared equally in the cabinet and in the field: The boldness of his enterprizes was no less remarkable than his personal valour in conducting them. He had the talent of attaching his friends by affability, and of gaining his enemies by address and clemency. The English, dazzled by the lustre of his character, still more than by that of his victories, were reconciled to the defects in his title: The French almost forgot that he was an enemy: And his care in maintaining justice in his civil administration, and preserving discipline in his armies, made some amends to both nations for the calamities inseparable from those wars, in which his short reign was almost entirely occupied. That he could forgive the earl of Marche, who had a better title to the crown than himself, is a sure indication of his magnanimity; and that the earl relied so entirely on his friendship is no less a proof of his established character for candour and sincerity. There remain in history few instances of such mutual trust; and still fewer where neither party found reason to repent it.

The exterior figure of this great prince, as well as his deportment, was engaging. His stature was somewhat above the middle size; his countenance beautiful; his limbs genteel and slender, but full of vigour; and he excelled in all warlike and manly exercises.[q] He left by his queen, Catharine of France, only one son, not full nine months old; whose misfortunes, in the course of his life, surpassed all the glories and successes of his father.

In less than two months after Henry's death, Charles VI. of France, his father-in-law, terminated his unhappy life. He had, for several years, possessed only the appearance of royal authority: Yet was this mere appearance of considerable advantage to the English; and divided the duty and affections of the French between them and the dauphin. This prince was proclaimed and crowned king of France at Poictiers, by the name of Charles VII. Rheims, the place where this ceremony is usually performed, was at that time in the hands of his enemies.

Catharine of France, Henry's widow, married, soon after his death, a Welsh gentleman, Sir Owen Tudor, said to be descended

[q] T. Livii, p. 4.

CHAPTER XIX

from the ancient princes of that country: She bore him two sons,
Edmund and Jasper, of whom the eldest was created earl of Richmond; the second earl of Pembroke. The family of Tudor, first
raised to distinction by this alliance, mounted afterwards the
throne of England.

The long schism, which had divided the Latin church for near
forty years, was finally terminated in this reign by the council of
Constance; which deposed the pope, John XXIII. for his crimes,
and elected Martin V. in his place, who was acknowledged by
almost all the kingdoms of Europe. This great and unusual act of
authority in the council gave the Roman pontiffs ever after a
mortal antipathy to those assemblies. The same jealousy, which
had long prevailed in most European countries, between the civil
aristocracy and monarchy, now also took place between these powers in the ecclesiastical body. But the great separation of the bishops in the several states, and the difficulty of assembling them,
gave the pope a mighty advantage, and made it more easy for him
to center all the powers of the hierarchy in his own person. The
cruelty and treachery, which attended the punishment of John
Huss and Jerome of Prague, the unhappy disciples of Wickliffe,
who, in violation of a safe-conduct, were burned alive for their
errors by the council of Constance, prove this melancholy truth,
that toleration is none of the virtues of priests in any form of
ecclesiastical government. But as the English nation had little or no
concern in these great transactions, we are here the more concise
in relating them.

Miscella-neous trans-actions.

The first commission of array, which we meet with, was issued
in this reign.[r] The military part of the feudal system, which was the
most essential circumstance of it, was entirely dissolved; and could
no longer serve for the defence of the kingdom. Henry, therefore,
when he went to France in 1415, impowered certain commissioners to take in each county a review of all the freemen able to
bear arms, to divide them into companies, and to keep them in
readiness for resisting an enemy. This was the era, when the feudal
militia in England gave place to one which was perhaps still less
orderly and regular.

We have an authentic and exact account of the ordinary revenue of the crown during this reign; and it amounts only to 55,714

[r] Rymer, vol. ix. p. 254, 255.

pounds 10 shillings and 10 pence a-year.[s] This is nearly the same with the revenue of Henry III. and the kings of England had neither become much richer nor poorer in the course of so many years. The ordinary expence of the government amounted to 42,507 pounds 16 shillings and 10 pence. So that the king had a surplus only of 13,206 pounds 14 shillings for the support of his household; for his wardrobe; for the expence of embassies, and other articles. This sum was nowise sufficient: He was therefore obliged to have frequent recourse to parliamentary supplies, and was thus, even in time of peace, not altogether independent of his people. But wars were attended with a great expence, which neither the prince's ordinary revenue, nor the extraordinary supplies were able to bear; and the sovereign was always reduced to many miserable shifts, in order to make any tolerable figure in them. He commonly borrowed money from all quarters; he pawned his jewels and sometimes the crown itself;[t] he ran in arrears to his army; and he was often obliged, notwithstanding all these expedients to stop in the midst of his career of victory, and to grant truces to the enemy. The high pay which was given to soldiers agreed very ill with his low income. All the extraordinary supplies, granted by parliament to Henry during the course of his reign, were only seven tenths and fifteenths, about 203,000 pounds.[u] It is easy to compute how soon this money must be exhausted by armies of 24,000 archers, and 6000 horse; when each archer had sixpence a-day,[w] and each horseman two shillings. The most splendid successes proved commonly fruitless, when supported by so poor a revenue; and the debts and difficulties, which the king thereby incurred, made him pay dear for his victories. The civil administration, likewise, even in time of peace, could never be very regular, where the government was so ill enabled to support itself. Henry till within a year of his death owed debts, which he had contracted when prince of Wales.[x] It was in vain that the parliament pretended to restrain him from arbitrary practices, when he was reduced to such necessities. Though the right of levying pur-

[s] Rymer, vol. x. p. 113. [t] Ibid. p. 190. [u] Parliamentary History, vol. ii. p. 168. [w] It appears from many passages of Rymer, particularly vol. ix. p. 258, that the king paid 20 marks a-year for an archer, which is a good deal above sixpence a-day. The price had risen, as is natural, by raising the denomination of money. [x] Rymer, vol. x. p. 114.

CHAPTER XIX

veyance, for instance, had been expressly guarded against by the Great Charter itself, and was frequently complained of by the commons, it was found absolutely impracticable to abolish it; and the parliament at length, submitting to it as a legal prerogative, contented themselves with enacting laws to limit and confine it. The duke of Glocester, in the reign of Richard II. possessed a revenue of 60,000 crowns, (about 30,000 pounds a-year of our present money,) as we learn from Froissard,[y] and was consequently richer than the king himself, if all circumstances be duly considered.

It is remarkable, that the city of Calais alone was an annual expence to the crown of 19,119 pounds;[z] that is, above a third of the common charge of the government in time of peace. This fortress was of no use to the defence of England, and only gave that kingdom an inlet to annoy France. Ireland cost two thousand pounds a year, over and above its own revenue; which was certainly very low. Every thing conspires to give us a very mean idea of the state of Europe in those ages.

From the most early times, till the reign of Edward III. the denomination of money had never been altered: A pound sterling was still a pound troy; that is, about three pounds of our present money. That conqueror was the first that innovated in this important article. In the twentieth of his reign, he coined twenty-two shillings from a pound troy; in his twenty-seventh year he coined twenty-five shillings. But Henry V. who was also a conqueror, raised still farther the denomination, and coined thirty shillings from a pound troy.[a] His revenue therefore must have been about 110,000 pounds of our present money; and by the cheapness of provisions, was equivalent to above 330,000 pounds.

None of the princes of the house of Lancaster ventured to impose taxes without consent of parliament: Their doubtful or bad title became so far of advantage to the constitution. The rule was then fixed, and could not safely be broken afterwards, even by more absolute princes.

[y] Liv. iv. chap. 86.   [z] Rymer, vol. x. p. 113.   [a] Fleetwood's Chronicon Preciosum, p. 52.

XX

HENRY VI

Government during the minority – State of France – Military operations – Battle of Verneüil – Siege of Orleans – The maid of Orleans – The siege of Orleans raised – The king of France crowned at Rheims – Prudence of the duke of Bedford – Execution of the maid of Orleans – Defection of the duke of Burgundy – Death of the duke of Bedford – Decline of the English in France – Truce with France – Marriage of the king with Margaret of Anjou – Murder of the duke of Glocester – State of France – Renewal of the war with France – The English expelled France

1422. Government during the minority.

DURING THE REIGNS of the Lancastrian princes, the authority of parliament seems to have been more confirmed, and the privileges of the people more regarded, than during any former period; and the two preceding kings, though men of great spirit and abilities, abstained from such exertions of prerogative, as even weak princes, whose title was undisputed, were tempted to think they might venture upon with impunity. The long minority, of which there was now the prospect, encouraged still farther the lords and commons to extend their influence; and without paying much regard to the verbal destination of Henry V. they assumed the power of giving a new arrangement to the whole administration. They declined altogether the name of *Regent* with regard to England: They appointed the duke of Bedford *protector* or *guardian* of that kingdom, a title which they supposed to imply less authority: They invested the duke of Glocester with the same dignity during the absence of his elder brother;[b] and in order to limit the power of both these princes, they appointed a council, without whose advice and approbation no measure of importance could be determined.[c] The person and education of the infant prince was committed to Henry Beaufort, bishop of Winchester, his great uncle and the legitimated son of John of Gaunt, duke of Lancaster; a prelate, who, as his family could never have any pretensions to the crown, might safely, they thought, be intrusted with that important charge.[d] The two princes, the dukes of Bedford and Glocester, who seemed injured by this plan of government, yet, being persons of great integrity and honour, acquiesced in any appointment, which tended to give security to the public; and as the wars in France appeared to be the object of greatest moment, they avoided every dispute which might throw an obstacle in the way of foreign conquests.

When the state of affairs between the English and French kings was considered with a superficial eye, every advantage seemed to be on the side of the former; and the total expulsion of Charles appeared to be an event, which might naturally be expected from the superior power of his competitor. Though Henry was yet in his infancy, the administration was devolved on the duke of Bedford, the most accomplished prince of his age; whose experience, prudence, valour, and generosity qualified him for his high office, and enabled him both to maintain union among his friends, and to gain the confidence of his enemies. The whole power of England was at his command: He was at the head of armies enured to victory: He was seconded by the most renowned generals of the age, the earls of Somerset, Warwic, Salisbury, Suffolk, and Arundel, Sir John Talbot, and Sir John Fastolfe: And besides Guienne, the ancient inheritance of England, he was master of the

State of France.

---

[b] Rymer, vol. x. p. 261. Cotton, p. 564.   [c] Cotton, p. 564.   [d] Hall, fol. 83. Monstrelet, vol. ii. p. 27.

capital, and of almost all the northern provinces, which were well enabled to furnish him with supplies both of men and money, and to assist and support his English forces.

But Charles, notwithstanding the present inferiority of his power, possessed some advantages derived partly from his situation, partly from his personal character, which promised him success, and served, first to controul, then to overbalance, the superior force and opulence of his enemies. He was the true and undoubted heir of the monarchy: All Frenchmen, who knew the interests, or desired the independance of their country, turned their eyes towards him as its sole resource: The exclusion given him, by the imbecillity of his father, and the forced or precipitate consent of the states, had plainly no validity: That spirit of faction, which had blinded the people, could not long hold them in so gross a delusion: Their national and inveterate hatred against the English, the authors of all their calamities, must soon revive, and inspire them with indignation at bending their necks under the yoke of that hostile people: Great nobles and princes, accustomed to maintain an independance against their native sovereigns, would never endure a subjection to strangers: And though most of the princes of the blood were, since the fatal battle of Azincour, detained prisoners in England, the inhabitants of their demesnes, their friends, their vassals, all declared a zealous attachment to the king, and exerted themselves in resisting the violence of foreign invaders.

Charles himself, though only in his twentieth year, was of a character well calculated to become the object of these benevolent sentiments; and perhaps from the favour which naturally attends youth, was the more likely, on account of his tender age, to acquire the good-will of his native subjects. He was a prince of the most friendly and benign disposition, of easy and familiar manners, and of a just and sound, though not a very vigorous understanding. Sincere, generous, affable, he engaged from affection the services of his followers, even while his low fortunes might make it their interest to desert him; and the lenity of his temper could pardon in them those sallies of discontent, to which princes in his situation are so frequently exposed. The love of pleasure often seduced him into indolence; but amidst all his irregularities the goodness of his heart still shone forth; and by exerting at intervals his courage and

CHAPTER XX

activity, he proved, that his general remissness proceeded not from the want, either of a just spirit of ambition, or of personal valour.

Though the virtues of this amiable prince lay some time in obscurity, the duke of Bedford knew, that his title alone made him formidable, and that every foreign assistance would be requisite, ere an English regent could hope to complete the conquest of France; an enterprize, which, however it might seem to be much advanced, was still exposed to many and great difficulties. The chief circumstance, which had procured to the English all their present advantages, was the resentment of the duke of Burgundy against Charles; and as that prince seemed intent rather on gratifying his passion than consulting his interests, it was the more easy for the regent, by demonstrations of respect and confidence, to retain him in the alliance of England. He bent therefore all his endeavours to that purpose: He gave the duke every proof of friendship and regard: He even offered him the regency of France, which Philip declined: And that he might corroborate national connexions by private ties, he concluded his own marriage with the princess of Burgundy, which had been stipulated by the treaty of Arras.

Being sensible, that next to the alliance of Burgundy, the friendship of the duke of Britanny was of the greatest importance towards forwarding the English conquests; and that, as the provinces of France, already subdued, lay between the dominions of these two princes, he could never hope for any security without preserving his connexions with them; he was very intent on strengthening himself also from that quarter. The duke of Britanny, having received many just reasons of displeasure from the ministers of Charles, had already acceded to the treaty of Troye, and had, with other vassals of the crown, done homage to Henry V. in quality of heir to the kingdom: But as the regent knew, that the duke was much governed by his brother, the count of Richemont, he endeavoured to fix his friendship, by paying court and doing services to this haughty and ambitious prince. *1423.*

Arthur, count of Richemont, had been taken prisoner at the battle of Azincour, had been treated with great indulgence by the late king, and had even been permitted on his parole to take a journey into Britanny, where the state of affairs required his presence. The death of that victorious monarch happened before Richemont's return; and this prince pretended, that, as his word was given personally to Henry V. he was not bound to fulfil it towards his son and successor: A chicane which the regent, as he could not force him to compliance, deemed it prudent to overlook. An interview was settled at Amiens between the dukes of Bedford, Burgundy, and Britanny, at which the count of Richemont was also present:[e] The alliance was renewed between these princes: And the regent persuaded Philip to give in marriage to Richemont his eldest sister, widow of the deceased Dauphin, Lewis, the elder brother of Charles. Thus Arthur was connected both with the regent and the duke of Burgundy, and seemed engaged by interest to prosecute the same object, in forwarding the success of the English arms.

While the vigilance of the duke of Bedford was employed in gaining or confirming these allies, whose vicinity rendered them so important, he did not overlook the state of more remote countries. The duke of Albany, regent of Scotland, had died; and his power had devolved on Murdac, his son, a prince of a weak understanding and indolent disposition; who, far from possessing the talents requisite for the government of that fierce people, was not even able to maintain authority in his own family, or restrain the petulance and insolence of his sons. The ardour of the Scots to serve in France, where Charles treated them with great honour and distinction, and where the regent's brother enjoyed the dignity of constable, broke out afresh under this feeble administration: New succours daily came over, and filled the armies of the French king: The earl of Douglas conducted a reinforcement of 5000 men to his assistance. And it was justly to be dreaded, that the Scots, by commencing open hostilities in the north, would occasion a diversion still more considerable of the English power, and would ease Charles, in part, of that load, by which he was at present so grievously oppressed. The duke of Bedford, therefore, persuaded the English council to form an alliance with James their prisoner; to free that prince from his long captivity; and to connect him with England, by marrying him to a daughter of the earl of Somerset and cousin of the young king.[f] As the Scottish regent,

---

[e] Hall, fol. 84. Monstrelet, vol. i. p. 4. Stowe, p. 364.   [f] Hall, fol. 86. Stowe, p. 364. Grafton, p. 501.

CHAPTER XX

tired of his present dignity, which he was not able to support, was now become entirely sincere in his applications for James's liberty, the treaty was soon concluded; a ransom of forty thousand pounds was stipulated;[g] and the king of Scots was restored to the throne of his ancestors, and proved, in his short reign, one of the most illustrious princes, that had ever governed that kingdom. He was murdered in 1437 by his traiterous kinsman the earl of Athole. His affections inclined to the side of France; but the English had never reason, during his life-time, to complain of any breach of the neutrality by Scotland.

But the regent was not so much employed in these political negociations as to neglect the operations of war, from which alone he could hope to succeed in expelling the French monarch. Though the chief seat of Charles's power lay in the southern provinces, beyond the Loire; his partizans were possessed of some fortresses in the northern, and even in the neighbourhood of Paris; and it behoved the duke of Bedford first to clear these countries from the enemy, before he could think of attempting more distant conquests. The castle of Dorsoy was taken after a siege of six weeks: That of Noyelle and the town of Rüe in Picardy underwent the same fate: Pont sur Seine, Vertus, Montaigu, were subjected by the English arms: And a more considerable advantage was soon after gained by the united forces of England and Burgundy. John Stuart, constable of Scotland, and the lord of Estissac had formed the siege of Crevant in Burgundy: The earls of Salisbury and Suffolk, with the count of Toulongeon, were sent to its relief: A fierce and well disputed action ensued: The Scots and French were defeated: The constable of Scotland and the count of Ventadour were taken prisoners: And above a thousand men, among whom was Sir William Hamilton, were left on the field of battle.[h] The taking of Gaillon upon the Seine, and of la Charité upon the Loire, was the fruit of this victory: And as this latter place opened an entrance into the southern provinces, the acquisition of it appeared on that account of the greater importance to the duke of Bedford, and seemed to promise a successful issue to the war.

Military operations.

The more Charles was threatened with an invasion in those provinces which adhered to him, the more necessary it became,

1424.

---

[g] Rymer, vol. x. p. 299, 300, 326.   [h] Hall, fol. 85. Monstrelet, vol. ii. p. 8. Holingshed, p. 586. Grafton, p. 500.

that he should retain possession of every fortress, which he still held within the quarters of the enemy. The duke of Bedford had besieged in person, during the space of three months, the town of Yvri in Normandy; and the brave governor, unable to make any longer defence, was obliged to capitulate; and he agreed to surrender the town, if, before a certain term, no relief arrived. Charles, informed of these conditions, determined to make an attempt for saving the place. He collected, with some difficulty, an army of 14,000 men, of whom one half were Scots; and he sent them thither under the command of the earl of Buchan, constable of France; who was attended by the earl of Douglas, his countryman, the duke of Alençon, the mareschal de la Fayette, the count of Aumale, and the viscount of Narbonne. When the constable arrived within a few leagues of Yvri, he found that he was come too late, and that the place was already surrendered. He immediately turned to the left, and sat down before Verneüil, which the inhabitants, in spite of the garrison, delivered up to him.[i] Buchan might now have returned in safety, and with the glory of making an acquisition no less important than the place which he was sent to relieve: But hearing of Bedford's approach, he called a council of war, in order to deliberate concerning the conduct which he should hold in this emergence. The wiser part of the council declared for a retreat; and represented, that all the past misfortunes of the French had proceeded from their rashness in giving battle when no necessity obliged them; that this army was the last resource of the king, and the only defence of the few provinces which remained to him; and that every reason invited him to embrace cautious measures, which might leave time for his subjects to return to a sense of their duty, and give leisure for discord to arise among his enemies, who, being united by no common band of interest or motive of alliance, could not long persevere in their animosity against him. All these prudential considerations were overborne by a vain point of honour, not to turn their backs to the enemy; and they resolved to await the arrival of the duke of Bedford.

27th Aug. Battle of Verneüil.

The numbers were nearly equal in this action; and as the long continuance of war had introduced discipline, which, however imperfect, sufficed to maintain some appearance of order in such

[i] Monstrelet, vol. ii. p. 14. Grafton, p. 504.

small armies, the battle was fierce, and well disputed, and attended with bloodshed on both sides. The constable drew up his forces under the walls of Verneüil, and resolved to abide the attack of the enemy: But the impatience of the viscount of Narbonne, who advanced precipitately, and obliged the whole line to follow him in some hurry and confusion, was the cause of the misfortune which ensued. The English archers, fixing their palisadoes before them, according to their usual custom, sent a volley of arrows amidst the thickest of the French army; and though beaten from their ground, and obliged to take shelter among the baggage, they soon rallied, and continued to do great execution upon the enemy. The duke of Bedford, meanwhile, at the head of the men at arms, made impression on the French, broke their ranks, chaced them off the field, and rendered the victory entirely complete and decisive.[k] The constable himself perished in battle, as well as the earl of Douglas and his son, the counts of Aumale, Tonnerre, and Ventadour, with many other considerable nobility. The duke of Alençon, the mareschal de la Fayette, the lords of Gaucour and Mortemar were taken prisoners. There fell about four thousand of the French, and sixteen hundred of the English; a loss esteemed, at that time, so unusual on the side of the victors, that the duke of Bedford forbad all rejoicings for his success. Verneüil was surrendered next day by capitulation.[l]

The condition of the king of France now appeared very terrible, and almost desperate. He had lost the flower of his army and the bravest of his nobles in this fatal action: He had no resource either for recruiting or subsisting his troops: He wanted money even for his personal subsistence; and though all parade of a court was banished, it was with difficulty he could keep a table, supplied with the plainest necessaries, for himself and his few followers: Every day brought him intelligence of some loss or misfortune: Towns, which were bravely defended, were obliged at last to surrender for want of relief or supply: He saw his partizans entirely chaced from all the provinces which lay north of the Loire: And he expected soon to lose, by the united efforts of his enemies, all the territories of which he had hitherto continued master; when an incident happened, which saved him on the brink of ruin, and lost

[k] Hall, fol. 88, 89, 90. Monstrelet, vol. ii. p. 15. Stowe, p. 365. Hollingshed, p. 588. [l] Monstrelet, vol. ii. p. 15.

the English such an opportunity for completing their conquests, as they never afterwards were able to recal.

Jaqueline, countess of Hainault and Holland, and heir of these provinces, had espoused John duke of Brabant, cousin german to the duke of Burgundy; but having made this choice from the usual motives of princes, she soon found reason to repent of the unequal alliance. She was a princess of a masculine spirit and uncommon understanding; the duke of Brabant was of a sickly complexion and weak mind: She was in the vigour of her age; he had only reached his fifteenth year: These causes had inspired her with such contempt for her husband, which soon proceeded to antipathy, that she determined to dissolve a marriage, where, it is probable, nothing but the ceremony had as yet intervened. The court of Rome was commonly very open to applications of this nature, when seconded by power and money; but as the princess foresaw great opposition from her husband's relations, and was impatient to effect her purpose, she made her escape into England, and threw herself under the protection of the duke of Glocester. That prince, with many noble qualities, had the defect of being governed by an impetuous temper and vehement passions; and he was rashly induced, as well by the charms of the countess herself, as by the prospect of possessing her rich inheritance, to offer himself to her as a husband. Without waiting for a papal dispensation; without endeavouring to reconcile the duke of Burgundy to the measures; he entered into a contract of marriage with Jaqueline, and immediately attempted to put himself in possession of her dominions. Philip was disgusted with so precipitate a conduct: He resented the injury done to the duke of Brabant, his near relation: He dreaded to have the English established on all sides of him: And he foresaw the consequences, which must attend the extensive and uncontrouled dominion of that nation, if, before the full settlement of their power, they insulted and injured an ally, to whom they had already been so much indebted, and who was still so necessary for supporting them in their farther progress. He encouraged, therefore, the duke of Brabant to make resistance: He engaged many of Jaqueline's subjects to adhere to that prince: He himself marched troops to his support: And as the duke of Glocester still persevered in his purpose, a sharp war was suddenly kindled in the Low Countries. The quarrel soon became personal

CHAPTER XX

as well as political. The English prince wrote to the duke of Burgundy, complaining of the opposition made to his pretensions; and though in the main he employed amicable terms in his letter, he took notice of some falsehoods, into which, he said, Philip had been betrayed during the course of these transactions. This unguarded expression was highly resented: The duke of Burgundy insisted, that he should retract it: And mutual challenges and defiances passed between them on this occasion.[m]

The duke of Bedford could easily foresee the bad effects of so ill-timed and imprudent a quarrel. All the succours, which he expected from England, and which were so necessary in this critical emergence, were intercepted by his brother, and employed in Holland and Hainault: The forces of the duke of Burgundy, which he also depended on, were diverted by the same wars: And besides this double loss, he was in imminent danger of alienating for ever that confederate, whose friendship was of the utmost importance, and whom the late king had enjoined him, with his dying breath, to gratify by every mark of regard and attachment. He represented all these topics to the duke of Glocester: He endeavoured to mitigate the resentment of the duke of Burgundy: He interposed with his good offices between these princes: But was not successful in any of his endeavours; and he found, that the impetuosity of his brother's temper was still the chief obstacle to all accommodation.[n] For this reason, instead of pushing the victory gained at Verneüil, he found himself obliged to take a journey into England, and to try, by his counsels and authority, to moderate the measures of the duke of Glocester.

There had likewise broken out some differences among the English ministry, which had proceeded to great extremities, and which required the regent's presence to compose them.[o] The bishop of Winchester, to whom the care of the king's person and education had been entrusted, was a prelate of great capacity and experience, but of an intriguing and dangerous character; and as he aspired to the government of affairs, he had continual disputes with his nephew, the protector; and he gained frequent advantages over the vehement and impolitic temper of that prince. The

[m] Monstrelet, vol. ii. p. 19, 20, 21.   [n] Monstrelet, p. 18.   [o] Stowe, p. 368. Hollingshed, p. 590.

duke of Bedford employed the authority of parliament to reconcile them; and these rivals were obliged to promise before that assembly, that they would bury all quarrels in oblivion.[p] Time also seemed to open expedients for composing the difference with the duke of Burgundy. The credit of that prince had procured a bull from the pope; by which not only Jaqueline's contract with the duke of Glocester was annulled; but it was also declared, that, even in case of the duke of Brabant's death, it should never be lawful for her to espouse the English prince. Humphrey, despairing of success, married another lady of inferior rank, who had lived some time with him as his mistress.[q] The duke of Brabant died; and his widow, before she could recover possession of her dominions, was obliged to declare the duke of Burgundy her heir, in case she should die without issue, and to promise never to marry without his consent. But though the affair was thus terminated to the satisfaction of Philip, it left a disagreeable impression on his mind: It excited an extreme jealousy of the English, and opened his eyes to his true interests: And as nothing but his animosity against Charles had engaged him in alliance with them, it counterbalanced that passion by another of the same kind, which in the end became prevalent, and brought him back, by degrees, to his natural connexions with his family and his native country.

About the same time, the duke of Britanny began to withdraw himself from the English alliance. His brother, the count of Richmond, though connected by marriage with the dukes of Burgundy and Bedford, was extremely attached by inclination to the French interest; and he willingly hearkened to all the advances which Charles made him for obtaining his friendship. The staff of constable, vacant by the earl of Buchan's death, was offered him; and as his martial and ambitious temper aspired to the command of armies, which he had in vain attempted to obtain from the duke of Bedford, he not only accepted that office, but brought over his brother to an alliance with the French monarch. The new constable, having made this one change in his measures, firmly adhered ever after to his engagements with France. Though his pride

[p] Hall, fol. 98, 99. Hollingshed, p. 593, 594. Polydore Virgil, p. 466. Grafton, p. 512, 519.   [q] Stowe, p. 367.

and violence, which would admit of no rival in his master's confidence, and even prompted him to assassinate the other favourites, had so much disgusted Charles, that he once banished him the
court and refused to admit him to his presence, he still acted with
vigour for the service of that monarch, and obtained at last, by his
perseverance, the pardon of all past offences.

In this situation, the duke of Bedford, on his return, found the *1426.*
affairs of France, after passing eight months in England. The duke
of Burgundy was much disgusted. The duke of Britanny had entered into engagements with Charles, and had done homage to
that prince for his dutchy. The French had been allowed to recover
from the astonishment, into which their frequent disasters had
thrown them. An incident too had happened, which served extremely to raise their courage. The earl of Warwic had besieged
Montargis with a small army of 3000 men, and the place was
reduced to extremity, when the bastard of Orleans undertook to
throw relief into it. This general, who was natural son to the prince
assassinated by the duke of Burgundy, and who was afterwards
created count of Dunois, conducted a body of 1600 men to Montargis; and made an attack on the enemy's trenches with so much
valour, prudence, and good fortune, that he not only penetrated
into the place, but gave a severe blow to the English, and obliged
Warwic to raise the siege.[r] This was the first signal action that
raised the fame of Dunois, and opened him the road to those great
honours, which he afterwards attained.

But the regent, soon after his arrival, revived the reputation of
the English arms, by an important enterprize which he happily
atchieved. He secretly brought together, in separate detachments,
a considerable army to the frontiers of Britanny; and fell so unexpectedly upon that province, that the duke, unable to make
resistance, yielded to all the terms required of him: He renounced
the French alliance; he engaged to maintain the treaty of Troye;
he acknowledged the duke of Bedford for regent of France; and
promised to do homage for his dutchy to king Henry.[s] And the
English prince, having thus freed himself from a dangerous en-

---

[r] Monstrelet, vol. ii. p. 32, 33. Hollingshed, p. 597.   [s] Monstrelet, vol. ii.
p. 35, 36.

emy who lay behind him, resolved on an undertaking, which, if successful, would, he hoped, cast the balance between the two nations, and prepare the way for the final conquest of France.

1428.
Siege of
Orleans.
The city of Orleans was so situated between the provinces commanded by Henry, and those possessed by Charles, that it opened an easy entrance to either; and as the duke of Bedford intended to make a great effort for penetrating into the south of France, it behoved him to begin with this place, which, in the present circumstances, was become the most important in the kingdom. He committed the conduct of the enterprize to the earl of Salisbury, who had newly brought him a reinforcement of 6000 men from England, and who had much distinguished himself, by his abilities, during the course of the present war. Salisbury, passing the Loire, made himself master of several small places, which surrounded Orleans on that side;[1] and as his intentions were thereby known, the French king used every expedient to supply the city with a garrison and provisions, and enable it to maintain a long and obstinate siege. The lord of Gaucour, a brave and experienced captain, was appointed governor: Many officers of distinction threw themselves into the place: The troops, which they conducted, were enured to war, and were determined to make the most obstinate resistance: And even the inhabitants, disciplined by the long continuance of hostilities, were well qualified, in their own defence, to second the efforts of the most veteran forces. The eyes of all Europe were turned towards this scene; where, it was reasonably supposed, the French were to make their last stand for maintaining the independance of their monarchy, and the rights of their sovereign.

The earl of Salisbury at last approached the place with an army, which consisted only of 10,000 men; and not being able, with so small a force, to invest so great a city, that commanded a bridge over the Loire, he stationed himself on the southern side towards Sologne, leaving the other, towards the Beausse, still open to the enemy. He there attacked the fortifications, which guarded the entrance to the bridge; and after an obstinate resistance he carried several of them: But was himself killed by a cannon ball as he was

[1] Monstrelet, vol. ii. p. 38, 39. Polyd. Virg. p. 468.

taking a view of the enemy." The earl of Suffolk succeeded to the command; and being reinforced with great numbers of English and Burgundians, he passed the river with the main body of his army, and invested Orleans on the other side. As it was now the depth of winter, Suffolk, who found it difficult, in that season, to throw up intrenchments all around, contented himself, for the present, with erecting redoubts at different distances, where his men were lodged in safety, and were ready to intercept the supplies, which the enemy might attempt to throw into the place. Though he had several pieces of artillery in his camp, (and this is among the first sieges in Europe, where cannon were found to be of importance,) the art of engineering was hitherto so imperfect, that Suffolk trusted more to famine than to force for subduing the city; and he purposed in the spring to render the circumvallation more complete, by drawing intrenchments from one redoubt to another. Numberless feats of valour were performed both by the besiegers and besieged during the winter: Bold sallies were made, and repulsed with equal boldness: Convoys were sometimes introduced and often intercepted: The supplies were still unequal to the consumption of the place: And the English seemed daily, though slowly, to be advancing towards the completion of their enterprize.

But while Suffolk lay in this situation, the French parties ravaged all the country around; and the besiegers, who were obliged to draw their provisions from a distance, were themselves exposed to the danger of want and famine. Sir John Fastolfe was bringing up a large convoy, of every kind of stores, which he escorted with a detachment of 2500 men; when he was attacked by a body of 4000 French, under the command of the counts of Clermont and Dunois. Fastolfe drew up his troops behind the waggons; but the French generals, afraid of attacking him in that posture, planted a battery of cannon against him, which threw every thing into confusion, and would have insured them the victory; had not the impatience of some Scottish troops, who broke the line of battle, brought on an engagement, in which Fastolfe was victorious. The

1429.

" Hall, fol. 105. Monstrelet, vol. ii. p. 39. Stowe, p. 369. Hollingshed, p. 599. Grafton, p. 531.

count of Dunois was wounded; and about 500 French were left on the field of battle. This action, which was of great importance in the present conjuncture, was commonly called the battle of *Herrings;* because the convoy brought a great quantity of that kind of provisions, for the use of the English army during the Lent season.[w]

Charles seemed now to have but one expedient for saving this city, which had been so long invested. The duke of Orleans, who was still prisoner in England, prevailed on the protector and the council to consent, that all his demesnes should be allowed to preserve a neutrality during the war, and should be sequestered, for greater security, into the hands of the duke of Burgundy. This prince, who was much less cordial in the English interests than formerly, went to Paris, and made the proposal to the duke of Bedford; but the regent coldly replied, That he was not of a humour to beat the bushes, while others ran away with the game: An answer, which so disgusted the duke, that he recalled all the troops of Burgundy, that acted in the siege.[x] The place however was every day more and more closely invested by the English: Great scarcity began already to be felt by the garrison and inhabitants: Charles, in despair of collecting an army, which should dare to approach the enemy's entrenchments, not only gave the city for lost, but began to entertain a very dismal prospect with regard to the general state of his affairs. He saw that the country, in which he had hitherto, with great difficulty, subsisted, would be laid entirely open to the invasion of a powerful and victorious enemy; and he already entertained thoughts of retiring with the remains of his forces into Languedoc and Dauphiny, and defending himself as long as possible in those remote provinces. But it was fortunate for this good prince, that, as he lay under the dominion of the fair, the women, whom he consulted, had the spirit to support his sinking resolution in this desperate extremity. Mary of Anjou, his queen, a princess of great merit and prudence, vehemently opposed this measure, which, she foresaw, would discourage all his partizans, and serve as a general signal for deserting a prince, who seemed

---

[w] Hall, fol. 106. Monstrelet, vol. ii. p. 41, 42. Stowe, p. 369. Hollingshed, p. 600. Polyd. Virg. p. 469. Grafton, p. 532.   [x] Hall, fol. 106. Monstrelet, vol. ii. p. 42. Stowe, p. 369. Grafton, p. 533.

himself to despair of success. His mistress too, the fair Agnes Sorel, who lived in entire amity with the queen, seconded all her remonstrances, and threatened, that, if he thus pusillanimously threw away the scepter of France, she would seek in the court of England a fortune more correspondent to her wishes. Love was able to rouze in the breast of Charles that courage, which ambition had failed to excite: He resolved to dispute every inch of ground with an imperious enemy; and rather to perish with honour in the midst of his friends, than yield ingloriously to his bad fortune: When relief was unexpectedly brought him by another female of a very different character, who gave rise to one of the most singular revolutions, that is to be met with in history.

In the village of Domremi near Vaucouleurs, on the borders of Lorraine, there lived a country girl of twenty-seven years of age, called Joan d'Arc, who was servant in a small inn, and who in that station had been accustomed to tend the horses of the guests, to ride them without a saddle to the watering-place, and to perform other offices, which, in well-frequented inns, commonly fall to the share of the men servants.[y] This girl was of an irreproachable life, and had not hitherto been remarked for any singularity; whether that she had met with an occasion to excite her genius, or that the unskilful eyes of those who conversed with her, had not been able to discern her uncommon merit. It is easy to imagine, that the present situation of France was an interesting object even to persons of the lowest rank, and would become the frequent subject of conversation: A young prince, expelled his throne by the sedition of native subjects, and by the arms of strangers, could not fail to move the compassion of all his people, whose hearts were uncorrupted by faction; and the peculiar character of Charles, so strongly inclined to friendship and the tender passions, naturally rendered him the hero of that sex, whose generous minds know no bounds in their affections. The siege at Orleans, the progress of the English before that place, the great distress of the garrison and inhabitants, the importance of saving this city and its brave defenders, had turned thither the public eye; and Joan, inflamed by the general sentiment, was seized with a wild desire of bringing relief to her sovereign in his present distresses. Her unexperienced

The maid of Orleans.

[y] Hall, fol. 107. Monstrelet, vol. ii. p. 42. Grafton, p. 534.

mind, working day and night on this favourite object, mistook the impulses of passion for heavenly inspirations; and she fancied, that she saw visions, and heard voices, exhorting her to re-establish the throne of France, and to expel the foreign invaders. An uncommon intrepidity of temper made her overlook all the dangers, which might attend her in such a path; and thinking herself destined by Heaven to this office, she threw aside all that bashfulness and timidity, so natural to her sex, her years, and her low station. She went to Vaucouleurs; procured admission to Baudricourt, the governor; informed him of her inspirations and intentions; and conjured him not to neglect the voice of God, who spoke through her, but to second those heavenly revelations, which impelled her to this glorious enterprize. Baudricourt treated her at first with some neglect; but on her frequent returns to him, and importunate solicitations, he began to remark something extraordinary in the maid, and was inclined, at all hazards, to make so easy an experiment. It is uncertain, whether this gentleman had discernment enough to perceive, that great use might be made with the vulgar of so uncommon an engine; or, what is more likely in that credulous age, was himself a convert to this visionary: But he adopted at last the schemes of Joan; and he gave her some attendants, who conducted her to the French court, which at that time resided at Chinon.

It is the business of history to distinguish between the *miraculous* and the *marvellous;* to reject the first in all narrations merely profane and human; to doubt the second; and when obliged by unquestionable testimony, as in the present case, to admit of something extraordinary, to receive as little of it as is consistent with the known facts and circumstances. It is pretended, that Joan, immediately on her admission, knew the king, though she had never seen his face before, and though he purposely kept himself in the crowd of courtiers, and had laid aside every thing in his dress and apparel which might distinguish him: That she offered him, in the name of the supreme Creator, to raise the siege of Orleans, and conduct him to Rheims to be there crowned and anointed; and on his expressing doubts of her mission, revealed to him, before some sworn confidents, a secret, which was unknown to all the world beside himself, and which nothing but a heavenly inspiration could have discovered to her: And that she demanded, as the

CHAPTER XX

instrument of her future victories, a particular sword, which was kept in the church of St. Catharine of Fierbois, and which, though she had never seen it, she described by all its marks, and by the place in which it had long lain neglected.[z] This is certain, that all these miraculous stories were spread abroad, in order to captivate the vulgar. The more the king and his ministers were determined to give into the illusion, the more scruples they pretended. An assembly of grave doctors and theologians cautiously examined Joan's mission, and pronounced it undoubted and supernatural. She was sent to the parliament, then residing at Poictiers; and was interrogated before that assembly: The presidents, the counsellors, who came persuaded of her imposture, went away convinced of her inspiration. A ray of hope began to break through that despair, in which the minds of all men were before enveloped. Heaven had now declared itself in favour of France, and had laid bare its outstretched arm to take vengeance on her invaders. Few could distinguish between the impulse of inclination and the force of conviction; and none would submit to the trouble of so disagreeable a scrutiny.

After these artificial precautions and preparations had been for some time employed, Joan's requests were at last complied with: She was armed cap-a-pee, mounted on horseback, and shown in that martial habiliment before the whole people. Her dexterity in managing her steed, though acquired in her former occupation, was regarded as a fresh proof of her mission; and she was received with the loudest acclamations by the spectators. Her former occupation was even denied: She was no longer the servant of an inn. She was converted into a shepherdess, an employment much more agreeable to the imagination. To render her still more interesting, near ten years were substracted from her age; and all the sentiments of love and of chivalry, were thus united to those of enthusiasm, in order to inflame the fond fancy of the people with prepossessions in her favour.

When the engine was thus dressed up in full splendor, it was determined to essay its force against the enemy. Joan was sent to Blois, where a large convoy was prepared for the supply of Orleans, and an army of ten thousand men, under the command of

---

[z] Hall, fol. 107. Hollingshed, p. 600.

St. Severe, assembled to escort it. She ordered all the soldiers to confess themselves before they set out on the enterprize: She banished from the camp all women of bad fame: She displayed in her hands a consecrated banner; where the Supreme Being was represented, grasping the globe of earth, and surrounded with flower de luces. And she insisted, in right of her prophetic mission, that the convoy should enter Orleans, by the direct road from the side of Beausse: But the count of Dunois, unwilling to submit the rules of the military art to her inspirations, ordered it to approach by the other side of the river, where, he knew, the weakest part of the English army was stationed.

Previous to this attempt, the maid had written to the regent and to the English generals before Orleans, commanding them, in the name of the omnipotent Creator, by whom she was commissioned, immediately to raise the siege and to evacuate France; and menacing them with divine vengeance in case of their disobedience. All the English affected to speak with derision of the maid and of her heavenly commission; and said, that the French king was now indeed reduced to a sorry pass, when he had recourse to such ridiculous expedients: But they felt their imagination secretly struck with the vehement persuasion, which prevailed in all around them; and they waited with an anxious expectation, not unmixed with horror for the issue of these extraordinary preparations.

As the convoy approached the river, a sally was made by the garrison on the side of Beausse, to prevent the English general from sending any detachment to the other side: The provisions were peaceably embarked in boats, which the inhabitants of Orleans had sent to receive them: The maid covered with her troops the embarkation: Suffolk did not venture to attack her: And the French general carried back the army in safety to Blois; an alteration of affairs, which was already visible to all the world, and which had a proportional effect on the minds of both parties.

29th April.

The maid entered the city of Orleans, arrayed in her military garb, and displaying her consecrated standard; and was received, as a celestial deliverer, by all the inhabitants. They now believed themselves invincible under her influence; and Dunois himself, perceiving such a mighty alteration both in friends and foes, consented that the next convoy, which was expected in a few days,

CHAPTER XX

should enter by the side of Beausse. The convoy approached: No sign of resistance appeared in the besiegers: The waggons and troops passed without interruption between the redoubts of the English: A dead silence and astonishment reigned among those troops, formerly so elated with victory, and so fierce for the combat.

The earl of Suffolk was in a situation very unusual and extraordinary; and which might well confound the man of the greatest capacity and firmest temper. He saw his troops overawed, and strongly impressed with the idea of a divine influence, accompanying the maid. Instead of banishing these vain terrors by hurry and action and war, he waited till the soldiers should recover from the panic; and he thereby gave leisure for those prepossessions to sink still deeper into their minds. The military maxims, which are prudent in common cases, deceived him in these unaccountable events. The English felt their courage daunted and overwhelmed; and thence inferred a divine vengeance hanging over them. The French drew the same inference from an inactivity so new and unexpected. Every circumstance was now reversed in the opinions of men, on which all depends: The spirit, resulting from a long course of uninterrupted success, was on a sudden transferred from the victors to the vanquished.

The maid called aloud, that the garrison should remain no longer on the defensive; and she promised her followers the assistance of heaven in attacking those redoubts of the enemy, which had so long kept them in awe, and which they had never hitherto dared to insult. The generals seconded her ardour: An attack was made on one redoubt, and it proved successful:[a] All the English, who defended the entrenchments, were put to the sword or taken prisoners: And Sir John Talbot himself, who had drawn together, from the other redoubts, some troops to bring them relief, durst not appear in the open field against so formidable an enemy.

Nothing after this success seemed impossible to the maid and her enthusiastic votaries. She urged the generals to attack the main body of the English in their entrenchments: But Dunois, still unwilling to hazard the fate of France by too great temerity, and sensible that the least reverse of fortune would make all the

[a] Monstrelet, vol. ii. p. 45.

present visions evaporate, and restore every thing to its former condition, checked her vehemence, and proposed to her first to expel the enemy from their forts on the other side of the river, and thus lay the communication with the country entirely open, before she attempted any more hazardous enterprize. Joan was persuaded, and these forts were vigorously assailed. In one attack the French were repulsed; the maid was left almost alone; she was obliged to retreat, and join the runaways; but displaying her sacred standard, and animating them with her countenance, her gestures, her exhortations, she led them back to the charge, and overpowered the English in their entrenchments. In the attack of another fort, she was wounded in the neck with an arrow; she retreated a moment behind the assailants; she pulled out the arrow with her own hands; she had the wound quickly dressed; and she hastened back to head the troops, and to plant her victorious banner on the ramparts of the enemy.

By all these successes, the English were entirely chaced from their fortifications on that side: They had lost above six thousand men in these different actions; and what was still more important, their wonted courage and confidence was wholly gone, and had given place to amazement and despair. The maid returned triumphant over the bridge, and was again received as the guardian angel of the city. After performing such miracles, she convinced the most obdurate incredulity of her divine mission: Men felt themselves animated as by a superior energy, and thought nothing impossible to that divine hand, which so visibly conducted them. It was in vain even for the English generals to oppose with their soldiers the prevailing opinion of supernatural influence. They themselves were probably moved by the same belief: The utmost they dared to advance, was, that Joan was not an instrument of God; she was only the implement of the Devil: But as the English had felt, to their sad experience, that the Devil might be allowed sometimes to prevail, they derived not much consolation from the enforcing of this opinion.

The siege of Orleans raised. 8th May.

It might prove extremely dangerous for Suffolk, with such intimidated troops, to remain any longer in the presence of so courageous and victorious an enemy; he therefore raised the siege, and retreated with all the precaution imaginable. The French resolved to push their conquests, and to allow the English no leisure to recover from their consternation. Charles formed a body of six

CHAPTER XX

thousand men, and sent them to attack Jergeau, whither Suffolk had retired with a detachment of his army. The siege lasted ten days; and the place was obstinately defended. Joan displayed her wonted intrepidity on the occasion. She descended into the fosse, in leading the attack; and she there received a blow on the head with a stone, by which she was confounded and beaten to the ground: But she soon recovered herself; and in the end rendered the assault successful: Suffolk was obliged to yield himself prisoner to a Frenchman called Renaud; but before he submitted, he asked his adversary, whether he were a gentleman. On receiving a satisfactory answer, he demanded, whether he were a knight. Renaud replied, that he had not yet attained that honour. *Then I make you one,* replied Suffolk: Upon which, he gave him the blow with his sword, which dubbed him into that fraternity; and he immediately surrendered himself his prisoner.

The remainder of the English army was commanded by Fastolfe, Scales, and Talbot, who thought of nothing but of making their retreat, as soon as possible, into a place of safety; while the French esteemed the overtaking them equivalent to a victory. So much had the events, which passed before Orleans, altered every thing between the two nations! The vanguard of the French under Richemont and Xaintrailles attacked the rear of the enemy at the village of Patay. The battle lasted not a moment: The English were discomfited and fled: The brave Fastolfe himself showed the example of flight to his troops; and the order of the garter was taken from him, as a punishment for this instance of cowardice.[b] Two thousand men were killed in this action, and both Talbot and Scales taken prisoners.

18th June.

In the account of all these successes, the French writers, to magnify the wonder, represent the maid (who was now known by the appellation of *the Maid of Orleans*) as not only active in combat, but as performing the office of general; directing the troops, conducting the military operations, and swaying the deliberations in all councils of war. It is certain, that the policy of the French court endeavoured to maintain this appearance with the public: But it is much more probable, that Dunois and the wiser commanders prompted her in all her measures, than that a country girl, without experience or education, could, on a sudden, become expert in a

[b] Monstrelet, vol. ii. p. 46.

profession, which requires more genius and capacity, than any other active scene of life. It is sufficient praise, that she could distinguish the persons on whose judgment she might rely; that she could seize their hints and suggestions, and, on a sudden, deliver their opinions as her own; and that she could curb, on occasion, that visionary and enthusiastic spirit, with which she was actuated, and could temper it with prudence and discretion.

The raising of the siege of Orleans was one part of the maid's promise to Charles: The crowning of him at Rheims was the other: And she now vehemently insisted, that he should forthwith set out on that enterprize. A few weeks before, such a proposal would have appeared the most extravagant in the world. Rheims lay in a distant quarter of the kingdom; was then in the hands of a victorious enemy; the whole road, which led to it, was occupied by their garrisons; and no man could be so sanguine as to imagine that such an attempt could so soon come within the bounds of possibility. But as it was extremely the interest of Charles to maintain the belief of something extraordinary and divine in these events, and to avail himself of the present consternation of the English; he resolved to follow the exhortations of his warlike prophetess, and to lead his army upon this promising adventure. Hitherto he had kept remote from the scene of war: As the safety of the state depended upon his person, he had been persuaded to restrain his military ardour: But observing this prosperous turn of affairs, he now determined to appear at the head of his armies, and to set the example of valour to all his soldiers. And the French nobility saw at once their young sovereign assuming a new and more brilliant character, seconded by fortune, and conducted by the hand of heaven; and they caught fresh zeal to exert themselves in replacing him on the throne of his ancestors.

The king of France crowned at Rheims.

17th July.

Charles set out for Rheims at the head of twelve thousand men: He passed by Troye, which opened its gates to him: Chalons imitated the example: Rheims sent him a deputation with its keys, before his approach to it: And he scarcely perceived, as he passed along, that he was marching through an enemy's country. The ceremony of his coronation was here performed[c] with the holy oil, which a pigeon had brought to king Clovis from heaven, on the first establishment of the French monarchy: The maid of Orleans

[c] Monstrelet, vol. ii. p. 48.

stood by his side, in complete armour, and displayed her sacred banner, which had so often dissipated and confounded his fiercest enemies: And the people shouted with the most unfeigned joy, on viewing such a complication of wonders. After the completion of the ceremony, the Maid threw herself at the king's feet, embraced his knees, and with a flood of tears, which pleasure and tenderness extorted from her, she congratulated him on this singular and marvellous event.

Charles, thus crowned and anointed, became more respectable in the eyes of all his subjects, and seemed, in a manner, to receive anew, from a heavenly commission, his title to their allegiance. The inclinations of men swaying their belief, no one doubted of the inspirations and prophetic spirit of the Maid: So many incidents, which passed all human comprehension, left little room to question a superior influence: And the real and undoubted facts brought credit to every exaggeration, which could scarcely be rendered more wonderful. Laon, Soissons, Chateau-Thierri, Provins, and many other towns and fortresses in that neighbourhood, immediately after Charles's coronation, submitted to him on the first summons; and the whole nation was disposed to give him the most zealous testimonies of their duty and affection.

Nothing can impress us with a higher idea of the wisdom, address, and resolution of the duke of Bedford, than his being able to maintain himself in so perilous a situation, and to preserve some footing in France, after the defection of so many places, and amidst the universal inclination of the rest to imitate that contagious example. This prince seemed present every where by his vigilance and foresight: He employed every resource, which fortune had yet left him: He put all the English garrisons in a posture of defence: He kept a watchful eye over every attempt among the French towards an insurrection: He retained the Parisians in obedience, by alternately employing caresses and severity: And knowing that the duke of Burgundy was already wavering in his fidelity, he acted with so much skill and prudence, as to renew, in this dangerous crisis, his alliance with that prince; an alliance of the utmost importance to the credit and support of the English government.

Prudence of the duke of Bedford.

The small supplies which he received from England set the talents of this great man in still a stronger light. The ardour of the English for foreign conquests was now extremely abated by time and reflection: The parliament seems even to have become sensible of the danger, which might attend their farther progress: No supply of money could be obtained by the regent during his greatest distresses: And men enlisted slowly under his standard, or soon deserted, by reason of the wonderful accounts, which had reached England, of the magic, and sorcery, and diabolical power of the maid of Orleans.[d] It happened fortunately, in this emergency, that the bishop of Winchester, now created a cardinal, landed at Calais with a body of 5000 men, which he was conducting into Bohemia, on a crusade against the Hussites. He was persuaded to send these troops to his nephew during the present difficulties;[e] and the regent was thereby enabled to take the field; and to oppose the French king, who was advancing with his army to the gates of Paris.

The extraordinary capacity of the duke of Bedford appeared also in his military operations. He attempted to restore the courage of his troops by boldly advancing to the face of the enemy; but he chose his posts with so much caution, as always to decline a combat, and to render it impossible for Charles to attack him. He still attended that prince in all his movements; covered his own towns and garrisons; and kept himself in a posture to reap advantage from every imprudence or false step of the enemy. The French army, which consisted mostly of volunteers, who served at their own expence, soon after retired and was disbanded: Charles went to Bourges, the ordinary place of his residence; but not till he made himself master of Compiegne, Beauvais, Senlis, Sens, Laval, Lagni, St. Denis, and of many places in the neighbourhood of Paris, which the affections of the people had put into his hands.

1430.

The regent endeavoured to revive the declining state of his affairs, by bringing over the young king of England and having him crowned and anointed at Paris.[f] All the vassals of the crown, who lived within the provinces possessed by the English, swore new allegiance and did homage to him. But this ceremony was cold and insipid, compared with the lustre which had attended the coronation of Charles at Rheims; and the duke of Bedford expected more effect from an accident, which put into his hands the person that had been the author of all his calamities.

The maid of Orleans, after the coronation of Charles, declared

---

[d] Rymer, vol. x. p. 459, 472.   [e] Ibid. vol. x. p. 421.   [f] Rymer, vol. x. p. 432.

CHAPTER XX

to the count of Dunois, that her wishes were now fully gratified, and that she had no farther desire than to return to her former condition, and to the occupations and course of life which became her sex: But that nobleman, sensible of the great advantages which might still be reaped from her presence in the army, exhorted her to persevere, till, by the final expulsion of the English, she had brought all her prophecies to their full completion. In pursuance of this advice, she threw herself into the town of Compiegne, which was at that time besieged by the duke of Burgundy, assisted by the earls of Arundel and Suffolk; and the garrison on her appearance believed themselves thenceforth invincible. But their joy was of short duration. The Maid, next day after her arrival, *24th* headed a sally upon the quarters of John of Luxembourg; she *May.* twice drove the enemy from their entrenchments; finding their numbers to encrease every moment, she ordered a retreat; when hard pressed by the pursuers, she turned upon them, and made them again recoil; but being here deserted by her friends, and surrounded by the enemy, she was at last, after exerting the utmost valour, taken prisoner by the Burgundians.[g] The common opinion was, that the French officers, finding the merit of every victory ascribed to her, had, in envy to her renown, by which they themselves were so much eclipsed, willingly exposed her to the fatal accident.

The envy of her friends on this occasion was not a greater proof of her merit than the triumph of her enemies. A complete victory would not have given more joy to the English and their partizans. The service of *Te Deum,* which has so often been profaned by princes, was publicly celebrated on this fortunate event at Paris. The duke of Bedford fancied, that, by the captivity of that extraordinary woman, who had blasted all his successes, he should again recover his former ascendant over France; and to push farther the present advantage, he purchased the captive from John of Luxembourg, and formed a prosecution against her, which, whether it proceeded from vengeance or policy, was equally barbarous and dishonourable.

There was no possible reason, why Joan should not be regarded *1431.* as a prisoner of war, and be entitled to all the courtesy and good usage, which civilized nations practise towards enemies on these

[g] Stowe, p. 371.

occasions. She had never, in her military capacity, forfeited, by any act of treachery or cruelty, her claim to that treatment: She was unstained by any civil crime: Even the virtues and the very decorums of her sex had ever been rigidly observed by her: And though her appearing in war, and leading armies to battle, may seem an exception, she had thereby performed such signal service to her prince, that she had abundantly compensated for this irregularity; and was on that very account, the more an object of praise and admiration. It was necessary, therefore, for the duke of Bedford to interest religion some way in the prosecution; and to cover under that cloak his violation of justice and humanity.

The bishop of Beauvais, a man wholly devoted in the English interests, presented a petition against Joan, on pretence that she was taken within the bounds of his diocese; and he desired to have her tried by an ecclesiastical court for sorcery, impiety, idolatry, and magic: The university of Paris was so mean as to join in the same request: Several prelates, among whom the cardinal of Winchester was the only Englishman, were appointed her judges: They held their court in Rouen, where the young king of England then resided: And the Maid clothed in her former military apparel, but loaded with irons, was produced before this tribunal.

She first desired to be eased of her chains: Her judges answered, that she had once already attempted an escape by throwing herself from a tower: She confessed the fact, maintained the justice of her intention, and owned, that if she could, she would still execute that purpose. All her other speeches showed the same firmness and intrepidity: Though harassed with interrogatories, during the course of near four months, she never betrayed any weakness or womanish submission; and no advantage was gained over her. The point, which her judges pushed most vehemently, was her visions and revelations and intercourse with departed saints; and they asked her, whether she would submit to the church the truth of these inspirations: She replied, that she would submit them to God, the fountain of truth. They then exclaimed, that she was a heretic, and denied the authority of the church. She appealed to the pope: They rejected her appeal.

They asked her, why she put trust in her standard which had been consecrated by magical incantations: She replied, that she put trust in the Supreme Being alone, whose image was impressed

CHAPTER XX

upon it. They demanded, why she carried in her hand that standard at the anointment and coronation of Charles at Rheims: She answered, that the person who had shared the danger, was entitled to share the glory. When accused of going to war contrary to the decorums of her sex, and of assuming government and command over men; she scrupled not to reply, that her sole purpose was to defeat the English, and to expel them the kingdom. In the issue, she was condemned for all the crimes of which she had been accused, aggravated by heresy; her revelations were declared to be inventions of the devil to delude the people; and she was sentenced to be delivered over to the secular arm.

Joan, so long surrounded by inveterate enemies, who treated her with every mark of contumely; brow-beaten and overawed by men of superior rank, and men invested with the ensigns of a sacred character, which she had been accustomed to revere, felt her spirit at last subdued; and those visionary dreams of inspiration, in which she had been buoyed up by the triumphs of success and the applauses of her own party, gave way to the terrors of that punishment to which she was sentenced. She publicly declared herself willing to recant; she acknowledged the illusion of those revelations which the church had rejected; and she promised never more to maintain them. Her sentence was then mitigated: She was condemned to perpetual imprisonment, and to be fed during life on bread and water.

Enough was now done to fulfil all political views, and to convince both the French and the English, that the opinion of divine influence, which had so much encouraged the one and daunted the other, was entirely without foundation. But the barbarous vengeance of Joan's enemies was not satisfied with this victory. Suspecting, that the female dress, which she had now consented to wear, was disagreeable to her, they purposely placed in her apartment a suit of men's apparel; and watched for the effects of that temptation upon her. On the sight of a dress, in which she had acquired so much renown, and which, she once believed, she wore by the particular appointment of heaven, all her former ideas and passions revived; and she ventured in her solitude to cloath herself again in the forbidden garment. Her insidious enemies caught her in that situation: Her fault was interpreted to be no less than a relapse into heresy: No recantation would now suffice, and no pardon could be granted her. She was condemned to be burned in the market-place of Roüen; and the infamous sentence was accordingly executed. This admirable heroine, to whom the more generous superstition of the ancients would have erected altars, was, on pretence of heresy and magic, delivered over alive to the flames, and expiated by that dreadful punishment the signal services which she had rendered to her prince and to her native country.

Execution of the maid of Orleans. 14th June.

1432. The affairs of the English, far from being advanced by this execution, went every day more and more to decay: The great abilities of the regent were unable to resist the strong inclination, which had seized the French to return under the obedience of their rightful sovereign, and which that act of cruelty was ill fitted to remove. Chartres was surprized, by a stratagem of the count of Dunois: A body of the English, under lord Willoughby, was defeated at St. Celerin upon the Sarte:[h] The fair in the suburbs of Cäen, seated in the midst of the English territories, was pillaged by de Lore, a French officer: The duke of Bedford himself was obliged by Dunois to raise the siege of Lagni with some loss of reputation: And all these misfortunes, though light, yet being continued and uninterrupted, brought discredit on the English, and menaced them with an approaching revolution. But the chief detriment, which the regent sustained, was by the death of his dutchess, who had hitherto preserved some appearance of friendship between him and her brother, the duke of Burgundy:[i] And his marriage soon afterwards, with Jaqueline of Luxembourg, was the beginning of a breach between them.[k] Philip complained, that the regent had never had the civility to inform him of his intentions, and that so sudden a marriage was a slight on his sister's memory. The cardinal of Winchester mediated a reconciliation between these princes, and brought both of them to St. Omers for that purpose. The duke of Bedford here expected the first visit, both as he was son, brother, and uncle to a king, and because he had already made such advances as to come into the duke of Burgundy's territories, in order to have an interview with him: But Philip, proud of his great power and independant dominions,

---

[h] Monstrelet, vol. ii. p. 100.   [i] Ibid. p. 87.   [k] Stowe, p. 323. Grafton, p. 554.

refused to pay this compliment to the regent: And the two princes, unable to adjust the ceremonial, parted without seeing each other:[1] A bad prognostic of their cordial intentions to renew past amity!

Nothing could be more repugnant to the interest of the house of Burgundy, than to unite the crowns of France and England on the same head; an event, which had it taken place, would have reduced the duke to the rank of a petty prince, and have rendered his situation entirely dependant and precarious. The title also to the crown of France, which, after the failure of the elder branches, might accrue to the duke or his posterity, had been sacrificed by the treaty of Troye; and strangers and enemies were thereby irrevocably fixed upon the throne. Revenge alone had carried Philip into these impolitic measures; and a point of honour had hitherto induced him to maintain them. But as it is the nature of passion gradually to decay, while the sense of interest maintains a permanent influence and authority; the duke had, for some years, appeared sensibly to relent in his animosity against Charles, and to hearken willingly to the apologies made by that prince for the murder of the late duke of Burgundy. His extreme youth was pleaded in his favour; his incapacity to judge for himself; the ascendant gained over him by his ministers; and his inability to resent a deed, which, without his knowledge, had been perpetrated by those under whose guidance he was then placed. The more to flatter the pride of Philip, the king of France had banished from his court and presence Tanegui de Chatel, and all those who were concerned in that assassination: and had offered to make every other atonement, which could be required of him. The distress, which Charles had already suffered, had tended to gratify the duke's revenge; the miseries, to which France had been so long exposed, had begun to move his compassion; and the cries of all Europe admonished him, that his resentment, which might hitherto be deemed pious, would, if carried farther, be universally condemned as barbarous and unrelenting. While the duke was in this disposition, every disgust, which he received from England, made a double impression upon him; the entreaties of the count of Richemont and the duke of Bourbon, who had married his two sisters, had weight; and he finally determined to unite himself to

Defection of the duke of Burgundy.

[1] Monstrelet, vol. ii. p. 90. Grafton, p. 561.

1433. the royal family of France, from which his own was descended. For this purpose, a congress was appointed at Arras under the mediation of deputies from the pope and the council of Basle: The duke of Burgundy came thither in person: The duke of Bourbon, the count of Richemont, and other persons of high rank, appeared as ambassadors from France: And the English having also been invited to attend, the cardinal of Winchester, the bishops of Norwich and St. David's, the earls of Huntingdon and Suffolk, with others, received from the protector and council a commission for that purpose.[m]

August. The conferences were held in the abbey of St. Vaast; and began with discussing the proposals of the two crowns, which were so wide of each other as to admit of no hopes of accommodation. France offered to cede Normandy with Guienne, but both of them loaded with the usual homage and vassalage to the crown. As the claims of England upon France were universally unpopular in Europe, the mediators declared the offers of Charles very reasonable; and the cardinal of Winchester, with the other English ambassadors, without giving a particular detail of their demands, immediately left the congress. There remained nothing but to discuss the mutual pretensions of Charles and Philip. These were easily adjusted: The vassal was in a situation to give law to his superior; and he exacted conditions, which, had it not been for the *1435.* present necessity, would have been deemed, to the last degree, dishonourable and disadvantageous to the crown of France. Besides making repeated atonements and acknowledgments for the murder of the duke of Burgundy, Charles was obliged to cede all the towns of Picardy which lay between the Somme and the Low Countries; he yielded several other territories; he agreed, that these and all the other dominions of Philip should be held by him, during his life, without doing any homage or swearing fealty to the present king; and he freed his subjects from all obligations to allegiance, if ever he infringed this treaty.[n] Such were the conditions, upon which France purchased the friendship of the duke of Burgundy.

[m] Rymer, vol. x. p. 611, 612.   [n] Monstrelet, vol. ii. p. 112. Grafton, p. 565.

CHAPTER XX

The duke sent a herald to England with a letter, in which he notified the conclusion of the treaty of Arras, and apologized for his departure from that of Troye. The council received the herald with great coldness: They even assigned him his lodgings in a shoemaker's house, by way of insult; and the populace were so incensed, that, if the duke of Glocester had not given him guards, his life had been exposed to danger, when he appeared in the streets. The Flemings, and other subjects of Philip, were insulted, and some of them murdered by the Londoners; and every thing seemed to tend towards a rupture between the two nations.[o] These violences were not disagreeable to the duke of Burgundy; as they afforded him a pretence for the farther measures which he intended to take against the English, whom he now regarded as implacable and dangerous enemies.

A few days after the duke of Bedford received intelligence of this treaty, so fatal to the interests of England, he died at Roüen; a prince of great abilities, and of many virtues; and whose memory, except from the barbarous execution of the maid of Orleans, was unsullied by any considerable blemish. Isabella, queen of France, died a little before him, despised by the English, detested by the French, and reduced in her later years to regard, with an unnatural horror, the progress and success of her own son, in recovering possession of his kingdom. This period was also signalized by the death of the earl of Arundel,[p] a great English general, who, though he commanded three thousand men, was foiled by Xaintrailles at the head of six hundred, and soon after expired of the wounds which he received in the action. *14th Sept. Death of the duke of Bedford.*

The violent factions, which prevailed between the duke of Glocester and the cardinal of Winchester, prevented the English from taking the proper measures for repairing these multiplied losses, and threw all their affairs into confusion. The popularity of the duke, and his near relation to the crown, gave him advantages in the contest, which he often lost by his open and unguarded temper, unfit to struggle with the politic and interested spirit of his rival. The balance, meanwhile, of these parties, kept every thing in *1436.*

---

[o] Monstrelet, vol. ii. p. 120. Hollingshed, p. 612. [p] Monstrelet, vol. ii. p. 105. Hollingshed, p. 610.

suspence: Foreign affairs were much neglected: And though the duke of York, son to that earl of Cambridge, who was executed in the beginning of the last reign, was appointed successor to the duke of Bedford, it was seven months before his commission passed the seals; and the English remained so long in an enemy's country, without a proper head or governor.

Decline of the English in France.

The new governor on his arrival found the capital already lost. The Parisians had always been more attached to the Burgundian than to the English interest; and after the conclusion of the treaty of Arras, their affections, without any farther controul, universally led them to return to their allegiance under their native sovereign. The constable, together with Lile-Adam, the same person who had before put Paris into the hands of the duke of Burgundy, was introduced in the night-time by intelligence with the citizens: Lord Willoughby, who commanded only a small garrison of 1500 men, was expelled: This nobleman discovered valour and presence of mind on the occasion; but unable to guard so large a place against such multitudes, he retired into the Bastile, and being there invested, he delivered up that fortress, and was contented to stipulate for the safe retreat of his troops into Normandy.[q]

In the same season, the duke of Burgundy openly took part against England, and commenced hostilities by the siege of Calais, the only place which now gave the English any sure hold of France, and still rendered them dangerous. As he was beloved among his own subjects, and had acquired the epithet of *Good*, from his popular qualities, he was able to interest all the inhabitants of the Low Countries in the success of this enterprize; and he invested that place with an army, formidable from its numbers, but without experience, discipline, or military spirit.[r] On the first alarm of this siege, the duke of Glocester assembled some forces, sent a defiance to Philip, and challenged him to wait the event of a battle, which he promised to give, as soon as the wind would permit him to reach Calais. The warlike genius of the English had at that time rendered them terrible to all the northern parts of Europe; especially to the Flemings, who were more expert in manufactures, than in arms; and the duke of Burgundy, being already foiled in some attempts

[q] Monstrelet, vol. ii. p. 127. Grafton, p. 568.   [r] Monstrelet, vol. ii. p. 126, 130, 132. Hollingshed, p. 613. Grafton, p. 571.

before Calais, and observing the discontent and terror of his own army, thought proper to raise the siege, and to retreat before the arrival of the enemy.[s] 26th June.

The English were still masters of many fine provinces in France; but retained possession, more by the extreme weakness of Charles, than by the strength of their own garrisons or the force of their armies. Nothing indeed can be more surprising than the feeble efforts made, during the course of several years, by these two potent nations against each other; while the one struggled for independence, and the other aspired to a total conquest of its rival. The general want of industry, commerce, and police, in that age, had rendered all the European nations, and France and England no less than the others, unfit for bearing the burthens of war, when it was prolonged beyond one season; and the continuance of hostilities had, long ere this time, exhausted the force and patience of both kingdoms. Scarcely could the appearance of an army be brought into the field on either side; and all the operations consisted in the surprisal of places, in the rencounter of detached parties, and in incursions upon the open country; which were performed by small bodies, assembled on a sudden from the neighbouring garrisons. In this method of conducting the war, the French king had much the advantage: The affections of the people were entirely on his side: Intelligence was early brought him of the state and motions of the enemy: The inhabitants were ready to join in any attempts against the garrisons: And thus ground was continually, though slowly, gained upon the English. The duke of York, who was a prince of abilities, struggled against these difficulties during the course of five years; and being assisted by the valour of lord Talbot, soon after created earl of Shrewsbury, he performed actions, which acquired him honour, but merit not the attention of posterity. It would have been well, had this feeble war, in sparing the blood of the people, prevented likewise all other oppressions; and had the fury of men, which reason and justice cannot restrain, thus happily received a check from their impotence and inability. But the French and English, though they exerted such small force, were, however, stretching beyond their resources, which were still smaller; and the troops, destitute of

[s] Monstrelet, vol. ii. p. 136. Hollingshed, p. 614.

pay, were obliged to subsist by plundering and oppressing the country, both of friends and enemies. The fields in all the north of France, which was the seat of war, were laid waste and left uncultivated.[t] The cities were gradually depopulated, not by the blood spilt in battle, but by the more destructive pillage of the garrisons:[u] And both parties, weary of hostilities, which decided nothing, seemed at last desirous of peace, and they set on foot negociations for that purpose. But the proposals of France and the demands of England, were still so wide of each other, that all hope of accommodations immediately vanished. The English ambassadors demanded restitution of all the provinces which had once been annexed to England, together with the final cession of Calais and its district; and required the possession of these extensive territories without the burthen of any fealty or homage on the part of their prince: The French offered only part of Guienne, part of Normandy, and Calais, loaded with the usual burthens. It appeared in vain to continue the negociation, while there was so little prospect of agreement. The English were still too haughty to stoop from the vast hopes which they had formerly entertained, and to accept of terms more suitable to the present condition of the two kingdoms.

The duke of York soon after resigned his government to the earl of Warwic, a nobleman of reputation, whom death prevented from long enjoying this dignity. The duke, upon the demise of that nobleman, returned to his charge, and during his administration a truce was concluded between the king of England and the duke of Burgundy, which had become necessary for the commercial interests of their subjects.[w] The war with France continued in the same languid and feeble state as before.

The captivity of five princes of the blood, taken prisoners in the battle of Azincour, was a considerable advantage which England long enjoyed over its enemy; but this superiority was now entirely lost. Some of these princes had died; some had been ransomed;

---

[t] Grafton, p. 562. [u] Fortescue, who, soon after this period, visited France, in the train of prince Henry, speaks of that kingdom as a desert in comparison of England. See his Treatise *de laudibus Angliae.* Though we make allowance for the partialities of Fortescue, there must have been some foundation for his account; and these destructive wars are the most likely reason to be assigned for the difference remarked by this author.
[w] Grafton, p. 573.

and the duke of Orleans, the most powerful among them, was the last that remained in the hands of the English. He offered the sum of 54,000 nobles[x] for his liberty; and when this proposal was laid before the council of England, as every question was there an object of faction, the party of the duke of Glocester, and that of the cardinal of Winchester, were divided in their sentiments with regard to it. The duke reminded the council of the dying advice of the late king, that none of these prisoners should on any account be released, till his son should be of sufficient age to hold, himself, the reins of government. The cardinal insisted on the greatness of the sum offered, which in reality was near equal to two thirds of all the extraordinary supplies, that the parliament, during the course of seven years, granted for the support of the war. And he added, that the release of this prince was more likely to be advantageous than prejudicial to the English interests; by filling the court of France with faction, and giving a head to those numerous malcontents, whom Charles was at present able with great difficulty to restrain. The cardinal's party, as usual, prevailed: The duke of Orleans was released, after a melancholy captivitiy of twenty-five years:[y] And the duke of Burgundy, as a pledge of his entire reconciliation with the family of Orleans, facilitated to that prince the payment of his ransom. It must be confessed, that the princes and nobility, in those ages, went to war on very disadvantageous terms. If they were taken prisoners, they either remained in captivity during life, or purchased their liberty at the price which the victors were pleased to impose, and which often reduced their families to want and beggary.

The sentiments of the cardinal, some time after, prevailed in another point of still greater moment. That prelate had always encouraged every proposal of accommodation with France; and had represented the utter impossibility, in the present circumstances, of pushing farther the conquests in that kingdom, and the great difficulty of even maintaining those which were already   *1443.*

---

[x] Rymer, vol. x. p. 764, 776, 782, 795, 796. This sum was equal to 36,000 pounds sterling of our present money. A subsidy of a tenth and fifteenth was fixed by Edward III. at 29,000 pounds, which, in the reign of Henry VI. made only 58,000 pounds of our present money. The parliament granted only one subsidy during the course of seven years, from 1437 to 1444.   [y] Grafton, p. 578.

made. He insisted on the extreme reluctance of the parliament to grant supplies; the disorders in which the English affairs in Normandy were involved; the daily progress made by the French king; and the advantage of stopping his hand by a temporary accommodation, which might leave room for time and accidents to operate in favour of the English. The duke of Glocester, high-spirited and haughty, and educated in the lofty pretensions, which the first successes of his two brothers had rendered familiar to him, could not yet be induced to relinquish all hopes of prevailing over France; much less could he see, with patience, his own opinion thwarted and rejected by the influence of his rival in the English council. But notwithstanding his opposition, the earl of Suffolk, a nobleman who adhered to the cardinal's party, was dispatched to Tours, in order to negociate with the French ministers. It was found impossible to adjust the terms of a lasting peace; but a truce for twenty-two months was concluded, which left every thing on the present footing between the parties. The numerous disorders, under which the French government laboured, and which time alone could remedy, induced Charles to assent to this truce; and the same motives engaged him afterwards to prolong it.[z] But Suffolk, not content with executing this object of his commission, proceeded also to finish another business, which seems rather to have been implied than expressed in the powers that had been granted him.[a]

28th May. Truce with France.

In proportion as Henry advanced in years, his character became fully known in the court, and was no longer ambiguous to either faction. Of the most harmless, inoffensive, simple manners; but of the most slender capacity: he was fitted, both by the softness of his temper, and the weakness of his understanding, to be perpetually governed by those who surrounded him; and it was easy to foresee, that his reign would prove a perpetual minority. As he had now reached the twenty-third year of his age, it was natural to think of choosing him a queen; and each party was ambitious of having him receive one from their hand; as it was probable, that this circumstance would decide for ever the victory between them. The duke of Glocester proposed a daughter of the count of Armagnac; but had not credit to effect his purpose. The cardinal

---

[z] Rymer, vol. xi. p. 101, 108, 206, 214.   [a] Ibid. p. 53.

and his friends had cast their eye on Margaret of Anjou, daughter of Regnier, titular king of Sicily, Naples, and Jerusalem, descended from the count of Anjou, brother of Charles V. who had left these magnificent titles, but without any real power or possessions, to his posterity. This princess herself was the most accomplished of her age both in body and mind; and seemed to possess those qualities, which would equally qualify her to acquire the ascendant over Henry, and to supply all his defects and weaknesses. Of a masculine, courageous spirit, of an enterprizing temper, endowed with solidity as well as vivacity of understanding, she had not been able to conceal these great talents even in the privacy of her father's family; and it was reasonable to expect, that, when she should mount the throne, they would break out with still superior lustre. The earl of Suffolk, therefore, in concert with his associates of the English council, made proposals of marriage to Margaret, which were accepted. But this nobleman, besides preoccupying the princess's favour by being the chief means of her advancement, endeavoured to ingratiate himself with her and her family, by very extraordinary concessions: Though Margaret brought no dowry with her, he ventured of himself, without any direct authority from the council, but probably with the approbation of the cardinal and the ruling members, to engage by a secret article, that the province of Maine, which was at that time in the hands of the English, should be ceded to Charles of Anjou her uncle,[b] who was prime minister and favourite of the French king, and who had already received from his master the grant of that province as his appanage.

Marriage of the king with Margaret of Anjou.

The treaty of marriage was ratified in England: Suffolk obtained first the title of marquis, then that of duke; and even received the thanks of parliament, for his services in concluding it.[c] The princess fell immediately into close connections with the cardinal and his party, the dukes of Somerset, Suffolk, and Buckingham;[d] who, fortified by her powerful patronage, resolved on the final ruin of the duke of Glocester.

This generous prince, worsted in all court intrigues, for which his temper was not suited, but possessing, in a high degree, the favour of the public, had already received from his rivals a cruel

1447.

[b] Grafton, p. 590. [c] Cotton, p. 630. [d] Hollingshed, p. 626.

mortification, which he had hitherto born without violating public peace, but which it was impossible that a person of his spirit and humanity could ever forgive. His dutchess, the daughter of Reginald, lord Cobham, had been accused of the crime of witchcraft, and it was pretended, that there was found in her possession a waxen figure of the king, which she and her associates, Sir Roger Bolingbroke a priest, and one Margery Jordan of Eye, melted in a magical manner before a slow fire, with an intention of making Henry's force and vigour waste away by like insensible degrees. The accusation was well calculated to affect the weak and credulous mind of the king, and to gain belief in an ignorant age; and the dutchess was brought to trial with her confederates. The nature of this crime, so opposite to all common sense, seems always to exempt the accusers from observing the rules of common sense in their evidence: The prisoners were pronounced guilty; the dutchess was condemned to do public penance, and to suffer perpetual imprisonment, the others were executed.[e] But as these violent proceedings were ascribed solely to the malice of the duke's enemies, the people, contrary to their usual practice in such marvellous trials, acquitted the unhappy sufferers; and encreased their esteem and affection towards a prince, who was thus exposed without protection, to those mortal injuries.

These sentiments of the public made the cardinal of Winchester and his party sensible, that it was necessary to destroy a man, whose popularity might become dangerous, and whose resentment they had so much cause to apprehend. In order to effect their purpose, a parliament was summoned to meet, not at London, which was supposed to be too well affected to the duke, but at St. Edmondsbury, where they expected that he would be entirely at mercy. As soon as he appeared, he was accused of treason, and thrown into prison. He was soon after found dead in his bed;[f] and though it was pretended that his death was natural, and though his body, which was exposed to public view, bore no marks of outward violence, no one doubted but he had fallen a victim to the vengeance of his enemies. An artifice, formerly practised in the case of Edward II. Richard II. and Thomas of Woodstock, duke of Glocester, could deceive no body. The reason of this assassination of the duke seems not, that the ruling party apprehended his

28th Feb. Murder of the duke of Glocester.

[e] Stowe, p. 381. Hollingshed, p. 622. Grafton, p. 587.　[f] Grafton, p. 597.

CHAPTER XX

acquittal in parliament on account of his innocence, which, in such times, was seldom much regarded; but that they imagined his public trial and execution would have been more invidious than his private murder, which they pretended to deny. Some gentlemen of his retinue were afterwards tried as accomplices in his treasons, and were condemned to be hanged, drawn and quartered. They were hanged and cut down; but just as the executioner was proceeding to quarter them, their pardon was produced, and they were recovered to life.[g] The most barbarous kind of mercy that can possibly be imagined!

This prince is said to have received a better education than was usual in his age, to have founded one of the first public libraries in England, and to have been a great patron of learned men. Among other advantages, which he reaped from this turn of mind, it tended much to cure him of credulity; of which the following instance is given by Sir Thomas More. There was a man, who pretended, that, though he was born blind, he had recovered his sight by touching the shrine of St. Albans. The duke, happening soon after to pass that way, questioned the man, and seeming to doubt of his sight, asked him the colours of several cloaks, worn by persons of his retinue. The man told them very readily. *You are a knave,* cried the prince; *had you been born blind, you could not so soon have learned to distinguish colours:* And immediately ordered him to be set in the stocks as an impostor.[h]

The cardinal of Winchester died six weeks after his nephew, whose murder was universally ascribed to him as well as to the duke of Suffolk, and which, it is said, gave him more remorse in his last moments, than could naturally be expected from a man hardened, during the course of a long life, in falsehood and in politics. What share the queen had in this guilt is uncertain; her usual activitiy and spirit made the public conclude with some reason, that the duke's enemies durst not have ventured on such a deed without her privity. But there happened soon after an event, of which she and her favourite, the duke of Suffolk, bore incontestibly the whole odium.

That article of the marriage treaty, by which the province of Maine was to be ceded to Charles of Anjou, the queen's uncle, had probably been hitherto kept secret; and during the lifetime of the

[g] Fabian Chron. anno 1447.   [h] Grafton, p. 597.

duke of Glocester, it might have been dangerous to venture on the execution of it. But as the court of France strenuously insisted on performance, orders were now dispatched, under Henry's hand, to Sir Francis Surienne, governor of Mans, commanding him to surrender that place to Charles of Anjou. Surienne, either questioning the authenticity of the order, or regarding his government as his sole fortune, refused compliance; and it became necessary for a French army, under the count of Dunois, to lay siege to the city. The governor made as good a defence as his situation could permit; but receiving no relief from Edmund duke of Somerset, who was at that time governor of Normandy, he was at last obliged to capitulate, and to surrender not only Mans, but all the other fortresses of that province, which was thus entirely alienated from the crown of England.

1448. The bad effects of this measure stopped not here. Surienne, at the head of all his garrisons, amounting to 2500 men, retired into Normandy, in expectations of being taken into pay, and of being quartered in some towns of the province. But Somerset, who had no means of subsisting such a multitude, and who was probably incensed at Surienne's disobedience, refused to admit him; and this adventurer, not daring to commit depredations on the territories either of the king of France or of England, marched into Britanny, seized the town of Fougeres, repaired the fortifications of Pontorson and St. James de Beuvron, and subsisted his troops by the ravages which he exercised on that whole province.[i] The duke of Britanny complained of this violence to the king of France, his liege lord: Charles remonstrated with the duke of Somerset: That nobleman replied, that the injury was done without his privity, and that he had no authority over Surienne and his companions.[k] Though this answer sought to have appeared satisfactory to Charles, who had often felt severely the licentious, independant spirit of such mercenary soldiers, he never would admit of the apology. He still insisted, that these plunderers should be recalled, and that reparation should be made to the duke of Britanny for all the damages which he had sustained: And in order to render an accommodation absolutely impracticable, he made the estimation

---

[i] Monstrelet, vol. iii. p. 6.   [k] Monstrelet, vol. iii. p. 7. Hollingshed, p. 629.

CHAPTER XX

of damages amount to no less a sum than 1,600,000 crowns. He was sensible of the superiority, which the present state of his affairs gave him over England; and he determined to take advantage of it.

No sooner was the truce concluded between the two kingdoms, than Charles employed himself, with great industry and judgment, in repairing those numberless ills, to which France, from the continuance of wars both foreign and domestic, had so long been exposed. He restored the course of public justice; he introduced order into the finances; he established discipline in his troops; he repressed faction in his court; he revived the languid state of agriculture and the arts; and in the course of a few years, he rendered his kingdom flourishing within itself, and formidable to its neighbours. Meanwhile, affairs in England had taken a very different turn. The court was divided into parties, which were enraged against each other: The people were discontented with the government: Conquests in France, which were an object more of glory than of interest, were overlooked amidst domestic incidents, which engrossed the attention of all men: The governor of Normandy, ill supplied with money, was obliged to dismiss the greater part of his troops, and to allow the fortifications of the towns and castles to become ruinous: And the nobility and people of that province had during the late open communication with France, enjoyed frequent opportunities of renewing connexions with their ancient master, and of concerting the means of expelling the English. The occasion therefore seemed favourable to Charles for breaking the truce. Normandy was at once invaded by four powerful armies; one commanded by the king himself; a second by the duke of Britanny; a third by the duke of Alençon; and a fourth by the count of Dunois. The places opened their gates almost as soon as the French appeared before them: Verneüil, Nogent, Chateau Gaillard, Ponteau de mer, Gisors, Mante, Vernon, Argentan, Lisieux, Fecamp, Coutances, Belesme, Pont de l'Arche, fell in an instant into the hands of the enemy. The duke of Somerset, so far from having an army, which could take the field, and relieve these places, was not able to supply them with the necessary garrisons and provisions. He retired with the few troops, of which he was master, into Roüen; and thought it sufficient, if, till the arrival of succours from England, he could save that capital from the general

State of France.

1449.

Renewal of the war with France.

4th Nov.

fate of the province. The king of France, at the head of a formidable army, fifty thousand strong, presented himself before the gates: The dangerous example of revolt had infected the inhabitants; and they called aloud for a capitulation. Somerset, unable to resist at once both the enemies within and from without, retired with his garrison into the palace and castle; which, being places not tenable, he was obliged to surrender: He purchased a retreat to Harfleur by the payment of 56,000 crowns, by engaging to surrender Arques, Tancarville, Caudebec, Honfleur, and other places in the higher Normandy, and by delivering hostages for the performance of articles.[l] The governor of Honfleur refused to obey his orders; upon which the earl of Shrewsbury, who was one of the hostages, was detained prisoner; and the English were thus deprived of the only general capable of recovering them from their present distressed situation. Harfleur made a better defence under Sir Thomas Curson the governor; but was finally obliged to open its gates to Dunois. Succours at last appeared from England under Sir Thomas Kyriel, and landed at Cherbourg: But these came very late, amounted only to 4000 men, and were soon after put to rout at Fourmigni by the count of Clermont.[m] This battle, or rather skirmish, was the only action fought by the English for the defence of their dominions in France, which they had purchased at such an expence of blood and treasure. Somerset, shut up in Caën without any prospect of relief, found it necessary to capitulate: Falaise opened its gates, on condition that the earl of Shrewsbury should be restored to liberty: And Cherbourg, the last place of Normandy which remained in the hands of the English, being delivered up, the conquest of that important province was finished in a twelvemonth by Charles, to the great joy of the inhabitants and of his whole kingdom.[n]

1450.

A like rapid success attended the French arms in Guienne; though the inhabitants of that province were, from long custom, better inclined to the English government. Dunois was dispatched thither, and met with no resistance in the field, and very little from the towns. Great improvements had been made, during this age, in the structure and management of artillery, and none in forti-

The English expelled France.

[l] Monstrelet, vol. iii. p. 21. Grafton, p. 643. [m] Hollingshed, p. 631.
[n] Grafton, p. 646.

CHAPTER XX

fication; and the art of defence was by that means more unequal, than either before or since, to the art of attack. After all the small places about Bourdeaux were reduced, that city agreed to submit, if not relieved by a certain time; and as no one in England thought seriously of these distant concerns, no relief appeared; the place surrendered; and Bayonne being taken soon after, the whole province, which had remained united to England since the accession of Henry II. was, after a period of three centuries, finally swallowed up in the French monarchy.

Though no peace of truce was concluded between France and England, the war was in a manner at an end. The English, torn in pieces by the civil dissensions which ensued, made but one feeble effort more for the recovery of Guienne: And Charles, occupied at home in regulating the government, and fencing against the intrigues of his factious son, Lewis the Dauphin, scarcely ever attempted to invade them in their island, or to retaliate upon them, by availing himself of their intestine confusions.

XXI

HENRY VI

Claim of the duke of York to the crown – The earl of Warwic – Impeachment of the duke of Suffolk – His banishment – and death – Popular insurrection – The parties of York and Lancaster – First armament of the duke of York – First battle of St. Albans – Battle of Blore-heath – of Northampton – A parliament – Battle of Wakefield – Death of the duke of York – Battle of Mortimer's Cross – Second Battle of St. Albans – Edward IV. assumes the crown – Miscellaneous transactions of this reign

1450. A WEAK PRINCE, seated on the throne of England, had never failed, how gentle soever and innocent, to be infested with faction, discontent, rebellion, and civil commotions; and as the incapacity of Henry appeared every day in a fuller light, these dangerous consequences began, from past experience, to be universally and justly apprehended. Men also of unquiet spirits, no longer employed in foreign wars, whence they were now excluded by the situation of the neighbouring states, were the more likely to excite intestine disorders, and by their emulation, rivalship, and animosities, to tear the bowels of their native country. But though these causes alone were sufficient to breed confusion, there concurred another circumstance of the most dangerous nature: A pretender to the crown appeared: The title itself of the weak prince, who enjoyed the name of sovereignty, was disputed: And the English were now to pay the severe, though late penalty, of their turbulence under Richard II. and of their levity in violating, without any necessity or just reason, the lineal succession of their monarchs.

All the males of the house of Mortimer were extinct; but Anne, the sister of the last earl of Marche, having espoused the earl of Cambridge, beheaded in the reign of Henry V. had transmitted her latent, but not yet forgotten claim to her son, Richard, duke of York. The prince, thus descended by his mother from Philippa, only daughter of the duke of Clarence, second son of Edward III. stood plainly in the order of succession before the king, who derived his descent from the duke of Lancaster, third son of that monarch; and that claim could not, in many respects, have fallen into more dangerous hands than those of the duke of York. Richard was a man of valour and abilities, of a prudent conduct and mild dispositions: He had enjoyed an opportunity of displaying these virtues in his government of France: And though recalled from that command by the intrigues and superior interest of the duke of Somerset, he had been sent to suppress a rebellion in Ireland; had succeeded much better in that enterprize than his rival in the defence of Normandy; and had even been able to attach to his person and family the whole Irish nation, whom he was sent to subdue.[o] In the right of his father, he bore the rank of first prince of the blood; and by this station, he gave a lustre to his title derived from the family of Mortimer, which, though of great nobility, was equalled by other families in the kingdom, and had been eclipsed by the royal descent of the house of Lancaster. He possessed an immense fortune from the union of so many successions, those of Cambridge and York on the one hand, with those of Mortimer on the other: Which last inheritance had before been augmented by an union of the estates of Clarence and Ulster, with the patrimonial possessions of the family of Marche. The alliances too of Richard, by his marrying the daughter of Ralph Nevil, earl

Claim of the duke of York to the crown.

[o] Stowe, p. 387.

of Westmoreland, had widely extended his interest among the nobility, and had procured him many connexions in that formidable order.

The family of Nevil was perhaps at this time the most potent, both from their opulent possessions and from the characters of the men, that has ever appeared in England. For besides the earl of Westmoreland, and the lords Latimer, Fauconberg, and Abergavenny; the earls of Salisbury and Warwic were of that family, and were of themselves, on many accounts, the greatest noblemen in the kingdom. The earl of Salisbury, brother-in-law to the duke of York, was the eldest son by a second marriage of the earl of Westmoreland; and inherited by his wife, daughter and heir of Montacute, earl of Salisbury, killed before Orleans, the possessions and title of that great family. His eldest son, Richard, had married Anne, the daughter and heir of Beauchamp, earl of Warwic, who died governor of France; and by this alliance he enjoyed the possessions, and had acquired the title, of that other family, one of the most opulent, most ancient, and most illustrious in England. The personal qualities also of these two earls, especially of Warwic, enhanced the splendour of their nobility, and encreased their influence over the people. This latter nobleman, commonly known, from the subsequent events, by the appellation of the *King-maker,* had distinguished himself, by his gallantry in the field, by the hospitality of his table, by the magnificence, and still more by the generosity of his expence, and by the spirited and bold manner which attended him in all his actions. The undesigning frankness and openness of his character rendered his conquest over men's affections the more certain and infallible: His presents were regarded as sure testimonies of esteem and friendship and his professions as the overflowings of his genuine sentiments. No less than 30,000 persons are said to have daily lived at his board in the different manors and castles which he possessed in England: The military men, allured by his munificence and hospitality, as well as by his bravery, were zealously attached to his interests: The people in general bore him an unlimited affection: His numerous retainers were more devoted to his will, than to the prince or to the laws: And he was the greatest, as well as the last, of those mighty barons, who formerly overawed the crown, and rendered the people incapable of any regular system of civil government.

The earl of Warwic.

CHAPTER XXI

But the duke of York, besides the family of Nevil, had many other partizans among the great nobility. Courtney, earl of Devonshire, descended from a very noble family of that name in France, was attached to his interests: Moubray, duke of Norfolk, had, from his hereditary hatred to the family of Lancaster, embraced the same party: And the discontents, which universally prevailed among the people, rendered every combination of the great the more dangerous to the established government.

Though the people were never willing to grant the supplies necessary for keeping possession of the conquered provinces in France, they repined extremely at the loss of these boasted acquisitions; and fancied, because a sudden irruption could make conquests, that, without steady counsels and a uniform expence, it was possible to maintain them. The voluntary cession of Maine to the queen's uncle, had made them suspect treachery in the loss of Normandy and Guienne. They still considered Margaret as a French woman and a latent enemy of the kingdom. And when they saw her father and all her relations active in promoting the success of the French, they could not be persuaded, that she, who was all powerful in the English council, would very zealously oppose them in their enterprizes.

But the most fatal blow, given to the popularity of the crown and to the interests of the house of Lancaster, was by the assassination of the virtuous duke of Glocester, whose character, had he been alive, would have intimidated the partizans of York, but whose memory, being extremely cherished by the people, served to throw an odium on all his murderers. By this crime, the reigning family suffered a double prejudice: It was deprived of its firmest support; and it was loaded with all the infamy of that imprudent and barbarous assassination.

As the duke of Suffolk was known to have had an active hand in the crime, he partook deeply of the hatred attending it; and the clamours, which necessarily rose against him, as prime minister and declared favourite of the queen, were thereby augmented to a ten-fold pitch, and became absolutely uncontrollable. The great nobility could ill brook to see a subject exalted above them; much more one who was only great grandson to a merchant, and who was of a birth so much inferior to theirs. The people complained of his arbitrary measures; which were, in some degree, a necessary consequence of the irregular power then possessed by the prince, but which the least disaffection easily magnified into tyranny. The great acquisitions, which he daily made, were the object of envy; and as they were gained at the expence of the crown, which was itself reduced to poverty, they appeared on that account, to all indifferent persons, the more exceptionable and invidious.

The revenues of the crown, which had long been disproportioned to its power and dignity, had been extremely dilapidated during the minority of Henry;[p] both by the rapacity of the courtiers, which the king's uncles could not controul, and by the necessary expences of the French war, which had always been very ill supplied by the grants of parliament. The royal demesnes were dissipated; and at the same time the king was loaded with a debt of 372,000 pounds, a sum so great, that the parliament could never think of discharging it. This unhappy situation forced the ministers upon many arbitrary measures: The household itself could not be supported without stretching to the utmost the right of purveyance, and rendering it a kind of universal robbery upon the people: The public clamour rose high upon this occasion, and no one had the equity to make allowance for the necessity of the king's situation. Suffolk, once become odious, bore the blame of the whole; and every grievance, in every part of the administration, was universally imputed to his tyranny and injustice.

Impeachment of the duke of Suffolk. This nobleman, sensible of the public hatred under which he laboured, and foreseeing an attack from the commons, endeavoured to overawe his enemies, by boldly presenting himself to the charge, and insisting upon his own innocence, and even upon his merits and those of his family in the public service. He rose in the house of peers; took notice of the clamours propagated against him; and complained, that, after serving the crown in thirty-four campaigns; after living abroad seventeen years without once returning to his native country; after losing a father and three brothers in the wars with France; after being himself a prisoner, and purchasing his liberty by a great ransom; it should yet be suspected, that he had been debauched from his allegiance by that enemy whom he had ever opposed with such zeal and fortitude, and that he had betrayed his prince, who had rewarded his services by the

[p] Cotton, p. 609.

CHAPTER XXI

highest honours and greatest offices, that it was in his power to confer.[q] This speech did not answer the purpose intended. The commons, rather provoked at his challenge, opened their charge against him, and sent up to the peers an accusation of high treason, divided into several articles. They insisted, that he had persuaded the French king to invade England with an armed force, in order to depose the king, and to place on the throne his own son, John de la Pole, whom he intended to marry to Margaret, the only daughter of the late John, duke of Somerset, and to whom, he imagined, he would by that means acquire a title to the crown: That he had contributed to the release of the duke of Orleans, in hopes, that that prince would assist king Charles in expelling the English from France, and recovering full possession of his kingdom: That he had afterwards encouraged that monarch to make open war on Normandy and Guienne, and had promoted his conquests by betraying the secrets of England, and obstructing the succours intended to be sent to those provinces: And that he had, without any powers of commission, promised by treaty to cede the province of Maine to Charles of Anjou, and had accordingly ceded it; which proved in the issue the chief cause of the loss of Normandy.[r]

It is evident, from a review of these articles, that the commons adopted without enquiry all the popular clamours against the duke of Suffolk, and charged him with crimes, of which none but the vulgar could seriously believe him guilty. Nothing can be more incredible, than that a nobleman, so little eminent by his birth and character, could think of acquiring the crown to his family, and of deposing Henry by foreign force, and, together with him, Margaret, his patron, a princess of so much spirit and penetration. Suffolk appealed to many noblemen in the house, who knew, that he had intended to marry his son to one of the co-heirs of the earl of Warwic, and was disappointed in his views, only by the death of that lady: And he observed, that Margaret of Somerset could bring to her husband no title to the crown; because she herself was not so much as comprehended in the entail, settled by act of parliament. It is easy to account for the loss of Normandy and Guienne,

[q] Cotton, p. 641.   [r] Cotton, p. 642. Hall, fol. 157. Hollingshed, p. 631. Grafton, p. 607.

from the situation of affairs in the two kingdoms, without supposing any treachery in the English ministers; and it may safely be affirmed, that greater vigour was requisite to defend these provinces from the arms of Charles VII. than to conquer them at first from his predecessor. It could never be the interest of any English minister to betray and abandon such acquisitions; much less of one, who was so well established in his master's favour, who enjoyed such high honours and ample possessions in his own country, who had nothing to dread but the effects of popular hatred, and who could never think, without the most extreme reluctance, of becoming a fugitive and exile in a foreign land. The only article, which carries any face of probability, is his engagement for the delivery of Maine to the queen's uncle: But Suffolk maintained, with great appearance of truth, that this measure was approved of by several at the council table;[s] and it seems hard to ascribe to it, as is done by the commons, the subsequent loss of Normandy and expulsion of the English. Normandy lay open on every side to the invasion of the French: Maine, an inland province, must soon after have fallen without any attack: And as the English possessed in other parts more fortresses than they could garrison or provide for, it seemed no bad policy to contract their force, and to render the defence practicable, by reducing it within a narrower compass.

The commons were probably sensible, that this charge of treason against Suffolk would not bear a strict scrutiny; and they, therefore, soon after, sent up, against him, a new charge of misdemeanors, which they also divided into several articles. They affirmed, among other imputations, that he had procured exorbitant grants from the crown, had embezzled the public money, had conferred offices on improper persons, had perverted justice by maintaining iniquitous causes, and had procured pardons for notorious offenders.[t] The articles are mostly general, but are not improbable: And as Suffolk seems to have been a bad man and a bad minister, it will not be rash in us to think, that he was guilty, and that many of these articles could have been proved against him. The court was alarmed at the prosecution of a favourite minister, who lay under such a load of popular prejudices; and an expedient was fallen upon to save him from present ruin. The king

[s] Cotton, p. 643.   [t] Cotton, p. 643.

summoned all the lords, spiritual and temporal, to his apartment:
The prisoner was produced before them, and asked what he could
say in his own defence: He denied the charge; but submitted to the
king's mercy: Henry expressed himself not satisfied with regard to
the first impeachment for treason; but in consideration of the
second for misdemeanors, he declared, that, by virtue of Suffolk's
own submission, not by any judicial authority, he banished him the
kingdom during five years. The lords remained silent; but as soon *His ban-*
as they returned to their own house, they entered a protest, that *ishment,*
this sentence should nowise infringe their privileges, and that, if
Suffolk had insisted upon his right, and had not voluntarily submitted to the king's commands, he was intitled to a trial by his peers
in parliament.

It was easy to see, that these irregular proceedings were meant
to favour Suffolk, and that, as he still possessed the queen's confidence, he would, on the first favourable opportunity, be restored
to his country, and be re-instated in his former power and credit.
A captain of a vessel was therefore employed by his enemies to
intercept him in his passage to France: He was seized near Dover;
his head struck off on the side of a long boat; and his body thrown *and*
into the sea.[u] No enquiry was made after the actors and accom- *death.*
plices in this atrocious deed of violence.

The duke of Somerset succeeded to Suffolk's power in the
ministry, and credit with the queen; and as he was the person,
under whose government the French provinces had been lost, the
public, who always judge by the event, soon made him equally the
object of their animosity and hatred. The duke of York was absent
in Ireland during all these transactions; and however it might be
suspected, that his partizans had excited and supported the prosecution against Suffolk, no immediate ground of complaint could,
on that account, lie against him. But there happened soon after an
incident, which roused the jealousy of the court, and discovered to
them the extreme danger, to which they were exposed, from the
pretensions of that popular prince.

The humours of the people, set afloat by the parliamentary
impeachment, and by the fall of so great a favourite as Suffolk,

[u] Hall, fol. 158. Hist. Croyland, contin. p. 525. Stowe, p. 388. Grafton, p.
610.

broke out in various commotions, which were soon suppressed; but there arose one in Kent, which was attended with more dangerous consequences. A man of low condition, one John Cade, a native of Ireland, who had been obliged to fly into France for crimes, observed, on his return to England, the discontents of the people; and he laid on them the foundation of projects, which were at first crowned with surprising success. He took the name of John Mortimer; intending, as is supposed, to pass himself for a son of that Sir John Mortimer, who had been sentenced to death by parliament, and executed, in the beginning of this reign, without any trial or evidence, merely upon an indictment of high treason, given in against him.[w] On the first mention of that popular name, the common people of Kent, to the number of 20,000, flocked to Cade's standard; and he excited their zeal by publishing complaints against the numerous abuses in government, and demanding a redress of grievances. The court, not yet fully sensible of the danger, sent a small force against the rioters, under the command of Sir Humphry Stafford, who was defeated and slain in an action near Sevenoke;[x] and Cade, advancing with his followers towards London, encamped on Black-heath. Though elated by his victory, he still maintained the appearance of moderation; and sending to the court a plausible list of grievances,[y] he promised, that, when these should be redressed, and when lord Say, the treasurer, and Cromer, sheriff of Kent, should be punished for their malversations, he would immediately lay down his arms. The council, who observed that nobody was willing to fight against men so reasonable in their pretensions, carried the king, for present safety, to Kenilworth; and the city immediately opened its gates to Cade, who maintained, during some time, great order and discipline among his followers. He always led them into the fields

---

[w] Stowe, p. 364. Cotton, p. 564. This author admires, that such a piece of injustice should have been committed in peaceable times: He might have added, and by such virtuous princes as Bedford and Glocester. But it is to be presumed, that Mortimer was guilty, though his condemnation was highly irregular and illegal. The people had at this time a very feeble sense of law and a constitution; and power was very imperfectly restrained by these limits. When the proceedings of a parliament were so irregular, it is easy to imagine, that those of a king would be more so.   [x] Hall, fol. 159. Hollingshed, p. 634.   [y] Stowe, p. 388, 389. Hollingshed, p. 633.

during the night-time; and published severe edicts against plunder and violence of every kind: But being obliged, in order to gratify their malevolence against Say and Cromer, to put these men to death without a legal trial,[z] he found, that, after the commission of this crime, he was no longer master of their riotous disposition, and that all his orders were neglected.[a] They broke into a rich house, which they plundered; and the citizens, alarmed at this act of violence, shut their gates against them, and being seconded by a detachment of soldiers, sent them by lord Scales, governor of the Tower, they repulsed the rebels with great slaughter.[b] The Kentishmen were so discouraged by the blow, that, upon receiving a general pardon from the primate, then chancellor, they retreated towards Rochester, and there dispersed. The pardon was soon after annulled, as extorted by violence: A price was set on Cade's head,[c] who was killed by one Iden, a gentleman of Sussex; and many of his followers were capitally punished for their rebellion.

It was imagined by the court, that the duke of York had secretly instigated Cade to this attempt, in order to try, by that experiment, the dispositions of the people towards his title and family:[d] And as the event had, so far, succeeded to his wish, the ruling party had greater reason than ever to apprehend the future consequences of his pretensions. At the same time, they heard that he intended to return from Ireland; and fearing that he meant to bring an armed force along with him, they issued orders, in the king's name, for opposing him, and for debarring him entrance into England.[e] But the duke refuted his enemies by coming attended with no more than his ordinary retinue: The precautions of the ministers served only to shew him their jealousy and malignity against him: He was sensible, that his title, by being dangerous to the king, was also become dangerous to himself: He now saw the impossibility of remaining in his present situation, and the necessity of proceeding forward in support of his claim. His partizans, therefore, were instructed to maintain, in all companies, his right by succession, and by the established laws and constitution of the kingdom: These questions became every day, more and more, the subject of conversation: The minds of men were insensibly sharpened

---

[z] Grafton, p. 612.   [a] Hall, fol. 160.   [b] Hist. Croyland, contin. p. 526.
[c] Rymer, vol. ix. p. 275.   [d] Cotton, p. 661. Stowe, p. 391.   [e] Stowe, p. 394.

against each other by disputes, before they came to more dangerous extremities: And various topics were pleaded in support of the
pretensions of each party.

*The par-
ties of
Lancaster
and
York.*

The partizans of the house of Lancaster maintained, that,
though the elevation of Henry IV. might at first be deemed somewhat irregular, and could not be justified by any of those principles
on which that prince chose to rest his title, it was yet founded on
general consent, was a national act, and was derived from the
voluntary approbation of a free people, who, being loosened from
their allegiance by the tyranny of the preceding government, were
moved, by gratitude, as well as by a sense of public interest, to
entrust the sceptre into the hands of their deliverer: That, even if
that establishment were allowed to be at first invalid, it had acquired solidity by time; the only principle which ultimately gives
authority to government, and removes those scruples, which the
irregular steps, attending almost all revolutions, naturally excite in
the minds of the people: That the right of succession was a rule
admitted only for general good, and for the maintenance of public
order; and could never be pleaded to the overthrow of national
tranquillity, and the subversion of regular establishments: That
the principles of liberty, no less than the maxims of internal peace,
were injured by these pretensions of the house of York; and if so
many re-iterated acts of the legislature, by which the crown was
entailed on the present family, were now invalidated, the English
must be considered, not as a free people, who could dispose of
their own government, but as a troop of slaves, who were implicitly
transmitted by succession from one master to another: That the
nation was bound to allegiance under the house of Lancaster by
moral, no less than by political duty; and were they to infringe
those numerous oaths of fealty, which they had sworn to Henry
and his predecessors, they would thenceforth be thrown loose
from all principles, and it would be found difficult ever after to fix
and restrain them: That the duke of York himself had frequently
done homage to the king as his lawful sovereign, and had thereby,
in the most solemn manner, made an indirect renunciation of
those claims, with which he now dares to disturb the tranquillity of
the public: That, even though the violation of the rights of blood,
made on the deposition of Richard, was perhaps rash and imprudent, it was too late to remedy the mischief; the danger of a dis-

CHAPTER XXI

puted succession could no longer be obviated; the people, accustomed to a government, which, in the hands of the late king, had been so glorious, and in that of his predecessor, so prudent and salutary, would still ascribe a right to it; by causing multiplied disorders, and by shedding an inundation of blood, the advantage would only be obtained, of exchanging one pretender for another; and the house of York itself, if established on the throne, would, on the first opportunity, be exposed to those revolutions, which the giddy spirit, excited in the people, gave so much reason to apprehend: And that, though the present king enjoyed not the shining talents, which had appeared in his father and grandfather, he might still have a son, who should be endowed with them; he is himself eminent for the most harmless and inoffensive manners; and if active princes were dethroned on pretence of tyranny, and indolent ones on the plea of incapacity, there would thenceforth remain in the constitution no established rule of obedience to any sovereign.

These strong topics, in favour of the house of Lancaster, were opposed by arguments no less convincing on the side of the house of York. The partizans of this latter family asserted, that the maintenance of order in the succession of princes, far from doing injury to the people, or invalidating their fundamental title to good government, was established only for the purposes of government, and served to prevent those numberless confusions, which must ensue, if no rule were followed but the uncertain and disputed views of present convenience and advantage: That the same maxims, which ensured public peace, were also salutary to national liberty; the privileges of the people could only be maintained by the observance of laws; and if no account were made of the rights of the sovereign, it could less be expected, that any regard would be paid to the property and freedom of the subject: That it was never too late to correct any pernicious precedent; an unjust establishment, the longer it stood, acquired the greater sanction and validity; it could, with more appearance of reason, be pleaded as an authority for a like injustice; and the maintenance of it, instead of favouring public tranquillity, tended to disjoint every principle, by which human society was supported: That usurpers would be happy, if their present possession of power, or their continuance for a few years, could convert them into legal princes; but nothing

would be more miserable than the people, if all restraints on violence and ambition were thus removed, and a full scope given to
the attempts of every turbulent innovator: That time indeed might
bestow solidity on a government, whose first foundations were the
most infirm; but it required both a long course of time to produce
this effect, and the total extinction of those claimants, whose title
was built on the original principles of the constitution: That the
deposition of Richard II. and the advancement of Henry IV. were
not deliberate national acts; but the result of the levity and violence
of the people, and proceeded from those very defects in human
nature, which the establishment of political society, and of an
order in succession, was calculated to prevent: That the subsequent entails of the crown were a continuance of the same violence and usurpation; they were not ratified by the legislature,
since the consent of the rightful king was still wanting; and the
acquiescence, first of the family of Mortimer, then of the family of
York, proceeded from present necessity, and implied no renunciation of their pretensions: That the restoration of the true order
of succession could not be considered as a change, which familiarized the people to revolutions; but as the correction of a former
abuse, which had itself encouraged the giddy spirit of innovation,
rebellion, and disobedience: And that, as the original title of Lancaster stood only, in the person of Henry IV. on present convenience, even this principle, unjustifiable as it was, when not
supported by laws, and warranted by the constitution, had now
entirely gone over to the other side; nor was there any comparison
between a prince utterly unable to sway the scepter, and blindly
governed by corrupt ministers, or by an imperious queen, engaged
in foreign and hostile interests; and a prince of mature years, of
approved wisdom and experience, a native of England, the lineal
heir of the crown, who, by his restoration, would replace every
thing on ancient foundations.

So many plausible arguments could be urged on both sides of
this interesting question, that the people were extremely divided in
their sentiments; and though the noblemen of greatest power and
influence seem to have espoused the party of York, the opposite
cause had the advantage of being supported by the present laws,
and by the immediate possession of royal authority. There were
also many great noblemen in the Lancastrian party, who balanced

CHAPTER XXI

the power of their antagonists, and kept the nation in suspence between them. The earl of Northumberland adhered to the present government: The earl of Westmoreland, in spite of his connexions with the duke of York, and with the family of Nevil, of which he was the head, was brought over to the same party; and the whole north of England, the most warlike part of the kingdom, was, by means of these two potent noblemen, warmly engaged in the interests of Lancaster. Edmund Beaufort, duke of Somerset, and his brother Henry, were great supports of that cause; as were also Henry Holland, duke of Exeter, Stafford, duke of Buckingham, the earl of Shrewsbury, the lords Clifford, Dudley, Scales, Audley, and other noblemen.

While the kingdom was in this situation, it might naturally be expected, that so many turbulent barons, possessed of so much independant authority, would immediately have flown to arms, and have decided the quarrel, after their usual manner, by war and battle, under the standards of the contending princes. But there still were many causes which retarded these desperate extremities, and made a long train of faction, intrigue, and cabal, precede the military operations. By the gradual progress of arts in England, as well as in other parts of Europe, the people were now become of some importance; laws were beginning to be respected by them; and it was requisite, by various pretences, previously to reconcile their minds to the overthrow of such an ancient establishment as that of the house of Lancaster, ere their concurrence could reasonably be expected. The duke of York himself, the new claimant, was of a moderate and cautious character, an enemy to violence, and disposed to trust rather to time and policy, than to sanguinary measures, for the success of his pretensions. The very imbecillity itself of Henry tended to keep the factions in suspence, and make them stand long in awe of each other: It rendered the Lancastrian party unable to strike any violent blow against their enemies; it encouraged the Yorkists to hope, that, after banishing the king's ministers, and getting possession of his person, they might gradually undermine his authority, and be able, without the perilous experiment of a civil war, to change the succession, by parliamentary and legal authority.

The dispositions, which appeared in a parliament, assembled soon after the arrival of the duke of York from Ireland, favoured

1451.
6th Nov.

these expectations of his partizans, and both discovered an un-usual boldness in the commons, and were a proof of the general discontents which prevailed against the administration. The lower house, without any previous enquiry or examination, without alleg-ing any other ground of complaint than common fame, ventured to present a petition against the duke of Somerset, the dutchess of Suffolk, the bishop of Chester, Sir John Sutton lord Dudley, and several others of inferior rank; and they prayed the king to remove them for ever from his person and councils, and to prohibit them from approaching within twelve miles of the court.[f] This was a violent attack, somewhat arbitrary, and supported but by few precedents, against the ministry; yet the king durst not openly oppose it: He replied, that, except the lords, he would banish all the others from court during a year, unless he should have occa-sion for their service in suppressing any rebellion. At the same time, he rejected a bill, which had passed both houses, for at-tainting the late duke of Suffolk, and which, in several of its clauses, discovered a very general prejudice against the mea-sures of the court.

1452.
The first armament of the duke of York.
The duke of York, trusting to these symptoms, raised an army of 10,000 men, with which he marched towards London; de-manding a reformation of the government, and the removal of the duke of Somerset from all power and authority.[g] He unexpectedly found the gates of the city shut against him; and on his retreating into Kent, he was followed by the king at the head of a superior army; in which several of Richard's friends, particularly Salisbury and Warwic, appeared; probably with a view of mediating between the parties, and of seconding, on occasion, the duke of York's pretensions. A parley ensued; Richard still insisted upon the re-moval of Somerset, and his submitting to a trial in parliament: The court pretended to comply with his demand; and that nobleman was put in arrest: The duke of York was then persuaded to pay his respects to the king in his tent; and on repeating his charge against the duke of Somerset, he was surprised to see that minister step from behind the curtain, and offer to maintain his innocence. Richard now found, that he had been betrayed; that he was in the hands of his enemies; and that it was become necessary, for his own

[f] Parliamentary History, vol. ii. p. 263.   [g] Stowe, p. 394.

safety, to lower his pretensions. No violence, however, was attempted against him: The nation was not in a disposition to bear the destruction of so popular a prince: He had many friends in Henry's camp: And his son, who was not in the power of the court, might still be able to revenge his death on all his enemies: He was therefore dismissed; and he retired to his seat of Wigmore on the borders of Wales.[h]

While the duke of York lived in this retreat, there happened an incident, which, by encreasing the public discontents, proved favourable to his pretensions. Several Gascon lords, affectionate to the English government, and disgusted at the new dominion of the French, came to London, and offered to return to their allegiance under Henry.[i] The earl of Shrewsbury, with a body of 8000 men, was sent over to support them. Bourdeaux opened its gates to him: He made himself master of Fronsac, Castillon, and some other places: Affairs began to wear a favourable aspect: But as Charles hastened to resist this dangerous invasion, the fortunes of the English were soon reversed: Shrewsbury, a venerable warrior, above fourscore years of age, fell in battle; his conquests were lost; Bourdeaux was again obliged to submit to the French king;[k] and all hopes of recovering the province of Gascony were for ever extinguished.

1453.
20th
July.

Though the English might deem themselves happy to be fairly rid of distant dominions, which were of no use to them, and which they never could defend against the growing power of France, they expressed great discontent on the occasion; and they threw all the blame on the ministry, who had not been able to effect impossibilities. While they were in this disposition, the queen's delivery of a son, who received the name of Edward, was deemed no joyful incident; and as it removed all hopes of the peaceable succession of the duke of York, who was otherwise, in the right of his father, and by the laws enacted since the accession of the house of Lancaster, next heir to the crown, it had rather a tendency to inflame the quarrel between the parties. But the duke was incapable of violent counsels: and even when no visible obstacle lay between him and the throne, he was prevented by his own scruples from

13th Oct.

1454.

[h] Grafton, p. 620.   [i] Hollingshed, p. 640.   [k] Polyd. Virg. p. 501. Grafton, p. 623.

mounting it. Henry, always unfit to exercise the government, fell at this time into a distemper, which so far encreased his natural imbecillity, that it rendered him incapable of maintaining even the appearance of royalty. The queen and the council, destitute of this support, found themselves unable to resist the York party; and they were obliged to yield to the torrent. They sent Somerset to the Tower; and appointed Richard lieutenant of the kingdom, with powers to open and hold a session of parliament.[l] That assembly also, taking into consideration the state of the kingdom, created him protector during pleasure. Men, who thus entrusted sovereign authority to one that had such evident and strong pretensions to the crown, were not surely averse to his taking immediate and full possession of it: Yet the duke, instead of pushing them to make farther concessions, appeared somewhat timid and irresolute even in receiving the power which was tendered to him. He desired, that it might be recorded in parliament, that this authority was conferred on him from their own free motion, without any application on his part: He expressed his hopes, that they would assist him in the exercise of it: He made it a condition of his acceptance, that the other lords, who were appointed to be of his council, should also accept of the trust, and should exercise it: And he required, that all the powers of his office should be specified and defined by act of parliament. This moderation of Richard was certainly very unusual and very amiable; yet was it attended with bad consequences in the present juncture, and by giving time to the animosities of faction to rise and ferment, it proved the source of all those furious wars and commotions which ensued.

The enemies of the duke of York soon found it in their power to make advantage of his excessive caution. Henry being so far recovered from his distemper, as to carry the appearance of exercising the royal power; they moved him to resume his authority, to annul the protectorship of the duke, to release Somerset from the Tower,[m] and to commit the administration into the hands of that nobleman. Richard, sensible of the dangers which might attend his former acceptance of the parliamentary commission, should he submit to the annulling of it, levied an army; but still without

1455.

[l] Rymer, vol. xi. p. 344.   [m] Rymer, vol. xi. p. 361. Hollingshed, p. 642. Grafton, p. 626.

advancing any pretensions to the crown. He complained only of the king's ministers, and demanded a reformation of the government. A battle was fought at St. Albans, in which the Yorkists were superior, and without suffering any material loss, slew about 5000 of their enemies; among whom were the duke of Somerset, the earl of Northumberland, the earl of Stafford, eldest son of the duke of Buckingham, lord Clifford, and many other persons of distinction." The king himself fell into the hands of the duke of York, who treated him with great respect and tenderness: He was only obliged (which he regarded as no hardship) to commit the whole authority of the crown into the hands of his rival.

First battle of St. Albans. 22d May.

This was the first blood spilt in that fatal quarrel, which was not finished in less than a course of thirty years, which was signalized by twelve pitched battles, which opened a scene of extraordinary fierceness and cruelty, is computed to have cost the lives of eighty princes of the blood, and almost entirely annihilated the ancient nobility of England. The strong attachments, which, at that time, men of the same kindred bore to each other, and the vindictive spirit, which was considered as a point of honour, rendered the great families implacable in their resentments, and every moment widened the breach between the parties. Yet affairs did not immediately proceed to the last extremities: The nation was kept some time in suspense: The vigour and spirit of queen Margaret, supporting her small power, still proved a balance to the great authority of Richard, which was checked by his irresolute temper. A parliament, which was soon after assembled, plainly discovered, by the contrariety of their proceedings, the contrariety of the motives by which they were actuated. They granted the Yorkists a general indemnity; and they restored the protectorship to the duke, who, in accepting it, still persevered in all his former precautions: But at the same time they renewed their oaths of fealty to Henry, and fixed the continuance of the protectorship to the majority of his son, Edward, who was vested with the usual dignities of prince of Wales, duke of Cornwal, and earl of Chester. The only decisive act, passed in this parliament, was a full resumption of all the grants which had been made since the death of Henry V. and which had reduced the crown to great poverty.

9th July.

" Stowe, p. 309. Hollingshed, p. 643.

1456.   It was not found difficult to wrest power from hands so little
tenacious as those of the duke of York. Margaret, availing herself
of that prince's absence, produced her husband before the house
of lords; and as his state of health permitted him at that time to act
his part with some tolerable decency, be declared his intentions of
resuming the government, and of putting an end to Richard's
authority. This measure, being unexpected, was not opposed by
the contrary party: The house of lords, who were many of them
disgusted with the late act of resumption, assented to Henry's
proposal: And the king was declared to be reinstated in sovereign
authority. Even the duke of York acquiesced in this irregular act of
the peers; and no disturbance ensued. But that prince's claim to
the crown was too well known, and the steps, which he had taken
to promote it, were too evident, ever to allow sincere trust and
confidence to have place between the parties. The court retired to
1457. Coventry, and invited the duke of York and the earls of Salisbury
and Warwic to attend the king's person. When they were on the
road, they received intelligence, that designs were formed against
their liberties and lives. They immediately separated themselves:
Richard withdrew to his castle of Wigmore: Salisbury to Mid-
dleham in Yorkshire: And Warwic to his government of Calais,
which had been committed to him after the battle of St. Albans,
and which, as it gave him the command of the only regular military
force maintained by England, was of the utmost importance in the
present juncture. Still, men of peaceable dispositions, and among
the rest Bourchier, archbishop of Canterbury, thought it not too
late to interpose with their good offices, in order to prevent that
effusion of blood, with which the kingdom was threatened; and the
awe, in which each party stood of the other, rendered the mediation for some time successful. It was agreed, that all the great
leaders on both sides should meet in London, and be solemnly
reconciled. The duke of York and his partizans came thither with
1458. numerous retinues, and took up their quarters near each other for
mutual security. The leaders of the Lancastrian party used the
same precaution. The mayor, at the head of 5000 men, kept a strict
watch, night and day; and was extremely vigilant in maintaining
peace between them.[o] Terms were adjusted, which removed not

[o] Fabian Chron. anno 1458. The author says that some lords brought 900
retainers, some 600, none less than 400. See also Grafton, p. 633.

CHAPTER XXI

the ground of difference. An outward reconciliation only was procured: And in order to notify this accord to the whole people, a solemn procession to St. Paul's was appointed, where the duke of York led queen Margaret, and a leader of one party marched hand in hand with a leader of the opposite. The less real cordiality prevailed, the more were the exterior demonstrations of amity redoubled. But it was evident, that a contest for a crown could not thus be peaceably accommodated; that each party watched only for an opportunity of subverting the other; and that much blood must yet be spilt, ere the nation could be restored to perfect tranquillity, or enjoy a settled and established government.

Even the smallest accident, without any formed design, was sufficient, in the present disposition of men's minds, to dissolve the seeming harmony between the parties; and had the intentions of the leaders been ever so amicable, they would have found it difficult to restrain the animosity of their followers. One of the king's retinue insulted one of the earl of Warwic's: Their companions on both sides took part in the quarrel: A fierce combat ensued: The earl apprehended his life to be aimed at: He fled to his government of Calais; and both parties, in every county of England, openly made preparations for deciding the contest by war and arms. *1459.*

The earl of Salisbury, marching to join the duke of York, was overtaken, at Blore-heath on the borders of Staffordshire, by lord Audley, who commanded much superior forces; and a small rivulet with steep banks ran between the armies. Salisbury here supplied his defect in numbers by stratogem; a refinement, of which there occur few instances in the English civil wars, where a headlong courage, more than military conduct, is commonly to be remarked. He feigned a retreat, and allured Audley to follow him with precipitation: But when the van of the royal army had passed the brook, Salisbury suddenly turned upon them; and partly by the surprize, partly by the division, of the enemies' forces, put this body to rout: The example of flight was followed by the rest of the army: And Salisbury, obtaining a complete victory, reached the general rendezvous of the Yorkists at Ludlow.[p] *Battle of Blore-heath 23d Sept.*

The earl of Warwic brought over to this rendezvous a choice body of veterans from Calais, on whom, it was thought, the fortune of the war would much depend, but this reinforcement occa-

[p] Hollingshed, p. 649. Grafton, p. 936.

sioned, in the issue, the immediate ruin of the duke of York's party. When the royal army approached, and a general action was every hour expected, Sir Andrew Trollop, who commanded the veterans, deserted to the king in the night-time; and the Yorkists were so dismayed at this instance of treachery, which made every man suspicious of his fellow, that they separated next day without striking a stroke:[q] The duke fled to Ireland: The earl of Warwic, attended by many of the other leaders, escaped to Calais; where his great popularity among all orders of men, particularly among the military, soon drew to him partizans, and rendered his power very formidable. The friends of the house of York in England kept themselves every where in readiness to rise on the first summons from their leaders.

1460.

After meeting with some successes at sea, Warwic landed in Kent, with the earl of Salisbury, and the earl of Marche, eldest son of the duke of York; and being met by the primate, by lord Cobham, and other persons of distinction, he marched, amidst the acclamations of the people, to London. The city immediately opened its gates to him; and his troops encreasing on every day's march, he soon found himself in a condition to face the royal army, which hastened from Coventry to attack him. The battle was fought at Northampton; and was soon decided against the royalists by the infidelity of lord Grey of Ruthin, who, commanding Henry's van, deserted to the enemy during the heat of action, and spread a consternation through the troops. The duke of Buckingham, the earl of Shrewsbury, the lords Beaumont and Egremont, and Sir William Lucie were killed in the action or pursuit: The slaughter fell chiefly on the gentry and nobility; the common people were spared by orders of the earls of Warwic, and Marche.[r] Henry himself, that empty shadow of a king, was again taken prisoner; and as the innocence and simplicity of his manners, which bore the appearance of sanctity, had procured him the tender regard of the people,[s] the earl of Warwic and the other leaders took care to distinguish themselves by their respectful demeanour towards him.

Battle of North-ampton. 10th July.

A parlia-ment. 7th Oct.

A parliament was summoned in the king's name, and met at Westminster; where the duke soon after appeared from Ireland.

[q] Hollingshed, p. 650. Grafton, p. 537.   [r] Stowe, p. 409.   [s] Hall, fol. 169. Grafton, p. 195.

CHAPTER XXI

This prince had never hitherto advanced openly any claim to the crown: He had only complained of ill ministers, and demanded a redress of grievances: And even in the present crisis, when the parliament was surrounded by his victorious army, he showed such a regard to law and liberty, as is unusual during the prevalence of a party in any civil dissentions; and was still less to be expected, in those violent and licentious times. He advanced towards the throne; and being met by the archbishop of Canterbury, who asked him, whether he had yet paid his respects to the king? he replied, that he knew of none to whom he owed that title. He then stood near the throne,[t] and addressing himself to the house of peers, he gave them a deduction of his title by descent; mentioned the cruelties by which the house of Lancaster had paved their way to sovereign power, insisted on the calamities which had attended the government of Henry, exhorted them to return into the right path, by doing justice to the lineal successor, and thus pleaded his cause before them as his natural and legal judges.[u] This cool and moderate manner of demanding a crown, intimidated his friends and encouraged his enemies: The lords remained in suspence;[w] and no one ventured to utter a word on the occasion. Richard, who had probably expected, that the peers would have invited him to place himself on the throne, was much disappointed at their silence; but desiring them to reflect on what he had proposed to them, he departed the house. The peers took the matter into consideration, with as much tranquillity as if it had been a common subject of debate: They desired the assistance of some considerable members among the commons in their deliberations: They heard, in several successive days, the reasons alleged for the duke of York: They even ventured to propose objections to his claim, founded on former entails of the crown, and on the oaths of fealty sworn to the house of Lancaster:[x] They also observed, that, as Richard had all along borne the arms of York, not those of Clarence, he could not claim as successor to the latter family: And after receiving answers to these objections, derived from the violence and power, by which the house of Lancaster supported their present possession of the crown, they proceeded to give a decision. Their sentence was calculated, as far as possible, to please both

[t] Hollingshed, p. 655.   [u] Cotton, p. 665. Grafton, p. 643.   [w] Hollingshed, p. 657. Grafton, p. 645.   [x] Cotton, p. 666.

parties: They declared the title of the duke of York to be certain and indefeasible; but in consideration that Henry had enjoyed the crown, without dispute or controversy, during the course of thirty-eight years, they determined, that he should continue to possess the title and dignity during the remainder of his life; that the administration of the government, meanwhile, should remain with Richard; that he should be acknowledged the true and lawful heir of the monarchy; that every one should swear to maintain his succession, and it should be treason to attempt his life; and that all former settlements of the crown, in this and the two last reigns, should be abrogated and rescinded.[y] The duke acquiesced in this decision: Henry himself, being a prisoner, could not oppose it: Even if he had enjoyed his liberty, he would not probably have felt any violent reluctance against it: And the act thus passed with the unanimous consent of the whole legislative body. Though the mildness of this compromise is chiefly to be ascribed to the moderation of the duke of York, it is impossible not to observe in those transactions visible marks of a higher regard to law, and of a more fixed authority, enjoyed by parliament, than has appeared in any former period of English history.

It is probable, that the duke, without employing either menaces or violence, could have obtained from the commons a settlement more consistent and uniform: But as many, if not all the members of the upper house, had received grants, concessions, or dignities, during the last sixty years, when the house of Lancaster was possessed of the government, they were afraid of invalidating their own titles by too sudden and violent an overthrow of that family; and in thus temporizing between the parties, they fixed the throne on a basis, upon which it could not possibly stand. The duke, apprehending his chief danger to arise from the genius and spirit of queen Margaret, sought a pretence for banishing her the kingdom: He sent her, in the king's name, a summons to come immediately to London; intending, in case of her disobedience, to proceed to extremities against her. But the queen needed not this menace to excite her activity in defending the rights of her family. After the defeat at Northampton, she had fled with her infant son to Durham, thence to Scotland; but soon returning, she applied to

[y] Cotton, p. 666. Grafton, p. 647.

the northern barons, and employed every motive to procure their assistance. Her affability, insinuation, and address, qualities in which she excelled; her caresses, her promises wrought a powerful effect on every one who approached her: The admiration of her great qualities was succeeded by compassion towards her helpless condition: The nobility of that quarter, who regarded themselves as the most warlike in the kingdom, were moved by indignation to find the southern barons pretend to dispose of the crown and settle the government: And that they might allure the people to their standard, they promised them the spoils of all the provinces on the other side of the Trent. By these means, the queen had collected an army twenty thousand strong, with a celerity which was neither expected by her friends, nor apprehended by her enemies.

The duke of York, informed of her appearance in the north, hastened thither with a body of 5000 men, to suppress, as he imagined, the beginnings of an insurrection; when, on his arrival at Wakefield, he found himself so much outnumbered by the enemy. He threw himself into Sandal castle, which was situated in the neighbourhood; and he was advised by the earl of Salisbury, and other prudent counsellors, to remain in that fortress, till his son, the earl of Marche, who was levying forces in the borders of Wales, could advance to his assistance.[z] But the duke, though deficient in political courage, possessed personal bravery in an eminent degree; and notwithstanding his wisdom and experience, he thought, that he should be for ever disgraced, if, by taking shelter behind walls, he should for a moment resign the victory to a woman. He descended into the plain, and offered battle to the enemy, which was instantly accepted. The great inequality of numbers was sufficient alone to decide the victory; but the queen, by sending a detachment, who fell on the back of the duke's army, rendered her advantage still more certain and undisputed. The duke himself was killed in the action; and as his body was found among the slain, the head was cut off by Margaret's orders, and fixed on the gates of York, with a paper crown upon it, in derision of his pretended title. His son, the earl of Rutland, a youth of seventeen, was brought to lord Clifford; and that barbarian, in

Battle of Wakefield. 24th Dec.

Death of the duke of York.

[z] Stowe, p. 412.

revenge of his father's death, who had perished in the battle of St. Albans, murdered, in cool blood, and with his own hands, this innocent prince, whose exterior figure, as well as other accomplishments, are represented by historians as extremely amiable. The earl of Salisbury was wounded and taken prisoner, and immediately beheaded, with several other persons of distinction, by martial law at Pomfret.[a] There fell near three thousand Yorkists in this battle: The duke himself was greatly and justly lamented by his own party; a prince who merited a better fate, and whose errors in conduct proceeded entirely from such qualities, as render him the more an object of esteem and affection. He perished in the fiftieth year of his age, and left three sons, Edward, George, and Richard, with three daughters, Anne, Elizabeth, and Margaret.

1461.

The queen, after this important victory, divided her army. She sent the smaller division under Jasper Tudor, earl of Pembroke, half brother to the king, against Edward, the new duke of York. She herself marched with the larger division towards London, where the earl of Warwic had been left with the command of the

Battle of Mortimer's Cross.

Yorkists. Pembroke was defeated by Edward at Mortimer's Cross in Herefordshire, with the loss of near 4000 men: His army was dispersed; he himself escaped by flight; but his father, Sir Owen Tudor, was taken prisoner, and immediately beheaded by Edward's orders. This barbarous practice, being once begun, was continued by both parties, from a spirit of revenge, which covered itself under the pretence of retaliation.[b]

Margaret compensated this defeat by a victory which she obtained over the earl of Warwic. That nobleman, on the approach of the Lancastrians, led out his army, re-inforced by a strong body of the Londoners, who were affectionate to his cause; and he gave

Second battle of St. Albans

battle to the queen at St. Albans. While the armies were warmly engaged, Lovelace, who commanded a considerable body of the Yorkists, withdrew from the combat; and this treacherous conduct, of which there are many instances in those civil wars, decided the victory in favour of the queen. About 2300 of the vanquished perished in the battle and pursuit; and the person of the king fell again into the hands of his own party. This weak prince was sure to be almost equally a prisoner whichever faction had the keeping

[a] Polyd. Virg. p. 510. [b] Hollingshed, p. 660. Grafton, p. 650.

CHAPTER XXI

of him; and scarce any more decorum was observed by one than by the other, in their method of treating him. Lord Bonville, to whose care he had been entrusted by the Yorkists, remained with him after the defeat, on assurances of pardon given him by Henry: But Margaret, regardless of her husband's promise, immediately ordered the head of that nobleman to be struck off by the executioner.[c] Sir Thomas Kiriel, a brave warrior, who had signalized himself in the French wars, was treated in the same manner.

The queen made no great advantage of this victory: Young Edward advanced upon her from the other side; and collecting the remains of Warwic's army, was soon in a condition of giving her battle with superior forces. She was sensible of her danger, while she lay between the enemy and the city of London; and she found it necessary to retreat with her army to the north.[d] Edward entered the capital amidst the acclamations of the citizens, and immediately opened a new scene to his party. This prince, in the bloom of youth, remarkable for the beauty of his person, for his bravery, his activity, his affability, and every popular quality, found himself so much possessed of public favour, that, elated with the spirit natural to his age, he resolved no longer to confine himself within those narrow limits, which his father had prescribed to himself, and which had been found by experience so prejudicial to his cause. He determined to assume the name and dignity of king; to insist openly on his claim; and thenceforth to treat the opposite party as traitors and rebels to his lawful authority. But as a national consent, or the appearance of it, still seemed, notwithstanding his plausible title, requisite to precede this bold measure, and as the assembling of a parliament might occasion too many delays, and be attended with other inconveniences, he ventured to proceed in a less regular manner, and to put it out of the power of his enemies to throw obstacles in the way of his elevation. His army was ordered to assemble in St. John's Fields; great numbers of people surrounded them; an harangue was pronounced to this mixed multitude, setting forth the title of Edward, and inveighing against the tyranny and usurpation of the rival family; and the people were then asked, whether they would have Henry of Lancaster for king? They unanimously exclaimed against the proposal. It was

[c] Hollingshed, p. 660.   [d] Grafton, p. 652.

Edward IV. assumes the crown.

then demanded, whether they would accept of Edward, eldest son of the late duke of York? They expressed their assent by loud and joyful acclamations.[e] A great number of bishops, lords, magistrates, and other persons of distinction were next assembled at Baynard's castle, who ratified the popular election; and the new king was on the subsequent day proclaimed in London, by the title of Edward IV.[f]

5th March.

In this manner ended the reign of Henry VI. a monarch, who, while in his cradle, had been proclaimed king both of France and England, and who began his life with the most splendid prospects that any prince in Europe had ever enjoyed. The revolution was unhappy for his people, as it was the source of civil wars; but was almost entirely indifferent to Henry himself, who was utterly incapable of exercising his authority, and who, provided he personally met with good usage, was equally easy, as he was equally enslaved, in the hands of his enemies and of his friends. His weakness and his disputed title were the chief causes of the public calamities: But whether his queen, and his ministers, were not also guilty of some great abuses of power, it is not easy for us at this distance of time to determine: There remain no proofs on record of any considerable violation of the laws, except in the assassination of the duke of Glocester, which was a private crime, formed no precedent, and was but too much of a piece with the usual ferocity and cruelty of the times.

Miscellaneous transactions of this reign.

The most remarkable law, which passed in this reign, was that for the due election of members of parliament in counties. After the fall of the feudal system, the distinction of tenures was in some measure lost; and every freeholder, as well those who held of mesne lords, as the immediate tenants of the crown, were by degrees admitted to give their votes at elections. This innovation (for such it may probably be esteemed) was indirectly confirmed by a law of Henry IV.;[g] which gave right to such a multitude of electors, as was the occasion of great disorder. In the eighth and tenth of this king, therefore, laws were enacted, limiting the electors to such as possessed forty shillings a-year in land, free from all burdens within the county.[h] This sum was equivalent to near twenty

[e] Stowe, p. 415. Hollingshed, p. 661.   [f] Grafton, p. 653.   [g] Statutes at large, 7 Henry IV. cap. 15.   [h] Ibid. 8 Henry VI. cap. 7. 10 Henry VI. cap. 2.

CHAPTER XXI

pounds a-year of our present money; and it were to be wished, that the spirit, as well as letter of this law, had been maintained.

The preamble of the statute is remarkable: "Whereas the elections of knights have of late, in many counties of England, been made by outrages and excessive numbers of people, many of them of small substance and value, yet pretending to a right equal to the best knights and esquires; whereby manslaughters, riots, batteries, and divisions among the gentlemen and other people of the same counties, shall very likely rise and be, unless due remedy be provided in this behalf, &c." We may learn from these expressions what an important matter the election of a member of parliament was now become in England: That assembly was beginning in this period to assume great authority: The commons had it much in their power to enforce the execution of the laws; and if they failed of success in this particular, it proceeded less from any exorbitant power of the crown, than from the licentious spirit of the aristocracy, and perhaps from the rude education of the age, and their own ignorance of the advantages resulting from a regular administration of justice.

When the duke of York, the earls of Salisbury and Warwic, fled the kingdom upon the desertion of their troops, a parliament was summoned at Coventry in 1460, by which they were all attainted. This parliament seems to have been very irregularly constituted, and scarcely deserves the name: Insomuch, that an act passed in it, "that all such knights of any county, as were returned by virtue of the king's letters, without any other election, should be valid, and that no sheriff should, for returning them, incur the penalty of the statute of Henry IV."[i] All the acts of that parliament were afterwards reversed; "because it was unlawfully summoned, and the knights and barons not duly chosen."[k]

The parliaments in this reign, instead of relaxing their vigilance against the usurpations of the court of Rome, endeavoured to enforce the former statutes enacted for that purpose. The commons petitioned, that no foreigner should be capable of any church preferment, and that the patron might be allowed to present anew upon the nonresidence of any incumbent:[l] But the king eluded these petitions. Pope Martin wrote him a severe letter

---

[i] Cotton, p. 664.   [k] Statutes at large, 39 Henry VI. cap. I.   [l] Cotton, p. 585.

against the statute of provisors; which he calls an abominable law,
that would infallibly damn every one who observed it.[m] The cardinal of Winchester was legate; and as he was also a kind of prime
minister, and immensely rich from the profits of his clerical dignities, the parliament became jealous lest he should extend the papal
power; and they protested, that the cardinal should absent himself
in all affairs and councils of the king, whenever the pope or see of
Rome was touched upon.[n]

Permission was given by parliament to export corn when it was
at low prices; wheat at six shillings and eight pence a quarter,
money of that age; barely at three shillings and four pence.[o] It
appears from these prices, that corn still remained at near half its
present value; though other commodities were much cheaper.
The inland commerce of corn was also opened in the eighteenth
of the king, by allowing any collector of the customs to grant a
licence for carrying it from one county to another.[p] The same year
a kind of navigation act was proposed with regard to all places
within the Streights; but the king rejected it.[q]

The first instance of debt contracted upon parliamentary security occurs in this reign.[r] The commencement of this pernicious
practice deserves to be noted; a practice, the more likely to become
pernicious, the more a nation advances in opulence and credit.
The ruinous effects of it are now become apparent, and threaten
the very existence of the nation.

[m] Burnet's Collection of Records, vol. i. p. 99. [n] Cotton, p. 593.
[o] Statutes at large, 15 Henry VI. cap. 2. 23 Henry VI. cap. 6. [p] Cotton,
p. 625. [q] Ibid. p. 626. [r] Ibid. p. 593, 614, 638.

XXII

EDWARD IV

---

*Battle of Touton – Henry escapes into
Scotland – A parliament – Battle of Hexham –
Henry taken prisoner, and confined to the Tower
– King's marriage with the Lady Elizabeth
Gray – Warwic disgusted – Alliance with
Burgundy – Insurrection in Yorkshire – Battle
of Banbury – Warwic and Clarence banished –
Warwic and Clarence return – Edward IV.
expelled – Henry VI. restored – Edward IV.
returns – Battle of Barnet, and death of
Warwic – Battle of Teukesbury, and murder of
prince Edward – Death of Henry VI. – Invasion
of France – Peace of Pecquigni – Trial and
execution of the duke of Clarence – Death
and character of Edward IV*

YOUNG EDWARD, now in his twentieth year, was of a temper well fitted to make his way through such a scene of war, havoc, and devastation, as must conduct him to the full possession of that crown, which he claimed from hereditary right, but which he had assumed from the tumultuary election alone of his own party. He was bold, active, enterprising; and his hardness of heart and sever-

1461.

ity of character rendered him impregnable to all those movements of compassion, which might relax his vigour in the prosecution of the most bloody revenges upon his enemies. The very commencement of his reign gave symptoms of his sanguinary disposition. A tradesman of London, who kept shop at the sign of the Crown, having said, that he would make his son heir to the Crown; this harmless pleasantry was interpreted to be spoken in derision of Edward's assumed title; and he was condemned and executed for the offence.[s] Such an act of tyranny was a proper prelude to the events which ensued. The scaffold, as well as the field, incessantly streamed with the noblest blood of England, spilt in the quarrel between the two contending families, whose animosity was now become implacable. The people, divided in their affections, took different symbols of party: The partizans of the house of Lancaster chose the red rose as their mark of distinction; those of York were denominated from the white; and these civil wars were thus known, over Europe, by the name of the quarrel between the two roses.

The licence, in which queen Margaret had been obliged to indulge her troops, infused great terror and aversion into the city of London and all the southern parts of the kingdom; and as she there expected an obstinate resistance, she had prudently retired northwards among her own partizans. The same licence, joined to the zeal of faction, soon brought great multitudes to her standard; and she was able, in a few days, to assemble an army sixty thousand strong in Yorkshire. The king and the earl of Warwic hastened, with an army of forty thousand men, to check her progress; and when they reached Pomfret, they dispatched a body of troops, under the command of lord Fitzwalter, to secure the passage of Ferrybridge over the river Are, which lay between them and the enemy. Fitzwalter took possession of the post assigned him; but was not able to maintain it against lord Clifford, who attacked him with superior numbers. The Yorkists were chased back with great slaughter; and lord Fitzwalter himself was slain in the action.[t] The earl of Warwic, dreading the consequences of this disaster, at a time when a decisive action was every hour expected, immediately

---

[s] Habington in Kennet, p. 431. Grafton, p. 791.   [t] W. Wyrcester, p. 489. Hall, fol. 186. Holingshed, p. 664.

CHAPTER XXII

ordered his horse to be brought him, which he stabbed before the whole army; and kissing the hilt of his sword, swore, that he was determined to share the fate of the meanest soldier.[u] And to shew the greater security, a proclamation was at the same time issued, giving to every one full liberty to retire; but menacing the severest punishment to those who should discover any symptoms of cowardice in the ensuing battle.[w] Lord Falconberg was sent to recover the post which had been lost: He passed the river some miles above Ferrybridge, and falling unexpectedly on lord Clifford, revenged the former disaster by the defeat of the party and the death of their leader.[x]

The hostile armies met at Touton; and a fierce and bloody battle ensued. While the Yorkists were advancing to the charge, there happened a great fall of snow, which, driving full in the faces of their enemies, blinded them; and this advantage was improved by a stratagem of lord Falconberg's. That nobleman ordered some infantry to advance before the line, and, after having sent a volley of flight-arrows, as they were called, amidst the enemy, immediately to retire. The Lancastrians, imagining that they were gotten within reach of the opposite army, discharged all their arrows, which thus fell short of the Yorkists.[y] After the quivers of the enemy were emptied, Edward advanced his line, and did execution with impunity on the dismayed Lancastrians: The bow however was soon laid aside, and the sword decided the combat, which ended in a total victory on the side of the Yorkists. Edward issued orders to give no quarter.[z] The routed army was pursued to Tadcaster with great bloodshed and confusion; and above thirty-six thousand men are computed to have fallen in the battle and pursuit:[a] Among these were the earl of Westmoreland, and his brother, Sir John Nevil, the earl of Northumberland, the lords Dacres and Welles, and Sir Andrew Trollop.[b] The earl of Devonshire, who was not engaged in Henry's party, was brought a prisoner to Edward; and was soon after beheaded by martial law at York. His head was fixed on a pole erected over a gate of that city; and the head of duke Richard and that of the earl of Salisbury were

Battle of Touton. 29th of March.

---

[u] Habington, p. 432.   [w] Hollingshed, p. 664.   [x] Hist. Croyl. contin. p. 532.   [y] Hall, fol. 186.   [z] Habington, p. 432.   [a] Holingshed, p. 665. Grafton, p. 656. Hist. Croyl. cont. p. 533.   [b] Hall, fol. 187. Habington, p. 433.

taken down, and buried with their bodies. Henry and Margaret had remained at York during the action; but learning the defeat of their army, and being sensible, that no place in England could now afford them shelter, they fled with great precipitation into Scotland. They were accompanied by the duke of Exeter, who, though he had married Edward's sister, had taken part with the Lancastrians, and by Henry duke of Somerset, who had commanded in the unfortunate battle of Touton, and who was the son of that nobleman killed in the first battle of St. Albans.

Henry escapes into Scotland. Notwithstanding the great animosity which prevailed between the kingdoms, Scotland had never exerted itself with vigour, to take advantage, either of the wars which England carried on with France, or of the civil commotions which arose between the contending families. James I. more laudably employed, in civilizing his subjects, and taming them to the salutary yoke of law and justice, avoided all hostilities with foreign nations; and though he seemed interested to maintain a balance between France and England, he gave no farther assistance to the former kingdom in its greatest distresses, than permitting, and perhaps encouraging, his subjects to enlist in the French service. After the murder of that excellent prince, the minority of his son and successor, James II. and the distractions incident to it, retained the Scots in the same state of neutrality; and the superiority, visibly acquired by France, rendered it then unnecessary for her ally to interpose in her defence. But when the quarrel commenced between the houses of York and Lancaster, and became absolutely incurable but by the total extinction of one party; James, who had now risen to man's estate, was tempted to seize the opportunity, and he endeavoured to recover those places, which the English had formerly conquered from his ancestors. He laid siege to the castle of Roxborough in 1460, and had provided himself with a small train of artillery for that enterprize: But his cannon were so ill framed, that one of them burst as he was firing it, and put an end to his life in the flower of his age. His son and successor, James III. was also a minor on his accession: The usual distractions ensued in the government: The queen-dowager, Anne of Gueldres, aspired to the regency: The family of Douglas opposed her pretensions: And queen Margaret, when she fled into Scotland, found there a people little less divided by faction, than those by whom she had been

CHAPTER XXII

expelled. Though she pleaded the connexions between the royal family of Scotland and the house of Lancaster, by the young king's grandmother, a daughter of the earl of Somerset; she could engage the Scottish council to go no farther than to express their good wishes in her favour: But on her offer to deliver to them immediately the important fortress of Berwic, and to contract her son in marriage with a sister of king James, she found a better reception; and the Scots promised the assistance of their arms to re-instate her family upon the throne.[c] But as the danger from that quarter seemed not very urgent to Edward, he did not pursue the fugitive king and queen into their retreat; but returned to London, where a parliament was summoned for settling the government.

On the meeting of this assembly, Edward found the good effects of his vigorous measure in assuming the crown, as well as of his victory at Touton, by which he had secured it: The parliament no longer hesitated between the two families, or proposed any of those ambiguous decisions, which could only serve to perpetuate and inflame the animosities of party. They recognized the title of Edward, by hereditary descent, through the family of Mortimer; and declared, that he was king by right, from the death of his father, who had also the same lawful title; and that he was in possession of the crown from the day that he assumed the government, tendered to him by the acclamations of the people.[d] They expressed their abhorrence of the usurpation and intrusion of the house of Lancaster, particularly that of the earl of Derby, otherwise called Henry IV. which, they said, had been attended with every kind of disorder, the murder of the sovereign and the oppression of the subject. They annulled every grant which had passed in those reigns; they reinstated the king in all the possessions, which had belonged to the crown at the pretended deposition of Richard II. and though they confirmed judicial deeds and the decrees of inferior courts, they reversed all attainders passed in any pretended parliament; particularly the attainder of the earl of Cambridge, the king's grandfather; as well as that of the earls of Salisbury and Glocester and of lord Lumley, who had been forfeited for adhering to Richard II.[e]

4th Nov. A parliament.

---

[c] Hall, fol. 137. Habington, p. 434.　　[d] Cotton, p. 670.　　[e] Cotton, p. 672. Statutes at large, 1 Edw. IV. cap. I.

Many of these votes were the result of the usual violence of party: The common sense of mankind, in more peaceable times, repealed them: And the statutes of the house of Lancaster, being the deeds of an established government, and enacted by princes long possessed of authority, have always been held as valid and obligatory. The parliment, however, in subverting such deep foundations, had still the pretence of replacing the government on its ancient and natural basis: But in their subsequent measures, they were more guided by revenge, at least by the views of convenience, than by the maxims of equity and justice. They passed an act of forfeiture and attainder against Henry VI. and queen Margaret, and their infant son, prince Edward: The same act was extended to the dukes of Somerset and Exeter; to the earls of Northumberland, Devonshire, Pembroke, Wilts; to the viscount Beaumont, the lords Roos, Nevil, Clifford, Welles, Dacre, Gray of Rugemont, Hungerford; to Alexander Hedie, Nicholas Latimer, Edmond Mountfort, John Heron, and many other persons of distinction.[f] The parliament vested the estates of all these attainted persons in the crown; though their sole crime was the adhering to a prince, whom every individual of the parliament had long recognized, and whom that very king himself, who was now seated on the throne, had acknowledged and obeyed as his lawful sovereign.

The necessity of supporting the government established will more fully justify some other acts of violence; though the method of conducting them may still appear exceptionable. John earl of Oxford and his son, Aubrey de Vere, were detected in a correspondence with Margaret, were tried by martial law before the constable, were condemned and executed.[g] Sir William Tyrrel, Sir Thomas Tudenham, and John Montgomery were convicted in the same arbitrary court; were executed, and their estates forfeited. This introduction of martial law into civil government was a high strain of prerogative; which, were it not for the violence of the times, would probably have appeared exceptionable to a nation so jealous of their liberties as the English were now become.[h] It was impossible but such a great and sudden revolution must leave the

---

[f] Cotton, p. 670. W. Wyrcester, p. 490.   [g] W. de Wyrcester p. 492. Hall, fol. 189. Grafton, p. 658 Fabian, fol. 215. Fragm. ad finem T. Sproti.
[h] See note [Q] at the end of the volume.

CHAPTER XXII

roots of discontent and dissatisfaction in the subject, which would require great art, or in lieu of it, great violence to extirpate them. The latter was more suitable to the genius of the nation in that uncultivated age.

But the new establishment still seemed precarious and uncertain; not only from the domestic discontents of the people, but from the efforts of foreign powers. Lewis, the eleventh of the name, had succeeded to his father, Charles, in 1460; and was led, from the obvious motives of national interest, to feed the flames of civil discord among such dangerous neighbours, by giving support to the weaker party. But the intriguing and politic genius of this prince was here checked by itself: Having attempted to subdue the independant spirit of his own vassals, he had excited such an opposition at home, as prevented him from making all the advantage, which the opportunity afforded, of the dissensions among the English. He sent however a small body to Henry's assistance under Varenne, Seneschal of Normandy;[i] who landed in Northumberland, and got possession of the castle of Alnewic: But as the indefatigable Margaret went in person to France where she solicited larger supplies; and promised Lewis to deliver up Calais, if her family should by his means be restored to the throne of England; he was induced to send along with her a body of 2000 men at arms, which enabled her to take the field, and to make an inroad into England. Though reinforced by a numerous train of adventurers from Scotland, and by many partizans of the family of Lancaster; she received a check at Hedgley-more from lord Montacute or Montague, brother to the earl of Warwic, and warden of the east Marches between Scotland and England. Montague was so encouraged with this success, that, while a numerous reinforcement was on their march to join him by orders from Edward, he yet ventured, with his own troops alone, to attack the Lancastrians at Hexham; and he obtained a complete victory over them. The duke of Somerset, and lords Roos, and Hungerford, were taken in the pursuit, and immediately beheaded by martial law at Hexham. Summary justice was in like manner executed at Newcastle on Sir Humphrey Nevil, and several other gentlemen. All those who were spared in the field, suffered on the scaffold; and the utter

1462.

1464.

25th April.

Battle of Hexham.
15th May.

---

[i] Monstrelet, vol. iii. p. 95.

extermination of their adversaries was now become the plain object of the York party; a conduct, which received but too plausible an apology from the preceding practice of the Lancastrians.

The fate of the unfortunate royal family, after this defeat, was singular. Margaret, flying with her son into a forest, where she endeavoured to conceal herself, was beset, during the darkness of the night, by robbers, who, either ignorant or regardless of her quality, despoiled her of her rings and jewels, and treated her with the utmost indignity. The partition of this rich booty raised a quarrel among them; and while their attention was thus engaged, she took the opportunity of making her escape with her son into the thickest of the forest, where she wandered for some time, over-spent with hunger and fatigue, and sunk with terror and affliction. While in this wretched condition, she saw a robber approach with his naked sword; and finding that she had no means of escape, she suddenly embraced the resolution of trusting entirely for protection to his faith and generosity. She advanced towards him; and presenting to him the young prince, called out to him, *Here, my friend, I commit to your care the safety of your king's son.* The man, whose humanity and generous spirit had been obscured, not entirely lost, by his vicious course of life, was struck with the singularity of the event, was charmed with the confidence reposed in him; and vowed, not only to abstain from all injury against the princess, but to devote himself entirely to her service.[k] By his means she dwelt some time concealed in the forest, and was at last conducted to the sea-coast, whence she made her escape into Flanders. She passed thence into her father's court, where she lived several years in privacy and retirement. Her husband was not so fortunate or so dexterous in finding the means of escape. Some of his friends took him under their protection, and conveyed him into Lancashire; where he remained concealed during a twelve-month; but he was at last detected, delivered up to Edward, and thrown into the Tower.[l] The safety of his person was owing less to the generosity of his enemies, than to the contempt which they had entertained of his courage and his understanding.

The imprisonment of Henry, the expulsion of Margaret, the execution and confiscation of all the most eminent Lancastrians,

[k] Monstrelet, vol. iii. p. 96.   [l] Hall, fol. 191. Fragm. ad finem Sproti.

CHAPTER XXII

seemed to give full security to Edward's government; whose title by blood, being now recognized by parliament, and universally submitted to by the people, was no longer in danger of being impeached by any antagonist. In this prosperous situation, the king delivered himself up, without controul, to those pleasures which his youth, his high fortune, and his natural temper invited him to enjoy; and the cares of royalty were less attended to, than the dissipation of amusement, or the allurements of passion. The cruel and unrelenting spirit of Edward, though enured to the ferocity of civil wars, was at the same time extremely devoted to the softer passions, which, without mitigating his severe temper, maintained a great influence over him, and shared his attachment with the pursuits of ambition, and the thirst of military glory. During the present interval of peace, he lived in the most familiar and sociable manner with his subjects,[m] particularly with the Londoners; and the beauty of his person, as well as the gallantry of his address, which, even unassisted by his royal dignity, would have rendered him acceptable to the fair, facilitated all his applications for their favour. This easy and pleasurable course of life augmented every day his popularity among all ranks of men: He was the peculiar favourite of the young and gay of both sexes. The disposition of the English, little addicted to jealousy, kept them from taking umbrage at these liberties: And his indulgence in amusements, while it gratified his inclination, was thus become, without design, a means of supporting and securing his government. But as it is difficult to confine the ruling passion within strict rules of prudence, the amorous temper of Edward led him into a snare, which proved fatal to his repose, and to the stability of his throne.

Jaqueline of Luxembourg, dutchess of Bedford, had, after her husband's death, so far sacrificed her ambition to love, that she espoused, in second marriage, Sir Richard Woodeville, a private gentleman, to whom she bore several children; and among the rest, Elizabeth, who was remarkable for the grace and beauty of her person, as well as for other amiable accomplishments. This young lady had married Sir John Gray of Groby, by whom she had children; and her husband being slain in the second battle of St. Albans, fighting on the side of Lancaster, and his estate being for

King's marriage with the lady Elizabeth Gray.

[m] Polyd. Virg. p. 513. Biondi.

that reason confiscated, his widow retired to live with her father, at his seat of Grafton in Northamptonshire. The king came accidentally to the house after a hunting party, in order to pay a visit to the dutchess of Bedford; and as the occasion seemed favourable for obtaining some grace from this gallant monarch, the young widow flung herself at his feet, and with many tears, entreated him to take pity on her impoverished and distressed children. The sight of so much beauty in affliction strongly affected the amorous Edward; love stole insensibly into his heart under the guise of compassion; and her sorrow, so becoming a virtuous matron, made his esteem and regard quickly correspond to his affection. He raised her from the ground with assurances of favour; he found his passion encrease every moment, by the conversation of the amiable object; and he was soon reduced in his turn to the posture and stile of a supplicant at the feet of Elizabeth. But the lady, either averse to dishonourable love from a sense of duty, or perceiving that the impression, which she had made, was so deep as to give her hopes of obtaining the highest elevation, obstinately refused to gratify his passion; and all the endearments, caresses, and importunities of the young and amiable Edward, proved fruitless against her rigid and inflexible virtue. His passion, irritated by opposition, and encreased by his veneration for such honourable sentiments, carried him at last beyond all bounds of reason; and he offered to share his throne, as well as his heart, with the woman, whose beauty of person, and dignity of character seemed so well to entitle her to both. The marriage was privately celebrated at Grafton:[n] The secret was carefully kept for some time: No one suspected, that so libertine a prince could sacrifice so much to a romantic passion: And there were in particular strong reasons, which at that time rendered this step, to the highest degree, dangerous and imprudent.

The king, desirous to secure his throne, as well by the prospect of issue, as by foreign alliances, had, a little before, determined to make application to some neighbouring princes; and he had cast his eye on Bona of Savoy, sister to the queen of France, who, he hoped, would, by her marriage, ensure him the friendship of that power, which was alone both able and inclined to give support and

[n] Hall, fol. 193. Fabian, fol. 216.

assistance to his rival. To render the negociation more successful, the earl of Warwic had been dispatched to Paris, where the princess then resided; he had demanded Bona in marriage for the king; his proposals had been accepted; the treaty was fully concluded; and nothing remained but the ratification of the terms agreed on, and the bringing over the princess to England.[o] But when the secret of Edward's marriage broke out, the haughty earl, deeming himself affronted, both by being employed in this fruitless negociation, and by being kept a stranger to the king's intentions, who had owed every thing to his friendship, immediately returned to England, inflamed with rage and indignation. The influence of passion over so young a man as Edward, might have served as an excuse for his imprudent conduct, had he deigned to acknowledge his error, or had pleaded his weakness as an apology: But his faulty shame or pride prevented him from so much as mentioning the matter to Warwic; and that nobleman was allowed to depart the court, full of the same ill-humour and discontent, which he brought to it.

Warwic disgusted.

Every incident now tended to widen the breach between the king and this powerful subject. The queen, who lost not her influence by marriage, was equally solicitous to draw every grace and favour to her own friends and kindred, and to exclude those of the earl, whom she regarded as her mortal enemy. Her father was created earl of Rivers: He was made treasurer in the room of lord Mountjoy:[p] He was invested in the office of constable for life; and his son received the survivance of that high dignity.[q] The same young nobleman was married to the only daughter of lord Scales, enjoyed the great estate of that family, and had the title of Scales conferred upon him. Catherine, the queen's sister, was married to the young duke of Buckingham, who was a ward of the crown:[r] Mary, another of her sisters, espoused William Herbert, created earl of Huntingdon: Anne, a third sister, was given in marriage to the son and heir of Grey, lord Ruthyn, created earl of Kent.[s] The daughter and heir of the duke of Exeter, who was also the king's niece, was contracted to Sir Thomas Gray, one of the queen's sons

1466.

[o] Hall, fol. 193. Habington, p. 437. Holingshed, p. 667. Grafton, p. 665. Polyd. Virg. p. 513. [p] W. Wyrcester, p. 506. [q] Rymer, vol. xi. p. 581. [r] W. Wyrcester, p. 505. [s] Ibid. p. 506.

by her former husband; and as lord Montague was treating of a marriage between his son and this lady, the preference given to young Gray was deemed an injury and affront to the whole family of Nevil.

The earl of Warwic could not suffer with patience the least diminution of that credit, which he had long enjoyed, and which, he thought, he had merited by such important services. Though he had received so many grants from the crown, that the revenue arising from them amounted, besides his patrimonial estate, to 80,000 crowns a-year, according to the computation of Philip de Comines;[t] his ambitious spirit was still dissatisfied, so long as he saw others surpass him in authority and influence with the king.[u] Edward also, jealous of that power which had supported him, and which he himself had contributed still higher to exalt, was well pleased to raise up rivals in credit to the earl of Warwic; and he justified, by this political view, his extreme partiality to the queen's kindred. But the nobility of England, envying the sudden growth of the Woodevilles,[w] were more inclined to take part with Warwic's discontent, to whose grandeur they were already accustomed, and who had reconciled them to his superiority by his gracious and popular manners. And as Edward obtained from parliament a general resumption of all grants, which he had made since his accession, and which had extremely impoverished the crown;[x] this act, though it passed with some exceptions, particularly one in favour of the earl of Warwic, gave a general alarm to the nobility, and disgusted many, even zealous, partizans of the family of York.

But the most considerable associate, that Warwic acquired to his party, was George, duke of Clarence, the king's second brother. This prince deemed himself no less injured than the other grandees, by the uncontrouled influence of the queen and her relations; and as his fortunes were still left on a precarious footing, while theirs were fully established, this neglect, joined to his unquiet and restless spirit, inclined him to give countenance to all the malcontents.[y] The favourable opportunity of gaining him was espied by the earl of Warwic, who offered him in marriage his elder daughter, and co-heir of his immense fortunes; a settlement

---

[t] Liv. 3. chap. 4.   [u] Polyd. Virg. p. 514.   [w] Hist. Croyl. cont. p. 539.
[x] W. Wyrcester, p. 508.   [y] Grafton, p. 673.

which, as it was superior to any that the king himself could confer upon him, immediately attached him to the party of the earl.[z] Thus an extensive and dangerous combination was insensibly formed against Edward and his ministry. Though the immediate object of the malcontents was not to overturn the throne, it was difficult to foresee the extremities, to which they might be carried: And as opposition to government was usually in those ages prosecuted by force of arms, civil convulsions and disorders were likely to be soon the result of these intrigues and confederacies.

While this cloud was gathering at home, Edward carried his views abroad, and endeavoured to secure himself against his factious nobility, by entering into foreign alliances. The dark and dangerous ambition of Louis XI. the more it was known, the greater alarm it excited among his neighbours and vassals; and as it was supported by great abilities, and unrestrained by any principle of faith or humanity, they found no security to themselves but by a jealous combination against him. Philip, duke of Burgundy, was now dead: His rich and extensive dominions were devolved to Charles, his only son, whose martial disposition acquired him the surname of *Bold,* and whose ambition, more outrageous than that of Lewis, but seconded by less power and policy, was regarded with a more favourable eye by the other potentates of Europe. The opposition of interests, and still more, a natural antipathy of character, produced a declared animosity between these bad princes; and Edward was thus secure of the sincere attachment of either of them, for whom he should chuse to declare himself. The duke of Burgundy, being descended by his mother, a daughter of Portugal, from John of Gaunt, was naturally inclined to favour the house of Lancaster:[a] But this consideration was easily overbalanced by political motives; and Charles, perceiving the interests of that house to be extremely decayed in England, sent over his natural brother, commonly called the bastard of Burgundy, to carry in his name proposals of marriage to Margaret, the king's sister. The alliance of Burgundy was more popular among the English than that of France; the commercial interests of the two nations invited the princes to a close union; their common jealousy

Alliance with the duke of Burgundy.

---

[z] W. Wyrcester, p. 511. Hall, fol. 200. Habington, p. 439. Hollingshed, p. 671. Polyd. Virg. p. 515.   [a] Comines, liv. 3. chap. 4, 6.

1468. of Lewis was a natural cement between them; and Edward, pleased with strengthening himself by so potent a confederate, soon concluded the alliance, and bestowed his sister upon Charles.[b] A league, which Edward at the same time concluded with the duke of Britanny, seemed both to encrease his security, and to open to him the prospect of rivalling his predecessors in those foreign conquests, which, however short-lived and unprofitable, had rendered their reigns so popular and illustrious.[c]

1469. But whatever ambitious schemes the king might have built on these alliances, they were soon frustrated by intestine commotions, which engrossed all his attention. These disorders probably arose not immediately from the intrigues of the earl of Warwic, but from accident, aided by the turbulent spirit of the age, by the general humour of discontent which that popular nobleman had instilled into the nation, and perhaps by some remains of attachment to the *Insurrection in
Yorkshire.* house of Lancaster. The hospital of St. Leonard's near York had received, from an ancient grant of king Athelstane, a right of levying a thrave of corn upon every plough-land in the county; and as these charitable establishments are liable to abuse, the country people complained, that the revenue of the hospital was no longer expended for the relief of the poor, but was secreted by the managers, and employed to their private purposes. After long repining at the contribution, they refused payment: Ecclesiastical and civil censures were issued against them: Their goods were distrained, and their persons thrown into jail: Till, as their ill-humour daily encreased, they rose in arms; fell upon the officers of the hospital, whom they put to the sword; and proceeded in a body, fifteen thousand strong, to the gates of York. Lord Montague, who commanded in those parts, opposed himself to their progress; and having been so fortunate in a skirmish as to seize Robert Hulderne their leader, he ordered him immediately to be led to execution; according to the practice of the times. The rebels, however, still continued in arms; and being soon headed by men of greater distinction, Sir Henry Nevil, son of lord Latimer, and Sir John Coniers, they advanced southwards, and began to appear formidable to government. Herbert, earl of Pembroke, who had received that title on the forfeiture of Jasper Tudor, was ordered

[b] Hall, fol. 169, 197. [c] W. Wyrcester, p. 5. Parliament. Hist. vol. ii. p. 332.

by Edward to march against them at the head of a body of Welsh-men; and he was joined by five thousand archers under the com-mand of Stafford, earl of Devonshire, who had succeeded in that title to the family of Courtney, which had also been attainted. But a trivial difference about quarters having begotten an animosity between these two noblemen, the earl of Devonshire retired with his archers, and left Pembroke alone to encounter the rebels. The two armies approached each other near Banbury; and Pembroke, having prevailed in a skirmish, and having taken Sir Henry Nevil prisoner, ordered him immediately to be put to death, without any form of process. This execution enraged, without terrifying, the rebels: They attacked the Welsh army, routed them, put them to the sword without mercy; and having seized Pembroke, they took immediate revenge upon him for the death of their leader. The king, imputing the misfortune to the earl of Devonshire, who had deserted Pembroke, ordered him to be executed in a like summary manner. But these speedy executions, or rather open murders, did not stop there: The northern rebels, sending a party to Grafton, seized the earl of Rivers and his son John; men who had become obnoxious by their near relation to the king and his partiality towards them; And they were immediately executed by orders from Sir John Coniers.[d]

Battle of Banbury.

26th July.

There is no part of English history since the Conquest, so ob-scure, so uncertain, so little authentic or consistent, as that of the wars between the two Roses: Historians differ about many material circumstances; some events of the utmost consequence, in which they almost all agree, are incredible and contradicted by records;[e] and it is remarkable, that this profound darkness falls upon us just on the eve of the restoration of letters, and when the art of Printing was already known in Europe. All we can distinguish with certainty through the deep cloud, which covers that period, is a scene of horror and bloodshed, savage manners, arbitrary executions, and treacherous, dishonourable conduct in all parties. There is no possibility, for instance, of accounting for the views and intentions of the earl of Warwic at this time. It is agreed, that he resided, together with his son-in-law, the duke of Clarence, in his govern-ment of Calais, during the commencement of this rebellion; and

[d] Fabian, fol. 217.   [e] See note [R] at the end of the volume.

that his brother Montague acted with vigour against the northern rebels. We may thence presume, that the insurrection had not proceeded from the secret counsels and instigation of Warwic; though the murder, committed by the rebels, on the earl of Rivers, his capital enemy, forms, on the other hand, a violent presumption against him. He and Clarence came over to England, offered their service to Edward, were received without any suspicion, were entrusted by him in the highest commands,[f] and still persevered in their fidelity. Soon after, we find the rebels quieted and dispersed by a general pardon granted by Edward from the advice of the earl of Warwic: But why so courageous a prince, if secure of Warwic's fidelity, should have granted a general pardon to men, who had been guilty of such violent and personal outrages against him, is not intelligible; nor why that nobleman, if unfaithful, should have endeavoured to appease a rebellion, of which he was able to make such advantages. But it appears, that, after this insurrection, there was an interval of peace, during which the king loaded the family of Nevil with honours and favours of the highest nature: He made lord Montague a Marquess, by the same name: He created his son, George, duke of Bedford:[g] He publicly declared his intention of marrying that young nobleman to his eldest daughter, Elizabeth, who, as he had yet no sons, was presumptive heir of the crown: Yet we find, that, soon after, being invited to a feast by the archbishop of York, a younger brother of Warwic and Montague, he entertained a sudden suspicion, that they intended to seize his person or to murder him: And he abruptly left the entertainment.[h]

1470.

Soon after, there broke out another rebellion, which is as unaccountable as all the preceding events; chiefly because no sufficient reason is assigned for it, and because, so far as appears, the family of Nevil had no hand in exciting and fomenting it. It arose in Lincolnshire, and was headed by Sir Robert Welles, son to the lord of that name. The army of the rebels amounted to 30,000 men; but lord Welles himself, far from giving countenance to them, fled into a sanctuary, in order to secure his person against the king's anger or suspicions. He was allured from this retreat by a promise of safety; and was soon after, notwithstanding this assur-

[f] Rymer, vol. xi. p. 647, 649, 650.   [g] Cotton, p. 702.   [h] Fragm. Ed. IV. ad. fin. Sprotti.

CHAPTER XXII

ance, beheaded, along with Sir Thomas Dymoc, by orders from *13th*
Edward.[i] The king fought a battle with the rebels, defeated them, *March.*
took Sir Robert Welles and Sir Thomas Launde prisoners, and
ordered them immediately to be beheaded.

Edward, during these transactions, had entertained so little
jealousy of the earl of Warwic or duke of Clarence, that he sent
them with commissions of array to levy forces against the rebels:[k]
But these malcontents, as soon as they left the court, raised troops
in their own name, issued declarations against the government,
and complained of grievances, oppressions, and bad ministers.
The unexpected defeat of Welles disconcerted all their measures;
and they retired northwards into Lancashire, where they expected
to be joined by lord Stanley, who had married the earl of Warwic's
sister. But as that nobleman refused all concurrence with them, *Warwic*
and as lord Montague also remained quiet in Yorkshire; they were *and*
Clarence
obliged to disband their army, and to fly into Devonshire, where *banished.*
they embarked and made sail towards Calais.[l]

The deputy-governor, whom Warwic had left at Calais, was one
Vaucler, a Gascon, who seeing the earl return in this miserable
condition, refused him admittance; and would not so much as
permit the dutchess of Clarence to land; though, a few days before,
she had been delivered on ship-board of a son, and was at that time
extremely disordered by sickness. With difficulty, he would allow
a few flaggons of wine to be carried to the ship for the use of the
ladies: But as he was a man of sagacity, and well acquainted with
the revolutions to which England was subject, he secretly apologized to Warwic for this appearance of infidelity, and represented
it as proceeding entirely from zeal for his service. He said, that the
fortress was ill supplied with provisions; that he could not depend
on the attachment of the garrison; that the inhabitants, who lived
by the English commerce, would certainly declare for the established government; that the place was at present unable to resist
the power of England on the one hand, and that of the duke of

[i] Hall, fol. 204. Fabrian, fol. 218. Habington, p. 442. Hollingshed, p. 674.
[k] Rymer, vol. xi. p. 652. [l] The king offered by proclamation a reward of
1000 pounds, or 100 pounds a year in land, to any that would seize them.
Whence we may learn that land was at that time sold for about ten years
purchase. See Rymer, vol. xi. p. 654.

Burgundy on the other; and that, by seeming to declare for Edward, he would acquire the confidence of that prince, and still keep it in his power, when it should become safe and prudent, to restore Calais to its ancient master.[m] It is uncertain, whether Warwic was satisfied with this apology, or suspected a double infidelity in Vaucler; but he feigned to be entirely convinced by him; and having seized some Flemish vessels, which he found lying off Calais, he immediately made sail towards France.

The king of France, uneasy at the close conjunction between Edward and the duke of Burgundy, received with the greatest demonstrations of regard the unfortunate Warwic,[n] with whom he had formerly maintained a secret correspondence, and whom he hoped still to make his instrument, in overturning the government of England, and re-establishing the house of Lancaster. No animosity was ever greater than that which had long prevailed between that house and the earl of Warwic. His father had been executed by orders from Margaret: He himself had twice reduced Henry to captivity, had banished the queen, had put to death all their most zealous partizans either in the field or on the scaffold, and had occasioned innumerable ills to that unhappy family. For this reason, believing that such inveterate rancour could never admit of any cordial reconciliation, he had not mentioned Henry's name, when he took arms against Edward; and he rather endeavoured to prevail by means of his own adherents, than revive a party, which he sincerely hated. But his present distresses and the entreaties of Lewis, made him hearken to terms of accommodation; and Margaret being sent for from Angers, where she then resided, an agreement was from common interest soon concluded between them. It was stipulated, that Warwic should espouse the cause of Henry, and endeavour to restore him to liberty and to re-establish him on the throne; that the administration of the government, during the minority of young Edward, Henry's son, should be entrusted conjointly to the earl of Warwic and the duke of Clarence; that prince Edward should marry the lady Anne, second daughter of that nobleman; and that the crown, in case of the failure of male issue in that prince, should descend to the duke of Clarence, to the entire exclusion of king Edward and his poster-

[m] Comines, liv. 3. cap. 4. Hall, fol. 205.   [n] Polyd. Virg. p. 519.

CHAPTER XXII

ity. Never was confederacy, on all sides, less natural or more evidently the work of necessity: But Warwic hoped, that all former passions of the Lancastrians might be lost in present political views; and that at worst, the independant power of his family, and the affections of the people, would suffice to give him security, and enable him to exact the full performance of all the conditions agreed on. The marriage of prince Edward with the lady Anne was immediately celebrated in France.

Edward foresaw, that it would be easy to dissolve an alliance, composed of such discordant parts. For this purpose, he sent over a lady of great sagacity and address, who belonged to the train of the dutchess of Clarence, and who, under colour of attending her mistress, was empowered to negociate with the duke, and to renew the connexions of that prince with his own family.[o] She represented to Clarence, that he had unwarily, to his own ruin, become the instrument of Warwic's vengeance, and had thrown himself entirely in the power of his most inveterate enemies; that the mortal injuries, which the one royal family had suffered from the other, were now past all forgiveness; and no imaginary union of interests could ever suffice to obliterate them; that even if the leaders were willing to forget past offences, the animosity of their adherents would prevent a sincere coalition of parties, and would, in spite of all temporary and verbal agreements, preserve an eternal opposition of measures between them; and that a prince, who deserted his own kindred, and joined the murderers of his father, left himself single, without friends, without protection, and would not, when misfortunes inevitably fell upon him, be so much as entitled to any pity or regard from the rest of mankind. Clarence was only one and twenty years of age, and seems to have possessed but a slender capacity; yet could he easily see the force of these reasons; and upon the promise of forgiveness from his brother, he secretly engaged, on a favourable opportunity, to desert the earl of Warwic, and abandon the Lancastrian party.

During this negociation, Warwic was secretly carrying on a correspondence of the same nature with his brother, the marquess of Montague, who was entirely trusted by Edward; and like motives produced a like resolution in that nobleman. The marquess

[o] Comines, liv. 3. chap. 5. Hall, fol. 207. Hollingshed, p. 675.

also, that he might render the projected blow the more deadly and incurable, resolved, on his side, to watch a favourable opportunity for committing *his* perfidy, and still to maintain the appearance of being a zealous adherent to the house of York.

After these mutual snares were thus carefully laid, the decision of the quarrel advanced apace. Lewis prepared a fleet to escort the earl of Warwic, and granted him a supply of men and money.[p] The duke of Burgundy, on the other hand, enraged at that nobleman for his seizure of the Flemish vessels before Calais, and anxious to support the reigning family in England, with whom his own interests were now connected, fitted out a larger fleet, with which he guarded the Channel; and he incessantly warned his brother-in-law of the imminent perils, to which he was exposed. But Edward, though always brave and often active, had little foresight or penetration. He was not sensible of his danger: He made no suitable preparations against the earl of Warwic:[q] He even said, that the duke might spare himself the trouble of guarding the seas, and that he wished for nothing more than to see Warwic set foot on English ground.[r] A vain confidence in his own prowess, joined to the immoderate love of pleasure, had made him incapable of all sound reason and reflection.

September.
Warwic
and
Clarence
return.

The event soon happened, of which Edward seemed so desirous. A storm dispersed the Flemish navy, and left the sea open to Warwic.[s] That nobleman seized the opportunity, and setting sail, quickly landed at Dartmouth, with the duke of Clarence, the earls of Oxford and Pembroke, and a small body of troops; while the king was in the north, engaged in suppressing an insurrection, which had been raised by lord Fitz-Hugh, brother-in-law to Warwic. The scene, which ensues, resembles more the fiction of a poem or romance than an event in true history. The prodigious popularity of Warwic,[t] the zeal of the Lancastrian party, the spirit of discontent with which many were infected; and the general instability of the English nation, occasioned by the late frequent revolutions, drew such multitudes to his standard, that, in a very few days, his army amounted to sixty thousand men; and was

[p] Comines, liv. 3. chap. 4. Hall, fol. 207.   [q] Grafton, p. 687.   [r] Comines, liv. 3. chap. 5. Hall, fol. 208.   [s] Comines, liv. 3. chap. 5.   [t] Hall, fol. 205.

CHAPTER XXII

continually encreasing. Edward hastened southwards to encounter him; and the two armies approached each other near Nottingham, where a decisive action was every hour expected. The rapidity of Warwic's progress had incapacitated the duke of Clarence from executing *his* plan of treachery; and the marquess of Montague had here the opportunity of striking the first blow. He communicated the design to his adherents, who promised him their concurrence: They took to arms in the night-time, and hastened with loud acclamations to Edward's quarters: The king was alarmed at the noise, and starting from bed, heard the cry of war, usually employed by the Lancastrian party. Lord Hastings, his chamberlain, informed him of the danger, and urged him to make his escape by speedy flight from an army, where he had so many concealed enemies, and where few seemed zealously attached to his service. He had just time to get on horseback, and to hurry with a small retinue to Lynne in Norfolk, where he luckily found some ships ready, on board of which he instantly embarked.[u] And after this manner, the earl of Warwic, in no longer space than eleven days after his first landing, was left entire master of the kingdom.

Edward IV. expelled.

But Edward's danger did not end with his embarkation. The Easterlings or Hanse-Towns were then at war both with France and England; and some ships of these people, hovering on the English coast, espied the king's vessels, and gave chace to them; nor was it without extreme difficulty that he made his escape into the port of Alcmaer in Holland. He had fled from England with such precipitation, that he had carried nothing of value along with him; and the only reward, which he could bestow on the captain of the vessel that brought him over, was a robe lined with sables; promising him an ample recompence, if fortune should ever become more propitious to him.[w]

It is not likely, that Edward could be very fond of presenting himself in this lamentable plight before the duke of Burgundy; and that having so suddenly, after his mighty vaunts, lost all footing in his own kingdom, he could be insensible to the ridicule which must attend him in the eyes of that prince. The duke, on his part, was no less embarrassed how he should receive the dethroned monarch. As he had ever borne a greater affection to the house of

[u] Comines, liv. 3. chap. 5. Hall, fol. 208.   [w] Comines, liv. 3. chap. 5.

Lancaster than to that of York, nothing but political views had engaged him to contract an alliance with the latter; and he foresaw, that probably the revolution in England would now turn this alliance against him, and render the reigning family his implacable and jealous enemy. For this reason, when the first rumour of that event reached him, attended with the circumstance of Edward's death, he seemed rather pleased with the catastrophe; and it was no agreeable disappointment to find, that he must either undergo the burthen of supporting an exiled prince, or the dishonour of abandoning so near a relation. He began already to say, that his connexions were with the kingdom of England, not with the king; and it was indifferent to him, whether the name of Edward or that of Henry were employed in the articles of treaty. These sentiments were continually strengthened by the subsequent events. Vaucler, the deputy governor of Calais, though he had been confirmed in his command by Edward, and had even received a pension from the duke of Burgundy on account of his fidelity to the crown, no sooner saw his old master, Warwic, reinstated in authority, than he declared for him, and with great demonstrations of zeal and attachment, put the whole garrison in his livery. And the intelligence, which the duke received every day from England, seemed to promise an entire and full settlement in the family of Lancaster.

Henry VI. restored. Immediately after Edward's flight had left the kingdom at Warwic's disposal, that nobleman hastened to London; and taking Henry from his confinement in the Tower, into which he himself had been the chief cause of throwing him, he proclaimed him king with great solemnity. A parliament was summoned, in the name of that prince, to meet at Westminster; and as this assembly could pretend to no liberty, while surrounded by such enraged and insolent victors, governed by such an impetuous spirit as Warwic, their votes were entirely dictated by the ruling faction. The treaty with Margaret was here fully executed: Henry was recognized as lawful king; but his incapacity for government being avowed, the regency was entrusted to Warwic and Clarence till the majority of prince Edward; and in default of that prince's issue, Clarence was declared successor to the crown. The usual business also of reversals went on without opposition: Every statute, made during the reign of Edward, was repealed; that prince was declared to be an usurper; he and his adherents were attainted; and in particular,

CHAPTER XXII

Richard duke of Glocester, his younger brother: All the attainders of the Lancastrians, the dukes of Somerset and Exeter, the earls of Richmond, Pembroke, Oxford, and Ormond, were reversed; and every one was restored, who had lost either honours or fortune, by his former adherence to the cause of Henry.

The ruling party were more sparing in their executions, than was usual after any revolution during those violent times. The only victim of distinction was John Tibetot, earl of Worcester. This accomplished person, born in an age and nation where the nobility valued themselves on ignorance as their privilege, and left learning to monks and schoolmasters, for whom indeed the spurious erudition, that prevailed, was best fitted, had been struck with the first rays of true science, which began to penetrate from the south, and had been zealous, by his exhortation and example, to propagate the love of letters among his unpolished countrymen. It is pretended, that knowledge had not produced, on this nobleman himself, the effect which so naturally attends it, of humanizing the temper, and softening the heart;[x] and that he had enraged the Lancastrians against him, by the severities which he exercised upon them, during the prevalence of his own party. He endeavoured to conceal himself after the flight of Edward; but was caught on the top of a tree in the forest of Weybridge, was conducted to London, tried before the earl of Oxford, condemned and executed. All the other considerable Yorkists either fled beyond sea, or took shelter in sanctuaries; where the ecclesiastical privileges afforded them protection. In London alone, it is computed, that no less than 2000 persons saved themselves in this manner;[y] and among the rest, Edward's queen, who was there delivered of a son, called by his father's name.[z]

Queen Margaret, the other rival queen, had not yet appeared in England, but on receiving intelligence of Warwic's success, was preparing with prince Edward for her journey. All the banished Lancastrians flocked to her; and among the rest, the duke of Somerset, son of the duke beheaded after the battle of Hexham. This nobleman, who had long been regarded as the head of the party, had fled into the Low Countries on the discomfiture of his friends;

---

[x] Hall, fol. 210. Stowe, p. 422.　[y] Comines, liv. 3. chap. 7.　[z] Hall, fol. 210. Stowe, p. 423. Holingshed, p. 677. Grafton, p. 690.

and as he concealed his name and quality, he had there languished in extreme indigence. Philip de Comines tells us,[a] that he himself saw him, as well as the duke of Exeter, in a condition no better than that of a common beggar; till being discovered by Philip duke of Burgundy, they had small pensions allotted them, and were living in silence and obscurity, when the success of their party called them from their retreat. But both Somerset and Margaret were detained by contrary winds from reaching England,[b] till a new revolution in that kingdom, no less sudden and surprising than the former, threw them into greater misery than that from which they had just emerged.

Though the duke of Burgundy, by neglecting Edward, and paying court to the established government, had endeavoured to conciliate the friendship of the Lancastrians, he found that he had not succeeded to his wish; and the connexions between the king of France and the earl of Warwic, still held him in great anxiety.[c] This nobleman, too hastily regarding Charles as a determined enemy, had sent over to Calais a body of 4000 men, who made inroads into the Low Countries;[d] and the duke of Burgundy saw himself in danger of being overwhelmed by the united arms of England and of France. He resolved therefore to grant some assistance to his brother-in-law; but in such a covert manner, as should give the least offence possible to the English government. He equipped four large vessels, in the name of some private merchants, at Terveer in Zealand; and causing fourteen ships to be secretly hired from the Easterlings, he delivered this small squadron to Edward, who, receiving also a sum of money from the duke, immediately set sail for England. No sooner was Charles informed of his departure, than he issued a proclamation inhibiting all his subjects from giving him countenance or assistance;[e] an artifice which could not deceive the earl of Warwic, but which might serve as a decent pretence, if that nobleman were so disposed, for maintaining friendship with the duke of Burgundy.

1471.

Edward, impatient to take revenge on his enemies, and to recover his lost authority, made an attempt to land with his forces, which exceeded not 2000 men, on the coast of Norfolk; but being

[a] Liv. 3. chap. 4.   [b] Grafton, p. 692. Polyd. Virg. p. 522.   [c] Hall, fol. 205.
[d] Comines, liv. 1. chap. 6.   [e] Comines, liv. 3. chap. 6.

CHAPTER XXII

there repulsed, he sailed northwards, and disembarked at Ravenspur in Yorkshire. Finding, that the new magistrates, who had
been appointed by the earl of Warwic, kept the people every where
from joining him, he pretended, and even made oath, that he came
not to challenge the crown, but only the inheritance of the house
of York, which of right belonged to him, and that he did not intend
to disturb the peace of the kingdom. His partizans every moment
flocked to his standard: He was admitted into the city of York: And
he was soon in such a situation, as gave him hopes of succeeding
in all his claims and pretensions. The marquis of Montague commanded in the northern counties; but from some mysterious reasons, which, as well as many other important transactions in that
age, no historian has cleared up, he totally neglected the beginnings of an insurrection, which he ought to have esteemed so
formidable. Warwic assembled an army at Leicester, with an intention of meeting and of giving battle to the enemy; but Edward,
by taking another road, passed him unmolested, and presented
himself before the gates of London. Had he here been refused
admittance, he was totally undone: But there were many reasons,
which inclined the citizens to favour him. His numerous friends,
issuing from their sanctuaries, were active in his cause; many rich
merchants, who had formerly lent him money, saw no other
chance for their payment but his restoration; the city-dames, who
had been liberal of their favours to him, and who still retained an
affection for this young and gallante prince, swayed their husbands and friends in his favour;[f] and above all, the archbishop of
York, Warwic's brother, to whom the care of the city was committed, had secretly, from unknown reasons, entered into a correspondence with him; and he facilitated Edward's admission into
London. The most likely cause, which can be assigned for those
multiplied infidelities, even in the family of Nevil itself, is the spirit
of faction, which, when it becomes inveterate, it is very difficult for
any man entirely to shake off. These persons, who had long distinguished themselves in the York party, were unable to act with
zeal and cordiality for the support of the Lancastrians; and they
were inclined, by any prospect of favour or accommodation offered them by Edward, to return to their ancient connexions.

25th
March.
Edward
IV. re-
turns.

11th
April.

[f] Comines, liv. 3. chap. 7.

However this may be, Edward's entrance into London, made him master not only of that rich and powerful city, but also of the person of Henry, who, destined to be the perpetual sport of fortune, thus fell again into the hands of his enemies.[g]

It appears not, that Warwic, during his short administration, which had continued only six months, had been guilty of any unpopular act, or had anywise deserved to lose that general favour, with which he had so lately overwhelmed Edward. But this prince, who was formerly on the defensive, was now the aggressor; and having overcome the difficulties, which always attend the beginnings of an insurrection, possessed many advantages above his enemy: His partizans were actuated by that zeal and courage, which the notion of an attack inspires; his opponents were intimidated for a like reason; every one, who had been disappointed in the hopes, which he had entertained from Warwic's elevation, either became a cool friend, or an open enemy to that nobleman; and each malcontent, from whatever cause, proved an accession to Edward's army. The king, therefore, found himself in a condition to face the earl of Warwic; who, being reinforced by his son-in-law, the duke of Clarence, and his brother the marquis of Montague, took post at Barnet, in the neighbourhood of London. The arrival of queen Margaret was every day expected, who would have drawn together all the genuine Lancastrians, and have brought a great accession to Warwic's forces: But this very consideration proved a motive to the earl rather to hurry on a decisive action, than to share the victory with rivals and ancient enemies, who, he foresaw, would, in case of success, claim the chief merit in the enterprize.[h] But while his jealousy was all directed towards that side, he overlooked the dangerous infidelity of friends, who lay the nearest to his bosom. His brother, Montague, who had lately temporized, seems now to have remained sincerely attached to the interests of his family: But his son-in-law, though bound to him by every tie of honour and gratitude, though he shared the power of the regency, though he had been invested by Warwic in all the honours and patrimony of the house of York, resolved to fulfil the secret engagements, which he had formerly taken with his brother, and to support the interests of his own family: He deserted to the king in

[g] Grafton, p. 702.   [h] Comines, liv. 3. chap. 7.

the night-time, and carried over a body of 12,000 men along with him.[i] Warwic was now too far advanced to retreat; and as he rejected with disdain all terms of peace offered him by Edward and Clarence, he was obliged to hazard a general engagement. The battle was fought with obstinacy on both sides: The two armies, in imitation of their leaders, displayed uncommon valour: And the victory remained long undecided between them. But an accident threw the balance to the side of the Yorkists. Edward's cognisance was a sun; that of Warwic a star with rays; and the mistiness of the morning rendering it difficult to distinguish them, the earl of Oxford, who fought on the side of the Lancastrians, was, by mistake, attacked by his friends, and chaced off the field of battle.[k] Warwic, contrary to his more usual practice, engaged that day on foot, resolving to show his army, that he meant to share every fortune with them; and he was slain in the thickest of the engagement:[l] His brother underwent the same fate: And as Edward had issued orders not to give any quarter, a great and undistinguished slaughter was made in the pursuit.[m] There fell about 1500 on the side of the victors.

14th April. Battle of Barnet, and death of Warwic.

The same day, on which this decisive battle was fought,[n] queen Margaret and her son, now about eighteen years of age, and a young prince of great hopes, landed at Weymouth, supported by a small body of French forces. When this princess received intelligence of her husband's captivity, and of the defeat and death of the earl of Warwic, her courage, which had supported her under so many disastrous events, here quite left her; and she immediately foresaw all the dismal consequences of this calamity. At first, she took sanctuary in the abbey of Beaulieu;[o] but being encouraged by the appearance of Tudor, earl of Pembroke, and Courtney, earl of Devonshire, of the lords Wenloc and St. John, with other men of rank, who exhorted her still to hope for success, she resumed her former spirit, and determined to defend to the utmost the ruins of her fallen fortunes. She advanced through the counties of Devon, Somerset, and Glocester, encreasing her army on each day's

---

[i] Grafton, p. 700. Comines, liv. 3. chap. 7. Leland's collect. vol. ii. p. 505.
[k] Habington, p. 449. [l] Comines, liv. 3. chap. 7. [m] Hall, fol. 218.
[n] Leland's Collect. vol. ii. p. 505. [o] Hall, fol. 219. Habington, p. 451.
Grafton, p. 706. Polyd. Virg. p. 528.

Battle of Teukes-bury. 4th May.

march; but was at last overtaken by the rapid and expeditious Edward, at Teukesbury, on the banks of the Severne. The Lancastrians were here totally defeated: The earl of Devonshire and lord Wenloc were killed in the field: The duke of Somerset, and about twenty other persons of distinction, having taken shelter in a church, were surrounded, dragged out, and immediately beheaded: About 3000 of their side fell in battle: And the army was entirely dispersed.

Murder of prince Edward. 21st May.

Death of Henry VI.

Queen Margaret and her son were taken prisoners, and brought to the king, who asked the prince, after an insulting manner, how he dared to invade his dominions? The young prince, more mindful of his high birth than of his present fortune, replied, that he came thither to claim his just inheritance. The ungenerous Edward, insensible to pity, struck him on the face with his gauntlet; and the dukes of Clarence and Glocester, lord Hastings and Sir Thomas Gray, taking the blow as a signal for farther violence, hurried the prince into the next apartment, and there dispatched him with their daggers.[p] Margaret was thrown into the Tower; King Henry expired in that confinement a few days after the battle of Teukesbury; but whether he died a natural or violent death is uncertain. It is pretended, and was generally believed, that the duke of Glocester killed him with his own hands:[q] But the universal odium, which that prince has incurred, inclined perhaps the nation to aggravate his crimes without any sufficient authority. It is certain, however, that Henry's death was sudden; and though he laboured under an ill state of health, this circumstance, joined to the general manners of the age, gave a natural ground of suspicion; which was rather encreased than diminished, by the exposing of his body to public view. That precaution served only to recal many similar instances in the English history, and to suggest the comparison.

All the hopes of the house of Lancaster seemed now to be utterly extinguished. Every legitimate prince of that family was dead: Almost every great leader of the party had perished in battle or on the scaffold: The earl of Pembroke, who was levying forces in Wales, disbanded his army, when he received intelligence of the

[p] Hall, fol. 221. Habington, p. 453. Hollingshed, p. 688. Polyd Virg. p. 530.
[q] Comines, Hall, fol. 223. Grafton. p. 703.

CHAPTER XXII

battle of Teukesbury; and he fled into Britanny with his nephew, the young earl of Richmond.[r] The bastard of Falconberg, who had levied some forces, and had advanced to London during Edward's absence, was repulsed; his men deserted him; he was taken prisoner and immediately executed:[s] And peace being now fully restored to the nation, a parliament was summoned, which ratified, as usual, all the acts of the victor, and recognized his legal authority.

6th Oct.

But this prince, who had been so firm, and active, and intrepid during the course of adversity, was still unable to resist the allurements of a prosperous fortune; and he wholly devoted himself, as before, to pleasure and amusement, after he became entirely master of his kingdom, and had no longer any enemy who could give him anxiety or alarm. He recovered, however, by this gay and inoffensive course of life, and by his easy, familiar manners, that popularity, which, it is natural to imagine, he had lost by the repeated cruelties exercised upon his enemies; and the example also of his jovial festivity served to abate the former acrimony of faction among his subjects, and to restore the social disposition, which had been so long interrupted between the opposite parties. All men seemed to be fully satisfied with the present government; and the memory of past calamities served only to impress the people more strongly with a sense of their allegiance, and with the resolution of never incurring any more the hazard of renewing such direful scenes.

1472.

But while the king was thus indulging himself in pleasure, he was rouzed from his lethargy by a prospect of foreign conquests, which, it is probable, his desire of popularity, more than the spirit of ambition, had made him covet. Though he deemed himself little beholden to the duke of Burgundy, for the reception which that prince had given him during his exile,[t] the political interests of their states maintained still a close connection between them; and they agreed to unite their arms in making a powerful invasion on France. A league was formed, in which Edward stipulated to pass the seas with an army, exceeding 10,000 men, and to invade the French territories: Charles promised to join him with all

1474.

[r] Habington, p. 454. Polyd. Virg. p. 531.   [s] Hollingshed, p. 689, 690, 691. Hist. Croyl. cont. p. 554.   [t] Comines, liv. 3. chap. 7.

his forces: The king was to challenge the crown of France, and to obtain at least the provinces of Normandy and Guienne: The duke was to acquire Champaigne and some other territories, and to free all his dominions from the burthen of homage to the crown of France: And neither party was to make peace without the consent of the other.[u] They were the more encouraged to hope for success from this league, as the count of St. Pol, constable of France, who was master of St. Quintin, and other towns on the Somme, had secretly promised to join them; and there were also hopes of engaging the duke of Britanny to enter into the confederacy.

The prospect of a French war was always a sure means of making the parliament open their purses, as far as the habits of that age would permit. They voted the king a tenth of rents, or two shillings in the pound; which must have been very inaccurately levied, since it produced only 31,460 pounds; and they added to this supply a whole fifteenth, and three quarters of another:[w] But as the king deemed these sums still unequal to the undertaking, he attempted to levy money by way of *benevolence*; a kind of exaction, which, except during the reigns of Henry III. and Richard II. had not much been practised in former times, and which, though the consent of the parties was pretended to be gained, could not be deemed entirely voluntary.[x] The clauses, annexed to the parliamentary grant, show sufficiently the spirit of the nation in this respect. The money levied by the fifteenth was not to be put into the king's hands, but to be kept in religious houses; and if the expedition into France should not take place, it was immediately to be refunded to the people. After these grants, the parliament was dissolved, which had sitten near two years and a half, and had undergone several prorogations; a practice not very usual at that time in England.

1475.
Invasion
of
France.

The king passed over to Calais with an army of 1500 men at arms, and 15,000 archers; attended by all the chief nobility of England, who, prognosticating future successes from the past, were eager to appear on this great theatre of honour.[y] But all their

[u] Rymer, vol. xi. p. 806, 807, 808, &c.   [w] Cotton, p. 696, 700. Hist. Croyl. cont. p. 558.   [x] Hall, fol. 226. Habington, p. 461. Grafton, p. 719. Fabian, fol. 221.   [y] Comines, liv. 4. chap. 5. This author says, (chap. II.) that the king artfully brought over some of the richest of his subjects, who, he knew, would be soon tired of the war, and would promote all proposals of peace, which, he foresaw, would be soon necessary.

sanguine hopes were damped, when they found, on entering the French territories, that neither did the constable open his gates to them, nor the duke of Burgundy bring them the smallest assistance. That prince, transported by his ardent temper, had carried all his armies to a great distance, and had employed them in wars on the frontiers of Germany, and against the duke of Lorrain: And though he came in person to Edward, and endeavoured to apologize for this breach of treaty, there was no prospect that they would be able this campaign to make a conjunction with the English. This circumstance gave great disgust to the king, and inclined him to hearken to those advances, which Lewis continually made him for an accommodation.

That monarch, more swayed by political views than by the point of honour, deemed no submissions too mean, which might free him from enemies, who had proved so formidable to his predecessors, and who, united to so many other enemies, might still shake the well-established government of France. It appears from Comines, that discipline was, at this time, very imperfect among the English; and that their civil wars, though long continued, yet, being always decided by hasty battles, had still left them ignorant of the improvements, which the military art was beginning to receive upon the continent.[z] But as Lewis was sensible, that the warlike genius of the people would soon render them excellent soldiers, he was far from despising them for their present want of experience; and he employed all his art to detach them from the alliance of Burgundy. When Edward sent him a herald to claim the crown of France, and to carry him a defiance in case of refusal: so far from answering to this bravado in like haughty terms, he replied with great temper, and even made the herald a considerable present:[a] He took afterwards an opportunity of sending a herald to the English camp; and having given him directions to apply to the lords Stanley and Howard, who, he heard, were friends to peace, he desired the good offices of these noblemen in promoting an accommodation with their master.[b] As Edward was now fallen into like dispositions, a truce was soon concluded on terms more advantageous than honourable to Lewis. He stipulated to pay Edward immediately 75,000 crowns, on condition that he should

29th Aug.

---

[z] Comines, liv. 4. chap. 5.   [a] Comines, liv. 4. chap. 5. Hall, fol. 227.
[b] Comines, liv. 4. chap. 7.

withdraw his army from France, and promised to pay him 50,000 crowns a year during their joint lives: It was added, that the dauphin, when of age, should marry Edward's eldest daughter.[c] In order to ratify this treaty, the two monarchs agreed to have a personal interview; and for that purpose, suitable preparations were made at Pecquigni near Amiens. A close rail was drawn across a bridge in that place, with no larger intervals than would allow the arm to pass; a precaution against a similar accident to that which befel the duke of Burgundy in his conference with the dauphin at Montereau. Edward and Lewis came to the opposite sides; conferred privately together; and having confirmed their friendship, and interchanged many mutual civilities, they soon after parted.[d]

Lewis was anxious not only to gain the king's friendship; but also that of the nation, and of all the considerable persons in the English court. He bestowed pensions, to the amount of 16,000 crowns a year, on several of the king's favourites; on lord Hastings two thousand crowns; on lord Howard and others in proportion; and these great ministers were not ashamed thus to receive wages from a foreign prince.[e] As the two armies, after the conclusion of the truce, remained some time in the neighbourhood of each other, the English were not only admitted freely into Amiens, where Lewis resided, but had also their charges defrayed, and had wine and victuals furnished them in every inn, without any payment's being demanded. They flocked thither in such multitudes, that once above nine thousand of them were in the town, and they might have made themselves masters of the king's person; but Lewis, concluding from their jovial and dissolute manner of living, that they had no bad intentions, was careful not to betray the least sign of fear or jealousy. And when Edward, informed of this disorder, desired him to shut the gates against them; he replied, that he would never agree to exclude the English from the place where he resided; but that Edward, if he pleased, might recal them, and place his own officers at the gates of Amiens to prevent their returning.[f]

Lewis's desire of confirming a mutual amity with England, engaged him even to make imprudent advances, which it cost him

[c] Rymer, vol. xii. p. 17. [d] Comines, liv. 4. chap. 9. [e] Hall, fol. 235.
[f] Comines, liv. 4. chap. 9. Hall, fol. 233.

CHAPTER XXII

afterwards some pains to evade. In the conference at Pecquigni, he had said to Edward, that he wished to have a visit from him at Paris; that he would there endeavour to amuse him with the ladies; and that, in case any offences were then commited, he would assign him the cardinal of Bourbon for confessor, who, from fellow-feeling, would not be over and above severe in the penances which he would enjoin. This hint made deeper impression than Lewis intended. Lord Howard, who accompanied him back to Amiens, told him, in confidence, that, if he were so disposed, it would not be impossible to persuade Edward to take a journey with him to Paris, where they might make merry together. Lewis pretended at first not to hear the offer; but on Howard's repeating it, he expressed his concern, that his wars with the duke of Burgundy would not permit him to attend his royal guest, and do him the honours he intended. "Edward," said he, privately to Comines, "is a very handsome and a very amorous prince: Some lady at Paris may like him as well as he shall do her; and may invite him to return in another manner. It is better that the sea be between us."[g]

This treaty did very little honour to either of these monarchs: It discovered the imprudence of Edward, who had taken his measures so ill with his allies, as to be obliged, after such an expensive armament, to return without making any acquisitions, adequate to them: It showed the want of dignity in Lewis, who, rather than run the hazard of a battle, agreed to subject his kingdom to a tribute, and thus acknowledge the superiority of a neighbouring prince, possessed of less power and territory than himself. But as Lewis made interest the sole test of honour, he thought that all the advantages of the treaty were on his side, and that he had overreached Edward, by sending him out of France on such easy terms. For this reason, he was very solicitous to conceal his triumph; and he strictly enjoined his courtiers never to show the English the least sign of mockery or derision. But he did not himself very carefully observe so prudent a rule: He could not forbear, one day, in the joy of his heart, throwing out some raillery on the easy simplicity of Edward and his council; when he perceived, that he was overheard by a Gascon, who had settled in England. He was immediately sensible of his indiscretion; sent a message to the gentleman; and

[g] Comines, liv. 4. chap. 10. Habington, p. 469.

offered him such advantages in his own country, as engaged him to remain in France. *It is but just,* said he, *that I pay the penalty of my talkativeness.* [h]

The most honourable part of Lewis's treaty with Edward was the stipulation for the liberty of queen Margaret, who, though after the death of her husband and son she could no longer be formidable to government, was still detained in custody by Edward. Lewis paid fifty thousand crowns for her ransom; and that princess, who had been so active on the stage of the world, and who had experienced such a variety of fortune, passed the remainder of her days in tranquillity and privacy, till the year 1482, when she died: An admirable princess, but more illustrious by her undaunted spirit in adversity, than by her moderation in prosperity. She seems neither to have enjoyed the virtues, nor been subject to the weaknesses of her sex; and was as much tainted with the ferocity, as endowed with the courage, of that barbarous age, in which she lived.

Though Edward had so little reason to be satisfied with the conduct of the duke of Burgundy, he reserved to that prince a power of acceding to the treaty of Pecquigni: But Charles, when the offer was made him, haughtily replied, that he was able to support himself without the assistance of England, and that he would make no peace with Lewis, till three months after Edward's return into his own country. This prince possessed all the ambition and courage of a conqueror; but being defective in policy and prudence, qualities no less essential, he was unfortunate in all his enterprizes; and perished at last in battle against the Swiss;[i] a people whom he despised, and who, though brave and free, had hitherto been in a manner overlooked in the general system of Europe. This event, which happened in the year 1477, produced a great alteration in the views of all the princes, and was attended with consequences which were felt for many generations. Charles left only one daughter, Mary, by his first wife; and this princess, being heir of his opulent and extensive dominions, was courted by all the potentates of Christendom, who contended for the possession of so rich a prize. Lewis, the head of her family, might, by a proper application, have obtained this match for the dauphin,

1477.

[h] Comines, liv. 3. chap. 10.   [i] Comines, liv. 5. chap. 8.

and have thereby united to the crown of France all the provinces of the Low Countries, together with Burgundy, Artois, and Picardy; which would at once have rendered his kingdom an overmatch for all its neighbours. But a man wholly interested is as rare as one entirely endowed with the opposite quality; and Lewis, though impregnable to all the sentiments of generosity and friendship, was, on this occasion, carried from the road of true policy by the passions of animosity and revenge. He had imbibed so deep a hatred to the house of Burgundy, that he rather chose to subdue the princess by arms, than unite her to his family by marriage: He conquered the dutchy of Burgundy and that part of Picardy, which had been ceded to Philip the Good by the treaty of Arras: But he thereby forced the states of the Netherlands to bestow their sovereign in marriage on Maximilian of Austria, son of the emperor Frederic, from whom they looked for protection in their present distresses: And by these means, France lost the opportunity, which she never could recal, of making that important acquisition of power and territory.

During this interesting crisis, Edward was no less defective in policy, and was no less actuated by private passions, unworthy of a sovereign and a statesman. Jealousy of his brother, Clarence, had caused him to neglect the advances which were made of marrying that prince, now a widower, to the heiress of Burgundy;[k] and he sent her proposals of espousing Anthony earl of Rivers, brother to his queen, who still retained an entire ascendant over him. But the match was rejected with disdain;[l] and Edward, resenting this treatment of his brother-in-law, permitted France to proceed without interruption in her conquests over his defenceless ally. Any pretence sufficed him for abandoning himself entirely to indolence and pleasure, which were now become his ruling passions. The only object, which divided his attention, was the improving of the public revenue, which had been dilapidated by the necessities or negligence of his predecessors; and some of his expedients for that purpose, though unknown to us, were deemed, during the time, oppressive to the people.[m] The detail of private wrongs naturally escapes the notice of history; but an act of tyranny, of which Ed-

---

[k] Polyd. Virg. Hall, fol. 240. Hollingshed, p. 703. Habington, p. 474. Grafton, p. 742. [l] Hall, fol. 240. [m] Ibid. 241. Hist. Croyl. cont. p. 559.

ward was guilty in his own family, has been taken notice of by all writers, and has met with general and deserved censure.

Trial and execution of the duke of Clarence.

The duke of Clarence, by all his services in deserting Warwic, had never been able to regain the king's friendship, which he had forfeited by his former confederacy with that nobleman. He was still regarded at court as a man of a dangerous and a fickle character; and the imprudent openness and violence of his temper, though it rendered him much less dangerous, tended extremely to multiply his enemies, and to incense them against him. Among others, he had had the misfortune to give displeasure to the queen herself, as well as to his brother, the duke of Glocester, a prince of the deepest policy, of the most unrelenting ambition, and the least scrupulous in the means which he employed for the attainment of his ends. A combination between these potent adversaries being secretly formed against Clarence, it was determined to begin by attacking his friends; in hopes, that, if he patiently endured this injury, his pusillanimity would dishonour him in the eyes of the public; if he made resistance and expressed resentment, his passion would betray him into measures, which might give them advantages against him. The king, hunting one day in the park of Thomas Burdet of Arrow, in Warwickshire, had killed a white buck, which was a great favourite of the owner; and Burdet, vexed at the loss, broke into a passion, and wished the horns of the deer in the belly of the person, who had advised the king to commit that insult upon him. This natural expression of resentment, which would have been overlooked or forgotten, had it fallen from any other person, was rendered criminal and capital in that gentleman, by the friendship in which he had the misfortune to live with the duke of Clarence: He was tried for his life; the judges and jury were found servile enough to condemn him; and he was publicly beheaded at Tyburn for this pretended offence.[n] About the same time, one John Stacey, an ecclesiastic, much connected with the duke, as well as with Burdet, was exposed to a like iniquitous and barbarous prosecution. This clergyman, being more learned in mathematics and astronomy than was usual in that age, lay under the imputation of necromancy with the ignorant vulgar; and the

---

[n] Habington, p. 475. Hollingshed, p. 703. Sir Thomas More in Kennet, p. 498.

court laid hold of this popular rumour to effect his destruction. He was brought to his trial for that imaginary crime; many of the greatest peers countenanced the prosecution by their presence; he was condemned, put to the torture, and executed.[o]

The duke of Clarence was alarmed, when he found these acts of tyranny exercised on all around him: He reflected on the fate of the good duke of Glocester in the last reign, who, after seeing the most infamous pretences employed for the destruction of his nearest connexions, at last fell himself a victim to the vengeance of his enemies. But Clarence, instead of securing his own life against the present danger, by silence and reserve, was open and loud in justifying the innocence of his friends, and in exclaiming against the iniquity of their prosecutors. The king, highly offended with his freedom, or using that pretence against him, committed him to the Tower,[p] summoned a parliament, and tried him for his life before the house of peers, the supreme tribunal of the nation.

1478.
16th Jan.

The duke was accused of arraigning public justice, by maintaining the innocence of men, who had been condemned in courts of judicature; and of inveighing against the iniquity of the king, who had given orders for their prosecution.[q] Many rash expressions were imputed to him, and some too reflecting on Edward's legitimacy; but he was not accused of any overt act of treason; and even the truth of these speeches may be doubted of, since the liberty of judgment was taken from the court, by the king's appearing personally as his brother's accuser,[r] and pleading the cause against him. But a sentence of condemnation, even when this extraordinary circumstance had not place, was a necessary consequence, in those times, of any prosecution by the court or the prevailing party; and the duke of Clarence was pronounced guilty by the peers. The house of commons were no less slavish and unjust: They both petitioned for the execution of the duke, and afterwards passed a bill of attainder against him.[s] The measures of the parliament, during that age, furnish us with examples of a strange contrast of freedom and servility: They scruple to grant, and sometimes refuse, to the king the smallest supplies, the most necessary for the support of government, even the most necessary for the

[o] Hist. Croyl. cont. p. 561. [p] Ibid. p. 562. [q] Stowe, p. 430. [r] Hist. Croyl. cont. p. 562. [s] Stowe, p. 430. Hist. Croyl. cont. p. 562.

maintenance of wars, for which the nation, as well as the parliament itself, expressed great fondness: But they never scruple to concur in the most flagrant act of injustice or tyranny, which falls on any individual, however distinguished by birth or merit. These maxims, so ungenerous, so opposite to all principles of good government, so contrary to the practice of present parliaments, are very remarkable in all the transactions of the English history for more than a century after the period in which we are now engaged.

18th Feb. The only favour, which the king granted his brother, after his condemnation, was to leave him the choice of his death; and he was privately drowned in a butt of malmesey in the Tower: A whimsical choice, which implies that he had an extraordinary passion for that liquor. The duke left two children, by the elder daughter of the earl of Warwic; a son created an earl by his grandfather's title, and a daughter, afterwards countess of Salisbury. Both this prince and princess were also unfortunate in their end, and died a violent death; a fate, which, for many years, attended almost all the descendants of the royal blood in England. There prevails a report, that a chief source of the violent prosecution of the duke of Clarence, whose name was George, was a current prophecy, that the king's sons should be murdered by one, the initial letter of whose name was G.[1] It is not impossible, but, in those ignorant times, such a silly reason might have some influence: But it is more probable, that the whole story is the invention of a subsequent period, and founded on the murder of these children by the duke of Glocester. Comines remarks, that, at that time, the English never were without some superstitious prophecy or other, by which they accounted for every event.

All the glories of Edward's reign terminated with the civil wars; where his laurels too were extremely sullied with blood, violence, and cruelty. His spirit seems afterwards to have been sunk in indolence and pleasure, or his measures were frustrated by imprudence and the want of foresight. There was no object, on which he was more intent, than to have all his daughters settled by splendid marriages, though most of these princesses were yet in their infancy, and though the completion of his views, it was obvious, must

[1] Hall, fol. 239. Holingshed, p. 703. Grafton, p. 741. Polyd. Virg. p. 537. Sir Thomas More in Kennet, p. 497.

CHAPTER XXII

depend on numberless accidents, which were impossible to be foreseen or prevented. His eldest daughter, Elizabeth, was contracted to the dauphin; his second, Cicely, to the eldest son of James III. king of Scotland; his third, Anne, to Philip, only son of Maximilian and the dutchess of Burgundy; his fourth, Catharine, to John, son and heir to Ferdinand, king of Arragon, and Isabella, queen of Castile.[u] None of these projected marriages took place; and the king himself saw in his life-time the rupture of the first, that with the dauphin, for which he had always discovered a peculiar fondness. Lewis, who paid no regard to treaties or engagements, found his advantage in contracting the dauphin to the princess Margaret, daughter of Maximilian; and the king, notwithstanding his indolence, prepared to revenge the indignity. The French monarch, eminent for prudence, as well as perfidy, endeavoured to guard against the blow; and by a proper distribution of presents in the court of Scotland, he incited James to make war upon England. This prince, who lived on bad terms with his own nobility, and whose force was very unequal to the enterprize, levied an army; but when he was ready to enter England, the barons, conspiring against his favourites, put them to death without trial; and the army presently disbanded. The duke of Glocester, attended by the duke of Albany, James's brother, who had been banished his country, entered Scotland at the head of an army, took Berwic, and obliged the Scots to accept of a peace, by which they resigned that fortress to Edward. This success emboldened the king to think more seriously of a French war; but while he was making preparations for that enterprize, he was seized with a distemper, of which he expired in the forty-second year of his age, and the twenty-third of his reign: A prince more splendid and showy, than either prudent or virtuous; brave, though cruel; addicted to pleasure, though capable of activity in great emergencies; and less fitted to prevent ills by wise precautions, than to remedy them, after they took place, by his vigour and enterprize. Besides five daughters, this king left two sons; Edward, prince of Wales, his successor, then in his thirteenth year, and Richard, duke of York, in his ninth.

1482.

9th April. Death and character of Edward IV.

[u] Rymer, vol. xi. p. 110.

XXIII

EDWARD V
AND RICHARD III

---

*Edward V. – State of the court – The
earl of Rivers arrested – Duke of Glocester
protector – Execution of Lord Hastings – The
protector aims at the crown – Assumes the
crown – Murder of Edward V. and of the duke
of York – Richard III. – Duke of Buckingham
discontented – The earl of Richmond –
Buckingham executed – Invasion by the earl
of Richmond – Battle of Bosworth –
Death and character of Richard III*

EDWARD V

*1483.
State of
the court.* **D**URING THE LATER YEARS of Edward IV. the nation, having,
in a great measure, forgotten the bloody feuds between the
two roses, and peaceably acquiescing in the established government, was agitated only by some court-intrigues, which, being
restrained by the authority of the king, seemed no wise to endanger the public tranquillity. These intrigues arose from the perpetual rivalship between two parties; one consisting of the queen

494

and her relations, particularly the earl of Rivers, her brother, and the marquis of Dorset, her son; the other composed of the ancient nobility, who envied the sudden growth and unlimited credit of that aspiring family.[w] At the head of this latter party was the duke of Buckingham, a man of very noble birth, of ample possessions, of great alliances, of shining parts; who, though he had married the queen's sister, was too haughty to act in subserviency to her inclinations, and aimed rather at maintaining an independant influence and authority. Lord Hastings, the chamberlain, was another leader of the same party; and as this nobleman had, by his bravery and activity, as well as by his approved fidelity, acquired the confidence and favour of his master, he had been able, though with some difficulty, to support himself against the credit of the queen. The lords Howard and Stanley maintained a connexion with these two noblemen, and brought a considerable accession of influence and reputation to their party. All the other barons, who had no particular dependance on the queen, adhered to the same interest; and the people in general, from their natural envy against the prevailing power, bore great favour to the cause of these noblemen.

But Edward knew, that, though he himself had been able to overawe those rival factions, many disorders might arise from their contests during the minority of his son; and he therefore took care, in his last illness, to summon together several of the leaders on both sides, and, by composing their ancient quarrels, to provide, as far as possible, for the future tranquillity of the government. After expressing the intentions, that his brother, the duke of Glocester, then absent in the north, should be entrusted with the regency, he recommended to them peace and unanimity during the tender years of his son; represented to them the dangers which must attend the continuance of their animosities; and engaged them to embrace each other with all the appearance of the most cordial reconciliation. But this temporary or feigned agreement lasted no longer than the king's life: He had no sooner expired, than the jealousies of the parties broke out afresh: And each of them applied, by separate messages, to the duke of Glocester, and endeavoured to acquire his favour and friendship.

[w] Sir Thomas More, p. 481.

This prince, during his brother's reign, had endeavoured to live on good terms with both parties; and his high birth, his extensive abilities, and his great services, had enabled him to support himself without falling into a dependance on either. But the new situation of affairs, when the supreme power was devolved upon him, immediately changed his measures; and he secretly determined to preserve no longer that neutrality which he had hitherto maintained. His exorbitant ambition, unrestrained by any principle either of justice or humanity, made him carry his views to the possession of the crown itself; and as this object could not be attained without the ruin of the queen and her family, he fell, without hesitation, into concert with the opposite party. But being sensible, that the most profound dissimulation was requisite for effecting his criminal purposes, he redoubled his professions of zeal and attachment to that princess; and he gained such credit with her, as to influence her conduct in a point, which, as it was of the utmost importance, was violently disputed between the opposite factions.

The young king, at the time of his father's death, resided in the castle of Ludlow, on the borders of Wales; whither he had been sent, that the influence of his presence might overawe the Welsh, and restore the tranquillity of that country, which had been disturbed by some late commotions. His person was committed to the care of his uncle, the earl of Rivers, the most accomplished nobleman in England, who, having united an uncommon taste for literature[x] to great abilities in business, and valour in the field, was entitled, by his talents, still more than by nearness of blood, to direct the education of the young monarch. The queen, anxious to preserve that ascendant over her son, which she had long maintained over her husband, wrote to the earl of Rivers, that he should levy a body of forces, in order to escort the king to London, to protect him during his coronation, and to keep him from falling into the hands of their enemies. The opposite faction, sensible that Edward was now of an age when great advantages could be made of his name and countenance, and was approaching to the age

---

[x] This nobleman first introduced the noble art of printing into England. Caxton was recommended by him to the patronage of Edward IV. See Catalogue of Royal and Noble Authors.

CHAPTER XXIII

when he would be legally intitled to exert in person his authority, foresaw, that the tendency of this measure was to perpetuate their subjection under their rivals; and they vehemently opposed a resolution, which they represented as the signal for renewing a civil war in the kingdom. Lord Hastings threatened to depart instantly to his government of Calais:[y] The other nobles seemed resolute to oppose force by force: And as the duke of Glocester, on pretence of pacifying the quarrel, had declared against all appearance of an armed power, which might be dangerous, and was nowise necessary, the queen, trusting to the sincerity of his friendship, and overawed by so violent an opposition, recalled her orders to her brother, and desired him to bring up no greater retinue than should be necessary to support the state and dignity of the young sovereign.[z]

The duke of Glocester, mean while, set out from York, attended by a numerous train of the northern gentry. When he reached Northampton, he was joined by the duke of Buckingham, who was also attended by a splendid retinue; and as he heard that the king was hourly expected on that road, he resolved to await his arrival, under colour of conducting him thence in person to London. The earl of Rivers, apprehensive that the place would be too narrow to contain so many attendants, sent his pupil forward by another road to Stony-Stratford; and came himself to Northampton, in order to apologize for this measure, and to pay his respects to the duke of Glocester. He was received with the greatest appearance of cordiality: He passed the evening in an amicable manner with Glocester and Buckingham: He proceeded on the road with them next day to join the king: But as he was entering Stony-Stratford, he was arrested by orders from the duke of Glocester:[a] Sir Richard Gray, one of the queen's sons, was at the same time put under a guard, together with Sir Thomas Vaughan, who possessed a considerable office in the king's household; and all the prisoners were instantly conducted to Pomfret. Glocester approached the young prince with the greatest demonstrations of respect; and endeavoured to satisfy him with regard to the violence committed on his uncle and brother: But Edward, much

The earl of Rivers arrested. 1st May.

---

[y] Hist. Croyl. cont. p. 564, 565.   [z] Sir T. More, p. 483.   [a] Hist. Croyl. cont. p. 564, 565.

attached to these near relations, by whom he had been tenderly educated, was not such a master of dissimulation as to conceal his displeasure.[b]

The people, however, were extremely rejoiced at this revolution; and the duke was received in London with the loudest acclamations: But the queen no sooner received intelligence of her brother's imprisonment, than she foresaw, that Glocester's violence would not stop there, and that her own ruin, if not that of all her children, was finally determined. She therefore fled into the sanctuary of Westminster, attended by the marquis of Dorset; and she carried thither the five princesses, together with the duke of York.[c] She trusted, that the ecclesiastical privileges, which had formerly, during the total ruin of her husband and family, given her protection against the fury of the Lancastrian faction, would not now be violated by her brother-in-law, while her son was on the throne; and she resolved to await there the return of better fortune. But Glocester, anxious to have the duke of York in his power, proposed to take him by force from the sanctuary; and he represented to the privy-council, both the indignity put upon the government by the queen's ill-grounded apprehensions, and the necessity of the young prince's appearance at the ensuing coronation of his brother. It was farther urged, that ecclesiastical privileges were originally intended only to give protection to unhappy men, persecuted for their debts or crimes; and were entirely useless to a person, who, by reason of his tender age, could lie under the burden of neither, and who, for the same reason, was utterly incapable of claiming security from any sanctuary. But the two archbishops, cardinal Bourchier, the primate, and Rotherham archbishop of York, protesting against the sacrilege of this measure; it was agreed, that they should first endeavour to bring the queen to compliance by persuasion, before any violence should be employed against her. These prelates were persons of known integrity and honour; and being themselves entirely persuaded of the duke's good intentions, they employed every argument, accompanied with earnest entreaties, exhortations, and assurances, to bring her over to the same opinion. She long continued obstinate, and insisted, that the duke of York, by living in the sanctuary,

[b] Sir T. More, p. 484.　　[c] Hist. Croyl. cont. p. 565.

CHAPTER XXIII

was not only secure himself, but gave security to the king, whose life no one would dare to attempt, while his successor and avenger remained in safety. But finding, that none supported her in these sentiments, and that force, in case of refusal, was threatened by the council, she at last complied, and produced her son to the two prelates. She was here on a sudden struck with a kind of presage of his future fate: She tenderly embraced him; she bedewed him with her tears; and bidding him an eternal adieu, delivered him, with many expressions of regret and reluctance, into their custody.[d]

The duke of Glocester, being the nearest male of the royal family, capable of exercising the government, seemed intitled, by the customs of the realm, to the office of protector; and the council, not waiting for the consent of parliament, made no scruple of investing him with that high dignity.[e] The general prejudice, entertained by the nobility against the queen and her kindred, occasioned this precipitation and irregularity; and no one foresaw any danger to the succession, much less to the lives, of the young princes, from a measure so obvious and so natural. Besides that the duke had hitherto been able to cover, by the most profound dissimulation, his fierce and savage nature; the numerous issue of Edward, together with the two children of Clarence, seemed to be an eternal obstacle to his ambition; and it appeared equally impracticable for him to destroy so many persons possessed of a preferable title, and imprudent to exclude them. But a man, who had abandoned all principles of honour and humanity, was soon carried by his predominant passion beyond the reach of fear or precaution; and Glocester, having so far succeeded in his views, no longer hesitated in removing the other obstructions, which lay between him and the throne. The death of the earl of Rivers, and of the other prisoners detained in Pomfret, was first determined; and he easily obtained the consent of the duke of Buckingham, as well as of lord Hastings, to this violent and sanguinary measure. However easy it was, in those times, to procure a sentence against the most innocent person, it appeared still more easy to dispatch an enemy, without any trial or form of process; and orders were accordingly issued to Sir Richard Ratcliffe, a proper instrument in

Duke of Glocester protector.

---

[d] Sir T. More, p. 491.   [e] Hist. Croyl. cont. p. 566.

the hands of this tyrant, to cut off the heads of the prisoners. The protector then assailed the fidelity of Buckingham by all the arguments capable of swaying a vicious mind, which knew no motive of action but interest and ambition. He represented, that the execution of persons so nearly related to the king, whom that prince so openly professed to love, and whose fate he so much resented, would never pass unpunished; and all the actors in that scene were bound in prudence to prevent the effects of his future vengeance: That it would be impossible to keep the queen for ever at a distance from her son, and equally impossible to prevent her from instilling into his tender mind the thoughts of retaliating, by like executions, the sanguinary insults committed on her family: That the only method of obviating these mischiefs was to put the sceptre in the hands of a man, of whose friendship the duke might be assured, and whose years and experience taught him to pay respect to merit and to the rights of ancient nobility: And that the same necessity, which had carried them so far in resisting the usurpation of these intruders, must justify them in attempting farther innovations, and in making, by national consent, a new settlement of the succession. To these reasons, he added the offers of great private advantages to the duke of Buckingham; and he easily obtained from him a promise of supporting him in all his enterprizes.

The duke of Glocester, knowing the importance of gaining lord Hastings, sounded at a distance his sentiments, by means of Catesby, a lawyer, who lived in great intimacy with that nobleman; but found him impregnable in his allegiance and fidelity to the children of Edward, who had ever honoured him with his friendship.[f] He saw, therefore, that there were no longer any measures to be kept with him; and he determined to ruin utterly the man, whom he despaired of engaging to concur in his usurpation. On the very day when Rivers, Gray, and Vaughan were executed, or rather murdered, at Pomfret, by the advice of Hastings, the protector summoned a council in the Tower; whither that nobleman, suspecting no design against him, repaired without hesitation. The duke of Glocester was capable of committing the most bloody and treacherous murders with the utmost coolness and indifference. On taking his place at the council-table, he appeared in the easiest

13th June.

_____

[f] Sir T. More, p. 493.

and most jovial humour imaginable. He seemed to indulge himself in familiar conversation with the counsellors, before they should enter on business; and having paid some compliments to Morton, bishop of Ely, on the good and early strawberries which he raised in his garden at Holborn, he begged the favour of having a dish of them, which that prelate immediately dispatched a servant to bring to him. The protector then left the council, as if called away by some other business; but soon after returning with an angry and enflamed countenance, he asked them, what punishment those deserved that had plotted against *his* life, who was so nearly related to the king, and was entrusted with the administration of government? Hastings replied, that they merited the punishment of traitors. *These traitors,* cried the protector, *are the sorceress, my brother's wife, and Jane Shore, his mistress, with others, their associates: See to what a condition they have reduced me by their incantations and witchcraft:* Upon which he laid bare his arm, all shrivelled and decayed. But the counsellors, who knew that this infirmity had attended him from his birth, looked on each other with amazement; and above all, lord Hastings, who, as he had, since Edward's death, engaged in an intrigue with Jane Shore,[g] was naturally anxious concerning the issue of these extraordinary proceedings. *Certainly, my lord,* said he, *if they be guilty of these crimes, they deserve the severest punishment. And do you reply to me,* exclaimed the protector, *with your ifs and your ands? You are the chief abettor of that witch, Shore: You are yourself a traitor: And I swear by St. Paul, that I will not dine before your head be brought me.* He struck the table with his hand: Armed men rushed in at the signal: The counsellors were thrown into the utmost consternation: And one of the guards, as if by accident or mistake, aimed a blow with a poll-ax at lord Stanley, who, aware of the danger, slunk under the table; and though he saved his life, received a severe wound in the head, in the protector's presence. Hastings was seized, was hurried away, and instantly beheaded on a timber-log, which lay in the court of the Tower.[h] Two hours after, a proclamation, well penned and fairly written, was read to the citizens of London, enumerating his offences, and apologizing to them, from the suddenness of the discovery, for the sudden execution of that nobleman, who was very popular among them:

Execution of lord Hastings.

[g] See note [S] at the end of the volume. [h] Hist. Croyl. cont. p. 566.

But the saying of a merchant was much talked of on the occasion, who remarked, that the proclamation was certainly drawn by the spirit of prophecy.[i]

Lord Stanley, the archbishop of York, the bishop of Ely, and other counsellors, were committed prisoners in different chambers of the Tower: And the protector, in order to carry on the farce of his accusations, ordered the goods of Jane Shore to be seized; and he summoned her to answer before the council for sorcery and witchcraft. But as no proofs, which could be received even in that ignorant age, were produced against her, he directed her to be tried in the spiritual court, for her adulteries and lewdness; and she did penance in a white sheet at St. Paul's, before the whole people. This lady was born of reputable parents in London, was well educated, and married to a substantial citizen; but unhappily, views of interest, more than the maid's inclinations, had been consulted in the match, and her mind, though framed for virtue, had proved unable to resist the allurements of Edward, who solicited her favours. But while seduced from her duty by this gay and amorous monarch, she still made herself respectable by her other virtues; and the ascendant, which her charms and vivacity long maintained over him, was all employed in acts of beneficence and humanity. She was still forward to oppose calumny, to protect the oppressed, to relieve the indigent; and her good offices, the genuine dictates of her heart, never waited the solicitation of presents, or the hopes of reciprocal services. But she lived not only to feel the bitterness of shame imposed on her by this tyrant, but to experience, in old age and poverty, the ingratitude of those courtiers, who had long solicited her friendship, and been protected by her credit. No one, among the great multitudes, whom she had obliged, had the humanity to bring her consolation or relief: She languished out her life in solitude and indigence: And amidst a court, inured to the most atrocious crimes, the frailties of this woman justified all violations of friendship towards her, and all neglect of former obligations.

The protector aims at the crown.

These acts of violence, exercised against all the nearest connexions of the late king, prognosticated the severest fate to his defenceless children; and after the murder of Hastings, the pro-

---

[i] Sir T. More, p. 496.

CHAPTER XXIII

tector no longer made a secret of his intentions to usurp the crown. The licentious life of Edward, who was not restrained in his pleasures either by honour or prudence, afforded a pretence for declaring his marriage with the queen invalid, and all his posterity illegitimate. It was asserted, that, before espousing the lady Elizabeth Gray, he had paid court to the lady Eleanor Talbot, daughter to the earl of Shrewsbury; and being repulsed by the virtue of that lady, he was obliged, ere he could gratify his desires, to consent to a private marriage, without any witnesses, by Stillington, bishop of Bath, who afterwards divulged the secret.[k] It was also maintained, that the act of attainder, passed against the duke of Clarence, had virtually incapacitated his children from succeeding to the crown; and these two families being set aside, the protector remained the only true and legitimate heir of the house of York. But as it would be difficult, if not impossible, to prove the preceding marriage of the late king; and as the rule, which excludes the heirs of an attainted blood from private successions, was never extended to the crown; the protector resolved to make use of another plea still more shameful and scandalous. His partizans were taught to maintain, that both Edward IV. and the duke of Clarence were illegitimate; that the dutchess of York had received different lovers into her bed, who were the fathers of these children; that their resemblance to those gallants was a sufficient proof of their spurious birth; and that the duke of Glocester alone, of all her sons, appeared, by his features and countenance, to be the true offspring of the duke of York. Nothing can be imagined more impudent than this assertion, which threw so foul an imputation on his own mother, a princess of irreproachable virtue, and then alive; yet the place chosen for first promulgating it was the pulpit, before a large congregation, and in the protector's presence. Dr. Shaw was appointed to preach in St. Paul's; and having chosen this passage for his text, *Bastard slips shall not thrive,* he enlarged on all the topics, which could discredit the birth of Edward IV. the duke of Clarence, and of all their children. He then broke out in a panegyric on the duke of Glocester; and exclaimed, "Behold this excellent prince, the express image of his noble father, the genuine descendant of the house of York; bearing, no less in the virtues of his

22d June.

---

[k] Hist. Croyl. cont. p. 567. Comines. Sir Thom. More, p. 482.

mind, than in the features of his countenance, the character of the gallant Richard, once your hero and favourite: He alone is entitled to your allegiance: He must deliver you from the dominion of all intruders: He alone can restore the lost glory and honour of the nation." It was previously concerted, that, as the doctor should pronounce these words, the duke of Glocester should enter the church; and it was expected that the audience would cry out, *God save King Richard;* which would immediately have been laid hold of as a popular consent, and interpreted to be the voice of the nation: But by a ridiculous mistake, worthy of the whole scene, the duke did not appear, till after this exclamation was already recited by the preacher. The doctor was therefore obliged to repeat his rhetorical figure out of its proper place: The audience, less from the absurd conduct of the discourse, than from their detestation of these proceedings, kept a profound silence: And the protector and his preacher were equally abashed at the ill success of their stratagem.

But the duke was too far advanced to recede from his criminal and ambitious purpose. A new expedient was tried to work on the people. The mayor, who was brother to Dr. Shaw, and entirely in the protector's interests, called an assembly of the citizens; where the duke of Buckingham, who possessed some talents for eloquence, harangued them on the protector's title to the crown, and displayed those numerous virtues, of which, he pretended, that prince was possessed. He next asked them, whether they would have the duke for king? and then stopped, in expectation of hearing the cry, *God save King Richard.* He was surprized to observe them silent; and turning about to the mayor, asked him the reason. The mayor replied, that perhaps they did not understand him. Buckingham then repeated his discourse with some variation; inforced the same topics, asked the same question, and was received with the same silence. "I now see the cause," said the mayor; "the citizens are not accustomed to be harangued by any but their recorder; and know not how to answer a person of your grace's quality." The recorder, Fitz-Williams, was then commanded to repeat the substance of the duke's speech; but the man, who was averse to the office, took care, throughout his whole discourse, to have it understood, that he spoke nothing of himself, and that he only conveyed to them the sense of the duke of Buckingham. Still the audience kept a profound silence: "This is wonderful obstinacy," cried the duke: "Express your meaning, my friends, one way or other: When we apply to you on this occasion, it is merely from the regard which we bear to you. The lords and commons have sufficient authority, without your consent, to appoint a king: But I require you here to declare in plain terms, whether or not you will have the duke of Glocester for your sovereign." After all these efforts, some of the meanest apprentices, incited by the protector's and Buckingham's servants, raised a feeble cry, *God save King Richard:*[1] The sentiments of the nation were now sufficiently declared: The voice of the people was the voice of God: And Buckingham, with the mayor, hastened to Baynard's castle, where the protector then resided, that they might make him a tender of the crown.

25th June.

When Richard was told, that a great multitude was in the court, he refused to appear to them, and pretended to be apprehensive for his personal safety: A circumstance taken notice of by Buckingham, who observed to the citizens, that the prince was ignorant of the whole design. At last, he was persuaded to step forth, but he still kept at some distance; and he asked the meaning of their intrusion and importunity. Buckingham told him, that the nation was resolved to have him for king: The protector declared his purpose of maintaining his loyalty to the present sovereign, and exhorted them to adhere to the same resolution. He was told, that the people had determined to have another prince; and if he rejected their unanimous voice, they must look out for one, who would be more compliant. This argument was too powerful to be resisted: He was prevailed on to accept of the crown: And he thenceforth acted as legitimate and rightful sovereign.

The protector assumes the throne.

This ridiculous farce was soon after followed by a scene truly tragical: The murder of the two young princes. Richard gave orders to Sir Robert Brakenbury, constable of the Tower, to put his nephews to death; but this gentleman, who had sentiments of honour, refused to have any hand in the infamous office. The tyrant then sent for Sir James Tyrrel, who promised obedience; and he ordered Brakenbury to resign to this gentleman the keys and government of the Tower for one night. Tyrrel, chusing three associates, Slater, Dighton, and Forest, came in the night-time to the door of the chamber where the princes were lodged; and sending in the assassins, he bade them execute their commission,

Murder of Edward V. and of the duke of York.

[1] Sir Thomas More, p. 496.

while he himself staid without. They found the young princes in bed, and fallen into a profound sleep. After suffocating them with the bolster and pillows, they showed their naked bodies to Tyrrel, who ordered them to be buried at the foot of the stairs, deep in the ground, under a heap of stones.[m] These circumstances were all confessed by the actors, in the following reign; and they were never punished for the crime: Probably, because Henry, whose maxims of government were extremely arbitrary, desired to establish it as a principle, that the commands of the reigning sovereign ought to justify every enormity in those who paid obedience to them. But there is one circumstance not so easy to be accounted for: It is pretended, that Richard, displeased with the indecent manner of burying his nephews, whom he had murdered, gave his chaplain orders to dig up the bodies, and to inter them in consecrated ground; and as the man died soon after, the place of their burial remained unknown, and the bodies could never be found by any search, which Henry could make for them. Yet in the reign of Charles II. when there was occasion to remove some stones and to dig in the very spot, which was mentioned as the place of their first interment, the bones of two persons were there found, which by their size exactly corresponded to the age of Edward and his brother: They were concluded with certainty to be the remains of those princes, and were interred under a marble monument by orders of king Charles.[n] Perhaps, Richard's chaplain had died before he found an opportunity of executing his master's commands; and the bodies being supposed to be already removed, a diligent search was not made for them by Henry, in the place where they had been buried.

RICHARD III

1483.

THE FIRST ACTS of Richard's administration were to bestow rewards on those who had assisted him in usurping the crown, and to gain by favours those, who, he thought, were best able to

[m] Sir T. More, p. 501.　[n] Kennet, p. 551.

CHAPTER XXIII

support his future government. Thomas, lord Howard, was created duke of Norfolk; Sir Thomas Howard, his son, earl of Surry; lord Lovel, a viscount, by the same name; even lord Stanley was set at liberty and made steward of the houshold. This nobleman had become obnoxious by his first opposition to Richard's views, and also by his marrying the countess dowager of Richmond, heir of the Somerset family; but sensible of the necessity of submitting to the present government, he feigned such zeal for Richard's service, that he was received into favour, and even found means to be entrusted with the most important commands by that politic and jealous tyrant.

But the person, who, both from the greatness of his services, and the power and splendor of his family, was best intitled to favours under the new government, was the duke of Buckingham; and Richard seemed determined to spare no pains or bounty in securing him to his interests. Buckingham was descended from a daughter of Thomas of Woodstock, duke of Glocester, uncle to Richard II. and by this pedigree, he not only was allied to the royal family, but had claims for dignities as well as estates, of a very extensive nature. The duke of Glocester, and Henry earl of Derby, afterwards Henry IV. had married the two daughters and co-heirs of Bohun, earl of Hereford, one of the greatest of the ancient barons, whose immense property came thus to be divided into two shares. One was inherited by the family of Buckingham; the other was united to the crown by the house of Lancaster, and after the attainder of that royal line, was seized as legally devolved to them, by the sovereigns of the house of York. The duke of Buckingham laid hold of the present opportunity, and claimed the restitution of that portion of the Hereford estate, which had escheated to the crown, as well as of the great office of constable, which had long continued by inheritance in his ancestors of that family. Richard readily complied with these demands, which were probably the price stipulated to Buckingham for his assistance in promoting the usurpation. That nobleman was invested with the office of constable; he received a grant of the estate of Hereford;[o] many other dignities and honours were conferred upon him; and the king thought himself sure of preserving the fidelity of a man, whose

[o] Dugdale's Baron. vol. i. p. 168, 169.

interests seemed so closely connected with those of the present government.

Duke of Buck- ingham discon- tented. But it was impossible, that friendship could long remain inviolate between two men of such corrupt minds as Richard and the duke of Buckingham. Historians ascribe their first rupture to the king's refusal of making restitution of the Hereford estate; but it is certain from records, that he passed a grant for that purpose, and that the full demands of Buckingham were satisfied in this particular. Perhaps, Richard was soon sensible of the danger which might ensue from conferring such an immense property on a man of so turbulent a disposition, and afterwards raised difficulties about the execution of his own grant: Perhaps, he refused some other demands of Buckingham, whom he found it impossible to gratify for his past services: Perhaps, he resolved, according to the usual maxim of politicians, to seize the first opportunity of ruining this powerful subject, who had been the principal instrument of his own elevation; and the discovery of this intention begat the first discontent in the duke of Buckingham. However this may be, it is certain, that the duke, soon after Richard's accession, began to form a conspiracy against the government, and attempted to overthrow that usurpation, which he himself had so zealously contributed to establish.

Never was there in any country an usurpation more flagrant than that of Richard, or more repugnant to every principle of justice and public interest. His claim was entirely founded on impudent allegations, never attempted to be proved, some of them incapable of proof, and all of them implying scandalous reflections on his own family, and on the persons with whom he was the most nearly connected. His title was never acknowledged by any national assembly, scarcely even by the lowest populace to whom he appealed; and it had become prevalent merely for want of some person of distinction, who might stand forth against him, and give a voice to those sentiments of general detestation, which arose in every bosom. Were men disposed to pardon these violations of public right, the sense of private and domestic duty, which is not to be effaced in the most barbarous times, must have begotten an abhorrence against him; and have represented the murder of the young and innocent princes, his nephews, with whose protection he had been entrusted, in the most odious colours imaginable. To endure such a bloody usurper seemed to draw disgrace upon the nation, and to be attended with immediate danger to every individual, who was distinguished by birth, merit, or services. Such was become the general voice of the people; all parties were united in the same sentiments; and the Lancastrians, so long oppressed, and, of late, so much discredited, felt their blasted hopes again revived, and anxiously expected the consequences of these extraordinary events. The duke of Buckingham, whose family had been devoted to that interest, and who, by his mother, a daughter of Edmund, duke of Somerset, was allied to the house of Lancaster, was easily induced to espouse the cause of this party, and to endeavour the restoring of it to its ancient superiority. Morton, bishop of Ely, a zealous Lancastrian, whom the king had imprisoned, and had afterwards committed to the custody of Buckingham, encouraged these sentiments; and by his exhortations the duke cast his eye towards the young earl of Richmond, as the only person who could free the nation from the tyranny of the present usurper.[p]

Henry, earl of Richmond, was at this time detained in a kind of honourable custody by the duke of Britanny; and his descent, which seemed to give him some pretensions to the crown, had been a great object of jealousy both in the late and in the present reign. John, the first duke of Somerset, who was grandson of John of Gaunt, by a spurious branch, but legitimated by act of parliament, had left only one daughter, Margaret; and his younger brother, Edmund, had succeeded him in his titles, and in a considerable part of his fortune. Margaret had espoused Edmund, earl of Richmond, half brother of Henry VI. and son of Sir Owen Tudor and Catharine of France, relict of Henry V. and she bore him only one son, who received the name of Henry, and who, after his father's death, inherited the honours and fortune of Richmond. His mother, being a widow, had espoused in second marriage Sir Henry Stafford, uncle to Buckingham, and after the death of that gentleman, had married lord Stanley; but had no children by either of these husbands; and her son, Henry, was thus, in the event of her death, the sole heir of all her fortunes. But this was not the most considerable advantage, which he had reason to expect from

The earl of Richmond.

[p] Hist. Croyl. cont. p. 568.

her succession: He would represent the elder branch of the house of Somerset; he would inherit all the title of that family to the crown; and though its claim, while any legitimate branch subsisted of the house of Lancaster, had always been much disregarded, the zeal of faction, after the death of Henry VI. and the murder of prince Edward, immediately conferred a weight and consideration upon it.

Edward IV. finding, that all the Lancastrians had turned their attention towards the young earl of Richmond, as the object of their hopes, thought him also worthy of his attention; and pursued him into his retreat in Britanny, whither his uncle, the earl of Pembroke, had carried him, after the battle of Teukesbury, so fatal to his party. He applied to Francis II. duke of Britanny, who was his ally, a weak but a good prince; and urged him to deliver up this fugitive, who might be the source of future disturbances in England: But the duke, averse to so dishonourable a proposal, would only consent, that, for the security of Edward, the young nobleman should be detained in custody; and he received an annual pension from England for the safe keeping or the subsistance of his prisoner. But towards the end of Edward's reign, when the kingdom was menaced with a war both from France and Scotland, the anxieties of the English court with regard to Henry were much encreased; and Edward made a new proposal to the duke, which covered, under the fairest appearances, the most bloody and treacherous intentions. He pretended, that he was desirous of gaining his enemy, and of uniting him to his own family by a marriage with his daughter, Elizabeth; and he solicited to have him sent over to England, in order to execute a scheme, which would redound so much to his advantage. These pretences, seconded, as is supposed, by bribes to Peter Landais, a corrupt minister, by whom the duke was entirely governed, gained credit with the court of Britanny: Henry was delivered into the hands of the English agents: He was ready to embark: When a suspicion of Edward's real design was suggested to the duke, who recalled his orders, and thus saved the unhappy youth from the imminent danger which hung over him.

These symptoms of continued jealousy in the reigning family of England both seemed to give some authority to Henry's pretensions, and made him the object of general favour and compas-

CHAPTER XXIII

sion, on account of the dangers and persecutions to which he was exposed. The universal detestation of Richard's conduct turned still more the attention of the nation towards Henry; and as all the descendants of the house of York were either women or minors, he seemed to be the only person, from whom the nation could expect the expulsion of the odious and bloody tyrant. But notwithstanding these circumstances, which were so favourable to him, Buckingham and the bishop of Ely well knew, that there would still lie many obstacles in his way to the throne; and that though the nation had been much divided between Henry VI. and the duke of York, while present possession and hereditary right stood in opposition to each other; yet, as soon as these titles were united in Edward IV. the bulk of the people had come over to the reigning family; and the Lancastrians had extremely decayed, both in numbers and in authority. It was therefore suggested by Morton, and readily assented to by the duke, that the only means of overturning the present usurpation, was to unite the opposite factions, by contracting a marriage between the earl of Richmond and the princess Elizabeth, eldest daughter of king Edward, and thereby blending together the opposite pretensions of their families, which had so long been the source of public disorders and convulsions. They were sensible, that the people were extremely desirous of repose after so many bloody and destructive commotions; that both Yorkists and Lancastrians, who now lay equally under oppression, would embrace this scheme with ardour; and that the prospect of reconciling the two parties, which was in itself so desirable an end, would, when added to the general hatred against the present government, render their cause absolutely invincible. In consequence of these views, the prelate, by means of Reginald Bray, steward to the countess of Richmond, first opened the project of such an union to that lady; and the plan appeared so advantageous for her son, and, at the same time, so likely to succeed, that it admitted not of the least hesitation. Dr. Lewis, a Welsh physician, who had access to the queen-dowager in her sanctuary, carried the proposals to her; and found, that revenge for the murder of her brother and of her three sons, apprehensions for her surviving family, indignation against her confinement, easily overcame all her prejudices against the house of Lancaster, and procured her approbation of a marriage, to which the age and birth, as well as the present situation of the parties, seemed so naturally to invite them. She secretly borrowed a sum of money in the city, sent it over to the earl of Richmond, required his oath to celebrate the marriage as soon as he should arrive in England, advised him to levy as many foreign forces as possible, and promised to join him, on his first appearance, with all the friends and partizans of her family.

The plan being thus laid upon the solid foundations of good sense and sound policy, it was secretly communicated to the principal persons of both parties in all the counties of England; and a wonderful alacrity appeared in every order of men, to forward its success and completion. But it was impossible, that so extensive a conspiracy could be conducted in so secret a manner, as entirely to escape the jealous and vigilant eye of Richard; and he soon received intelligence, that his enemies, headed by the duke of Buckingham, were forming some design against his authority. He immediately put himself in a posture of defence by levying troops in the North; and he summoned the duke to appear at court, in such terms as seemed to promise him a renewal of their former amity. But that nobleman, well acquainted with the barbarity and treachery of Richard, replied only by taking arms in Wales, and giving the signal to his accomplices for a general insurrection in all parts

October. of England. But at that very time there happened to fall such heavy rains, so incessant and continued, as exceeded any known in the memory of man; and the Severne, with the other rivers in that neighbourhood, swelled to a height which rendered them impassable, and prevented Buckingham from marching into the heart of England to join his associates. The Welshmen, partly moved by superstition at this extraordinary event, partly distressed by famine in their camp, fell off from him; and Buckingham, finding himself deserted by his followers, put on a disguise, and took shelter in the house of Banister, an old servant of his family.

Buck- But being detected in his retreat, he was brought to the king at
ingham Salisbury; and was instantly executed, according to the summary
executed. method practised in that age.[q] The other conspirators, who took arms in four different places, at Exeter, at Salisbury, at Newbury, and at Maidstone, hearing of the duke of Buckingham's mis-

[q] Hist. Croyl. cont. p. 568.

fortunes, despaired of success, and immediately dispersed themselves.

The marquis of Dorset and the bishop of Ely made their escape beyond sea: Many others were equally fortunate: Several fell into Richard's hands, of whom he made some examples. His executions seem not to have been remarkably severe; though we are told of one gentleman, William Colingbourne, who suffered under colour of this rebellion, but in reality for a distich of quibbling verses, which he had composed against Richard and his ministers.ʳ The earl of Richmond, in concert with his friends, had set sail from St. Malo's, carrying on board a body of 5000 men, levied in foreign parts; but his fleet being at first driven back by a storm, he appeared not on the coast of England till after the dispersion of all his friends; and he found himself obliged to return to the court of Britanny.

The king, every where triumphant, and fortified by this unsuccessful attempt to dethrone him, ventured at last to summon a parliament; a measure which his crimes and flagrant usurpation had induced him hitherto to decline. Though it was natural, that the parliament, in a contest of national parties, should always adhere to the victor, he seems to have apprehended, lest his title, founded on no principle, and supported by no party, might be rejected by that assembly. But his enemies being now at his feet, the parliament had no choice left but to recognize his authority, and acknowledge his right to the crown. His only son, Edward, then a youth of twelve years of age, was created prince of Wales: The duties of tonnage and poundage were granted to the king for life: And Richard, in order to reconcile the nation to his government, passed some popular laws, particularly one against the late practice of extorting money on pretence of benevolence.

*1484.
23d of
Jan.*

All the other measures of the king tended to the same object. Sensible, that the only circumstance, which could give him security, was to gain the confidence of the Yorkists, he paid court to the

ʳ The lines were:

> The Rat, the Cat, and Lovel that Dog,
> Rule all England under the Hog.

Alluding to the names of Ratcliffe and Catesby; and to Richard's arms, which were a boar.

queen-dowager with such art and address, made such earnest protestations of his sincere good-will and friendship, that this princess, tired of confinement, and despairing of any success from her
former projects, ventured to leave her sanctuary, and to put herself and her daughters into the hands of the tyrant. But he soon
carried farther his views for the establishment of his throne. He
had married Anne, the second daughter of the earl of Warwic, and
widow of Edward prince of Wales, whom Richard himself had
murdered; but this princess having born him but one son, who
died about this time, he considered her as an invincible obstacle to
the settlement of his fortune, and he was believed to have carried
her off by poison; a crime for which the public could not be supposed to have any solid proof, but which the usual tenor of his
conduct made it reasonable to suspect. He now thought it in his
power to remove the chief perils, which threatened his government. The earl of Richmond, he knew, could never be formidable
but from his projected marriage with the princess Elizabeth, the
true heir of the crown; and he therefore intended, by means of a
papal dispensation, to espouse, himself, this princess, and thus to
unite in his own family their contending titles. The queen-dowager,
eager to recover her lost authority, neither scrupled this alliance,
which was very unusual in England, and was regarded as inces-
tuous; nor felt any horror at marrying her daughter to the mur-
derer of her three sons and of her brother: She even joined so far
her interests with those of the usurper, that she wrote to all her
partizans, and among the rest to her son, the marquis of Dorset,
desiring them to withdraw from the earl of Richmond; an injury
which the earl could never afterwards forgive: The court of Rome
was applied to for a dispensation: Richard thought, that he could
easily defend himself during the interval, till it arrived; and he had
afterwards the agreeable prospect of a full and secure settlement.
He flattered himself, that the English nation, seeing all danger
removed of a disputed succession, would then acquiesce under the
dominion of a prince, who was of mature years, of great abilities,
and of a genius qualified for government; and that they would
forgive him all the crimes, which he had committed, in paving his
way to the throne.

But the crimes of Richard were so horrid and so shocking to
humanity, that the natural sentiments of men, without any politi-

CHAPTER XXIII

cal or public views, were sufficient to render his government unstable; and every person of probity and honour was earnest to prevent the scepter from being any longer polluted by that bloody and faithless hand which held it. All the exiles flocked to the earl of Richmond in Britanny, and exhorted him to hasten his attempt for a new invasion, and to prevent the marriage of the princess Elizabeth, which must prove fatal to all his hopes. The earl, sensible of the urgent necessity, but dreading the treachery of Peter Landais, who had entered into a negociation with Richard for betraying him, was obliged to attend only to his present safety; and he made his escape to the court of France. The ministers of Charles VIII. who had now succeeded to the throne after the death of his father Lewis, gave him countenance and protection; and being desirous of raising disturbance to Richard, they secretly encouraged the earl in the levies, which he made for the support of his enterprize upon England. The earl of Oxford, whom Richard's suspicions had thrown into confinement, having made his escape, here joined Henry; and enflamed his ardour for the attempt, by the favourable accounts which he brought of the dispositions of the English nation, and their universal hatred of Richard's crimes and usurpation.

The earl of Richmond set sail from Harfleur in Normandy with a small army of about 2000 men; and after a navigation of six days, he arrived at Milford-Haven in Wales, where he landed without opposition. He directed his course to that part of the kingdom, in hopes that the Welsh, who regarded him as their countryman, and who had been already prepossessed in favour of his cause by means of the duke of Buckingham, would join his standard, and enable him to make head against the established government. Richard, who knew not in what quarter he might expect the invader, had taken post at Nottingham, in the center of the kingdom; and having given commissions to different persons in the several counties, whom he empowered to oppose his enemy, he purposed in person to fly, on the first alarm, to the place exposed to danger. Sir Rice ap Thomas and Sir Walter Herbert were entrusted with his authority in Wales; but the former immediately deserted to Henry; the second made but feeble opposition to him: And the earl, advancing towards Shrewsbury, received every day some reinforcement from his partizans. Sir Gilbert Talbot joined

1485.
Invasion by the earl of Richmond.
7th August.

him with all the vassals and retainers of the family of Shrewsbury: Sir Thomas Bourchier, and Sir Walter Hungerford, brought their friends to share his fortunes; and the appearance of men of distinction in his camp made already his cause wear a favourable aspect.

But the danger, to which Richard was chiefly exposed, proceeded not so much from the zeal of his open enemies, as from the infidelity of his pretended friends. Scarce any nobleman of distinction was sincerely attached to his cause, except the duke of Norfolk; and all those who feigned the most loyalty were only watching for an opportunity to betray and desert him. But the persons, of whom he entertained the greatest suspicion, were lord Stanley and his brother Sir William; whose connexions with the family of Richmond, notwithstanding their professions of attachment to his person, were never entirely forgotten or overlooked by him. When he empowered lord Stanley to levy forces, he still retained his eldest son, lord Strange, as a pledge for his fidelity; and that nobleman was, on this account, obliged to employ great caution and reserve in his proceedings. He raised a powerful body of his friends and retainers in Cheshire and Lancashire, but without openly declaring himself: And though Henry had received secret assurances of his friendly intentions, the armies on both sides knew not what to infer from his equivocal behaviour. The two rivals, at last, approached each other, at Bosworth near Leicester; Henry at the head of six thousand men, Richard with an army of above double the number; and a decisive action was every hour expected between them. Stanley, who commanded above seven thousand men, took care to post himself at Atherstone, not far from the hostile camps; and he made such a disposition as enabled him on occasion to join either party. Richard had too much sagacity not to discover his intentions from these movements; but he kept the secret from his own men for fear of discouraging them: He took not immediate revenge on Stanley's son, as some of his courtiers advised him; because he hoped that so valuable a pledge would induce the father to prolong still farther his ambiguous conduct: And he hastened to decide by arms the quarrel with his competitor; being certain, that a victory over the earl of Richmond would enable him to take ample revenge on all his enemies, open and concealed.

22d Aug.
Battle of
Bosworth.

CHAPTER XXIII

The van of Richmond's army, consisting of archers, was commanded by the earl of Oxford: Sir Gilbert Talbot led the right wing; Sir John Savage the left: The earl himself, accompanied by his uncle, the earl of Pembroke, placed himself in the main body. Richard also took post in *his* main body, and entrusted the command of his van to the duke of Norfolk: As his wings were never engaged, we have not learned the names of the several commanders. Soon after the battle began, lord Stanley, whose conduct in this whole affair discovers great precaution and abilities, appeared in the field, and declared for the earl of Richmond. This measure, which was unexpected to the men, though not to their leaders, had a proportional effect on both armies: It inspired unusual courage into Henry's soldiers; it threw Richard's into dismay and confusion. The intrepid tyrant, sensible of his desperate situation, cast his eye around the field, and descrying his rival at no great distance, he drove against him with fury, in hopes, that either Henry's death or his own would decide the victory between them. He killed with his own hands Sir William Brandon, standard-bearer to the earl: He dismounted Sir John Cheyney: He was now within reach of Richmond himself, who declined not the combat; when Sir William Stanley, breaking in with his troops, surrounded Richard, who, fighting bravely to the last moment, was over-whelmed by numbers, and perished by a fate too mild and honour- *Death,* able for his multiplied and detestable enormities. His men every where sought for safety by flight.

There fell in this battle about four thousand of the vanquished; and among these the duke of Norfolk, lord Ferrars of Charltey, Sir Richard Ratcliffe, Sir Robert Piercy, and Sir Robert Brackenbury. The loss was inconsiderable on the side of the victors. Sir William Catesby, a great instrument of Richard's crimes, was taken, and soon after beheaded, with some others, at Leicester. The body of Richard was found in the field, covered with dead enemies, and all besmeared with blood: It was thrown carelessly across a horse; was carried to Leicester amidst the shouts of the insulting spectators; and was interred in the Gray-Friars church of that place.

The historians who favour Richard (for even this tyrant has met *and char-* with partizans among the later writers) maintain, that he was well *acter of* qualified for government, had he legally obtained it; and that he *Richard* committed no crimes but such as were necessary to procure him *III.*

possession of the crown: But this is a poor apology, when it is confessed, that he was ready to commit the most horrid crimes, which appeared necessary for that purpose; and it is certain, that all his courage and capacity, qualities in which he really seems not to have been deficient, would never have made compensation to the people for the danger of the precedent, and for the contagious example of vice and murder, exalted upon the throne. This prince was of a small stature, humpbacked, and had a harsh disagreeable countenance; so that his body was in every particular no less deformed than his mind.

Thus have we pursued the history of England through a series of many barbarous ages; till we have at last reached the dawn of civility and sciences, and have the prospect, both of greater certainty in our historical narrations, and of being able to present to the reader a spectacle more worthy of his attention. The want of certainty, however, and of circumstances, is not alike to be complained of throughout every period of this long narration. This island possesses many ancient historians of good credit; as well as many historical monuments; and it is rare, that the annals of so uncultivated a people, as were the English as well as the other European nations, after the decline of Roman learning, have been transmitted to posterity so complete, and with so little mixture of falsehood and of fable. This advantage we owe entirely to the clergy of the church of Rome; who, founding their authority on their superior knowledge, preserved the precious literature of antiquity from a total extinction;[s] and under shelter of their numerous privileges and immunities, acquired a security, by means of the superstition, which they would in vain have claimed, from the justice and humanity of those turbulent and licentious ages. Nor is the spectacle altogether unentertaining and uninstructive, which the history of those times presents to us. The view of human manners, in all their variety of appearances, is both profitable and agreeable; and if the aspect in some periods seems horrid and deformed, we may thence learn to cherish with the greater anxiety

[s] See note [T] at the end of the volume.

CHAPTER XXIII

that science and civility, which has so close a connexion with virtue and humanity, and which, as it is a sovereign antidote against superstition, is also the most effectual remedy against vice and disorders of every kind.

The rise, progress, perfection, and decline of art and science, are curious objects of contemplation, and intimately connected with a narration of civil transactions. The events of no particular period can be fully accounted for, but by considering the degrees of advancement, which men have reached in those particulars.

Those who cast their eye on the general revolutions of society, will find, that, as almost all improvements of the human mind had reached nearly to their state of perfection about the age of Augustus, there was a sensible decline from that point or period; and man thenceforth relapsed gradually into ignorance and barbarism. The unlimited extent of the Roman empire, and the consequent despotism of its monarchs, extinguished all emulation, debased the generous spirits of men, and depressed that noble flame, by which all the refined arts must be cherished and enlivened. The military government, which soon succeeded, rendered even the lives and properties of men insecure and precarious; and proved destructive to those vulgar and more necessary arts of agriculture, manufactures, and commerce; and in the end, to the military art and genius itself, by which alone the immense fabric of the empire could be supported. The irruption of the barbarous nations, which soon followed, overwhelmed all human knowledge, which was already far in its decline; and men sunk every age deeper into ignorance, stupidity, and superstition; till the light of ancient science and history had very nearly suffered a total extinction in all the European nations.

But there is a point of depression, as well as of exaltation, from which human affairs naturally return in a contrary direction, and beyond which they seldom pass either in their advancement or decline. The period, in which the people of Christendom were the lowest sunk in ignorance, and consequently in disorders of every kind, may justly be fixed at the eleventh century, about the age of William the Conqueror; and from that aera, the sun of science, beginning to re-ascend, threw out many gleams of light, which preceded the full morning, when letters were revived in the fifteenth century. The Danes and other northern people, who had so long infested all the coasts, and even the inland parts of Europe, by their depredations, having now learned the arts of tillage and agriculture, found a certain subsistance at home, and were no longer tempted to desert their industry, in order to seek a precarious livelihood by rapine and by the plunder of their neighbours. The feudal governments also, among the more southern nations, were reduced to a kind of system; and though that strange species of civil polity was ill fitted to ensure either liberty or tranquillity, it was preferable to the universal licence and disorder, which had every where preceded it. But perhaps there was no event, which tended farther to the improvement of the age, than one, which has not been much remarked, the accidental finding of a copy of Justinian's Pandects, about the year 1130, in the town of Amalfi in Italy.

The ecclesiastics, who had leisure, and some inclination of study, immediately adopted with zeal this excellent system of jurisprudence, and spread the knowledge of it throughout every part of Europe. Besides the intrinsic merit of the performance, it was recommended to them by its original connexion with the imperial city of Rome, which, being the seat of their religion, seemed to acquire a new lustre and authority, by the diffusion of its laws over the western world. In less than ten years after the discovery of the Pandects, Vacarius, under the protection of Theobald, archbishop of Canterbury, read public lectures of civil law in the university of Oxford; and the clergy every where, by their example as well as exhortation, were the means of diffusing the highest esteem for this new science. That order of men, having large possessions to defend, was, in a manner, necessitated to turn their studies towards the law; and their properties being often endangered by the violence of the princes and barons, it became their interest to enforce the observance of general and equitable rules, from which alone they could receive protection. As they possessed all the knowledge of the age, and were alone acquainted with the habits of thinking, the practice, as well as science of the law, fell mostly into their hands: And though the close connexion, which without any necessity they formed between the canon and civil law, begat a jealousy in the laity of England, and prevented the Roman jurisprudence from becoming the municipal law of the country, as was the case in many states of Europe, a great part of it was se-

CHAPTER XXIII

cretly transferred into the practice of the courts of justice, and the imitation of their neighbours made the English gradually endeavour to raise their own law from its original state of rudeness and imperfection.

It is easy to see what advantages Europe must have reaped by its inheriting at once from the ancients, so complete an art, which was also so necessary for giving security to all other arts, and which, by refining, and still more, by bestowing solidity on the judgment, served as a model to farther improvements. The sensible utility of the Roman law both to public and private interest recommended the study of it, at a time when the more exalted and speculative sciences carried no charms with them; and thus the last branch of ancient literature, which remained uncorrupted, was happily the first transmitted to the modern world. For it is remarkable, that in the decline of Roman learning, when the philosophers were universally infected with superstition and sophistry, and the poets and historians with barbarism, the lawyers, who, in other countries, are seldom models of science or politeness, were yet able, by the constant study and close imitation of their predecessors, to maintain the same good sense in their decisions and reasonings, and the same purity in their language and expression.

What bestowed an additional merit on the civil law, was the extreme imperfection of that jurisprudence, which preceded it among all the European nations, especially among the Saxons or ancient English. The absurdities which prevailed at that time in the administration of justice, may be conceived from the authentic monuments which remain of the ancient Saxon law; where a pecuniary commutation was received for every crime; where stated prices were fixed for men's lives and members; where private revenges were authorized for all injuries, where the use of the ordeal, corsnet, and afterwards of the duel, was the received method of proof, and where the judges were rustic freeholders, assembled of a sudden, and deciding a cause from one debate or altercation of the parties. Such a state of society was very little advanced beyond the rude state of nature: Violence universally prevailed, instead of general and equitable maxims: The pretended liberty of the times, was only an incapacity of submitting to government: And men, not protected by law in their lives and properties, sought shelter, by their personal servitude and attachments under some powerful chieftain, or by voluntary combinations.

The gradual progress of improvement raised the Europeans somewhat above this uncultivated state; and affairs, in this island particularly, took early a turn, which was more favourable to justice and to liberty. Civil employments and occupations soon became honourable among the English: The situation of that people rendered not the perpetual attention to wars so necessary as among their neighbours, and all regard was not confined to the military profession: The gentry, and even the nobility, began to deem an acquaintance with the law a necessary part of education: They were less diverted than afterwards from studies of this kind by other sciences; and in the age of Henry VI. as we are told by Fortescue, there were in the inns of court about two thousand students, most of them men of honourable birth, who gave application to this branch of civil knowledge: A circumstance which proves, that a considerable progress was already made in the science of government, and which prognosticated a still greater.

One chief advantage, which resulted from the introduction and progress of the arts, was the introduction and progress of freedom; and this consequence affected men both in their *personal* and *civil* capacities.

If we consider the ancient state of Europe, we shall find, that the far greater part of the society were every where bereaved of their *personal* liberty, and lived entirely at the will of their masters. Every one, that was not noble, was a slave: The peasants were sold along with the land: The few inhabitants of cities were not in a better condition: Even the gentry themselves were subjected to a long train of subordination under the greater barons or chief vassals of the crown; who, though seemingly placed in a high state of splendor, yet, having but a slender protection from law, were exposed to every tempest of the state, and by the precarious condition in which they lived, paid dearly for the power of oppressing and tyrannizing over their inferiors. The first incident, which broke in upon this violent system of government, was the practice, begun in Italy, and imitated in France, of erecting communities and corporations, endowed with privileges and a separate municipal government, which gave them protection against the tyranny of the barons, and which the prince himself deemed it prudent to

CHAPTER XXIII

respect.[1] The relaxation of the feudal tenures, and an execution somewhat stricter, of the public law, bestowed an independance of vassals, which was unknown to their forefathers. And even the peasants themselves, though later than other orders of the state, made their escape from those bonds of villenage or slavery, in which they had formerly been retained.

It may appear strange, that the progress of the arts, which seems, among the Greeks and Romans, to have daily encreased the number of slaves, should, in later times, have proved so general a source of liberty; but this difference in the events proceeded from a great difference in the circumstances, which attended those institutions. The ancient barons, obliged to maintain themselves continually in a military posture, and little emulous of elegance or splendor, employed not their villains as domestic servants, much less as manufacturers; but composed their retinue of free-men, whose military spirit rendered the chieftain formidable to his neighbours, and who were ready to attend him in every warlike enterprize. The villains were entirely occupied in the cultivation of their master's land, and paid their rents either in corn and cattle and other produce of the farm, or in servile offices, which they performed about the baron's family, and upon the farms which he retained in his own possession. In proportion as agriculture improved, and money encreased, it was found, that these services, though extremely burdensome to the villain, were of little advantage to the master; and that the produce of a large estate could be much more conveniently disposed of by the peasants themselves, who raised it, than by the landlord or his bailiff, who were formerly accustomed to receive it. A commutation was therefore made of

---

[1] There appear early symptoms of the jealousy, entertained by the barons against the progress of the arts, as destructive of their licentious power. A law was enacted, 7 Henry IV. chap. 17. prohibiting any one who did not possess twenty shillings a year in land from binding his sons apprentices to any trade. They found already that the cities began to drain the country of the labourers and husbandmen; and did not foresee how much the encrease of commerce would encrease the value of their estates. See farther, Cotton, p. 179. The kings, to encourage the boroughs, granted them this privilege, that any villain, who had lived a twelvemonth in any corporation and had been of the guild, should be thenceforth regarded as free.

rents for services, and of money-rents for those in kind; and as men, in a subsequent age, discovered, that farms were better cultivated where the farmer enjoyed a security in his possession, the practice of granting leases to the peasant began to prevail, which entirely broke the bonds of servitude, already much relaxed from the former practices. After this manner, villenage went gradually into disuse throughout the more civilized parts of Europe: The interest of the master, as well as that of the slave, concurred in this alteration. The latest laws which we find in England for enforcing or regulating this species of servitude, were enacted in the reign of Henry VII. And though the ancient statutes on this subject remain still unrepealed by parliament, it appears, that, before the end of Elizabeth, the distinction of villain and freeman was totally, though insensibly abolished, and that no person remained in the state, to whom the former laws could be applied.

Thus *personal* freedom became almost general in Europe; an advantage which paved the way for the encrease of *political* or *civil* liberty, and which, even where it was not attended with this salutary effect, served to give the members of the community some of the most considerable advantages of it.

The constitution of the English government, ever since the invasion of this island by the Saxons, may boast of this preeminence, that in no age the will of the monarch was ever entirely absolute and uncontrouled: But in other respects the balance of power has extremely shifted among the several orders of the state; and this fabric has experienced the same mutability, that has attended all human institutions.

The ancient Saxons, like the other German nations, where each individual was enured to arms, and where the independance of men was secured by a great equality of possessions, seem to have admitted a considerable mixture of democracy into their form of government, and to have been one of the freest nations, of which there remains any account in the records of history. After this tribe was settled in England, especially after the dissolution of the Heptarchy, the great extent of the kingdom produced a great inequality in property; and the balance seems to have inclined to the side of aristocracy. The Norman conquest threw more authority into the hands of the sovereign, which, however, admitted of great controul; though derived less from the general forms of the consitution, which were inaccurate and irregular, than from the inde-

CHAPTER XXIII

pendant power enjoyed by each baron in his particular district or province. The establishment of the Great Charter exalted still higher the Aristocracy, imposed regular limits on royal power, and gradually introduced some mixture of Democracy into the constitution. But even during this period, from the accession of Edward I. to the death of Richard III. the condition of the commons was nowise eligible; a kind of Polish Aristocracy prevailed; and though the kings were limited, the people were as yet far from being free. It required the authority almost absolute of the sovereigns, which took place in the subsequent period, to pull down those disorderly and licentious tyrants, who were equally averse from peace and from freedom, and to establish that regular execution of the laws, which, in a following age, enabled the people to erect a regular and equitable plan of liberty.

In each of these successive alterations, the only rule of government, which is intelligible or carries any authority with it, is the established practice of the age, and the maxims of administration, which are at that time prevalent, and universally assented to. Those who, from a pretended respect to antiquity, appeal at every turn to an original plan of the constitution, only cover their turbulent spirit and their private ambition under the appearance of venerable forms; and whatever period they pitch on for their model, they may still be carried back to a more ancient period, where they will find the measures of power entirely different, and where every circumstance, by reason of the greater barbarity of the times, will appear still less worthy of imitation. Above all, a civilized nation, like the English, who have happily established the most perfect and most accurate system of liberty that was ever found compatible with government, ought to be cautious in appealing to the practice of their ancestors, or regarding the maxims of uncultivated ages as certain rules for their present conduct. An acquaintance with the ancient periods of their government is chiefly *useful* by instructing them to cherish their present constitution, from a comparison or contrast with the condition of those distant times. And it is also *curious,* by shewing them the remote, and commonly faint and disfigured originals of the most finished and most noble institutions, and by instructing them in the great mixture of accident, which commonly concurs with a small ingredient of wisdom and foresight, in erecting the complicated fabric of the most perfect government.

NOTES TO THE SECOND VOLUME

NOTE [A], p. 89

Rymer, vol. ii. p. 216, 845. There cannot be the least question, that the homage usually paid by the kings of Scotland was not for their crown, but for some other territory. The only question remains, what that territory was? It was not always for the earldom of Huntingdon, nor the honour of Penryth; because we find it sometimes done at a time when these possessions were not in the hands of the kings of Scotland. It is probable, that the homage was performed in general terms without any particular specification of territory; and this inaccuracy had proceeded either from some dispute between the two kings about the territory and some opposite claims, which were compromised by the general homage, or from the simplicity of the age, which employed few words in every transaction. To prove this we need but look into the letter of king Richard, where he resigns the homage of Scotland, reserving the usual homage. His words are, *Saepedictus W. Rex ligius homo noster deveniat de omnibus terris de quibus antecessors sui antecessorum nostrorum ligii homines fuerunt, et nobis atque haeredibus nostris fidelitatem jurarunt.* Rymer, vol. i. p. 65. These general terms were probably copied from the usual form of the homage itself.

It is no proof that the kings of Scotland possessed no lands or baronies in England, because we cannot find them in the imperfect histories and records of that age. For instance, it clearly appears from another passage of this very letter of Richard, that the Scottish king held lands both in the county of Huntingdon and elsewhere in England; though the earldom of Huntingdon itself was then in the person of his brother, David; and we know at present of no other baronies, which William held. It cannot be expected that we should now be able to specify all his fees which he either possessed or claimed in England; when it is probable that the two monarchs themselves and their ministers would at that very time have differed in the list: The Scotish king might possess some to which his right was disputed; he might claim others, which he did not possess: And neither of the two kings was willing to resign his pretensions by a particular enumeration.

NOTES TO THE SECOND VOLUME

A late author of great industry and learning, but full of prejudices, and of no penetration, Mr. Carte, has taken advantage of the undefined terms of the Scotch homage, and has pretended that it was done for Lothian and Galloway, that is, all the territories of the country now called Scotland, lying south of the Clyde and Forth. But to refute this pretension at once, we need only consider, that if these territories were held in fee of the English kings, there would, by the nature of the feudal law, as established in England, have been continual appeals from them to the courts of the lord Paramount; contrary to all the histories and records of that age. We find, that, as soon as Edward really established his superiority, appeals immediately commenced from all parts of Scotland: And that king, in his writ to the king's-bench, considers them as a necessary consequence of the feudal tenure. Such large territories also would have supplied a considerable part of the English armies, which never could have escaped all the historians. Not to mention that there is not any instance of a Scotch prisoner of war being tried as a rebel, in the frequent hostilities between the kingdoms, where the Scottish armies were chiefly filled from the southern counties.

Mr. Carte's notion with regard to Galloway, which comprehends, in the language of that age, or rather in that of the preceding, most of the south-west counties of Scotland; his notion, I say, rests on so slight a foundation, that it scarcely merits being refuted. He will have it (and merely because he will have it) that the Cumberland, yielded by king Edmund to Malcolm I. meant not only the county in England of that name, but all the territory northwards to the Clyde. But the case of Lothian deserves some more consideration.

It is certain, that in very ancient language, Scotland means only the country north of the friths of Clyde and Forth. I shall not make a parade of literature to prove it; because I do not find that this point is disputed by the Scots themselves. The southern country was divided into Galloway and Lothian; and the latter comprehended all the south-east counties. This territory was certainly a part of the ancient kingdom of Northumberland, and was entirely peopled by Saxons, who afterwards received a great mixture of Danes among them. It appears from all the English histories, that the whole kingdom of Northumberland paid very little obedience to the Anglo-Saxon monarchs, who governed after the dissolution of the heptarchy; and the northern and remote parts of it seem to have fallen into a kind of anarchy, sometimes pillaged by the Danes, sometimes joining them in their ravages upon other parts of England. The kings of Scotland, lying nearer them, took at last possession of the country, which had scarcely any government; and we are told by Matthew of Westminster, p. 193. that king Edgar made a grant of the territory to Kenneth III. that is, he resigned claims, which he could not make effectual, without bestowing on them more trouble and expence than they were worth: For these are the only grants of provinces made by kings; and so ambitious and active a prince as Edgar would never have made presents of any other kind. Tho'

Matthew of Westminster's authority may appear small with regard to so remote a transaction; yet we may admit it in this case, because Ordericus Vitalis, a good authority, tells us, p. 701. that Malcolm acknowledged to William Rufus, that the Conqueror had confirmed to him the former grant of Lothian. But it follows not, because Edgar made this species of grant to Kenneth, that therefore he exacted homage for that territory. Homage and all the rites of the feudal law were very little known among the Saxons; and we may also suppose, that the claim of Edgar was so antiquated and weak, that, in resigning it, he made no very valuable concession, and Kenneth might well refuse to hold, by so precarious a tenure, a territory, which he at present held by the sword. In short, no author says, he did homage for it.

The only colour indeed of authority for Mr. Carte's notion is, that Matthew Paris, who wrote in the reign of Henry III. before Edward's claim of superority was heard of, says that Alexander III. did homage to Henry III. *pro Laudiano et aliis terris.* See page 555. This word seems naturally to be interpreted Lothian. But, in the first place, Matthew Paris's testimony, though considerable, will not outweigh that of all the other historians, who say that the Scotch homage was always done for lands in England. Secondly, if the Scotch homage was done in general terms (as has been already proved), it is no wonder that historians should differ in their account of the object of it, since, it is probable, the parties themselves were not fully agreed. Thirdly, there is reason to think that *Laudianum* in Matthew Paris does not mean the Lothians, now in Scotland. There appears to have been a territory, which anciently bore that or a similar name, in the north of England. For (1) The Saxon Chronicle, p. 197. says, that Malcolm Kenmure met William Rufus in Lodene in England. (2) It is agreed by all historians, that Henry II. only reconquered from Scotland the northern counties of Northumberland, Cumberland, and Westmorland. See Newbriggs, p. 383. Wykes, p. 30. Hemingford, p. 492. Yet the same country is called by other historians Loidis, comitatus Lodonensis, or some such name. See M. Paris, p. 68. M. West. p. 247. Annal. Waverl. p. 159. and Diceto, p. 531. (3) This last mentioned author, when he speaks of Lothian in Scotland, calls it Loheneis, p. 574, though he had called the English territory Loidis.

I thought this long note necessary in order to correct Mr. Carte's mistake, an author whose diligence and industry has given light to many passages of the more ancient English history.

NOTE [B], p. 90

Rymer, vol. ii. p. 543. It is remarkable that the English chancellor spoke to the Scotch parliament in the French tongue. This was also the language commonly made use of by all parties on that occasion. Ibid. passim. Some of the most considerable among the Scotch, as well as almost all the English barons, were of French origin; they valued themselves upon it; and pretended to despise the language and manners of the island. It is difficult to

NOTES TO THE SECOND VOLUME

account for the settlement of so many French families in Scotland, the Bruces, Baliols, St. Clairs, Montgomeries, Somervilles, Gordons, Frasers, Cummins, Colvilles, Umfrevilles, Mowbrays, Hays, Maules, who were not supported there, as in England, by the power of the sword. But the superiority of the smallest civility and knowledge over total ignorance and barbarism, is prodigious.

NOTE [C], p. 94

See Rymer, vol. ii. p. 533. where Edward writes to the King's Bench to receive appeals from Scotland. He knew the practice to be new and unusual; yet he establishes it as an infallible consequence of his superiority. We learn also from the same collection, p. 603, that immediately upon receiving the homage, he changed the style of his address to the Scotch king, whom he now calls *dilecto & fideli,* instead of *fratri dilecto & fideli,* the appellation which he had always before used to him; see p. 109. 124. 168. 280. 1064. This is a certain proof, that he himself was not deceived, as was scarcely indeed possible, but that he was conscious of his usurpation. Yet he solemnly swore afterwards to the justice of his pretensions, when he defended them before pope Boniface.

NOTE [D], p. 108

Throughout the reign of Edw. I. the assent of the commons is not once expressed in any of the enacting clauses; nor in the reigns ensuing, till the 9 Edw. III. nor in any of the enacting clauses of 16 Rich. II. Nay even so low as Hen. VI. from the beginning till the 8th of his reign, the assent of the commons is not once expressed in any enacting clause. See preface to Ruffhead's edit. of the Statutes, p. 7. If it should be asserted, that the commons had really given their assent to these statutes, though they are not expressly mentioned; this very omission, proceeding, if you will, from carelessness, is a proof how little they were respected. The commons were so little accustomed to transact public business, that they had no speaker, till after the parliament 6th Edw. III. See Prynne's preface to Cotton's abridg. Not till the first of Richard II. in the opinion of most antiquaries. The commons were very unwilling to meddle in any state affairs, and commonly either referred themselves to the lords, or desired a select committee of that house to assist them, as appears from Cotton. 5 E. III. n. 5; 15 E. III. n. 17; 21 E. III. n. 5; 47 E. III. n. 5; 50 E. III. n. 10; 51 E. III. n. 18; 1 R. II. n. 12; 2 R. II. n. 12; 5 R. II. n. 14, 2 parl. 6 R. II. n. 14; parl. 2. 6 R. II. n. 8. &c.

NOTE [E], p. 109

It was very agreeable to the maxims of all the feudal governments, that every order of the state should give their consent to the acts which more immediately concerned them; and as the notion of a political system was not then so well understood, the other orders of the state were often not consulted on these occasions. In this reign, even the merchants, though no public body, granted the king impositions on merchandize, because the first payments came out of their pockets. They did the same in the reign of Edward III. but the commons had then observed that the people paid these duties, though the merchants advanced them; and they therefore remonstrated against this practice. Cotton's abridg. p. 39. The taxes imposed by the knights on the counties were always lighter than those which the burgesses laid on the boroughs; a presumption, that in voting those taxes, the knights and burgesses did not form the same house. See Chancellor West's enquiry into the manner of creating peers, p. 8. But there are so many proofs, that those two orders of representatives were long separate, that it is needless to insist on them. Mr. Carte, who had carefully consulted the rolls of parliament, affirms, that they never appear to have been united till the 16th of Edward III. See Hist. vol. ii. p. 451. But it is certain that this union was not even then final: In 1372, the burgesses acted by themselves, and voted a tax after the knights were dismissed. See Tyrrel, Hist. vol. iii. p. 734. from Rot. Claus. 46 Edw. III. n. 9. In 1376, they were the knights alone, who passed a vote for the removal of Alice Pierce from the king's person, if we may credit Walsingham, p. 189. There is an instance of a like kind in the reign of Richard II. Cotton, p. 193. The different taxes voted by those two branches of the lower house, naturally kept them separate: But as their petitions had mostly the same object, namely, the redress of grievances, and the support of law and justice both against the crown and the barons, this cause as naturally united them, and was the reason why they at last joined in one house for the dispatch of business. The barons had few petitions. Their privileges were of more ancient date: Grievances seldom affected them: They were themselves the chief oppressors. In 1333, the knights by themselves concurred with the bishops and barons in advising the king to stay his journey into Ireland. Here was a petition which regarded a matter of state, and was supposed to be above the capacity of the burgesses. The knights, therefore, acted apart in this petition. See Cotton, abridg. p. 13. Chief baron Gilbert thinks, that the reason why taxes always began with the commons or burgesses was, that they were limited by the instructions of their boroughs. See Hist. of the Exchequer, p. 37.

NOTE [F], p. 109

The chief argument from ancient authority, for the opinion that the representatives of boroughs preceded the forty-ninth of Henry III. is the famous petition of the borough of St. Albans, first taken notice of by Selden, and then by Peyt, Brady, Tyrrel, and others. In this petition, presented to the parliament in the reign of Edward II. the town of St. Albans asserts, that though they held *in capite* of the crown, and owed only, for all other service, their attendance in parliament, yet the sheriff had omitted them in his writs; whereas both in the reign of the king's father, and all his predecessors, they had always sent members. Now, say the defenders of this opinion, if the commencement of the house of commons were in Henry III.'s reign, this expression could not have been used. But Madox, in his History of the Exchequer, p. 522, 523, 524, has endeavoured, and with great reason, to destroy the authority of this petition for the purpose alleged. He asserts, first, that there was no such tenure in England as that of holding by attendance in parliament, instead of all other service. Secondly, That the borough of St. Albans never held of the crown at all, but was always demesne land of the abbot. It is no wonder, therefore, that a petition which advances two falsehoods, should contain one historical mistake, which indeed amounts only to an inaccurate and exaggerated expression; no strange matter in ignorant Burgesses of that age. Accordingly St. Albans continued still to belong to the abbot. It never held of the crown, till after the dissolution of the monasteries. But the assurance of these petitioners is remarkable. They wanted to shake off the authority of their abbot, and to hold of the king; but were unwilling to pay any services even to the crown: Upon which they framed this idle petition, which later writers have made the foundation of so many inferences and conclusions. From the tenor of the petition it appears, that there was a close connection between holding of the crown, and being represented in parliament: The latter had scarcely ever place without the former: Yet we learn from Tyrrel's Append. vol. iv. that there were some instances to the contrary. It is not improbable, that Edward followed the roll of the earl of Leicester, who had summoned, without distinction, all the considerable boroughs of the kingdom; among which there might be some few that did not hold of the crown. Edward also found it necessary to impose taxes on all the boroughs in the kingdom without distinction. This was a good expedient for augmenting his revenue. We are not to imagine, because the house of commons have since become of great importance, that the first summoning of them would form any remarkable and striking epoch, and be generally known to the people even seventy or eighty years after. So ignorant were the generality of men in that age, that country burgesses would readily imagine an innovation, seemingly so little material, to have existed from time immemorial, because it was beyond their own memory, and perhaps that of their fathers. Even the parliament in the reign of Henry V. say, that Ireland had, from the beginning of time, been subject to the crown of England. (See Brady.) And surely, if any thing interests the people above all others, it is war and conquests, with their dates and circumstances.

NOTE [G], p. 238

This story of the six burgesses of Calais, like all other extraordinary stories, is somewhat to be suspected; and so much the more as Avesbury, p. 167, who is particular in his narration of the surrender of Calais, says nothing of it: and on the contrary extols in general the king's generosity and lenity to the inhabitants. The numberless mistakes of Froissard, proceeding either from negligence, credulity, or love of the marvellous, invalidate very much his testimony, even though he was a contemporary, and though his history was dedicated to queen Philippa herself. It is a mistake to imagine, that the patrons of dedications read the books, much less vouch for all the contents of them. It is not a slight testimony, that should make us give credit to a story so dishonourable to Edward, especially after that proof of his humanity, in allowing a free passage to all the women, children, and infirm people, at the beginning of the siege; at least, it is scarcely to be believed, that, if the story has any foundation, he seriously meant to execute his menaces against the six townsmen of Calais.

NOTE [H], p. 243

There was a singular instance about this time of the prevalence of chivalry and gallantry in the nations of Europe. A solemn duel of thirty knights against thirty was fought between Bembrough, an Englishman, and Beaumanoir, a Breton, of the party of Charles of Blois. The knights of the two nations came into the field; and before the combat began, Beaumanoir called out, that it would be seen that day *who had the fairest mistresses*. After a bloody combat the Bretons prevailed; and gained for their prize, full liberty to boast of their mistresses' beauty. It is remarkable, that two such famous generals as Sir Robert Knolles, and Sir Hugh Calverley, drew their swords in this ridiculous contest. See Pere Daniel, vol. ii. p. 536, 537, &c. The women not only instigated the champions to those rough, if not bloody frays of tournament; but also frequented the tournaments during all the reign of Edward, whose spirit of gallantry encouraged this practice. See Knyghton, p. 2597.

NOTE [I], p. 259

This is a prodigious sum, and probably near the half of what the king received from the parliament during the whole course of his reign. It must be remarked, that a tenth and fifteenth (which was always thought a high grant) were, in the eighth year of his reign, fixed at about 29,000 pounds: There were said to be near 30,000 sacks of wool exported every year: A sack of wool was at a medium sold for five pounds. Upon these suppositions it would be easy to compute all the parliamentary grants, taking the list as they stand in Tyrrel, vol. iii. p. 780: Though somewhat must still be left to conjecture. This king levied more money on his subjects than any of his predecessors; and the parliament frequently complained of the poverty of the people, and the oppressions under which they laboured. But it is to be remarked, that a third of the French king's ransom was yet unpayed when war broke out anew between the two crowns: His son chose rather to employ his money in combating the English, than in enriching them. See Rymer, vol. viii. p. 315.

NOTE [J], p. 288

In the fifth year of the king, *the commons complained of the government about the king's person, his court, the excessive number of his servants, of the abuses in the*

Chancery, King's Bench, Common Pleas, Exchequer, and of grievous oppressions in the country, by the great multitudes of maintainers of quarrels, (men linked in confederacies together) *who behaved themselves like kings in the country, so as there was very little law or right, and of other things which they said were the cause of the late commotions under Wat Tyler.* Parl. Hist. vol. i. p. 365. This irregular government, which no king and no house of commons had been able to remedy, was the source of the licentiousness of the great, and turbulency of the people, as well as tyranny of the princes. If subjects would enjoy liberty, and kings security, the laws must be executed.

In the ninth of this reign, the commons also discovered an accuracy and a jealousy of liberty, which we should little expect in those rude times. "It was agreed by parliament," says Cotton, p. 309, "that the subsidy of wools, wool fells, and skins, granted to the king until the time of Midsummer then ensuing, should cease from the same time unto the feast of St. Peter *ad vincula;* for that thereby the king should be interrupted for claiming such grant as due." See also Cotton, p. 198.

NOTE [K], p. 296

Knyghton, p. 2715, &c. The same author, p. 2680, tells us, that the king, in return to the message, said, that he would not for their desire remove the meanest scullion from his kitchen. This author also tells us, that the king said to the commissioners, when they harangued him, that he saw his subjects were rebellious, and his best way would be to call in the king of France to his aid. But it is plain, that all these speeches were either intended by Knyghton merely as an ornament to his history, or are false. For (1) when the five lords accuse the king's ministers in the next parliament, and impute to them every rash action of the king, they speak nothing of those replies which are so obnoxious, were so recent, and are pretended to have been so public. (2) The king, so far from having any connexions at that time with France, was threatend with a dangerous invasion from that kingdom. This story seems to have been taken from the reproaches afterwards thrown out against him, and to have been transferred by the historian to this time, to which they cannot be applied.

NOTE [L], p. 301

We must except the 12th article, which accuses Brembre of having cut off the heads of twenty-two prisoners, confined for felony or debt, without warrant or process of law: But as it is not conceivable what interest Brembre could have to treat these felons and debtors in such a manner, we may presume that the fact is either false or misrepresented. It was in these men's power to say any thing against the persons accused: No defence or apology was admitted: All was lawless will and pleasure.

They are also accused of designs to murder the lords: but these accusations either are general, or destroy one another. Sometimes, as in article 15th, they intend to murder them by means of the mayor and city of

London: Sometimes, as in article 28th, by trial and false inquests: Sometimes, as in article 28th, by means of the king of France, who was to receive
Calais for his pains.

NOTE [M], p. 303

In general, the parliament in those days never paid a proper regard to
Edward's statute of treasons, though one of the most advantageous laws
for the subject that has ever been enacted. In the 17th of the king, *the dukes
of Lancaster and Glocester complain to Richard, that Sir Thomas Talbot, with others
of his adherents, conspired the death of the said dukes in divers parts of Cheshire, as
the same was confessed and well known; and praying that the parliament may judge
of the fault. Whereupon the king and the lords in the parliament judged the same
fact to be open and high treason: And hereupon they award two writs, the one to the
sheriff of York, and the other to the sheriffs of Derby, to take the body of the said Sir
Thomas returnable in the King's bench in the month of Easter then ensuing. And
open proclamation was made in Westminster-hall, that upon the sheriff's return, and
at the next coming in of the said Sir Thomas, the said Thomas should be convicted
of treason, and incur the loss and pain of the same: And all such as should receive
him after the proclamation should incur the same loss and pain.* Cotton, p. 354.
It is to be observed, that this extraordinary judgment was passed in a time
of tranquillity. Though the statute itself of Edward III. reserves a power
to the parliament to declare any new species of treason, it is not to be
supposed that this power was reserved to the house of lords alone, or that
men were to be judged by a law *ex post facto*. At least, if such be the meaning
of the clause; it may be affirmed, that men were at that time very ignorant
of the first principles of law and justice.

NOTE [N], p. 308

In the preceding parliament, the commons had shewn a disposition very
complaisant to the king; yet there happend an incident in their proceedings, which is curious, and shews us the state of the house during that
period. The members were either country gentlemen, or merchants, who
were assembled for a few days, and were entirely unacquainted with
business; so that it was easy to lead them astray, and draw them into votes
and resolutions very different from their intention. Some petitions, concerning the state of the nation, were voted; in which, among other things,
the house recommended frugality to the king, and for that purpose,
desired, that the court should not be so much frequented as formerly by
bishops and *ladies*. The king was displeased with this freedom: The commons very humbly craved pardon: He was not satisfied unless they would
name the mover of the petitions. It happened to be one Haxey, whom the
parliament, in order to make atonement, condemned for this offence to
die the death of a traitor. But the king, at the desire of the archbishop of
Canterbury, and the prelates, pardoned him. When a parliament in those
times, not agitated by any faction, and being at entire freedom, could be
guilty of such monstrous extravagance, it is easy to judge what might

be expected from them in more trying situations. See Cotton's Abridg. p. 361, 362.

NOTE [O], p. 319

To show how little credit is to be given to this charge against Richard, we may observe, that a law in the 13 Edw. III. had been enacted against the continuance of sheriffs for more than one year: But the inconvenience of changes having afterwards appeared from experience, the commons in the twentieth of this king, applied by petition that the sheriffs might be continued; though that petition had not been enacted into a statute, by reason of other disagreeable circumstances, which attended it. See Cotton, p. 361. It was certainly a very moderate exercise of the dispensing power in the king to continue the sheriffs, after he found that that practice would be acceptable to his subjects, and had been applied for by one house of parliament: Yet is this made an article of charge against him by the present parliament. See art. 18. Walsingham, speaking of a period early in Richard's minority, says, *But what do acts of parliament signify, when, after they are made, they take no effect; since the king, by the advice of the privy council, takes upon him to alter, or wholly set aside, all those things, which by general consent had been ordained in parliament?* If Richard, therefore, exercised the dispensing power, he was warranted by the examples of his uncles and grandfather, and indeed of all his predecessors from the time of Henry III, inclusive.

NOTE [P], p. 325

The following passage in Cotton's Abridgment, p. 196, shows a strange prejudice against the church and churchmen. *The commons afterwards coming into the parliament, and making their protestation, shewed, that for want of good redress about the king's person in his household, in all his courts, touching maintainers in every county, and purveyors, the commons were daily pilled, and nothing defended against the enemy, and that it should shortly deprive the king and undo the state. Wherefore in the same government, they entirely require redress. Whereupon the king appointed sundry bishops, lords and nobles, to sit in privy-council about these matters: Who since that they must begin at the head, and go at the request of the commons, they in the presence of the king charged his confessor not to come into the court but upon the four principal festivals.* We should little expect that a popish privy-council, in order to preserve the king's morals, should order his confessor to be kept at a distance from him. This incident happened in the minority of Richard. As the popes had for a long time resided at Avignon, and the majority of the sacred college were Frenchmen, this circumstance naturally encreased the aversion of the nation to the papal power: But the prejudice against the English clergy cannot be accounted for from that cause.

NOTE [Q], p. 460

That we may judge how arbitrary a court, that of the constable of England was, we may peruse the patent granted to the earl of Rivers in this reign, as it is to be found in Spellman's Glossary in verb. *Constabularius* ; as also, more fully in Rymer, vol. xi. p. 581. Here is a clause of it: *Et ulterius de uberiori gratia nostra eidem comiti de Rivers plenam potestatem damus ad cognoscendum, & procedendum, in omnibus, & singulis, causis et negotiis, de et super crimine lesae majestatis, seu super occasione caeterisque causis, quibuscunque per praefatum comitem de Rivers, ut constabularium Angliae—quae in curia constabularii Angliae ab antiquo,* viz. *tempore dicti domini Gulielmi conquestoris seu aliquo tempore citra tractari, audiri, examinari, aut decidi consueverant, aut jure debuerant, aut debent, causasque et negotia praedicta cum omnibus et singulis emergentibus, incidentibus & connexis, audiendum, examinandum, et fine debito terminandum, etiam* summarie et de plano, sine strepitu et figura justitiæ, sola facti veritate inspecta, *ac etiam manu regia, si opportunum visum fuerit eidem comiti de Rivers, vices nostras, appellatione remota.* The office of constable was perpetual in the monarchy; its jurisdiction was not limited to times of war, as appears from this patent, and as we learn from Spellman: Yet its authority was in direct contradiction to *Magna Charta;* and it is evident, that no *regular* liberty could subsist with it. It involved a full dictatorial power, continually subsisting in the state. The only check on the crown, besides the want of force to support all its prerogatives, was, that the office of constable was commonly either hereditary or during life; and the person invested with it, was, for that reason, not so proper an instrument of arbitrary power in the king. Accordingly the office was suppressed by Henry VIII. the most arbitrary of all the English princes. The practice, however, of exercising martial law, still subsisted; and was not abolished till the petition of Right under Charles I. This was the epoch of true liberty, confirmed by the Restoration, and enlarged and secured by the Revolution.

NOTE [R], p. 469

We shall give an instance: Almost all the historians, even Comines, and the continuator of the annals of Croyland, assert that Edward was about this time taken prisoner by Clarence and Warwic, and was committed to the custody of the archbishop of York, brother to the earl; but being allowed to take the diversion of hunting by this prelate, he made his escape, and afterwards chaced the rebels out of the kingdom. But that all the story is false appears from Rymer, where we find, that the king, throughout all this period, continually exercised his authority, and never was interrupted in his government. On the 7th of March 1470, he gives a commission of array to Clarence, whom he then imagined a good subject; and on the 23d of the same month, we find him issuing an order for apprehending him. Besides, in the king's manifesto against the duke and earl, (Claus. 10 Edward IV. m. 7, 8.) where he enumerates all their treasons, he mentions no such fact: He does not so much as accuse them of exciting young Welles's rebellion: He only says, that they exhorted him to continue in his rebellion. We may judge how smaller facts will be misrepresented by historians, who can in the most material transactions mistake so grossly. There may even some doubt arise with regard to the proposal of marriage made to Bona of Savoy; though almost all the historians concur in it, and the fact be very likely in itself: For there are no traces in Rymer of any such embassy of Warwic's to France. The chief certainty in this and the preceding reign arises either from public records, or from the notice taken of certain passages by the French historians. On the contrary, for some centuries after the conquest, the French history is not complete without the assistance of English authors. We may conjecture, that the reason of the scarcity of historians during this period, was the destruction of the convents, which ensued so soon after: Copies of the more recent historians not being yet sufficiently dispersed, these histories have perished.

NOTE [S], p. 501

Sir Thomas More, who has been followed, or rather transcribed, by all the historians of this short reign, says, that Jane Shore had fallen into connexions with lord Hastings; and this account agrees best with the course of the events: But in a proclamation of Richard's, to be found in Rymer, vol. xii. p. 204, the marquis of Dorset is reproached with these connexions. This reproach, however, might have been invented by Richard, or founded only on popular rumour; and is not sufficient to overbalance the authority of Sir Thomas More. The proclamation is remarkable for the hypocritical purity of manners affected by Richard: This bloody and treacherous tyrant upbraids the marquis and others, with their gallantries and intrigues as the most terrible enormities.

NOTE [T], p. 518

Every one that has perused the ancient monkish writers, knows, that, however barbarous their own style, they are full of allusions to the Latin classics, especially the poets. There seems also in those middle ages to have remained many ancient books, that are now lost. Malmesbury, who flourished in the reign of Henry I. and king Stephen, quotes Livy's description of Caesar's passage over the Rubicon. Fitz-Stephen, who lived in the reign of Henry II. alludes to a passage in the larger history of Sallust. In the collection of letters, which passes under the name of Thomas a Becket, we see how familiar all the ancient history and ancient books were to the more ingenious and more dignified churchmen of that time, and consequently how much that order of men must have surpassed all the other members of the society. That prelate and his friends call each other Philosophers in all the course of their correspondence, and consider the rest of the world as sunk in total ignorance and barbarism.